Bombay to Bloo

CW00972391

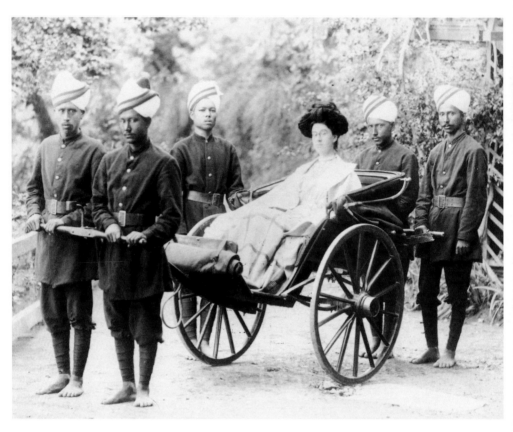

Frontispiece: Pippa Strachey in a rickshaw in India,
surrounded by her liveried rickshawmen

Bombay to Bloomsbury

A Biography of the Strachey Family

BARBARA CAINE

OXFORD

UNIVERSITY PRESS

OXFORD

UNIVERSITY PRESS

Great Clarendon Street, Oxford OX2 6DP

Oxford University Press is a department of the University of Oxford.
It furthers the University's objective of excellence in research, scholarship,
and education by publishing worldwide in

Oxford New York

Auckland Cape Town Dar es Salaam Hong Kong Karachi Kuala Lumpur
Madrid Melbourne Mexico City Nairobi New Delhi Shanghai Taipei Toronto

With offices in

Argentina Austria Brazil Chile Czech Republic France Greece
Guatemala Hungary Italy Japan Poland Portugal
Singapore South Korea Switzerland Thailand Turkey Ukraine Vietnam

Oxford is a registered trade mark of Oxford University Press
in the UK and in certain other countries

Published in the United States
by Oxford University Press Inc., New York

British Library Cataloguing in Publication Data

Data available

Library of Congress Cataloging in Publication Data

Data available

ISBN 0-19-9250340

1 3 5 7 9 10 8 6 4 2

Typeset by Kolam Information Services Pvt. Ltd, Pondicherry, India
Printed in Great Britain
on acid-free paper by
Biddles Ltd
King's Lynn, Norfolk

In memory of
Peggy Caine (1921–2002)
and Rhona Ovedoff (1922–2002)

Preface

I have been researching and writing this book on the Stracheys for nearly a decade. In part, the length of time the project has taken reflects the changes it has undergone since I began. Initially, I was concerned primarily to explore the lives and activities of the Strachey women. Jane Maria Strachey and her daughters and daughters-in-law offer one of the few examples of a family in which there were two generations of feminist activists across the nineteenth and early twentieth centuries. The younger Strachey women, moreover, offered a variety of different ways of thinking about the emancipation of women as some were interested in careers, and in combining careers with marriage and motherhood, while others saw emancipation in sexual rather than political terms. As I read through the material, however, I realized that it was impossible to separate the lives of the Strachey women from their father, brothers, and husbands. The richness of the material made me decide rather to extend the scope of the work and to encompass the whole family, including its best known member, Lytton.

I have retained my original plan of attempting to combine collective biography with a history of attitudes, beliefs, and ideas. However, the expanded scope of the book has inevitably expanded this discussion, making questions about modernity, and the ways in which a significant Victorian family understood and dealt with the excursions of some of its younger members into a variety of new ideas, approaches, and ways of life central. Jane Strachey remained the matriarch of the family until her death in 1928. While she, like her husband, embraced a range of advanced and 'modern' ideas and attitudes in her youth, she became increasingly conservative in her final years. Her children remained devoted to her, and indeed often to the family values and traditions that she endorsed so strongly and of which she was so very proud. What interests me particularly are the ways in which the younger Stracheys dealt with their desire for a new kind of life and their rejection of many Victorian values while still enmeshed within a familial framework. Conversely, I am interested in the extent to which even the most radical of the younger Stracheys took a pride in their family name and heritage, and in the ways in which this limited or served to mediate the ways in which they accepted or understood the modernity that some of them espoused. The book thus includes both a number of biographical chapters, seeking to explore their life experiences in thematic ways, and a number of chapters dealing with their involvement in India and in British imperialism, in feminism, in changing approaches to gender and sexuality, and in literature and British intellectual life generally.

In the course of the researching and writing of this book, many individuals and institutions have helped me. The History Department at Monash University has provided a most congenial environment in which to undertake the research and to write and many colleagues have contributed to it. I want to thank all my colleagues, particularly David Garrioch, Ian Copland, Jane Drakard, and Maria Nugent. I have received invaluable assistance in doing the research from Julie Burbidge, Lesley Sutherland, and especially from Barbara Russell who not only helped me to find material, but also compiled the new family trees. The work of other scholars and the memoirs of those who knew the Stracheys have been extremely important in this work and I wish to thank Michael Holroyd, Bill Lubenow, Frances Partridge, Peter Stansky, and the late Barbara Strachey for sharing with me their personal knowledge of the Stracheys and the results of their own extensive research into Bloomsbury.

A number of friends have indulged or shared my preoccupation with the Stracheys over many years, offering very helpful suggestions and critical insights that they may well find incorporated into the book. I wish particularly to thank Sally Alexander, Christine Battersby, Ellen Dubois, Jane Caplan, Joan Landes, Moira Gatens, Leela Gandhi, Vivian Gornick, Jose Harris, Jeri Johnson, Alison Light, Ruth McMullen, Ros Pesman, Rosemary Pringle, and Ellen Ross. Ruth Poisson and Sophie Watson both offered the generous hospitality that makes doing research in London such a pleasure—and Sophie Watson and Russell Hay were wonderful companions in the many months that I spent poring over Strachey papers in the British Library. Their interest in the unfolding Strachey story, and Sophie's links to this Bloomsbury world, added greatly to my enjoyment of the research. I owe very special thanks to two other friends. Glenda Sluga has shared my interest in this project from the beginning, offering many insights from her own extensive knowledge of the history of feminism and of questions of gender in relation to nationalism, and imperialism. Pauline Nestor has helped immeasurably with the writing of the book. I have discussed almost every aspect of it with her, often over very pleasant dinners, and her critical intelligence and sense of humour have been invaluable.

As a family that prided itself on its administrative capacities and traditions, the Stracheys were, for the most part, very good keepers of records. Hence the archival material is both extensive and rich. It is now widely dispersed and I have used the resources of many different libraries. I thank the staff and the trustees of the following libraries for assistance and for access to the material in their collections: the Oriental and India Office Library for access to the Strachey papers, the Lytton papers, and the Salisbury papers; the Manuscript Room in the British Library for access to the Strachey papers, the Keynes papers, and the Havelock Ellis papers; the Women's Library for access to the Papers of Jane Maria, Pernel and Philippa Strachey, and to their Autograph Letter Collections; the British Institute of Psycho-Analysis for access to their collection of Strachey papers and their correspondence files; the Berg Collection in the New York Public Library, the Harry Ransom Center at the University of Texas, and the University of Princeton Library for the Strachey papers that they hold. I thank the University of Sussex Library for access to the Papers of Leonard Woolf; the Provost and Scholars of King's College, Cambridge for access to the Papers of Maynard Keynes; the Principal of Newnham College for access to the college records, and the Lilley Library at the University of Indiana for access to the Papers of Ray Strachey in the Hannah Whitall Smith Collection. I thank the Bibliothèque Nationale for access to the correspondence of Dorothy Bussy, Andre Gide, and Roger Martin du Gard. I also wish to thank the archivists at St Paul's School in London, at Clifton College, at Balliol College and Lady Margaret Hall in Oxford, and at Newnham College for their helpful responses to my queries about the Stracheys.

For permission to publish extracts from the letters of Lytton Strachey, I thank the Strachey Trust and the British Society of Authors. For permission to publish the picture of Jane and Richard Strachey in India, I thank the Oriental and India Office Library at the British Library. For their help in supplying me with Strachey pictures and for permission to publish the Strachey photographs and the sketches by Ray Strachey that I have chosen from their collection, I thank the National Portrait Gallery. For supplying the print and for permission to publish the portrait of Lady Strachey by Dora Carrington, I thank the National Portrait Gallery of Scotland.

In writing this book, I have benefited greatly from the opportunity to give papers at a number of different seminars and thank all those involved for the helpful comments and suggestions. I wish particularly to thank the Feminist History and the Psychoanalysis and History seminars at the Institute of Historical Research in London; the History seminars at Bryn Mawr, Pennsylvania State University, Monash University, the University of Sydney, the Research School of Social Sciences at the Australian National University, and the Women's' Studies Seminar at UCLA.

Giselle Antmann and Carla Lipsig-Mummé read sections of the manuscript and David Garrioch, Pauline Nestor, and Glenda Sluga read it in its entirely. I thank them all for their extremely helpful comments and suggestions.

I wish to express my immense gratitude to the Australian Research Council for the Large Grants that enabled me both to do much of the research for this book and to take time off teaching in order to write it.

I would like to thank Ruth Parr and Anne Gelling and the editorial and marketing teams at Oxford University Press for their enthusiasm for this project—and for their patience. I want also to thank Lucy Bland whose report and comments on the manuscript were invaluable.

Finally I want to thank my family. My own siblings, Geoffrey, Diana, and Louise Caine, continue to give me insights into both the complexity and the rewards of family relationships. Larry Boyd, as always, not only offers love and support, but keeps our life and our home going through all my absences and neglect of even my share of domestic and family responsibilities. Tessa and Nicholas Boyd-Caine offer the affection, interest, and scepticism that enable one to maintain a sense of reality in the midst of absorption into other lives and times. My mother, Peggy Caine, and my aunt, Rhona Ovedoff, have shared my interest in history and biography generally, and in the Stracheys and Bloomsbury in particular, for decades. It a great source of sadness to me that neither of them lived to see this book finished, and I dedicate it to their memory.

B.C.
Melbourne 2003

Contents

List of Illustrations

between pp. 238 and 239

Frontispiece: Pippa Strachey in a rickshaw in India, surrounded by her liveried rickshawmen

1. The Stracheys and friends in Simla, *c*.1860s

2. a) John and Richard Strachey
   b) Sir Richard Strachey in full dress uniform, *c*.1870s
   c) Portrait of Sir Richard Strachey by Simon Bussy, *c*.1900

3. a) Jane Strachey, *c*.1860
   b) Portrait of Jane Strachey by Dora Carrington, 1920

4. Family groups:
   a) Four generations of women: Jane Strachey with her mother, daughter, and granddaughter, *c*.1880s
   b) Richard Strachey and his daughters, *c*.1890s

5. The Strachey family, *c*.1890s

6. The Strachey children, *c*.1890s

7. a) Dick Strachey
   b) Ralph Strachey
   c) Margaret Strachey with her sons, Dick and John, 1908
   d) Ralph Strachey with the same sons, Dick and John, *c*.1911

8. a) Dorothy, Simon, and Jamie Bussy, *c*.1912
   b) Dorothy Bussy, *c*.1930
   c) Simon Bussy, *c*.1930

9. a) Pippa Strachey in the Women's Land Army outfit she loved to wear in the country, *c*.1918
   b) Pippa Straachey in more formal attire

10. a) Pernel Strachey
    b) Pernel and Pippa Strachey, *c*.1930

xii

11. a) Ray Strachey (nee Costelloe), 1911
     b) Oliver Strachey, 1911
     c) Ray Strachey, self-portrait
     d) Oliver Strachey, playing solitaire, *c*.1914

12. a) Lytton Strachey as a child
     b) James Strachey as a child
     c) James and Lytton Strachey, *c*.1905

13. a) Marjorie Strachey, *c*.1900
     b) Marjorie and Lytton Strachey playing chess, 1920s

14. Ray Strachey's sketches.
     a) Lytton Strachey
     b) Alix Strachey

15. a) Alix Strachey, *c*.1960s
     b) James Strachey, *c*.1960s

16. a) Lytton and Pernel Strachey
     b) Jane Strachey with her granddaughter, Barbara

Abbreviations

ALC	Autograph Letter Collections
BC	New York Library, Berg Collection
BIP	British Institute of Psychoanalysis
BL	British Library Manuscript Collection
BN	Bibliothèque Nationale
HRC	Harry Ransom Center
IO	British Library Oriental and India Office Collections
KC	King's College
LL	Lilley Library, University of Indiana
NC	Newnham College Archives
NUWSS	National Union of Women's Suffrage Societies
PUL	Princeton University Library
SUL	Sussex University Library
UCL	University College Library
WL	Women's Library
WSPU	Women's Social and Political Union

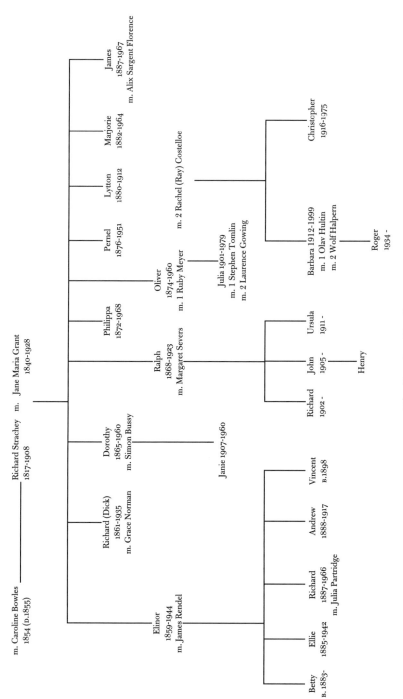

Richard Strachey m. Jane Maria Grant
1817-1908   1840-1928

m. Caroline Bowles
1854 (D.1855)

Elinor
1859-1944
m. James Rendel

Richard (Dick)
1861-1935
m. Grace Norman

Dorothy
1865-1960
m. Simon Bussy

Ralph
1868-1923
m. Margaret Severs

Philippa
1872-1968

Oliver
1874-1960
m. 1 Ruby Meyer

Pernel
1876-1951

Lytton
1880-1912

Marjorie
1882-1964

James
1887-1967
m. Alix Sargent Florence

Betty
b. 1883-

Ellie
1885-1942

Richard
1887-1966
m. Julia Partridge

Andrew
1888-1917

Vincent
b.1898

Janie 1907-1960

Richard
1902 -

John
1905 -

Ursula
1911 -

Henry

Julia 1901-1979
m. 1 Stephen Tomlin
m. 2 Laurence Gowing

m. 2 Rachel (Ray) Costelloe

Barbara 1912-1999
m. 1 Olav Hultin
m. 2 Wolf Halpern

Christopher
1916-1975

Roger
1934 -

The Strachey Family

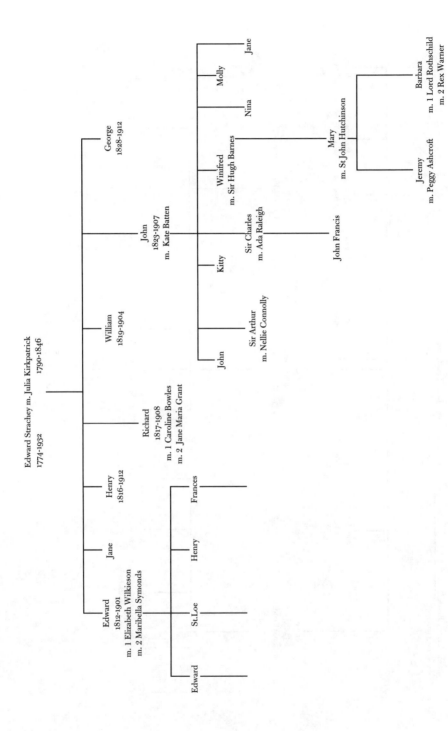

The Extended Strachey Family

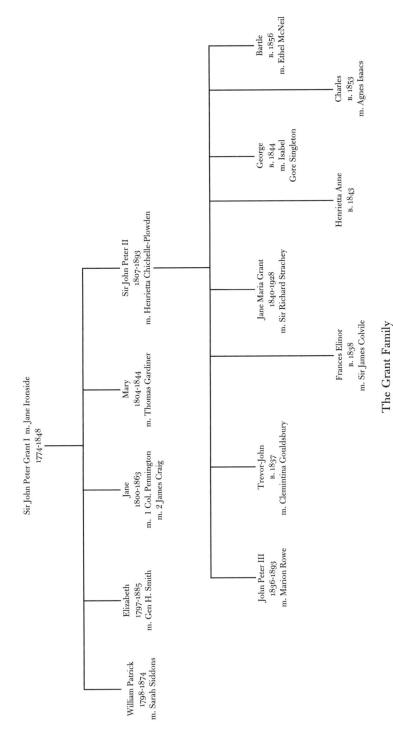

The Grant Family

Sir John Peter Grant I m. Jane Ironside
1774-1848

William Patrick
1798-1874
m. Sarah Siddons

Elizabeth
1797-1885
m. Gen H. Smith

Jane
1800-1863
m. 1 Col. Pennington
m. 2 James Craig

Mary
1804-1844
m. Thomas Gardiner

Sir John Peter II
1807-1893
m. Henrietta Chichelle-Plowden

John Peter III
1836-1893
m. Marion Rowe

Trevor-John
B. 1837
m. Clemintina Gouldsbury

Frances Elinor
B. 1838
m. Sir James Colvile

Jane Maria Grant
1840-1928
m. Sir Richard Strachey

Henrietta Anne
B. 1843

George
B. 1844
m. Isabel
Gore Singleton

Charles
B. 1853
m. Agnes Isaacs

Bartle
B. 1856
m. Ethel McNeil

Introduction

This book began as a study of the Strachey women and grew out of my research on the history of English feminism. As I was working through the records of the women's suffrage movement in 1994, I came increasingly to think that the story of Jane Strachey and her daughters, Philippa and Pernel, offered a rare insight into British feminist interests and activities spanning two generations and more than half a century, from the 1890s until the 1950s. An added interest was provided by one of Jane's daughters-in-law, Ray Strachey, whose book, *The Cause*, still remains one of the best-known histories of the British women's movement. Ray married into the Strachey family in 1911, bringing into the Strachey story both a woman who combined a working life with marriage and a particularly close female friendship. Her devotion to Pippa Strachey was far more important in her life than was her brief interest in Oliver Strachey, the man that she married. Indeed, it is hard not to see her as marrying him largely because of her desire to connect herself closely to his sister. Not all the Strachey women were feminists, however, and the youngest two, Marjorie and Alix, provide an interesting contrast to the others. Marjorie, the youngest Strachey daughter, was both a black sheep and a casualty within the family. 'Gumbo' as she was known to Vanessa Bell and others within Bloomsbury, was renowned for her high spirits, her eccentricity, and her complete lack of ordinary social graces. There was always something slightly paradoxical about her as she combined what Virginia Woolf referred to as 'a peculiar touch of genius in being blatantly obscene' with an extraordinarily rigid

1

moral code.[1] She was a source of both amusement and embarrassment to family and friends and, unlike her older sisters, seems never quite to have worked out what she wanted to do or how she wanted to live. Alix Sargent Florence was similar in age to Marjorie. She married James, the youngest Strachey son. Unlike Ray, she never became close to the other Strachey women. Along with her close friend, Dora Carrington, Alix was one of the group of young women Virginia Woolf described as 'Bloomsbury Crop heads'. She was a thoroughly modern young woman who pursued James Strachey relentlessly for some years until he finally agreed to marry her. For the rest of her life, she worked alongside him translating the work of Sigmund Freud and of other prominent psychoanalysts including Melanie Klein. Alix was very much an 'emancipated woman', but one who regarded the feminism of her own mother and of the other Strachey women as boring, irrelevant, and outmoded.

The differences amongst the Strachey women would, I thought, allow me to explore not only some of the changes and developments within organized feminist activity, but also to show the difficulties feminists faced in attracting younger women to their cause. A study of the Strachey women would also require discussion of women's college and university life in the early twentieth century, and of the ways in which the first generation of British career women set about organizing their personal and professional lives. In the case of Ray Strachey, this meant balancing a career with children and a family. Alix and Marjorie Strachey also raised other questions about the ways in which self-consciously 'modern' women in the early twentieth century rejected their feminist antecedents. They served at the same time to link the Stracheys more closely into Bloomsbury and to raise more generally questions about the connection between feminism and English modernism.

As I read more and more of the voluminous family correspondence, however, the idea of discussing the Strachey women without encompassing the Strachey men became impossible. Jane Strachey had been a devoted and much beloved wife. She adored her husband and confided in him. He was both her most intimate companion and her most regular and important correspondent. It is thus impossible to understand her feminism, her public life, or her connection with her daughters without dealing also with her marriage. This was equally the case with both Ray and Alix Strachey, women whose very connection with the Strachey family came through marriage. Indeed, as I came to see, the contrast between the various Strachey marriages was itself a fascinating subject. Richard and Jane Strachey had an exemplary companionate marriage of a particularly Victorian kind. By contrast, Oliver and Ray, and later James and Alix, had 'modern' marriages, in which infidelity and sexual experimentation were accepted, taken for granted, and sometimes openly discussed. Even those Strachey women who did not marry could not be adequately depicted without discussing their close relationships to their father and brothers. Lytton and Ralph Strachey were both immensely important to Pippa, for example, and her story cannot be told without them. Like so many other recent feminist historians, I found, as I delved more and more into the family, that questions about gender, about how masculinity and femininity were understood and changed within the family, were central to any analysis of it. Indeed, one of the most interesting themes here centres on the changing place of men and women within the family as the Stracheys, which had been very much a patriarchal family in the nineteenth century, came effectively to be headed by Pippa, a single daughter, in the twentieth.

Expanding the focus to include the whole family also brought more clearly to the fore the central importance of the family's Indian connections and its imperial outlook. The Stracheys traced their involvement in India back to the days of Robert Clive in the late eighteenth century and their imperial heritage was something they valued very highly. Richard Strachey spent almost forty years in India and played a significant role in establishing the system of public works that was so central to British control of the subcontinent in the later nineteenth century. His wife, Jane Grant, also came from an imperial family. They married in Calcutta in 1859 and were still there when their first child was born in the following year. The Strachey's Indian experiences, their sense of close connection with other 'Anglo-Indian' families, and their ideal of service to the British Raj were central to their lives and to their sense of personal identity.[2] They took it for granted that their sons would follow their father into Indian service.

The Strachey children in turn grew up in a world dominated by India. Their mother attempted from their earliest years to imbue her children with a sense of imperial duty and splendour. Kipling took his place, alongside Virgil and Goethe, in her compilation of *Nursery Lyrics* and she urged her sons to read *The Lives of Indian Officers*. The older children had a particularly intimate sense of their connection with India. Several of them spent part of their infancy there and they heard constantly about it in the periods during which they remained in Britain while their parents were in

India. They grew up imbued with their mother's sense of the immense ability and significance of their father to the Raj—and indeed, with a sense that the government of India and the India Office depended entirely upon him and his brother, John. Oliver expressed this feeling clearly in the letter he wrote congratulating his father on his appointment to the chairmanship of the East India Railway in 1888. 'It is very surprising that you are going to be Chairman of the East India Railway Company & appears to me rather rapid', he wrote. 'I can't think how they'll do without you at the India Office, but as long as they've got uncle John, I suppose they can scramble on.'[3]

Richard Strachey's role in India was a source of great pride to his children, but it also caused them considerable disruption and unhappiness. His years in India made necessary long periods of separation from the family. Indeed, the younger Stracheys had almost no experience of a settled home life until Richard resigned from his Indian post in the 1870s. Moreover, while everyone in the family relished their father's success, it carried a high cost for some. For the older Strachey sons in particular, India was primarily the place in which their father had made his name and set the pattern that they were expected to follow. They were destined from childhood to follow him into Indian service. None of them approached his success, however, or felt as closely connected to India as he had done, and their India was a harder, harsher, and lonelier place than that known to their parents. They found themselves stationed in isolated territories, far not only from home, but also from the main centres of the Raj, and all questioned frequently what they were doing there.

Going to India divided the Strachey sons not only from the wider society, but also from their families. Richard and Jane Strachey were always surrounded by family in India, and were at one with their own parents and siblings in their imperial beliefs. This was not the case for their children, some of whom never set foot in India. Oliver, the third Strachey son, protested at being sent to India—and managed to stay there for quite a short time. Lytton and James, the two younger sons, absolutely rejected the idea of Indian or any other form of imperial service. Far from inspiring them, the example of their older brothers confirmed their sense that going to India was the worst possible thing that could happen to them. Lytton expounded at some length on his sense of 'the horror of the solitude and the wretchedness of every single creature out there',[4] and of the effects of spending years and years away from civilization. He used his brothers as an

4

example in seeking to dissuade one of his friends from applying for imperial service. 'I've seen my brothers and what's happened to them', he wrote, 'and it's sickening to think of.'[5]

The failure of the two older brothers to make their mark in India left them vulnerable and isolated both in India and back in Britain. As the last of the family to go to India, and as unhappy exiles there, they mark a midway point in the change of the Stracheys from an imperial Victorian family to a modern Edwardian one. The criticisms of imperialism becoming widespread amongst some liberals and progressives within Britain were even evident in the Strachey family in the early twentieth century. By 1911, both Lytton and James were involved with groups who rejected imperial values as central to their sense of themselves as 'modern' and advanced young men. They came increasingly to regard their older siblings who believed in or were involved with the empire as reactionary beings from another age. But there were marked changes even amongst those older siblings who did not question the virtues of imperial rule. The single Strachey sisters, for example, who had benefited from some of the expanding opportunities for women in the later nineteenth century, led new kinds of lives that incorporated professional and public activities and a strong sense of autonomy. Their approach to life was almost unthinkable to the brothers who had begun married life in India and accepted the values of the Raj.

India functioned in a very different way for Elinor and Dorothy, the oldest two sisters, who spent some of their childhood and adolescent years there, years which were in some ways as enjoyable and as magical as those of their mother. They enjoyed possibly a closer companionship with their mother in India than any of the Stracheys ever knew back home, and were warmly welcomed by their parents' friends. Their participation in Raj society was pleasurable and exciting, and opened to them, as it did to their mother, aristocratic circles that they did not meet in Britain. Following her mother here, as elsewhere, Elinor Strachey married into another 'distinguished Anglo-Indian' family and maintained through her husband an ongoing connection with India. But she did not ever live there after childhood. Pippa was the only Strachey daughter to visit India as an adult, and doing so changed her life. Imperial life offered her, as it did other feminists, not only adventure and excitement, but also a sense of power and authority. Unlike her brothers, Pippa Strachey managed to mobilize the family name and influence when she was in India, thus ensuring that she had an extremely enjoyable time. An unexpected family crisis required her to act as head of the extended family, and the ease with which she did so effectively established her in this position for life. The extended trip to India she made in 1900 thus gave her the confidence to leave the sphere of family and home and embark on a public life.

Even those Stracheys like Lytton and James who sought entirely to reject the familial imperial framework were unable to do so. Unlike their older siblings, they were both closely involved with individuals who were strongly opposed both to particular imperial policies and to the whole foundation of imperialism. Two of Lytton's closest friends, Leonard Woolf and Maynard Keynes, wrote to him respectively from the India Office and from Ceylon, expressing their growing opposition to imperial claims and practices. It is perhaps these conflicting pressures that explain a paradox evident some years later. In 1920, Lytton Strachey managed to write a family portrait in which there was no reference to India or to any connection with it.[6] Two years later, he demanded that his older brothers exert all their influence as Anglo-Indians on his behalf to enable him to become a member of the Oriental Club![7] He saw it as the ideal place to get over the strain he felt after writing *Queen Victoria*—and it was a place where he could comment satirically on the other nabobs, while giving free rein to his own orientalist imagination. Interesting and complex as it is, the question of how to deal with the Stracheys' Indian history within this work was a difficult one. It is here, more than in any other aspect of their lives, that one faces a complete contrast between their view of themselves and the assessment of later generations. Richard Strachey, like his brother John, is a familiar figure in much of the postcolonial writing of recent decades. The Strachey brothers were very powerful figures in establishing the administrative framework of the Raj. They shared to the full the late Victorian sense of the importance and the virtues of the British Empire—and its sense of Indian inferiority, incompetence, and backwardness that made it possible to see themselves as dedicated rulers, bringing enlightenment and good government to a benighted people. The Stracheys valued their own contributions to India very highly indeed, although the consequences of their approach to finance and to public works have been seriously questioned since. In this study, I have attempted both to show and to explore their imperial beliefs and attitudes, and to offer a critical analysis of them in the light of recent postcolonial scholarship.

Just as expanding the focus to include the whole family brought their Indian involvement into greater prominence, so too it altered the way in which other aspects of the Strachey story could be told. Feminism, for example, was important not just to the Strachey women, but also to the men. Jane Strachey's enthusiasm for the cause and that of her daughters necessarily meant that Richard and his sons had some involvement too, although they sometimes found the enthusiasm of their womenfolk a little hard to bear. Richard certainly supported Jane's demands for a first-class education for their daughters and took great pride in their educational successes—which were considerably more notable than were those of their sons. Here, too, gender became an interesting issue, as the Strachey family offers a rare insight into the very different experiences of boys and girls or young men and women both at school and at university in the later nineteenth and early twentieth centuries.

As it now stands, the book is as much a family as a feminist biography. It takes as its starting point the marriage of Richard Strachey and Jane Grant in India in 1859, and ends with the death of Pippa, the last of their children, just over one hundred years later. It is also a history of the Stracheys, linking their lives and activities to several of the central themes of British imperial, cultural, and social history across the period. This is not to suggest that the Stracheys were in any way a typical upper middle class family. On the contrary, they were clearly exceptional in their intelligence and in their contribution to imperialism and to British intellectual and cultural life. Their very prominence in imperial administration and science in the nineteenth century, however, or in feminism and women's education, in the study of biography, and in new approaches to sexuality in the twentieth, links their lives and ideas and with broader historical developments.

To emphasize the ways in which this work combines biography and history, I have chosen a thematic rather than a chronological structure. The first chapter deals with the Stracheys and India and explores the importance of imperialism and of their connection with India across the two generations. This is followed by a number of biographical chapters that follow a pattern now widespread amongst those writing family or collective biographies by organizing chapters around life stages: childhood, education, adult life, careers, etc. This enables the stories of each individual to be told while at the same time allowing one to see the changes that occurred within the family over time. The oldest Strachey child was nearly thirty years older than her youngest sibling and there were many changes, not only within the family, but in the wider society, which affected their daily lives. These chapters are followed by ones dealing with the Stracheys' ideas and with their intellectual, political, and literary activity. They focus on their understanding of gender and of 'modernity', their involvement in feminism, and their literary activity.

The history of the family as an institution was a popular field in the 1960s and 1970s as the rise of social history brought a new emphasis on an institution seen as basic to any society and historical period. Recently family history has been subject to considerable scrutiny and criticism, however. Feminists continue to point out not only how significant the family was and often still is in the oppression of women, but how hard it is to hear women's voices within a familial framework that usually privileges a male head. The constant study of the family, moreover, has been seen as reifying it and as continuing to privilege a particular normative model of the family—rather than to explore the many different ways in which people organize their emotional, sexual, and economic lives. The language of family, as many scholars have shown, serves to suggest that something that is complex, shifting, and varied, and often imaginary is permanent and real. The use of surnames to designate a family, as Leonore Davidoff has recently argued, rather than providing an accurate listing or statement of relationship and connection, creates imagined families which express our desire for unity and attachment to others.[8] Names are used to indicate boundaries between belonging and not belonging. But the entities to which the names apply rarely fit together in any coherent or functional way.

I want to draw on some of this recent literature, by exploring the complex and changing ways in which the Stracheys understood and thought about themselves as a 'family', and to show the importance to them of the Strachey name. Richard and Jane Strachey were extremely conscious both of their heritage and of their extensive familial connections. Extended family was integral to their lives and they frequently lived and worked with siblings and cousins. The value they placed on the Strachey name encompassed its place within an extended kinship network and social world, much of which could be seen at Jane Strachey's regular Sunday afternoon 'at homes' where the extended family always gathered. There, as Lytton Strachey later recalled, Grants, Battens, Plowdens, Ridpaths, and many other imperial families that had marital connections with the Stracheys could regularly be seen.⁹ The children of Richard and Jane Strachey, by contrast, made no attempts to maintain contact with other branches of the family. Indeed, while all of them remained close to particular siblings, some of the younger ones rarely even saw their older brothers and sisters and felt little sense of kinship with them at all. For their own support in daily life, many found or created alternate family groups: Pernel among the women dons of Cambridge, for example, and Lytton Strachey among his Bloomsbury friends.

While the younger Stracheys may not have cared as much as their mother did about maintaining all their family connections, they shared absolutely her sense of the importance of their name and a strong sense of what a 'Strachey' was. All of them cherished a sense of the longevity and distinction of the Strachey name and took pride in their imperial and intellectual heritage. They also took a great interest in political and public affairs and prided themselves on being well read and knowledgeable about contemporary literary and cultural developments. The family's intellectual framework shifted markedly across the nineteenth century. Few of the younger Stracheys shared their father's mathematical or scientific interests, feeling more at home with their mother's literary ones. Indeed, by the end of the nineteenth century, the family library was probably their most important possession and it was reading and their passion for amateur theatricals that bound them most closely to each other. A continuation of Richard's mathematical interests was still evident, primarily in the games and puzzles that he devised for and engaged in with his sons although increasingly crossword puzzles took over as the family's preferred recreational activity.

This shift in family interest and outlook was accompanied by other changes which are evident in the changing resonances of the name Strachey and its meaning and significance to those who bore it. The Strachey name always evoked particular ideas, activities, and achievements as well as a sense of family. In the nineteenth century, as Virginia Woolf noted, the Stracheys were regarded by others and by themselves primarily as 'a distinguished Anglo-Indian family'.¹⁰ According to *The Times* of 1882, Richard Strachey and his brother, Sir John, were amongst the very few Indian officials whose names were generally known to the British public. They were regarded then, as they still are by some contemporary historians, as a dominating force in determining the policy and outlook of the

Raj.[11] Their name had resonance in scientific and literary circles too. It thus ensured a certain degree of prominence and brought younger members of the family social contacts wherever they were. At the same time, it carried both obligations and expectations which could be a considerable burden. Indeed, it sometimes seems as if the older sons were crushed beneath its weight.

By the early twentieth century, however, the family's imperial glory was coming to an end and the Strachey name came to be associated with quite other attitudes and activities. As Lytton Strachey became prominent, it was his wit and demeanour that the name came to evoke. His high-pitched voice, dandified dress, and demand for sexual tolerance and freedom of sexual expression made him as notable a figure in Cambridge in the early years of the twentieth-century as it was later to do in Bloomsbury.[12] He seemed to many to typify early twentieth century British 'modernity' in his life, his attitudes, his dress and his demeanour—as well as in his critical and satirical analysis of Victorian England. There were others too who added their contribution to a linking of the Strachey name with modernity. For those connected to the British psychoanalytic community, the name Strachey was inseparable from James and Alix's work of translating Freud and thus disseminating his ideas. The Strachey approach to Freud has become increasingly controversial in recent years, but it dominated the twentieth-century understanding of psychoanalysis. For feminists and feminist historians, the name is an important one too. It brings immediately to mind Ray Strachey, author of *The Cause*, perhaps the most vivid and triumphal account of English feminist achievements ever written, and a dominating presence in the inter-war British women's movement.[13]

III

Anyone seeking to write about the Stracheys has for a start to come to terms with the many Strachey stories and impressions that abounded within the family itself as well as in Bloomsbury and the wider British literary world. One of the most engaging of these was provided by Leonard Woolf, who spent many evenings with them in the early years of the twentieth century when he and Lytton Strachey were students at Cambridge. The Stracheys, Woolf wrote, 'stand out in my memory as much the most remarkable family I have ever known, an extinct phenomenon which has passed away and will never be known again'. Woolf was struck by the ways in which the family's history was a continuous living thing. He noted particularly their sense of close connection with the British Raj and with British politics and literature from the eighteenth century to the present. At dinner, someone might mention George IV or Warren Hastings as if they knew him. 'I felt', commented Woolf, 'that whereas I was living in 1902, they were living in 1774–1902 . . . The atmosphere of the dining-room at Lancaster Gate was that of British history and of the comparatively small ruling middle class which for the last 100 years had been the principal makers of British history.'

The level of intelligence in each son and daughter and in the father and mother was incredibly, fantastically high. They were all, like their mother, passionately intellectual, most of them with very quick minds and lively imaginations . . . Their chief recreation was conversation and they adored conversational speculation which usually led to argument. When six or seven Stracheys became involved in an argument over the dinner table, as almost always happened, the roar and rumble, the shrill shrieks, the bursts of laughter, the sound and fury of excitement were deafening and to an unprepared stranger paralysing.[14]

Leonard Woolf's sense of the intelligence, intellectual vitality, and sense of fun evident in the Stracheys was shared by many. Ray Strachey, for example, who became increasingly anti-social around the time of the First World War, eschewed all Bloomsbury and other entertainments, but could never resist a Strachey family party.

Not everyone felt like this, however, and Leonard Woolf and Ray Strachey's pictures are very different from that drawn by Virginia Woolf. 'There are three words knocking about in my brain to use of Stracheys', she wrote in 1918:

a prosaic race, lacking magnanimity, shorn of atmosphere. As these words have occurred automatically, & will tease me till written down, I daresay there is some truth in them. It is an air, a vapour, an indescribable taste of dust in the throat, something tickling & irritating as well as tingling & stimulating. But then one must combine with this a great variety of mental gifts & gifts of character—honesty, loyalty, intelligence of a spiritual order . . . when I think of a Strachey, I think of someone infinitely cautious, elusive and unadventurous. To the common stock of our set they have added phrases, standards & witticisms, but never any new departure; never an Omega, a Post Impressionist movement, nor even a country cottage, a Brunswick Square, a printing press.[15]

Virginia Woolf's view of the rigidity and even the aridity of the Stracheys was echoed by David Garnett. While her closest contact with the family came through Lytton, Garnett's first contact was with Lytton's younger brother, James. 'I was immediately struck in him', Garnett later recalled, 'by what I later discovered was a very marked characteristic of the whole family: an astonishing inelasticity of values, a rigid adherence to certain limitations which they have imposed upon themselves ... To know Stracheys well, one has to be ready to accept the atmosphere in which they live.'[16] In Garnett's view, the Stracheys also insisted on imposing their views and truths upon those they were with. His autobiography contains several incidents in which either James or Lytton Strachey were present, and in the course of which they managed absolutely to insist that others accepted their values, their ideas of appropriate behaviour, and above all a general sense of the importance of catering to their particular needs and demands. Invariably this meant a reduction in animal spirits and fun—and a turn to more serious intellectual matters. When Garnett first met James Strachey, he had been on a walking holiday with Noel Olivier, a close friend of James, and two of her sisters. They were a group of carefree young people, enjoying the countryside and showing little concern for decorum or for following the normal middle-class family patterns in terms of proper meals or daily programme. They met James at a country cottage where he was convalescing after a brief illness. James 'immediately transformed our party and, by tea-time, my careless companions were scarcely recognisable; the body was forgotten, the mind supreme'. The group did tease James a little, but the teasing was mixed with respect—and recognition of the need to ensure that James's health and comfort were assured. Between every meal, 'a glass of ovaltine was prepared and administered to James as though it were a sacrificial rite'.[17]

Although often serious and always intellectual, the Stracheys were not lacking in either a sense of humour or a capacity for enjoyment. On the contrary, the sense of a 'Strachey atmosphere' owed much to a number of shared family pastimes that were enjoyed by all. Reading was of course the most important activity for the Stracheys—and their habit of reading at table when guests were not invited was a source of considerable comment amongst their friends. But the Stracheys also shared a passion for many different puzzles and games. Richard Strachey devised mathematical puzzles that he sent to his sons, but these were augmented by others. Oliver loved bridge and both played and wrote about it for many years. The others all took to crosswords and acrostics with immense enthusiasm. Their importance was perhaps underlined by the role they played in times of extremity. Thus Pippa spent hours doing crossword puzzles with her blind mother in Jane Strachey's final years—as indeed she did with Lytton in his final days. Not all Strachey pastimes were intellectual ones, however. Music and dancing were also important to them—and almost every member of the family played a musical instrument. Indeed, a piano was an absolute requisite of any Strachey home. Pernel bought one when she was at Newnham, and both Oliver and Ralph insisted on having pianos with them in India. But here too, one can see the ways in which family and tradition structured Strachey pastimes. Thus the dance that they took up with most enthusiasm was the Scottish reel. Leonard Woolf recalled the time when Pippa decided that the younger Stracheys and their friends 'should all be taught by her to dance Highland dances' and arranged evening parties 'at which about twenty young people ... practised this difficult art under the lively and exacting tuition of Pippa'.[18]

These shared pleasure, like their enjoyment of discussion and argument, all contributed to a sense of the Stracheys as sharing a number of characteristics. Amongst their friends and associates, as indeed within the family itself, the very utterance of the Strachey name always conjured up not just particular people, but also specific qualities. There was little agreement as to what these qualities were, from whom they were inherited, or how important a part they played in anyone's lives, although most people included the very slender Strachey body and the Strachey spectacles. But everyone who knew the Stracheys had a favourite set. Many members of the extended Strachey family insisted that all Stracheys inherited the qualities that went with the name through the paternal line.[19] Lytton Strachey sometimes shared this view, reducing his friends to mirth when he insisted that James, the least organized or commanding of men, had inherited from their father the qualities of a great imperial administrator.[20] His sisters, by contrast, like Leonard Woolf, saw the distinctive qualities of Lytton and of themselves as ones that came through the Grant family from their mother.[21]

IV

The Stracheys' sense of their own history, tradition, and importance is of great assistance to anyone wanting to write about them. They were inveterate and in some cases immensely talented letter-writers and, as a significant family with a long tradition of imperial administration, they tended to keep the letters and documents which came into the household. Thus for the most part, the correspondence of Richard and Jane Strachey with each other, with their children and with their extended families and friends are extant. This family tradition of keeping papers passed down at least to some of their children and Pippa, Dorothy, Lytton, and James kept most of their letters. Some of this correspondence is already quite well-known, especially that of Lytton Strachey with his Bloomsbury friends; James with Rupert Brooke and with his wife, Alix; and Dorothy Bussy with André Gide.[22] But there are other wonderful collections of letters which remain largely unexplored. The letters of Pippa Strachey to her mother and her siblings, for example, bring vividly to life her travels in India, her work in the women's movement, and her relationships with some of her siblings. In a similar way, the letters James received from his long-time lover Noel Olivier make wonderful reading. Inevitably there are gaps in the correspondence, however. Letters that came into the Strachey home were kept, but not always those that went to children living elsewhere. Lytton and James Strachey kept all their correspondence, but other members of the family were less certain of the significance of their lives, or less stable in their domestic environments or simply less careful. Thus there are few of the family's letters to or indeed of any other letters of Elinor, Dick, Ralph, Oliver, or Marjorie in their adult years. While they were frequent letter-writers, few of the Stracheys kept diaries. As a result, one has little insight into their own introspections or into feelings and thoughts which they did not regard as suitable for direct communication. But this absence is itself significant: the lack of diary keeping is an indication of the disinclination for introspection amongst many members of the family. Pippa, for example, would have found it quite as difficult to express her feelings in words to herself as she did to anyone else. The tensions around the very question of keeping a diary are articulated well by one Strachey sister-in-law, Ray. She kept a diary intermittently, wanting somewhere to record things and feeling that the discipline of regular reporting was a good thing. But she was never able to confide to it directly matters that were of greatest moment to her— and hinted at rather than addressing them directly. She constantly reiterated her fears that members of her family would try to find and read it, but these fears were closely connected to her own intense dislike of any form of intimate revelation. By contrast, Dorothy Bussy, the most emotional of the Stracheys, poured out her doubts, anxieties, and many different sources of anguish regularly in the pages of her journal.

The question of how one reads the many letters is a difficult one. Some of them were public performances, intended to be read aloud or passed from one member of the family to another. Others, like those between Lytton and James, were very intimate and frank, intended only for their immediate recipient. But even here, as Maynard Keynes once commented to Lytton, there was both fear and excitement in the possibility that letters detailing criminal homosexual activity just might fall into the hands of Pippa—and thus demonstrate to their older sisters the daring and risky nature of their modern lives.

Absence of letters, like the absence of diaries, is also important. Silence itself sometimes indicates how relationships worked. Pippa, for example, wrote to and received letters from her siblings frequently. It was she who remained in contact even with the oldest brother, Dick, when few others had anything to do with him. Marjorie, by contrast, was often left without letters, even when there were major family crises—and she in turn seems to have communicated only rarely with her siblings. Thus while the coverage of different members of the family is uneven, the silences sometimes suggest something about the closeness to or distance of individuals from their parents and siblings.

The letters and diaries of people beyond the family are also important in writing about the Stracheys. The most useful are those of Virginia Woolf. She knew the family well and was on terms of quite close friendship with many of them, including their mother. Woolf was fascinated by the Strachey Anglo-Indian heritage, one which she shared, but at a rather greater remove than they. Her emphasis on the importance of the Indian experience within the family, and on its almost mythical status in the life of their mother is something which I wish to explore in detail. She attempted often to characterize individual members of the Strachey family and sometimes to depict the family as a whole. Her comments are sometimes wonderfully insightful and even when open to question, serve to indicate how various members of the family were seen within the Bloomsbury world.

What Woolf's diaries offer in terms of insight into the Stracheys in the period from 1915 until her own death in 1941, Frances Partridge offers for the years after that. Although she became most closely connected with Lytton Strachey through her relationship with Ralph Partridge in the 1920s, Frances Partridge had other connections with the family as well. Julia, the daughter of Oliver Strachey, had been her best friend since her school days and one of her sisters married into the Rendel family. After the death of Ralph, Frances Partridge took a room in the home of Alix and James Strachey and did some work on their translation of Freud. It was James and Alix with whom she remained most closely in touch, but she saw several of the other Stracheys too in their final years.

Both Virginia Woolf and Lytton Strachey are important figures in this study, not just because of the insights their letters and other writings offer into the lives of the Stracheys, but because of their importance in the development of modern biographical writing. Between them, they transformed the writing of biography as well as bringing to the fore major discussions about the literary problems of biography, the question of how to relate public and private life, and the importance of evaluation and impression in biographical writing. As others have commented before, while their differing but always imaginative approaches offer inspiration, their many critical comments on the work of others serves as a dire warning to anyone foolhardy enough to address their lives.

An Anglo-Indian Family

It is impossible to overstate the importance of India in the lives of the Stracheys. Both Richard and Jane Strachey described themselves as 'Anglo-Indians' and took immense pride in the term. They used it, of course, in its nineteenth-century sense as one referring, not to those born in India of mixed British and Indian descent, but rather to those English families and individuals who spent time engaged in imperial service in India. Thus their sense of themselves as Anglo-Indian was inseparable from their sense of connection to Britain's imperial mission. Jane Strachey made this absolutely clear in a speech she made to the Lyceum Club in London in 1910. 'My family and my husband's family', she explained, 'belong to that class of Anglo-Indians whose lives have been spent in the arduous and noble service of rescuing the natives of India from intolerable oppression & in building up such an example of government by foreign conquerors as the world has never before seen.'[1]

Service in India was very much a family tradition in the nineteenth century for both Richard Strachey and for his wife. '*Our* connection with India', Jane had told her audience at the Lyceum club, 'stretches continuously from the days of Clive and Warren Hastings to the present day.' As family records make clear, Richard Strachey's grandfather, Henry Strachey, was the first member of the family to go to India as secretary to Robert Clive in 1764. Henry's son, Edward, followed his father to India as a company writer for the East India Company in 1793. While there, he married Julia Kirkpatrick, daughter of another Anglo-Indian family in 1808. Edward Strachey returned home in 1811, becoming an Assistant Examiner of Correspondence concerning judicial matters in the East

India Company a few years later. He held a position of considerable authority and importance, working alongside James Mill. His sons were educated at various East India Company colleges before following him into Indian service.[2]

Richard Strachey was thus destined to go to India from his infancy. As a man with an interest in science and engineering, he found in India a range of possibilities not available to him back home. In the early decades of the nineteenth century, the East India Company had become convinced of the need to develop railways and canals, both to modernize India and to ensure their own better control of it. Richard Strachey played a major part in developing this programme. He remained in India for more than thirty years, visiting Britain during that time, but usually only for quite short periods. When he finally returned 'home' in the 1870s, he continued to be engaged in the development and management of Indian public works, in a range of different forms of scientific investigation of Indian astronomy, botany, and geology, and in general questions of British policy in India. India thus dominated every aspect of his intellectual activity as well as his professional and public life.

His wife, Jane Grant, spent far less time in India than he, but felt just as closely connected to it. She too came from a family with a long tradition of imperial service, and took particular pride in the distinguished career of her father, Sir John Peter Grant, Lieutenant-Governor of the Central Provinces in the 1850s. She was conceived in India and born on the ship taking her mother back home to Britain. She visited her father in Calcutta twice in her childhood, and met and married her husband there. She was in India also for the birth of her first child. Thus India, while not her home for long, was the location of the most important and exciting events in her life.

The Stracheys took particular pride in the importance of their contribution to the British Raj. Richard Strachey and his brother John were regarded as the most significant imperial administrators within their own family and both received considerable public acknowledgement. Whenever the opportunity arose, moreover, they paid fulsome tribute to each other. In the preface to his book on *India: Its Administration and Progress*, John Strachey outlined his sense of the contribution that had been made by Richard.

In my belief, there are few men living who have done so much, often in ways unknown to the outside world, for the improvement of Indian administration. It is to him that India owes the extension of railways and canals which has been crowned with such extraordinary success, which has increased to an incalculable extent the wealth of the country, and has profoundly altered its condition.[3]

Self-congratulatory as this was, it expressed a view to be found elsewhere in Britain at the time. The Stracheys were not universally admired or liked, but their importance in British India was generally recognized. Richard Strachey's obituary in *The Times* offers a good illustration.

When his eminent civilian brother Sir John passed away less than two months ago, we remarked that he had inspired and influenced the Indian Policy of the greater part of the Victorian era to a degree and over a period approached by no other member of the Indian Civil Service and indeed only rivalled by his elder brother Sir Richard. The great achievements of Sir John in the sphere of ordinary administration and finance were at least equalled by Sir Richard in that of providing the Dependency with those great public works which have so beneficently transformed the face of the country and the conditions of life there.[4]

The celebration of the Strachey role in India, so evident during the apogee of imperialism, has, of course been replaced by a much more critical assessment in recent years, when the impact of their ideas on Indians has come to be assessed and their racial views and assumptions critiqued. Their part in determining British financial policy and in the establishment of public works has come under particular scrutiny. The unquestioned belief that the new system of canals and railways developed in the nineteenth century was a great benefit to India has been undermined by contemporary historians, geographers, agricultural experts, and economists seeking to explain the current agricultural problems faced by India—and the decline in Indian life expectancy and per capita income across the nineteenth century. New questions have thus come to be asked about Richard Strachey's approach to Indian irrigation and agriculture. Few doubt that the irrigation canals he advocated 'transformed the face of the country', but many now question whether this transformation was either necessary or beneficial. The 'improvements so praised by the British', Dione and Macleod point out, 'were sometimes brought at great cost to local inhabitants. Irrigation canals often proved breeding grounds for malaria, and railways led to deforestation and erosion.'[5] The canals and the new scale of agriculture served moreover to increase salinity levels in water. Far from reducing food scarcity, market-driven agriculture increased it, leading as it did to the export of rice and grain when they could attain high prices abroad—even when there was dearth and famine within India itself.[6]

The Stracheys' role in relation to the terrible Indian famine of the late 1870s has been particularly subject to question. Richard was the chair of the commission set up to investigate the causes of this famine and to lay down guidelines to avoid its repetition. His report, issued in 1880–1, was welcomed by the government of India who wrote to

express their sense of the admirable manner in which the Commission performed a task of unusual difficulty and magnitude, and record their opinion that they have laid a lasting foundation for the administration of famine relief, and that their proposals will suggest means of economising the strength and resources of the state, and of largely reducing human death and suffering.[7]

Terrible famines continued in India, however, exacerbated, many would argue, by the very measures the Stracheys advocated. Imperial Famine Codes were never seriously directed towards reducing the suffering of famine victims. On the contrary, they were framed by utilitarian and free-market policies that made 'economizing the strength and resources of the state' the primary concern and explicitly excluded the possibility of inter-ventions directed towards assisting the suffering population. The appalling late nineteenth-century famines, Mike Davis has recently argued, were a result not simply of drought and lack of food, but of food being priced in ways that made it unobtainable to the poor. The death tolls of these famines occurred because of the 'fatal meshing of extreme events between the world climate system and the late Victorian world economy'.[8] The Famine Codes promulgated in response, and Davis singles out particularly those drawn up by Richard Strachey, offered little but justifications for existing British policy that led to what Davis regards as a 'late Victorian holocaust' in terms of its toll in human life and suffering, with devastating and destructive consequences for India.[9]

The contrary case has also received vigorous support, however. The report of Strachey's Famine Commission, Jean Dreze has recently argued, despite its ideological underpinnings, was 'by any standard, an adminis-trative and intellectual masterpiece, and it embodied a considerable dose of experience, scholarliness and wisdom'. The brief of the Famine Commis-sion was to

collect with the utmost care all information which may assist future administrators in the task of limiting the range or mitigating the intensity of these calamities. The Commission applied itself vigorously to this task, and its report remains to this day a goldmine of information on previous famines in British India, as well as a most edifying treatise on the possible measures to prevent them.[10]

Strachey's interests in India extended way beyond the area of his formal profession. In addition to engineering and public works, he had extensive scientific interests, including botany, geology, geography, astronomy, and meteorology. In the 1850s, he travelled in the Himalayas. During this time, he studied the glaciers of Kumaon, establishing the existence of a series of Palaeozoic beds. His observations, published by the Geological Society in London in 1851, provided the first British description and analysis of the geological structure of the Himalayas. Strachey also provided an account of his journey and the terrain he covered for the Royal Geographical Society. As a later writer in the *Journal of the Royal Geographical Society* commented in his obituary on Strachey, the information 'acquired by Strachey in that first excursion across the Himalayas—information geological, botanical, relating to glaciers and snowfall . . . has never been exceeded by any one traveller'.[11] And indeed, it was not only these disciplines to which he contributed: in later years, Strachey participated in the debates about aqueous vapour in the atmosphere which exercised the British Meteorological Council and he played a significant part in establishing the meteorological study of India.[12] He also drew on his explorations of the Himalayas in the foundation series of lectures in geography which he gave at Cambridge University in 1876. Richard Strachey thus played a part in accumulating what has come to be called the 'imperial archive' and in bringing information about India within the broad framework of nineteenth-century science.[13] His work was available not only to the British government and to members of the several learned societies, including the Royal Society, of which he was a fellow, but also to general readers: he wrote the articles on 'Asia' and the 'Himalayas' for the *Encyclopaedia Britannica*.

The Indian world of Jane Strachey too has been interrogated in new ways within the postcolonial framework. Her imperial life was celebrated in her own time and after, most particularly in relation to her claim to have been 'in the counsels of the men who governed India'.[14] Her specialist knowledge of India was welcomed within the women's suffrage movement because it made her effective in opposing the anti-suffrage claim that enfranchising women would upset Indians and thus threaten the empire.[15] She was thus one of those many late Victorian and Edwardian feminists who have been the subject of recent feminist critiques, for embracing imperial ideas and values and disregarding entirely the way that imperialism itself often exacerbated the oppression of women.[16] Jane Strachey did not take up the plight of Indian women as her own 'special burden': on the contrary, she expressed almost no interest in or concern for Indian women at all, apparently regarding them as almost too low in the scale of civilization to warrant attention. Instead, living in India served to exalt her sense of her own power and status and of the importance of her feminist cause.

❧ I ❧

Richard Strachey had been destined for a career in India from the moment of his birth. Born at the Strachey family seat of Sutton Court in Somerset in 1817, he was the third of the six sons of Edward and Julia Strachey. There is little information available about his childhood or early education. The few extant letters to him from his mother indicate that she was both affectionate and demonstrative and that he was a caring and loving son. The family atmosphere, however, was probably heavily masculine. Richard was close in age to his five brothers and had only one living sister. (A number of other daughters were born to the family when he was already in his teens, but none survived.)

Like his older brothers, Richard was educated at an East India Company college. His interest in science and engineering made the military academy at Addiscombe seem the appropriate place for him and he went there in 1834, at the age of 17. From his early childhood, Richard Strachey had been regarded as exceptionally intelligent and he came top of his class at Addiscombe. His later difficulties in dealing with official expectations and requirements were already evident, however. He was refused the Sword of Honour to which his marks entitled him, because of his open criticism of the drill sergeant. As was to happen often in his later life, he had to stand by and watch the honour awarded to the person who had come second to him in the examinations.

Strachey left Addiscombe with a commission as second lieutenant in the Bombay Engineers in 1836 and sailed for India the following year. There are no extant letters describing either his voyage out to India or his feelings about the early years of his military life there. His dislike of military life and of Raj society in later years, and his generally anti-social disposition make it hard to imagine him enjoying barrack life or ever developing any kind of *esprit de corps* with his fellow officers, and his later letters make clear that he sought to be free of army ties or military responsibilities as early as he could. As an engineer, Strachey was involved in very little direct military activity. From the moment he arrived in India, he was involved in canal construction, first at Poona, then on the Jumna, and by the early 1840s, on the Ganges.

Although the life of a soldier was not to his taste, when called upon in this capacity Richard Strachey showed the same high level of ability as he did in all things. His major military engagement occurred in the mid-1840s when he was required to participate in the Sutlej Campaign of the Sikh War. He was charged with both intelligence and engineering work. He had to establish the number and position of the enemy forces, to devise a battle strategy, and to construct the bridge over the Sutlej which enabled the British forces to enter the Punjab. Strachey received a medal with clasp for his services in the Sutlej Campaign, but this did not quite compensate him for the inconvenience and irritation suffered. At the battle of Aliwal, his horse was shot from under him. He was shocked, but uninjured. He needed the horse to be replaced. Yet, no matter how clearly he attempted to explain to the military bureaucracy that he could not carry out the reconnaissance tasks he had been assigned without a horse, the army command insisted that, as he was not in the cavalry, it would not replace the animal![17]

Shortly after the end of the war, in 1846, Strachey became ill with recurrent attacks of fever, and was forced to transfer to the hill station of Naini Tal. Like so many other prominent Victorians, he refused to regard illness as a reason for idleness and immediately began learning about botany and geology as a prelude to exploring the Himalayas in the area close to Tibet. He managed in the course of these explorations to catalogue all the local flora, sending samples, each carefully ticketed with notes of the locality and elevation at which it was found, to the Hookerian Herbarium (now at Kew gardens), the British Museum, and to the Linnean Society.

Strachey returned to England for five years in 1850, using this time to classify his Kumaon Collection and to write up his researches. He was back in India in 1856 and was appointed as assistant to John Peter Grant, Lieutenant-Governor of the Central Provinces. Grant had met Strachey earlier and been very impressed by his abilities. They cemented the relationship when Strachey later married Jane, Grant's daughter. Grant wanted him to assist in all the areas of responsibility that he was expected to undertake as lieutenant-governor and Strachey thus gained very diverse experience. He worked with Grant during the Mutiny of 1857, assisting him with military strategy, but charged particularly with the task of replacing the railway station at Allahabad which had been destroyed by the mutineers.

Working with Grant provided the break Strachey needed from the army and in the following years, he began to take on an increasingly important role in public works. In 1858, he was appointed consultant engineer to government for railways. This position brought him a considerable increase in income. A few years later, in 1862, this position was expanded and he was made secretary to the government for public works. These positions were both responsible and wide-ranging, enabling him to become involved in a variety of different fields. ' I am still quite busy', he wrote to his wife from the Public Works Office in 1862.

I am now still hard at work on budgets. I have written an essay on Agricultural Societies in India—Mr Laing is going to take it and I will send you the papers to see— I have also been cooking up sundry other things—The Museum is I hope soon likely to become a reality. I have started an attempt to improve the Hooghly ... Then we have schemes for giving Local Governments more complete powers to spend money from certain sources to encourage self government as far as possible. Further there are several plans afloat to start branch Railways which will be important if they come to anything. On the whole I am as busy as a hive of bees.[18]

While Strachey often disliked the people he had to work with, he was fortunate in that there was a close fit between his views and the general direction of Indian policy in the mid and later nineteenth century. The 1830s, as David Washbrook and others have commented, were marked by a growing self-confidence among the British public and policy-makers in the 'world-destiny' of their own imperial project and by a major shift in British thinking about how to approach India. The long-standing belief that the British should uphold the ancient laws, customs, and religion of India and avoid any violent innovations was giving way to a new set of ideas much more hostile to Indian customs and demanding the transformation of Indian institutions and beliefs and, for some, the conversion of Indians themselves.[19] James Mill's influential *History of British India* had interrogated and criticized those who venerated Indian culture and traditions, arguing that, if properly applied, the principle of utility demonstrated that Indian religions and customs were primitive, riddled with superstition, and able only to produce social degradation.[20]

Strachey arrived in India just at the end of the viceroyalty of Lord William Cavendish Bentinck (1828–35). Bentinck had enthusiastically endorsed Mill's ideas and sought to modernize India along the lines approved by the utilitarians. He set about codifying laws and attempting to reform the judiciary. Bentinck also sought to establish a new system of westernized education, to reform the system of land tenure and to introduce a new system of finance. The practice of suttee, which he and many other reforming administrators saw as the ultimate embodiment of the ways in which Indian traditional practices disregarded human life, was another target of his reforming zeal.[21]

Like many others educated in East India Company colleges, Strachey had been schooled in utilitarian principles from an early age and believed passionately in the need to bring order and system to India. His own immediate interest in questions of science and technology were addressed in the 1830s, but became more and more important in the mid-1850s when Bentinck's concern with institutional reform systems was replaced with a new interest in the possibilities evident in railway expansion. Lord Dalhousie, viceroy from 1848 to 1857, declared that the railways, telegraphs, and an organized postal system were 'the three great engines of social improvement in India', and immediately set about introducing the former and reorganizing the latter.[22] He, too, was a follower of Bentham, and set his own approach to westernization on a permanent footing by the establishment of a separate Public Works Department for the government of India in 1854.

The widespread belief that railways and the telegraph would 'regenerate' the Indian people, lifting them out of what their British rulers perceived as their state of 'passivity' and 'indolence', while at the same time rendering them more governable and more responsive to imperial imperatives, was if anything reinforced by the uprising of Indian troops against the British in 1857. There was concern after the Mutiny that some of the reforms of the 1830s, especially those which had sought to alter Indian customs, had resulted in the alienation of the landowning classes from the Raj. New efforts were now made to conciliate the landowners—while at the same time demonstrating that British rule had been established and would be maintained by military force. Public works became ever more important. Indeed, as Benita Parry has argued, they became the base of the administrator's creed in the later nineteenth century, as the British sought to impose western influence on India through the building or canals, railways, roads, and bridges and through attempts to control famine and other natural disasters.[23]

Although his work in India was interesting, demanding, and well paid, by the early 1860s Richard Strachey had hoped to be able to return home to England. He was now married and the father of a growing family, and the strains of imperial life told on both him and his wife. He had hoped that his position of secretary to the government in public works would be his last job in India and that he and his wife could settle permanently in England when he left this job in 1865. Then in his late 40s, Richard Strachey was entitled to a distinguished service pension and had sufficient savings to support the family temporarily. His ambition was to gain a seat on the India Council which he felt would enable him to use his extensive knowledge of India to influence government policy.[24] He was created CSI in 1866. His plans for staying in England did not materialize, however, as the seat on the India Council was not forthcoming. Moreover, in June 1866, the Agra Bank in which his savings—as well as those of his brothers Henry and John—were invested went into liquidation.[25] The day on which the bank failure was announced, 6 June, continued to be known in the family as 'Black Friday' and it was a grim one for the Stracheys who had no family money to fall back upon.[26] There was only one possible course of action. 'I suppose you will have to come back to India', John Strachey wrote to Richard, on receiving this terrible news, though 'what you can get I have no idea'.[27]

Richard returned to India at the end of that year and found employment immediately. He went first to Bombay and from there was called on to inspect all the great irrigation works of India with a view to establishing a uniform system of irrigation.[28] This tour strengthened Strachey's already firm conviction about the need for more extensive irrigation works. After visiting Sindh, he wrote to Lord Cranbourne, the Secretary of State for India, that a complete transformation of 'the present rude system of irrigation' was essential if there were to be any progress there. The current practice of raising water by bullock-drawn water-wheels was wasteful and made any form of agriculture more expensive than it was in areas with better water supplies. This in turn kept Sindh outside the market economy that Strachey advocated.

The whole condition of affairs . . . would be changed if in this rainless district a proper provision of irrigation were made. Then Sindh would be in a position to supply a vastly larger quantity of produce for exportation, with the great advantage of fair proximity to the sea and short land carriage. The prospect of a railway then would be as certain as it is now hopeless.[29]

The following year, in July 1867, Strachey was appointed inspector general of irrigation works. This was a new position and one that he effectively designed. Some years earlier, he had written to the Secretary of State for India arguing that it was imperative that such a position be established and his letter, outlining the functions of this inspector, became the basis for defining his new role. He was charged with oversight of all government work in regard to irrigation, including superintending all planning and all business that arose from local governments and administration. He was also required to survey and inspect work already done. 'It appears to the Governor General in Council', said the document that Strachey had drafted laying down his role, that

while preserving the general control of the Secretary in the Public Works Depart-ment, it will be expeditious to entrust considerable powers to the Inspector General of Irrigation, and the more so since the officer who has been selected for the post is one who has held positions of high responsibility and in whom the government of India may place a special degree of confidence.[30]

Although he had a lot of power, he constantly complained of how slowly things developed and how much opposition any new scheme faced.[31]

Indeed, Strachey often depicted himself as constantly being thwarted by others in the Indian administration who were too stupid or rigid or to do what he asked—and what was clearly necessary. 'Sometimes', he wrote to his wife, 'I feel very flat about it all I don't exactly doubt myself, but somehow I see that I don't fit into the machine. I think I am too revolu-tionary, too logical, to be approved by my neighbours except by my *nearest* and *dearest one*.'[32] There is no question that he often felt justifiably frustrated by the rigidity, the 'masterly inactivity', and the insistence on tedious bureaucratic procedure that characterized much of the administra-tion of British India. On one occasion, a scheme he wanted was rejected on the grounds that he had communicated to the India Council in London a decision taken by the government of India by telegraph. Perhaps, he suggested to the viceroy, the India Council would like the government of India 'to destroy the telegraph, or order that it should never be used. What on earth is supposed to be the use of telegraphs and railways and the like if they are not just to hasten the conveyance of messages etc.'[33]

Nonetheless, while Strachey bristled when he was faced with bureau-cratic rigidity, he too could behave in an extremely bureaucratic and high-handed way. Some of those he worked with complained that, as secretary to the government of India for public works, he intervened excessively in local schemes and denied anyone else any of the autonomy he sought for himself. Strachey talked often about the need for decentralization, and especially for local governments to be able to fund and carry out their own schemes. But in the eyes of Bartle Frere, head of the Bombay government, Strachey worked rather to foster central control. Frere had to submit his proposals for public works to Strachey who rejected both the budget and the plan on the grounds that the list of items was too extensive, the budget outlay suggested excessive—and that the precise form in which such submissions should be made had been disregarded. Frere was outraged by both the substance and the tone of Strachey's reply. He complained both to the viceroy, Lord Elgin, and to the Secretary of State that Strachey was ignorant of local needs, ruthless in his determination to control every detail of public works himself, and extraordinarily rude and unpleasant in his dealings with others.[34] 'Rely on it, my dear Strachey,' Frere wrote,

you cannot be both superintending Engineer of every work in India, and also Secretary in the P. W. D. to the Gov't of India. You may very well ensure that not a work is commenced throughout India till you have been satisfied as to the minutest detail of plan and estimate. But you will find this will end in the paralysis of the P. W. D. You wish to ensure a maximum of work and efficiency and a minimum of expense. The means you adopt will ensure the reverse. All our money will go in establishments and designs and writing; the work done will be a minimum.[35]

Even Jane Strachey, devoted though she was to her husband, suggested that his manner might be overbearing: 'is it not something queer that the person who has striven more for economical management of Indian finance than any one in India, should have the reputation of being a dangerous spend thrift? Indian Brunel indeed! Bismarck is much nearer the mark.'[36]

Strachey held the position of Secretary of Public Works for five years, after which time he returned home. Although pleased to be back home in England, he was neither ready to relinquish his influence on Indian developments nor to retire in the early 1870s. He continued to seek a seat on the India Council, but his long history of criticism of that body did not make him welcome there. As an interim measure, Lord Salisbury, the Secretary of State for India, appointed him Inspector of Railway Stores in the India Office. Despite its unassuming title, this position gave Strachey oversight of all Indian railway developments. Here too there were some difficulties: Strachey held many of those who worked at the India Office in contempt, feeling that they lacked any actual knowledge of India and hence any idea about how to administer it. He found his new position interesting, but was still concerned that the complete system of irrigation he had sought to develop had not been completed. He pondered the possibility of returning to India to do this, but was advised against it. After talking this idea over, Lord Salisbury wrote to tell him of his 'conviction that there is a party or rather a clique, not numerous but active and tolerably influential, who, if you went back to India would meet you with the most determined opposition'.

The fact is honourable to you—for it is the fate of every stringent and resolute administrator, especially under an absolute government to excite a class of determined enemies. But it would make a renewal of your official career in India very irksome to you : & would go far to neutralise the advantage which your great abilities would bring to the public service.[37]

Finally, the long-awaited seat on the India Council was granted. Richard Strachey's appointment illustrates the changing nature of the India Council in the later decades of the nineteenth century. Indian government, from 1858 onwards, had been a responsibility shared somewhat uneasily between the viceroy or governor-general in Calcutta and the Secretary of State for India in London. As the British government demanded closer scrutiny of Indian affairs, the role of the Secretary of State for India grew more onerous and more important. Incumbents of this office tended to draw heavily on retired Indian administrators to make up the India Council. Their advice, as Anil Seal argues, 'was as skilled as it was sometimes dated'.[38] In offering Strachey a seat on the Council, Salisbury made clear his sense that this was a position of importance. 'Your action upon the management of public works', he wrote, 'will be less direct; but it will be more continuous & it will tend to give something like unity to the policy personnel in the future.'[39] Richard Strachey replied with his customary graciousness, that it 'has been my fortune—I may say my good fortune long to have held opinions which have kept me in the feeling that I am a member of a minority. I frankly accept the necessities of that position.'[40] He took his seat on the India Council the following year, in January 1875.

Strachey's position on the India Council in London was no sinecure. In 1877, he was sent back to India to arrange the terms for the purchase of the East India Railway. While there, he was prevailed upon to chair an inquiry into the causes of the devastating famine that engulfed the Deccan plateau. As we have seen, Strachey's role in relation to famine has been the source of much critical comment. It is worth looking at it in some detail because it reveals much about his relationship with the government of India and his approach to Indian administration. Richard Strachey's appointment as chair of the Inquiry into the Famine of 1878 had been suggested by his brother, John, then finance member on the viceroy's council. The appointment was strongly approved by the viceroy, Lord Lytton. This close family connection had been noted by the British government too—and seen as precluding the possibility of Richard Strachey becoming involved in the commission. Neither the viceroy nor John Strachey saw Richard's appointment as improper, however. In justifying his decision to appoint him to the commission, Lord Lytton emphasized to Lord Cranbrook, the Secretary of State for India, that Richard Strachey was 'no respecter of persons, but maketh his criticisms to rain upon the just and unjust with celestial disregard of human blessings or cursings'.[41] At the same time, Lord Lytton and John Strachey saw this appointment as one that would enable Richard to resume his earlier role as overseer of Indian public works (thereby replacing the current inspector whose ideas did not accord with their own).[42] Richard in turn agreed to take on the commission because he thought that in doing so he could assist his brother and the viceroy better to resist the criticism to which they were being subjected as details of the famine became known in Britain.[43]

Their shared involvement in the famine question continued what had always been a very close working relationship between Richard and John Strachey. John, who had met with success earlier than Richard, had always done his best to support and promote his older brother. Richard in turn was prepared to sacrifice income and the comfort of his family to support and assist John. John's very close relationship with Lord Lytton was also important. The friendship between them was intense: Lytton once told Richard Strachey that, of all the men he knew, John Strachey was the one he would most like as a brother. It is notable that Richard himself seems never to have made close friendships with other men with the ease of his brother, but John's friends nonetheless became part of Richard's close world.

The framework in which the Commission into the Famine was set up precluded the possibility that it would be critical of the approach the Government of India had taken to the famine. Indeed, Richard Strachey shared fully the beliefs of his brother and of Lord Lytton that famine relief should be limited, that no assistance should be sought from England, and that Indian taxes must provide the only finance to deal with the famine.

Rejecting the idea that the famine was a catastrophic event that needed special measures, Strachey accepted the views of his brother and Lord Lytton that there should be no famine relief given except to those prepared to undertake public works. In essence, famine relief was administered in accordance with the guidelines set down by the Poor Law of 1834.[44] Both Stracheys shared Lord Lytton's contempt for the idea that charitable aid should be made available to famine victims.[45]

Strachey's understanding of famine had been evident for decades. He saw it as a result of the Indian climate, and as amenable to amelioration only through better irrigation and larger scale agriculture. Throughout the period during which the commission gathered information in areas devastated by famine, he showed to the full his capacity to ignore appalling immediate suffering and hardship, concentrating rather on what he saw as the underlying principles that needed to be grasped. Like many of those schooled in economic liberalism and utilitarianism in the nineteenth century, he saw the danger of pauperization through indiscriminate almsgiving as a much greater evil than physical suffering or even starvation.[46] The famine and the suffering of its victims had no appreciable effect on him— indeed, there is not a single comment in his letters about it.

Strachey remained in India for longer than he had intended. As soon as the Commission into the Famine had finished collecting its information, he took over the role of his brother John as Finance Minister on the governor-general's council to enable John to return to England for an eye operation. As we will see, this decision did not please his wife—but it did satisfy his own sense of loyalty to his brother.

On his return to England in 1880, Strachey resumed his seat on the India Council which he retained until 1889. Although he was now in his late 70s, his resignation from the India Council did not indicate an intention to retire. On the contrary, he relinquished his seat on the India Council in order to take up another and more onerous position as chairman of the board of directors of the East India Railway. As one would expect, Strachey's approach to the position of chairman was very much an executive one. He went out to India almost immediately after his appointment, instituted inquiries into all aspects of the operation of the company, and set about a major restructure. He introduced new ways of doing business as well as new services. At the same time, he attempted to find ways of increasing the speed of the trains by establishing new lines and investigating which source of coal proved most efficient.[47]

Strachey's work was made extremely difficult by the fact that the EIR was ultimately under the authority of the British government who determined the railway budget and particularly the amount that could be spent on capital works. The parsimony of the government and its refusal to permit money to be borrowed by local government or statutory bodies for capital works had long been a source of frustration to Strachey, and continued to be one. In his chairman's address for 1890, he pointed out that the 3 lakhs which had been allocated for capital outlay for the EIR, a railway extending over 1,500 miles with a capital of about 50 crores of rupees 'is hardly more than illusory'. But the government would not budge. Nonetheless, by the time he finally retired, there was general agreement amongst the other directors, the shareholders, and even newspapers like *The Pioneer*, which was often critical of Strachey, that his chairmanship had been a triumph.[48] Strachey continued as chairman for nearly two decades. Deafness and physical frailty finally compelled him to resign as chair in January 1907. On his resignation, the board of directors wrote to him to express their regrets at his departure and their sense of what he had contributed. They praised the standard of efficiency that characterized his chairmanship and noted that the 'receipts of the undertaking have increased from Rs 299,91.510 in the year 1889 to Rs 505,74. 773 in 1905'.[49] This view was endorsed by the company's historian who argued that for the ten years prior to Strachey's appointment, the company 'had remained in a state of torpor', and that Strachey brought a new vision which saw business and profits increase dramatically.[50]

India had been the source both of Richard Strachey's fame and of his fortune. His role as an imperial administrator in India produced a very comfortable income, but he bore little resemblance to the eighteenth-century nabobs who left India with a vast fortune. At the time of his marriage, he explained to Jane that his income was approximately £1,000 per annum. At that time, the salary of a skilled artisan was around £100 per annum, and that of a respectable middle-class shop keeper around £400. Thus this income placed the Stracheys well within the professional upper middle class, although it still made financial care necessary if they were to have the home, the carriage, and the other accoutrements required within the upper middle-class society in which they mixed. Richard's salary increased markedly when he was made secretary to the government for public works in 1862. The government had settled his pay, he explained to Jane, by giving me the same as Secretary to Govt of India in the Military Department. This will be 2500 rupees staff salary plus military pay & allowances which will be 1100 Rupees—overall 3600 Rs in place of 3000. But also proposed to make staff salary 2750 Rs & then if I get that & become full Colonel in which rank the military pay will be nearly 1300 Rs the whole pay will be over 4000Rs a month so that in fact I shall get as much as I want. I am perfectly satisfied that it has been settled and think it very fair.[51]

With an exchange rate of approximately 10 rupees to the pound, Strachey was now talking about an income of about £400 per month—or £4,800 per year—and was thus moving into the bracket of the upper middle class businessmen, leading professionals, senior government and imperial officials, and politicians with whom he worked.[52] This was augmented in 1866 with a small pension of £100 per annum for distinguished military service.[53] It was this large income that encouraged Strachey to invest heavily in the Agra Bank, in the hopes that he might soon be able to live independently of a regular salary. As we have seen, the collapse of the bank in 1867 ended this dream and made it necessary for him to return to India to find work. He did so, but at a lower salary than he had earned before. Nonetheless, his 3,000 rupees per month was a very reasonable sum.[54]

Strachey's salary was not quite so high after he returned to England in the 1870s. His first appointment as inspector of railway stores at the India Office brought a salary of £1,000 in addition to his army pay. 'Though I don't think it too much,' he wrote to his father-in-law, 'it does well enough.'[55] Four years later, when he was granted the coveted seat on the India Council the £1,200 he received as payment for this office enabled him to retire from the army[56] With his military pension, his total salary at this time was £1,756.[57] This was augmented by a considerable portfolio of shares and some investments in land.[58] Strachey's salary underwent one more significant change after this: it increased to £2,000 per annum when he became chairman of the EIR, and it continued at this rate for the seventeen years he was in the chair, although it dropped significantly when he retired.

Richard Strachey's retirement brought a marked diminution of income. This was not a result of any scheme by board and shareholders of the East India Railway. On the contrary, they made very clear their strong desire to express their appreciation of Strachey's outstanding role as chairman through a generous pension. They were not, however, allowed to do so. The British Government refused to allow Strachey any form of pension or terminating pay. The question of his pay rested not with the EIR, but rather with John Morley, Secretary of State for India. On Strachey's retirement, the board of the East India Railway wrote to Morley requesting the payment of a substantial pension, or a one-off grant of £5,000 'for the eminent services rendered by General Strachey'. Morley refused, insisting that he objected in principle to any form of termination payment for Strachey.[59] It is hard to understand his rationale. Military personnel and civil servants routinely received pensions and a national insurance scheme was already being discussed. Nor does it seem likely that there were personal grounds. Although Morley and Strachey were not particularly friendly, they certainly met socially—and like so many of Richard Strachey's colleagues, Morley was on very friendly terms with Jane Strachey. What seems most likely is that this was a remnant of a nineteenth-century sense that public office should be voluntary and unpaid. The decision had serious consequences for the Strachey family, however. Richard was left with a military pension of £756 per annum, to which was added the interest on his shares. This was far from penury, but it was not a sufficient income to maintain the family home in Lancaster Gate. The family sold up their home, said farewell to their large and expansive family life, and moved to the much smaller house in Belsize Park Gardens where Richard Strachey died.

II

Richard Strachey's interest in India was matched by that of his wife. Her descriptions of India and of life in the Raj, however, have an effusiveness and enthusiasm quite unknown to him. His Indian letters deal almost entirely with his career and his public activities. Jane Strachey's letters and memoirs about India, by contrast, centre primarily on her private and social life. Indeed, Jane's sense of India was inseparable from the close contact it offered first with an adored father and then with a beloved husband. Her first visit to India in 1852, she later recalled, was 'the most important epoch of my life'. The minute she arrived, 'the dull period of suppression and monotony was over, the gate of life in its infinite variety was thrown open'. She had come at the age of 12 to see her father, John Peter Grant, then Secretary to the Government of Bengal. Grant, Jane insisted, had 'the highest reputation of any civilian of his time.'[60] He included his daughter in all his social dealings with senior administrators and government officials, making very clear both his affection and his respect for her intellectual capacity. His house at 8 Elysium Row was only a short walk from the seat of government in Calcutta and this proximity increased Jane's sense of being closely involved in the political centre of the Raj. This pleasure in feeling that she was at the centre of imperial government and society was all the more remarkable by contrast to the rather dreary boarding school life Jane lived back home in Britain.

On her second trip to India in 1858, Jane met and married Richard Strachey, a close friend and sometime assistant to her father. Their mutual attraction was almost instantaneous and their courtship very brief. Jane Strachey's admiration for her husband was closely connected to her belief in the great importance of Britain's imperial mission. 'I must say first how proud it makes me that you should talk to me of your work', she wrote to Richard, early in their married life, 'I think that your present position is the one which possesses for the present the most latent power of good for India.'[61] As we will see, Jane soon took a central role in Richard's career. A woman of considerable intelligence and compelling charm, she had immense social skills and negotiated with great ease the upper echelons and elaborate rituals of Raj society.

Jane Strachey's sense that her time in India marked the high points in her life was made possible by the fact that she was rarely there for very long. She made three trips out after the one in 1858 during which she married and was there for approximately two years each in 1862–3, 1868–9, and finally in 1877–8. Her periods of time in Indian were sufficient for her to feel settled, but never long enough to acquire a sense of the ordinary daily routine that dominated her life in England in the 1870s and 1880s. For the most part, she spent her time in Simla, thus avoiding the extreme heat of the Indian summer and living in a world which seemed in its geographical features, its architecture, and its social ritual almost as much British as it was Indian. Her first home as a married woman was in Simla and she thus began her married life in its congenial climate, assisted by many servants and surrounded by the busy whirl of Raj society.

After a rather slow start, Jane's first Simla season was one of almost unalloyed delight. There were regular balls where she danced for hours— taking particular pride in her capacity to produce inexpensive dresses made of 'white holland' that were much admired, but were able to withstand the rigours of Indian balls better than lace and tulle.[62] She set up a croquet club which met weekly—and was soon playing on the croquet lawn that she and Richard had made in the front of their house. She began to give her own dinner parties which she thoroughly enjoyed. The high point of the season was the staging of Sheridan's play, *The Rivals*, in her house. She played Mrs Malaprop and assured her sister that she was not at all nervous—and ultimately that the production was a triumph.[63] Jane also learnt to ride and the season ended with a two-week excursion into the surrounding hills. Jane was ecstatic about this wonderful adventure. Accompanied by Richard and several friends, she rode her lovely grey pony as they explored the foothills of the Himalayas. Indian servants carted everything necessary for their comfort and made camp every evening where they could sit around campfires in the evening, singing and telling ghost stories. It was 'one of the pleasantest fortnights I ever spent' she told her sister, 'the outdoor gipsy life and the agreeable party of people who all suited each other' made it extremely pleasurable.[64]

Richard Strachey seems to have entered fully into Jane's social activities in Simla, but this was unusual. In her later trips to India, while she continued to enjoy the social activities of Raj life, he withdrew into his former habits of ignoring them. When Jane made her next trip to India in 1869, she attended many social gatherings without him. He was loath to attend functions which required him to wear dress uniform—and thus would not go with Jane when she attended the opera as part of the entourage of Lord Mayo, the new governor-general.[65] In a similar way, when the Duke of Edinburgh visited Calcutta some months later, Richard avoided the large welcome ball. It was to be 'a Fancy Ball', Jane explained to her son Dick, 'not even uniforms being allowed; so I suppose your Papa will not go, for he says nothing will induce him to put on a fancy dress. Uncle John has got a very pretty one of black velvet . . . & he is going in that.'[66]

There seems little doubt that much of the pleasure of India for Jane Strachey came from the contact it brought with genteel and even aristocratic society. Both her own and her husband's families had come from the landed gentry, although as Lytton Strachey later remarked, the families had declined since the eighteenth century. By the mid-nineteenth century, Richard and Jane Strachey were very much an upper middle class professional couple, dependent on Richard's earning capacity, rather than members of the gentry. Richard Strachey was very much at home in this social world, which included the men of science amongst whom he chose his close friends. Jane Strachey too had many friends at home, but she clearly relished the close contact with the upper classes that India offered. One of the things that gave her most pleasure when she settled in Simla in 1863 was the fact that the home she and Richard rented in 1863 was considered the best in the town, considerably better than Peterhoff, the house of Lord Elgin, then viceroy.[67]

Although Jane engaged in amateur theatricals with Lord Elgin in the early 1860s, the viceregal family to whom she became closest were the Lyttons. She was not the only member of the Strachey family for whom this was the case. Lytton had worked closely with John Strachey from the time he arrived in India as viceroy in 1875 and the two men became very close friends. Lytton courted Richard Strachey when he went out to India to purchase the land for the East India Railway in 1877 and when Jane went out a year later to join her husband, she and the viceroy became very close friends. Living as they did in Simla and surrounded by gossip and sexual intrigue, their relationship did not pass unnoticed. Indeed, Lytton, drove out with Jane Strachey in his carriage so often as to raise questions about whether or not they were having an affair. This conjecture seems to me extremely unlikely, however. Although Lytton was a noted womanizer, Jane Strachey was so devoted a Victorian wife and so conscientious a mother as to make it unlikely that she could even contemplate a sexual relationship with another man. Moreover, the fact that she asked Lytton to be her son's godfather, and that he agreed, makes it even more improbable. Lytton once sent her a note containing a popular limerick in Simla entitled 'the husband', but this in itself seems to confirm her innocence.

> The husband is a fearful beast
> He comes when you expect him least:
> He comes by day, he comes by night
>   But never when you want him quite.

Their intimacy seems really to have centred on their shared literary interests. Jane knew a number of writers and was immensely well read. Lord Lytton, who published under the name 'Owen Meredith', sent her his poems for comment and made use of her extensive literary connections. As soon as she had returned to England, he wrote to remind her 'that you had kindly promised and vowed on my behalf two things rather generally necessary to my salvation i.e. to endeavour to find out confidentially from Kegan Paul what he gave Tennyson for his last volume (or what is

Tennyson's average price) and ask Cross what George Eliot got for the *Spanish Gipsy*'.[68] It is notable, however, that close as she became to the Lyttons and to others in the viceregal entourage while in India, and careful as she always was to nurture and develop all her social contacts, once back in Britain, she had little contact with the aristocratic families that had made up her Indian world. An occasional letter was exchanged between the Stracheys and the Lyttons, but there seem to have been no meetings. The relatively small world of senior government officials in British India clearly allowed for close social contacts across class lines in ways that were not possible in England. Moreover, Richard Strachey, whose work had involved constant contact with aristocratic viceroys in India, had no reason to maintain any professional contact with them once they were all back home. Back in Britain, then, the often unspoken but nonetheless powerful social codes that separated upper middle class from aristocratic families served to distance the Stracheys from some of the people who had been integral to their Indian world. Dorothy later commented on this in 1942, when she registered her great sense of loss on hearing of the death of Betty Balfour, one of the Lytton daughters. Betty, she told André Gide, 'was from a different social and intellectual world from mine'. However, 'fortune' had thrown them together in when they found themselves in India at the age of 22 and they managed to maintain a friendship until Betty married Gerald Balfour. In the intervening years, she had sent Dorothy an occasional letter, but like their parents, they had never met.[69]

Jane Strachey's enjoyment of Indian life and her sense of excitement about it needs to be set against the hardship it imposed on her and on her family. Her marriage to Richard Strachey involved all the usual trials and difficulties of imperial marriage. There were long periods of separation, not only when Richard was in India while Jane was in England, but even when she was in India. She stayed in Simla for many months while he was required to remain in Calcutta, or to travel around the country inspecting the various irrigation and railway schemes for which he was responsible. She was often lonely and had to deal with family crises and tragedies, including the deaths of three babies, without her husband. There were separations also from her children. Like other Raj families, the Stracheys took it for granted that school-age children should remain in England. Hence Jane was often separated from her children. This separation was made easier by the fact that the children either lived with or at least spent vacation time with Jane's sister, Elinor Colevile. Hence she was assured that they were always loved and cared for. Nonetheless, as many of the letters Jane wrote to her husband and sister indicate, there were periods of acute misery. In her letters to her children, as in her later recollections, however, all of this is lost in a romantic haze.

Jane Strachey's romance was unquestionably an imperialist and orientalist one. She was almost intoxicated by her sense of India as an exotic place and by her vision of Britain (with Richard Strachey playing a leading part) as bringing civilization and good government to the benighted natives. But it was also in a certain way a feminist one as her marriage brought her a sense of being close to the centres of power, and indeed of exercising considerable power herself. She was her husband's adviser and confidante, reading over and commenting on almost all of his reports and dispatches and often making significant suggestions and alterations. Richard in turn depended heavily both on her judgement and on her literary skills. Thus, as Virginia Woolf noted, and as Jane herself made clear in her speech to the Lyceum Club, what remained the most valuable part of her Indian life was the sense that she 'was in the counsels of the men who governed India'.[70] In her later years, Virginia Woolf recalled, Jane Strachey loved to tell stories of her past experiences in India: 'of Lord Lytton and his sky blue dressing gown; of Lord Roberts helping to mend her sewing machine; of Lawrence and Outram . . . of Pattles and Prinseps; of bygone beauties and scandals— . . . of Indian Society fifty years, eighty years ago'. It was this close connection with imperial power above all that made her Indian years the high point in a life divided into 'the part of the excited illuminated play' with the rest of it 'merely trudging along the prosaic streets, with nothing to look forward to'.[71]

III

The Stracheys may have felt somewhat differently about the social world of the Raj, but they were as one in their views about the Indian subcontinent and its peoples, or about what was to them the more important question of India's place in the British Empire. Thomas Metcalfe has recently offered an interesting analysis of the tensions evident within imperial ideology in India between the notion of Indians as similar to Europeans and that of them as completely different.[72] The Stracheys offer an illustration of precisely this tension. On the one hand, they often argued that there were almost no resemblances between Indians and Europeans. At the same time, they saw India as different from contemporary Britain primarily because it was backward, and needed to follow the same path as Europe to modernity—thus suggesting that the differences between Britain and India were merely contingent and could be removed.

It was John Strachey, rather than Richard, who offered general comments on the nature of Indian religion, society, and culture and who sought to explain the differences between Indians and Britons in terms of their intellectual and moral qualities. John Strachey's views on India are frequently cited in current works exploring the ideology underlying British imperialism. Mrinalini Sinha, for example, quotes his insistence that 'there is not, and never was an India, or even any country of India . . . no Indian nation, no "people of India", but only a conglomeration of mutually antagonistic groups' to explain how the classification of native 'types' was assimilated into a mechanism for disciplining the colonial population and justifying imperial rule.[73] In his view, Indian customs were so barbaric, the conflict between its different religious and racial groups so intense, and the capacity of its rulers so limited that its only hope lay in 'the long continuance of the . . . strong government of Englishmen'.[74] Richard wrote some essays, but he tended to confine himself to matters of finance or to public works, leaving the broader analysis to his younger brother. However, as John Strachey made clear in the second edition of their jointly authored work, *The Finances and Public Works of India*, the views of the two brothers were indistinguishable. 'It is not worth while', he insisted,

to explain the shares in the book which belong respectively to my brother and myself. The opinions we hold on the subjects discussed are so much in unison, and have been so constantly formed in close personal communication, that for our own part distinctions are superfluous. When the first person is used, it may mean either the one or the other of the authors.[75]

Many of Richard's comments on Indian agriculture, irrigation, and transport bear out this view. After his tour of Sindh in 1867, he told his wife that 'the country is nearly in the same state materially as in the days of Alexander, the canals about the same and the cultivation of wealth to match. No doubt the people are tamer and the things a shade better.'[76] The burden of his comment was directed towards the British administrators who had done nothing to improve the situation. He took it for granted that agriculture and irrigation in India needed to be reformed so that they conformed to British standards.[77]

The Strachey's sense of Indian backwardness and their acceptance of a very hierarchical approach to imperial administration ensured that their relations with Indians were very distant. They were not among that small minority of British officials who engaged in friendly intercourse with Indians.[78] On the contrary, they exemplify the growing distance between Indians and their British rulers that became so marked after 1857. Richard Strachey received a few ceremonial statements of thanks from Indians he had known and worked with from time to time, along with letters seeking his assistance in matters of employment. But all serve simply to underline his distance from his Indian employees and their sense of him as a potential benefactor.

This sense of superiority to the Indians over whom they ruled is frequently evident in Jane Strachey's letters to their children. She described Richard's formal meetings with Indians in some of them, but always in terms which emphasized how exotic, strange, and childlike the Indians were, and how very much they lacked basic British ideas about decorum or businesslike conduct. 'On Monday some fine native gentlemen came to see your papa', she wrote to her oldest son Dick in 1868:

they had on very gay clothes, & their ponies had very gay saddles & bridles. They brought Papa a letter from their Rajah (or prince) about a canal which is being made throughout his country. The letter is not at all like an English one; there are big gold spots over the paper it is written on and instead of being in an envelope, it is in a bag of red silk, which is covered by another bag of white muslin, & then tied by a gild string from which hangs a thick gold seal.[79]

A few months later, she reported from Simla that 'a great Rajah has come to live in a house close to ours'. But this event was a subject of comic comment, not the prelude to any kind of social contact. The rajah had brought a 'a great train of followers, who make such a noise all day & all night; they blow horns and strike their tom-toms & worse than all there is a band of music played by natives, & they play the times all wrong'. The rajah always insisted that the band play to him while he ate dinner, 'because the Governor General has a band at his dinner & he thinks it very fine'.[80]

In view of the number of years that Richard and Jane Strachey were in India, their continued distance from Indian life is very marked. Many historians have commented on the ways in which social interaction between British officials and settlers and Indians declined in the course of the nineteenth century, and most particularly after the Indian mutiny of 1857. In part, this reflected a growing sense of British superiority to all Indian beliefs and social customs which contrasted markedly with the much greater enthusiasm for Indian religious beliefs and culture in the eighteenth century.[81] It reflected also the growth in size and the change in composition of the British community as women were sent out to India throughout the nineteenth century in order to ensure that British men were provided with wives and with a social life that resembled that they would lead back home.[82] As we will see, the Strachey family offers a striking illustration of this shift, for in the eighteenth century several members of the family were captivated by Indian customs—and some sought Indian wives. There is little indication, moreover, that the Victorian Stracheys engaged in either of the two different activities in which British men and women entered into relationships with Indians: sexual liaisons for men—and feminist projects for women. Richard Strachey was in India for nearly fifteen years before he entered his first brief marriage with Carolyn Bowles in 1854. But there is simply no indication as to whether or not he had an Indian mistress or any form of sexual relationship with Indian women—or indeed with other British women, prior to this. As one would expect, and like most other British military officers in India, his letters are entirely silent on sexual matters and it is hard to guess what this silence conceals. Strachey's letters to his wife suggest that he was a passionate man and that theirs was a passionate sexual relationship. At the same time, Richard Strachey's stern sense of duty, his long working hours, and his generally unsociable predisposition make it plausible that he remained celibate before marriage. One can more easily imagine him sharing the view of a fellow agnostic, Frederick Harrison, that 'a man who cannot learn self-control is a cad . . . a foul man . . . anti-social . . . a beast', than slipping into a cantonment and paying for a prostitute or engaging in any kind of flirtation.[83]

Jane Strachey was an ardent feminist in her later years, but she engaged in no feminist activity in India. Indeed, she never commented in any way on the lives of Indian women, nor did she see any connection between them and her feminist concerns. In 1867, she was fired with enthusiasm by John Stuart Mill's parliamentary speech in support of women's suffrage. 'If I were stopping in England for good', she wrote to Richard, 'I should go in hot and strong for this cause; as it is, it does not seem of much use'.[84] Her own focus on political questions seemed far removed from anything to do with Indian women—and she had little enthusiasm for anything philan-thropic. She later recommended working with women in zenanas to one of her daughters-in-law, but it was not an activity in which she engaged herself. On the contrary, as she foreshadowed in 1867, Jane delayed her involvement in the women's movement until she was settled finally in England in the 1880s.

For all this, however, the Strachey world was surrounded by questions about sexual relationships between English officials and Indians. Inter-racial marriages occurred within the family and needed to be dealt with. This is one of many areas where one can see a marked contrast between the romantic India of Jane Strachey's imagination and the realities of the imperial world which she inhabited and whose values she ardently upheld. Her romance of India included the possibility of Anglo-Indian love affairs and marriages—especially in the distant past. In 1860, she wrote to her father of a meeting with 'Mrs Phillips, a cousin of Richard who lived with his father and mother when he was a year old'.

She is still pretty and very kind and gentle and I have lost my heart to her. Her birth is rather romantic: her father was Col. Kirkpatrick Resident of Hyderabad; her mother was a relation of the Nizam's, and fell in love with the handsome Englishman through a purdah; so he ran away with, and married her. However it is rather like sending coals to Newcastle to send a tale like that to India.[85]

'Mrs Phillips', or Kitty Kirkpatrick as she was known prior to her marriage, had been quite a notable London figure some decades earlier. In 1822, at the age of 20, she was beautiful, exotic, and wealthy, and the subject of much interest in London society. Thomas Carlyle was greatly smitten by her and many years later still recalled their first meeting. There was

the dash of a brave carriage driving up and entry of a strangely complexioned young lady with soft brown eyes and floods of bronze-red hair, really a pretty-looking, smiling, amiable though most foreign bit of magnificence and kindly splendour...her birth, as I afterwards found, an Indian romance, mother a sublime Begum, father a ditto English official, mutually adoring, wedding, living withdrawn in their own private paradise, a romance famous in the East.[86]

She was widely regarded as the original for the character of Blumine in his novel, *Sartor Resartus*. Carlyle's picture of her origin and parentage involved a strong measure of fantasy. For the original marriage between the colonel and the begum, while romantic, was also short-lived and tragic, as is made clear in William Dalrymple's *White Mughals*, which explores the Kirkpatrick story in considerable detail.[87] James Achilles Kirkpatrick was indeed pursued by and then married the young Begum Khair un-Nissa and the couple were deeply in love. Kirkpatrick, however, died within five years of their marriage. He sent two children born to the couple to England shortly before his death, and their mother never saw or heard of them again. Her life after the death of Kirkpatrick was one of considerable difficulty and hardship. She was cast out by her own kin after her marriage—and treated extremely shabbily by the colleagues and friends that Kirkpatrick had expected to care for her. She died in 1813, still in her early 30s. The two children lived with their grandfather Colonel James Kirkpatrick, alongside various cousins, some of whom also were of mixed race parentage.[88] The son, named Mir Ghulam Ali by his parents, but known in England as William George Kirkpatrick, died while still in his 20s, in 1828. Kitty, who had been called Noor un-Nissa by her parents, married Captain James Winslow Phillips, had seven children, was well accepted in English society—and in her adult years established a connection with her Indian grandmother.[89]

The Kirkpatrick story fascinated others in the Strachey family as well as Jane. But it was she who undertook the research needed to establish the marital alliances and the children of the Kirkpatricks. She was always interested in genealogical questions and documented the marital alliances of many members of the Grant and Strachey family.[90] It was she to whom Richard's oldest brother, Edward Strachey, turned in the 1880s when he wished to write an essay on James Achilles Kirkpatrick.[91] It is hard not to see something of her fantasy in both the title and the content of the article that Edward Strachey ultimately wrote, 'The Romantic Marriage of James Achilles Kirkpatrick, Sometime British Resident at the Court of Hyderabad'.[92] Strachey paints a moving picture of the passionate attachment between Kirkpatrick and his wife, and he was touched also by the fact that their daughter re-established contact with her grandmother. He knew nothing, however, of the widowhood of Khair un-Nissa. Jane Strachey seems very much to have shared his views and her fascination extended not only to James Achilles and his wife, but also to his dashing father—whom she always called 'the handsome colonel', an appellation which seemed to accept and even condone his irregular life and his many amours.

This early inter-racial marriage was noted by a later generation of Stracheys as well. Half a century later, John Strachey commented on it in his book, *The End of Empire*. But his comment was very different in tone from Jane's—and directed towards a different end: he used this story to illustrate the growing distance between English rulers and their Indian subjects in the course of the nineteenth century. 'During the eighteenth and early nineteenth centuries,' he wrote,

two of my collateral ancestors , Colonel Kirkpatrick and Edward Strachey, had married what the late nineteenth-century British would, so offensively, have called native women. Kirkpatrick had married a Bengali lady of a distinguished family and Strachey a Persian princess, in each case, so far as the family records go, without exciting the least adverse comment or injuring their careers in any way. How unthinkable such alliances would have been to my great uncles, Sir John and Sir Richard Strachey, who were members of the Governor-General's Council in the eighteen-seventies.[93]

John Strachey, jun., was of course correct. Such a marriage would have been unthinkable to his great-uncles. Indeed, Jane Strachey, who was fascinated by this earlier liaison, was shocked when her favourite brother, Trevor Grant, married a 'Eurasian woman', Clementina Gouldsbury. Clementina's Indian grandmother had married an Englishman, as had her mother. Her skin was very pale and her upbringing English, but in the eyes of the Stracheys and the Grants, she was 'black'. Trevor Grant's letter to Jane announcing his engagement makes very clear the contrast between Jane's sense of the romance of earlier mixed marriages and her disapproval of actual current ones. 'You have heard me, and I have heard you, express a very decided opinion on the subject of dark blood.' He wrote,

But think better of it if you can old girl. It really is a relief to me to know that she is not by any means pretty—you will be quit at once of the charge of doing a foolish thing for the sake of a pretty face. I asked Clementina to marry me because she is so good that she commands the respect of all who know her; because her tastes are so right; and because I felt she is just such a lady as I've never seen in India outside my father's house, & just such a woman as I felt would make me, or any man, a good wife. If it were not for the fact of blood, there could not be a person not only less objectionable but more suitable.[94]

Jane apparently wrote back to indicate her acceptance of the match, but Trevor could not show her letter to Clementina because of a sentence in it about her dark blood. 'Poor good girl', he wrote to his sister, '—its her misery night and day—though of course we neither of us ever refer to it.'[95] Jane and Richard were joined by Jane's sister Elinor in accepting the marriage as inevitable. 'It is not an agreeable connection at all,' wrote Elinor, 'but as the girl herself is good and well educated we ought not to mind'. In time, Jane became quite friendly with her new sister-in-law.

Their mother, Henrietta Grant, was a different proposition, however. 'She wrote to me very severely about it [the marriage]', wrote Elinor to Jane, '& said . . . that he [Trevor] had known for many a year that she would never receive or own in any way a black daughter-in law. And I am afraid she will not.'[96] And indeed, although in later years they corresponded, Lady Grant never actually met this daughter-in-law. Clementina Grant did not travel to England, and Trevor Grant returned only after her death.

But while Trevor and Clementina Grant remained in India, efforts were made to reclaim their sons. Trevor's questionable marriage followed an unhappy history in which he had been constantly in debt and unable to secure appropriate employment. This pattern continued after his marriage and the letters which he and his wife sent the family in England tell a tale of continuous financial hardship, of distressing illness amongst the children, and of difficult relationships between some of the children and their parents. As if begging Jane to intercede, Clementina frequently expressed fears that her sons would not survive in the Indian climate. And Jane, a practical woman, accustomed to managing her own and often her mother's family, did just that. She visited Trevor and his family frequently and took his sons back to England, the oldest when he was only 4. The extended family lost no time in linking the boys with their British heritage: Jane's sister, Elinor Colvile, insisted for example, on buying young Trevor a green kilt![97] The sons of Trevor and Clementina seem to have grown up almost entirely in the care of extended family or at boarding school. Trevor Grant, who had been an irresponsible and spendthrift young man, was a predictably irresponsible father. He did not provide adequate money for his sons and often left Richard and Jane reluctantly to make what they saw as parental decisions. Nor were the sons ever reunited or reconciled with their parents. The oldest died quite young and the other three struggled into adulthood in England, doing badly at school, having great difficulty finding jobs, and always in a state of penury. They were pitied, but kept at a distance by the rest of the family and ultimately disinherited by their father, who left his money to his Strachey nieces and nephews rather than to his own needy Eurasian offspring.

While Jane Strachey established quite a close bond with her sister-in-law, she seems not to have established relationships with any other Indian or Eurasian women. In her own household there was a clear hierarchy of Indian and British employees, which continued even when she was forced to recognize its failings. On one occasion, for example, Jane acknowledged that the Indian ayah was far more devoted to and concerned about her children than was their English nurse. The nurse, it transpired, had been whipping the 2-year-old Ralph,

> perpetually on his hands, & has done so once at least elsewhere—given him a regular whipping. The ayah came to me crying, and said he had been whipped three times; I asked Davin, & she denied it, and as one prefers taking an English woman's word to a native's I said no more about it. Yesterday I heard him crying & went to see what it was about; he was in the jampan with Davin leaning over him, as I came up she gave him three or four hard smacks on one hand, & before I had time to interfere did the same to the other: I was very angry, & she appeared rather ashamed; it was merely because he cried at leaving the ayah.[98]

While the nurse was dismissed, there were no further comments on the ayah—and far from reconsidering her attitudes, Jane entrusted her baby to another English nurse in the home of her sister-in-law when she left Ralph in India a few months later.

The general question of relations between Indians and the British was one to which Richard Strachey gave far more thought than did his wife. He had arrived in India in the 1830s when the ideal of developing close contact between British rulers and their Indian subjects was widely espoused, and while others came to question it, he continued to favour this approach after the Mutiny. When Sir Bartle Frere was about to leave India in 1867, Richard wrote to Jane that he thought Frere 'above the common run of men...What he has done most good in is the advancement of social intercourse with the natives and stimulating education amongst them. It is a singular sight to see the native ladies at various parties & driving in their carriages.'[99]

For all this, Richard Strachey believed in only very limited possibilities for interaction between British and Indians, or for the acknowledgement of Indians within the Raj. John Strachey applauded the efforts of Lord Lytton to limit the access of Indians to the Covenanted Civil Service. His particular loathing of educated Bengalis made him question the very possibility that the competitive examination, deemed the best way of finding good candidates in England, could work in India. 'It is notorious', he insisted, 'that in their case, mere intellectual acuteness is no indication of ruling power. In vigour, in courage, and in administrative ability, some of the race of Indians most backward in education are well known to be superior to other races which intellectually are more advanced.'[100] Appointment of Indians to any civil service position could only take place if it could be guaranteed that they would not in any way undermine 'the safety of our dominion'. Strachey felt it reasonable to throw open some of the judicial service to Indians. But it was always necessary to bear in mind

the excessive disinclination of Englishmen . . . to be placed in any way under the authority of natives. This is not a feeling that there is any use in arguing about or regretting . . . As a matter of fact Englishmen will not obey natives, & it is equally true that it would be difficult to find half a dozen natives in the whole country who, if placed in charge of important duties, would possess the qualifications necessary for dealing with independent Englishmen. It is at the present time as natural for a native to obey as it is for an Englishman to command.[101]

At least a decade before the controversy over the Ilbert Bill, a measure that would have given Indian magistrates the capacity to preside over cases involving British men and women, John Strachey was in no doubt of the impossibility of giving Indian magistrates any form of authority over British settlers and clearly his sympathies lay with his own countrymen.[102] Both he and Richard ultimately adhered closely to the views of John's great friend, Fitzjames Stephen concerning the need to ensure that all positions of authority in India were held by Europeans.

We cannot foresee the time in which the cessation of our rule would not be the signal for universal anarchy and ruin, and it is clear that the only hope for India is the long continuance of the Benevolent but strong government of Englishmen. Let us give to the Natives the largest possible share in the administration . . . But let there be no hypocrisy about our intention to keep in the hands of our own people those executive posts . . . on which . . . our actual hold of the country depends.[103]

Richard Strachey's adherence to this approach was made clear in the 1890s when, as chairman of the vast EIR, he oversaw its policy regarding its Indian employees. He acknowledged the grievances felt by Indian employees over their low rates of pay, but did little to offer solutions. As a concerned employer, he was prepared to develop educational provision for all the children of EIR employees. But, just as the EIR paid its European, its 'East Indian', and its 'native' employees differently, and kept then completely separated from each other, so too it offered different kinds of education in three different school systems for the children of each group.[104]

The rights of Indian women were of little interest to Jane Strachey, and of even less to her husband and brother-in-law. When it came to regulating prostitution, the needs of the Indian army outweighed any question of the rights of Indian women. This question was battled out in the 1880s in the wake of the repeal of the Contagious Diseases Acts in Britain. Under pressure from abolitionists, Lord Cross, the Secretary of State for India, proposed new regulations in 1888 which abandoned the earlier practice of requiring prostitutes in India to register and to undergo periodic examination, proposing instead that anyone 'reasonably suspected' of being contagious should be excluded from the cantonment.[105] Richard Strachey, along with his brother John, registered their dissent, arguing that the India Council would be remiss in its duty 'if it abstained from protesting against the issue of orders which are certain to cause grave injury to the health of the British Army and to serious loss of military strength'.[106]

Jane Strachey made no comments on the question of contagious diseases legislation, either in India or in Britain. But it would seem likely that she agreed with her husband. There was no sexual radicalism in her feminism, and it always fitted neatly into her imperial framework. As we have seen, she had no particular sympathy for or interest in Indian women, and much concern about the health of the British army. Nor could she see the demand for women's rights in Britain as having any connection with India. This issue came to the fore in the first decade of the twentieth century, when the needs of the empire, and the impossibility of asking Indian men to accept government by British women was a constantly repeated theme of anti-suffragists. 'The adoption of female suffrage in England', argued a widely circulated anti-suffrage pamphlet, 'would be a long step towards the disintegration of the British Empire in India, and should be steadily opposed by all who have imperial interests at heart.'[107] Faced with the combined might of ex-viceroys, Lords Cromer and Curzon, who added their weight to the Anti-Suffrage League, the leader of the National Union of Women's Suffrage Societies, Millicent Garrett Fawcett called on Lady Strachey to respond. As one whose support for the British Empire was quite as passionate as her support for women's suffrage, and who believed that Britain was far superior in all its institutions and social arrangements to any other country, Lady Strachey found this view ludicrous. 'Is it to be seriously contended that we are to model our own Constitution with reference to the beliefs & prejudices & superstitions of any or all of the races & tribes over whom our Empire extends?' she asked in a letter to *The Times* on this subject in 1908.

If so there will be a great deal more to be done than merely to refuse the suffrage to women. The democratic principle is unintelligible and repulsive to the Sikh, the Pathan, the Rajput & the average Hindu or Mussulman. Are we therefore to disfranchise the working man in England, or even to abolish parliamentary government altogether?[108]

The real point, she insisted, was that Indian loyalty depended, not on parliamentary changes in Britain, but rather on how the British Government dealt with India, and 'on the wisdom with which we there respect ideals of life altogether contrary to our own, wherever it is possible to do so without outraging justice and humanity'.

Jane Strachey's rejection of the idea that women's suffrage would threaten the British Empire meant also that she rejected the idea that there was any connection between the demand for women's suffrage and that for self-government amongst British colonies. It was not the case that she was blind to the connection between the idea of national independence and the demand of women for political rights. In her attempt to make clear to Richard how strongly she felt about women's suffrage, she argued that, 'what the freedom of Italy is to an Italian, such ought to be the cause of women to a woman'.[109] But none of this applied to India. While others whom she knew, including Beatrice Webb, came to see a connection between the demand for women's rights, on the one hand, and that for self-government and an end to imperial control, on the other, Jane Strachey rejected any such connection. Unlike Italy, India, in her view, was not a nation—and hence could make no claims to independence. 'The vast number of peoples, languages and religions which were included within this geographical framework, the hostility between the two major groups, Hindus and Muslims, and the war-like and lawless conduct of others made the very idea of self-government ludicrous.' Like Lord Balfour, she felt Indians inherently unsuited to exercise political rights. The history of India, one of successive layers of conquest, served only to underline the lack of any earlier development of appropriate political institutions. Britain, 'the most recent conqueror, however differed from its predecessors, in having been used not for destruction but for preservation, not to impose our own beliefs but to safeguard impartially the various creeds and customs of those beneath our sway'. The withdrawal of Britain would result in chaos and collapse, violent struggle between Hindu and Muslim and the wholesale relapse into crime: 'To foresee the possible destruction at the hands of our own countrymen of all that has been accomplished, & the return to misery of those for whom our lives have been spent is a thought that is almost unbearable.'[110]

An Imperial Marriage

Richard and Jane Strachey exemplify the companionate Victorian middle-class marriage that has been of so much interest to historians in the past few decades. Once thought of as an absolutely patriarchal institution, in which a dominant and powerful husband had complete control over a subordinate wife, Victorian marriage has come in recent years to be seen as both more complex and more varied than this simple model suggests.[1] This is not to suggest that husbands did not have considerable legal power over the person, property, and children of their wives, but rather to recognize that many women exerted immense influence over their husbands and that personal affection often served to mitigate the extreme nature of patriarchal power. In a similar way, in place of an idea of Victorian women as sexually ignorant and innocent, accepting with resignation their 'marital duty', recent research has suggested that shared sexual passion was evident in many marriages. All of this has led to widespread recognition of the many different ways in which Victorian men and women negotiated close, affectionate, and fulfilling relationships within the unbending structures of the law.[2]

The Strachey marriage offers an example of such negotiation. In a formal sense, theirs was a conventional imperial marriage between an almost middle-aged husband and a very much younger wife. Richard Strachey was closer in age to Jane's father, John Peter Grant, to whom he had acted as secretary in the early 1850s, than he was to Jane herself. Jane in turn followed her older sister, Elinor, in finding a husband many years her senior amongst her father's entourage. The Grants had the highest possible view of Richard Strachey and his marriage to their daughter was welcomed.

In a well-established imperial pattern, this marriage cemented already existing ties of kinship as Richard's brother, John Strachey, had recently married one of Jane's cousins.[3] It thus offered no challenge to conventional expectations in terms of age structure or family background. Nor did the Stracheys offer any overt challenge to, or even question, established male prerogatives and female duties. Richard Strachey managed all the family finances and determined where and how they lived. Jane organized their domestic and social life and supervised their children. In a way that was rather more unusual, however, Richard, depended heavily on his wife, both emotionally and intellectually. She was his confidante and adviser in every aspect of his professional life. She in turn had many intellectual, literary, and social interests of her own, some of which she expected him to share.

Over time, even the considerable age disparity between them undermined rather than reinforced a conventional sexual hierarchy. Richard Strachey was a widower of 42 when he married the 19-year-old Jane Grant. At first, he saw himself as both husband and teacher. This view changed fairly rapidly, as he began to acknowledge Jane's wisdom and intelligence and to become more interested in her literary pursuits. The authority which greater age gave him in the early years of the marriage, moreover, was reversed in the later ones and few portraits of the Stracheys omit some reference to the ways in which, in the last thirty years of their marriage, Jane Strachey became the dominant figure in the family, as her literary and musical interests, her growing enthusiasm for feminism, and her many artistic and literary friends set the tone of the household. Richard, increasingly isolated by deafness, was always much beloved, but he was relegated to the periphery of family life.

By marrying Richard Strachey, Jane imposed upon herself the life of constant movement and frequent absences from husband and children which had been the lot of her own mother and which imperial marriage always demanded. Their periods of separation from each other were painful to both Jane and Richard. This 'is a very unnatural state of existence', Jane wrote at one point, '& very odd that when by chance two perfectly congenial persons are joined together by holy matrimony they should be separated by devilish circumstance'.[4] The magical glow that Jane's cast over the 'Indian years' in her later recollections required the erasure of some of the difficult and painful episodes of her earlier life when she had had to deal with loneliness and misery and with the illness and even deaths of children, sometimes en route to India and thus without either Richard or the support of her English family.

For all their closeness, one has a sense that the frequent absences that so pained the Stracheys also helped maintain the harmony of their marriage. While they shared many intellectual interests and political and social views, there were fundamental differences between them in temperament and in their approach to the wider social world. Jane's letters to Richard always make clear how much she missed him, but they indicate also how very much she enjoyed her busy social life in his absence and list the many dinners, parties, and musical events she hosted or attended, often in the company of her older sister. She accepted readily, and with amused resignation, Richard's refusal to participate in Raj society when she was in India, but this may well have become harder to deal with had it been a constant factor in her life. Jane Strachey never criticized her husband in her correspondence, nonetheless his many demands took their toll. Jane managed well enough when it came to his constant need to be praised and to have his sense that he was inadequately recognized and rewarded assuaged. Some career decisions, especially those made in conjunction with his brother, but requiring her to change her plans suddenly and to make new arrangements for their large family, were rather harder to accept. In later years, there were several occasions when, having first agreed to spend the summer in London, Richard would suddenly decide that it was imperative that he go to the country—and Jane would have to drop everything else she was doing to find a house that he would like.

The long periods that Jane and Richard Strachey spent away from each other are of course invaluable to the historian. Without them, one would know little of the inner dynamic and texture of the Stracheys' marriage. The comments of their children offer no hint of the closeness evident in the frequent and long letters that Jane and Richard wrote each other when they were apart. The expressions of deep affection in all their letters, interspersed with detailed accounts of all their activities, reading, and ideas, give one a very clear idea both of how much the Stracheys cared for each other and of how many interests and concerns they shared. Their letters to each other serve also to characterize the Stracheys. Jane's spontaneous outpourings contrast quite strongly with the much greater formality of Richard's prose. A couple of their wedding anniversary letters serve as a good example. 'My dearest Richard', wrote Jane on their eleventh wedding anniversary in 1869,

Your letter this morning was the next best thing to having you. Do you think anybody else was ever so happy in each other? I know very well that I have the best of it, & daresay your happiness would be increased if I had a scientific turn. I, at any rate am a great deal more in love with you now, than I was eleven years ago, though I was very fond of you then, but an ignorant goose of nineteen could not be expected to know what a valuable possession you were.[5]

Richard's anniversary letter to her some years later is very different from this, not in its affection, but rather in its cast of thought. 'Dearest Janie', he wrote,

let me first do honour to the day which 19 years ago took us together to Barrackpoor and which dearest wife now finds me more loving and more sensible of your real worth than ever, though unfortunately divided from you by half the globe—Sweet cat I am constantly wanting your help and countenance—whether I am doing my work or lying awake at night in spite of Gregory—However it is better so with the knowledge that we have done what is right than otherwise without such a feeling.[6]

Although devoted to each other, Jane and Richard Strachey did not enjoy the kind of privacy that is expected in a modern marriage. They were rarely alone as a couple. Even before the advent of their own large family, they were usually surrounded by extended family. They stayed with siblings for long periods in the early years of their marriage and their own home was constantly full of siblings, nieces and nephews, and cousins. On one occasion when Jane and Richard found themselves without any other company, Jane commented in a letter to one of her daughters that it 'feels very queer to have luncheon alone'.[7] The Stracheys were fond of many of their close relatives—and of course they could not have managed their imperial life without them. Jane's parents, her older sister, Elinor Colevile, and her brother Trevor were central figures in the Stracheys' lives, as were Richard's brothers, especially John. But there were vast numbers of close and distant cousins who were also regular visitors to the Strachey home and were part of Jane and Richard's daily life.

Both Richard and Jane Strachey lived to an advanced age. Richard died in 1908, when he was 91. Jane outlived him by twenty years, dying at the age of 88 in 1928. The Stracheys were remarkable not just for their longevity, but for the duration of their active lives. When they returned from India in the 1870s, it was not to retire, but rather to become absorbed in a host of new activities. Richard not only continued his Indian activities, but also extended and developed his scientific interests and became closely involved in the Royal Society. Jane gave birth to her last child just before she turned 50—and then turned her attention to editing and writing a series of books, to giving lessons and drama readings in schools and to interested groups of women, and to the women's movement.

❦ I ❦

The Stracheys' long and happy marriage was not without its problems. Richard Strachey was not an easy man and, despite his great devotion to his wife, one has a sense that his impatience and 'peppery' temperament were not entirely absent from this intimate relationship. 'I sometimes think now that you are so far away', he wrote to Jane in the first year of their marriage, when he had to go to Bangalore while she remained in Calcutta, 'that I ought to have been more loving which you were with me. And I suppose that I really did love you then as much as now—as much as possible—though the pain of separation makes me now think I might have been more affectionate in appearance.'[8]

It was his hypochondria, rather than his short temper, that caused the greatest initial difficulties, however. Almost immediately after he married Jane, Richard began to suffer from what others took to be an attack of the dyspepsia, but which he imagined to be a terminal illness. His health had never been robust and he had sometimes succumbed to fevers in India that made it necessary for him to go north to a hill station to escape the heat. This time, however, he believed himself to be seriously ill and in danger of his life. Thus in the first year of their marriage, while Jane waited to communicate to him the exciting news of her first pregnancy, Richard was writing increasingly frantic letters to her parents expressing despair at the thought he might never see her again. He did not want her to leave Calcutta to come to him in Bangalore, he wrote, fearing that she would arrive only to find him already dead![9] Several members of the family felt that Richard's response to his illness was hysterical. His brother-in-law James Colvile, for example, wrote rather gently to suggest his belief 'that your view of your health has been tinged by the depression which is an incident of dyspepsia' and his 'expectation that we shall soon hear a better account of you'.[10] Eventually this attack of dyspepsia passed, and although both his general health and his digestive system were always the source of some anxiety, Richard does not seem to have been as fearful about his health and his future ever again.

It is impossible to explain precisely why he should have reacted so strongly to the symptoms of dyspepsia at this time—and hard not to see it as indicating fear or at least anxiety about his marriage. There was perhaps some reason for this: Jane Grant was Richard Strachey's second wife and her predecessor, Caroline Bowles, had died within a few months of coming out to India with him in 1855. He was apparently severely affected by this loss. Both his own family and that of his first wife were anxious about him and sought constant reassurance that he was recovering from this bereavement. All of them were overjoyed when he became engaged to Jane.[11] Richard too appeared to be intensely happy when he and Jane married, but it is possible that he feared another sudden and tragic ending, and made himself the centre of a potential tragedy to pre-empt the possible loss to himself of another wife. Jane's parents were well acquainted with her strength, intelligence, organizing ability, and charm, and had no doubt of her capacity to manage this marriage. Her father, who was devoted to Richard, felt that Jane was all he needed to complete his life. 'You must look after him and keep him idle and enjoying himself strolling about and insisting on his own opinion over the fire', he wrote, on hearing that the doctors had said that there was nothing the matter with Richard 'except derangement caused by overwork...He is well worth taking care of...Your society will make him "jolly" which is what he wants.'[12]

In later years, Jane Strachey's children often commented on her lack of interest in their emotional lives and relationships. 'She never had a notion of what any of us children were doing or thinking,' wrote her daughter Dorothy, 'and intrigues of the most obvious and violent nature might be, and indeed were, carried on under her very nose without her having the smallest suspicion of them.'[13] This capacity to ignore the drama of daily life, and to maintain her own equanimity in the face of constant emotional storms, was a very important quality in her marriage. Richard Strachey later appeared to his children as the calm one who maintained the even tenor and balance of daily life. In his correspondence with his wife, however, one sees him as a man in constant need of reassurance and support as he felt himself unrecognized and inadequately rewarded in his work and constantly prey to ill health. In reading the letters of Richard and Jane Strachey, one sometimes feels an echo of Virginia Woolf's *To the Lighthouse* with its portrait of Mr Ramsay and of the Victorian patriarch as hysteric.

This is not to suggest that Jane herself received no support in her marriage, or that she was not sometimes a difficult person. On the contrary, once Richard got over his initial anxieties, he was clearly an affectionate and devoted husband, and one in whom Jane felt able to confide. Her emotional reserve had been a matter of some concern to Elinor Colevile, who felt that it had been both a cause and a symptom of the difficulties experienced by their parents. 'It is the greatest comfort in the world', she wrote to Jane, to tell one's husband 'all the troubles and difficulties . . . & if I might give one piece of advice, it would be to tell him everything—I am sure it is a happy and a wise plan—one always feels right then. But I daresay you do, only dearest you are reserved you know—but don't be so with your husband.'[14] Jane scarcely needed this prompting. From the start of their marriage, she seems to have enjoyed telling Richard all about her life and concerns. She tried to keep a journal for him when he was away, 'for it is such a comfort to sit down and write to you . . . I shall tell you everything, however trivling as Mr Garrod says, but I know you will like that.'[15] Her letters to him also suggest that Richard was the only person to whom Jane was prepared to show weakness and sorrow. 'Dear Richard', she wrote in one of her saddest letters, describing the funeral of her baby daughter, Olivia, 'I don't like to write you nothing but sadness—but you know what kind of person I am & that I can't bear any one else to see me cry.'[16] Richard too was saddened by this news. 'You know dearest darling that I feel with you & for you, as thoroughly as possible', he wrote in response to Jane's letter, 'and it adds no little to my grief that I was away when this ill fortune arrived—& that you had to bear it all alone'.[17] He in turn sent constant expressions of love and of longing in his letters, making clear that he regarded Jane as 'my other self' and confided to her all his feelings, plans, ambitions, and disappointments.

Although her children found Jane extremely hard to deal with in her later years, there is no indication that Richard did so. After Richard's death, both Lytton and James Strachey found that their mother's high-pitched shrieking laughter and her passion for jokes and funny stories made it almost impossible for them to stay in her house.[18] How Richard Strachey felt about these things is not possible to discern. His deafness certainly protected him from some of them—and it is at least likely that he shared Jane Strachey's fascination with the minutiae of Indian life and politics to a greater extent than his children did.

Richard's frequent expressions of his longing to 'hold my sweet Janie in my arms' suggest a strong physical and sexual bond within the Strachey marriage. Although Dorothy Strachey regarded her parents as lacking any element of sensuality, and Lytton believed that large Victorian families were a product of will rather than desire, other evidence suggests a very different picture.[19] The letters of Jane and Richard Strachey do not, of course, actually discuss any aspect of their sexual relationship, but they certainly make explicit their physical affection. 'You are to remember that I am always thinking about you dearest Janie', Richard wrote in one of their absences. 'I wake in the night & hear the clock strike—and I calculate what my cat is doing—just going to bed—or lying fast asleep—and I want to come and hug & kiss her all up.'[20]

The emotional tenor of the Strachey marriage is easiest to discern in the first decade of their marriage, the time in which they were most often apart and hence corresponded constantly. Their letters are more sporadic after Richard retired from the army in 1871. This is not to say that they were always together. On the contrary, they were frequently separated as Richard often travelled in pursuit of scientific interests, while Jane spent a lot of time with her own siblings. These absences tended to be short, however, and their letters to each other during them dealt with practical details rather than with personal feelings. As with any marriage, one has a sense that as the years wore on, a settled affection replaced the intensity of feeling evident in their early letters. But their closeness and importance to each other seems to have continued throughout their lives.

One important part of this centred on the large number of intellectual interests the Stracheys shared. Both had a particularly Victorian concern for self-improvement. In the early stages of their marriage, it was Jane who was the more anxious to extend her intellectual understanding. Like many other upper middle-class Victorian women, she had been sent to a small private school which offered a very limited curriculum. She had a strong sense of the inadequacy of her own formal education and a great desire to remedy it. Richard, as an older man, already established as a scientist and an important administrator, provided assistance and support. He assumed a somewhat tutelary tone in his letters, losing no time in pointing out to Jane the merits of a scientific approach to all questions. Jane was very willing to be tutored. After the birth of their first son in 1862, she was determined,

to begin steadily to improve my mind, on account of my boy; not of course that I am likely directly to teach him anything recondite whilst he is under my care, but that if my mind is rational it must influence his rationally. This resolution has been much strengthened by reading an essay of Sydney Smith's on 'Female Education'.[21]

Her reading programme centred on the works of John Stuart Mill. She began with his *Political Economy* and went on to work her way also through *Utilitarianism* and *Representative Government*. Richard was delighted both with her efforts and with her response to her reading. 'What you write about the Mill is very good', he wrote in response to her comments on *Political Economy*,

& what you say you feel is what you should feel. I have repeatedly said to you Madame that you must *submit* yourself to be taught—accept provisionally what the masters of science tell you—and learn how to understand fully and judge for yourself. You will not submit yourself to *me*—I hope you may be more tractable to Mr Mill. Be good and stick to your resolution of eschewing rubbish & of making yourself the wise cat you can be—and you will not only make me proud and happy but in the end satisfy yourself more too.[22]

Richard's letters to Jane sometimes resemble notes for a lecture rather than intimate communications with a spouse. 'Yes indeed', he wrote to her shortly after their marriage,

the so called positivism is the back bone of modern progress; and when you get to the bottom of it what does it all mean, but that you should not accept as worthy of belief anything for which there is not proper proof. Leave off assuming and supposing your faith, and so far as you can get at facts, build exclusively on them. Train your mind to distinguish a fact from an hypothesis or an assumption.[23]

Jane was not perturbed by his tone. She endorsed his views on positivism and wondered whether she might take up mathematics in her desire to 'give myself a systematic education even now'.[24] She read philosophy and history energetically, preparing herself for a year in Edinburgh in 1867 by reading Hume. She shared her husband's enthusiasm not only for science, but for the scientists whom he numbered amongst his close friends. After spending a week with some of them, including Hooker, Lubbock, and Tyndall in the later 1860s, she was, she wrote, 'forever convinced . . . of the superiority of science in developing worthy & charming men!'[25]

Jane was not simply a passive recipient of ideas, information, and instruction, however. On the contrary, the Strachey correspondence suggests a shifting balance even in their intellectual relationship almost from the start. Jane was fluent in French and Italian and read widely in both French and English literature. Under her guidance, Richard began to do so too, interspersing his reading of government reports and scientific papers with George Sand and Michelet. His reading of Auguste Comte in the early 1860s prompted him to 'perceive that the tendency of my own education & instincts has been to exalt unduly the value of the sciences'.[26] Under Jane's guidance he began also to follow French political developments and to discuss them with her. 'Your letters are as wise and as good as possible,' he wrote a few years after their marriage, 'and I think I may learn as much from you as you from me.'[27]

Jane had a deep desire to be involved in all her husband's interests and activities and an absolute passion for public affairs and Richard came more and more to depend on her critical insight. 'Every paper written by my husband was brought to me to read over before it was finally dealt with', she later recalled, 'and verbal criticisms were freely allowed and generally adopted'.[28] This statement is amply borne out in their correspondence, which frequently deals with papers and articles that Richard was writing and that he wanted her to read. Even dispatches which he wrote for the government on technical matters went first to her. In 1880, for example, he sent her a draft of the dispatch he was writing for the Secretary of State on railway estimates. 'I want your intelligence brought to bear on it *at once*', he wrote, 'therefore send me back your views as early as possible.'[29]

It was not only Jane's ideas and knowledge that Richard came to depend on, but also her social skills.[30] She was, he noted in the entry on the Stracheys that he provided for Francis Galton in 1900, 'generally reputed to be highly intelligent and with considerable social gifts. Great literary knowledge and powers of criticism.'[31] Shortly after they married, she began to make him participate more in social life, something he tended to ignore when he was by himself. Her sociability and charm gave her a much better sense than he of how to manage his professional world and she constantly advised him on how to deal with colleagues and superiors. Like his brother John, Jane reminded Richard of the need for small courtesies and social niceties, especially to those in authority who had the power to decide his fate.[32] Richard was well aware of the value of her social assistance. 'You tell me all about the parties', he wrote on one occasion when she was in London while he was in Calcutta. 'In fact I hardly ever go out—I find that some how or other when I do I get wrong and so shirk it. But I am not much troubled with invitations as I never call & have no Janie to make herself agreeable for me.'[33]

Jane Strachey was an extremely supportive wife, but she in turn expected Richard to share and understand her interests and concerns, including her growing interest in feminism. Both Stracheys read Mill and endorsed his ideas about utilitarianism and about scientific method. Jane was also strongly attracted to Mill's arguments in support of women's suffrage. She signed the petition in support of women's suffrage which he presented to Parliament shortly after his election in 1867, although she took no part in the early campaign for women's suffrage in Britain. 'I hope you will read J. S. Mill's speech for women' she wrote to Richard after Mill had made his first speech in the House of Commons supporting women's suffrage, 'don't you think 75 is a very respectable minority? And the nonsense talked on the other side was most encouraging. If I were stopping in England for good, I should go in hot and strong for this cause; as it is, it does not seem of much use.'[34] Richard advised caution before leaping into feminist campaigns, but he certainly accepted Jane's ideas about the need for a proper education for their daughters. All were sent to the best school Jane could find, with the youngest two going also to university—and Richard relished their academic success.

Like most Victorian feminists, Jane Strachey combined a strong sense of the need for political and legal change in the status of women with an equally strong adherence to conventional ideas about the necessary differences in the nature and the role of men and women.[35] Like many middle-class women with large families, she happily relinquished domestic duties to her daughters as soon as she possibly could. But she never questioned her wifely duties. While Jane often offered Richard advice, and clearly lived for the most part much as she chose, she never made overt demands or issued instructions. Hence in the final years of their marriage, when he was in his 80s and in need of assistance in getting up and going to bed, it was never Jane who indicated to him that bed time had come and that his nurse was waiting for him, but rather one of her daughters.

❧ II ☙

The Stracheys became parents soon after their marriage. Jane and Richard married on 4 January 1859 and by May of that year Jane was already pregnant. Her first child, Elinor, was born in December. Thereafter, children continued to appear at more or less regular intervals for the next thirty years. Jane gave birth to six children in the 1860s and to three in each of the following two decades. Ten of her thirteen children survived into

61

adult life, making quite a large family even by the standards of the Victorian upper middle class and an exceptionally large one within the Stracheys' circle of family and friends. Jane's sister, Elinor, had only one child and her brothers, like Richard's, had families of five or six children. Jane's continual child bearing was a source of concern to the family and sometimes of distress to herself. 'I am very sorry to say that number 7 is on the road and may be expected in November', she wrote to her mother in June 1869. 'I have not told a creature yet . . . because I thought they would have hardly recovered from Ralph yet—as I am sure I haven't. In fact I have been in a disgusted frame of mind as it puts all my winter plans out of joint.'[36] The family could not refrain from comment when the babies kept arriving. Was the strange name Pernel, given to Jane's tenth child, a reference to her 'perennial pregnancies', asked her sister-in-law, Kate Strachey?[37] 'We are all glad to know that your last troubles passed with satisfactory results', her mother wrote, after the birth of James in 1887, 'and hope it may be the last time we will have to send you congratulations on such an occasion.'[38]

The advent of children both underlined the constant separations that were an invariable part of imperial marriage and sometimes made them longer and harder. Jane was often miserable when she was away from Richard in the early years of their marriage and became very distressed when pregnancy threatened to make their separations even longer. They were together for the birth of their first two children, Elinor born in India in 1859 and Dick born when they returned to England in 1861. The following year, however, Richard returned to India without Jane. She was again pregnant and was prevailed upon by the family to have the baby at home. She could not endure the idea that she might have to remain there for a long time. 'Mama said if I had a bad confinement I might not be allowed to go to India for two years,' she wrote to Richard in January 1862, 'so when I came up to bed I cried and cried at the bare idea like any goose.'[39] This confinement was not difficult, however, and Jane booked a passage to India for herself, three children and two nannies when the new baby was just three months old. This baby daughter did not survive the voyage, however, and after several days of acute illness with fever and diarrhoea died and was buried at sea in November 1862. 'It is dreadful to think her father has never seen her', she wrote to her sister, Elinor, the day after her death,[40] and Richard grieved that she had to bear this blow alone.[41]

Two more children died in the 1860s, and Richard was absent on these occasions too. This was particularly hard when Olivia, Jane's favourite baby, died suddenly in Scotland in 1867. Richard had been in England for the birth of Olivia, but had to return to India soon after. Jane adored Olivia. 'I think I was more fond of her than of any babies whilst they were babies,' she wrote sadly to Richard after her death. The death itself was sudden and unexpected: the bright and alert baby suddenly became ill, stopped eating, and died within a matter of days. Jane was devastated. She took all the children to Olivia's funeral, where the 6-year-old Dick had to stand in for his father and act as head of the family. Olivia's death made her very anxious about the other children. 'I get so nervous at night', she wrote to Richard, 'and wake up thinking I hear someone tap at the door to say one of them is ill. This will wear off, & is simply the result of the shock, for it was very sudden to me; one day she seemed well, & the next day she was dead.'[42] Jane did not mention the loss of Olivia in any subsequent letters. Nonetheless it continued to have an impact on her and on her children. Dorothy, who had been born a year before Olivia, was clearly overshadowed by her and dominated by this memory. 'Only the day before she was taken ill,' Jane wrote to Richard, Kew, her maid, 'said to me You seem to think much more of her ma'am than you did of Miss Dolly'. Dorothy did not mention Olivia in her extant correspondence, but she took the name Olivia both as her pseudonym and as the eponymous title of her only novel.[43] Even Lytton was affected. He was not born until thirteen years after Olivia's death, but wrote a poem addressed to this dead baby when he was 10. Olivia's death was followed two years later by that of another baby, Roger. This time Jane seemed rather less upset. 'About six weeks ago my troubles came to a head,' she wrote to her father when she was in India in 1869,

& I was prematurely confined of a little boy, who lived a few hours, & was christened Roger; I had not expected the child to be born alive, but when I heard him cry & saw him which I did for a few seconds in the intervals of unconsciousness, I thought it was all right, & it was a shock to me to find that he had died & was buried without my knowing anything about it.[44]

Despite the concerns of her mother, Jane occasionally gave birth to children in India without ill effect. Roger died in India, but before this Ralph had arrived without excessive difficulty or complications. As the years passed, however, Jane had to leave her older children behind when she went out to Richard in India. Like other imperial families, the Stracheys thought it necessary that their children be educated in England where they would have appropriate instruction, attend the right kinds of school, and learn the discipline that seemed so hard to establish in India. Dick and Elinor were both deemed to be of school age in 1867. Jane was very anxious about leaving them behind and hated the idea of her son, who was only 6, having to go to boarding school and be cared for by strangers. When the Coleviles suggested that both the children stay with them, Jane was so relieved that she 'could hardly keep from crying the rest of the day'.[45]

Although the main reason she went to India was to be with her husband, Jane was separated from Richard for long periods even there. Richard's supervision of railways, irrigation, and other public works required constant travel around India and much time based in Calcutta. Jane, like the other Raj wives, stayed in the cooler climate of Simla. Life without Richard in India was sometimes more difficult than it was at home as Jane lacked the companionship of her own immediate family. When she was there in 1867, she shared a house in Simla with her sister-in-law, Kate Strachey, and '5 children under 5 years old to look after'. This was not an altogether easy arrangement. 'Kate Strachey and I are spending the winter up here whilst our husbands are together in Calcutta', Jane wrote to her father. 'Kate is stouter and less impetuous, but very good natured and was very kind to me when I was ill. She does not take much interest in my particular crotchets, so I air them less frequently than I should perhaps like to do—that however is a negative disadvantage. Positively we get on very well indeed.'[46] One has a sense that she was shedding the best possible light on a difficult situation and passing on to more pleasant topics, however, as Kate was an ardent opponent of women's suffrage and shared few of Jane's interests. She and Richard certainly agreed 'that life is not worth having under existing conditions',[47] and they were both relieved when he was finally able to retire from his government position in the early 1870s.

Child bearing continued to dominate Jane's life in the next two decades and she gave birth to Pippa in 1872, followed by Oliver in 1874 and Joan Pernel in 1876. The Stracheys were now back home, but the idea that they were permanently settled in Britain proved to be illusory. As we have seen, Richard Strachey's trip to India to organize the purchase of the East India Railway extended until 1879. Jane was very unhappy about Richard's prolonged absence and resented having to disrupt her own family again in order to go out to join him. She felt Richard was putting John's needs above those of his own family, but her protests were in vain.[48]

In 1879, Richard and Jane returned from India and this time they settled permanently back home. Jane was now 40, but her family was by no means complete. She gave birth to Lytton in 1880, followed by Marjorie in 1882, and finally James in 1887. There is some suggestion that Jane herself was becoming exhausted with child bearing by this stage. In the letter she sent in 1882 to congratulate Jane on the birth of the new baby who bore her husband's surname, Edith Lytton wrote, 'even if the dear little boy was not wanted before he came, it is such a blessing when all the suffering is over, and I know that you love babies so am sure you are happy altogether'.[49] As it turned out, it was the last two sons, Lytton and James, whom Jane considered the most remarkable of her children and to whom she was most devoted. Her affection for these two sons was widely recognized in the family and it is clearly evident in her letters to them. While all the other children were addressed alternately as 'dear' and 'dearest', 'Jembeau' (the name James was given as a child) was always addressed as 'darling' in letters overflowing with affection. Jane's relationship with Lytton was slightly different and it was their shared love of literature that made the special bond that is evident in their correspondence. Their letters were sequenced through a literary game: the reciting of consecutive lines of a comic poem. Poor Marjorie, the daughter sandwiched between these two adored sons, never got a look in.

The pattern of imperial life meant that the Strachey children were very much Jane's responsibility. It was she who oversaw their care in infancy, and supervised their early education. She felt 'more like a schoolmistress than ever', she wrote to her father in 1866, with six children to look after, only four of whom were her own. The other two were the children of Richard's brother John and his wife, Kate Strachey. She had employed a daily governess, but the young woman 'is quite unable to teach anything at all. She is pretty and good natured, and I daresay the children will do pretty well when Richard goes, & I can be more in the school room seeing what they are about.'[50] It was she too who made all the decisions about their schooling and activities throughout their childhood and adolescence. Richard sent instructions and advice, but it was Jane who had the final say. This in turn meant that the children played a rather larger part in her life than they did in Richard's. They were often close companions with whom she spent a great deal of time. This was so particularly when she was in India, but it was evident in Britain as well. Jane Strachey was not a conventional mother. She was rarely involved in or concerned with the direct physical care of her children. Indeed, it is notable that it was when they were staying with her sister, Elinor Colevile, that the familial problem of spinal weakness was both diagnosed and treated. Nonetheless, her letters provide a detailed summary of their interests, activities, and comments and she enjoyed their company and both encouraged and entered into many of their activities.

By contrast, Richard was often absent and seems to have been much less involved in the children's lives. His letters suggest that the constant presence of children was sometimes a nuisance, interfering with his relationship with his wife. 'How are we to behave when I get back to Italy?', he asked in December 1870, when he was returning from India and Jane was taking the children there to meet him. 'Will you send the children to England via Malta & we go alone by Vienna and Dresden back? I think this would have merit . . . I funk the Railway back with all that tribe . . . we shall have no peace of mind which otherwise would not be disturbed.'[51] This is not to suggest that Richard Strachey was not a concerned father, but as we will see, his absences, his formality of speech, and his sense of family heritage and of duty all made him sometimes both demanding and distant, especially in relation to his sons.

III

While children were central to the Strachey marriage right from the start, establishing a home was not. Richard's Indian career meant that they led a somewhat peripatetic existence for several years, moving back and forth from Britain to India without a settled home in either place. They stayed with relatives or rented houses for short spells in London, Simla, and Edinburgh throughout the 1860s. Jane Strachey's lack of domestic skills and interest and of aesthetic sense and taste have been much commented upon both by her children and by those who have written about them.[52] These qualities, however, served her very well in the years when she had no capacity to establish her own home and had to make do with whatever offered. She greatly enjoyed the elegance and splendour of the grand house that she and Richard rented in Simla in 1861, with its large drawing room and garden. But she managed equally well when forced to live in dreary surroundings. In 1867, she rented a house in Edinburgh for a year for herself and her children. The house was very dirty, she wrote to her father, 'the furniture rather dreadful; faded worked screen and mechanical clocks and stuffed parrots which distressed Richard very much, but as he is to live there only a month or so, I don't think he need mind.'[53] Jane spent her time in Edinburgh reading Hume and Mill, singing in a choir, and becoming interested in the cause of women's suffrage—and never commented on the house again.

Nonetheless, Jane took some pride in her capacity for domestic management in the early years of her marriage. It was mostly her financial competence and capacity to get the most out of her money that gave her pleasure. 'We have settled in our own house and I am deep in household business,' she wrote to her father when she and Richard were renting their first home in England in 1860.

I keep the bills regularly and in beautiful order, and shall be able to furnish you with any statistics concerning them that you may require. We have 4 servants: nurse, housemaid, cook and man. I find them all in everything and give the nurse £16; the housemaid £14; the cook £18 and the man £40. It is certainly a saving to give them beer as by paying ready money you get a 9 gallon cask for 9/- where as retail it is 2d a pint. I allow a pint a day to the women and a quart to the man; also cheaper to give them washing as washer woman will do it cheaper if she has the whole house.

Jane regretted the limitations of her cook, who 'can do plain things, but not side dishes which are necessary to use up the joints when there are only 2 in the family', and who had no common sense.[54]

The life of constant movement that followed Jane's marriage was not a novelty. She had become accustomed to this pattern from early childhood, as her mother too moved from relative to relative in the time she was at home and not with her husband in India. Jane in turn had spent time either at boarding school, or staying with relatives. The amount of movement that her life had entailed was evident in her comment that, when the Stracheys moved into Stowey House in Clapham in 1872, it 'was the first time that I had ever spent more than two years in the same house'.[55] The Stracheys bought this house after Richard finally retired from the Indian army. Jane had now to furnish a large family home and rather enjoyed going to auctions to purchase the many things needed. She took great pride in some of her purchases, but here too her concerns were financial ones. 'It was before the days when Sheraton became so fashionable', she later recalled, and she made a considerable profit on her own liking for his work. 'I bought a really beautiful table of his . . . I paid £18 for it, and when forty-seven years afterwards, I had to sell it, it went for £3,000.'[56]

In 1884 the Stracheys moved to 69 Lancaster Gate, a house apparently found for them by their oldest daughter, Elinor Rendel, who was already married by this time and lived close by. This house, in which they lived for twenty-four years, is the one with which they are most closely identified largely through the descriptions of it provided by Lytton Strachey and his friends. It was, Lytton noted, using a favourite Strachey adjective, a 'portentous place', remarkable both for its physical size, extreme ugliness, and appalling design. There was a basement with a vast drawing room above and then four floors of bedrooms, many of which were small and dark. Its dark narrow passage had ochre walls and a 'tessellated floor of magenta and indigo tiles'. The house was also extremely inconvenient, with one bathroom and a lavatory 'in an impossible position midway between the drawing-room and the lowest bedroom floors . . . to reach which, one had to run the gauntlet of stairs innumerable, and whose noises of rushing waters were all too audible in the drawing-room just below'. Despite its vast size, it had too few rooms, so that while Sir Richard had a sitting-room and the daughters shared a tiny room, Jane Strachey had no room of her own.[57] Jane Strachey was well aware of the ugliness of the house, but by this time seems rather to have given up the idea that it was her responsibility to do anything about it. In 1894 she wrote to tell Lytton that 'we have decided to improve the appearance of the dining room walls whose hideousness has at last got beyond bearing'. They planned to reduce the height by putting up a black moulding with a decorative paper below. There had been great difficulty in settling on the wall paper, but finally they found one everyone liked, although Jane was sure it was 'contrary to all artistic principles'.[58]

In Lytton Strachey's view, an important element in the family home in Lancaster Gate, with its vast and dominating drawing room, was its capacity to contain the Stracheys' extended family. 'The drawing room', he wrote,

was a family room . . . and the family combinations and permutations within it were very various . . . It was on Sunday afternoons, when my mother was invariably at home, that the family atmosphere, reinforced from without, reached its intensest and its oddest pitch. Then the drawing-room gradually grew thick with aunts and uncles, cousins and connections, with Stracheys, Grants, Rendels, Plowdens, Battens, Ridpaths, Rowes. One saw that it had been built for them—it held them all so nicely, so naturally, with their interminable varieties of age and character and class.[59]

The capacity to entertain these vast numbers of people and indeed the whole vital tenor of life of 69 Lancaster Gate came to an end when their financial situation forced the Stracheys to move to a much smaller house in Belsize Park Gardens in 1907. Duncan Grant, who had lived with them in Lancaster Gate and visited Belsize Park Gardens often, commented on the contrast between the noise, vitality, and constant excitement of Strachey life at Lancaster Gate and the dullness of Belsize Park Gardens. By the time the family moved there, Pernel and Marjorie were both living away from home and so the family itself was much smaller. Richard Strachey too had withdrawn completely and spent most of his time in his own room, and there was none of the liveliness or sociability that had characterized the Stracheys in the past.

❧ IV ❧

The close ties to extended family that Lytton Strachey saw as so significant in explaining 69 Lancaster Gate were evident in every aspect of the Strachey's lives. Jane and Richard Strachey both came from fairly large families: Richard had four brothers and one sister, while Jane had five brothers and two sisters. They had both had very close ties to particular siblings in their early life and these remained extremely important throughout their married life. Richard's close bond with his brother John was matched by Jane's close relationship with her older sister, Elinor Colevile, and her brother, Trevor Grant. In addition, Jane's parents were extremely important figures in the Stracheys' lives.

The relationships between the Stracheys and their siblings were not particularly unusual either in their closeness or in their alternating pattern of demand and support. Jane Strachey's parents, however, made somewhat excessive demands. For the most part, these were a consequence of their very unhappy marriage. Both Jane Strachey and her sister, Elinor Colevile, had been aware of their parents' unhappiness from childhood and consciously attempted to establish relationships with their own husbands that were different from those of their father and mother. The problem of their parents' marriage could not be avoided, however, and in the early years of their own married lives, Jane and Elinor and their husbands were called upon to assist in negotiating the marital affairs of the older Grants.

There are few papers to indicate exactly what occurred, but it is clear that the Grant marriage had long been a difficult one. Henrietta Grant was a great beauty, but her letters suggest that she was also moody, demanding, nervous, sometimes depressive, and singularly incompetent when it came to ordinary domestic and familial responsibilities. John Peter Grant, although adored by his daughters, Jane and Elinor, seems to have been peremptory, impatient, and unkind to his sons—and probably also to his wife. Gossip, originating with one of Henrietta and John's grandsons, Duncan Grant, suggests that Henrietta succumbed to the charm of other men in the long periods of time in India when she was separated from Grant—and that two of Henrietta's children were fathered by someone other than her husband.[60] This story accords with references in Sir James Colevile's letters to the Grants' 'terrible and painful past'.[61] Jane Strachey's letters to Richard Strachey also contain a slightly cryptic comment about the fact that when she went to be churched after the birth of her third child in 1862, her mother insisted on accompanying her—and the clerk 'who knows the real state of the case' was very put out.[62]

Grant spent many years in India without his wife and when he was about to leave permanently in 1862 made it clear that he did not wish to live with her again. He had no intention of involving them both in the scandal that would follow from a divorce and proposed to maintain a facade of marriage and to provide financially for his wife and all the children. Grant confided in both his sons-in-law, Richard Strachey and Sir James Colevile (who were old friends), and then in his two older daughters. 'He has no intention of altering the status of the children', Richard wrote to Jane, after discussing Grant's plans with him, and it 'may be necessary to get your mother not to object. If there is any tendency to deal harshly with your mother, I am quite certain that the best remedy is to be found in the influence that you and Elinor could produce—persist if necessary until you are successful.'[63]

James Colevile and Richard Strachey both seem to have accepted that this separation, while regrettable, was inevitable. 'I don't think that with their two tempers', Colevile wrote to Strachey, '& the memory of that terrible and painful past daily coming up between them, that their life would be anything but daily martyrdom. And for martyrdom neither has much vocation.'[64] But Jane did not want her parents to separate and her mother, Henrietta Grant, did not want a separation either. She wrote begging her husband to reconsider and to attempt a reconciliation. In September, Jane, who had just given birth to their third child, wrote to tell Richard that 'Papa has been here, mama begging him to let her be with him. I have been saying what I can. All very unhappy and I don't know what will be the end of it.'[65] The next time she wrote to Richard, however, Jane reported that she was now very happy. 'Papa has agreed to a trial reconciliation.' By October, the Grants were formally reconciled and remained together until the death of John Peter Grant in 1893. He remained deeply attached to Jane and Richard and when he inherited the Rothiermurchus Estate from his older brother hoped that they would settle and build a house there. After investigating the cost, Richard decided it was impossible. 'Words cannot express my intense disappointment at you having abandoned the scheme of building a house at Rothiermurchus', his father-in-law wrote, on hearing his decision. 'But I think you have not taken into your calculations the certainty that you could at any time dispose of the house without loss . . . can you not review the question in this light?' 'Can you not come to us again to stay this year', he added, 'I want you to give me a lesson in astronomy.'[66] It was perhaps just as well the Strachey did not take up this suggestion: while Jane's parents papered over their differences, they did not establish a harmonious relationship and their life continued to be filled with disagreement and disputes. Henrietta Grant, who often came off worst in verbal clashes, retaliated by rationing her husband's food. In his final years, visitors expressed some concern that she planned to starve him to death![67]

Grant was prepared to live with his wife, and to provide financial support for her sons—but he had no inclination to look after them. Henrietta felt that the task was impossible for her to undertake—and concurred with her husband in seeking to hand the parental responsibilities over to the Stracheys. 'If you are still disposed to be troubled with the entire control and responsibility of Charlie and Bartle for Sir John', Henrietta Grant wrote to Richard in 1873, 'I am willing to make over to you every atom of authority I am supposed to have over them. If you accept I will consider myself at once effaced and all matters regarding them will be between you and Sir John . . . I only ask one thing that I may be spared all consultations on, and even knowledge of, your arrangements.'[68] Sir John in turn wrote to Richard of his son Bartle, that,

I hereby make him over to you as your slave. He has been spoilt and like other spoilt boys is bad and unmanageable. I am afraid Woolwich will be as much beyond his stupid head as India has been beyond Charlie's. Still I suppose he had better try as the education for Woolwich is likely to be as generally useful when he is thrust on his own resources as any other . . . And I hereby make Charlie over to your command—And I think it very good of you to be troubled with such a brace of ne'er do wells.[69]

Richard supervised the Grant sons and saw them into the established family path of Indian service—for which they seem to have been little better suited than were his own sons. But the need to oversee Jane's family did not end there. In the 1890s, Jane helped to organize art classes and provided a home for her nephew, Duncan Grant, while his parents were in India. As we have seen, she and Richard also took some responsibility for the 'East Indian' sons of her brother, Trevor Grant. Jane also made arrangements for her younger sister, Henrietta, who was intellectually disabled and needed to be provided with a home and care.

It was fortunate for the Stracheys that not all their familial relationships were as demanding as those with Jane's parents and brothers. On the contrary, there were others from which the Stracheys derived considerable support. Foremost among these was that with Jane's older sister and her husband, Lady Elinor and Sir James Colevile.[70] The Coleviles offered their home as a base for the Stracheys when they first went to England after their marriage. Elinor was Jane Strachey's closest friend and companion and the two women read, shopped, and entertained together as well as sharing all the details and many of the responsibilities of their daily life. Elinor's husband, Sir James Colevile, seems also to have felt a little like an older brother to both Richard and Jane. When Richard departed from England in 1862, it was Colevile who accompanied him to Dover and saw him onto the steamer. Prior to that, Colevile had taken Richard Strachey to meet Lord Elgin who was to be the next viceroy.[71] He took care of Richard's family, keeping him fully informed about the state of Jane's health when she was pregnant and later joining with Elinor in offering to care for all the Strachey children when Richard and Jane were in India.

The Coleviles offered other forms of support too. Elinor Colevile clearly regarded Jane as her intellectual leader, but was in no doubt of her superiority when it came to matters of taste. She had no hesitation in giving Jane advice on fashion and dress, bringing her own seamstress to sort out Jane's wardrobe, buying her many items of clothing—and absolutely insisting on providing the train and supervising Jane's toilette when she had a royal audience.[72] The Strachey children all adored the Colevile home, appreciating the elegance and beauty that 'Aunt Lell' always created around herself, and relishing the shopping sprees and holidays that she offered them. This relationship was not one-sided, however. Jane Strachey spent months staying with her sister in 1876 when Elinor Colevile was faced with the devastating loss of her only child, as she did again when Elinor's husband died in 1880.

The extent to which Jane's sibling relationships were woven into her marriage were made absolutely clear after Richard's death. 'I have not been able to brace myself to write to you before', she wrote to her sister, Elinor, a week after his death,

though the knowledge of your understanding, & of the love you had for him, has been a great stand-by for me in these heavy hours. It is a wonderful thing to be able to say that in the long years we have all passed together, there has never been a passing cloud of disagreement or misunderstanding. You have been the best sister that ever lived and he loved you as truly as a brother.[73]

For Jane herself, these ties became ever more important in her widowhood. It was Elinor Colevile with whom she went away to recover after Richard's death, and Elinor and their brother Trevor were her frequent companions in subsequent years. All were by then widowed and they often travelled together or stayed in each other's homes.

Jane Strachey's close ties to her sister had their counterpart in Richard's relationship with his brother John. As we have seen, their careers in India were closely enmeshed and they remained on intimate terms throughout their lives. Richard made his home with John when Jane was not in India and, on at least one occasion, John and Kate Strachey looked after Richard and Jane's children in India. This is one of the few areas where one sees Richard as possibly slightly easier going than Jane. Richard maintained a very close and cordial relationship with Jane's family, undertaking any task demanded of him, and apparently very happy both to stay with the Coleviles and to support Jane's relationship with them. Jane was not quite prepared to reciprocate. She was happy enough to see Richard's family, but absolutely refused the suggestion that she and Richard share a home with John and Kate Strachey in Calcutta. She did not feel any close affinity with her sister-in-law and was not prepared to put herself in a situation where she was always in her company. Thus while Jane was prepared to support Richard's relationships with his family, neither she nor her children felt as close to the Stracheys as they always did to the Grants. Richard certainly maintained his ties, not only with John, but with his other brothers too. Here too, Jane Strachey passed her responsibility on to her daughters, particularly Pippa, who spent a lot of time with her Strachey relatives. Indeed, Pippa nursed some of her Strachey uncles and aunts in much the same way as she did her own parents—and with a patience and skill quite unknown to her mother!

V

Like many upper middle-class professional couples, the Stracheys enjoyed an active social and public life in addition to their private and domestic one. As we have seen, their life in India centred on the elite of the Raj society, and they dined. engaged in amateur theatricals, and played croquet with viceroys and their entourages. Back in England, they did not mix with quite such elevated folk, but rather with upper middle-class professionals like themselves. As the earlier comments on Jane Strachey's social skills suggest, it was she rather than Richard who established their friendship network. Jane Strachey made close friends with neighbours, people met on holidays, the teachers and principals of the children's schools, musicians whose concerts she attended, and artists and writers, as well as the scientists and political figures whom she met in the course of her husband's work or through family connections.

Jane's sense of the importance of social connections meant that she took care to cultivate many of the people she met. She shared with her sister Elinor an enthusiasm for establishing relationships with prominent writers and musicians, and they numbered the Carlyles, Browning, and George Eliot amongst their close acquaintances. Both George Eliot and her partner George Henry Lewes seem to have been greatly attracted to Jane. 'My dear Mrs Strachey', Lewes wrote in 1872, when Jane was looking for a permanent home in London, 'I so much desire to have you as a neighbour that if you will send me some word what style of house, how many rooms, & about what rent you contemplate I will ransack St John's Wood & Regent's Park, get you word to view any that seem promising & so take some of the bother from your hands.'[74] Jane later regretted that her own sense of inadequacy as a letter-writer made her shy away from complying with Eliot's request that they correspond. But she took some pride in hearing from George Eliot's widower, J. W. Cross, that he had found a note to her in Eliot's writing portfolio.[75] 'It is the last thing written by her hand on that fatal last

Sunday . . . I can scarcely bear to part with it' he wrote, 'but it belongs to you.'[76]

In her great liking of people and her enjoyment of many different kinds of social life, Jane Strachey was very different from her husband. Richard enjoyed going to his club and liked to see his friends and family, but disliked the triviality of parties and the demands of many formal social situations. In their later years, Richard seems to have accepted the pace which Jane sought in social life without complaint. 'We have now to go out to 3 garden parties in a row and then dinner', she wrote to Lytton, in 1889—when Richard was 80—and this was not an uncommon occurrence.[77] There was rarely a week without several dinner parties and some other social events. A decade later, in 1898, she wrote to James of a planned 'at home' party on 29 March, to which she had 'invited about 300 people—so they won't have room to stand if they all come—but they won't'.[78]

Some of Jane Strachey's friendships had a considerable impact on the family. The most significant of these was probably Marie Souvestre, whom she met in Italy in 1871, and to whose schools she subsequently sent her daughters. This relationship was an interesting one with an emotional complexity to which Jane Strachey seems to have been completely oblivious. After their first meeting in Florence, Jane wrote to Richard of the 'charming French woman she had met, with a fine intellect, virile head & countenance, & most excellent political views'. The invasion of France by Prussian troops meant she 'was driven away with her charges from Fontainebleau & has come here to settle'.[79] Mlle Souvestre, daughter of the French writer, Emile Souvestre, was the proprietor of a well-known girls' school, Les Ruches in Fontainebleau. As a passionate Francophile, Jane shared her distress at the fate of France during the Franco-Prussian War and saw her almost daily. 'You cannot think what excellent charming women both she and her friend M'elle Dussant are', she wrote to Richard. 'M'elle Souvestre in particular reminds me of one of Georges Sand's liberal-minded well-balanced heroines—& she is extremely handsome. She generally comes here every Wednesday evening—she knows almost everyone worth knowing in France.' When peace and stability were finally restored to France with the advent of the Third Republic, Mlle Souvestre returned to Fountainebleau and continued to run her school there. The two oldest Strachey daughters, Elinor and Dorothy, were now added to her list of pupils.

The school did not continue in France, however. It had been run as a partnership between Mlle Souvestre and her very close friend, and possibly lover, Lina Dussant and in the course of the 1880s, both their personal relationship and their business partnership came to an end. Both women wrote to Jane Strachey and Lina Dussant's letters express clearly her jealousy and her belief that Jane had displaced her in Marie Souvestre's affection.[80] Jane strongly denied this. The school was in financial difficulties, however, and once Lina Dussant decided to withdraw from it, it closed. Marie Souvestre now too made it clear that Jane was her closest friend and greatest support, but Jane took this in her stride, making Mlle Souvestre a central figure in the life of the whole family. A couple of years later, in the mid-1880s, Marie Souvestre opened a new school, Allenswood, in Wimbledon. The Stracheys were patrons, along with several other well-known upper middle-class liberal families, including those of Frederick Harrison and John Morley, all of whom sent their daughters there. Jane Strachey remained closely involved with the school, attending regularly and doing public readings of English literature.

While Jane's friendship network was the more extensive and expressive, this does not mean that Richard Strachey was friendless. His dislike of Raj society was in marked contrast to his great enjoyment of the society of fellow scientists. He rarely missed a meeting of any of the scientific societies of which he was a member, and numbered several leading Victorian scientists amongst his close friends. Joseph Hooker, with whom he and Jane travelled in the United States in the early 1870s, was perhaps the closest. But T. H. Huxley, John Tyndall, George Darwin, and Francis Galton were also close friends with whom Strachey dined at the Athenaeum and whom he often visited.

Richard Strachey had enjoyed a public life centred on the world of science in addition to his professional one before his marriage and continued with it afterwards. The importance of his botanical work in the Himalayas in the 1850s resulted in his election as a Fellow of the Royal Society in 1854 and of the Linnaean Society in 1859. But he became very much more prominent in the scientific world when he returned to England to live in 1871. Strachey was a polymath and he participated in many different scientific societies and bodies including Kew Gardens, the Royal Geographical Society, and the Meteorological Committee of the Royal Society. He participated in the management and administration both of the specialist societies: he was president of the Royal Geographic

Society in 1887–9, for example. He was a member of the Council of the Royal Society in 1872–4, 1880–1, 1884–6, and 1890–1, and vice-president in 1880–1 and again in 1885–6. During his presidency of the Royal Geographical Society, he worked to promote the teaching of geography and delivered a series of foundation lectures on it at Cambridge University. He was also a member of the special committee of the Royal Society set up in 1884 to investigate the eruption of Krakatoa in the previous year.

Richard Strachey's standing in the scientific community and the public nature of his work was well attested. He was sent as one of the Royal Society representatives to the Prime Meridian Conference in Washington in 1884, which formally established Greenwich Observatory as the site of the Prime Meridian. He was elected one of the secretaries at that conference, and his approach to establishing the Prime Meridian was the one accepted by the conference. In these later years, Strachey was also appointed to scientific bodies outside England, as corresponding member to the Belgian Society Royale de Medecine Publique in 1889, for example. These years were the ones in which Richard Strachey gained his major honours: an honorary doctorate at Cambridge in 1892; the Royal Society Medal in 1897, and the Symons Medal from the Royal Meteorological Society, of which he was chairman, in 1905. He had been created CSI in 1886 and, having declined the KCSI a number of times, was gazetted GCSI in 1897.

Jane Strachey gloried in her husband's successes, reporting them with great excitement to their absent children, and relishing all the social activities associated with them. The Cambridge honorary degree, the first university degree within the family, was an event of immense significance. New dresses were purchased for Dorothy and Pippa, and the family party which included Aunt Lell all piled into the train which was late, giving Richard just time to change into his robes before the official lunch. The proceedings were in Latin, Jane wrote to Lytton, so she could only follow 'a little of what was said about papa. He was one of a par nobile fratrum who had rendered great service to India had covered that country with canals & railways, geography, geology the Krakatoa eruption "good old General" from the gallery Ricardum Strachey—& that's all.'[81] After Richard received his GCSI, Jane and her daughters were presented to the queen. 'The reason we are going to a drawing room', she explained to James, 'is that it is considered a proper mark of respect, after the Queen has given your Papa an honour.' Not prepared to leave her sister to her own devices on this important occasion, Elinor Colevile gave Jane 'such a splendid train that all the dressmakers are in ecstasies over it'.[82]

The last Strachey child was born in 1887 and immediately after this Jane too began to expand her array of intellectual and public activities. She was nearly 50, but was in extremely good health and now had adult daughters who were able to help with household supervision and child care. Some years before this, Jane had begun her own forays into literary activity. She had always read to her children and encouraged them to read both French and English literature, to write their own newspapers, and to act in and produce their own plays. Her interests both in the intellectual development of her children and in literature inspired her first work, *Lay Texts for the Young in English and French*, which was published in 1886. Directed specifically to children aged between 7 and 14, the period during which 'the moral faculties begin to develop', the book aimed to train the growing impulses of the young. 'It behoves the young', she wrote in the preface, 'to learn in what manner the great and wise among men have considered human affairs, and to kindle at their torches that flame of generous enthusiasm which is the life of virtue'.[83] This work was followed by a selection of *Nursery Lyrics*, and then by a more ambitious anthology, *Poets on Poetry* in 1894.

Jane Strachey's letters from the late 1880s and early 1890s, especially those to Lytton, suggest that she had immense energy and a certain restlessness now that she was no longer preoccupied with child care. This led her to experiment with a host of different things. In 1890, she began to learn shorthand and tried to 'practise vigorously whilst my hair is being done and at all moments of the day'.[84] She also began to learn how to make parchment volumes, which was 'fascinating though laborious'.

Jane had always been a wonderful reader, with an immense knowledge of poetry and drama which she loved reciting. She passed her love of amateur theatricals on to her children and their productions were often, in Jane's view, better than those of the professional companies they saw in the West End. In 1890, Jane extended her activities by running classes for young women. I 'have had one or two readings with my young ladies', she wrote to Lytton, '& read them a new play last time, which pleased us all very much. By Dryden, "All for Love, or the world well lost". We also have a class here twice a week to be taught French pronunciation by a former actress of the Theatre Franchise. Have to learn by heart & recite different things.'[85] She also undertook new literary activities. The death of her father in 1893, and the research she did into his family in order to assist in the biography of him written by Walter Seton-Kerr, is sometimes credited with arousing the interest that led to her best-known work, her edition of the memoir of her aunt, Elizabeth Grant Smith, published as *Memoir of a Highland Lady* in 1898. As soon as this was finished, she began to work on an annotated calendar. She was 'reading for it a history of the British Navy', she wrote to Lytton, 'which is the most fascinating subject it is possible to imagine. I strongly advise you to study it when you get the chance'.[86]

At the turn of the twentieth century, Richard Strachey's activities began to wane. He was now in his 80s and was becoming increasingly deaf. He found the constant bustle of London hard to manage—and was knocked down several times by cabs or bicycles. He continued to go to his office and to the Royal Society, but his health and his impaired hearing meant that he also spent large amounts of time at home, working in his study—or reading novels. Jane was still in her 60s, and apart from occasional colds enjoyed robust health. Her public activities expanded dramatically in these years, as she took a close interest in the school and university activities of her daughters, continued her readings and became more and more prominent in the women's movement. As we will see, much of her public life had a family dimension as she shared her suffrage enthusiasm with her daughters and often worked closely with them in the women's movement. Her public activities became increasingly important in the early years of her widowhood, offering an alternative focus once Richard was no longer there.

Strachey Childhoods

The ten children of Richard and Jane Strachey enjoyed the privileged world of upper middle-class family life. Their world was large and varied one, with many homes and an extensive cast of characters. The extended family who were so important to their parents figured largely in their lives too, and their parents' friends and interests were often incorporated into their early lives. Theirs was not the most settled of childhoods, however, as Richard and Jane Strachey did not establish a permanent family home until their oldest children were almost in their teens. Hence the four oldest children moved around frequently between temporary rented accommodation and the homes of relatives. Even when Stowey House was purchased in 1872, the children did not spend all their time there. Summers often involved lengthy visits to Rothiermurchus, the Grant family estate in Scotland, or to other Strachey or Grant relatives in different parts of the country. Moreover, the entire family was dispersed in the late 1870s, when Jane went out again to be with Richard in India. The two older daughters, Elinor and Dorothy, accompanied their mother, but the other children all made a new home base with the Coleviles. The lives of the three youngest children were more settled as they grew up in the house in Lancaster Gate where the family moved in the mid-1880s.

Like other upper middle-class children, all the younger Stracheys spent their early days in nurseries, cared for by nannies who were supervised by their mother or another female relative. Although money was a constant concern for the Stracheys in the 1860s, there was never the slightest possibility that they would manage without a maid for Jane and a nanny who bathed, dressed, and fed the children and dealt with their daily needs.

In India, there was often an ayah with an English nanny to oversee what she did and to take the children out. In England, there was sometimes a governess to oversee early lessons. As was the case in many large families, the older daughters took over both domestic responsibilities and the care of younger siblings as soon as they were in their late teens. Both Jane Strachey and the rest of the family recognized that her lack of interest or skill in domestic matters meant that this arrangement was conducive to the peace and comfort of all!

Strachey childhoods were relatively gentle by Victorian standards. The children were generally expected to be obedient, and Jane Strachey was extremely critical of nephews and then grandchildren whom she considered to be excessively indulged. Neither she nor Richard approved either of corporal punishment or of any other kind of harsh discipline, however, and there is no suggestion of any of the children being beaten or severely punished at home. At the same time, neither Jane nor Richard were demonstrative parents. They expressed their own affection for each other, and often that for their children, verbally through the use of feline diminutives: they were both cats and the children often pussies.[1] Physical affection between them and their children seems to have been rare, however, although it was sometimes supplied by others. In later years, Lytton Strachey remembered his sister Dorothy giving him hundreds of kisses when he was a small boy.[2]

While not concerned particularly about their daily needs, Jane Strachey was immensely interested in the physical and more particularly the mental development of her children and kept careful notes of the precise point at which they began to walk and talk. Dick, her oldest son 'walked alone on the 24th aged 18 months 4 days', she wrote to Richard in 1862, noting also that this was '3 days sooner than El did. He can say mama beautifully, but says it to everything.'[3] She often listed the children's verbal accomplishments too, to keep Richard fully informed of their progress. Jane spent a lot of time with her children, regarding them as companions and entering into their activity with great enthusiasm. She oversaw their early education at home and as soon as they were able to read and write encouraged them to produce their own newspapers and to engage in amateur theatricals. Their cultural activities were taken very seriously: the Strachey Papers at the British Library include a number of beautiful handwritten journals and newspapers, as well as manuscripts of plays and printed programmes and handbills for plays staged at home.[4] Jane, who had what Leonard Woolf regarded as the most beautiful voice he had ever heard, also read aloud to her children, working her way through the Greek classics as well as many works of French and English literature.[5] She was also intensely interested in music and several of her children shared this passion, attending concerts and playing musical instruments. Jane was not entirely happy when Oliver took this further, composing music which she felt compelled to have published and also to play.[6] Dancing was a favoured pastime too and Jane, later helped by Pippa, taught the Scottish reel not only to her own children, but to many of their friends.[7] Jane Strachey was the central figure in the lives of her children, but Richard was by no means an uncaring father. He corresponded with the children and spent time with them whenever he could, especially in their adolescent years. He shared the family passion for crosswords, acrostics, and mathematical puzzles and devised many for them. He also travelled with the children both in Britain and sometimes on the Continent.

Religion was not a central ingredient in Strachey childhoods. Richard was an agnostic and, despite occasional acts of religious conformity when staying in the country, Jane was too.[8] Like many Victorian agnostics, however, their very lack of religious faith made them place a heavy emphasis on morality.[9] They had a strong sense of duty which they attempted to impart to their young. Their letters to their children, especially to their older sons, were filled with exhortations, stressing the importance of their setting examples to younger siblings and giving them directions as to how they should behave in order to live up to their father's example and prevent disappointment to their parents and themselves.

Like many Victorian families, this was one in which there were very clear favourites, and in which some children received vastly more parental, and especially maternal, care and affection than others. Family letters make it clear that Elinor was a great favourite who overshadowed not only her next sister Dorothy, but also her brother Dick. Jane Strachey's loss of her favourite baby, Olivia, seems also to have cast something of a pall over the birth of Ralph, her second son. Pippa, Oliver, and Pernel seem each to have found a way to be cared for and taken notice of, without ever quite matching up either to Elinor or to their younger brothers. When it came to the last three children, however, it is absolutely clear that Jane was entranced by her two sons, but had little time for her daughter, Marjorie. She regarded Lytton as the cleverest child she had ever seen and relished his sharpness of perception and witty turn of phrase. James, although not as brilliant as his brother, possessed charm, an outgoing temperament, and a capacity for quaint and unusual observations that captivated his mother. He was universally recognized as her favourite child. Poor Marjorie could offer nothing to compete. She was regarded as noisy, bumptious, and lacking in grace from her earliest years—and was never under any illusion as to the nature of her mother's feelings for her. Even when she was at school, Marjorie frequently commented, on how rarely Jane wrote to her—and how little she liked her company.

While there were obvious similarities in the broad pattern of their childhood, there were also significant differences in the lives and experiences of the younger Stracheys. The thirty-year time span across which their births occurred meant that they were born at very different stages in the long marriage of their parents and belonged effectively to different historical periods. Those born in the 1860s remained in some ways mid-Victorians. They began life as the children of a very young mother and a father still trying to establish his place in the government of India. They were children also in the period when the Stracheys underwent the great financial catastrophe that accompanied the collapse of the Agra Bank and necessitated a complete change in their father's plans. By the time the next three appeared in the 1870s, Richard Strachey had recouped his fortune, settled back home, and effectively made his name. Although still dominated by the family's imperial heritage and by a Victorian sense of duty, there was more scope for them to follow new lines and to choose new careers or life patterns. The children of the 1880s, Lytton, Marjorie, and James, all partook in some ways of the *fin de siècle*. Victorian ideas of duty, family, and responsibility were alien to them all and they experimented with new kinds of occupations, relationships, and ways of life. They were born to a mature and very well established couple who were widely recognized as central figures in the intellectual and social life of London. At the same time, they began life with a father who was in his 60s, prominent in the world of science and imperial administration, but rather less central at home. He was rather like a grandfather to them all while their mother, now beginning her own literary and public life, dominated their world. They also had adult siblings. While their brothers were usually absent at school and then went out to India, their older sisters, especially Dorothy and Pippa, were the ones who supervised their home and managed their daily needs. Their oldest sister, Elinor, married early in the 1880s and Marjorie and James often took their place in her nursery alongside nieces and nephews who were the same age or older than they.

Despite the many descriptions of the activities of the Strachey children, interpreting their inner lives and emotions is a difficult task. Family letters tend to focus on their physical developments, their funny sayings, and their school achievements. There was little knowledge of, or interest in, the feelings of children amongst their parents and relatives. In the later part of the nineteenth century, there was considerable discussion about childhood, but few of the new anxieties or the new views then being promulgated about the best ways to treat children seem to have penetrated the Strachey family. There is no suggestion in the correspondence of Richard or Jane Strachey that they read or had any interest in the newly emerging field of mental physiology in the 1870s or of the new developments in psychology, and its preoccupation with the problem of adolescents in the 1880s.[10] The ideas of Darwin and Huxley were important in the Strachey world, but the concerns about how to rear and educate children expressed by the 'alienist' Henry Maudsley or the psychologist James Sully were never mentioned.

It is impossible to write about Victorian childhoods now without drawing on some of the insights offered by psychology and psychoanalysis. This is the more interesting in view of the later involvement of James and Alix Strachey in translating not only the work of Freud, but also that of Melanie Klein. Nonetheless, while it is interesting to speculate about the younger Stracheys in terms of Freud's ideas on infantile sexuality and Oedipal struggles, and to hypothesize about the impact of parental absences, on the one hand, or demands and expectations, on the other, there is still no adequate theoretical framework within either psychology or psychoanalysis for examining the kind of family constituted by the Stracheys. The importance of birth order on children has been the subject of discussion amongst psychologists since the early twentieth century. However, the importance of siblings to each other, and their role in each other's psychic and emotional life has only recently become a matter of widespread discussion.[11] There is now a considerable literature on sibling relationships in the twentieth century, but few people have attempted to apply it to large mid-Victorian families, in which there were not three or four children—but rather ten. Nor has there been any theoretical discussion of the psychic foundations of families in which older siblings had the primary care of younger ones, in which nannies were central, and in which aunts and uncles were constant and significant figures in children's lives, stepping in to replace absent parents and providing

84

affectionate and familiar alternate homes. Anne McClintock has explored the erasure of the figure of the nanny from Freud's accounts of his own childhood—and also from his theoretical discussions.[12] All of this means that much of the following discussion of Strachey childhoods is necessarily tentative.

Nevertheless, it seems hard to overestimate the importance of sibling relationships amongst the Strachey children. There are several different aspects of these ties that need to be taken into account. First of all, there is the role of older sisters in the care and upbringing of younger siblings. Dorothy's role in Lytton's life is particularly important here, as is Elinor's in the life of Marjorie. In addition, some of the Strachey children formed very close bonds with those nearest to them in age. Jane Strachey encouraged particularly the development of close brother and sister pairs, attempting to educate children together in their early years and to ensure that they were companions in vacations. Elinor and Dick were just one year apart, and established very close ties in the early years they spent together, often away from their parents. Ralph and Pippa made another such pair and in their case the intimacy extended well into adult life. Oliver and Pernel made a third pair, despite their immense differences in personality and outlook. Dorothy lacked any close bond to a brother, although she was very close to Elinor throughout her life. Marjorie too, although she adored Lytton and was sometimes his childhood companion, never enjoyed the intimacy or affection that was evident amongst the others. It was rather James who, as the baby of the family, had no obvious partner who established a close bond with Lytton.

Apart from Dorothy and Lytton and, to an extent, James, the Strachey children were as restrained in writing about emotion as were their parents. They inhabited the same Victorian world in which familial duty and respect and devotion to parents were assumed to exist. Nonetheless it seems clear that they had rather different feelings about their parents and their parental home. Elinor, Pippa, and Ralph seem always to have loved their home and their parents and to have felt little conflict within this relationship. By contrast, both Lytton and James expressed intense feelings of alienation and distress at home. Lytton's feelings have been much written about, but they were possibly equalled by those of his sister, Pernel, who left home as soon as she possibly could and seems to have found family holidays and residences extremely trying. Marjorie too seems rarely to have felt much at home within the family.

❧ I ❧

From the moment they married, the Stracheys were very keen to produce an heir. As it turned out, however, at least until the 1880s, it was their daughters rather than their sons who were the great source of pleasure and of pride. Elinor, their first child, was warmly welcomed despite her sex and rapidly established a very firm place within the family. Indeed, even when the longed for son, Dick, appeared a year later, Elinor, unusually for a Victorian girl, experienced no diminution in importance. She was clearly an assertive child who made her demands very clear. 'El gets very jealous if she is not sufficiently noticed', wrote Jane to Richard shortly after the birth of Dick and Jane responded by ensuring that she gave Elinor the attention that she wanted.[13] Elinor seems to have been an ideal daughter. Jane's letters constantly refer to her as a charming child, both manageable and entertaining and admired by everyone. At the age of 3, when Elinor accompanied her to India, Jane found her an excellent companion, amusing, precocious, and well able to participate in her mother's social life. She 'perfectly appreciates the compliment of the Chief saying she has beautiful eyes', Jane told her sister, and has 'very decided views'. She had 'no hesitation in naming her first 3 partners when I asked her whom she would dance with when she went to balls'. When Richard said to her 'You are a queer little Kitten!', she replied 'I'm edzackly [sic] like you Papa!'[14]

In contrast with Elinor, the early life of Dick seems to have been somewhat troubled. Jane's anxiety about her own inadequacies in dealing with a son may have contributed to this. Elinor was a source of unalloyed pleasure, but the minute Dick was born, she began attempting to repair her own defective education. 'I am determined', she explained to Richard, 'to begin steadily to improve my mind, on account of my boy; not of course that I am likely directly to teach him anything recondite whilst he is under my care, but that if my mind is rational it must influence his rationally.'[15] There are few letters describing Dick's early months. However, within a very short time it seems clear that he did not measure up to his parent's expectations. There is no report on Dick as glowing as those about his older sister, but Jane worried about his 'wilfulness' when he was just over one year old.[16] Jane had to cope with Dick's infancy without her husband Shortly after he was born, Richard had to return to India, leaving Jane with the two children in England Jane missed her husband dreadfully and the constant presence and anxieties of her own mother made life difficult for everyone.[17] Jane in turn may have been depressed in ways that had an impact on her baby son.

Dick's childhood continued to be a hard one. There is little information about him in the course of his first trip out to India, but when Jane and the children returned to Britain in 1867, he was already expected to assume his place as head of the family when his father was absent. The first such occasion occurred after the death of Jane's fourth child, Olivia. Dick, then aged 6, was required to replace his father at her funeral. 'It was very sweet of you', Richard Strachey wrote to Jane, 'to make Dick tell me that he went with you to Olivia's funeral instead of me. I cannot thank you enough for the loving thoughts & the way of telling it me.'[18] While Richard was moved by this approach, one wonders about the impact that the death of this baby sister and the immense responsibility of replacing his father had on Dick himself. Poor Dick faced obligations at every turn. He was the recipient of more letters from his father than any other Strachey child, and Richard sent him a stream of chatty and affectionate letters with detailed descriptions and wonderful illustrations of his work and of the Indian countryside. They also contained constant injunctions to work hard and be diligent. 'I was very glad to find you could write me a letter so well', Richard wrote to his son in 1867,

and I hope you will go on learning both to read and write & do sums very fast and diligently. It will make your Mamma & me fonder of you and better pleased with you to know that you are not idle. It is right to attend to your lessons in lesson time and to play as much as you like in play time. But it is not right to play when you ought to be doing lessons. You must too remember to be good and kind to your Mamma & sisters & cousins, and also to . . . everyone else about.[19]

The following year, Jane returned to India, leaving Elinor and Dick with the Coleviles. There was no detailed discussion of why it was necessary for Dick (then aged 7) or El (aged 9) to remain 'back home'. It was simply taken for granted that now they were old enough to begin their education, they should stay in England. The Stracheys were very fortunate to have family willing to assist them. The possibility of boarding school for Dick and of having to find someone unknown to care for El was certainly mooted, but unlike Rudyard Kipling or many other imperial children they were not left unhappily with strangers. The Coleviles offered to take both children as companions to their own son, Andrew.[20] As Jane well knew, her children were cherished and well cared for in the Colevile's luxurious home.

Elinor was very happy with the Coleviles and clearly enjoyed dominating both her brother and their cousin. Shortly after the young Stracheys arrived, Elinor Colevile wrote to Jane about an episode when she had found Andrew crying, and discovered that 'El had knocked him as he passed . . . Andrew is so gentle with her and pegs into Dick if he hurts her, while El hits them both as hard as she can, and she is much the strongest of the lot. She is fond of power, the monkey.'[21] El's tomboyishness and even her capacity to be something of a bully did nothing to reduce the enthusiasm of the Coleviles at having her with them. It is clear too that she outshone Dick in their eyes. 'I can't tell you what happiness it is having them', Elinor Colevile wrote to her sister soon after the children had moved in, 'they are such darlings. It is very pleasing to James too, he is very much devoted to El & he sees how much happier Andrew is now he has these companions.'[22]

While Elinor flourished, Dick developed a distressing habit of constantly bursting into tears. He raised this matter with his parents, and their response was predictable. Neither of them suggested even the possibility that Dick was distressed or in an emotional state that needed to be addressed, and Jane offered rather what she saw as a practical remedy. 'In your last letter you ask Papa to advise you what to do to stop yourself crying when once you have begun', she wrote. 'I don't think he will be able to because he never cried when young. His brothers and sisters used to call him happy Dick. But when I was a little girl, I used to be just like you and found it very difficult to stop myself crying & now advise you to make yourself think of something else, or count backwards from 10 or hop etc.' [23] The arrival of Dick's first baby brother later in that year brought a new set of exhortations. 'Do you know, Dick,' wrote his mother,

I think Master Ralph's arrival will be of more consequence to you than to anyone else. You see you are much older than he is & will be quite big whilst he is still small, & he will naturally think a great deal of what his big brother does; if you are hard-working & well-behaved and get a good name for yourself at school, it will help very much to make Ralph do the same, but then you must begin to be all this at once so as to have got into good habits by the time he is able to understand; fancy how dreadful it would be if instead of saying I must try to be as wise & good as brother Dick he had to say I must try not to be as lazy & good for nothing as brother Dick. But I don't think there is any fear of that, is there my darling? No you will be the best of boys to your papa and me.[24]

Dick did not respond to all these suggestions and instructions quite as his parents might have wished and when Jane was finally reunited with her children after a three year absence, she found him particularly hard to deal with. He would not do his lessons or anything she asked unless she stood over him—or stayed with him while he did it. On one occasion, Jane reported to Richard, she smacked him and sent him to bed. Later, she went in to talk to him and he sobbed pitifully. After that he was good and did what she asked, provided he could sleep in her room.[25] Lytton Strachey was far too young to have known anything about his oldest brother's childhood. But there is something uncomfortably similar to Dick's childhood in Lytton's depiction in *Queen Victoria* of the relentless driving of Edward VII by his royal parents.[26]

There are few letters from Jane referring to the birth of her next daughter, Dorothy, in 1865. This very silence suggests that Dorothy, like Dick, suffered in comparison with the forthright, self-confident, and engaging Elinor. Dorothy Strachey did not cause Jane the kind of concern that Dick did, but nor was she a source of great pleasure. By the time Dorothy was 2, Jane was impressed by the extent of her language and described her to Richard as 'sweet and delightful' and 'universally admired'.[27] Other letters, however, describe her as awkward and 'still of a timid disposition'. When Dorothy was 4, Jane described her to her own father, Sir John Peter Grant, in terms which make the comparison with Elinor absolutely clear. Dolly was 'not a bad little thing. But not so sensible as her eldest sister was at her age.' Even her appearance suggested a lesser Elinor, as she 'looks like El, but less so'.[28]

Poor Dorothy was squeezed between two beloved daughters. She was preceded by the wondrous Elinor and closely followed by the precious Olivia. Dorothy's birth may not have been worthy of note, but Olivia's in 1867 certainly was. She 'is a most lovely creature', Jane wrote to her father shortly after Olivia's birth, 'although very disappointing on account of her sex'.[29] Jane loved Olivia dearly. 'I think I was more fond of her than of any babies whilst they were babies', she wrote to Richard.[30] Olivia did not survive, however, and Dorothy's childhood was probably overshadowed even more by the death of Olivia, who was not quite one year old when she suddenly became ill and died, than it had been by her birth.

The next child to arrive was a boy, Ralph, who was born in India in 1868. The lack of sons in the family as compared with daughters was becoming a matter of concern to the Stracheys by the mid-1860s and Ralph's arrival was very welcome. Jane regarded him, however, as her one truly ugly child. 'He is rather plain', she wrote to her father in 1869, '(though getting better looking every day) and already exhibits a great deal of what is called, I don't know why, "character".'[31] Fortunately for Ralph, his 'character' did not cause anxiety in the way in which Dick's wilfulness had. It is possible that his early months too were overshadowed by Olivia's death. Although ostensibly welcoming her new son, Jane Strachey left him earlier than she had any of her other children. For reasons that are never made clear in the Strachey correspondence, Ralph was left in India in 1870 when Jane went to Italy to be reunited with her mother and the two older children. Dorothy accompanied her mother back to Europe, but Ralph, who was only 2, remained in the home of his aunt and uncle, John and Kate Strachey, and in the care of their nanny. This separation also meant that Ralph did not establish a close tie with his older sister, Dorothy. When he was restored to his family again in Italy, he resented Dorothy. Later in 1871, the two children stayed with their grandmother she commented that Ralph was 'the most jealous little cat that ever was . . . He can't endure nurse Moss to pet Dolly, and insisted that she is a very uggery [sic] baby.' In the eyes of his grandmother, Ralph was 'ridiculously neat and clean and it is amusing to see him trot around the room putting the chairs in their places and making the room tidy (just as I do) & then he surveys it & says "now clean" '.[32]

No one minded Ralph's jealousy of his sister and he exhibited few other forms of behaviour which caused concern. Hence letters to him contain fewer exhortations than do those to his older brother. Nonetheless, he was made aware of his duties and responsibilities. The birthday greetings he received in 1880 are a case in point. 'Twelve years old is one of the epochs of life I think', wrote his mother, '& I hope you are beginning to feel somewhat of a responsible being now, & to understand that life is to each of us very much what we make it. I am sure you will try to please your father by being such a son as he has a right to expect.'[33]

II

The separation of Richard and Jane Strachey for much of the 1860s meant that the early childhood of Elinor, Dick, and Dorothy was constantly described in their letters. For most of the 1870s, however, they were together in England and what the children born of that period gained from having both parents and a home, the historian loses by the absence of letters about them. Jane's mother and sister were also constantly present and so there are few letters to them describing the first years of Pippa, Oliver, and Pernel.

Pippa, who was born in 1872, seems to have established herself as a pivotal member of the family very early on. Ralph, who disdained Dorothy, seems immediately to have become devoted to her. He was regarded as her slave by the time she was 2. In the occasional handwritten journal, *Our Paper*, devised by Jane and the Strachey children and written throughout the 1870s, Pippa was the only member of the family to whom a poem was dedicated. Written by Elinor and Dorothy, the little poem 'Our Pippa' certainly suggests that she was a child of considerable significance within the family:

> From little Ralph to clumsy Seethe,
> From Hammond unto Mary.
> We do not think it waste of breath
> To praise our little fairy
>
> Ralph is a martyr to her will,
> She startles Noll[34] from dozes,
> Her laugh is like the gurgling till
> Her cheeks are red as roses
>
> Our little Pippin Queen is she,
> Her subjects all adore her,
> She's lovely, we do all agree,
> Although she is a roarer
>
> Long live our little Pippin Queen,
> And may she never alter,
> Nor will her subjects 'twill be seen,
> In their allegiance falter.[35]

Oliver was born two years after Pippa and Pernel two years after that. There are almost no comments about their births or early childhood years—and Oliver and Pernel were not described in the family paper. The earliest extended discussion of these children was that provided by their aunt, Elinor Colevile, when they stayed with her 1878–80, during Jane's unexpected trip to India. On this occasion, the Coleviles looked after almost all the Strachey children. Dorothy and Elinor accompanied Jane, but the three youngest children all stayed with the Coleviles, and were joined there during the school holidays by Ralph. Elinor Colevile reported regularly on their development and activities to their mother.

The letters of Pippa and Oliver to their parents from this time make clear that for them, as for their older siblings, staying with 'Aunt Lell' meant being immersed in a world of luxury and treats. Visits to the zoo, extravagant teas, and holidays by the seaside were all things that she offered. Moreover, unlike their mother, the Coleviles were always very concerned about the health of their young charges—perhaps excessively so: they had lost their only and much beloved son, Andrew, in 1876, and so were on the lookout for any evidence of constitutional weakness. All the young Stracheys had scarlet fever while staying with the Coleviles, and afterwards Elinor Colevile was anxious about the general frailty and tendency to stoop evident in Oliver and Ralph.[36] Special exercises were prescribed by their doctor for the boys. Pippa and Pernel did not need them as they both seemed much more robust.

Much of Elinor Colevile's correspondence to Jane Strachey centres on the need to buy all the children new clothes, a task which she loved—and in the course of which she greatly exceeded the budget agreed on with the Stracheys. In the clothes-buying expeditions, it was Pernel whom she singled out as 'a true daughter of Eve', who loved 'pretty clothes and tries them on with the greatest patience and delight'.[37] Pernel's intelligence and articulateness were also noticed. She 'is quite an old child now and most delightful talks so prettily, and the girls say & so does Maggie that she is amazingly clever and forward for her age'.[38] Pippa was apparently less interested in clothes, but already popular and finding it easy to make friends. She is 'dining at Beaufort Gardens today to meet her young man Frank Wedderburn who pays her a great deal of attention', wrote Lady Colevile when Pippa was 7.[39]

There are few comments on Oliver Strachey's early childhood either from his mother or from his aunt. But his cleverness and musical talents were evident early and Jane Strachey's many amused and admiring comments on Oliver as an adolescent point to her deep affection for him.[40] He was 'looking very spruce with magnificent pale peony in his buttonhole', she wrote to Lytton in 1890 when she, Pernel, and Pippa visited him at Eton.[41] In her view, no one was ever bored in Oliver's presence.[42] Oliver's early life was spent in close companionship with Pernel. It was she with whom he often holidayed, whom he most wanted to see at school, and to whom he wrote most often.[43] Their shared enjoyment of music was clearly a strong common bond which more than made up for their other differences in temperament—for Pernel was perhaps the most conscientious student amongst all the Stracheys, while Oliver's failure ever to apply himself to work was the stuff of family legend.

❧ III ❧

The last three Strachey children, Lytton, Marjorie, and James, were all born in the 1880s. Here too, the fact that Richard and Jane Strachey were settled in England and living with their older daughters means that letters about the children in their very early years are scarce. Jane Strachey was in her 40s and clearly beginning to yearn for time to pursue her own literary and public interests by the time Lytton was born in 1880. As we have seen, her friends were well aware of her ambivalence about these last pregnancies. Fortunately, she was able to rely heavily on her older daughters in caring for them, and it is from their letters, particularly those of Dorothy and Elinor, that one gets the earliest glimpses of the childhoods of Lytton, Marjorie, and James.

Although Jane Strachey wrote few letters describing Lytton in his earliest years, it is clear that she was entranced by his intelligence and regarded him from early childhood as her most remarkable child. She corresponded with him regularly when he was away at school, keeping him fully informed of all family developments and most particularly about her own activities. He entered very fully into her writing and publishing activities and expressed great interest in the political developments in both France and Britain in which she was absorbed. Jane Strachey's letters to him are affectionate and confiding in tone—and his in turn exhibit a rather charming precocity and a use of hyperbole that often mirrored Jane's own. 'How exciting it is that Dick is going to be married so soon!', he wrote at the age of 16 in 1896 on hearing of his oldest brother's engagement. 'How will the creatures live, do you suppose?'[44] His sayings and his funny letters were always circulated amongst the family.

While there is little material on Jane's response to the birth and early years of Lytton, there is even less about Marjorie who was born two years later. Much has been written about the way that Lytton suffered when displaced by James, unquestionably his mother's favourite child, but what is even more noticeable is the lack of any significant place for poor Marjorie.[45] Jane relished Lytton's amusing sayings and stories and related them to others with great pleasure. But there were few affectionate stories about Marjorie. She 'is as rollicking as ever', Dorothy wrote to their mother when Marjorie was 2. 'She is making daily progress in talking. I think she will be as great a chatterbox as Lytton.'[46] Jane Strachey did not ignore Marjorie entirely: her letters to Lytton often mention taking Marjorie to children's parties or other outings as well as commenting on her poor health. But one rarely senses either pleasure or pride in her daughter in these comments.

It is noticeable, too, that Marjorie apparently flourished when she was away from home. She was a difficult child to feed and her eating was always a problem at home. There was no sign of this, however, when she was staying either with Aunt Lell or with her older sister, Elinor. 'Marjorie is extremely well and seems to be quite happy with us,' she wrote to her mother in 1891. 'Her appetite has greatly improved and I really think couldn't be better. She has never refused to eat her meat and always has two helpings of pudding and an egg at breakfast and tea and plenty of milk. She is very good indeed and not a bit of trouble so I hope you will leave her here as long as you can.'[47] Marjorie also found close companionship in the home of Elinor Rendel. Elinor had her first child in 1883, just a year after the birth of Marjorie, and a second child was born shortly after. Marjorie established closer ties with Elinor's two daughters, Ellie and Betty Rendel than she did with any of her own siblings and remained close to them throughout her life. Marjorie's difficulties did not grow less in adolescence. She was as bumptious as ever, her father commented, when she was 12. Jane Strachey's letters to Lytton throughout the 1890s contain a litany of Marjorie's difficulties: she needed bands for her teeth, seemed backward at school, and was forever losing her glasses.[48] It was a relief to send her off to school—and unlike the other Strachey children, she was sometimes left there through the holidays.

Although Marjorie and Lytton were set up as a pair in childhood, this seems never really to have developed into a close relationship. They sometimes went out together, but Lytton rarely wrote to Marjorie from school. While Ralph wrote his most intimate letters to Pippa, and Oliver sent his to Pernel, Lytton's most regular and his most important letters home were written not to Marjorie, but to his mother. Marjorie in turn was very much aware of the closeness of this relationship and of the importance to it of their shared literary interests, and this served to emphasize how rarely her mother wrote to her. 'Your conduct is perfectly disgraceful,' Marjorie wrote to her mother during her first year at Allenswood School in 1895. 'You have not written me one letter all this term.'[49] In later years, Marjorie was often left entirely out of the familial communications loop. She was not told that Oliver was going to India, for example, until he had already left. 'I expect Dorothy has told you of my astonishment & horror on learning that Oliver was off on his travels', she wrote somewhat reproachfully to her mother. 'I really think I might have been told by somebody, but I suppose everybody thought everybody else had told me. I am still ignorant of what he is going to do when he has reached the happy land.'[50]

While Marjorie received few letters, Jane Strachey lavished them on her youngest son. James was generally known as 'Jembeau' (Jem for short) in childhood and always to his mother. It was clear from the start that Jane adored him. She filled her letters to her other children with stories of his doings, stressing his charm and the wit that was evident even in his infancy. Every aspect of his life was of interest to her, and she was concerned always for him to be seen at his best. When Elinor brought him a suit that one of her sons had grown out of, Jane wrote to Lytton that James 'looked so absurd that I have quite determined not to put him into knickerbockers but shall alter the fashion of his petticoats into something a little more boyish'.[51] Jane was very amused at James's interest in worsted work and cross-stitch and wrote to tell Lytton of the trip she made with him to Bournemouth when he was 4.

The Old ladies in the boarding house admired Jem, couldn't get over astonishment at his sitting down to do cross stitch. They surrounded him with exclamations on his beauty, cleverness & good behaviour, so that if he had not had a tolerable sense of humour, he might have been quite upset; as it was he just looked at me out of the tail of his eye and grinned.[52]

Two years later, she reported to Lytton that Marjorie, who had just started at Allenswood, felt herself very backward in French. By contrast, Jembeau then aged 7, 'now repeats an anecdote (in French) about Frederick the Great in the most ravishing manner'.[53] Lytton may not have cared overly for this flow of glowing reports about his younger brother, but they kept on coming. Oliver composed music for him and Pippa travelled with and looked after him. As we will see, he was also the only son to attend a local school. Although he spent some years at boarding school in his prep years, James went to St Paul's in London where he was occasionally a weekly boarder, but mostly a day pupil able to return to his mother each night.

The affection evident in Jane Strachey's comments about James is evident also in her letters to him. He was the only Strachey who was always addressed as 'darling' by his mother. James in turn sent back a series of charming and amusing letters from his prep school. Unlike the stilted and perfunctory missives of Dick and Ralph, James's letters home, like Lytton's, were charming and affectionate and filled with news and stories guaranteed to interest his mother. Again like Lytton, he took a great interest in her activities, especially in her writing. 'There is a little boy here, whom I think you have spoken to,' he wrote, when he was 10, 'whose name is Russell, whose parents read *The Highland Lady* with joy! The boy beat me in Latin by 4 marks!'[54] Like Lytton, James did well at school, so that his regular reporting back of his position in class was a source of pleasure and pride—rather than the pain it was to Dick. For all this, there was some questioning within the family as to how much James himself benefited from the intensity of his mother's love. Jane Strachey herself commented on her lack of skill or interest in domestic management, and her daughters felt the house ran much more smoothly under their care than under hers. Dorothy was horrified when Jane decided to care for James when he was sent home from school with mumps at the age of 15. 'Mama proposes to nurse James herself', she wrote to Pippa, 'so if you value either safety or comfort I strongly recommend you not to return just yet!'[55]

School Days

The Stracheys were an unusual Victorian family in their belief that the education of daughters was almost as important as was that of their sons. Hence all the Strachey children went to school. For the most part the boys spent a longer time there, starting off as boarders at a preparatory schools when they were 7 or 8 and moving on to a public schools in their early teens. James followed the usual course in terms of a preparatory school, but then became the only one to attend a secondary day school. The daughters' preparatory schooling was either done at home or in local day schools. Thus while they too went to boarding school in their teens, they were usually away from home for less time than their brothers.

It was Jane Strachey who had to make the decision as to where and how the children should be educated. This was a singularly difficult task and one in which she received little help. Richard Strachey was in India when this issue had to be resolved for the older children, but even when he returned, he had little to say. Nor was there any family tradition to fall back upon. Neither the Stracheys nor the Grants had any connection with particular public schools and the immense expansion in the range of both public and private schools in the mid-nineteenth century meant that there was vast array of choice. Jane Strachey's limited formal education offered little as a basis for making this decision for her children. She relied on the comments and suggestions of friends and acquaintances, on chance contacts, and on her own views and intuitions. It was rare for two of the Strachey sons to attend the same school, and sometimes this did indicate her dissatisfaction. One does, however, need to bear in mind her own sense of the different needs and abilities of her sons, and the changing expectations of their parents regarding future careers. It was taken for granted that the oldest sons, Dick and Ralph, would follow their father into the Indian army, and the schools sought for them were thus ones with a military connection that would lead on to the Woolwich Military Academy or Sandhurst. Perhaps it was the poor results Dick achieved at Woolwich, and the spinal problems that made a military career impossible for Ralph that led Jane to question this approach. When schooling for Oliver was thought about, while Indian service remained the goal, it was the Indian Civil Service rather than the army that was the focus. This required a public school followed by university, and so Oliver went to Eton and then briefly to Balliol. When it came to Lytton, Jane Strachey apparently sought to avoid an ordinary public school and to find something that would meet his particular needs and develop his outstanding abilities. As Michael Holroyd has argued, however, her actual decisions seem hard to comprehend.[1] Why she chose to send a son whose intelligence and pronounced literary interests she appreciated, and whose delicate constitution was a source of great concern, to the recently opened Abbotsholme, with its Spartan syllabus, cold baths, and heavy manual labour is almost impossible to explain. In the case of James, other things seem to have come into play. He was sent away to preparatory school, but perhaps because of her own wish to have him with her at home he moved from there to St Paul's.

The education of the Strachey daughters was both more uniform than that of the sons and of a far higher quality. As a woman with deep regrets about her own inadequate education, Jane Strachey took the question of educating her daughters very seriously indeed. As we will see, her own close involvement in feminist campaigns did not really begin until the 1890s. Nonetheless she took a great interest in the feminist debates of the late 1860s and 1870s concerning the need for better secondary education for girls and for the opening of university entrance examinations to them.[2] Although there were some that offered a serious academic education, Jane Strachey did not send her daughters to English schools.[3] In 1870, just as their schooling was becoming a matter of importance, she had met and established a close friendship with Marie Souvestre. The girls' schools Mlle Souvestre ran were internationally recognized and were attended by the daughters of many prominent British, French, and American families. Her best known pupil, and the one who has left the clearest account of her school days, was Eleanor Roosevelt.[4] At Fontainbleau in France, Mlle

Souvestre ran a 'finishing' school which offered languages, literature, history, science, and music as well as an introduction to French society, intellectual life, and theatre. In the 1880s when she moved to London and established Allenswood in Wimbledon, although the curriculum remained much the same, the school began to take pupils at a younger age and to keep them for longer. All the Strachey daughters attended these schools, the older two in France, the younger two in London, and Pippa for a term in each place.[5]

The Strachey's decision to send their daughters to school was not one supported by all their friends. On the contrary, they were frequently advised not to do so—especially by those with whom they had become friendly in India. Lady Lytton, wife of the one-time viceroy, had become close to the Stracheys in India and continued to correspond with them when they all returned to England. Dorothy was a particular favourite of the Lyttons and visited them regularly. After one visit, Lady Lytton wrote to tell Jane Strachey how much they had all enjoyed Dorothy's visit—and to express her hope that Dorothy would not return to Fontainbleau, so that they could all see her more often.

I am sure she could continue to study at anything she wishes to learn, and it would do her good to be at home with you and help you with the other children, and it would cheer and encourage her before going out into the world. She is so meek and gentle now and I think school life and the discipline is rather apt to take away the individual character and brightness.[6]

There was nothing of the Spartan regime of cold rooms, bad food, and general discomfort common to so many English girls' schools at Allens-wood, however. There, as at Les Ruches, the girls were comfortably housed and well fed. Pupils described their wonderful meals at length in letters home.[7] Dorothy Strachey later suggested that educating her pupils' palates and introducing them to the excellence of French food was part of Mlle Souvestre's overall curriculum.[8] In England, the girls were also introduced to visiting French intellectuals, and kept abreast of political developments. They were not, however, prepared for university entrance. This had no place in Mlle Souvestre's curriculum and those who chose to go there had either to work up the necessary subjects themselves, or to attend a college designed for the purpose. For the most part, however, the underlying foundation that she provided enabled her students to pass university entrance examinations with ease.

The anxiety the Stracheys expressed about their oldest son, Dick, in his early years increased during his schooldays. Indeed, Dick's education was the subject of far more parental concern and anxiety than was that of any of his siblings. Jane began investigating schools for him very early. In 1868, when he was only 7, she spent a couple of days at Rugby. She was very interested to see the boys there, thinking all the while 'of our poor Dick turned adrift into such a world'.[9] She made it her business to call on and dine with the headmaster, but in the end decided against sending her sons there. Dick went first to Richmond House, a small prep school at Worthing and then, on the recommendation of its headmaster, to Wellington College. Established in 1853, Wellington College was one of the new Victorian public schools. Dick's headmaster at Richmond House liked its emphasis on science and mathematics and believed that 'they have achieved happy medium between old and new methods of education'. He felt that the situation of the school was 'healthy and likely to suit Dick'.[10] Dick would need a particular kind of school, he explained to Jane.

He is a boy of decided ability and when he applies his mind to any subject he can get on with it. He is perhaps more defective in mere acts of memory, such as learning by heart than in anything else. He is easily discouraged if things do not go quite smoothly with him he loses heart (& sometimes, to a slight degree, temper) but when he feels a rising tide under him he takes redoubled interest in what he is about, and often shows considerable promise.[11]

Despite this recommendation, Dick did not have an easy time at Wellington. His teachers there commented constantly on his lack of enthusiasm and application. Early in his first term, his housemaster asked Jane 'to write & stir up your little boy'. There was no definite fault to find with him, but he wasn't doing as well as he might, and there was a chance he would not be promoted to the next form. 'I wouldn't trouble you', the housemaster added revealingly, 'but I know how anxious you are about your respectable member of society'.[12] Dick's disinclination to work made Jane worried about having him at home over the vacations. She compared him unfavourably with his sisters. I wish Dorothy was a boy, she exclaimed to Richard after describing her anxieties about Dick. 'She would do us credit!' Dorothy had just taken honours in four school subjects at this point, in grammar, history, geography, and physiology.[13] Just before Jane came to join him in India in 1878 Richard Strachey demanded that she take some form of action to address Dick's school results. 'Lecture Dick well before you leave. He is in truth my only cause of anxiety—the more so in that I feel it is almost impossible to do more than let him have his own way for good or bad.'[14] Dick did not keep his mother's letters, but there can be little doubt either that Jane would have heeded the call 'to stir him up', or that it proved to be completely ineffective. The subsequent correspondence between Dick and his parents and between his housemaster and his mother makes it clear that, while he occasionally did well and even won a prize, his progress was a constant cause of concern. He was denied promotion to the next class several times. Languages, at which his mother excelled, were a particular problem. In his final year at Wellington, it was agreed that he should give up drawing to allow extra time and help for French and German.[15] Years later, when he was given the task of translating the first four lines of Thomson's *Seasons* into French, he could not do it and Jane did it for him.[16]

Dick completed his undistinguished schooling by failing to gain entry to the Woolwich Military Academy which his parents had seen as the next step he needed to take to establish a successful career in the Indian army. Indeed, although he never articulated a disinclination to go to India, it is hard not to see something of this in his approach both to school and to his later military training. He failed the entrance examination to Woolwich Military Academy twice—and even when he finally passed, managed to miss the deadline for applications![17] His low place in his year when he finally went to Woolwich caused his father to reflect gloomily that there was not 'much appearance of the Strachey tendency being carried on into the future through my offspring'.[18] Dick in turn made clear his sense of the burden he felt when faced with the constant questioning about his future. 'Tell Elinor I can sympathise with her having to tell everyone how she likes India', he wrote to his mother when Jane and her two older daughters were visiting India in 1878. 'Everybody I meet says to me "Oh what are you doing now; where are you studying?" Then "Oh yes, what are you going up for? Woolwich—oh that is for the army isn't it? Yes, do you hope to get into the engineers? When do you go up for examinations" etc. Etc.'[19] Dick ultimately failed to get into any of the engineering regiments, going instead into the Rifle Brigade and then to India as a junior officer in 1881.

Although Jane Strachey worried a great deal about Dick, she sometimes seemed to recognize that he was placed under heavy pressure, especially by his father, and that lecturing him constantly was not the best way to deal with the situation. 'Do not forget to write to Dick', she admonished her husband after Dick had written explaining his failure to gain admission to the officers's corps at Woolwich. 'He was perfectly open and straightforward in his letter to you, & it is not very encouraging if you only rave in return.'[20]

Whether it was Dick's lack of success that made them question the merits of Wellington, or for some other reason, none of the other Strachey sons were sent there. The next two sons, Ralph and Oliver, both began at Summerfield prep school in Oxford. After that, Ralph spent two years at Clifton College, where he won a scholarship to cover his tuition. Ralph was a very much better student than his older brother, but he too was frequently subject to maternal exhortations to work hard, to do well, and to make both his father and his school proud of him. The family was thrilled when Ralph came second in the school examination and received a scholarship in 1884. 'Everybody here was very much excited by the news', wrote his oldest sister Elinor, 'and I expect if I had been at Stowy I should have found Pippin standing on her head. I think it very nice to have such a distinguished brother.'[21] His mother's congratulations, however, were tempered by her anxieties and filled with warnings and instructions about the need for him to keep up the standard of his work. 'I suppose you are more left to yourself . . . than you were at Summerfield,' she wrote, when Ralph began studying at Clifton in 1884, ' & so you must learn to keep yourself up to the mark. Remember that a scholar is expected to be a credit to the School.'[22]

The imperative of going out to India seems to have taken precedence over everything else in Ralph's education. He left school before he had completed the sixth form, apparently in order to undertake the special coaching that was deemed necessary to enable him to go to Woolwich and hopefully then to obtain a commission in the Royal Engineers. Jane Strachey looked on this almost as if it were a sacred mission. 'We have received an excellent report of your first month', she wrote to him, 'and they seem to think that if you work as well before and after you get into Woolwich you have an excellent chance of the Engineers. If so, oh be joyful!—but I would think you have no spare time to lose.'[23] Unfortunately, Ralph's health and physical strength were deemed inadequate by the army medical board. He had left Clifton College before completing his secondary schooling and they wanted him back 'I feel most keenly for your and Ralph's disappointment about his profession,' wrote his housemaster, and for the increased anxiety which his delicacy will bring upon you: but I am also personally most sorry that we are to lose him from this house: nor am I alone in feeling this. Every one who has come across him has a good word for him and in his own circles he will be much missed. I do hope he may come back in September to prepare for his new life and do half work here; we will keep a place open for him.[24]

But Ralph did not return to school. Instead in 1886 he went to Cooper's Hill near Staines, an engineering college that would prepare him to go out to India as a railway engineer.

Life at Cooper's Hill seemed to agree with Ralph. 'I am getting on beautifully', he wrote to his mother shortly after he arrived there. 'I will describe the day':

First of all you are woken at the unearthly hour of seven—breakfast at half-past. This consists of fish, or eggs &c, and bread and butter, tea or coffee. Chapel from 8 to a quarter past about. Then from half past eight to half past 12 there are lectures (two) and then luncheon of meat, bread, cheese, beer. From 1 to 3 there is a lecture or private study, and up to about 4 there is generally something hovering about such as workshop gym or chemical lab. At 7 comes dinner which is a most sumptuous and elaborate meal of soup, fish, entree, joint and sweet... This is the best place for food I've ever been at. There is an hour's lecture after dinner and lights go out at eleven only my gas is perpetual.[25]

There was a marked change in familial expectations and ideas by the time it came to considering Oliver's education. Although India was still part of the general framework of Oliver's youth and education, it seems to have been thought of in rather vaguer terms and to have lacked a specific focus or set of objectives. This was possibly because Oliver's wit and his early interest in games, drama, and music gave him a rather different standing within the family, as well as making it unlikely that he would be either an engineer or a soldier. He followed Ralph to Summerfield and his reports from this prep school indicate that he was seen as a sunny and talented child. He deserved an 'excellent report on all counts: conduct, character, progress and health' wrote his housemaster in his second year there. 'I never saw him brighter or happier. He is in a class with a number of clever boys—constantly changing places. Oliver is delightful to teach in Mathematics and well on for his age. I am hoping to make a double scholar out of him. He practices very assiduously his music and seems to me to have rather a talent.'[26] Oliver was good both at languages and mathematics. He was often top of his form in French and towards the top in mathematics. Family correspondence suggests that he spent five very happy years at Summerfield.

For all his ability, however, Oliver missed out on the scholarship to Clifton and in 1888, at the age of 14, was sent to Eton. It is not clear why this prestigious school was chosen, or whether Jane needed to plan a special campaign to gain a place for him there. He remained at Eton for four years, however, and thoroughly enjoyed it. Oliver's liking for music and drama was not accompanied by any distaste for the rough and tumble of school life. The bullying and brutality of Eton, which appalled some of his contemporaries, rather appealed to him. Watching boys being flogged, was a nauseating experience for Roger Fry but one Oliver greatly enjoyed.[27] 'I held down the other day,' he wrote to his mother. 'When a boy gets birched, 2 boys hold up his shirt and I was fagged to be one of them. It is rather an extraordinary custom isn't it. I being very blood-thirsty enjoyed it immensely!'[28] Like his younger brothers, Oliver preferred the extracurricular activities to lessons. He tried out for essay competitions (usually without success) and wrote home enthusiastically about school musicals and plays. But he rarely mentioned either his school work or his results. He was recognized as very clever, but he lacked application. In 1892, when a Mr Smith was employed as a tutor to prepare Oliver for the Oxford entrance exams, Jane wrote to tell Richard that he 'he spoke almost with enthusiasm of Oliver's cleverness'. Mr Smith added, however, that Oliver

had not a notion of what work meant and must have been completely idle for the last year at least. He seemed to think that was nothing he might not do if he could be got fully to exert himself—& then said I or even without it—he's as clever as that. (And to think that the boy will never do anything! For that is my conviction) He said Oliver's head was so very clear—& that he had great powers of concentration—that he was excellent at mathematics though his knowledge was below the mark—& that he possessed a true literary aptitude. It had been suggested that his chess be cut off as too engrossing. Smith said no—he should be allowed to enjoy it and the piano.[29]

Mr Smith's efforts were successful and Oliver was admitted to Oxford. As we will see, however, his approach to work did not improve, and he left within a year.

II

Although the Stracheys took the education of their daughters very seriously, it is harder to establish precisely how each daughter was educated than is the case with the sons. There are no letters or records providing precise details of their early education. In her semi-autobiographical novel, *Olivia*, Dorothy Bussy described being sent, at the age of 13, to a London boarding school 'kept by an eminent woman of the Wesleyan persuasion', who had promised her mother that she would not try to convert her daughter. Nonetheless, the constant talk of hell fire and damnation and the lack of any intellectual stimulus apparently made the narrator of *Olivia* absolutely miserable.[30] There is no indication, however, as to whether her older sister, Elinor, also attended this school or how long she spent there. Such schools do not seem to have figured in the lives of her younger sisters. Jane Strachey's letters suggest rather that a governess was employed at home for both Pippa and Pernel, and that Pippa in turn gave the youngest daughter, Marjorie, her first lessons.

Although all the girls spent some time at one or other of Mlle Souvestre's schools, even some of these years are shrouded in mystery. Family letters during the girls' school days are sparse and the coverage uneven. There are detailed letters from Elinor and Pernel about their time with Mlle Souvestre, but there are no school letters at all from Dorothy and very few from Pippa and Marjorie. This is the more frustrating because there are some mysteries concerning both the relationship between the Stracheys and Mlle Souvestre, and the school lives of Dorothy and Pippa. In Dorothy's case, this is underlined by the length and intensity of her involvement with the school. She was a pupil for some years and was then employed by Marie Souvestre as a teacher for a number of years until her marriage to Simon Bussy. Marie Souvestre and her school are moreover the subject of Dorothy's one novel, *Olivia*. In Pippa's case, the mystery centres rather on her very brief schooling: she attended school for only a couple of terms while each of her sisters was there for several years.

The education of both Dorothy and Pippa seems to have been affected by the breakdown in the relationship between Marie Souvestre and her partner, Caroline Dussant, and the consequent closing of Les Ruches. The close friendship of these two women with Jane Strachey enables one to chart the relational breakdown.[31] The financial details concerning Les Ruches and its closure, like the actual setting up of Allenswood in Wimbledon, are impossible to ascertain, however. They were small private schools, operating at a time when there was little regulation or formality involved in private education. The schools no longer exist and there are no remaining records. Thus while one is able to supplement the meagre family letters about Ralph's time at Clifton, or James' at St Paul's through the school archives, no such resource is available for those who went to one of Mlle Souvestre's schools.

Family correspondence suggests that the Strachey daughters had somewhat different experiences at school. The length of time that they spent there, the things they learnt, and their feelings about school differed considerably from one daughter to another. Elinor was the first to go to school, travelling to Les Ruches in Fontainebleau when she was 15. Jane Strachey accompanied her and helped her to settle her in. Elinor's letters home suggest that she was very happy at school. She enjoyed a close and cordial relationship with both Marie Souvestre and Caroline Dussant, studying French with the former and German and physiology with the latter. In addition, she had lessons in music and history and greatly enjoyed the cultural and social life of Les Ruches.[32] Marie Souvestre did not believe in the frequent examinations that were the central feature of English boys' schools, and Elinor pursued her studies at her own pace and apparently with ease.

Elinor greatly admired Mlle Souvestre, although there is a touch of irony in some of her descriptions. 'Miss Souvestre is more beautiful than ever', she wrote in one of her early letters home, 'I sit opposite her at dinner, and I look at her all the time, she is dressed all in black with nice puffy sleeves, with a dark peacock blue bow under her chin, I think she looks just like a beautiful strong cart horse'.[33] But for her, this was an unproblematic relationship. She remained in close contact with Mlle Souvestre after she left school, attending school dances and functions as often as she could. She regarded Mlle Souvestre as a family friend, inviting her to her wedding and keeping up her social contact for many years. In March 1894, for example, she informed her mother that Marie Souvestre was coming to lunch with her.[34]

Here, as in every other part of her life, Dorothy Strachey seems to have had a rather more difficult and traumatic time. This was not entirely of her own making. While Elinor was at Les Ruches, it was a successful school run by a harmonious partnership. In the early 1880s, after she had left, but while Dorothy was still there, the personal and the business partnership between Marie Souvestre and Caroline Dussant broke down in an extremely bitter and acrimonious way. Caroline Dussant insisted that Marie Souvestre had no understanding of their financial situation and that her plans to borrow money to extend the school threatened them with bankruptcy.[35] Marie Souvestre, in turn, believed that Caroline's physical frailty and lack of emotional balance were making her act so destructively that the continuation of the school was unviable.[36] Les Ruches closed its doors in 1883 and, with the help of her English friends, Marie Souvestre moved to England.[37]

Their correspondence makes very clear the importance of Jane Strachey in the lives of both Marie Souvestre and Caroline Dussant. Indeed Dussant insisted that Jane Strachey had effectively replaced her in Marie Souvestre's affection, and was now the one who needed to proffer advice. Jane Strachey absolutely denied this. 'That Marie has always had a strong respect for my judgement, I do not deny', she wrote in response.

But to talk of my having had any 'influence' with regard to the matters which had been in dispute between you is absurd; I knew nothing of those differences of opinion in the management of Les Ruches, which formed the grounds of your complaints against her. I was long unaware of your growing disunion; Marie never breathed a word of it to me till long after I had heard it from you.[38]

'It is not in my power', she concluded her letter, 'to replace to her the friend with whom she shared all feelings, thoughts and interests for twenty years.'[39] While Jane Strachey may have regarded Marie Souvestre as but one amongst many quite close friends, this was not quite how Marie Souvestre herself saw it. When her school finally closed in France, she regarded Jane as the only fixed point in her 'vie errante'. She had always felt the need of a close and trusted friend to whom she could unbosom herself, she explained, and Jane Strachey was now the one.[40]

It is unlikely that Dorothy was ignorant of or unaffected by these events. In November 1882, Marie Souvestre wrote to Jane Strachey commenting on Dorothy's progress, and expressing her wish to have Dorothy return for the following school year—the last that Les Ruches was open. She wanted to ensure that Dorothy excelled in French writing as well as speech, so that she would have the great pleasure of believing that she had enriched the life of one of her dear friend's children.[41] Life at the moment was very hard, she added, and it was Dorothy who supplied the greatest interest and the brightest spot.[42]

None of Dorothy's school letters survive, so it is impossible to know what she made of the drama through which Marie Souvestre was living. Letters from some of the other pupils who were at Les Ruches at this time do suggest that the crisis in which its two leading teachers were engulfed and the threatened closure of the school were completely unknown to many pupils, particularly the younger ones taught by teachers other than Mlles Souvestre and Dussant.[43] But Dorothy was then 17 or 18, and a senior girl who clearly worked closely with Souvestre. Dorothy's novella, *Olivia*, moreover takes as its subject the breakdown in the emotional relationship between two women who run a school and the school's subsequent closure. *Olivia* has attained something of cult status as a lesbian school novel and is now standard reading in most gay and lesbian studies courses. It offers a powerful depiction of the passionate infatuation of a young girl for her school mistress, and of her devastation when she is caught up in the bitter termination of the relationship between the school mistress and her long-time business partner and lover.

Dorothy was adamant that the book was a work of art, not a memoir, and it clearly does not offer a simple description of her own schooldays.[44] The central story in *Olivia* differs in many significant details from events at Les Ruches. Quarrels and terrible fights there might have been at Les Ruches, as well as accusations and a divisive taking of sides by other staff and senior students. There was no suicide, however, and far from going off into a lonely exile after the death of Mlle Cara, as Dorothy has Mlle Julie do in *Olivia*, Marie Souvestre went on to open another school that was every bit as successful as the first. Mlle Dussant was replaced, moreover, by a new personal and professional partner, Mlle Samia. Nor was the hopeless infatuation described in *Olivia*, and the horror of being cast out forever from the world of the beloved teacher, part of Dorothy's own experience. On the contrary, Dorothy taught for several years at Allenswood, and when she left to marry a French artist and settle in France, Marie Souvestre helped both Dorothy and her husband to establish themselves. She also paid Dorothy 'a handsome sum every year'.[45] Dorothy in turn came to England when either Mlle Samia or Marie Souvestre needed her help.[46] Marie Souvestre's death left a great hole in Dorothy's life. Every time she looked at the paintings her husband was doing for a major art exhibition, Dorothy wrote to Pippa, 'I think how wretched it is that there is no Miss Souvestre to tell it to and that if Simon is successful half the pleasure of it will be gone.'[47]

It is interesting to note that Marjorie Strachey, who read an early draft of the manuscript before it was published, regarded *Olivia* as offering a picture of Allenswood, Mlle Souvestre's school in London, where Marjorie was a pupil in the 1890s. In her view, the relationship described in the novel was not that between Mlle Souvestre and Mlle Dussant, but rather the later one between Mlle Souvestre and Mlle Samia with whom she ran Allenswood. 'It seems to me a curious mixture', she wrote to Pippa, after reading the manuscript.

A great many facts appear to be incorrect . . . Kissing when one said good night? (Very odd—so important in her account—yet we certainly never did anything but shake hands) desks? Monitors? No mention of the morning room . . . I think on the other hand she has got the general atmosphere well. Signorina's devilishness and sinister influence on MS—the story of the row over the piece of paper is very typical. Also the curiously mixed emotions of work with Miss S—terror and terrific intellectual stimulus and enjoyment.[48]

This last point is particularly interesting because Dorothy's account centres on Mlle Julie's gifts as a teacher and on her capacity to arouse in her students the most intense passion.

The novel certainly offers one a clear sense of the magnetism and fascination of Marie Souvestre and of the emotional intensity and drama that drew her pupils into passionate personal and working relationships, but it cannot be used as a basis for inferring Dorothy's own school experiences. It is, however, interesting to speculate on the rather curious interplay of relationships between Jane Strachey, Marie Souvestre, and Dorothy. That Marie Souvestre saw her own devotion to Dorothy in part as a gift to Jane was doubtless extremely difficult for Dorothy to accept. She was well aware that she was not one of Jane's favoured daughters, and she suffered deeply from her own emotional intensity and her sense of the lack of corresponding emotions amongst other members of her family. It is possible that one of the many things that Dorothy achieved in writing *Olivia* was the capacity to tell a story of her school days in a way that made it her own—and from which her mother was completely excluded.

The end of Les Ruches in 1883 and the time lag between that and the opening of Allenswood may have had even more impact on the school life of the next Strachey daughter, Pippa. The brevity of her own school life was a mystery even to Pippa herself. 'For some unknown reason', she wrote in an autobiographical note towards the end of her life,

I did not have anything like the formal education that was given to my sisters, all four of whom spent their school years with Miss Souvestre that most unusual and inspiring of Head Mistresses. She was as a matter of fact my godmother, and was always very kind to me, but I spent no more than two terms with her, one at the age of ten at Fontainebleau and the other at the age of 14 or 15 at Allenswood in Wimbledon.[49]

The brevity of Pippa's schooling has always troubled those interested in the lives of the Stracheys. There have been suggestions that it occurred because the Strachey family was in financial straits at this time, and could not afford to send Pippa to school.[50] This seems unlikely: Richard Strachey had a seat on the India Council in the mid-1880s when Pippa was of school age, so the family was quite comfortable financially. Marie Souvestre was herself a wealthy woman, far more dependent on the Stracheys for friendship and contacts than for money. Pippa, moreover, was her god-daughter and it is impossible to believe that she would not have given a place to her had it been sought. There are no records to show exactly when Allenswood opened. What seems most likely is that, in the years between the closing of Les Ruches and the opening of Allenswood, Jane Strachey simply did not get around to finding Pippa another school. Her closeness to Pippa in later years also make it possible that Jane Strachey so enjoyed having this parti-cular daughter at home that she preferred to let her continue having lessons with her younger sister, Pernel, rather than sending her away to a school.

Pippa was at Allenswood briefly in 1888. Her few remaining letters home are filled with requests for things she needs: 'a dirty clothes bag, a tin of biscuits and a bible and prayer book', rather than with any details of her daily life.[51] Lack of schooling did not leave Pippa completely unedu-cated: she was well read and was apparently employed to teach the young-est children by Mlle Souvestre as well as being responsible for Marjorie's early lessons. But it ruled out the possibility of university for her, some-thing which was often commented on by her and her friends as a source of great regret.

Both Pernel and Marjorie attended Allenswood. Their letters suggest that it had become somewhat larger and slightly more impersonal now that it was established in London, and that Marie Souvestre's teaching role was supplemented by a large variety of others. There are no descriptions of the meals with her or the outings that figure so largely either in *Olivia*, or in Elinor's letters. Marie Souvestre continued to give the girls her wonderful readings of French literature, but there were also many other teachers, as well as an ever-increasing emphasis on organized games and exercise. 'Perhaps you would like to hear what happens every day', Pernel wrote to her mother, shortly after her arrival at Allenswood in February 1891:

We get up at half past 7 and breakfast is at 8. We generally finish at half past and prayers are at quarter to 9 sometimes in French and sometimes in German. After that our letters are given us. From 9 to 10 we have our walk & from 10 to 1 lessons.

At 1 we have lunch and from 2 to 3 we go for another walk & from 3 to 7 we work but at 4 we have 10 minutes for biscuits and milk. At 7 we have tea and after tea we may do anything we like except do lessons. On Thursdays we have a singing class from 9 to 10 . . . I am in the firsts. I am doing a Prelude and Fugue of bach & a march & a Valse by Dvorak. I have a music lesson every Thursday.[52]

Mlle Souvestre had a gymnasium built in 1892 and gymnastics were soon very popular.[53] Marie Souvestre's continued to read the girls all the classic French tragedies and comedies. Through Pernel, she asked Jane Strachey to come to the school to read some of the great English drama, including Jane's old favourite, 'She Stoops to Conquer'.[54] School was a comfortable and even a familial place for Pernel who was much envied by the other girls at Allenswood because Dorothy was then a teacher there, bringing a sense of the family with her.

While Pippa was at school for only two terms, Marjorie Strachey spent at least six years at Allenswood. She was younger than any of the others when she went in 1892, aged 10, and she remained there until 1898. Like her sisters, Marjorie studied languages and was enthralled by Mlle Souvestre's reading. It was not Racine that provided the introduction to French drama, but Molière, and in her later years Mlle Souvestre also read the novels of Victor Hugo. Marjorie loved the visits to the theatre that were part of the French curriculum. 'I have seen her! I have seen the "grande Sarah"', she wrote to her mother after a visit to Sarah Bernhardt in 1895. 'She is the most exquisite person that ever existed. She was completely transformed from the awkward horror playing croquet on Sunday, to an exquisite Princess of the middle ages as graceful as anything and simply fascinating. Her voice is the best part of her. There is something in it which makes it lovely & exquisite beyond description.'[55] Marjorie loved acting and participated in both French and German plays at school. She was very pleased when organised sport was introduced to the school. In 1898, a hockey field was installed. 'Isn't it exquisite about the hockey?', she wrote to her mother, 'Our sticks came today and we played for the first time this afternoon. It is the most fascinating game I have ever played.'[56] Cricket was also played on the hockey field and, true to form, Mlle Souvestre employed 'a professional from Lords' to give the girls cricket lessons.[57] Marjorie enjoyed playing cricket, but hockey remained 'the best game in the world'. There were other new activities at Allenswood in the 1890s, notably photography. It was 'the latest craze . . . All day we have been doing nothing but printing and fixing photographs' Marjorie wrote. 'Two of the girls have kodaks and are constantly taking photographs regardless of the expense.'[59]

Allenswood seemed to be changing in other ways too. Marjorie became friendly with a Jewish girl at school and was horrified by the amount of anti-Semitism and the general unpleasantness to which her friend, Ethel Lewis, was subjected. She had very little understanding of what Judaism was. 'Why do foolish people try to insult Jews?', she asked.

One of the girls called Ethel Lewis is of Jewish nationality and the way she is treated is abominable. She has a very Jewish face & that is how they found out. Unfortunately I never knew she was being annoyed till tonight as they never do it in my presence. She has not been baptised because her parents (who died when she was a child) wanted to leave her free. Of course it is very inconvenient especially as she is really an agnostic. Do you think she ought to be baptised and confirmed for convenience sake or stick to what she believes (or doesn't believe) at the cost of disgusting things happening to her and being treated generally badly? Aren't there difficulties at college? She is clever and wants to go there.[59]

Marjorie continued her friendship with Ethel Lewis after they both left Allenswood. Although the Stracheys were vocal opponents of the behaviour of the French military to Alfred Dreyfus, they included few Jews within their own social circle, but they certainly did nothing to discourage their children's friendship. Marjorie's friendship with Ethel Lewis occurred at about the same time that Lytton began taking Leonard Woolf home, and while there is now considerable discussion about Bloomsbury anti-Semitism in relation to Woolf, he always felt completely welcome in the Strachey home.[60] At the same time, it is interesting to note that it was Marjorie, rather than Lytton, who first became conscious of and concerned about British anti-Semitism through its impact on her friend.

There was just a hint of criticism of the school amongst Marjorie's contemporaries. 'We had a debate last night,' she wrote to her mother in 1898, 'and came to the conclusion that gossip is too prevalent in Allenswood—because we were so ignorant of outside affairs and so had nothing else to talk about. We have therefore made a petition asking to have bits of newspapers read to us and presented it to Miss Boyce. I wonder if anything will come of it.'[61] Marjorie left Allenswood shortly after, and never commented on the result of this petition.

Just as Pippa's short time at school may have been an indication of her value to her mother, one has a sense that Marjorie's lengthy stay reflected her mother's desire get her out of the way. Her school life kept her very much away from home. She was rarely visited at school, she spent some of her holidays there—and it somehow always seemed hard to arrange to have her met at the station. When Elinor first went to Les Ruches, Jane Strachey went with her, just as she later accompanied Pernel to Newnham. Marjorie, however, was accompanied by her older sisters rather than her mother. Marjorie liked school, indeed it may well have been preferable to home. She had older sisters employed there and got on well with her teachers. But one has a sense, nonetheless, that Jane Strachey relinquished her responsibilities for Marjorie to the school with great relief.

❦ III ❦

Unfortunately for the younger Strachey sons, although they knew Marie Souvestre and found her interesting and stimulating, no masculine equivalent of their sisters' school was ever available. Nor was Jane Strachey satisfied that the education of her older sons was appropriate for the far more talented younger two. Hence she tried a series of new ventures for them. Their schooling was not intended to provide them with any specific career, but rather to allow them to develop their considerable intellectual capacities. Their mother seemed concerned to provide them both with schooling that not involve dull conformity or an ordinary routine. On Lytton some of the stranger experiments were made and it was also he, of all the Strachey children, who seems to have been most miserable during his school years. By contrast, Jane's major concern in regard to her younger and favourite son, James, was to keep him close to home.

Lytton Strachey began his education at a Hyde Park kindergarten in 1887. He was accompanied by Marjorie. Even at the age of 7 both his charm and his exceptional intelligence was noted—and here, as at home, he completely eclipsed his unfortunate sibling. When Jane notified the kindergarten that she planned to take the children away, she received a letter from its head expressing deep regret. 'Although I cannot help feeling that you are right and that the children's lessons would be more regular if taken at home', wrote the headteacher, he was 'very distressed at the prospect of parting with Giles: he is so very bright and intelligent and such a good boy. I shall miss him sadly.'[62] There was no comment about the loss of Marjorie.

The question of Lytton's health was always one that had to be taken into account in his schooling and it determined where he would go next. Rather than sending him to a large preparatory school, the Stracheys decided to send him to a private tutor. They chose Henry Forde, a Dickensian character, in the view of Michael Holroyd, who supervised a small group of boarders in his own home. In 1889, at the age of 9, Lytton Strachey became one of his pupils. One of the attractions of Forde was the fact that he lived near Poole harbour in Dorset, which meant that Lytton could also gain the benefits of the sea air regarded as so very healthy by his parents and their contemporaries, and certainly he enjoyed sea bathing. Forde was extremely impressed by Lytton's literary abilities, 'his ear for, and . . . knack of hitting off queer and picturesque phrases and turns of expression', and thought he might well turn out to be a writer. He felt that his education 'should be chiefly directed to giving him help to evolve himself, not forcing him into ordinary moulds'.[63] Lytton remained with Forde for nearly five years. Forde himself felt that Lytton made good progress under his tuition— though not as good as he might have, had his health been better. Well aware of the limits of Forde's capabilities, and in pursuit of this last goal, Jane Strachey sent Lytton on a long sea voyage which took him to Egypt and Cape Town and which she believed would benefit his health. He returned healthy enough to leave Forde and Dorset and move to a more demanding school.

For his next phase of schooling, Jane chose the New School at Abbotsholme. This was unquestionably the strangest of all her educational decisions. John Reddie, its head, was a dynamic and idealistic man, filled in equal measure with zeal and eccentricity. His New School was designed to arrest the decline he saw throughout society with an educational formula that included arduous physical, mental, and spiritual training. The school was small, with only about forty pupils when Lytton went. It was situated in a large country house in Derbyshire. Each day was divided into three parts, with mornings devoted to school work, afternoons to sport and physical labour, and evenings to music, poetry, art, and social activities. Although Reddie's belief that 'Education spells Empire' doubtless appealed to Jane Strachey, as did his energy and idealism, it was extraordinary that she should send her most fragile child to a school so committed to making boys endure physical hardship and arduous physical labour. Dr Reddie's enthusiasm for new forms of community and social interaction between the boys was not equalled by his interest in literature—and

Lytton's writing skills were of little interest to him. Lytton himself tried hard to cope with the drills and athletics, the cold baths, the boxing matches fought outside even in the snow, and the heavy agricultural labour. But his health was not equal to the regime and he remained there for less than a year.[64]

Lytton Strachey went from the New School to Leamington College, where he spent another three miserable years. There was little of Reddie's enthusiasm or arduous routine here. It was replaced, as Holroyd suggests, with 'the more traditional philistinism' of a minor public school. Initially Lytton was subjected to bullying, but that passed and he was soon engaged in many different activities. His lessons continued to be interrupted by bouts of ill health. When he was well enough, however, he did engage in many extracurricular activities, including amateur theatricals, editing the school magazine, skating, and cycling. He also developed an interest in botany through growing plants in his window box, became head of his house, and began to read Gibbon.[65] Although Lytton experienced his first serious infatuations with other boys at Leamington, the school offered neither intellectual challenges nor any real source of friendship and after three years he wanted to leave. It's 'too relaxing and the tuition is not up to the mark', he explained to his mother.[66] As he was only 17, too young for Oxford or Cambridge, Lytton then sat the entrance examinations which enabled him to attend Liverpool University College in 1898. Walter Raleigh, the King Alfred Professor of English Literature, was a family connection, and offered Lytton hospitality. But the Liverpool years too were bleak and lonely, offering neither intellectual stimulus nor the companionship which Lytton craved.[67]

There was a very marked difference between Lytton's experience of schooling and that of his younger brother, James. While Jane Strachey seems to have gone out of her way to find unusual institutions for Lytton, James went to perfectly orthodox schools. He began his education at home with a governess under the supervision of Pippa. His health was not a cause of concern and, at the age of 10, he was sent to Hillbrow Preparatory School in Rugby. The school was somewhat spartan, but it was a small one in which James seems to have been well treated. When he had a slight headache, he was sent early to bed in a room close to the matron—and then kept in bed the following day.[68] James was a good although not an outstanding pupil in his prep school: he reported his position in class in his weekly letter to his mother and was usually in the top three in Latin, Greek,

French, and English, although lower in mathematics. Jane Strachey was very concerned that James should excel at school, and became anxious whenever he was not top of his form. For the most part, however, he did well enough at school to satisfy her maternal pride.

Unlike Lytton, who suffered in his school days from awful loneliness, James had close companions. Ironically, it was these very companions who were later to cause him grief and unhappiness. James had been preceded at Hillbrow by his cousin, Duncan Grant, who became a close friend, although he was not able subsequently to return James's intense devotion. At Hilbrow James also met and became friends with Rupert Brooke, thus establishing the unhappy friendship that dominated his late adolescence and his university life.

When James's time at Hilbrow drew to a close, it was agreed that he should attend St Paul's in London. There was general enthusiasm for this idea. 'I shall like going to St Paul's School very much', he wrote to his mother.[69] The teachers at his school were equally pleased. 'His work is already good', the head of Hilbrow wrote to Jane, 'at St Paul's he will develop into a scholar'.[70] Duncan Grant did not accompany James to St Paul's immediately, but came a year later and the cousins spent the next two years there together. During his first three years at St Paul's, James was a weekly boarder, staying at High House in Brook Green and going home for weekends. During his final years, he lived at home all the time.

Although James won a scholarship to St Paul's, his record there was not an outstanding one. On the contrary, the high places that had characterized him at Hilbrow were rarely in evidence. Moreover, the passivity and the long silences that were so characteristic of him as an adult were already noted. Everyone at school seemed to like James, but no one seemed able to establish what he liked or what he thought or felt. His house master, Mr Cholmely, had to rely on the fact that 'he looks more comfortable', when writing to tell his mother how he was settling in. He had placed James next to the school captain in the dormitory, he explained to Jane, because he believed him 'to be a very kindly person with some sense of responsibility'. He had decided, moreover, not to press James in the matter of games. 'I am sending him to the gymnasium (which he seems to like) twice a week, & to play fives by way of outdoor exercise; & when the school bath is in order, he can learn to swim.'[71] James continued to do well at St Paul's, winning a senior school scholarship for his final years. But his school reports always suggest that his teachers thought more effort was possible. 'Classics do not I fear hold the first place in his interests', wrote his Latin teacher in his final year at school—but others were equally hard pressed to find what did. His literary taste and sense of style were always commended, as was his capacity for doing translation. But there seems often to have been a sense amongst his teachers that 'he might do very much better, if he would take the trouble'.[72]

University Life

Although they are closely associated with the world of established English universities, particularly Cambridge, the Stracheys, unlike the families of some of Lytton's close friends, the Stephens, for example, or the Keynes, had no traditional connection with the English universities. One or two Stracheys with a particular interest in mathematics had gone to Cambridge in the sixteenth or seventeenth centuries, but they were rare exceptions.[1] Until the second half of the nineteenth century, British universities with their largely classical curriculum offered little to a family interested primarily in science, engineering, and imperial administration. Indeed, the changing place of Cambridge in the Strachey family in the late nineteenth and early twentieth centuries offers a striking illustration of the growing importance of universities in British scientific and professional life. In the mid-nineteenth century, both Oxford and Cambridge underwent considerable reform. The traditional classical curriculum was subjected to stringent criticism by those interested in developments in the sciences, and more broadly by a middle class that sought a university education that would better prepare their sons for professional life.[2] The outstanding scientific education available at German universities raised questions about the scholarly standards and the academic approach in England.[3] At the same time, a number of able young academics and fellows sought to reform curricula and teaching practices, and to incorporate a new degree structure in Britain. The question of university reform was considered sufficiently important for the appointment of two Royal Commissions in the 1850s and 1870s. As a result, in the second half of the nineteenth century, both Oxford and Cambridge, in Harold Perkin's words, 'were transformed in a generation from clerical-run seminars for gentlemen into professionalised institutions . . . operated by career dons for the sons of the landed and professional classes preparing for careers in the public service, including politics, the home and Indian Civil Services, colonial government, and the liberal professions'.[4]

Richard Strachey's involvement with Cambridge was connected both to his interest in science and to Indian administration. From the 1850s onwards, Cambridge had begun to offer a tripos in the natural sciences.[5] Strachey had many friends amongst Cambridge scientists and kept in touch with new developments in scientific research. His close involvement with the activities of the Royal Society after he returned to England in the early 1870s also brought more direct ties to Cambridge. As president of the Royal Society of Geographers, Richard Strachey delivered the foundation lectures in geography at Cambridge in 1876. The introduction of competitive examinations for entry to the Indian Civil Service in the 0850s was also important. Once this happened and both Oxford and Cambridge became significant recruitment centres for the ICS,[6] many senior Indian administrators kept a close eye on what was happening at the universities. As a member of the India Council, Richard Strachey protested vehemently against the fact that Colonel Osborne, a man critical of the Raj, had been invited to give lectures on Indian history at Cambridge in 1881. 'It will be a great scandal if he is permitted', he wrote to his wife.

I have stumbled on a number of the *Statesman* here with an article on this very subject by Osborne in which he says the result of British Rule has been ruin and destruction of all sense of rights in perpetuity on land and so forth. This is the man selected to lecture to the young men going out as Civilians! I have said to Maine they might as well get Parnell to lecture on Irish History.[7]

Strachey was critical of some aspects of Cambridge, but he now clearly felt himself to be an important player in it. His connection with Cambridge was cemented through the award to him of an honorary doctorate in 1892.[8]

Although the sending of their younger children to universities was accompanied by a new approach to questions about their future and their careers, this is not to suggest that India and the family's imperial heritage was ignored or forgotten. On the contrary, imperial questions were extremely important especially to Pernel and Lytton during their university lives, as both of them became closely involved in studying Indian languages or history—and in propagating imperial views.

For Jane Strachey, of course, as a woman growing up in the 1840s and 1850s, a university education would have been at best a utopian dream.[9] She too became closely involved with Cambridge in her adult life, however as a result of her husband's work and of her own feminism. She had been in India when the battles to establish colleges for women at Oxford and Cambridge began in the later 1860s, and took little part in them.[10] When she returned, however, and especially when she began to involve herself in feminist agitation in the 1880s, she took a very marked interest in the women's colleges. The many friends the Stracheys had in Cambridge made that the centre of her interest, while her close association with Millicent Garrett Fawcett made Newnham rather than Girton the college to which she was most committed. Her financial donations and her public speeches made her a welcome and frequent guest there in the late 1880s and the 1890s.

It was perhaps as much the growing sense of connection that Richard and Jane Strachey developed with the work of the universities in the late 1880s and 1890s as their own inclinations that made a university education an automatic choice for the four younger Strachey children. No thought seems to have been given to the idea of university for the older siblings. This is readily understandable in regard to the older Strachey sons. It was always assumed that Dick and Ralph would follow their father into the Indian army and this in turn meant that they were directed towards military colleges. It is slightly harder to understand, however, in relation to the older daughters. Hitchin, the forerunner to Girton, had taken its first students in 1869 and Newnham opened its doors in 1871, but they seem not to have been considered for Elinor, Dorothy, or Pippa. Elinor, although apparently very clever, never seems to have given a thought to any life possibility apart from marriage. Dorothy's academic abilities, however, especially her interest in languages, would have made her an ideal student. She continued studying at home for years after she finished school, and was establishing a career for herself in teaching when she married. It was she, moreover, who taught Pernel the Latin and Greek she needed to get into Cambridge. Neither Elinor nor Dorothy ever seemed to mind not having attended universities, and this is scarcely surprising. The worlds in which they mixed as adults were not ones in which university education itself was of much concern. It was Pippa who suffered most in the transition. She was much closer to her younger siblings and their Cambridge friends than were either Elinor or Dorothy, and was always aware, as indeed were they, of her lack of a university education. Both Lytton and James commented frequently on the divide that going to Cambridge created within the family. Pippa, to whom they were both deeply attached, was in Lytton's view 'a singularly reactionary woman' as a result 'of not having gone to Cambridge'. Pernel, who had gone, was 'infinitely more advanced'.[11]

Despite the growing connection of Richard and Jane Strachey with Cambridge, it was not automatic that their younger children would all go there. Jane Strachey never quite gave up the hope that all her sons would follow their father to India, thinking that perhaps the younger ones would make up to Richard for the disappointing careers of their older brothers. Balliol College at Oxford was regarded as the best preparation for those planning to sit the ICS entry exam. Hence Oliver Strachey was sent there and Jane had hoped that Lytton would go too.[12] Oliver lasted only one term at Balliol, however, and Lytton, to his great relief, was not offered a place. By the time James was ready for university, Balliol seems to have faded out of the picture entirely. Here, as elsewhere, Marjorie was the odd one out. At the very time that Cambridge was becoming central in the Strachey lives and the family was becoming known there, she was sent to Oxford, where her results never quite lived up to her own desire or expectations.

Although women began to attend universities in the late nineteenth century, the lives they led there were very different from those of men. When the women's colleges were first set up, there was considerable anxiety from staff and governing boards to ensure that they did not attract even a hint of scandal. Hence propriety governed every aspect of their lives.[13] Women students thus had none of the freedom that men enjoyed, They attended classes regularly and were not free to go out and about around town, to go away on reading parties, or to engage in much social and sexual experimentation. The constraints and the close supervision that many of the first generation of college women had to endure had eased off a little by the turn of the century, but they were still severe. This certainly imposed limits on some of the activities of women students, but it also meant that they were often more closely involved with and attached to their college and the college communities than were their male counterparts. In the case of the Stracheys, it also meant they were more interested and involved in their actual course of studies Women tended also to be engaged in college debates about contemporary political and social questions rather more than their male counterparts, and to become more involved in social and political organizations.

It was not only the sisters of the younger Strachey men and their friends who went to university, but also their wives. Dick and Ralph, the older Strachey sons, would have been appalled at the idea of marrying a woman with a university education. They seem hardly ever to have met one, and there was certainly no suggestion that they could have contemplated life with a woman of independent views. Oliver too was of this way of thinking when he first married in 1901. Within a decade, all of this had changed. The friends of the younger Strachey sisters were mainly women who had been to university and it was one of them, Ray Costello, who became Oliver's second wife. James, as the youngest of the Stracheys, almost reversed the expectation of his older siblings. He seems scarcely to have known or been close to a woman who had not gone to university—and it was almost inevitable that he would marry one who had.

I

The importance of university in the lives of his younger siblings could not have been anticipated by the response of Oliver, the first of the Stracheys to attend university, to his time at Oxford. Oliver hated Balliol and did not last even a year there. He was regarded as very clever both within the family and at school. His intellectual ability was not accompanied by any inclination to applying himself to serious work—and the extracurricular activities at which he excelled at school did not prepare him for university life. He had never done quite as well as expected at school examinations, and he found even the small amount of work required of him at university intolerable.[14] His letters home are filled with details about his study of the clarinet and his views on the concerts he attended. He hardly ever mentioned any aspect of his work, or even what he was reading. On the rare occasion that his academic work was mentioned, it was in the form of a funny story. 'Oliver sends very amusing letters from Oxford' wrote Jane Strachey to Lytton, shortly after he had begun.

He has to write an essay every week. One was on Falstaff & one on bimetallism. They are sent to master who makes comments. Oliver gave his Falstaff essay to a young German named Richter who matriculated with him. Richter copied it out word for word & showed it to his tutor who said that though there were no actual grammatical inaccuracies, it was easy to see that it was written by a German![15]

Oliver's time at Balliol was too short for him to develop any serious engagement with it. The Strachey letters are vague about exactly when he left, or why. Family rumour has it that he was sent down because a letter referring to a homosexual liaison was found in his room.[16] Oliver's well-known heterosexual promiscuity made the very idea of his involvement in a homosexual relationship a subject of much mirth to later generations of Stracheys. Nor is there evidence of any kind to support it. Balliol College records indicate that he was there only from January to March of 1893, but they offer no reason for his departure.[17] College records were often silent on matters of discipline and delicacy, and it does seem clear that Oliver had been in some kind of trouble. As soon as he left Oxford, Oliver was sent on a supervised round the world trip—a common way of dealing with young men 'sent down' for sexual misconduct at the time.[18] George Bushnell, the man appointed to accompany Oliver, sent Richard Strachey regular re-ports, some of which suggest that Oliver's heterosexual proclivities were already a source of some concern. In August 1893, Bushnell reported to Richard Strachey from Brisbane. They had been warmly welcomed by the governor, Sir Henry Norman (for whom Dick Strachey was working) and other British settlers.

Your son is most certainly benefiting in every way by his travels. However it is impossible for him to pursue his reading except in a desultory way, with our continual change of scene and abode. He is 5 foot 11 in tall, & has filled out considerably. He is still very interested in the young lady, whom I mentioned in a former letter, but I think this interest is waning somewhat.[19]

On his return, Oliver refused to resume his study at Balliol. His round the world voyage may not have improved his morals, but it certainly increased his courage and enabled him to write to tell his parents 'something that I'm afraid will annoy you'.

Put shortly it is that I want to give up the Indian Civil Service & go in for music. I know that I ought to have said this long ago if at all, and that it will be throwing away all the money that has been spent on me for the last two years—But the fact is I have again and again been on the point of saying this and have refrained first because I know you do not like the idea and are anxious to see me settled ... My idea is to learn the piano & then give lessons. I know it will be very hard work & you will perhaps say I have always been idle; but there is a difference between working at something that interests you and something that does not. Further it will be a life of poverty & I am extravagant to a degree—I can only say that since I have grown up I have improved in this respect—truly I was an absolute infant until I began my voyage round the world I have changed since in many ways.[20]

Although bitterly disappointed, Jane and Richard Strachey accepted his decision and supported Oliver for a year in Vienna. They recognized his musical enthusiasm, but Jane did not share his own assessment of his talent. 'Oliver has written another sonata for piano & violin I regret to say,' she wrote to Lytton while Oliver was in Vienna in 1896. She believed it was 'far superior to the last. It has gone to Mr Hubert Parry for an opinion on it. Several large breakers are to be seen ahead.'[21] In the event she was correct: after a year in Vienna, it was clear that Oliver would not be able to make his career in music. He attempted to return to Oxford, but failed the entrance examination. Jane Strachey was bitterly disappointed. Her letters to Oliver do not survive, but his reply, while demonstrating well his fecklessness, suggests that she did not spare his feelings on this occasion. 'I scarcely know what to say in reply to your letter', he wrote:

You use very hard words which I do not really think I have deserved. I certainly did not expect to come out as badly as I did in the examination, though I knew I was not nearly up to the mark—I do not suppose you are sorrier than I about the result. Moreover I really did do my best, though I don't suppose you will believe it if you have no confidence left in my sense of honour—As regards the Greek, of course you know the o is not an absolute o—they take off a certain deduction of marks. I did not cut any of the papers, and I did the best I could in them.[22]

After this failure, and a series of talks with his mother in which, as she explained to Pippa, 'I tried to rub it into to him that he had cut himself off from every source of profitable employment', Oliver was apparently very grateful that his father was able to find him a position in India![23]

II

Nothing could have been less like Oliver's messy and uninspiring university career than Pernel's. Even her admission to Newnham was a triumph. Her schooling at Allenswood had provided her with an excellent grounding in modern languages, music, and the humanities. She had learnt nothing, however, of the mathematics, Greek, and Latin required for the Cambridge 'Little Go', or entrance examination. She acquired all that she needed in a few weeks of intensive study under the guidance of her older sister, Dorothy. Both Jane and Richard were thrilled. 'Is not Pernel's success graced?', wrote Jane to her husband 'I feel so elated I can hardly contain myself. She actually was in the 2nd out of 4 classes in the classics division, & 3 months ago did not know the Greek alphabet! To say nothing of her having to tackle logic and mathematics at the same time.' Jane noted also the debt they all had to Dorothy—suggesting, as she so often did, a possible course of action for Richard. 'Don't you think Dorothy deserves a testimonial for her excellent conduct in giving up so much of her holidays to coaching her? I know she wants a watch, & I think it would be very graceful of you to present her with one.'[24] Richard too was delighted. I don't know which to admire most:', he wrote to Pernel, 'the diligence and intelligence displayed by you and Dorothy in preparing you for your battle with the Giant Little-Go—or the wonderful stupidity of the system of education of the other sex which hardly accomplishes in 8 or 9 years what you did in as many weeks. The world is a curious affair.'[25] Oliver too was impressed. The tutors attempting to prepare him for the first part of his Oxford tripos 'bowed their heads and prayed to their Creator to send them such pupils', he wrote to Pernel. 'Most of us have failed once or twice at Smalls or the Little Go and are still struggling for it.'[26]

Newnham had grown too large for its original house by the time Pernel arrived, and had moved to its current location in Sidgwick Avenue.[27] The Queen Anne style halls designed in the 1880s by Basil Champneys had recently been completed and she was allocated a large room in Clough Hall which she loved.[28] It was furnished, with 'a bed, small table, a bureau, a chest, 3 chairs, a book case. There is a cupboard to hang clothes in with a blue and white cretonne curtain. the bed is draped in the same stuff as also the cushion of the arm chair.'[29] Her mother, who had come with her to help her settle in at Newnham, purchased an additional chest of drawers, a large table she needed—and rented the piano which was an essential item for all Stracheys. Eleanor Sidgwick was the principal when Pernel first arrived and, although the Sidgwicks and the Stracheys were not close friends, they had many acquaintances and interests in common and both Jane and Pernel were warmly welcomed.[30]

At Cambridge, as at school, Pernel was very keen to make sure that those at home knew and understood in detail the pattern of her daily life. She was the first Strachey daughter to attend Cambridge, and her letters describing Newnham to her older sisters, Pippa and Dorothy, have something of the feel of an anthropologist writing home from an exotic and alien world. On her first morning in college, she reported, a gong rang at 8 and

I scurried into the hall where everyone assembled for prayers and breakfast. The prayers were most comique. At a given signal the door was flung open and the housekeeper followed by a train of about 12 housemaids marched in. They advanced to the dais and all knelt down together resting their arms on the dais. We all followed suit. I had breakfast at Miss Stephen's table. Food is put at one table, drink at another, you forage for yourself and there is no waiting ... one must try never to sit next to the same person at any meal. When you have done you simply get up and stalk off which seems very odd.[31]

Pernel's constant use of the term 'weird' and the exaggerated Strachey language that she employed to describe her surroundings and the college staff emphasize the novelty of this world. 'I have just come in from dinner which is a weird meal', she wrote to Pippa soon after her arrival. 'Tonight I sat on the platform. Mrs Sidgwick was on the one side of me and Miss Stephen (the senior tutor) on the other. You come into the hall when the gong sounds and your name is stridently shouted out. This means you are to sit on the dais.'[32] Pernel never quite grew accustomed to the ritual of the late night cocoa. 'In one minute and a half', she wrote to Pippa, three weeks after she had arrived,

I have got to go to a hideous entertainment called a cocoa; you are given one spoonful of powdery cocoa and one spoonful of 'cow' that is condensed milk. These you mix together in a cup till they look like mud; boiling water is then poured on, the next process being to try and drink it. Weird cakes are also passed around. At 10 o'clock at night this depresses me somewhat.[33]

Although nervous and rather shy, it is clear that Pernel very soon felt at home at Newnham and began both to establish her own social circle and to participate in the activities of the dons and older students. Following the tradition of discussion and reading circles at men's colleges, tutors at the women's colleges set up groups of their own. Unlike the men's colleges, however, where these groups were hallowed by tradition, in the women's colleges they seemed eccentric. 'If you think my conduct at all odd', wrote Pernel to Dorothy,

it is a sign that I am pre-destined to become a don of this august institution Yesterday Miss Stephen came up to me and solemnly said she was coming to see me at tea as she had something to say to me ... What do you think it was? It appears that the lunatic dons have a Society for reading to oneself in company which meets on Fridays at 2.0 clock in the afternoon. The only rule is that there are to be no rules (which is really exceedingly confusing); the Society meets in the room of one of the members & nobody ever knows *which* room it will be in— the game is to find out &, as Miss Stephen said, if you want to be sure of finding it, the only plan is to have it in your own room. She then went on to say that though the idea is to read silently, sometimes you may talk & always you may sleep. The members are all dons (but not all dons are members) also there are to be 3 students of whom *I* am to be one. You may imagine that I was extremely flattered if somewhat alarmed. I feel as though I ought to present myself wrapped in a sheet with a candle in my hand The only line I know which adequately represents the scene as I imagine it is:—pretty apart sat Partite in part of a Spartan apartment.[34]

For all her disclaimers, Pernel threw herself into college life with enthusiasm and was soon writing home about the many societies with which she was involved. There was a musical group called the Sharp Practice Society, and a discussion group called the Sunday Society. In her second year at college, there was yet another 'weird new society' formed by the dons. 'Its object', she explained to Pippa, 'is to learn as many new languages as possible, none of them to be known perfectly but only smatteringly. We have begun with Spanish.'[35] It would seem that Persian was added too: the following year, Ralph Strachey reported to Pippa that 'Pernel's elegant . . . epistle caused great excitement among the pundits of Dehri who declared that such high flown Persian has seldom been seen out of Hafiz'.[36] One has a sense from all of this that, right from the start, Pernel felt that the world of the dons would become her own, and that her college tutors in turn saw her as one of themselves.

Pernel's Indian interests were always part of her life at Newnham. They were evident not only in her interest in learning Persian, but also in the role she took in college debates and in the mock parliament set up to discuss political questions. Like all her siblings in their younger days, Pernel followed the family line, defending the British government in India, upholding particularly the Tory line against Little Englanders. 'It may interest you to hear that I have been made Secretary of State for India', she wrote to Lytton on 1897. 'Last week I had to speak to a motion censuring the policy of H. M's govt in India. Of course I had to stick up for the old Forward policy . . . but it was rather depressing because nobody knew *anything* whatever about the subject, consequently voted blindly against the govt.'[37]

As a young woman from a feminist family, Pernel also became closely involved in the battle for the admission of women to Cambridge degrees.

'Everyone here is very busy despatching circulars to MAs', she wrote to her mother during the 1897 campaign. 'This afternoon we spent 2 hours in folding up attractive appeals and invitations to lunch and sticking them in envelopes. Voting is on 21 May: Do bring your influence to bear on Sir Alexander [Rendel].'[38] For all the Stracheys' hard work, however, this campaign was as unsuccessful as its predecessors had been and women were not admitted to Cambridge degrees until 1946.[39]

Although interesting in many ways, the lives of Newnham women were severely policed. Many lessons were given in the college and the strict rules about chaperonage and hours allowed little scope to move outside. While some women students rebelled, Pernel did not. She occasionally commented on the limitations of her own experience. 'I sometimes wish I could get more practice in talking to men—it is a thing I cannot do in the least', she wrote to Lytton, after an agonizing evening in which she had tried to talk to the brother of the college principal, Arthur Clough.[40] But she did not pursue this wish—and spent her time happily with a close network of women friends. The Stracheys were a progressive family in some ways, but they shared the concerns of the college when it came to questions about moral and social conventions for women. When Pernel sought permission to go away on a reading party, an activity greatly favoured in later years by her brothers, and quite unproblematic for them, many questions were asked. 'Who would be going on the reading party?' asked her mother, when Pernel suggested one such reading party in 1898. 'You are too vague', she wrote in response to Pernel's next letter. 'Who is the friend, what is her age, where are you going, how long is it for? ... Of course I don't doubt your discretion for a moment—as far as that goes you might wander alone—but your experience is small and mine induces me to doubt that here below, everything is for the best in the best of all possible worlds.'[41] Ultimately Pernel was allowed to go— but neither Lytton nor James ever had to cope with this level of inter-rogation.

Unlike all her brothers, Pernel was an extremely conscientious student, concerned always about her position in class. She enrolled in history and politics when she first started at Newnham, regarding Lord Acton's lectures on the French Revolution as the highlight of her degree. 'We have all fallen deeply in love with Lord Acton who is without doubt the most charming person of the age', she wrote to Pippa.[42] But she disliked the second year course which involved political economy, political science, and early constitutional history, and came to see that languages were her forte. At the end of her second year, she changed to the newly formed tripos in medieval and modern languages. Her parents accepted and even encouraged this move. I am 'most grateful to you and Papa for having been so kind', she wrote when her mother indicated their support for her decision. 'If any of us ever are of any use in the world it will be entirely owing to you; you are wonderful in every way.'[43]

While Pernel clearly felt at home and wished to stay at Newnham, it is difficult to trace her intellectual developments or interests. In part this may be a result of the limited nature of her remaining correspondence. While Lytton Strachey discussed his ideas and his reading with James and many of his friends, there seem to be no extant letters from Pernel to her friends. Her family letters, mainly to Pippa and Dorothy, were designed for sisters who had not themselves been at Cambridge and tend to describe the tenor of her daily life rather than saying anything about her ideas or her reading. Nonetheless, it seems unlikely either that Pernel found her time at Cambridge as intellectually stimulating as did Lytton, or that she underwent the intellectual and emotional awakening that he experienced there. One has a sense rather that Cambridge extended her knowledge of history and languages, but without altering in any fundamental way her intellectual outlook. Sometimes she was very critical of the lectures and classes she attended. She was revolted, she wrote to Lytton in 1897, at the way in which Goethe's poems were paraphrased into prose.

The lecturer is always talking about 'penetrating into the poet's workshop' by comparing original and corrected versions of a poem. It is of course rather interesting to do this but as for thinking that it helps you to understand the working of a poet's mind—this appears to be ridiculous. But then I always look upon an artist as a person possessed by an outside daemon or priest sitting in an inner sanctuary and not as evolving painfully out of himself in a workshop![44]

This romantic view of poetry was similar to that of her mother, nor is there any suggestion in her letters of any reading or discussions that challenged the imperialist framework that she had imbibed at home.

Pernel's college friends were both introduced to and integrated into the family. The classicist, Jane Ellen Harrison, who became a close family friend, succumbed immediately to the charm of Lady Strachey when Pernel invited her home. 'After dinner, Mamma, Jane & I retired into Pippa-Dorothy's room', Pernel wrote to Lytton, after Jane's first visit.

Southey was read aloud for a short time after which every topic under the sun of art, literature, ethics, morals & philosophy was discussed with intense vivacity by Mamma & Jane while I crouched on the sofa in a literary attitude. Miss Harrison simply loved mamma—it was a most charming spectacle—& Mamma was in her very best form. There they sat smoking cigarettes & talking like mad.[45]

Subsequently, Jane Harrison holidayed with Pernel, on one occasion taking an ailing Lytton to a rest-cure in Sweden.

The fact that women's colleges were still small and very new made the final examinations into a major community event. Pernel sent Pippa wonderful descriptions of the way examination candidates were treated at Newnham. 'There was quite a large gang of examinees', she wrote,

& everyday we drove or bicycled or walked to the scene of torment which was the same as the Little-go rooms. In its normal state it is a mission room of some kind so its walls are covered with texts & banners telling you to Press forward and look upward . . . Stationed on a dais is a Member of the University who was there to deal out papers & to see that we did not cheat: and at a small table which was covered with sal volatile and eau do cologne sat a female invigilator ready to remove us if we fainted or had hysterics. Can you visualise the scene? On the first morning we were accompanied to doom by a swarm of Dons who pressed flowers into our hot hands, a favourite being rosemary.[46]

Examinees were given every attention. After the morning examinations, there was a special 'Tripos lunch: viz lamb cutlets, asparagus and goose-berry tarts then coffee'. After the final afternoon session, there was 'an exquisite tea'. 'Never have I felt so important and grand before', wrote Pernel. 'Everyone was always holding our hands, feeling our pulses, tucking us up when we went to bed.' They were even given the ultimate luxury a women's college could provide: a cup of tea in bed![47]

Pernel did very well, exceeding the expectations of her teachers by gaining a first, despite having worked at the medieval and modern language tripos for only a year. 'I feel very much honoured that you should allow me to share in Pernel's success,' her tutor wrote to Jane Strachey in 1898, 'even though for truth's sake I must disclaim a part therein! . . . We are all delighted at her distinguished performance—a performance which I should hardly have thought possible for any one, a year ago.'[48] But of course, although qualifying for a first, as a woman, Pernel did not ever receive a Cambridge degree.

Pernel was the only one of the Stracheys to undertake graduate work. Before she left Cambridge, in 1899, it was settled, she explained to Pippa, 'that after this I am to go in for the new French Doctorate called the Doctorate of the University of Paris. You sit in Paris for a year and write a thesis showing original research Ha! Ha!'[49] Jane Strachey accompanied Pernel to Paris, settling her initially in the home of her old friends, the Guieysse family, where they met Dorothy's future husband, the painter, Simon Bussy. Pernel was very relieved to have her mother with her, 'The French language is too horribly difficult', she wrote to Lytton, 'Mamma needless to say is simply miraculous and flows in wit and humour regardless of everything. Complete silence will reign when she leaves.'[50] As it turned out, Pernel had been misinformed about what she needed to do in Paris. 'At one moment,' she wrote to Pippa,

I thought my hitherto brilliant career was completely wrecked but by dint of eating dirt all is now well. yesterday I went to report myself and met Mrs Williams wreathed in smiles and amiability: she proposed that I should spend the rest of this year in preparing for the Guild Exam. The advantages of this seem to be (a) immense practice in writing the language (b) a good deal of reading which may lead to a thesis (c) a Certificate signed by University professors.

The disadvantages are (a) general tedium (b) potential and momentary abandonment of thesis. I may mention that what enrages me is that I was led to believe that 1 year would suffice for the business of the doctorate: it now seems that 2 are indispensable. This being so perhaps I *had* better go in for this exam; anyhow of course if I find a thesis or if I find that I am wasting my time I can at any moment leave off.[51]

The summary of Pernel's career in the Newnham records suggests that she did not in fact undertake any examination in France. However, the 'studies in Paris' combined with the Newnham results qualified her to teach French and German in England, which she did first at Royal Holloway College, and then later back at Newnham.

❧ III ❧

Pernel's experiences at Cambridge could scarcely have been more different from those of Lytton and James. While her Cambridge life was dominated by her studies and completely integrated with that of her college, neither of them took any interest in the former or had much to say about the latter. Lytton was immensely excited about going to Cambridge. 'Ho! Ho! Ho!', he wrote to his mother, with uncharacteristic enthusiasm. 'How proud

I was as I swept the streets of Cambridge yesterday, arrayed for the first time in cap & gown! To my great surprise and delight the gown is blue! Lovely!'[52] But as this suggests, it was the university as a whole and its associations that appealed to him rather than his college. Lytton and James both went to Trinity, but they had rooms there rather than being closely involved in college life—and there is rarely any mention of college activities in their correspondence. There are no descriptions of college meals or rituals, and few comments on teachers, classes, or exams. Indeed, where Pernel's life at Cambridge centred absolutely on Newnham, the lives of Lytton and James had little to do either with Trinity or with any other aspect of Cambridge as an institution.

Both Lytton and James had been considered very able during their school years. Lytton continued to be thought of as brilliant by many of his tutors. Neither he nor James were seriously engaged in the work required for their degrees, however. Lytton did some work on his final dissertation, although the second class he was awarded made it clear to his tutor that he had done little of the 'task work, books to be got up and definite facts to remember' required by his history tripos.[53] James did even less—indeed, he seems to have done no work at all at Cambridge and was awarded third class honours, regarded by himself and his friends as equivalent to a fail.

Lytton Strachey's Cambridge life has been discussed in considerable detail before, not only by his biographer Michael Holroyd, but also by Robert Skidelsky in his biography of Keynes, by Leonard Woolf in his own autobiography, and by S. P. Rosenbaum and others interested in the origins of Bloomsbury.[54] All of these accounts make very clear the way that Cambridge transformed Lytton's life, as indeed it did the lives of the other young men he met there. The lack of connection to the formal life of Cambridge did not mean a lack of intellectual stimulus or personal development. On the contrary, Lytton and his friends, all of whom had experienced years of tedium and unhappiness at unsuitable schools, found in Cambridge an intellectual and emotional home. But it was one provided largely by each other.

Lytton Strachey's immense charm and capacity to form friendships first became evident in his time at Cambridge. Within a few weeks of his arrival, he had begun to establish some of those close and intense friendships that lasted throughout his life. He met Thoby Stephen, Leonard Woolf, Clive Bell, and Saxon Sydney-Turner very shortly after he arrived and a year later became friends also with Maynard Keynes. These close friends, along with the many others that he made there, were all struck by his combination of extraordinary intelligence, breadth of knowledge, and vast intellectual curiosity, on the one hand, and his capacity for deep feeling on the other. Long talks on the sofa with Lytton, in which anything could be discussed and which helped to clarify everything about about life, often constituted the main event of the evening for Leonard Woolf and for Thoby Stephen, both of whom responded to Lytton's capacity for absolute honesty and frankness.[55]

It was not the formal lectures or lessons he was supposed to attend, but rather these friendships and the reading and discussion groups he joined that provided the intellectual stimulus Lytton found at Cambridge. He read widely in many fields: literature and history at the beginning, but then increasingly also in aesthetics and philosophy. His Cambridge friends met frequently and engaged in almost continuous conversation. Reading parties and holidays extended their close social and intellectual contact into vacation times. The social and the intellectual high point of Lytton's Cambridge life came in his third year, when he was elected to the most elite of all Cambridge discussion groups, the Apostles. This venerable society, formally known as the 'Cambridge Conversazione Society' had existed for almost 100 years by the time he was elected. No Apostle ever resigned and many of those who had graduated and left the university returned for its meetings. It was there that Lytton Strachey and his friends came into close contract with the older men who had such immense influence on them: Bertrand Russell, J. E. McTaggart, and especially G. E. Moore.[56] The Apostles had their own elaborate language and rituals. Most of them were agnostics, but their rituals, like their name, were filled with Christian symbolism. The Apostolic system, Michael Holroyd argues, was a parody of religion, but its language and symbolism enhanced its members' sense of themselves as a select and almost sacred brotherhood.[57] Those designated as potential members were 'Embryos' whose election brought birth into the world of enlightenment; their initiation involved a ceremony in front of the Ark; those Apostles who had settled down to definite opinions were known as 'Angels'. This was supposedly a secret society, but there was little really secret about a group that was so highly celebrated amongst British intellectuals. Jane Strachey was thrilled when Lytton, and then later James, wrote to tell her of their election.[58]

Membership of the Apostles had an immense impact on Lytton Stra-chey, and he in turn became a dominating force in establishing new directions for the society. The weekly evenings, and the requirement that members offer papers for discussion encouraged him to discuss and explore many questions that he had never before had a chance to raise. The strongest Apostolic traditions centred on the importance of candour, the value of intellectual integrity, and a concern with truth rather than material rewards. It was in the twenty papers he delivered to the Apostles that Lytton began to interrogate accepted religious ideas, to question the Victorian morality which had been so central in his youth, and to explore new approaches to sexuality and to art. But Lytton also interpreted 'candour' in a way that had not quite been done before, and demanded far more openness of discussion on questions about sexuality and bodily functions in particular. In one paper imagining a 'new heaven, new earth', he discussed the possibility of a society in which there was no censorship—not even on subjects such as defecation. In so doing, he 'broke one of the last Apostolic taboos'.[59] In a similar way his interrogation of the intimate male friendships that had always characterized the society, and his insist-ence on recognition of the sexual elements in them brought to the fore issues about sexuality that had previously been ignored.

Lytton was elected to the Apostles in 1903, the final year of his degree. But he continued to be closely involved in the Society for some years after that. Indeed, it was when he had finished his own undergraduate work that he became best known at Cambridge. He was based there for several years, working intermittently on the dissertation on Warren Hastings that he hoped might gain him a college fellowship.[60] For some of those years, he was secretary to the Apostles, a position that gave him considerable power to demand acceptance of his own views about the need for greater sexual tolerance—and even to include questions about sexual attractiveness in assessing which of the younger undergraduates should be selected as 'embryos'.

For all his apparent insistence on breaking Victorian taboos, however, one can already see in Lytton's Cambridge days both the nature and the limits of his desire to break with Victorian convention. The papers he read to the Apostles allowed him to question many accepted religious, moral, and sexual ideas and values, but he was less inclined to analyse or even to think about the broad political, social, and economic frameworks in which they were located. He sought and established great freedom in the discussion of sexuality, especially homosexuality, and he found amongst his friends the sense of comradeship and community that brought an end to his earlier terrible loneliness. But there were many ideas, values, and beliefs that he had derived from his family and retained at Cambridge. One can see this clearly even in Lytton's reaction to the person whom he and his friends regarded as the greatest and most influential man they encountered at Cambridge, G. E. Moore. Lytton and his friends were almost spell-bound by Moore, as much by his physical presence and personal charm as by his intellectual gifts. Leonard Woolf regarded Moore as 'the only great man whom I have ever met or known in the world', and Lytton clearly agreed.[61] Moore's unworldliness and intellectual rigour set the standard they wanted to achieve, and his influence was extended and consolidated in 1903 with the publication of his *Principia Ethica*.

The meaning and significance of Moore's work have been the subject of extensive debate—as have the ways in which it was taken up by Lytton Strachey and his friends. Shortly after its publication, Lytton wrote to tell Moore how wonderful he thought his book. It had 'wrecked and shattered all writers on Ethics from Aristotle and Christ to Herbert Spencer and Mr Bradley', and 'laid the true foundation of Ethics'. What appealed to Lytton most was not the theoretical approach that Moore took to ethics, but rather the more impressionistic writing of the last two chapters, in which Moore ventured to express his own views about 'Ethics in relation to conduct' and about 'the ideal'. It was here that Moore discussed the importance of personal relationships, describing 'certain states of con-sciousness which may be roughly described as the pleasures of human intercourse and the enjoyment of human objects' as being 'the most valuable things which we know or can imagine'. In many ways Moore was setting down as a general principle what Strachey had already come to feel in his own life. As Michael Holroyd says, he gave Lytton and his friends 'a method for trusting to intuition rather than rules, and a language for evaluating human relationships'.[62]

Moore's impact clearly derived from the ways in which his ideas served to undermine and thus helped Lytton to reject the imperatives of duty, earnestness, and self-sacrifice that had been so fundamental to the Victor-ians generally and to his own parents in particular. While he cast off some of the values he had found particularly oppressive both in his home and in the wider society, however, he retained others. His reading of Moore allowed him to give what he saw as the appropriate weight to friendship, but it did not in any way cause him to question the imperial values with which he had been brought up. Indeed, at the very time he was waxing lyrical about Moore, he was also working on the defence of Warren Hastings for his fellowship dissertation. There was no necessary contradiction here, for Moore's ethics, as understood by Lytton Strachey, were determinedly apolitical. But there is something ironic about the fact that Lytton Strachey, while reading and worshipping Moore, was also deeply immersed in the writings of his uncle, John Strachey and of Fitzjames Stephen—men for whom empire and duty were everything, and whose commitment to Victorian morality was absolute. Lytton Strachey was far less politically involved, or even concerned, than either his family or his friends. It is interesting here to note his relative lack of interest in issues like the Dreyfus affair—despite the fact that his family at home, and Leonard Woolf as a Jew at Cambridge, were deeply disturbed by it.[63]

In his Cambridge days, as in later years, it was primarily the demand for personal and sexual freedom, and a new approach to questions about friendship and about intimacy, that defined Lytton's Strachey's break with the world of established convention. While he retained many conventional values, these became rather less noticeable because of his insistence on the need for recognition and acknowledgement of his own homosexuality, and of sexuality more generally. Indeed, the freedom to acknowledge and discuss his own and others' sexuality was one of the most significant things that Cambridge had to offer Lytton. There is a striking contrast between Pernel Strachey's celibate life at Newnham and Lytton's Cambridge life in which sex was everywhere. There was more discussion of sexual freedom than actual experimentation, especially in his undergraduate years. Although his letters to both James and Maynard Keynes are full of references to buggery and rape, his belief in the 'higher sodomy', and his own extreme self consciousness, privileged unconsummated same-sex desire over any actual sexual encounter. What mattered was the acknowledgement of sexuality and of sexual desire, and the freedom to sexualize the everyday world in a way far removed from romantic convention.[64]

Lytton Strachey's continued connection with Cambridge after he had completed his undergraduate degree was made both closer and more complicated by his close bond with his younger brother, James. Lytton had organized James's entry to Cambridge in 1905, when James was just 18. James followed Lytton's footsteps in many respects. He took over his rooms and established relationships with many of his friends. As a result of Lytton's patronage, he had the unusual honour of being elected an Apostle in February 1906, the middle of his first year. As Lytton had done, he wrote of his initiation into the Society to his mother.

I am now fairly established in my new role, and have made the acquaintance of nearly all my brothers now resident in Cambridge. I have examined the Ark and gone through the mystic ceremonies of initiation. I have eaten the Lord's Supper. Finally I have stood on the Sacred hearthrug. The last is, of course, the most alarming function. At the first meeting a whole covey of angels alighted and fixed me with their circle of eyes as I addressed the Society. By the way, we are all rather scandalised by the elaborate account of us in the new *Life of Sidgwick* just published. Have you seen it?[65]

Unlike Lytton, however, James found neither easy companionship nor any obvious form of intellectual stimulation at Cambridge. He took even less interest in any form of academic work than Lytton had done, and devoted far less energy to reading or discussion. This was not because James lacked intellectual interests or rigour: he was already keen on and knowledgeable about music and would soon develop strong political views even before the emergence of his intense interest in psychoanalysis. But, for him, there was no intellectual spark at Cambridge. His perfunctory letters to his doting mother offer little indication that he read or thought about anything. Occasionally, he mentioned attending a lecture; more often he referred to his poor results and his lack of any sense of what he wanted to do.[66] Even admittance to the Apostles was of less significance to James than it had been to Lytton, and seems not to have contributed in the same way to his intellectual development. He must have written some papers or discussed some ideas at its meetings, but neither he nor anyone else ever referred to them.

Although fond of and very protective towards his younger brother, Lytton did not find it easy to have his life invaded and appropriated by him. He hated what James did to his room. It is 'grotesquely changed', he wrote to Leonard Woolf after visiting James in 1905, and is now 'an art nouveau symphony in green and white, with James, very prim & small, sitting in the extreme corner of the sofa, which is covered with green sack cloth. He's got a pianola too, with which he played us the 5th Symphony.'[67] To Keynes he commented that the room 'was ever so much more depressed and depressing than it was when I had it'.[68] Lytton found James's passivity and lack of energy both irritating and worrying. Pippa maintained that James was 'absolutely lazy in body and mind' and Lytton agreed. 'What's so sickening', he wrote to Keynes, 'is that there doesn't seem to be anything that can be done. Any definite act of interference, advice, etc., would simply be to commit the sins of the parentage which Russell and Norton so rightly condemn.'[69]

What bothered Lytton most about James was something he could not tell Pippa. He felt that James's apathy and depression were closely bound up with his long-standing and hopeless passion for his old school mate, Rupert Brooke. They had been together at Hillbrow prep school and then met again at Cambridge where they developed an intermittently close, but very difficult relationship. Brooke, although aggressively heterosexual, had occasional sexual encounters with men. He had no wish for a sexual relationship with James, however, to whom he was often cold and very hostile.[70] Lytton outlined his concerns and his feelings to Duncan Grant.

I am dreadfully shattered about James. Look where I will, I can see no sort of loop-hole in an atmosphere of inconceivable gloom. Its really appalling. He seems to me to be almost in despair, which is a shocking state for anyone at his age to be in. Its like a reversal of nature. As for blaming him, it would be ridiculous; but sometimes when I'm alone with him I do feel inclined to shriek out loud from irritation and terror—yes terror, for the atmosphere eats into one's bones, and I at any rate begin to feel at last that perhaps after all everything is a ghastly fraud. The grand & fundamental disease is that he takes no interest whatever in anything but the few people whom he happens to admire or be in love with—which of course is simple death.

James did 'nothing but dream of Rupert over a solitary fire which goes out because he's too lazy to put on coals'.[71] Lytton sometimes feared that James might be suicidal. 'I had a dreadful interview with him last night', he wrote to Duncan, 'in which he said that he could hardly bear his life here, and I could think of nothing to say or do.' Lytton felt responsible for James, but disinclined to devote his whole life to him.

If I gave up most of my existence to the business, I suppose something might be done, but I can't: I can't live in Cambridge, and I can't be always thinking of James. In the meantime I expect a pretty sickening storm is brewing over his work. Mama will have a sad shock, and what line—what conceivable line is one to take? Damn! Damn! Damn![72]

James was presumably suffering from one of the recurrent periods of intense depression that later led him to seek psychoanalysis. He acknowledged all Lytton's concerns and saw his situation in very similar terms, but could do nothing about it. 'I do no work, and am mostly in trances, though I read a little',[73] he reported in 1907. His life was completely dominated by his feelings for Brooke and his paralysing anxiety that Brooke was going to terminate their friendship. He also shared Lytton's anxiety about the likely result—and about their mother's reaction. 'I'm in despair again', he wrote to Lytton after doing the exams for the first part of his tripos.

I've done two out of four papers . . . and I've certainly failed. I don't think there's the least chance of my getting even a third. So I shan't be able to come up next year; I believe it's a college rule that you have to take the general, but anyhow its not likely Mama would let me go on. I saw it coming all along, and it frightened me, but I did nothing: and sometimes I forgot about it. Perhaps ineffectualness is an essential part of me—it seems to me very contemptible—but circumstances have made it *very* especially hard to do things this term.[74]

As it turned out, some of the anxiety was unnecessary: Rupert Brooke finally made clear to James how much he liked him as a friend and how important the friendship was to him. But it was too late. 'If I'd been as unworried about him as I am now at the beginning of the term', James wrote to Lytton, 'I think I might have done a good deal of work. But the large thing will have happened, if I'm never to come back.'

James did manage to scrape a third in these exams and stayed at Cambridge. Nor did the settling of his relationship with Brooke make him any more inclined to work. Rather, it set him free to engage in sexual relationships with other undergraduates, and in ways that sometimes shocked his older brother. Lytton and Keynes had talked much about sex and sexuality, but their conduct was still dominated by ideas about the 'higher sodomy' in which desire was as much aesthetic and spiritual as physical, and was rarely if ever consummated. Intensity of feeling mattered far more than any form of action. For James and his friends, by contrast, sex was to be performed and not just discussed. In the last two years that James was at Cambridge, Robert Skidelsky has argued, 'homosexual intrigues were played out with new openness'.[75] After an annual dinner of the Carbonari, a radical King's College Society formed by Rupert Brooke, Maynard Keynes reported to Lytton that 'James and George (Mallory) now stroke one another's faces in public'.[76]

Lytton Strachey's letters do not give a complete picture of James, however. For James did develop some interests at Cambridge that were of a rather different kind from those of his brother. Indeed, it is interesting to note the way that James's inertia seemed to disappear when he was pursuing activities in which Lytton had not been involved. Unlike Lytton, he was interested in politics, attending a Fabian Society Summer School with Rupert Brooke in 1908, and then continuing to do so without him for several more years.[77] As we will see, it was here that he met both Noel Olivier and Alix Sargant-Florence, the two women who became the dominant figures in his emotional life. Beatrice Webb who attended and sometimes oversaw the Fabian summer schools was very critical of James and his friends. They lacked discipline and commitment—and were disinclined to offer the respect she expected.[78] However, the Fabian Society brought James into a political world very different from that of his family and established the framework for his later political outlook.

⚜ IV ⚜

While James was following Lytton's footsteps at Cambridge, Marjorie was forging her own way in the new world of Somerville College, Oxford. There is far less information about her university life than there is about any of the others. She was not close to her siblings, and did not send anyone the detailed descriptions of college life that Pernel had sent to Pippa, or Lytton exchanged with James. She wrote occasionally to her mother, but her letters were tremulous and anxious. One has the sense that she was not certain that her letters would be welcomed, and she had none of the ease that her siblings show in writing to their mother.

As if to prolong her period of dependence, Marjorie was an undergraduate in two different institutions. In 1901, when Pernel was engaged as a tutor there, she enrolled at Royal Holloway College in London where she spent two years reading French (for which she received a prize) and Greek history.[79] Although the college was in London, not terribly far from Lancaster Gate, Jane Strachey seems not to have visited her there even once. 'I suppose Pernel has told you I have new rooms this term', Marjorie wrote to Jane in her second term. 'They are nicer than the last lot. My bedroom . . . is about 4 times as big as the old one and next to room where linen is kept so very warm. My study looks into the quadrangle.'[80]

While Jane took little interest in Marjorie, Marjorie herself was often required to know in detail about her mother's increasingly important public life. Her first year at Royal Holloway, 1902, saw the passage of the

Education Bill that abolished school boards leaving authority for education with county or borough councils. This legislation was of great concern to the Women's Movement because women had been very prominent on a number of school boards, but they were not able to serve as county or borough councillors and thus lost their role in local education. Jane Strachey had recently become president of the Women's Local Government Society, which had been campaigning for more than a decade for legislation to enable women to stand as local councillors and redoubled its efforts now. This whole issue was a matter of great interest at Royal Holloway, wrote Marjorie to her mother, and 'I have been asked to supply information on the women question, all owing to the circular on the subject of your meeting which was put on our notice board. Could you tell me a few remarks to make on the subject, or would it entail too much labour?'[81] Marjorie remained at Royal Holloway until 1904. She made a number of friends there and spent some of her vacations visiting France and Denmark with one of the tutors, Miss Pechinet.

The years at Royal Holloway were followed by several more at Somerville. Marjorie was 22 when she went there, the age James had been when he left Cambridge. There is no indication in family letters why she went to university so late or why she should have gone to Oxford rather than Cambridge. Not only had Pernel been to Newnham, but Elinor's daughters, Ellie and Betty Rendel, to whom Marjorie was very close, went there too. Indeed, Ellie Rendel was at Newnham in the very years that Marjorie was at Somerville.

The shabbiness of Jane's treatment of Marjorie, and the contrast with her treatment of her other children, was particularly marked in Marjorie's university years. Although Oxford was much less well known to the Stracheys than Cambridge, Marjorie was not accompanied by her mother when she first went there. 'I have now fairly settled into my room', she wrote to her mother a short time after arriving. It is a 'nice one with bow window and a fireplace. This place is more like a house than Holloway; the rooms are furnished simply but appropriately; all inhabitants are friendly and most know someone I do.'[82] Perhaps the fact that Jane was not herself a familiar figure in Oxford, as she was in Cambridge, had something to do with this. The principal, Miss Maitland, had not realized who she was, Marjorie reported, 'till the other night when she came to my room and saw your photograph. She then instantly said "Oh yes, I have frequently opposed her on committees!"'[83]

141

Nonetheless, there were family connections in Oxford and, almost as soon as she arrived, Marjorie began a round of calls. Walter Raleigh had left Liverpool to take up the first chair of English Literature there and she attended his inaugural lecture. It was 'enthralling', she reported, 'full of wit and humour & like Lytton in his methods'.[84] Although not often visited by her family, Marjorie was sent wine—which was greatly superior in quality to college supplies. She worked hard, although she found her routine arduous. Only three of Marjorie's classes were offered at Somerville and the others were spread throughout Oxford. She had to buy a bicycle to be able to get to them all. She seems not to have been involved in any kind of discussion group, but she did join the Somerville Bach choir as well as singing hymns to people in the Radcliffe Infirmary.[85]

Despite her earnest endeavours, Marjorie did not manage to get a first. 'I hope the result is satisfactory', she wrote in the letter she sent her mother telling her that she had been awarded a second class degree.

I have talked to Miss Pope and she was very nice. She says that all my work has been quite good and some of it first class, but the proportion of papers in which I could show my best work was not big enough for it to run to a first. Also I was exhausted by the examination and in the last paper had a headache and had to come out half way through and it was one of my good papers.[86]

To Marjorie's great relief, Jane regarded this as an excellent result. But, although Marjorie's results were acceptable, unlike Pernel, she had not made Somerville her home or found there the life she wished to pursue. On the contrary, when she left Oxford at the age of 26, Marjorie, like Lytton and James, was still utterly at a loss as to what to do in the future.

Modern Marriages

In his short memoir, 'Lancaster Gate', Lytton Strachey described the marriage of his sister Dorothy to Simon Bussy in 1903 as an event that brought to an end a number of Victorian traditions and shook the world of his parents to its foundations.[1] It was Dorothy's choice of a husband that was most shocking. Simon Bussy was a French artist who was well known to the Stracheys. Indeed, he had stayed in their home. But he had never been thought of as a possible husband for one of their daughters. For all her love of French literature and culture, Jane Strachey had never seriously contemplated herself or any member of her family actually becoming French. But there was also an issue of profession and social class. Not only was Bussy an impecunious painter, struggling to establish a name for himself, he was also the son of a shoe-maker, and while this artisan class was very important in the history of nineteenth- and early twentieth-century French art, it was not one with which the Stracheys had ever had any contact. The sense of shock felt by Richard and Jane Strachey on hearing of this engagement was evident in the way they announced it. 'You will doubtless be more astonished than pleased', Jane Strachey wrote to Lytton, 'to hear that Dorothy is engaged to marry S. Bussy. She is very bent on it, and of course must do as she chooses.'[2] 'Oh la! la!' she added as a postscript. As if to symbolize its distance from prior family tradition, this wedding was not celebrated in a church.[3] The Stracheys were agnostic. But up until this point at least, their sense of propriety had made church weddings obligatory. But this marriage and the two that followed it involved civil ceremonies. They were matters of private concern rather than public commitment, and the private celebrations signalled both the end of a family tradition and the advent of something quite new.

While the marriages that preceded Dorothy's had conformed to Strachey tradition in terms of how they were formalized, few had replicated precisely the pattern of Richard and Jane Strachey. One can see rather a series of shifts, as the oldest Strachey child followed almost exactly the pattern of her parents, while the next three show a gradual breakdown of mid-Victorian marital expectations and approaches. As we have seen, the marriage of Richard and Jane Strachey typified the highest form of Victorian companionate marriage, the kind extolled by some nineteenth-century feminists and warmly praised by many current historians, because of its combination of affection, respect, and shared interests, on the one hand, and close integration into the wider family and community, on the other. In the next generation, one begins to see this pattern disintegrate, either because there was no real companionship and sharing of interests, or because the young couple was not able to integrate itself into the wider family and community. In the later marriages, a new pattern emerged. The idea of companionate marriage remained, but it was redefined. The Victorian middle-class ideal, in which the husband was the bread winner and very much head of the household, gave way to one in which husband and wife could be equal partners. The supportive Victorian wife gave way to one whose career and professional activities were as important as her husband's. In the later Strachey marriages, too, there was also much greater sexual and emotional freedom.

The growing independence of Strachey wives reflected some of the broader legal changes of the second half of the nineteenth century. Most important amongst these was the married Women's Property Act of 1882 which gave women control of all their property, whether earned or inherited.[4] This legislation was passed in the year that Elinor, the oldest Strachey daughter, married, but it had little impact on her life. By the early twentieth century, however, it was extremely important as it underlay the financial control that both Dorothy and Ray Strachey exercised in their marriages. It enabled them and Alix Strachey to lead the lives they chose. While married women's property was important to the Stracheys, they took no notice of the changing legal or judicial approaches to child custody. There was only one divorce within the family, that of Oliver from his first wife in 1908. On this occasion, despite the recognition of women's rights in the Child Custody Act of 1886, and the increasing tendency for women in divorce cases to be granted regular access to their children, Oliver took upon himself all the privileges of the wronged Victorian husband in depriving his first wife not only of custody, but of any contact with their daughter.[5] Despite their strong feminist convictions, neither his mother, his sisters, nor his second wife uttered any protest at this brutal act.

Even before the twentieth-century Strachey wives began to demand independence, one can see a marked decline in the power and command of Strachey husbands. Richard Strachey was unquestionably a patriarchal figure. He was, as we have seen, in many ways a benevolent patriarch, willing to be guided by his much beloved wife, and often generous to his children. But, at least until he was well in to his 80s, there was never any question about his pre-eminence within the family. The first marriage amongst his children, that of Elinor to James Rendel, followed this pattern quite closely, with James very definitely the family head and also a successful public figure. But this was the only Strachey marriage to do so. None of the sons of Richard Strachey can be described in patriarchal terms. Financial difficulties or the inability to establish successful careers was one factor here, although certainly not the only one. Neither Dick nor Oliver were able to set up the homes or establish their wives in the manner expected of men of their social class. But even Ralph, who was financially quite well off when he married, never managed to assert himself as a family head, or to oversee the destinies of his wife and children. One can see here something of the ways in which Victorian domesticity, with its emphasis on women as central to family life and to the care of children undermined the role of fathers. But there were also the question of individual personality. As his son later recalled, Ralph's gentleness and indecision left him always prey to the whim and vagaries of his wife—and when he was engulfed by marital and familial difficulties, it was his sister Pippa who was called on to resolve them.[6] In Oliver's case too, it was not so much financial difficulties as the refusal to accept responsibility for his family that was the real issue. Oliver removed their child from his first wife. But having done so, he took no interest in her whereabouts, her welfare, or her well-being. He established a successful career in intelligence early in his second marriage, but this was not accompanied by any new sense of familial authority. On the contrary, Oliver was an engaging occasional companion to the children of his second marriage—an improvement perhaps on the complete lack of interest he showed in the child of his first. But he never took on in any way the role of a father. Oliver's behaviour can be seen as part of the 'discernible male revolt against domesticity' that John Tosh and others have found within the middle class towards the end of the nineteenth century.[7] But it merged into the pattern established by Ralph whereby it was the Strachey women who had to establish homes, manage finances, and take on all responsibility for the children of husbands or of brothers.

I

Elinor Strachey continued the pattern she had established early on as the model daughter into adulthood. On 3 Feb 1882, when Elinor was just 22, Jane Strachey wrote to Ralph in great excitement about the 'great event here: James Rendel has arrived and proposed to Elinor & she has accepted'.[8] In the best Victorian tradition, she married both early and well, for no one could have been a more welcome suitor than Rendel. The son of Sir Alexander Rendel, consulting engineer to the India Office, and a friend and close colleague of Richard Strachey's, James himself had been called to the Bar in 1880 and was already a successful lawyer. Much of his work was connected with Indian railways and he was soon to become a director of the Southern Punjab Railway and chairman of the Assam and Bengal Railway.[9]

While Jane's delight in Elinor's marriage is very evident, there is little information either from Elinor or from her children about the nature or the dynamics of this marriage. Elinor left neither a diary, nor the intense and emotional letters that we have from some of her other sisters to close friends. Nor are there sufficient letters to or from James Rendel to give one any very clear sense of him. There are suggestions in the later recollections of Ray Strachey and Frances Partridge that the Rendel marriage involved a certain amount of verbal sparring and argument, but there is little indication as to whether this was a source of enjoyment to the couple, or a sign of tension. Frances Partridge, who came to know Elinor well in her later years, maintains Elinor was regarded as the cleverest of the younger Stracheys, and that she had a great love of languages and wrote poetry that she regarded as too poor to publish.[10] But there is no other evidence to support this—nor, for all her ability, is there any suggestion that Elinor ever sought an alternative life to that of marriage and the care of a family. On the contrary, she seemed both to value it and to try at every opportunity to get her sisters and then her daughters to follow suit. There is one letter that offers a very slight hint that her economic dependence troubled her. In 1912, Jane Strachey proposed that, as her share of the limited Strachey family money, Elinor should be given the proceeds of a pearl necklace which Jane sold for £2,000. Elinor was thrilled. 'Dear mama, What a splendid price you got for the pearls!' she wrote. 'I feel rather overwhelmed by your generosity & as if I did not deserve such a gift. I hope it is not very swinish of me to accept it. It will be so pleasant to feel I have something of my very own! Jim is always rather enraged when I say this—but it is a genuine feeling.'[11] But the very tone of this letter suggests that while having some money of her own was a lovely treat, this was not because she felt in any way materially deprived or uncared for by her husband.

Just as Elinor was the model daughter, so her husband was the model son-in-law. Jim Rendel was on terms of great ease and intimacy with the Stracheys. He was their legal adviser, constantly called on to deal with marriage settlements, wills, and other legal matters. He not only offered his home to Elinor's siblings, but was prepared to move with her and their children into Lancaster Gate to look after Richard Strachey when Jane wanted to go away. The whole Rendel family was helpful and hospitable to the Stracheys. In 1896, when the foul drains at Lancaster Gate were declared a health hazard and the Stracheys had to move out to have them replaced, the Rendels took charge. James's father, Sir Alexander, oversaw all the work, and he and his wife invited all the Stracheys who had been staying at Lancaster Gate to stay with them. Jim Rendel was also very generous to the Stracheys. When Dick Strachey's Indian regiment was disbanded in 1908, he was put on half pay—which made it hard for him to return home. This happened at the very time when Sir Richard's retirement from the EIR left the rest of the Strachey family in somewhat straitened circumstances. Jim Rendel resolved the problem. 'It would give both Elinor and myself the greatest pleasure in the world to let Dick have any money that is necessary to get him home from India', he wrote to Jane Strachey, as soon as Dick's return was mooted. He also made it clear that he was offering a gift not a loan. 'I have been cleaning up my aunt's affairs and have a good balance unemployed and so giving the money will make no difference to us whatsoever.'[12] Jane Strachey in turn was devoted to him: he was named alongside several others in her will as people whom she wanted to choose something as a memento—but there was also a little note expressing her wish that 'my dear Jim' would choose something 'really good'.[13] It would seem that Jim Rendel, even more than his wife, was comfortable with a late Victorian outlook, and retained all his life the sense of social values and appropriate conduct that came from his imperial upper middle class family. In the early 1930s, Dorothy Strachey, who was having her annual holiday with the Rendels wrote to André Gide that Rendel was 'most terribly upset by modern manners and morals'. As one who sympathized with modern ways, she spent all her time 'trying to keep out of heated arguments into which he is always trying to force me'. But, she added, 'he's a dear all the same'.[14]

Just as marriage had come easily to Elinor Rendel, so too did motherhood. Her first daughter was born just a year after she married, in 1883, and was followed in quite rapid succession by another daughter and three sons. James Rendel's successful career ensured that Elinor had comfortable homes, first in Lancaster Gate and then in Rickettswood in Surrey, with substantial nurseries and nursery staff. She was deeply attached to her children, but as she was relieved of the need to provide basic care, her time was devoted to organizing outings, parties, and other pleasant activities for them.

As was often the case in large Victorian families, the children of the oldest daughters were born at much the same time as were their youngest siblings. Elinor and her mother were sometimes pregnant together, and certainly shared their experiences of motherhood. Elinor's first baby was born when Marjorie Strachey was just one year old, and two more Rendel babies appeared before the birth of James, the youngest of the Strachey children. This shared motherhood seems to have increased the closeness of Jane Strachey to her oldest daughter. Jane's letters describing her role in Elinor's first confinement certainly suggests a level of intimacy rare between her and her children. 'I sleep on a sofa at the bottom of her bed,' she wrote to Pippa, '& have had to feed her with milk, beef-tea and medicine every two hours through the night; but now she is well enough to do without so much feeding. The baby is a perfect gem, & as good as gold.'[15] Elinor played a considerable role in the early lives of her youngest siblings. Both Marjorie and James (referred to by Elinor's children as 'uncle baby') often inhabited her nursery and were included in her plans and activities. Elinor's letters to her mother suggest not only that she was happy to have them, but that she felt they were better cared for and less difficult to manage in her home than in their own. Marjorie in particular, never a favourite of her mother's, was always welcome at the Rendels.

Every aspect of Elinor's life fostered her closeness to her mother. They shared family interests, on the one hand, and feminist ones on the other. For Elinor was an ardent suffragist and held meetings in her own home, as well as joining her mother, sisters, and daughters in suffrage marches.[16] She also shared Jane Strachey's interest in the Women's Local Government Society. But this very closeness put Elinor out of step with her sisters. She was the only Strachey daughter to assume that marriage and family life were the necessary and most desirable things for a woman. Hence almost from the moment that she was married, she tried to find marriage partners for her sisters—bewailing their lack of interest in her endeavours. To her great regret, her own daughters followed their aunts' pattern, pursuing careers rather than marriage: 'I can't help feeling sorry there are no little Betties or Ellies', she wrote to her mother, 'being still old fashioned enough to think Husbands are good things'.[17]

The contrast evident between the childhoods of Elinor and Dick Strachey continued in their married life. Both marriage and children had come easily to Elinor, while Dick struggled for the former—and failed completely to provide the latter. As a young man, he lacked all the qualities that had made James Rendel so desirable a match, and had to wait years before he was able to persuade the father of the woman he loved to allow her to marry him. While he was serving as *aide-de-camp* to Sir Henry Norman, the governor of Queensland, Dick fell in love with Norman's daughter Grace. Norman forbade the match: both Dick's lack of income and the fact that he was not a Churchman made him unacceptable as a husband. But Norman also made it clear that Dick could not remain in the household, feeling as he did about Grace. So poor Dick was deprived of both his job and his beloved. A year and a half after he had arrived in Brisbane, Dick wrote to his mother to explain that he had to come home.

The fact is that I have fallen over head & ears in love with Grace Norman; the worst of it is that I can't doubt that she if possible is worse hit than I am, and that I am told that it is impossible—that nothing can come of it, and that I must go away without seeing her again. I am half mad just now and when I think of the poor girl and her state of mind everything seems a thousand time worse. Why can't something be said or done to give some hope?[18]

The young couple were determined, however, and after a three-year separation and a series of meetings between Jane Strachey and Lady Norman, Sir Henry finally dropped his objections. He was not happy about the marriage. On the contrary, Dick reported, 'he was very gloomy—

and said he thought Grace would have a hard time, but he seemed reconciled on the whole'.[19] The wedding was held in December 1895 after which Dick and Grace went back to India.

Norman's forebodings proved well founded: Dick and Grace seem to have been well suited, and to have had a harmonious marriage. But Dick's ongoing difficulties in the army and their inability to have children meant that theirs was often a narrow and limited life, lacking the close social contact, the extensive social connections, or the intellectual vitality of that of many of the other Stracheys. They were very comfortable, Dick wrote to his father,

out here in our little hut as weather is delightful and the place lovely. Have flower beds with sweet peas and nasturtiums . . . I have made up my mind not to apply for anything at present. We are very comfortable here. I think we can live very economically now we have settled down—hotel life rather drained me—but don't want another move at present . . . Grace is a splendid manager and we live like fighting cocks on the most ridiculous sum.[20]

Their letters always suggest marital contentment, but they are absolutely silent on the childlessness that one assumes would have been the great tragedy in both their lives. For Dick, this appears as a final cruel irony, underlining his inadequacy—especially as compared with his extraordinarily virile and fertile father who was still producing children in his 70s. For a woman as completely immersed in the duties of wifedom as Grace, it is hard not to see motherhood as an expectation. Their silence makes it impossible to know anything about the source of their childlessness, or whether they attempted to do anything about it—nor were there any comments about it in other family correspondence. But it certainly increased their isolation.

Although Dick was close to his mother and to Elinor in his early years, after his marriage neither he nor Grace was ever on really easy or intimate terms with his family. It was impossible for Grace to establish close ties with her sisters-in-law. She lacked their education or interests, and was resolutely opposed to women's suffrage or indeed, to any form of women's independence. In a family of feminists, Grace's comments on her husband read almost like a parody of Victorian femininity. 'I mean to try and make him [Dick] such a good wife that he may be repaid for all the bother he has had about me,' she wrote to Jane Strachey, after her engagement to Dick was formalized, and hope 'that you all may never repent welcoming me, so kindly, into the family. I am quite certain that Dick will make me a far better husband than I deserve, and that it will be my own fault, if I am unhappy.'[21] Twenty-five years later, when Jane sent her a present to celebrate their silver wedding anniversary, Grace replied in a similar style:

I don't really feel I ought to take presents from Dick's mother as a reward for having lived with him for 25 years, Rather the reverse—for *you* made him into the adorable perfect husband that he is and it would be fitter that I should give you a handsome present as some little token of gratitude for 25 years of happiness.[22]

Over the years, Dick and Grace's infrequent letters to Jane Strachey and to Pippa suggest that while they remained happy together, they were increasingly embittered by Dick's failure ever to gain the promotions which they both thought he deserved. This became more and more marked after their return to England in 1908. Dick worked in the War Office where he constantly watched colleagues obtaining honours and promotions that were denied to him. Dick suffered from an increasing range of physical ailments during these years, particularly neuralgia and sleeplessness. By contrast, Grace emerged from his shadow, becoming very active in voluntary work to support the war effort. But she too was clearly often depressed: after Christmas with her own mother in 1916, she wrote to her mother-in-law about what a nice change it had been. 'Mother always spoils us so and we come away with a happier outlook'.[23] When Dick retired in 1918, he and Grace had a trip to Majorca which they referred to as a 'second honeymoon'. They remained together for another seventeen years. But their contact with the rest of the family was so limited that there is no information in the family papers concerning the final decades of their married life.

II

Both Ralph and Oliver met their wives and married in India, and their weddings occurred only a few months apart. Oliver married first, in 1900, and Ralph followed a year later, in October of 1901. The two brothers had become very close while in India, and each was the best man at the other's wedding. They were alike too in having chosen to marry women who came from backgrounds and social classes different from their own—and very much outside the Strachey social world. That there was so little family comment on these marriages—as compared with Dorothy's—suggests perhaps a certain resignation: Oliver had already shown a marked inability to meet familial expectations, while Ralph, who had always been a dutiful son and brother, was so unhappy in India that it seems likely that everyone was very relieved when they thought his marriage might bring this to an end. Oliver certainly was. 'Ralph's engagement has just transpired', he wrote to his father in 1900, '& pleased I am, I must say. I have met Maggie in Calcutta and thought her charming. Also I believe it is just what will do Ralph good; he has always struck me as rather deserted so to speak, isolated perhaps I mean.'[24]

Ralph's marriage, unfortunately did not bring him the companionship he so desperately needed. Indeed, neither his nor Oliver's marriage was successful. They differed markedly from each other, however, both in the cause of unhappiness and in how it was dealt with. Ralph's married life was often miserable, and he spent a lot of time alone and away from his wife and children. But he never seems to have contemplated ending the marriage, or attempting a new life with someone else. By contrast, Oliver's marital unhappiness was made evident to all in the infidelity of his wife—and resulted in a divorce that shocked the family at least as much as Dorothy's marriage had done. Despite its similarity with Ralph's marriage at the start, the way that Oliver's marriage ended and the very different second marriage he made after it make it more appropriate to discuss his marital life separately from Ralph's—and in connection with the other 'modern' Strachey marriages: those of Dorothy and Simon and James and Alix.

In some ways, Ralph's miserable marriage suggests the final and dismal end of the nineteenth-century Strachey marriage pattern. He was a devoted and responsible husband, well able to support his wife and children financially and concerned about them. Unfortunately, his dependent wife, Margaret, had too limited an education to share any of his interests, and was mentally too unstable either to manage their children or to oversee a home. It seems very likely that there was something else happening here too, and that the complexity of Ralph's relationships with his family of origin made it difficult for him to commit himself to marriage. Of all the childhood pairs that Jane Strachey established amongst her children, the closest was that involving Ralph and Pippa. While the other two close pairs, Elinor and Dick, and Oliver and Pernel, ceased to function as close units in their adult years, Ralph and Pippa remained very close. The care that Pippa took of Ralph during his school days continued as she packed his things and oversaw all his preparations when he went out to India. She kept his photograph near her and wrote to him frequently. Pippa in turn was the repository of all Ralph's feelings, of his hopes, fears, and desires. In the many letters in which he lamented his loneliness and isolation in India, he suggested a visit from her as the one great solution. Many years later, Ralph's older son, Richard, suggested that, although there was no suggestion of incest in physical terms, emotionally Ralph was married to Pippa in a way that made any other marriage impossible. Pippa herself said and wrote nothing, but her affection for Ralph was known to all. The letters between Ralph and Pippa were always restrained in their emotional expression, but they did as young adults sometimes discuss an ideal future in which they would live together forever. When Ralph destroyed this possibility by becoming engaged, he couldn't bring himself to tell Pippa what he had done. Although he wrote to Pippa far more frequently than he did to anyone else, Ralph left it to his mother to tell her of his engagement. It was only after she had written to congratulate him that Ralph felt able to discuss the engagement with Pippa and his sense of awkwardness is palpable in the letter he sent her detailing 'the beastly thing'. 'You are the only person who saves my life,' he wrote, 'and if I wasn't abominably greedy I should never want anybody else.'[25]

Ralph might have been close to Pippa, but she certainly did not set a pattern for what he sought in a wife. It would have been hard to find someone more different from her or his other sisters than Margaret Severs, the woman he married. There are few details about her early life available, and the most detailed picture of it is that contained in the autobiography of her son. According to him, Margaret Severs came from a middle-class provincial family with few intellectual or social pretensions. Her father was a solicitor in Bedford with a small practice and a limited income. He was concerned to educate his sons, but not his daughter.[26] Margaret's ignorance was a constant source of comment amongst Stracheys. Margaret had apparently received a small amount of religious instruction, but even here there were amazing gaps. Lytton and James reported conversations in which, for example, Margaret expressed surprise at discovering that Judaism was not a branch of Christianity. But Margaret's limited intelligence and general knowledge, or so her son insists, were accompanied both by an absolute adherence to conventional middle-class social views and values and a conviction 'that she was always right'. Once her mind was made up, there was no changing it. 'Her vanity, her pride, her loquacity', wrote her son, 'were never to be moderated by my father or anybody else'.[27]

Lacking opportunities in England, all of Margaret's brothers had sought their fortune in India. She had joined them after her father's death, and was seeking an eligible husband in India. Ralph Strachey was eagerly pounced on by her family.

Ralph seems to have had very little experience with women prior to meeting Margaret. As he rarely mentioned it to Pippa, beyond noting that he had met Margaret and thought her 'rather nice', one has little sense of how the relationship developed. He seems to have been a little tentative: Ralph met Margaret when he was staying briefly in Calcutta in June 1900 and it took more than a year (a long time in India) for him to propose. Pippa was in India for much of that time and spent some of it with Ralph. But he said little to her of his plans. She was travelling on her own in August 1901 when the engagement occurred and, as I have said, was not informed of it until she received a letter from her mother. Shortly after finding out about the engagement, Pippa met Margaret and was charmed by her appearance.

From the photographs I had imagined that she was going to be rather short and stumpy instead of which she turns out to have a slim & highly elegant figure & looks taller than Ralph though really about an inch less. Her hair is quite dark & done on the top of her head in a ringlety & miniaturesque manner. Her eyes are the leading feature of the countenance large and dark and beautifully shaped. She is generally seen with a ribbon round her neck . . . her taste in the clothing department all that could be desired.[28]

But Pippa could not quite say the same about her 'mental and moral attributes'. Margaret 'is a simple infant', she wrote to her mother,

3 years of age full of life and full of glee, charmed with herself & her novel situation, enraptured with her new clothes, gloating over her wedding cake, madly excited as every new present rolls in & altogether slightly intoxicated by the circumstances. She has hitherto led an extremely sequestered existence in the wilds of Behar . . . She is evidently now bursting out into joy and my only alarm is that the realities of life at Lilloah may come as a slight shock.[29]

Pippa attended the wedding, but despite Ralph's entreaties refused to accompany the happy couple on their honeymoon. Her forebodings about Margaret's inability to deal with the realities of life were not unjustified. Margaret's extreme nervousness and anxiety attacks soon became a matter of concern. Shortly after their first son was born, Margaret went with him and a nurse to the hills to escape the summer heat. Once there, she became obsessed with the idea that the nurse was ill-treating her baby, and Ralph had to go and collect them, thereby forfeiting the considerable amount he had paid for Margaret's accommodation. Ralph took Margaret back to England for the birth of their second child in 1905. But her anxiety increased: shortly after the arrival of the new baby, Ralph wrote to tell Pippa that while the baby was well, Margaret was 'extremely nervous and jumpy—it gives her fits to see Dicky (then aged 3) walk across the room for fear of his falling down and injuring himself for life &c.' Ralph thought that 'the best thing will be to remove her entirely from the sphere of the infants until she has somewhat recovered her nerves'. This involved weaning the baby early, but both Ralph and the nurse felt it essential that this be done and Margaret given some respite.[30]

Margaret remained in England for some years after this, while Ralph went back to his work as assistant engineer on the East India Railway. Her letters to Jane Strachey at this time suggest that she was in a continuing state of agitation in which she found the supervision of servants and the care of a house almost impossible. She was almost paralysed with fear when there was any suggestion that the children were ill and wrote constantly asking one or other of the Stracheys to come to help her, particularly when a child had to be taken to the doctor.

Margaret rejoined Ralph in 1908, leaving the two sons in England under Pippa's supervision. She was in India in 1911 when Ursula, their third child and only daughter, was born, but returned to England the following year. Margaret's increasing incapacity was a growing source of concern to everyone. By 1912, Pippa and Oliver's second wife, Ray, had taken charge of the children, and Pippa had agreed to Ralph's request also to supervise the management of his and Margaret's finances. The boys stayed at boarding school while Ray Strachey provided a home for Ursula—and both Pippa and Ray attempted to keep Margaret as far from the children as they could. Margaret spent some time in private nursing homes. Ralph lived a lonely life in these years. He finally became chief engineer of the EIR in 1913, a position of some importance. But he gave up his house in India, finding it cheaper and easier to live at his club. He was desperate to get back to England, but could not find employment there, and so remained miserably lonely in India while his sister looked after his wife and children. Ralph had no capacity or resources to deal with this situation. He wrung his hands over his domestic life, but took no steps to alter it. In a similar way, although he wrote letters seeking alternative employment in Britain, others made clear to him that he would never find it unless he was prepared to take the risk of coming home so that he was on the spot when opportunities arose.

Ralph finally retired from the East India Railway in 1917 and returned home. He spent as much time as he could with Margaret, but her frequent collapses meant that she was often in a nursing home. Unlike Dick, Ralph remained very close to his family and wished to see them often. But Margaret's volatile state, and the many 'bad days' on which she was unable to see anyone interfered with these plans. Ralph had only a few years back home in England. He died of carcinoma of the liver in 1923. There was no obituary for him and few comments after his death. Ray Strachey, who knew him well, wrote one of them. Ralph, she said, had something Christlike about him. He was 'too good, and so very lovable. Just to be in the room with him was good, though he was often dreadfully dull, & always inexpressive, & sometimes dreadfully unhappy.'[31]

❧ III ❧

Although it was her marriage that shocked her parents, even prior to it Dorothy had had a relationship they would not have approved, had they known of it. In her late adolescent and early adult days, Dorothy was pursued by a number of young men. None were of any interest, she later explained to André Gide, because she was already passionately attached to a married cousin, Sidney Foster. For much of her 20s and 30s, she explained to Gide

I lived in intimate daily intercourse with a man whom I passionately loved. Circumstances (curiously enough) gave us every opportunity, every facility for the completest freedom, but we both resolved not to use it—that is *he* resolved and I consented . . . But in spite of that he was a perfect, an exquisite lover. I can't imagine that any woman can ever have been loved more tenderly, more ardently, more wholly. And he made me happy—more than happy—contented . . . He knew that the only real bitterness is not to believe that one is loved.[32]

Dorothy's depiction of this earlier romance as an idyllic unconsummated love affair owes more to her desire to show Gide—with whom she was in love at the time she wrote it—that for her, at least, passionate feeling did not require sexual fulfilment, than to accurate recollection. She might have depicted herself as happy and content during this earlier relationship, but family letters written at the time suggest otherwise. 'Dorothy is at present suffering from the most terrific depression I have ever witnessed' wrote Pernel to Pippa in 1892, when Dorothy was 28, 'she never speaks a word and sits immersed in gloom all day long. I think you had better write . . . it might act as a tonic to her poor demented brain.'[33] So miserable was Dorothy that her parents suggested a trip to India, where she had been happy as a child, as a way to cheer her up, but she declined. How much the family knew of the cause of Dorothy's depression is unclear. Jane Strachey, as Dorothy and others remarked, seemed always oblivious to the emotional dramas in her children's lives. But there was clearly some recognition. Dorothy was scarcely discreet: her letters to her sisters refer quite often to her 'dear Sidney' and seek information about him. Moreover when Foster died in 1907, just before Dorothy gave birth to her only child, the family led by Jane Strachey agreed that the news should be kept from her. A week after Janie's birth, she later told Gide, as soon as she felt strong enough, she wrote to Foster to tell him her news—and to seek his forgiveness. But just when she had finished the letter, her husband came to tell her of Foster's death. 'So he never got the letter,' she wrote, 'and Janie's cradle was watered by a good many tears.'[34]

Although Dorothy's engagement to Simon Bussy had come as a complete surprise to the Stracheys, they had known Bussy for quite some time. He had first met Jane and Pernel Strachey in 1899 when Pernel was undertaking her postgraduate work in Paris. Pernel had boarded initially with the Guieysse family, old friends of Jane Strachey's, and Bussy, a friend of their artist son-in-law, Auguste Bréal, was staying there. On first meeting him, Pernel described Bussy as the 'weirdest' member of a weird household. 'He is very small and rather like a frog to the outward view', she explained to Lytton, 'but his hair and other arrangements are all ultra-French. He is charming, loves mamma, and goes into hysterics of joy whenever she speaks.'[35] The Stracheys purchased some of Bussy's paintings, and were particularly delighted with a portrait he did of Pernel. Four years later, when he had decided to visit England, he was invited to stay at their home.

Dorothy too regarded Bussy as 'weird' when they first met. 'The chief amusement at present,' she wrote to Pippa shortly after he had come to stay,

is the visit of Bussy who is established here with a room full of pictures. He is a sweet and charming person—though withal weird—and he amuses me intensely. We have long conversations on every mortal subject and I find that the obscurity of a foreign language is a great help to freedom of intercourse. It is possible and even natural I find to say things in French that I would rather be dead than mention in English. He is very harrowing and piteous though a poor little object and quite forlorn in London.[36]

Bussy became even more pitiful and forlorn a few months later when he had an accident with a spirit lamp and burnt his face, hands, and hair very badly. Fortunately he escaped eye damage, but had to be brought back to the Strachey home to recover. He 'is a wretched sight with hair burnt off, no eyebrows or moustache & red scars on his face', Pernel reported, and he needed considerable nursing—that Dorothy provided.[37] It was during this time that Dorothy described Bussy to Lytton as 'a charmer' and by February 1903, they were engaged.

The Strachey habit of using diminutives served to tame and domesticate Simon Bussy, as it did all outsiders. And yet, although small and vulnerable, and not financially successful, Simon Bussy was certainly not unknown in the world of French art. A student of Gustave Moreau, Bussy had exhibited in France not only in the official Salon but also at a successful one-man show.[38] He was a rival of Roualt for the position of first place amongst Moreau's students and a close friend of Henri Matisse, then still struggling for recognition. Bussy's years in Paris in the late 1880s and 1890s had seen him establish himself as a central figure in the bohemian Parisian artistic world. He had lived for some years with a beautiful woman called Leona, whom he often painted. In the mid-1890s, Bussy had decided to turn his back on the experiments in colour and new techniques which Matisse was following, choosing rather to focus his attention on detailed and miniature paintings of animals and birds. He alternated between his animal studies and portraits of family and friends. Bussy was a widely respected painter, although never quite attaining the success he sought. But to the Stracheys, he was always 'Poor Simon'.

The Bussys left for France as soon as they were married. They spent some time with Simon's parents and then with the Guieysse family at Beaulieu, near Roquebrunne on the French Riviera. While exploring the surrounding countryside, Dorothy and Simon found *La Souco*, the house at Roquebrunne where they decided to live. Family legend has it that Richard Strachey purchased the house for them. Dorothy's letters to her parents describing the house make it perfectly clear that, while she was very grateful to her father for the allowance he paid her, she and Simon paid for the house. 'I wish I could tell you something about the charming house we have seen at Roquebrunne,' she wrote him in May 1903, 'but we are waiting for the carpenter to come down in his terms and he has made no sign at present. It is by far the nicest place we have seen and has a great many advantages so I earnestly hope we can get it.'[39] The carpenter was asking 20,000 francs, a fair price. 'We think of giving 12 or 14,000 to begin with and paying off the rest in yearly instalments', she explained to her mother. 'We have now got 23,000 odd in the bank, so that if things are at all prosperous it oughtn't to be too difficult and if they aren't we think we shall be able to let at an advantage.'[40] 'Roquebrunne is a most beautiful place', Dorothy wrote a little later to her mother.

where there are not many villas at present but where they are just beginning to build. A new tram line connecting it with Monaco and Mentone is to be opened this winter, and the water company's water is to be laid on in a year or two. Our house is in a situation where it is impossible to build in front and spoil the view as the ground is too steep. The garden is already laid out in little terraces and planted with a good many vegetables.[41]

Dorothy's knowledge of the Bussy financial affairs was important because it was she who managed them. She also provided a considerable amount of their income. The allowance that her family gave was an important part of this, and it was supplemented also by a small allowance paid her by Marie Souvestre for whom she had worked for well over a decade by the time of her marriage. Mlle Souvestre had also attempted to help Dorothy establish herself in France by introducing her to people who might want her to do translations for them. Dorothy used her home, her teaching experience, and her fluency in French as additional ways of earning money. She provided lessons for some of the local children, took in paying guests, and offered French tuition and accommodation to the children of English family and friends.

As with the other Strachey marriages, the precise nature of the Bussy relationship is hard to ascertain. Simon and Dorothy were rarely apart, and there are no extant letters from each to the other. Dorothy, who was by far the most emotional and introspective of the Stracheys, kept a journal, but it seems not to have survived. Her letters to her family and friends keep people informed of Simon's activities, but rarely say anything more reveal- ing. Lytton Strachey commented first on how extraordinarily undemon- strative Dorothy and Simon were during their engagement. 'Je ne comprend pas ca!', he wrote to Leonard Woolf. 'They part in the drawing room, in public, without a word. Goodbye they say to each other. Good bye I say to you.'[42] But the year after their marriage, when he visited them in France, he was irritated rather by their demonstrativeness. 'I must say that I am sometimes a little annoyed at their affectionateness' he wrote to Woolf. 'Wouldn't you be? Two people loving each other so much there's something selfish in it.' But Lytton was uncomfortable with their hetero-sexuality and found any sign of affection discomforting. 'Couples on the road with their silly arms round their stupid waists irritate me in the same way', he added. 'I want to shake them.'[43]

The comments on Simon in Dorothy's letters suggest that she was always closely involved in his work, and that their daily life was a satisfying one. Simon seems to have been very self-sufficient, wanting nothing so much as long days to paint in his studio. When the Bussys travelled to London, he spent the days at the zoo, studying the animals he was later to paint. Theirs seems to have been a companionable marriage, but not a particularly passionate one. This was probably just as well for when Dorothy was passionately attached to anyone, the intensity of her feelings made life extremely uncomfortable both for herself and for them, as Dorothy herself acknowledged. In her letter to André Gide describing her earlier involvement with Sidney Foster, she insisted that the first five years after the birth of her daughter, Janie, were the happiest in her life. Sidney Foster was dead and so she was finally released from that entangle-ment 'and I thought I was done with passion and was at peace. But that was false, for my passion then was for Janie, and even that which they say is the *purest* of loves . . . well it was very like all the others.'[44] This is an extraor-dinary admission—pointing at one and the same time to her lack of passion for Simon—and to the deeply painful and difficult relationship she had with her daughter.

Dorothy watched over Janie, who was born in 1907, with an eagle eye. Although fluent in French and much enamoured of French life, Dorothy insisted that her daughter have an English upbringing, with early meals eaten separately from the adults, cold daily baths, and early bedtimes. Zoum Walter, the daughter of Simon Bussy's close friend, Vanden Eeckhoudt, recalled in later years her horror at watching Janie's nurse put her into a cold bath as a child.[45] The nurse might bathe Janie, but it was Dorothy who taught her lessons and watched every step she took. Zoum also commented that, had it not been for the time she spent in Roquebrunne as a child, Janie would have had a completely isolated childhood.[46] Occasionally English cousins came to stay, but here too

Dorothy was always involved in any relationship Janie formed. Many of Dorothy's letters to Gide demonstrate the intensity of her involvement in Janie's life—and explain why Janie's friends, like Vanessa Bell, felt so bitterly that she had been deprived of her own life and enslaved to her mother's needs and demands.

While this relationship with her daughter filled the early years of Dorothy's marriage, it was soon supplemented by her attachment to Gide. They met in England in 1918, and became friends when Dorothy agreed to help Gide improve his English. This led to a professional and personal relationship that continued until Gide's death. In time, Dorothy became Gide's major English translator, but even before this she fell deeply in love with him. This painful relationship can be followed only too easily through the extensive correspondence between them. Dorothy declared her love constantly, even obsessively in a stream of letters that continued for decades. Their relationship has been the source of quite extensive discussion amongst Gide scholars, and it is one that poses a number of questions.[47] Dorothy was well aware of Gide's homosexuality, and indeed established close friendships with some of his lovers. But none of this lessened the intensity of her feelings. Gide in turn was deeply attached to Simon Bussy, whom he regarded as a fount of intelligence and calm good sense. He was clearly fond of Dorothy whom he not only relied on in his work, but also integrated into his own close network of friends. Their relationship, however, was an intensely uncomfortable one, in which Dorothy alternated between self-abasement on the one hand, and excessive demands for recognition and affection on the other. Gide in turn tried to parry her demands, maintaining always a tone of friendship, but seeking to continue their friendship while avoiding the intimacy that she sought.

Correspondence was an integral part of this relationship—and it is hard not to see some of Dorothy's letters as allowing her the opportunity to express and even, as it were, to perform her passionate feelings and yearnings in ways which carried no risk or threat to her daily life. The violence of her passion was glorious—as well as frustrating. For one as intensely emotional as she seems to have been, an epistolary passion was the only one that could possibly be reconciled with any form of ordered daily life. In Gide's case too, there are questions that need to be asked. While his friends and his biographer have argued that 'he showed great dignity in a delicate situation', there is more to it than that.[48] Eric Marty has suggested that Gide himself became very much caught up not only with

Dorothy's letters, but also with his desire that she should write about him in her journal and keep a record of his life. Marty is surely correct in suggesting that there was something perverse about Gide's preparedness and even desire to maintain this relationship, 'playing with another as a way to assure himself of his posthumous image'.[49]

Although based mainly in France, Dorothy retained very close ties to her family. She and Simon visited England every summer except for the war years. During this time, Dorothy spent some weeks always in the family flat, with a few more at the country home of her closest sister, Elinor. When the Bussys were not in England, many of the Stracheys were to be found at Roquebrunne. Dorothy's home was both a holiday destination and a nursing home for her mother and siblings. Pippa and Pernel, neither of whom had robust health, often went there to recover from various illnesses or from complete exhaustion. But it was also a favourite holiday destination for them, as it was for Marjorie Strachey, for Ray, and sometimes for Alix and James.

❧ IV ❧

While Dorothy Strachey managed to maintain the fabric of daily life even while suffering intense extra-marital passions, Oliver had no such restraint. Moreover while Dorothy's life was dominated by long-standing and un-consummated passions, Oliver's centred rather on a series of short-term sexual liaisons. As we have seen, Oliver's susceptibility to young women was well known even when he was very young. It was a source of concern when he was sent on his extended voyage in the early 1890s and again when he went to Vienna in 1896. Shortly after he arrived there to pursue his musical career, Oliver wrote to tell his mother of his wish to marry a young woman called Laura Findlay. His mother very sensibly had insisted that he tell her parents of this plan—and the marriage did not occur. But there was no such reprieve the next time. Within months of his arrival in India in 1899, Oliver had met and decided to marry Ruby Meyer, 'I fell a victim almost at once', he explained to his sister and confidante, Pernel.

Ruby Meyer was even further outside the Strachey framework than Simon Bussy. Her father was German tradesman, making a living in India as a contractor for building supplies, and Oliver's growing friendship with her gave rise to critical comment within the Anglo-Indian community.

'I can hardly make you realize the snobbishness of it,' he wrote to Pernel, 'but people who make bricks, and Germans, are quite out of society.'[50] Although Oliver's letters to Pernel suggest that this relationship would have been more acceptable in England, he must have known this was not the case. Everything he said of Ruby made clear how very different her family was from his own. He was fond of her mother, he wrote, although, 'she frequently stumbles in matters of taste'. He liked her sisters—although one was married to a very violent man who made her own and the family's life miserable. Ralph too was aware of the difficulties, both in terms of Oliver's financial situation and in terms of his choice. He had tried to talk to Oliver, Ralph reported to Pippa. Oliver 'perceived the disadvantages but is bent on proceeding. He is also in terror of the effect the news will have on Par and Mar.' Ruby, Ralph assured Pippa, 'is *quite all right*',—and, he added, one of her sisters had married a 'quite respectable man'.[51]

Oliver's description of Ruby suggests that in addition to their difference of background, they had almost nothing in common. Ruby 'is most reserved', Oliver wrote to Pernel,

and will sit speechless by the hour . . . she does not care much for reading, nor does she play the piano or sing; but she has a sense of humour, also a healthy mind She has the reputation in her own family as well as outside of being made of ice; this is all bosh, but she is not particularly demonstrative & doesn't fall in love with many people either male or female.[52]

It is hard to imagine Pernel being delighted by this description!

Oliver and Ruby married in January 1900, with Ralph as best man and Pippa as bridesmaid. Pippa was very taken with Ruby and they soon became good friends. Oliver's letters to the family and Ralph's reports suggested that Oliver and Ruby settled happily into domestic life, relishing the arrival of their daughter, Julia, in 1901. Oliver was unhappy in his work, however, and they went back to England soon after Julia's birth where he sought alternative employment. There was nothing that offered him either security or an income as high as that he received in India back home and he returned to India. Ruby followed, and soon after a son was born. From that point on matters steadily deteriorated. Ruby left Oliver for another man and in 1908 the couple divorced. Both Oliver's letters home and Ralph's suggest that it was entirely Ruby who was at fault. She was depicted by them as an unreliable and faithless wife, refusing to follow Oliver's wishes as to where they should live, giving birth to one son of whom he was not the father, and finally leaving him for another man.

The fullest account of the breakdown of this marriage, and the one that became the Strachey family version, was that written by Ralph to Pippa in October 1908. Oliver had just received a letter from Ruby, he wrote, 'to tell him she was in Lahore with a man called Hunter and asking him to divorce her'. Ruby was pregnant, and Oliver now explained to Ralph that he was not the father of Ruby's first son, Rupert, who had been born in 1907. Oliver had known earlier about Ruby's adultery, he explained, but had chosen to forgive her. Ralph felt very sympathetic to Oliver.

He has taken it very bravely and will get through all right. I think it is a relief to him in a way to feel that there is now an end to a state of affairs which must have kept him continually on the rack when she was living with him. My dear, she has behaved like a beast. After Oliver's wonderful generosity the other time she refused to stay at home with Julia but came out to him dead against his wishes, and . . . would hardly speak to him and went about wearing the other man's ring and a locket with his picture on one side and the baby's on the other. When she went to Mussoori she must have started this new intrigue immediately—a baby is expected in February.[53]

The Strachey family responded to the news of Oliver's impending divorce in very different ways—and ones that illustrate quite well their very different views about sexual morality. James was very amused by the horror felt by his mother and sisters, although even he felt that Ruby's behaviour was beyond the pale. 'There was a shock awaiting me here when I arrived this morning from the Horners,' he wrote to Lytton

Marjorie was even more in mourning than usual, with an air of general horror. On the landing in a terrific voice—'Have you heard the news?'—my mind, of course, flew at once to death—it was the only possible thing, I thought, after such an introduction. I said I'd heard nothing, and she replied 'Oh' in a voice of such sepulchral gloom that not only death but death in its most ghastly forms hovered before my imagination. Dragging me into my room, and shutting the door, she then said, 'Ruby'—and I knew at once she was dying of cancer in the tongue at the very least, and waited horror struck, when the awful truth was announced as follows—'She's got to be divorced!' It was all I could do to prevent myself exploding with laughter, I tried, but I couldn't take it as she wished it, and she finally left the room enraged. Very odd indeed, this femininity! Her ladyship, however, showed more sense and by her account the affair does seem a trifle stiff. Poor Oliver will I'm afraid be wrecked. He hopes to return in January, In the meantime Ruby and Mr Hunter are wrapped in one another's arms in Mussoori—wherever that may be, and Oliver is to get a divorce so that (after 6 months) they may marry.[54]

Regarded by himself, his family, and the law as the wronged party, Oliver took revenge on Ruby in an absolutely savage way. He divorced her, but demanded and was granted not only sole custody of their daughter, Julia, but also the termination of any contact between Julia and her mother. Ruby was not even allowed to let Julia know she was still alive. These arrangements were not ones required by law. Oliver would certainly have been granted custody, but for the most part, in Edwardian divorce cases, non-custodial mothers were allowed contact with their children—regardless of their sexual conduct. Ruby did not contest the divorce: she later claimed that she had not known at the time that she had any rights in the matter.

Oliver was perfectly well aware that his divorce settlement was brutal—and that his own conduct was not above criticism. He made this clear in a very strange convoluted and apologetic letter he sent Pippa shortly after the divorce. As was her wont, Pippa had become close friends with Ruby, and Oliver feared that she may have been angry with him about the divorce. Pippa had not answered Oliver's earlier letter, he wrote.

I suppose you found it too difficult and painful to do so. You being especially Ruby's friend I can well see it. In fact I cannot but imagine you as blaming me in ways impossible of course the whole thing is beyond discussion. Only I will say that since I last parted from you I do not see how better I could have acted than I have.

Of course, before,—in the earlier stages—dear Pippa I really cannot—I could only say so much less than I mean—and be afraid it would convey so much *more*. I resign—But [3 words crossed out] . . . I have been hundreds of times—But yet forgivable—She would not—And so, as I suppose hated also to be forgiven . . . the only thing is that she has refused to have any more of me . . . and that is both my defence and the evidence against me. All these things, with all the details which are the worst part, go on round and round; and on top of course the fact that she is the one who suffers. But still I will say I do not plead guilty. I do wish you'd write and blow me up or something.[55]

Oliver's conclusion suggests that he knew what he had done to Ruby, but that others would deal with it. 'If as I hope you are still Ruby's friend,' he ended his letter, 'please write to her occasionally news of Julia'.

Ruby herself had written to Pippa, telling her of her acute distress at losing Julia and asking Pippa to look after her. 'Its all my fault, & yet I can't feel that it is—& I can't *bear* the thought of Julia being torn away from me—she seem to be so absolutely my very own, & it seems so dreadfully cruel to take her away from me like this.'[56] While accepting that her own behaviour had been thoughtless, Ruby indicated that she and Oliver had been unhappy almost from the start—and suggested, echoing Oliver's strange comments to Pippa, that Oliver might have strayed from his wife in his very early married days. Perhaps this whole divorce settlement was for the best, Ruby suggested, 'as Oliver and I were unhappy for such a long time, & though both of us tried to come together again we both failed hopelessly'. It is not clear whether or not Pippa wrote to Ruby, but Jane Strachey did, keeping up for at least some years the practice of sending regular letters informing her of Julia's health and progress. Jane Strachey herself found the divorce extremely difficult, and was particularly concerned that, as Oliver had not repudiated Ruby's sons, 'the two spurious children' might have a distant claim on the Strachey family estate.[57]

Having removed Julia from her mother, Oliver took almost no further interest in her. Julia herself has written about the misery of her childhood. She was wrenched suddenly away from a life in India in which she was doted on by her parents, loved by her ayah, and regarded as charming, and delightful—and sent back to England where she was looked after by a very fierce old nanny in the Rendel family nursery. No one had any time to devote to Julia and everyone in England regarded her as a problem: a child needing constant care and supervision, but always miserable and singularly lacking in charm. No one seemed willing to recognize the trauma she had suffered or to offer her any affection or support. Julia's lifelong dislike of and bitterness towards the Stracheys is made very clear in her own autobiography, and one cannot but feel that it was entirely justified.[58]

Many years later, Ruby re-established contact with Julia, although they never enjoyed a close relationship. Time and the long separation obviously had something to do with this, but so did their very different personalities. After years of thinking about and longing for her mother, Julia had the extreme disappointment of finding Ruby to be a woman with whom she shared no intellectual or artistic interests and who lived in a world completely dominated by sexual liaisons, travel, gossip, and fashion. It was to Julia, however, that Ruby gave her story of the marriage. She feared that Oliver would have said terrible things about her, she explained, and wanted Julia to understand her version of events. While Oliver's story emphasizes Ruby's sexual promiscuity and dishonesty, Ruby presented him as far the more promiscuous of the two, and as selfish, callous, and cowardly as well. Ruby had married Oliver when she was only 18, she explained to Julia, and found herself married to a man who infected her with a sexually transmitted disease in their first sexual encounter. She was soon pregnant and feared for the health of her baby. After Julia, was born, Ruby insisted, she followed the custom of many European women and took her to the hills for short time. When she returned, Oliver was engrossed in an affair with a young married woman whom she named only as 'May'. When May's husband was transferred to another military post, Oliver brought May and her sister home, giving them the bedroom that he and Ruby had shared, and forcing Ruby to sleep on a small verandah. Every night, Ruby told Julia, the two girls would get straight into bed after dinner and Oliver and his friend Dr Holmes would accompany them. Ruby was sometimes invited to join them, 'so as not to be too lonely all by myself in the drawing room. I only went once, but the sight of 4 of them in bed together was so revolting I could never face it again.'[59]

According to Ruby, Oliver followed May back to Britain, but once there lost interest in her and became involved again with Laura Findlay, the woman he had wanted to marry in Vienna. Ruby was asked to participate in this new relationship too: to sleep with Laura's husband, who had grown bored with his paid mistress, so that he ceased to bother Laura. While Laura's husband apparently accepted her relationship with Oliver, May's did not and threw her out when she became pregnant with Oliver's child. Oliver himself washed his hands of May, Ruby insisted, and it was she who had visited May and given her what little money she had. It was only after all of this, Ruby maintained, that she succumbed to the attentions of another man, 'the most heavenly handsome creature I've ever seen'—and to whom she became pregnant.[60] Back in India, both Oliver and Ruby engaged in other sexual relationships, but remained formally together until, or so Ruby says, Oliver wrote to tell her that she had overstayed her welcome in his house and he wished her to leave. The one point where Ruby's story meets Oliver's is in her account of his apologizing to her after this, and asking that she come back and remain with him. But Ruby refused, choosing instead to go off 'with the first man who asked me to— because he was rich and in a good position'. But she couldn't bear him either, and subsequently found several other partners, some of whom she married.

Ruby's account makes Oliver sound like the drunken, diseased, promiscuous roué so common in the 'new woman' novels of the 1890s. Although much time had elapsed between the end of her marriage and the writing of her letters, her account of Oliver's conduct is certainly not implausible.

Oliver's desire for multiple and changing partners, his complete irrespon-
sibility towards Julia and his later children, and his propensity to drink are
all documented elsewhere. As we will see, there is much more to be said
about Oliver's interest in sex and his desire for sexual experimentation.
Ruby found this disgusting, and it is only too easy to imagine that Oliver
was extremely demanding and selfish as a sexual partner. Some of the
family, like his mother, regarded him as charming. But Lytton and his
domestic companion, Dora Carrington, commented often on his selfishness. They found him a difficult guest, refusing to pay his share of bills,
imposing on them women they disliked, and offering no assistance in the
house or garden.

Oliver moved back and forth between India and England after his
divorce, going back home for an extended period in 1911. It was in that
year that he married for the second time. Nothing could have been more
different from Oliver's first marriage and his first wife, than his second.
While Ruby was young woman with little education and no family connections, Ray Costelloe had been a university friend of both Marjorie
Strachey and of the oldest daughter of Elinor Strachey, Ellie Rendel. Ray
was a woman of independent means and extensive connections within
Anglo-American intellectual and professional circles and indeed in both
Britain and Europe. Her grandmother, Hannah Whitall Smith, was an
important evangelical and feminist. Her uncle, Logan Pearsall was a well-
known writer, while her aunt, Alys Pearsall, had married Bertrand Russell.
Ray's mother, Mary Costelloe, had left her family when Ray was a small
child to live with and then to marry the art historian and connoisseur,
Bernard Berenson. This divorce had not meant that Ray lost her mother,
however. For while Ray and her sister lived with their grandmother, Mary
visited them every year and Ray in turn spent time at the Berenson's
luxurious *Villa I Tatti* in Florence. Ray and her mother remained in
constant contact throughout Ray's adult life.

Even before she met Oliver, Ray had established a close relationship
with his family. Ellie Rendel had been a friend of Ray's both at school and
at Newnham and had taken Ray often to visit her family. Ray was entranced
by the Stracheys. Her letters to her mother are filled with reports on their
hilarious dinner parties, their interesting conversations, their sharp political
insights—and best of all to Ray, their complete lack of interest in fashion.
Ray's letters to her mother describing her affection for Lady Strachey and
her growing intimacy with Marjorie and Pippa give one the sense that Ray

had fallen in love with the family, and was just waiting for the means to connect herself formally with it.[61] This was provided by Oliver. Ray met Oliver at the Stracheys' home in Belsize Park Gardens in April 1911. They got on well from the start and suddenly, a month after they had met, they became engaged. This was not because either Ray's feelings or Oliver's were particularly intense. On the contrary, although they got on very well and enjoyed talking to each other and corresponding, their relationship seemed set to develop in a very leisurely way with quite infrequent meetings until Ray faced one of the great crises of her life: the sudden death of her grandmother. Ray had lived all her life with Hannah, whose love and devotion to her had been very important. Her grandmother, she explained to Oliver,

was always in the same place, always interested and always approving. She was always on my side, no matter how foolish a side it might be, and everything that happened to me had its understanding echo with her. She never made a claim of any sort, wether for attention or affection and we all knew that what she really wanted was for each of us to please ourselves in every way.

You can see what an awful blank she leaves. It is like losing the one safe sure thing—far worse than coming to an end of a belief in God.[62]

Two weeks later, Ray and Oliver were engaged. He suggested that she had proposed to him, and this seems very likely to have been the case.[63] But this was an unromantic affair. The engagement happened, Ray explained to her sister Karen, when 'we were happily situated between the sewage system and the lunatic asylum at Littlemore. The place was so romantic that it couldn't be avoided.'[64]

The Stracheys were relieved—if not overjoyed—by this marriage. Rachel Costelloe, Jane Strachey wrote to her sister, was 'very nice girl, good and intelligent, whom we have long been acquainted with and like very much'. Her family was 'well to do', and fortunately 'Rachel has a little money of her own'. The speed of the whole affair was what shocked Jane Strachey. 'It rather takes your breath away', she confided to her sister, 'but he was bound to marry, and I am thankful it is somebody so respectable'. As an afterthought she noted that 'Costelloe is an *Irish* name, not Jewish as it sounds.'[65] Jane Strachey assured her sister that Ray's family was 'enchanted at the match', but this was far from being the case. 'It is what grandma would call a poor prospect for Ray', wrote Mary Berenson to her sister, Alys Russell, and her brother, Logan Pearsall Smith:

They *had* to get married, of course [or they could not have lived together openly], but she said the other day it was a pity, and I half think if it were to do again I should be tempted to offer the Vilino and seclusion without the formality of the Registry Office. It is very hard to know. But I simply cannot think she will be happy with Oliver.[66]

Oliver's lack of career prospects bothered Mary as did his connection with Bloomsbury. Ray had always kept her mother fully informed of the sexual beliefs and behaviours of her Bloomsbury friends and, while no stranger herself to marital infidelity and intrigue, Mary found their open disregard of marital relationships and their homosexual proclivities hard to accept. Ray argued that it was much better to have the young men engaged in sexual relationships with each other than frequenting prostitutes, but Mary, as she confided to Berenson, felt that their approach to life was 'awful— horripilent, as thee says'.[67] At the same time Mary was well aware that Ray had found in the Stracheys a congenial family, and commented frequently on the way Ray shut herself 'up into the Strachey shell'.[68]

Ray's engagement produced a number of crises amongst her close female friends. Ellie Rendel, in particular, seems to have experienced a breakdown when it occurred and Oliver's sister, Marjorie, was also distraught. Both women were prescribed rest-cures. Ray had also to cancel a trip around England she had agreed to make with the American feminist and public speaker, the Revd Anna Shaw, who had also become intensely fond of her. Ray, whose closest relationships were always with women, couldn't bear passion or emotional demands even from them. These difficult relationships with her close women friends made Ray feel that life 'seems to be a rather complicated business'. By contrast, the lack of passion or intensity in her relationship with Oliver was a relief. 'There is nothing complicated or difficult about you or me' she assured him. 'The odd thing is that there never will or can be. I wonder if we shall find it dull—always agreeing so well and going the same way?'[69]

For those who know Ray Strachey as a feminist writer and activist, there is something deeply disturbing about her marriage to Oliver. It is unlikely that she knew anything of the detailed story of his sexual past which his first wife later revealed, but it seems hard to believe she had no sense of it. She certainly did know both about his divorce settlement and about his daughter—and expressed concern about neither. Ray did nothing to make up for Oliver's neglect of Julia, insisting only that she should not be required to take any responsibility for her. When it was no longer possible for Julia to remain with the Rendels, it was arranged that she should go to stay with Ray's aunt, Alys Russell. At the time, Alys Russell was in a state of acute distress as her marriage to Bertrand Russell was coming to an end. She was thus a miserable companion for poor Julia. Ray was perfectly aware of this, but sent Julia there nonetheless. Both Alys Russell and Ray's mother, Mary Berenson, were very critical of Ray and Oliver's behaviour to Julia. 'I honestly think that [Ray and Oliver] are neglecting Julia', Alys wrote to Mary Berenson. 'However, that they evidently mean to do always, & I shall cease thinking about it and look on myself as her mother.'[70] Ray attempted to exonerate herself, often by insisting that Julia was impossible. Her letters make it perfectly clear that she was determined to avoid having to care for Julia—and prepared to do anything that was necessary to ensure her own freedom.[71] The contrast between her absolute and callous disregard of Julia and her deep engagement with her own children is very marked.

Ray's marriage was inevitably somewhat more complicated than she anticipated. But her overall sense that this was a marriage of companionship and convenience did turn out to be the case. From Oliver's point of view, there were great advantages—not least the end of any thought that he should have to sacrifice himself to an uncongenial occupation. He did make one attempt to enter the civil service after their marriage, but was relieved that it was unsuccessful. 'This of course alters our arrangements', he wrote to his mother when he heard that he had not been offered a civil service post. But he had decided not to seek another position.

We have always thought we should like to work together, and as we have enough means to live quietly and do so, we intend to take seriously the Indian History—at which we can work together with great advantage—Ray has over £500 a year, with a practical certainty of ample later on to provide for any family—I daresay I could add an occasional bonus by writing. So long as there is enough to provide for ourselves and children, the important thing is to have some regular work, as useful and congenial as may be—and it is not often that husband and wife are so luckily constituted as to be able to work together—We both think it would be foolish to look for some uncongenial office job for me, that would not bring in more than a hundred or two and would spoil so pleasant a prospect as joint work.[72]

Ray and Oliver went to India shortly after their marriage and began to think seriously about their Indian history project. Ray tried hard to persuade Bernhard Berenson to finance it. Berenson paid Ray quite a generous allowance, but he was not prepared to do more. To Ray's distress, he

171

refused to believe that Oliver was a talented writer who had simply lacked the opportunity to show his true ability! As one might have expected, the writing project did not last, and Ray and Oliver produced only one slim volume.[73]

Ray became pregnant while she and Oliver were in India and they returned to England for the birth of Barbara, their first child, in 1913. The unusual approach that Ray had shown to her engagement and her marriage continued with the anticipation of motherhood. She had had been deeply involved in suffrage work before her marriage and resumed it, despite her pregnancy, as soon as she returned. The baby had to be fitted in to her busy round of meetings and then, after August 1914, around the work she was doing with Pippa, coordinating the relief work undertaken by the National Union of Women's Suffrage Societies during the war. Oliver, too, who had completely lacked direction before the war, found his vocation during it. He had always been extremely good at crosswords and acrostics, and a family friend in the War Office who saw his potential as a code-breaker and recruited him for military intelligence. As a result, Oliver and Ray were often apart during the war. They corresponded constantly and were clearly on good terms. Ray, who had very much wanted to have two children, became anxious at her failure to become pregnant again at once. She suffered a couple of miscarriages and then for a year or two seemed unable to conceive. She was becoming deeply distressed about this until a doctor removed a fibroid—and told her to relax. Finally, in 1916, she gave birth to Christopher, her second child.

To her mother's great distress, and although she adored Christopher, Ray resumed work very shortly after Christopher's birth. In December 1916, she explained to her mother that she was going to attempt to continue working both on the suffrage and in the area of women's employment—and by January was back in the thick of it. 'Your letter lamenting that I should go on doing politics reached me in the midst of a most interesting series of events which I will describe to you' she wrote to Mary in January 1917. 'It is no use supposing that I can sit down & wait during the war, or while such interesting things are waiting to be done, for I simply can't do it. It would stick in my conscience too, even if it didn't stick in my inclinations!'[74] Christopher timed his arrival very well, she added, choosing 'the slack months at the end of the Asquith administration'. This set the pattern for Ray's future married life, centred as it was on care of her children, on the one hand, and her work on the other—with time for her extended family in between. There was increasingly little space in her life for Oliver.

There are no details about precisely how the sexual and intimate side of Ray and Oliver's marriage came to an end, but effectively their marriage was over by 1918. Oliver's relationship with Inez Ferguson was an accepted thing within Bloomsbury in that year. He took her to stay at Lytton's house and she was his regular companion at Bloomsbury evenings. Ray seems to have minded very little. She saw Oliver frequently, and in 1921, wrote to tell Pippa Strachey that,

I have given up my tacit objection to encountering Inez Ferguson & propose in future to join—when I want to—parties or dinners which she attends. I shall go once to dine with her too, to make all clear. There is no sense in making social difficulties to no purpose, I think. And I find I have no interior objection to this course. It will make life easier for Oliver, and different for me—so why not be obliging?[75]

Throughout this time, and in subsequent years, Ray and Oliver remained on excellent terms. They often lived apart: Ray built herself a mud brick house in Sussex, while Oliver shared a home in London with Julia for some years. But Ray supervised Oliver's finances and oversaw the running of his home. In 1926, moreover, she and Oliver moved into a house together, and continued to share a London base until Ray's death in 1941. Their daughter, Barbara Strachey, recalls them as getting on well and creating a very harmonious environment for their children. Oliver visited Ray in the country, sometimes taking his current partner with him—and Ray was completely unconcerned.[76]

Ray found Oliver's partners easier to deal with because she too had an emotional life separate from him. For most of the time it centred on her children, on the one hand, and on Pippa Strachey, on the other. Ray had always been fond of Pippa, but became increasingly attached to her during the 1920s. She worked closely with her—and indeed maintained that she had continued to work for the women's movement after the war largely because it guaranteed this daily contact, Often too, Ray would drop in on Pippa in the evening, and regarded these visits as 'an hour of sunlight in the day'.[77] Pippa was the centre of Ray's life during these years, as her diary makes clear. Ray cared for her far more than she ever did Oliver, and found Pippa's failure to return her affection deeply distressing.[78] Ray attempted to watch over Pippa, ensuing that she had sufficient rest, taking her on holiday, and looking after her when Pippa's health collapsed as she combined her own professional life with nursing Jane Strachey through her final years.

Ray's life was a very full one during these years. She was the only one of the Strachey wives who combined a significant career with children, but she also differed from all the other Strachey women in terms of her apparently limitless energy. She described herself sometimes as a 'juggler' with several different balls to be kept always in the air.[79] But while her life was sometimes difficult, one feels that she relished the sense of herself as a modern woman, racing around London in her motor car. The car was probably essential in view of the amount of dashing about that she did in order to encompass her work and family obligations each week, before returning to the mud house in the country each weekend.[80] This lifestyle had been financed by the Berensons until the end of the 1920s, but during the Depression the regular allowance she had received from Bernard Berenson and the irregular but substantial amounts of money sent by her mother more or less came to an end. Ray had now to undertake paid work, which she added to the unpaid work she did for the London Society for Women's Service and a number of other feminist organizations. Her children were constantly in need of care and support during this time, as was her mother, whose relationship with Bernard Berenson was becoming increasingly difficult.[81] Ray was buoyed up in these years by her love of Pippa—but this made it all the harder for her when Pippa refused, even after Jane Strachey died, to move in and live with Ray. 'I am exceedingly disappointed that P decided not to come and live in the top part of my house', she confided to her diary. 'I dare say her decision was wise from every point of view. But I had somehow fancied she might come and was cast down.'[82] Ray couldn't sleep when Pippa made this decision—and came closer to a physical breakdown than ever before. She recovered from this disappointment in time, and some years later confided to her diary that she had now made a new friend, entered only as 'Molly' who became a regular companion on holidays and spent a lot of time at her home in the country.

IV

While Ray and Oliver negotiated a marriage which gave him sexual freedom and her the chance to have both children and an independent career, it was the final Strachey marriage, that of James and Alix Sargant-Florence, that encompassed fully the framework of an open modern marriage for both partners. James and Alix had lived together for a short time before they married and both had had sexual relationships with others. This pattern continued after their marriage. But sexual infidelity seems never to have threatened either their domestic harmony or their close companionship, based as it was as much on shared work as on mutual affection.

Although his years at Cambridge were dominated by homosexual passions, James Strachey's sexual orientation changed apparently just after he left Cambridge. At the Fabian Summer School in 1910, he met both Alix Sargant-Florence and Noel Olivier—the two women who became the central figures in his emotional and sexual life. Although James took an immediate liking to Alix, it was Noel Olivier with whom he was initially smitten and who dominated his life throughout his 20s. James's change in sexual object choice did not immediately bring a change in sexual orientation. In falling in love with Noel Olivier, he chose a woman who was also being pursued by Rupert Brooke and hence kept him closely linked to Brooke.[83] Moreover while James shifted his attention to women, he did not adopt a masculine approach or demeanour. He adored Noel, but did not so much engage in pursuit, as declare his love and wait for her to pursue him. She saw him always as adopting a passive and feminine role, waiting anxiously for her to move. Her letters refer constantly to his meekness and devotion—characteristics which aroused her to acts of marked cruelty, after which she felt very contrite.[84] It was Noel who took the lead, assisting him in the use of condoms and introducing him to heterosexual intercourse. And throughout all these years, Noel followed her intellectual and professional inclinations and qualified as a doctor, while James wandered aimlessly around.

While James was engrossed with Noel Olivier, Alix Sargant-Florence began pursuing him. Like Ray Costelloe, Alix had been educated at Newnham. She was a few years younger than Ray, and her university life, which occurred in the years just before the First World War, seems to have involved less feminist politics than Ray's had done, and rather more social and sexual experimentation. Alix was the daughter of a painter who had persuaded her to try art school before university. [85] There, she had met Dora Carrington, who became a close friend and introduced her independently of James to the Bloomsbury world. After she settled in London in 1915, Alix was pursued by both Harry Norton and David Garnett. Just as James adopted a feminine approach to relationships, Alix adopted a masculine one. She had no interest in the passionate, even violent, desire for her expressed by Garnett, nor was she interested in the attentions of Norton. Instead, she chose to woo the indifferent James.[86]

Alix travelled in Europe immediately after she left university in 1914 and was in Russia when war broke out. She managed to get back to England early in 1915. It was then that she decided that she wanted James as a partner and set about pursuing him with grim determination. Alix arranged dinners and reading parties at her mother's house in Marlow. She planned weekends in the country and finally invited him also to come and share her flat. These years between 1915 and 1920 were filled with drama and distress, as James, who liked Alix, alternated time with her with his continued pursuit of Noel. Alix was no retiring violet—and she made very public both her passion and her constant pain. She had been ill at university and suffered now from both physical and mental collapses. Dora Carrington seemed to be constantly carting her off to the country to rest. Carrington's letters and diaries provide a wonderful picture of Alix and of her pursuit of James. Carrington loved Alix dearly, and described at length her moodiness and self-dramatisation, her rejection of fresh air and exercise, her love of coffee, cigarettes, and open fires—and her generosity and charm.[87] 'I am here with Alix—who has a passion for weeding paths' she wrote to Lytton Strachey in March 1918.

I get on with her better than anybody really—we spent all the evening grousing against the Strachey frères . . . a complete history of all you people from the beginning—James never turned up to lunch today and I had cooked a repast the like of which has never been seen in Tidmarsh before! Alix has just gone to meet him now 4.20. Very soon I shall know whether I am to be coupled up with that enraged Black Bear for the next week—or spend a tolerably peaceful weekend.[88]

James did arrive eventually at about half-past five, Carrington wrote, 'so the black Bear smiles & dances round her pole'. The relationship between Alix and Carrington in these years was made even closer by the fact that both were in love with Stracheys who did not return their affection. Carrington was also a little bit in love with Alix. 'Oh Alix.' she once wrote, 'I wish you were a Sappho. We might have had such a happy life without these Stracheys.'[89] Ultimately, however, James succumbed. Even Virginia Woolf, whose diaries provide a continuous sardonic commentary on the scenes that accompanied Alix's pursuit of James, conceded that she deserved to win. Woolf felt, however, that this was a marriage deprived of interest because so many emotional battles had been fought before it occurred.[90]

James and Alix married in 1920. Theirs, too, was a marriage without ceremony, undertaken essentially because they had decided to go on an extended European tour, with a long stop in Vienna where James hoped to meet Freud and to begin psychoanalysis. The marriage was enthusiastically welcomed by Jane Strachey, although it was a small and very quiet affair. Despite his initial lack of interest, it is clear that shortly after their marriage, James came not only to accept Alix's devotion, but to love her deeply himself. He wrote long letters expressing this love and telling her of his loneliness whenever they were separated. Alix, who had taken a certain grim pleasure in her pursuit of him, was initially uneasy about this turn of events. 'Well, what am I to say about the most important part of your letter?', she asked, when he had written of his longing for her while he was away in Germany with Lytton in 1922.

The *absolute* truth is that it gives me an anxiety—hysteria—fixation neurosis, in a slight degree. You mustn't, you really mustn't be more fond of me than is suitable or I shall very soon sink under the ground or cease to exist in some way or other. It would be terrible to think one would never have another chance of pining away in secret—or in public—especially when one thinks how badly one did it and how ungrateful one was at the time. I do so like running after you, you see, like the awful perverted woman I am.[91]

But in time Alix came to accept, enjoy, and depend on James's devotion. Their extensive correspondence from the period 1924-5, when she was in Berlin undergoing analysis, while James stayed in London, suggests a very intimate and affectionate relationship.[92] Alix had not enjoyed her first direct encounter with analysis. When she and James were in Vienna, although James had been Freud's primary patient, Freud had agreed to see her when she began suffering from anxiety attacks. Although he was too busy to give her regular appointments, he refused to refer her to anyone else and fitted her in when he felt he had time. Alix had hated this and decided that, while she wanted to undergo analysis, she had to do so alone. She went to Berlin to be analysed by Karl Abrahams in 1924, but insisted that James stay in London so that she could concentrate all her energy on her analysis. James missed Alix terribly and had constantly to fight against his desire to go to join her there. He took to listening to Berlin radio as a way of feeling closer to her life.

Although not entirely explicit, their letters do suggest that theirs was a marriage of companionship rather than one with much sexual intimacy. In 1925, for example, Alix wrote to James expressing her delight that he was proposing to resume analysis in England. She was pleased, she said 'for I've always had a sort of superstition that your own inhibitions do queer your pitch, even tho' unconsciously with your patients'. As an afterthought, and in parenthesis, she added '(as for the mere fucking business it is absolute "Wuscht" [sic] to me. One can always begin by buying a candle & end by hiring a human candelabra, if necessary). Well, I see I'm going off on a vulgar line. So goodbye dearest James, I love you always. Yrs Alix'.[93] This line was pursued also in an earlier letter: 'If and when I come back I'm bursting with vaginal libido,' Alix promised James when she was in Berlin in 1925, 'I'll keep myself going with candles and bananas . . . if that is what is partly in your mind'.[94]

The idea that their was not a passionately sexual marriage is re-enforced by the ease with which they both accepted the end of any sexual exclusiveness. Alix seems to have taken the first step. As an advanced young woman who had always eschewed feminine clothing and manners, and who moved in circles that advocated sexual freedom, Alix rather assumed that she ought to have a relationship with a woman. There were always women friends who were in love with her, but she could not respond. In Berlin, she bewailed her inability to fall in love with women, even when the opportunity offered. But after she returned to England in the late 1920s, she finally had a lesbian relationship with a woman only ever referred to as Nancy M.[95] Little is known about Nancy or about the relationship between her and Alix. As ever, Carrington provides the most revealing comments. Having always been a little in love with Alix herself, Carrington was very unhappy about this new relationship, and confided to her diaries her misery when it interfered with the intimacy between herself and Alix. Carrington had been badly hurt in the course of her own lesbian relationship with Henrietta Bingham shortly before this, and she found Alix's and Nancy's happiness in each other's company almost unbearable.[96] Although there is a suggestion in Lytton's letters of some tension and difficulty between Alix and James at this time, they remained close. Alix spent several weeks holidaying with Nancy in 1929 and 1930, but wrote regularly and affectionately to James.

There was a playful quality about their relationship, as Frances Partridge observed when she and Ralph met up with James and Alix in Avignon shortly after Lytton Strachey's death in 1930. As always, James and Alix were concerned to protect themselves from the cold and 'arrived buttoned-up and fur coated as if they were off to the Antarctic'.

They seem a very solid pair when confronting the world 'abroad'. James is the dominating one of the two, and carried a neat list of places and times, Alix is a complying but wayward child—chooses pigeon though (or because) it is the most expensive dish on the menu and insists on sitting up in a cafe drinking grenadine when James wants to go to bed.[97]

Alix's relationship with Nancy seems only to have lasted for a year or two. There is no mention of it after 1930. But it served in some ways as a prelude to James's much longer affair with Noel. James and Noel Olivier had never lost contact. Indeed, Noel, who married at about the same time as James and Alix, was often called as their doctor throughout the 1920s and 1930s. In the late 1930s, however, Noel fell suddenly in love with James. They had a passionate affair which extended from 1937 until the early stages of the Second World War. James was anything but meek or passive in this relationship—and sex was very much what it was about. 'The weather here is rather hot—over 90 degrees for 4 days' he wrote to Noel from a psychoanalytic conference in Paris in 1938. 'I quite like it, all the same. The only difficulty is that it makes me extremely lustful. I keep imagining you're here with me in the most provocative shapes. In fact I'm thinking of going off to the Follies Bergere tonight. But that won't make up for you not being really here with me.'[98] James wrote to Noel almost daily and went to see her as often as he could. (Fortunately for them both, she lived close to Glyndebourne—and as James wrote occasional programme notes and attended regularly, he was often around.) James's only stipulation when he visited was that Noel guaranteed she would be able to come to his room at night.

In its second phase, the relationship between James and Noel was completely different from what it had been previously. Having inherited Lytton Strachey's copyrights, James was comfortably off and he lent Noel and her husband substantial sums of money.[99] Moreover it was Noel who was the one more smitten, while he seemed more able to take or leave this relationship. Ultimately it seems to have been James who brought an end to it, visiting and writing less and less often as he became more and more preoccupied with work and with his translations of Freud.[100] There can be no doubt that Alix knew about this relationship. James kept all of Noel's letters and neither they nor his time with her seems to have been a secret.

While Alix and James remained childless, there has been some suggestion that Noel and James had a child together, and that Noel's youngest child, Angela Richards, who worked with James and then Alix in their final translation of Freud, was James's daughter. It was certainly she to whom James left his share of the Freud royalties—and it was Alix who insisted that this bequest be recognized and who extended the bequests to Angela in her own will.[101] Thus not only did James's relationship with Noel seem not to have disrupted Alix and James's domestic harmony, Alix seems rather to have accepted it as something for which she too had responsibility.

Single Life

Marriage was by no means the universal pattern amongst the younger Stracheys. It was considerably less common than it had been in the families of their parents: only one of Jane Strachey's siblings had been single, and none of Richard's. By contrast, four of their ten children remained unmarried. In addition, Dorothy married when she was nearly 40, and hence was single for a significant part of her adult life. Jane Strachey would have dearly loved to see all her children married and Elinor and Lytton constantly kept an eye out for eligible young men for their sisters. Lytton too was under constant maternal pressure to find a spouse—which was a source of amusement to him and his friends. When marriages did not occur, however, everyone was philosophical about it.

The lives of the unmarried Stracheys offer a rich insight into the different ways in which a single life was understood and could be lived at the turn of the nineteenth and twentieth centuries. This is most obviously the case in regard to the women. The Strachey women were beneficiaries of half a century of feminist debate about and campaigns for single women. The census of 1851 revealed that there were some 205,000 unmarried women—approximately 12 per cent of the female population—and while the percentage remained much the same until the First World War, the absolute numbers grew until, by 1911, they had reached more than half a million. Recognition of how very large the number of single women was in the British population in the mid-nineteenth century had led to extensive and often angry discussion about 'superfluous' or 'redundant' women and what to do with them.[1] Feminists had fought strongly against this view, stressing the many important forms of philanthropic and other social work that single women could do, urging the need for paid work, especially for middle-class women, and insisting that single women could lead important and purposeful lives. The examples of Florence Nightingale, Mary Carpenter, and Louisa Twining helped make their point and by the end of the nineteenth century, although single women could not entirely escape what the feminist journal, *The Freewoman* called 'the shadow of the spinster', they could lead full and rewarding lives.[2]

The single Strachey women were in some ways transitional figures between the silent and long-suffering single Victorian daughter, relinquishing her own desires and interests to serve parental and family needs, and the independent modern single woman. Those daughters who remained at home were expected to take over the domestic responsibilities of their mother, supervising servants, looking after younger siblings, and sometimes caring not only for their ageing and ailing parents, but also for their aunts and uncles. Pippa especially was called on for this purpose. At the same time, the careers of the daughters were treated with the utmost respect: thus Lytton, as a writer with no fixed hours, was expected to take occasional turns caring for his mother, but Pernel as principal of Newnham was not. Her work at Newnham took precedence over family duties and it was accepted that her holiday time was necessary for her own recreation. The daughters who remained at home also worked and followed their own interests. Dorothy was a teacher and a scholar of languages until she married. Even Pippa, who undertook the major role of caring for Jane and Richard Strachey in their final years, had a busy working life as a full-time feminist activist. 'Pippa is overwhelmed with work,' Jane Strachey wrote to James in 1914,

> & all I see of her is 10 mins before she goes to the office. She is now in the thick of it. The Annual meeting yesterday, today and tomorrow, with the London Society fighting for its life, a London Society reception for delegates tonight, the tremendous Albert Hall meeting tomorrow night, & 2 London by-elections on hand. She is to have a holiday when all is over—if she is not over too!'[3]

Moreover, while Pippa was constantly in demand from all members of the family, she was regarded not as the family drudge but rather as its head. She managed her mother, dealt with all the crises of her siblings, organized the family finances, and determined everyone's inheritance.

It is noticeable that, while the Strachey family respected its single women, the world of Bloomsbury did not. On the contrary, Bloomsbury manifested in many ways its scorn for spinsters. The sense of the close connection between sexual freedom and modernity, the fascination with sexuality, and the belief that their own open discussion of sexual behaviour was evidence of their higher level of civilization which was so marked amongst Lytton's Bloomsbury friends was accompanied by a measure of contempt for those single women who carried with them the taint of virginity. Just as Vanessa and Clive Bell had disparaged Virginia Woolf's single women friends, and dismissed or ignored the unmarried sisters of Roger Fry, so too they and the rest of Bloomsbury looked somewhat askance at the single Strachey women.[4]

While the Strachey women could all take advantage of the new opportunities for employment and independence available to women, their lives still demonstrate the extent to which the meaning of the term 'single' was gendered. For the Stracheys, as for most other women, 'single' continued to imply celibate, as it had done throughout the nineteenth century. Marjorie had one sexual liaison, and Pippa certainly had one emotional entanglement. These, however, were very brief episodes in essentially celibate lives. By contrast, single men throughout the nineteenth century had been assumed to have some form of a more or less clandestine sexual life. The growing awareness of homosexuality in the later part of the nineteenth century of course raised questions about whether the secret life of men centred on women or other men, as was the case with Lytton Strachey. He was constantly involved in some form of sexual intrigue from the time he was at Cambridge. As a man, he was allowed not only sexual freedom, but also the opportunity to establish his very unorthodox home with Dora Carrington. His mother refused ever to talk about it, but there was no question of her or anyone else preventing it.

I

It was Pippa, the oldest of the unmarried daughters, who took on the major responsibility for running the Strachey home and caring for Richard and Jane throughout their final years. She took on this task when Dorothy married in 1903 and maintained it until the death of Jane Strachey in 1928. Despite her often arduous labour, Pippa never felt herself to be, and was certainly not seen or treated by others as, the family drudge. She was 31 at the time she took on this responsibility and had lived a remarkably care-free life until that point. In her 20s, Pippa seems to have had a more privileged and leisurely life than her sisters. Her limited education was an ongoing source of grief to her, but it seems to have obviated the need for her to do anything much to support herself. All the other single Strachey women either continued their education at university, or engaged in paid work after their school days. Pippa did neither. When she was at home, she enjoyed a busy social life, with frequent dinners, dances, picnics, and boating expeditions. She loved sport and was an enthusiastic cyclist. Music was important to her too, and she was in constant demand as a violinist for string quartets. Her life was not entirely free of work: she apparently gave Marjorie her first school lessons, and worked for a short time with the youngest girls at Allenswood. For much of the 1890s, however, while Dorothy taught at Mlle Souvestre's, ran private classes, and taught herself Greek and Latin, Pippa divided her time between visits to her close friends, the Croalls, European travel, and perfecting her skills as a cyclist. 'I suppose we shall see you back before the resurrection comes', her father wrote in November 1893, when she was visiting the Croalls yet again.

Pippa's competence and charm meant that she was much in demand as a travel companion, both within the family and outside it. She visited Italy with her uncle and aunt, Sir John and Lady Kate Strachey, and Paris with her godmother, Mlle Souvestre.[5] One has a sense here that Pippa was so much the centre of family life that neither she nor anyone else wanted her time to be devoted to anything else. 'I don't want you to go on with Allenswood,' wrote Dorothy shortly after she had moved to France after her own marriage, 'because if you do you will never be able to come and I really feel sometimes as if I couldn't exist without your coming for a long time.'[6]

The ease of Pippa's life in the 1890s was possible because Dorothy remained at home until 1903 and undertook almost all domestic responsibilities. Jane Strachey relinquished household supervision to her daughters as soon as she could, and Dorothy's letters throughout the 1880s make it clear that she took primary responsibility for Lytton and then Marjorie when they were young, as well as managing most other domestic concerns. She ran the household, sorted out where everyone was supposed to be and how they should get there and made sure that medical and other appointments were kept. Dorothy seemed not to mind these domestic tasks, provided that she had the company of her siblings. When they were all away, she complained to Pippa that life was horrible and that she got extremely depressed.[7] Unlike Pippa, however, she did sometimes resent the expectations that she would also look after extended family. 'The blot on my existence', she complained in 1893, 'is having to read to Grand Papa. I simply loathe it and I feel it is vile of me.'[8]

When she was at home in the 1890s, Pippa helped Dorothy and took over her share of domestic tasks. It was she, for example, who dealt with the great drain crisis. Although Elinor assured the Stracheys that the drains had recently been done when they first looked at 69 Lancaster Gate, they were always a source of some concern. The plumbing in the house was noisy and inconvenient, there were sometimes offensive odours and there was a general sense throughout the early 1890s that the drains might be causing Richard's persistent ill health. Richard Strachey rejected this idea and while Jane mentioned the need to call in a sanitary inspector from time to time, she did nothing about it. When Richard and Jane went to France in 1896, however, Pippa and Dorothy together called in the sanitary inspector. His report, Pippa told her mother,

is exceedingly unsatisfactory . . . the main drain has been found to be in a very bad state—leaking violently & not properly connected with the sewer. Jim (Rendel) came round this morning & has taken away the report to ask Sir Alexander's opinion as to what ought to done, but evidently papa ought not to come back to the house in its present condition.[9]

Jane and Richard Strachey were rather relieved to be away. Between them, Pippa and the Rendels managed everything, keeping Richard constantly informed as to the proceedings and the cost. 'It is a fearful business and most of it falls on you poor creatures at home,' Jane wrote to Pippa. 'But I don't see what is to be done . . . As far as I can see it would be no use our coming home in the middle of it, & your papa is disposed to stay on here as it is really doing him good . . . It is really dreadful to leave it all upon you.' This sense that Pippa and Dorothy had been left an onerous task did not, however, stop both Jane and Richard sending a constant stream of requests to be sent books they wanted, bills, and prospectuses for Dorothy's classes.[10]

Pippa's life changed dramatically in the years after 1903. She had come back from India determined to establish a career. Dorothy's marriage, however, left her in charge of the Strachey household, and at a time when Richard, now in his 80s, was increasingly frail and in need of care. The Strachey family always had servants, although their number diminished when Richard Strachey retired. Pippa was thus not involved in the physical demands of housekeeping, but her family duties were onerous and became more and more so. She nursed her father through his final days in 1908. The older Stracheys all regarded Pippa as angelic—and one can see why. Her response to her parents, especially to their needs and demands in their last years, is one that suggests a nineteenth-century dutiful daughter rather than a twentieth-century career woman. Not only did she not seem to mind nursing them, she treated it almost as a privilege. Many years after the death of Richard Strachey, she described her feelings when it had happened to Roger Fry

After days & nights of watching him struggling it was a relief, just for a short time, to know it had stopped & a comfort to see the beauty of his face. So triumphant it looked & magnificent. But that was a very short time & afterwards there was nothing but dreariness & desolation. Besides affection ending I felt as one would if all the books one depends on were suddenly swept out of existence. Does your sister Agnes feel as hopelessly lost as I did? I expect so, but in a different way because she probably doesn't feel as I did outraged by the waste of all that human store. The stores they accumulated with such desperate toil vanish before the breath is out of their bodies, leaving only such queer marks of having been there.[11]

After Richard Strachey's death, Pippa assumed primary responsibility for her mother. Both Lytton and James regarded living with their mother as unbearable in these years. They loathed the way that meal times were dominated by her incessant stories of the past, interspersed with jokes from *Home Chat* and *Tit-Bits*. They particularly hated the loud shrieking that ensued when Marjorie was home or when other female Strachey cousins visited. But Pippa, whom both Lytton and James often described as the only tolerable member of the family, bore all with grace and good humour. She was well aware of her mother's eccentricities, and often had to negotiate with her on behalf of her siblings. But she never complained, not even in the final years when Jane Strachey was very difficult indeed. On the few occasions when Pippa left her mother to take a holiday, she wrote loving letters every day. 'How sad it is that you cannot be transported by a waving wand to this delightful spot', she wrote while holidaying at *La Souco* with Ray early in 1928. 'How I wish you could be here with your knitting & your patience in the loggia darling mama. I feel very much at sea without you & it will be a lovely moment when I see you again—not now far off though we don't know yet when the day will be.'[12]

It was not only her mother who made demands on Pippa. Many of her siblings did too. Almost all her brothers turned to her when in need. Ralph needed constant emotional support and practical help as well. By 1911, when it had become clear that his wife could neither stay with him in India nor manage her family in England, it was Pippa who took over the care of their financial affairs and the supervision of their sons, visiting his wife in Brighton and the two boys at school. During these years Lytton made heavy demands, calling frequently on Pippa to nurse him, to travel with him, or just to visit to cheer him up. She typed his play and his manuscripts, ordered his library books and generally helped keep his life in order. James too called on Pippa, when Alix fell ill while they were in Vienna in 1922. Pippa was particularly needed in the event of illness or other difficulty—and this sense of her as a strong and sympathetic person was shared by her nieces and nephews as well as her siblings. 'Darling Pippa', her niece Janie Bussy wrote in the 1920s, 'I wish you were still here; we all miss you so much. It is terrible the way people one and all cling to you in moments of despair. But it is really your fault for being the most sympathetic person in the whole world.'[13] Pippa met all these demands, but always had her own work to do as well. It is scarcely surprising that she sometimes collapsed!

Pippa's single state has been a source of much comment both from Strachey friends and acquaintances and amongst later historians. She, far more than either Pernel or Marjorie, had inherited Jane Strachey's immense charm and social skills and was regarded always as an attractive and engaging companion. Pippa made friends with ease wherever she was. In the course of one visit to Oliver at Eton, Jane Strachey reported to Lytton that Pippa had made friends with twenty-three people! She struck up friendships everywhere, even amongst people with whose views she strongly disagreed. In 1913, she went on a cruise alone and thoroughly enjoyed it. 'My friends are all of the male persuasion,' she reported to her mother, 'but some of them like me as much as I like them.' To her horror, she discovered after ten days that,

I have become fondly attached to a famous leader of anti-suffragism . . . He is, as a matter of fact, a well known figure in London literary and dramatic circle & there was absolutely no excuse for my not having tumbled to him sooner . . . Yesterday evening the veil of besottedness was suddenly riven by some stray remark & I beheld him in his true light! . . . am now too much attached to be put off by learning that he started the Men's Anti League.[14]

Pippa's charm made it inevitable that she would have suitors, and there were several in her youth. In her autobiography, Mary Stocks recalls that her uncle Herbert Rendel 'loved her [Pippa Strachey] exclusively and ardently for many years, but alas, she did not love him'.[15] Pippa's charm was recognized by Lytton Strachey and his friends who deemed her the ideal mate for their beloved G. E. Moore. They spent months trying to arrange a match without success.[16] But Pippa was no more interested in Moore than she was in any of the other young men who pursued her. Indeed, it seems unlikely that she ever seriously contemplated an alternative life to that of the daughter at home.

The one relationship about which Pippa was serious was that with Roger Fry during and immediately after the First World War. Fry had been a friend of Oliver Strachey and come to know the rest of the family in the early 1890s. He visited the Strachey home often and sometimes lent them Durbins, his home, for the summer holidays. He also stayed with the Bussys in France and it was there that his friendship with Pippa developed. Fry spent some time at *La Souco* in May and June 1915 trying to recover from the intense misery he felt after Vanessa Bell ended their relationship. Pippa was there too and offered sympathy and affection at a time when they were badly needed. They became close friends. 'All that valley from the Williamsons to Mentone seems to me to belong to you,' Fry wrote when he left *La Souco*.

I thought in my sleepy early morning fashion of how extraordinary you are. Yes you have got rooted very deep somehow which makes it so pleasant to lean against your trunk in the chequered shade, my dear subsidiary olive tree. But I don't think you know quite how extraordinary your generosity is, giving so much the casual air of someone who gives one a light for one's cigarette. *C'est pas banal tu sais.* Anyhow I know that you gave me a kind of new belief in myself in my power to create life around me which I thought was gone altogether.[17]

For Fry, as Frances Spalding suggests, this was an *amitié amoureuse* which helped him through one of the hardest periods of his life.[18] Pippa clearly made no demands of him, but this relationship was of far greater importance to her than it was to him. Its significance is evident, not just in the letters themselves, but also in the fact that she kept these letters all her life in a sealed parcel. There was no real possibility that the relationship could develop any further. Pippa was already in her 40s when she became close to Fry—and he usually chose much younger women as lovers. But the question of age was important in other ways too: Pippa had grown up in the 1870s and 1880s and, for all her charm, exuded a strong sense of Victorian womanhood. It is hardly conceivable that someone as physically and emotionally restrained as Pippa Strachey could have deal with Fry's sensuality, sexual energy, and demand for emotional honesty.

Fry was not only prepared to discuss his own feelings, but made Pippa articulate hers as well. This in turn led him to some remorse at the realization that he had made her suffer—and to distress when it appeared that she was avoiding him. Pippa did suffer in this relationship, but self-deprecating as ever, she always insisted that her suffering was a very minor thing. 'At its darkest moments it never gets beyond a middling grey & you needn't imagine that it ever comes within a range of comparison with your sort of gloom.' She insisted that she had no wish for him to be in love with her, although,

I sometimes wd like things which probably could only happen if you were, but that is quite different and simply illogical. I truly don't want you to be dearest angel. And when I am imagining things that would be nice, I don't in irresponsible dreams dream that. I only want you friendly. There isn't any worry about greater flights & as this, strange to say, is a fact, it solves the whole situation.[19]

Fry felt some guilt at the realization that she had been hurt in the course of their friendship. He alternated between insisting that he had never for a moment been dishonest about his feelings—and recognizing that his need for her was such that, even though he did know she felt more for him than he for her, he didn't want to acknowledge it.

It is hard to work out how important this relationship was to Pippa. Dorothy was the only member of family ever to mention it—and even she was not sure quite what it had involved. Pippa suffered from periodic breakdowns in health in the years in which she was close to Fry, but this occurred at other times too and it is hard to know exactly what was involved here. Pippa's health had never been robust: her debility and exhaustion were probably caused as much by the stress she faced with constant suffrage work and ever-increasing family demands as by her feelings about Fry. While she was deeply attached to him, this does not seem to have been a relationship that broke her heart. Rather it offered her a deep and affectionate friendship that allowed other imaginative possibilities without disturbing a way of life that was firmly set. Moreover, the confessions of feelings in their letters enabled Pippa to be more frank and open with Fry than she was with anyone else. This correspondence was the only place in all Pippa's writings where she allowed herself to express exasperation with her mother or her brothers—or to admit how much she relished the power she had within the family.

While Pippa Strachey may have nourished a hopeless passion for Roger Fry, she was herself the subject of an equally hopeless passion from her sister-in-law Ray. Passion is perhaps too strong a word for either woman, both of whom eschewed emotional intensity and preferred a life of calm friendship. But certainly Ray's strongest feelings, apart from those for her children, were for Pippa. As we have seen, from the start, Ray's marriage to Oliver was as much the expression of her desire to be a member of the Strachey family as it was an indication of a desire for Oliver himself. She was devoted to Pippa before she met Oliver—and this devotion lasted a great deal longer. The two women worked closely together in the suffrage movement, in the organiza-tion of the relief programme of the NUWSS and in the field of women's employment during the war, and in the London Society for Women's Service promoting the cause of women's employment after the war. They were neighbours, as the house in which Ray and Oliver lived in Hampstead was very close to the Strachey home in Belsize Park Gardens. Soon after her marriage, Ray got into a habit which she continued for much of her life of visiting Pippa almost every evening after dinner. Ray's diaries make very clear both the strength of her attachment to Pippa—and her sense of the need to keep it hidden. 'There is only one person in the world I feel free to talk openly with about my own feelings,' she wrote in the mid-1920s, '& that is P and even with her I don't talk about my feelings for her. (But that's more because she wouldn't like it than because I shouldn't). Otherwise I prefer to keep them to myself.'[20] 'P' is mentioned constantly in the diary, and Ray went so far as to insist that her real reason for engaging in feminist activity was because it brought her into daily contact with Pippa.

Pippa watched Ray's competence and energy with a mixture of awe and amusement. 'Ray has come to spend Sunday', she wrote to Roger Fry from the hotel where she and Pernel were having their vacation, '& with her usual efficiency has just succeeded in toasting several slices of thin bread and butter with the aid of tea spoons in the lounge of this fashionable hotel.'[21] Ray was a strong swimmer, and Pippa wrote admiringly to her mother of her aquatic prowess when they were holidaying together at Cavalere in the south of France in 1928. Ray

plays all sorts of games in the water with the other two English ladies. Her industry is most marvellous. She writes away at a tremendous pace at a book for several hours every day & at moments when other people would sink into a novel she sets to work upon her carpet with which she has made so much progress that it has become a great heavy role which would break the back of the strongest but which she tucks under her arm and carries nimbly over hills and down dales for the sake of putting in a few stitches at resting places.

She had much to thank Ray for. It was Ray who came closest to offering her the service of a wife, keeping her company, helping to amuse her mother, constantly monitoring her health and her level of exhaustion, and taking her away on holidays when they were needed. Pippa in turn clearly enjoyed Ray's company, and was a little in awe of her vitality, competence, and strength. She felt temporarily bereft when Ray left her at Cavalieres in 1928—although her sense of humour did not desert her. 'I have just seen Ray driving off in a motor car clasping to her heart a small flask of cognac bestowed upon her as a parting present by the hotel owner who was captivated by her charms', she wrote to her mother. 'The waiter, deeply sympathising with my forlorn state & with equal discrimination of character pressed *tea* upon me to console me.' The conclusion of this letter also reveals the limitations of Pippa's feelings about Ray. 'Theseus in the form of Ray has deserted me', she wrote, 'but in a short time Bachus–Pernel will appear on the horizon.'[22]

Ray's recollection of this holiday in her dairy show how differently the two women were positioned in relation to each other. 'I dashed off to join P at Cavaliere', she noted in June 1928, 'left the office to itself, & embarked on one of the most heavenly months I've ever spent. P was still ill, leading a very quiet existence and mostly resting.' The place she noted 'was heavenly, the bathing perfect, the countryside lovely'. Ray was very clear that 'the chief joy of being at Cavalieres was being with P, day after day. Her elusiveness needs a good deal of time to break through—& it comes over her again very fast. But I made some rifts in it, —& she has not closed them up again—though its now just a year since that time.'[23] The holiday had taken place shortly before Jane Strachey's death. Ray had long cherished a secret hope this event would lead to the final break up of the Strachey family home, and that Pippa would then go to live with her. But this was not to be. Just as Pippa welcomed the arrival of Pernel after Ray left Cavalere, so too she planned to maintain the family home and to share it with Pernel when she finally retired from Newnham College. Ray was a close and excellent companion, but she was never quite equal in importance to parents or beloved siblings.

⁓ II ⁓

While Pippa Strachey remained at home, Pernel chose the other alternative which so many educated upper middle-class women found attractive in the late nineteenth and early twentieth centuries: life in an all-women institution. She was one of the independent women depicted so clearly by Martha Vicinus, who found in a women's college both the work she loved and the community that sustained her.[24] Early in her student life, as we have seen, Pernel was selected by the women dons at Newnham for membership of their discussion and language-learning groups. They clearly saw in her someone whom they would welcome into their world. She depicted their activities with some irony for Pippa's entertainment, but clearly found these women deeply engaging. Several of the dons whom she regarded as either bizarre or intimidating in her student days, including Miss Clough and Miss Tukes, became her close friends and Newnham itself was her home for forty of her seventy-five years.

Although her letters are filled with the expressions of affection and respect which are the common currency of Strachey family letters, Pernel seems to have found family life, especially when her siblings were absent, hard to deal with. She was happy to take her friends home and watch them succumbing to her mother's charm, apparently without resentment. But Pernel seems to have spent as little time living at home as possible. Even when she undertook family responsibilities, they were away from home. Thus in 1911, she and Jane Harrison accompanied Lytton to Sweden where he was supposed to undertake a cure.[25] In a similar way, Pernel sometimes took Pippa away when she was ill or exhausted. But she chose always to take Pippa away for holidays rather than to replace her at home. Pernel did assume some familial responsibilities for which Pippa seemed disinclined. Thus it was she who kept an eye on Marjorie, their youngest sister, when Marjorie was having a particularly difficult time. Pernel seems to have supervised Marjorie in her time at Royal Holloway and, in later years, she often invited her to stay at Newnham when Marjorie was depressed and at a loose end.[26] Pernel also travelled with Marjorie—possibly an act of real generosity, as Pernel had many friends with whom to spend holidays, while Marjorie did not.

Although nineteenth-century feminists liked to insist that education only made women better at and more devoted to domestic tasks, many educated women suggested that this was a lie. Pernel Strachey certainly seems never to have wished to undertake any domestic tasks. Indeed, it is very likely that one of the attractions of college life for her was that it obviated the need for domestic management. Pernel was the only Strachey daughter who escaped entirely from domestic responsibilities at home. Marjorie had one or two disastrous short spells of running the home, but Pernel had none. Nor does she seem to have been particularly concerned about creature comforts. Newnham students later recalled that the stodgy dinner of beef and vegetables followed by prunes and custard which is so central a feature of *A Room of One's Own* was not absolutely typical: Virginia Woolf had been late—and so the dinner was drier than usual. But all the students agreed that Newnham food was not for gourmets.[27] Pernel herself never commented on it. She had few hedonistic traits and regarded meals as a daily necessity rather than a source of pleasure.

While both Dorothy and Pippa had an extensive social life in London, and enjoyed the company of young men, Pernel never did. Male company was always something she found hard to manage. Her preference clearly from an early age was for the society of women. She had had friends at school and from the moment that she first went to Newnham, she began to establish the network of close female friendships that lasted throughout her life. 'Nothing would ever induce me to marry', she told Virginia Woolf after a visit to Asheham in 1918, and Woolf believed her. 'Indeed', she wrote, 'I should fancy that her bachelor life, with many woman friends and a great many books, & lectures to prepare on French literature suit her perfectly.'[28] Woolf never for a moment thought that any of Pernel's friendships had sexual or erotic undertones, and it would seem she was right. The emotional intensity and the lesbian overtones in the relationships of several of the dons who were Pernel's friends have often been discussed, most recently in relation to Jane Harrison and Hope Mirlees.[29] But there is no suggestion that Pernel had a particular friend who might be thought of as a partner. It was Pippa whom she thought of as a domestic companion—and with whom she did indeed live when she retired. Up until that time, hers was a celibate life that found its focus in the organized community of a women's college and in the social circles all around it.

❧ III ❧

While Pippa lived in the bosom of the family, and Pernel found an alternative community in Newnham College, in her personal as in her professional life, Marjorie Strachey lived always on the margins. Unlike her older sisters, she seems very much to have wanted marriage and a family rather than to have chosen a single life. For several years, she cherished the dream of marrying the MP, Josiah Wedgwood, and found his rejection intensely painful. Nor did she establish a successful career. Hence she lacked both the focus and direction that comes from dedication to work— and the comforts of a secure income. Marjorie often faced financial struggle and a level of physical hardship and loneliness unknown to the rest of her family.

The Strachey family was rarely a source of companionship and support for Marjorie. She had never been close to her mother and had few close sibling ties. Both Elinor and Pernel showed older sisterly concern for Marjorie and sometimes invited her to stay. Elinor's home was probably the place where Marjorie felt most welcome and she spent time there consistently throughout her life. But she was never an integral part of Pernel's world in the way that Pippa was. Marjorie also attempted to maintain contact with Lytton and James, although their contact was often awkward. Lytton and James both found her something of an embarrassment. Her loud voice, desire to write poetry that she made them read, and her occasional insistence on rigid moral values, made her a difficult person for them to have around. Lytton sometimes got on well with Marjorie, but generally moaned when she wanted to stay with him, or even to take accommodation close by. He and James loathed Marjorie's evening parties—and sometimes rather cruelly organized competing ones designed to draw her guests away. It is notable too that Pippa, who kept in close contact with everyone else, rarely wrote to Marjorie and almost never commented on her.

None of this is really surprising. Marjorie was possibly the oddest member of a family renowned for its eccentricities—and one whose own eccentricities were out of kilter with those of the others. All the Stracheys shared certain notable traits in addition to their high-pitched voices, thin angular bodies, and powerful spectacles. They were known for their propensity to argue constantly at the tops of their voices and to use exaggerated and high-flown terms like 'weird' or 'portentous' to describe mundane objects. Marjorie was far more boisterous and energetic than her siblings, and prone to extraordinary bodily display and excess. She loved to dance, but this sometimes led to naked displays at evening parties. She had what Virginia Woolf described as a 'gift for obscenity' and developed a way of reciting nursery rhymes in such a way as to make them appear obscene, which she did as a party piece.[30] She was the only Strachey to gain substantial weight as an adult and her size, along with her habit of wearing outlandish clothes, contributed to her status of an outsider. It was taken for granted within the family that Marjorie's behaviour would always be outrageous and attract attention. 'Marjorie...went with Duncan to Hampstead Heath yesterday,' Jane Strachey wrote to Pippa in 1908, '& was so fascinated by the step-dancing going on there, that she nearly set off on a reel with Duncan; luckily the music did not suit, and she did nothing worse than fire three times with a rifle at the jumping balls & hit each time amid the applause of the crowd.'[31] A few years later, when Jane Strachey was staying in the country with her sister, Elinor Colevile, she informed James that Marjorie was expected the next day. 'I suppose she will prance down the high street in black satin tights & bare feet, to 4 different and simultaneous tunes. What will your aunt Lell say!'[32]

While neither Pippa nor Pernel sought a married life, Marjorie clearly did. But this too eluded her—and indeed, her emotional life seems to have been a very meagre one. There is talk of one or two unsuccessful liaisons, but no serious relationships. While visiting Dorothy Bussy in France in 1905, Marjorie had had a brief romance with Albert Guieysse, the son of Jane Strachey's old friend. It is not clear exactly what happened, but whatever it was, the Guieysse family was very upset, and Jane Strachey had to write several tactful letters to restore peace.[33]

The most painful episode in Marjorie's life was her relationship with the Liberal MP, Josiah Wedgwood. They went out together for a short while during the First World War and clearly had an affair. Wedgwood was married, and Marjorie had hoped that he would marry her once he divorced. But this was not to be. This relationship was an insignificant interlude in Wedgwood's life and the moment his divorce was finalized he married someone else. What makes this whole thing sadder is that this relationship seems to have been deliberately set up as a cruel practical joke at Marjorie's expense. According to Virginia Woolf, the scheme was originated by her sister, Vanessa Bell, and Ottoline Morrell, but with the full knowledge of Keynes and probably Lytton Strachey as well.

For Marjorie herself, this sad affair dragged on for some time. She was still occasionally seeing Wedgwood in 1917 and continued to hope he would marry her until his marriage put it quite out of the question. This affair was a watershed, or so some like the Woolfs thought. 'Doesn't

Conrad say that there's a shadow line between youth and middle age?',
asked Virginia Woolf, after seeing Marjorie in 1919,

Well since I saw her last she has crossed it into the smoother greyer waters
beyond. She has just had notice to leave her school on account of her short
sight. In old days this would not have mattered much; she would have been on
with something new; but when I spoke of her as the acrobat flying from trapeze to
trapeze she shook her head; no that is all over. She now has her two rooms in
Kensington, lives on her earnings, comes home & is glad to be quiet there, glad to
find her charwoman has lit the fire—Things haven't turned out well...The
prospect is drearier than I could face in my own case. I begin to see, now, how
my friends' lives are shaping. It looks a little as if Marjorie was to be one of the
failures—not that I rank marriage or success in a profession as success. Its an
attitude of mind—the way one looks at life.[34]

Overcoming this great personal tragedy was made harder for Marjorie
because there was neither an active career, nor a settled and stable world
to which she could retreat. Some of the family attempted to help her
through this painful period. Pernel arranged for her to spend time at
Cambridge where she had 'a great social success with the young ladies'
and seemed quite cheerful. 'We never allude to painful subjects', she wrote
to Lytton, 'and she busily reads about Charlemagne, the Goths and the
Dark Ages when she is not teaching eurhythmics or cataloguing the
Library.'[35]

Marjorie, who was in her mid 30s when this affair occurred, still had no
profession or regular income. Once the possibility of a life with Wedgwood
came to an end, she had to work out what to do to earn her own living.
Marjorie's infrequent letters to her family make it hard to paint a detailed
picture of her subsequent life. But it seems to have involved a series of
moves from lodgings to small flats, with occasional spells in the family
home. Lytton helped subsidize her from time to time, when she was not
earning adequately to pay her rent. She spent some time with Jane Strachey
in the 1920s, when Pippa needed a break. During the Second World War,
she moved to Hazelmere and lived there with her oldest sister, Elinor
Rendel, and her cousin, Ellie.

Although Marjorie had some friends, her social and emotional life
outside the family remains also a bit of a mystery. She seems not to have
had anything resembling the large circle of other single women with whom
Pernel spent her time. She loved parties and continued to give them
throughout the 1920s—happily spending her small savings on them.

'Marjorie is giving another party on Friday week', wrote James Strachey to his wife Alix, in 1924. It was on a much smaller scale than the last one: '(a mere 30 guests) & at Oliver's this time. In spite of her woe-tasting proclivities she says she finds she's now got savings to the amount of £50 in hand & I suppose is going to blow them.'[36] But James was appalled at the guest-list. It contains 'an incredible miscellaneous riff-raff of Marjorie's "friends" ', he told Alix, 'my cousin Allis Grant . . . Nannie Niemeyer, 2 sons of Augustus John, Ellie (Rendel), Mr McFarlane . . . etc., all intermingled with select Bloomsbury. The woman is crazed.'[37] James may have been a little jaundiced: Virginia Woolf, who was at this party, recorded it in her diary as one 'which being undress and very easy going gave me a great deal of pleasure'.[38] Nonetheless, while Marjorie saw something of her family, especially the Rendels, and dined sometimes with the Woolfs and others in Bloomsbury, one has a sense of her as being very isolated. There are no discussions or descriptions of close friends or regular companions—and several comments about her being alone. Unlike the others, she also travelled alone. In March 1929, Ray Strachey wrote to tell her mother that Marjorie was setting off to Jerusalem, via Athens and Constantinople. 'She would be exceedingly grateful for any introductions in Baghdad (she has plenty for Jerusalem, where she has been before) & would much like to know your movements in case her own cross them at any point & you could exchange handshakes. She is going by herself, is busy learning Arabic in Preparation! Rather her than me!'[39] Other family papers make it clear that Marjorie had hoped that Pernel would accompany her, but that when this plan fell through she was forced either to relinquish her travel plans or to go alone. In her final years, Marjorie drew closer to the family. She kept in contact with cousins and nieces and nephews, and finally returned to live with Pippa in Gordon Square.

IV

While the single Strachey daughters serve to demonstrate, rather than challenge, the range of accepted models for single women in the early twentieth century, Lytton Strachey lived an entirely different single life. He was deeply critical of the formality, the silences, and the lack of any kind of personal intimacy that was evident in many Victorian middle and upper middle class homes, including of course his own. Indeed, as we will see, through his intimacy with Vanessa and Clive Bell, he played a significant role in setting up very different kinds of relationships between married couples and their friends whereby friends were admitted even into the marital bedroom.

As one determined to articulate his own homosexual desires and interests and to attempt to push the boundaries of propriety, Lytton Strachey's life obviously incorporated sexual expression and activity in ways almost unthinkable to his sisters. For him, being single was the condition that permitted free homosexual relations rather than containing any suggestion of celibacy. Hence his single life was one that involved a succession of sexual relationships. None of these was successful and, as several historians have noted, there was far more sexual anguish than sexual pleasure in his life.[40] Perhaps the more markedly different aspect of his life was that some of it involved sharing a house with a woman to whom he was not married—and hence setting up a domestic arrangement almost unthinkable to his Victorian forebears. His mother refused ever to mention the fact that he lived with Dora Carrington.

As with so much else in his life, Lytton's concerns about where and how he should live became a matter of great importance to his friends. Lytton's charm, including both the wit, sharpness of intellect, breadth of knowledge, and incomparable conversational skills, on the one hand, and his emotional vulnerability and capacity for deep unhappiness on the other, combined to ensure that his state of well-being was always of great moment to his large circle of friends. Many of them shared his desire for a new form of domestic life that would encompass a kind of intimacy that included a closeness to friends and the sharing of daily and intimate concerns and experiences in a way utterly foreign to the upper middle-class Victorian and Edwardian families from which they came. Hence while the question of where and how the Strachey daughters should live was a matter of concern only to themselves and their family, when it came to Lytton, all of Bloomsbury was involved.

For all his ostensible desire to avoid it, Lytton Strachey was often to be found back in the family home. Michael Holroyd has depicted vividly his unhappiness in this female-dominated world from which he had to hide his emotional life and sexual interests, and which offered him little that was pleasurable in terms either of aesthetic surroundings or companionship. 'I'm feeling pretty wild here' he wrote to James, shortly after moving back into Lancaster Gate in 1904. 'If one were sarcastic what an account one could give of one's dinner table!'[41] Everything about family life appalled him. The lack of aesthetic taste or domestic comfort, the presence of a vast range of eccentric relatives, the peculiar habits of his parents. The Strachey home at Lancaster Gate was widely recognized as appallingly ugly and uncomfortable. But life at home did not improve for Lytton when they left it in 1908 and moved to Belsize Park. As his letters make clear, one of the hardest things for Lytton about living at home was the presence of his mother. During the earlier days (with only Pippa and Marjorie in the house), he wrote to James when he had just gone back to Belsize Park Gardens in 1912, 'I simply couldn't make out what the objections were to living there always. Then on Monday her ladyship landed, and—whisk!— the bands of the body were breaking, and all came in sight.'[42] Jane Strachey's presence in these years was difficult for Lytton for many reasons. He found his mother's incessant chatter and love of jokes tedious, her political and social ideas completely out of tune with his own, and her relationships with the other women in the family often boisterous in the extreme. 'I've just had to beat a retreat from the after-dinner drawing room', Lytton wrote to James one evening. 'Marjorie in full swing with Ellie and mama. Affectation effreey [sic]. It's really filthy. I've practically decided to leave.'[43]

Lytton Strachey was extraordinarily passive and helpless when faced with this situation, however, and it is hard not to see his inertia, even paralysis, when it came to planning to leave home, as stemming in part from his intense emotional ties both to his family and to his home. However irritating his mother was, and despite her complete inability to understand anything about his sexuality or his emotional life, he remained devoted to her. He continued to share his love of literature more with her than anyone else. His sisters were important too. He might have he found Marjorie hard to bear, but he was heavily dependent on Pippa. She was one of the great consolations in his life after Cambridge. 'My chief horror', he wrote to Leonard Woolf in 1906, 'is that there is no one to talk to. What I find so shocking with everybody now, except Pippa and Duncan, is that they simply don't attempt to bring themselves into one's state of mind.'[44] In the years preceding the First World War, Lytton spent much time with Pippa and she was part of both his domestic and his social life. She accompanied him to many Bloomsbury evenings as well as hosting enter-tainments with him in the Strachey home. Lytton sometimes commented that Pippa was 'unconscious' and marvelled at the way she could have lengthy conversations with Duncan Grant or Maynard Keynes without any apparent realization of the way that they, like Lytton, were engrossed in a homosexual world. He regarded her as 'reactionary' and felt that, having not been to university herself, she lacked the intellectual framework which he and his friends took for granted. Nonetheless, he continued not only to depend and to rely on her, but to find her company and her practical skills and knowledge absolutely invaluable.

For many years, Lytton's life was dominated by a sense of the need to leave home. A few schemes were suggested: the possibility of sharing a place with Leonard Woolf when he returned from Ceylon, or more immediately of sharing one with his younger brother, James. But nothing came of them. Money was a constant problem. Lytton resented his financial dependence, especially after he gave up his regular contributions to the *Spectator* in 1909. He sometimes felt that he ought not to accept his annual £50 allowance, especially with the decline in family income that followed his father's retirement in 1907. But, as he wrote to Leonard Woolf, 'I think equally its my duty to write plays if I possibly can, in the hope that I'll eventually have enough to live on.'[45] However it was clearly not just lack of money that kept him at home. When he finally did leave home in 1917, he was still dependent on his familial allowance and was able to move into a new home only because he was supported by a group of family and friends. What seems to have prevented him moving out earlier was rather lack of will and organizing ability, on the one hand, and dependence on the care and comfort that his family provided on the other. Lytton's health was never robust and whether or not some of his illnesses were psychosomatic, they were nonetheless debilitating and made him heavily dependent on female care. It was thus only when an alternative to the care he received from his family was offered by Dora Carrington that he was able to leave home.

Lytton met Dora Carrington, a young art student, when they were both visiting Vanessa Bell in 1915. Their strange intense affection for each other, which intrigued their friends, as it has their biographers, developed almost immediately, and they soon agreed that Carrington should find them a house to share. Although he had done nothing towards it himself, Lytton admonished Carrington for her dilatoriness. Finally, in 1917, she found the 'romantic and lovely' Mill House in Tidmarsh. Payment for the lease of the house was provided by a small Bloomsbury consortium consisting of

Oliver and Lytton Strachey, Harry Norton, Saxon Sydney-Turner, and Maynard Keynes. They regarded it not only as a home for Lytton, but also as a potential rural retreat for themselves. By December 1917, Carrington had succeeded in making the house comfortable and she and Lytton moved in. Their early years there, Michael Holroyd argues, were the happiest of their lives.[46]

In moving into a house with Carrington, Lytton Strachey was simultaneously maintaining a customary and very traditional way of life—and embarking on a radically new one. The idea of an unmarried man and woman sharing a house was an extremely novel one that shocked conventional opinion. At the same time, of course, Lytton was replicating in his house with Carrington the kind of domestic care he was accustomed to at home. He was well aware of his dependence and would not, as he confessed to Clive Bell, have been able to face living in a country cottage alone. But 'female companionship I think may make it tolerable'.[47] Carrington, as both Michael Holroyd and Gretchen Gerzina have shown, worked hard to make the house and Lytton's life as comfortable as possible. She too combined a traditional female role with a very new one, supervising all housekeeping responsibilities, devoting herself to finding ways to ensuring and improving Lytton's health and comfort, making the house an immensely inviting one for visitors. She created an exciting modern decor and a garden that made their home visually pleasing, and she ensured that their home was sufficiently welcoming and informal to allow the new kinds of relationships and the new forms of sociability so beloved of Bloomsbury. In one of her rather acid comments on Lytton Strachey, Virginia Woolf commented on his caution and conservatism and lack of initiative and vitality. The Stracheys, she argued, had never added significantly to 'the common stock of our set . . . Even in the matter of taking Tidmarsh, Lytton had to be propelled from behind, & his way of life in so far as it is unconventional, is so by the desire and determination of Carrington.'[48] After five or six years, the beauty of the Mill House could no longer make up for the inconvenience of its small rooms, or constant damp and in 1923, a lease was taken on the larger and more comfortable Ham Spray. Lytton was by then a successful author and able to manage the rent on the new house which remained his base until his death in 1932.

While Lytton Strachey sought a new openness in relation to sexuality, this was often evident more in conversation and in his taste in art and literature than it was in his relationships. Although the emphasis on the 'higher sodomy' that had been so prevalent in Cambridge days was giving way to a new interest in buggery and other forms of sexual intercourse amongst and some of Lytton's friends, questions about the nature of love and anxieties about physical intimacy remained. They were clearly evident in Lytton's first, and most devastating passion, that for his younger cousin, Duncan Grant, which dominated his life throughout the first decade of the twentieth century, and from which he never quite recovered. Duncan Grant had more or less taken up residence in the Strachey house in Lancaster Gate in 1902. Lytton, however, was mainly at Cambridge then and only really came to know and to become attracted to him in 1905. Duncan came from a world very different from Lytton and his lack of interest in Lytton's intellectual pursuits, on the one hand, combined with his intelligence, charm, his beauty, and talent gave Lytton a sense of the possibilities of a quite different kind of relationship from those he had thought about in Cambridge. 'I've managed since I saw you last to catch a glimpse of Heaven', he wrote to Keynes after he had fallen in love with Duncan. This relationship was always difficult and uneasy, however. Grant did not reciprocate Strachey's passion, and though often fond of him, and sometimes prepared to show some physical affection, could never pretend to feel anything like the devotion expressed by Lytton. Duncan was based in Paris where he was studying art for much of this time and his meetings with Lytton were irregular and often difficult. Their relationship was never a satisfactory one and was punctuated by constant pain for Lytton as Duncan engaged in sexual relationships with other young men. Although it had almost petered out by 1907, Lytton was devastated when in the course of the following year Duncan fell in love with Maynard Keynes. The relationship between Keynes and Grant lasted little over a year, but its impact was felt by Lytton throughout the rest of his life. It brought to an end his close friendship with Keynes as well as separating him permanently from any intimacy with Grant.

The unsatisfactory pattern evident in Lytton's relationship with Duncan Grant continued in his later life. He had several other sexual relationships, none of which had quite the intensity or desperation of this first love, although all were complicated and painful. Michael Holroyd has detailed Strachey's two other important relationships: that with Henry Lamb, just before the war, and the much more distressing one with Roger Senhouse in the 1920s. In between, there were many other flirtations and mild flings. In addition, he was for many years deeply in love with Ralph Partridge, who in turn was in love with Dora Carrington. Lytton seemed quite prepared to have Partridge as part of his life without any kind of physical relationship.[49] Although much is always made of Carrington's devotion to a man who was never inclined to have a sexual relationship with her, it is also evident that Strachey shared with her a capacity for relationships in which intense desire did not require sexual fulfilment. Although Lytton's relationships were always painful and unfulfilled, they were deeply engrossing—rather too much so for his friends: Virginia Woolf commented acidly on Lytton's 'harem' which consisted of Carrington and several young men in the early 1920s, resenting the ways in which, whenever he had a new love, he seemed unavailable to his old friends.[50]

Sibling Ties

Sibling ties were of central importance to the Stracheys, as they were to all large Victorian and Edwardian families. Both Jane Grant and Richard Strachey came from large families and were extremely close to some of their siblings and the same thing was true of their own ten children. Jane made a point of encouraging the development of close ties amongst her children from their earliest years. She was particularly keen to establish brother and sister pairs amongst those children who were close in age, organizing shared holidays for these pairs, and expecting the girls always to take particular care of brothers who were sent away to school. These childhood relationships changed form in late adolescent and adult life as some early companions drifted apart while different pairs were formed. In some cases, the brother–sister pairs were replaced by same-sex ones. Thus while Dick and Elinor, Pippa and Ralph, and Oliver and Pernel formed pairs in childhood, in adult life some of the closer ties were those between Elinor and Dorothy, Pippa and Pernel, and Ralph and Oliver. These relationships changed again during the Stracheys' final years, as siblings clung to each other in old age and in death. Pippa, Pernel, Oliver, and James were all present at Lytton's deathbed, for example, and it was they rather than the companions of later years whose company he wanted. Moreover, many of the Stracheys spent their final years back in the family home: Pernel moved there when she retired from Newnham in the 1940s, and Dorothy, Oliver, and Marjorie also returned to Gordon Square towards the end of their lives.

There was more to the sibling ties of the Stracheys than merely the question of close companionship amongst some and greater distance between others. All of these individual relationships occurred within a general familial framework that included both a general sense of connection and a range of shared values, beliefs, and assumptions. These changed noticeably over time and the bond that bound the younger Stracheys in the twentieth century was very different from that which had been important to the Victorian Stracheys and the Grants. The strong commitment to Britain's imperial project and the sense of having a special place within it, combined with a particular knowledge of India and of the nature and some of the hardships of imperial life, was a constant theme of the letters between the older Stracheys and the Grants and served to bind them all together. This was certainly not the case in the next generation. On the contrary, while the Indian experience of Dick, Ralph, and Oliver gave them a sense of kinship with each other, it served to separate them absolutely from their siblings, all of whom were engrossed in other interests and activities. Even those, like Elinor, Dorothy, and Pippa, who were interested in the family's Indian history and experience, regarded it as a kind of background, and rarely carried it, in the way their mother had done, into their other political or literary activities.

Some at least of the younger Stracheys felt a significant bond with all their siblings. To some extent this centred on shared familial character-istics. Their similarity of physical appearance was important here, and many people commented on the long spindly bodies, the small features, the short-sighted eyes encased in glasses, and the well-known high-pitched voice with its shrill laughter. The Strachey voice seems to have originated only in the 1890s and as it was a feature of many of the younger Stracheys, but was never referred to in relation to their parents. There were also mental characteristics and shared interests. Foremost amongst these was the love of discussion, debate, and voluble argument that occurred when-ever the younger Stracheys were assembled. There were also a number of very distinctive Strachey verbal mannerisms and speech patterns, most notable of which was their use of a highly exaggerated language. Strachey conversations, like their letters are filled with references to 'portentous' events and places, on the one hand, and to 'horrors', and 'fatalities', on the other. They described themselves as 'enraged', when they had been slightly inconvenienced; the people that they meet are more often than not 'weird', 'lunatic'—or at the very least 'wretched creatures'. Ruin and the end of the world are everywhere.[1] To this colourful approach to things in general were added a few special terms, the best known of which was 'filth packets', a term that encompassed family customs and traditions including both physical objects and forms of behaviour. The Strachey language and capacity for telling amusing stories underlay their frequent enjoyment of each other's company and also helped make many family occasions entertaining.

Although Lytton Strachey always depicted his family life as rather dour and gloomy, others saw it in a very different light. Duncan Grant, who lived with the Stracheys for some time in 1902 at Lancaster Gate, found them fascinating and insisted that their family life was characterized by high spirits and enjoyment. Like Leonard Woolf, he was aware of Sir Richard Strachey as a silent presence, 'a symbol of all that was good and wise and dignified and beautiful', sitting patiently beside his wife at one end of the drawing room in the evening, while at the other end of the room, around the piano, there was 'a noisy hurly burly'.

James, Marjorie and I, with Pippa playing the accompaniment, shouted songs from 'patience', 'HMS Pinafore', or the latest Gaiety Comic Opera. Dorothy in those days was dressed very smartly and might come in late from a fashionable dinner party . . . Pippa was perhaps my favourite in the family, always it seemed ready to talk to me of fascinating subjects. Then there was often Pernel, quiet, observant and witty, and Marjorie, high spirited and often shocking, with outrageous views.[2]

In Grant's view, this vitality was greatly reduced when the Stracheys moved to Belsize Park Gardens in 1907. However, Ray Strachey, who met them after this, was entranced by the Stracheys and continued for years to think that there was nothing more amusing than a Strachey family party. Others expressed a similar view. 'It is astonishing how much more amusing I find my own family than other people's', wrote Dorothy Strachey in 1946—and her comment would have been echoed by almost all her siblings.[3]

While the younger Stracheys might have found each other amusing, this was a light overlay underneath which lay their lifelong need to negotiate and deal with each other in order for each individual to establish a place for themselves within the family. Some of the recent theoretical work of sociologists and psychologists is quite helpful here in suggesting possible links between personality and position in the family. Frank Sulloway's concept of the 'sibling niche' to describe the particular space within its family that a child might find and develop as its own is particularly useful.[4] Drawing on the discussions on birth order and their relation to personality pioneered by Alfred Adler, Sulloway suggests that older children are likely to claim priority within a family, to see and identify themselves in relation to parents, and then to demand recognition by late comers of their own pre-eminence and expertise.[5] Faced with this situation, younger children are more likely to seek out new interests and to 'diversify' as a way of claiming parental interest and involvement. Each child thus seeks a particular niche in which they will be unique, and from which they can make a claim for familial recognition.[6] This idea of differentiation in order to establish a 'niche' provides a useful framework for analysing the apparent ease with which some of the younger Stracheys established a particular place for themselves, in contrast to the immense difficulty evident in others, some of whom found it almost impossible. Elinor, Dorothy, Pernel, Pippa, Oliver, Lytton, and James, one might argue, all managed to differentiate themselves from each other using their particular characteristics to find a special niche. By contrast, Marjorie, like Dick and Ralph, conspicuously failed to do so and they were always somewhat awkwardly placed within the family.

Some of the younger Stracheys were of course interested in psycho-analysis, and it too is helpful in thinking about their sibling ties, although sometimes in rather indirect ways. Freud, as many later commentators have noted, paid relatively little attention to siblings. He mentioned them frequently, as Juliet Mitchell has recently shown, but rarely offered any theoretical comments.[7] They appear in his work mainly as the vehicles through which children come to recognize the genital differences between boys and girls: it was primarily through seeing her brother's penis that a girl came to understand what she lacked. But siblings seem hardly to affect the fundamental relationships between parents and children either in his theoretical framework or in his case studies. Nonetheless, his insistence on infantile sexuality and on the sexual underpinnings of the family romance could be easily adapted to sibling ties, and especially at a time when the question of incest was being discussed amongst social investiga-tors exploring working-class homes.[8]

The advent of psychoanalysis also seems to help explain the changing nature of sibling ties and the changing ways in which sibling relationships were understood amongst the generation of Richard and Jane Strachey, on the one hand, and that of their children, particularly their younger chil-dren, on the other. What seems most important in looking at the Stracheys is not so much that psychoanalysis offered specific insight into sibling feelings and relationships, but rather that it had brought a new way of thinking about family ties which allowed for the possibility of infantile sexual feelings, incestuous overtones, and profound ambivalence towards parents and siblings. For the older Stracheys, all sibling relationships took their place within a broader social and familial context. For the younger Stracheys, by contrast, while the family name still mattered, there was little sense of connection to the wider family, and relatively little contact between some of the older and younger siblings. On the other hand, there was an increasing recognition of the complexity of the relationships amongst those who did remain close to each other. Even before the 1920s, the existence of sexual undertones and emotional conflict in sibling relationships was becoming recognized. Thus, unlike their parents, the younger Stracheys were often aware of the ways in which sexual jealousy, desire, and disappointment featured in their feelings for each other, and of the intensity and the conflict which was often integral to their closest sibling ties.

❧ I ☙

It was not only particular siblings, but also their entire family of origin that was important to both Richard and Jane Strachey. Richard kept in close contact with all his brothers and his sister, visiting the family seat frequently and hosting family dinners and weekends. In a similar way, Jane Strachey maintained contact with all of her siblings. They regularly attended the Strachey Sunday afternoon 'at homes' and were often united during regular summer holiday visits to the Doune House, Aviemore. Richard and Jane also undertook a supervisory role in regard to Jane's younger brothers who spent some time living in their home. Jane's niche within her own family was that of the most competent and organized daughter, and even in adult life she often assumed responsibility for the others. Her intervention to ensure that her nephew, Duncan Grant, was sent to art school rather than into the army was replicated as she intervened to organize the schooling or activities of other nephews and nieces.[9]

The broad pattern of sibling ties amongst the older Stracheys was both fundamental to and enhanced by their imperial interests and by the time they spent together. Their shared interest and involvement in the Raj was a constant topic of Strachey and Grant conversation and it served also to increase their involvement in each other's lives as they took responsibility for each other's children or provided mutual support in the constant movement from England to India that was part of imperial life. Here, too, we have seen the ways in which particular ties were fostered between

Richard and John Strachey, on the one hand, and Jane Strachey and Elinor Colevile on the other. Richard took more pride in figuring alongside John as one of 'the Strachey brothers', who together dominated Indian policy in the later nineteenth century, than he did in any separate or individual achievement. In 1877, for example, when Richard had gone out to India to oversee the purchase of the East India Railway, and remained to work on the Famine Commission, he wrote to his wife about the work he had been doing with his brother. Richard had been writing a plan for railways, while John was working on a restructure of imperial finances which incorporated their shared belief in free trade. 'We have got rid of the sugar duties', he wrote,

and struck out nearly half the items of the Imperial Tariff—taken duty off coarser sorts of cotton manufacture and laid the train for the total extinction of input customs duties.

On the whole we shall not leave Calcutta without having done a very good stroke of work. How good very few people will really appreciate . . . The Indian newspapers will howl at all we have done I don't doubt but this is of no moment. We shall be safe in London and Manchester—& what has been done cannot be undone till a much stronger man comes than there is any sign of at present who shall dare to take the other side with a view to upsetting the Strachey brothers.[10]

The views of Richard and John Strachey on most imperial questions were identical, their work was complementary, and they could even take over each other's administrative roles when necessary.

The relationship between 'the Strachey brothers' was in some ways an unusual one. John was the younger brother and, for much of the time, the more successful. He was appointed Collector of Oude in the 1850s, and was a senior Indian administrator when Richard was still struggling for recognition. John Strachey often advised Richard on how to conduct his life. But Richard seems never to have felt any jealousy or resentment. On the contrary, he devoted himself to supporting and defending his brother whenever necessary. Not only did he replace him in India when John needed to return home in the late 1870s, but when John was criticized for financial incompetence over errors in the budget and costing of the Afghan Wars undertaken by Lord Lytton while he was Lytton's financial adviser, Richard spent months writing in his defence.[11]

One has a sense that this was the one sibling relationship amongst the older Stracheys that had the potential to threaten marital ties. Jane Strachey, while accepting the importance of her husband's siblings, certainly felt that her husband was excessive in his devotion and preparedness to sacrifice not only himself, but also his immediate family, to his brother. She was particularly unhappy in the late 1870s when her family arrangements had to be completely altered to suit John. Richard, who had initially gone to India for only a few months, decided to remain there, for some years if necessary, to enable his brother to retain his position on the Governor-General's Council while he returned to England for an eye operation. John's financial comfort depended on his retaining this position until he was eligible for a pension. Richard was prepared to do anything needful to further his brother's interests, even though, as his wife complained, this involved breaking up their family yet again and incurring considerable financial hardship. 'I am sorry you are not pleased with the turn things have at last taken in respect to me', he wrote in response to Jane's letter complaining of the hardship that his decision to support his brother had imposed on her and their family.

But though there is much truth in what you say I don't see that I could decently have done otherwise than I have actually done in present circumstances—I quite admit that the whole thing is a great nuisance & that we should have been much happier at home. But the position is a peculiar one, & as you know I have ideas of duty which cannot be smothered.[12]

Ultimately Jane was aware that she had little choice but to accept this arrangement. Moreover, she knew her husband's sense of duty also extended to her and her siblings, for some of whom he took considerable pains. And of course when Jane went to join her husband in India, it was her own sister, Elinor Colevile, who eased her path, providing a home for all the young Stracheys and keeping an eye also on the older ones who were at school.

Richard Strachey's death in 1908 signalled the end of one particular phase of family life. By this time, several of his brothers and some of Jane's too had died and the Victorian world of the Stracheys had come to an end. The change in the nature of family life was symbolized by their move from the large house at Lancaster Gate, with its vast drawing room, made to contain the whole extended family, to the much smaller one, with a modest drawing room, in Belsize Park Gardens.[13]

II

All the Stracheys of the next generation took great pride in their name and shared characteristics, and had a pronounced sense of family. Many of them also maintained close ties with some of their siblings. But they had little if any of their parents' sense of these ties as fitting within a broader family network. Lytton, James, Marjorie, and Pernel had almost no contact with their two older brothers. Indeed, Lytton and James regarded them as belonging almost to a different species. Marjorie remained on very close terms with their oldest sister, Elinor, but in their adult years Lytton and James had little to do with her either. For the younger Stracheys, there were occasional gatherings and dinners, and some members of the family met at country weekend parties or on holidays, but these meetings were much less frequent than had been the case in the nineteenth century and there were always conspicuous absences.

Their sense of family and their imperial interests might have enhanced the sibling relationships of the older Stracheys, but they served rather to divide the next generation. Being in India together established a bond between Dick, Ralph, and Oliver, but even this was limited. Ralph and Oliver supported each other through marital difficulties in India, and Dick stayed with Oliver when he was first in London after his return from India—and helped him to get his job in intelligence during the First World War. But there was only infrequent contact after this and there is no sense that it enabled them to provide any significant support and companionship for each other. Oliver spent far more time with Lytton than he did with Ralph, and Ralph in turn found his greatest supports amongst Pippa and Ray when he came home. Dick remained isolated from them all.

It was University that set the framework for the adult lives of the younger Stracheys, Pernel, Lytton, Marjorie, and James, and India was in many ways alien to them all. Their educational experience, moreover, was so different from the military and engineering colleges where Dick and Ralph were educated, or the world of British India in which they worked, as to make any form of conversation difficult. Dick and Ralph seem to have had no contact with Pernel and Marjorie and to have figured in the lives of Lytton and James as the embodiment of the conservative Victorian imperial world they sought so strongly to reject, rather than as significant individuals. Oliver was the one brother who sought to cross this chasm, and to maintain close ties with his younger brothers both while he was in India and when he returned. But this was a difficult task. Oliver spent more than a decade working in India between the late 1890s and 1911, interspersed with several trips home. He wrote frequently to Lytton and tried hard to enter into his younger brother's world, reading the books he liked, and even entering into a correspondence with G. E. Moore. Oliver was a talented musician and was also clever, with a great interest in both philosophy and sex, but his ideas never meshed with those of Lytton and James. 'You may imagine the very painful time I've been having with him', James wrote to Lytton in 1911 when Oliver was staying in the family home in Belsize Park Gardens.

The conclusion I've come to is that the man *won't do*. He hasn't got his values right . . . of course he's so frightfully out of date just now. It'll need *you* to make him believe in modern life. He's plunged into life, indeed, of a sort—but unerringly he's chosen the Bloomsbury backwater . . . My dear, he's a regular bore with his metaphysics and music. I don't believe he understands either.[14]

James's response was very precious, but he had had a difficult time with this brother, who disliked Lytton's unpublished erotic poems, commented tactlessly on the portrait of Rupert Brooke in James's room, and turned the family library, which was James's refuge, into his 'smoking room'. At the same time, Oliver's extensive sexual interests and experience were quite helpful to James. Oliver had over several years written to Lytton about sexual matters, but as his interests were entirely heterosexual Lytton rarely even bothered to reply. For James, who was just beginning to contemplate heterosexual relations, Oliver's frankness was a godsend and he was grateful for the sex education, particularly in relation to contraception, Oliver provided. Nonetheless, Oliver's masculine bonhomie was deeply alien to James. Lytton was sympathetic, but pointed out that, once home from India, Oliver changed as he 'moved into date'.[15] James was not convinced. 'Such a clever man, but so *limited*', he commented to Lytton after an evening spent with Oliver in the following year, and Lytton clearly agreed.[16] Nonetheless, Oliver persevered. He was one of the group who contributed the money that enabled Lytton to set up his home with Carrington at Mill House in 1917. Having done so, however, Oliver claimed his entitlement to visit whenever he wanted. As Carrington acidly remarked, he was less assiduous when it came to paying his share of domestic expenses. Moreover, he brought a sequence of female companions she didn't like—and never offered any help in the garden.

Although they too had had different experiences and early lives, there was less division amongst the sisters. University itself was less divisive for the women and did not destroy sibling bonds. Elinor, although she never went to university, sent her daughters there and took a close interest in it.

Dorothy, after all, had coached Pernel to enable her to go to Newnham, and they saw each other often afterwards, and Pippa and Pernel retained extremely close ties, despite the fact that Pippa had never attended the institution to which her sister devoted her life.

Sibling ties were generally more important to the Strachey sisters than to their brothers and, in so far as anyone attempted to hold all the Stracheys together in the twentieth century, it was the three oldest sisters: Elinor, Dorothy, and Pippa. Elinor, who belonged very much to the mid-Victorian world of her mother, took very seriously her position as oldest sister. Her values and lifestyle were very different from those of her younger siblings, but she maintained what contact she could with them. She shared some of the interests of her younger sisters, participating in the feminist demonstrations organized by Pippa. She even offered support to Lytton, attending the tribunal when he appeared before it as a conscientious objector, as well as providing financial support to Dick. Lytton and James may have regarded her as something of a dinosaur, but even they sometimes joined their siblings around her table when she invited them all to lunch.

Elinor's closest adult bond was with Dorothy, and here too there was something reminiscent of the older Stracheys in the ways that their relationship encompassed their entire families. Dorothy spent several weeks each year in Elinor's country home, usually accompanied by Simon and Janie, while Elinor's sons in turn went to stay with the Bussys so that Dorothy could teach them French.[17] Elinor also remained close to Marjorie, although the fact that Marjorie confided in Elinor about her personal life, including her relationship with Josiah Wedgwood, seemed extraordinary to Lytton and James.[18] Her home was often a refuge for Marjorie in adult life as it had been in childhood.

Dorothy maintained ties with many of her siblings. She was particularly close to Elinor, Pippa, and also to Ray, but she was in frequent touch with the others. Her home played a crucial role in this. There is no record of Dick or Ralph doing so, but all the other Stracheys visited the idyllic Bussy home at Roquebrune many times, in search of health or for recreation. Dorothy also took in many of their Bloomsbury friends, often as paying guests. Her home and her home-making capacity clearly contributed to her particular niche within the family and their world, but this was augmented by her involvement in the world of modern French art and culture. Her passionate interest in literature, her knowledge of contemporary French developments, and her deeply painful and complicated emotional life gave her a greater sympathy with the intellectual projects and the personal relationships of her younger siblings than was possible for the others close to her in age. Her easy acceptance of homosexuality was important too and Lytton, who carefully kept his sexual life hidden from Pippa, was very relaxed in discussing it with Dorothy. He didn't divulge the details that are in his letters to James, but he certainly let her know about his feelings for Duncan Grant, and about the general tenor of sexual his life.[19]

It was Pippa Strachey who maintained the closest ties with all her siblings, and for whom sibling ties were most important. Her niche was that of the centre of the family, caring for parents, nursing ailing siblings, keeping in touch with everyone—and attempting always to make life as pleasant and as comfortable as it could be both for herself and for others. It was she who corresponded most frequently with Dick, informing all the others, including her mother, about Dick's life and activities. She remained immensely close to Ralph, helping him through all his familial difficulties. In addition, she was in constant contact with Dorothy, Pernel, Lytton, and James. Pippa did not have very much specific contact with Oliver, but her closeness to Ray would have made his life and activities well known to her as well. Marjorie was the one who seemed to have least of a relationship with Pippa. They almost never wrote to each other when absent, although they did spend time together in the family home.

Pippa was extremely important in the lives of her siblings too. Part of this derived from her close relationship with her mother. As Jane Strachey aged and became both more conservative and more difficult, it was Pippa who was called on to negotiate with her to obtain either the money that her siblings needed, or to gain acceptance of their activities. It was she who broke the news to Jane of Oliver's planned marriage to Ray Costello, a marriage that was not altogether welcome after the trauma of his divorce.[20] In a similar way, when James was suffering from severe depression in 1913 and wanted his mother to finance a trip to Vienna for him, it was Pippa whom he consulted and whom he asked to break the news to his mother.[21] Pippa was more than merely a channel to her mother, however, as almost all her siblings relied on her completely whenever they were in difficulties. Lytton sought her help whenever he was ill, James regarded her as the most dependable and companionable of his siblings besides Lytton, Pernel saw her as providing the companionship she would need when she retired from Newnham. Although Pippa was considerably older than Lytton and his friends, and very different in outlook and demeanour, she was usually welcome amongst her younger siblings and their friends. She was a frequent guest in the homes Lytton shared with Carrington—and never subject to the critical comments made of Oliver. 'I hope Pippa will come down on Saturday', Carrington wrote to Lytton in 1920. 'God preserve us from Oliver and Inez.'[22] A month later, when she had been staying in the Strachey household in Gordon Square, Carrington waxed lyrical over Pippa. 'I love your sister Pippa so much,' she wrote to Lytton. 'That's what I call a triumph. To be such a perfect character and radiate happiness after forty.'[23]

It is noticeable that those Strachey sisters who held the siblings together did so very much by playing a conventional and somewhat Victorian sisterly role. They kept house and acted as hostesses, nursed the brothers who were sick, and generally offered companionship and support. The expectations placed on sisters without any obvious reciprocity also caused some strain in the face of changing opportunities and expectations for women in the early twentieth century. Like other Victorian feminist families, the Stracheys supported the idea of education for their daughters and believed in women's rights, but never questioned the differences in the customary behaviour of men and women. In the next generation, however, as some of the Strachey women struck out on different paths from their mother, their expectations of their brothers changed—and there was more than a little distress when the brothers themselves refused to recognize their claims.

Lytton was the focus of most of the tension over changing expectations for women. Unlike James, who made few demands upon his sisters, Lytton constantly sought their help and support in his work and his domestic life, and especially when he was ill. He saw himself very much as a 'modern' man in terms of his sexuality and his way of life, but this did not transform his ideas about his sisters. The conservatism of Lytton Strachey's social and political values has been commented on before, most particularly in terms of his relationships with and ideas about women.[24] In regard to his sisters, these values and attitudes made him exploitative and sometimes cruel. Lytton was often financially generous to his sisters: he paid Marjorie a small allowance in the 1920s, and sent Dorothy a quite substantial cheque in 1931 when he received some unexpected royalties at a time when she was in severe financial straits.[25] This generosity, however, was not matched either by recognition of his sisters' needs and independent interest, or by any recognition of or help with their work. Lytton noted and chronicled the suffrage work of his sisters, but, unlike Oliver and James, rarely took any part in it. He and James found it much harder to accept that their commitment to women's suffrage involved other political ideas as well. They regarded it as an affront to themselves and as an additional hardship to find that Pippa supported the war effort and thus would not sympathize with or make much of their stance as conscientious objectors. They still demanded strategic advice from her about what they should do—and of course they received it. At the same time, as we will see, Pippa did extract a price from Lytton for all her hard work and support.

It is in regard to Dorothy Bussy, however, that one sees more clearly Lytton's extreme selfishness to his sisters, and his refusal to reciprocate their support. When the Bussys were first living in France, Dorothy wrote several articles on French literature and sought Lytton's help in getting them published. The articles no longer exist and one has no idea of their quality. Nonetheless, Dorothy's translations and her novella, *Olivia*, indicate some literary capacity. But Lytton seems to have done little. The thing she found really galling, however, was his refusal to write a preface for or even to read her English translation of André Gide's novel, *La Porte Etroite*. Shortly after meeting Gide in 1919, Dorothy had translated this novel of her own accord and without telling Gide. He was pleased with the translation when she showed it to him, but she was very nervous about it and wanted Lytton's views on both its accuracy and literary merit. Lytton refused even to look at it. Instead of offering help, she told Gide, he was horrid. 'Having lately read the French, he can't bring himself to read it again in English. I had really believed he would be more friendly and am hurt as well as disappointed. But Lytton doesn't easily face being bored.'[26] Lytton had earlier asked Dorothy to write to Gide about the prospects of selling a French translation of his own work, so her disappointment seems reasonable enough. Moreover he expected her to oversee the French translation of both *Eminent Victorians* and *Queen Victoria*, to correct them, and to ensure that they had not lost their distinctive literary qualities—although he would not lift a finger to help her become their translator.[27]

III

The relationships of Pippa Strachey with her siblings illustrate both the continuities across the generations and also some of the changes. In her concern to hold the family together and to assist and support her siblings, Pippa harks back to her mother and to Victorian ideas and values. At the same time, she was sometimes prepared to articulate the pain, the hurt, and the conflict that underlay sibling ties in ways which point to a far more modern sense of family connections. I do not want to suggest that jealousy and hurt were not felt in earlier sibling relationships, but rather that they were not spoken about—or were encompassed in a language of duty and appropriate behaviour. In the twentieth century, the undertones of sibling ties amongst the Stracheys came to be recognized and discussed in ways that had been unthinkable for the previous generation. Pippa is the most interesting figure here, perhaps because, as the sister who did not marry and who remained at home, so much of her own emotional life was focused on her siblings. This is not to say that Pippa had no other close ties: as we have seen, she was deeply attached to Roger Fry and it is sometimes in her very frank and uninhibited letters to Fry, rather than in the letters to her siblings, that her anger and her desires in regard to her family were expressed.

It is scarcely surprising that some of Pippa's darker feelings were directed towards Ralph and his family. She never commented on this relationship, or on the way in which her closeness to Ralph was altered by his marriage. Ralph himself seems to have had no insight into his own feelings, or into hers, nor was he able to see that there might be a conflict for Pippa in relation to his marriage. He was unable to tell her about his engagement, yet once his mother had broken the news, pleaded with her to accompany him and his wife on their honeymoon. When his marriage became difficult, he turned at once to her, telling her of his problems and anxieties, and seeking her support for himself and her help for his wife and children. Pippa offered affection and advice, as she had done since child-hood. In response to his requests, she also took over the supervision of his family and of his financial affairs. Initially, Ralph's wife, Margaret, also looked to Pippa for support, begging her to visit, to accompany Margaret when she took the children to see medical specialists, and to help with her home. In later years, however, Margaret Strachey came to believe that Pippa had destroyed her family, taken away her sons, and managed their money in ways which deprived her of the kind of life she wanted.[28]

Margaret Strachey was unquestionably disturbed and unstable: she was so terrified of harm coming to her children that she feared even letting them walk across a room in case they injured themselves. Despite her anxiety

about their health, her terror of noise and traffic made it impossible for her
to take them to a doctor without help. Pippa, assisted by her sister-in-law,
Ray Strachey, managed Ralph's family. Pippa organized boarding schools
for his sons, while Ray offered a home to Ursula, his daughter. Margaret
clearly could not manage the children or her finances—but she was not
entirely wrong in her reading of the pleasure Pippa took in taking control of
her family. Pippa's family letters never suggest such a thing, but there is
more than a hint of it in a letter she wrote to Roger Fry in 1917. She could
not visit Fry as he wished in on her holiday, she wrote, because she had

to relieve my sister-in-law Margaret of her family duties till the end of September.
I have been carrying on a frenzied campaign in these regions & and just touching
success though of course it may still come to nothing. Still I have kidnapped her
child & established it in a school, have dismissed all her servants, & have obtained
complete control over her bank account. So something's done. Also I've arranged
for her departure to a cure at Matlock on Thursday. Will she be got off? Who can
say? I think so and when that's done I've got to let her house & pack up her goods
& send the boys back to their different schools & see that they've got their vests &
things. All of which I'm not at all bright at—except the letting of the house. I feel a
martyr of course but am borne up by pride in the job.[29]

Although it had no such overt sexual overtones, Pippa's relationship with
Lytton was possibly even more complex and painful than that with Ralph.
Lytton clearly had some ambivalence about Pippa: he was attached to
her, relied on her, and often enjoyed her companionship. But he was
always aware of their differences in outlook and in values, and he
was always engaged in trying to conceal from her the details of his personal
and sexual life.[30]

   Pippa's refusal to acknowledge his sexuality was possibly an irritant to
Lytton, precisely because he relied so much upon her. When he returned
to live with his family after graduating from Cambridge, Pippa was his main
domestic solace. He talked to her about his work, his concerns about
James, and sometimes even about his friends and his plans for the Apostles.
She went with him to dinners, to the theatre, and sometimes on holidays as
well. They went together to Bloomsbury entertainments: to parties and to
the 'Friday Club' as well as organizing evening parties at home.[31] Lytton
had some admiration for Pippa's administrative ability and for the flair she
showed in organizing suffrage marches and demonstrations. But he often
treated her ideas with contempt, and made clear his sense that he regarded
her not only as less educated than he, but also as reactionary.

Lytton's intellectual self-confidence, and his arrogant sense of himself as an advanced modern man living in the midst of an old-fashioned Victorian family was not always concealed from Pippa. She felt her own lack of education profoundly, but did not always accept her brother's assessment either of himself or of her. Even when she was in her 40s, Lytton's assumption of superiority provoked violent rages in her. Here too, Roger Fry was the recipient of her confidences and she wrote to him in 1918 of 'a violent quarrel' she had had with Lytton on the subject of prostitutes. 'He first invented my ideas on the subject and then abused me in the most violent terms for holding them', she wrote to Fry.

I was so angry that I was unable to do anything but screech abuse and hurl my shoes across the passage—unluckily not at his head. The attack was entirely founded upon my beginning a remark to the effect that they—the prostitutes in the streets—didn't seem to me very tempting. The remark was leading on to something else but the use of the shocking word tempt implies of course moral blame & anybody in such a state of ignorant out of date mischievous prejudice is to [sic] permitted even to finish a sentence. Goodness me my fury has made me quite incoherent again! I daresay you'll catch my meaning though. I really can't put in nots. Anyhow so we parted & so as you see I remain—that is convinced that I am *not* the most narrow minded and unable to see beyond the end of my nose, of the two of us.[32]

In addition to her occasional bouts of rage, Pippa also harboured a deep hurt that Lytton had somehow caused and that she saw as having funda-mentally affected her life. Characteristically she refused to talk to him about it, although she did let him know that it had occurred. In 1919, Lytton sent Pippa a copy of *Eminent Victorians* with a bunch of violets attached. Somehow this gesture loosened at least her pen and in what was ostensibly a letter of thanks, she told him of her years of sadness.

Something dreadful happened once between us which shattered me as much as any love affair. My nerve I daresay is gone but not anything else. If I feel ill there are only two people I can bear to think of being with and those are you and Pernel. I don't know why I'm saying this. For such a long time I loved you so happily & always I Love you so much that it wouldn't be a thing to speak of—but alas dearest creature it is.[33]

Pippa offered no details as to what exactly this 'dreadful' thing had been and Lytton was understandably distressed. 'Your letter has upset me terribly', he wrote in reply.

I am quite in the dark, and never dreamt that anything had happened of the sort. What can it have been? I am acid at times—I fear too much so—perhaps for feeling myself such a heretic—and you have lately been involved in interests rather remote from mine; but I have never felt the slightest doubt about our fundamental affection, or that it had altered. Without you, my life would have been impossible.[34]

He sought details, but they were not forthcoming. 'I didn't mean to worry you', Pippa replied, somewhat disingenuously.

I can't think what uneasy demon made me write that letter. After concealing it carefully all these years why did I suddenly speak of it?
    As for explaining it's difficult. It would mean I believe a disquisition on my life history. But it was only the starting point that was your fault—all the rest was mine & your part was quite accidental as it were & mine went on because when I'm hurt I can't recover. It happened before we left number 69. Something perfectly trivial which I'm sure you forgot the next day sent me off inquiring into the foundations of belief and it crumbled & I felt miserable & let other things get involved & withdrew into the wilderness. It was all my own arrangement & I suppose it was much the same as what happens to people who lose faith in their religion I mean in its spreading effect as well as in the innocence of the Trinity.
    When I was alone in the house last summer I came home one night & found *Eminent Victoria* & a bunch of flowers. It pleased me so very much. But I couldn't write to thank you because of all the complicated things which wanted to come out at the same time. Now there won't be any more of that & I shall be more comfy for having told you if only you aren't worried by it. Perhaps it won't convey anything to your mind. Don't be worried because I never could have written if I hadn't been practically cured.[35]

Pippa's use of her favourite term 'comfy' in this last letter functions ironically to underline how uncomfortable the situation really was. But, having broached the subject and ensured that Lytton was aware of it, she provided no further clues as to what it was that so upset her. Nor was there any hint or suggestion in any other correspondence. Lytton seems to have made no further attempts to find out what had upset her, either through asking her again or through raising the subject with Pernel. Pippa's use of the image of a 'loss of faith' and of 'wandering in the wilderness' is rather curious here. The Stracheys had been agnostics since the mid-nineteenth century, and the Victorian drama of loss of religious faith was certainly not a feature of their lives, nor was it a common theme after the First World War. It is tempting in some ways to see all of this as having something to do with Lytton's sexuality, and more particularly with his relationship with

Duncan Grant that began in Lancaster Gate. But there is no direct evidence to support this.

This particular correspondence demonstrates the complexity, intensity, and importance of some of Pippa's family relationships—and their distance from the selfless sister so beloved by the Victorians.[36] Her siblings had the capacity to cause her immense unhappiness. But she did not suffer in silence, extracting a powerful revenge. Lytton was left with a strong sense of his inability to know this sister on whom he depended so heavily. 'Pippa seems to be bearing up pretty well', he wrote to Dorothy, after a few weeks after their mother's death, 'but it is never very easy to be sure'.[37] It is perhaps ironic that even Pippa's relationships with her in-laws were complicated, as we have seen in regard to both Margaret, Ralph's wife, and to Ray Strachey.

It was Pernel with whom Pippa had the longest lasting and probably the easiest of her sibling relationships. Their closeness was evident quite early in their lives: it was to Pippa that Pernel sent her detailed accounts of both school and university life. Pippa took an immense interest in Pernel's life and work at Newnham. She informed the others about progress on the building fund to extend Newnham, and she sometimes chivvied Ray and Alix, as Newnham graduates, to appear at important occasions. This was also a reciprocal relationship in the ways that those between Pippa and her brothers were not. Lytton occasionally expressed concern about Pippa, but his letters, like Ralph's, are usually filled with his own needs and demands. Pernel, by contrast, looked after Pippa too. She took her to Roquebrunne when her health broke down in the early stages of the First World War and seems on a number of other occasions to have nursed her through illness or sorrow. Theirs was an overtly affectionate relationship, in which intimacy was evident in nicknames: Pippa was sometimes 'Moossoo' and sometimes 'Miss', Pernel in turn was sometimes 'Darling Pernie' or 'Dearest Joy'.

While this relationship was never ostensibly troubled, however, it is hard not to see it as having an underlying tension of its own. Pernel, after all, as an academic, typified in the most extreme form what Pippa had missed in not having a sufficient schooling to be able to attend university. It is also notable that Pernel rarely wrote to Pippa about her friends: she discussed them and their activities with Lytton and with Virginia Woolf. But she wrote to Pippa mainly about college matters or other members of the family. Pippa's letters to Pernel seem also to have become more and more affectionate after the deaths of Lytton and then of Ralph. It was in the

1920s that the plan for Pippa and Pernel to live together when Pernel retired seems to have become the subject for discussion, turning the ageing process into one of pleasure and anticipation, rather than pain.

While Pippa's sibling relationships were sometimes made painful by intense emotion that was only half expressed, there were other siblings for whom the open recognition of complex feeling and even shared sexual involvements ultimately brought greater familiarity and complete ease. This was the case between Lytton and James, the two Stracheys who were perhaps most completely integrated into each other's adult lives. As we have seen, this was not always an easy relationship: although devoted to James, Lytton felt some resentment at the way in which James followed him to Cambridge, taking over his rooms—and altering them in ways that made Lytton profoundly uncomfortable. He was often anxious about James during the latter's student days. James's lethargy and depression, his refusal to work or even to read, and his obsession with Rupert Brooke all caused Lytton considerable concern. Lytton also felt that James was excessively dependent on him and wanted constant support that he did not always feel able or inclined to provide.

Lytton's occasional resentment is not hard to understand. Not only did James want to enter into his university life and friendship network, he also wanted to share his love life. This became evident when James professed his love to Duncan Grant at the very time that Lytton was attempting to negotiate his own relationship with Grant. James had been at school with Duncan Grant, and had been quite close to him in childhood and adolescence. But it was not until February 1906, when Lytton's feelings for Grant were well known, that he felt a need to declare his love. Duncan Grant in turn wrote to tell Lytton that James had 'told me he was in love with me. I didn't know what to do or say except to feel sorry for him—indeed I almost burst into tears. He seemed more or less resigned, said he must leave at once but that it had relieved him to tell me.'[38] According to Grant, James had been afraid that Lytton might be angry, although he did not feel that there was any problem himself. Using the language of the 'higher sodomy' as it had been used earlier by Lytton and Maynard Keynes, James argued that he could be in love with many people, while feeling no lustful desire for them. Indeed, as James made clear, he did not see that his feelings for Grant would in any way interfere with the relationship between Grant and Lytton.

In some ways James was right. The fascination with sexual desire and intrigue that dominated the homosexual world that Lytton and James inhabited both in Cambridge and in London in the first decade of the twentieth century was expressed more in letters than in actual sexual encounters. Desire was rarely consummated and buggery written vastly more often than it was performed. Within this framework, the mere expression of homosexual desire was a source of immense excitement, as well as being assumed to be everywhere. It was thus both less surprising that James should have been in love with Lytton's lover than might have been the case elsewhere—and less damaging. Lytton did mind the close friendship between James and Duncan Grant, but he did not see it as involving a betrayal and it did not in any way lessen his confidential relationship with James. It was from James that he sought comfort and solace when Grant fell in love with Maynard Keynes and brought his tortuous relationship with Lytton to an end.

But this was not the only occasion on which Lytton and James desired each other's partners. Lytton's deep concern about the debilitating effect on James of his long-standing infatuation with Rupert Brooke did not prevent Lytton from beginning his own flirtation with Brooke. In a similar way, he became very interested in one of the men who was actually James's lover: George Mallory. The Strachey brothers were not bound by their shared sexual interests in as deep and painful a way as were Vanessa Bell and Virginia Woolf; rather they served to establish a kind of intimacy between them which allowed for the easy discussion of all other relationships.[39] This sharing of sexual interests came to an end anyway around 1910, when James transferred his sexual attentions to women. Ironically, the brothers moved together away from the shared homosocial world of Cambridge and early Bloomsbury into a post-war one in which they both set up homes with women. James's wife, Alix Sargant-Florence was one of Dora Carrington's closest friends, and the easy companionship of Lytton and James was enhanced rather than diminished when Lytton and Carrington set up house.

The very close tie between Lytton and James continued throughout their adult life. James was a frequent visitor to Lytton's home, Ham Spray, both with and without Alix, and Lytton in turn became increasingly interested in the psychoanalytic work he undertook. There are fewer letters between them in the 1920s, but one senses that this is because of their regular meetings and their use of the telephone rather than any lack of contact. In some ways, the dynamic within this relationship changed in these years. Lytton had been in many ways the leader in their early years. However, this changed during the First World War, when James, as the one who was politically more interested and informed, became the one who first articulated an opposition to the war. James's involvement in psychoanalysis continued this pattern as it was he who introduced Lytton to the ideas of Freud. But Lytton's emotional dominance continued, composed as it was both of James's affection for his older brother and of his sense of Lytton's immense talent. Lytton, moreover, had many close friends, while James seems to have had very few. Hence Lytton loomed very large in his brother's life. James, as several people noted, could not bear any kind of criticism of Lytton. Frances Partridge regarded Lytton as 'one of the household gods' in James's home, alongside Freud, Mozart, and Stanislavsky, and noted that James became inarticulate with rage when there was even a hint of anything less than adulatory said about Lytton.[40] Lytton may not have placed James on a pedestal, but his affection and sense of closeness was evident not only throughout his life, but also in his death. It was James to whom Lytton left the bulk of his estate, thus ensuring a comfortable life for James and Alix for the rest of their days.

IV

The changing patterns of education and occupation, like the changing ideas about women and the new forms of sexuality in which some of the Stracheys were involved, all served to break down the pattern of sibling bonds that had existed amongst the Victorian Stracheys. At the same time, some of these very things increased the closeness and mutual dependence of the younger Stracheys in their final years. As the parents of a very large family, Richard and Jane Strachey had children to nurse them through their final years. Pippa took the largest role, nursing both her father and her mother. But Dorothy, Marjorie, and Lytton all helped out, as of course did Ray particularly towards the end of Jane Strachey's life. Four of the younger Stracheys remained single, and two of those who married (Dick and James) were childless. Thus it was to each other that many of the Stracheys looked as they aged. Lytton first showed the dependence on siblings at the end of life, even for one well provided with close friends. While Carrington and Ralph Partridge hovered around, it was Pippa who remained by his bedside during his final illness, alternating sometimes with James, while Oliver and Pernel stayed close by. But in his case, it was only at the very end that siblings came to the fore. For some of the others, there were years of domestic companionship in old age.

It was Pippa who had maintained the necessary framework that enabled the Stracheys to be together by insisting on keeping the family home in Gordon Square after the death of her mother in 1928. Pernel joined her there after she retired from Newnham in 1941. Oliver joined them in 1944. Ray's death in 1941 deprived him of the wife who had overseen his home and so, when he was forced by age and ill health to leave Bletchley Park, he returned to Gordon Square. Marjorie, too moved into Gordon Square after the Second World War, and, as soon as it was possible to leave France, Dorothy Bussy came too. Simon Bussy developed senile dementia a few years later and had to be sent to a nursing home. So Dorothy made her own home base alongside her siblings.

By the 1950s, Pippa who was in her 70s was no longer able to run the home. Her nieces, Jane Bussy and Barbara Strachey were engaged in constant battle to keep the furniture in a state of reasonable repair, to remove papers, and to keep the house habitable. Nonetheless, the family home served as the major residence for five of the ten Stracheys for most of their final years. The younger generation of Stracheys thus come to illustrate, almost to exemplify, the modern pattern of sibling relationships throughout the life cycle that is of so much interest currently among social workers and family theorists. Amongst them sibling–sibling relationships were a 'sub-system', as important as and often semi-independent from spouse–spouse or parent–child systems.[41] Like many other siblings, they were each other's first socializing agent and peer contact, and their relationships with each other underwent a continuous process of development that occurs throughout the life span, outlasting both their relationships with their parents and, in some cases, with their marital partners.[42]

Work, Income, and Changing Career Patterns

The changing social status of the Strachey family, particularly the decline from the landed origins of his parents in the eighteenth century to their professional upper middle-class position in the nineteenth, was a subject of great interest and some regret to Lytton Strachey.[1] He was impressed by the energy and the will evident in his parents and their contemporaries, but disliked their values, their taste, and many aspects of their way of life—symbolized as it was for him by the family's massive, 'portentous', ugly, and inconvenient house at 69 Lancaster Gate. Like his siblings, Lytton Strachey enjoyed the time spent at Jane Grant's family estate of Rothiemurchus, near Aviemore in Scotland, and probably felt some nostalgia at the possibility it seemed to suggest of a leisured life with an independent income that would have enabled him more freely to pursue his artistic and literary interests, free from both the need to earn a living and to be dependent on the very small allowance that his family was able to provide.

As Lytton was probably aware, these views were not ones that his father shared. Richard Strachey had been born on his own family's small estate, Sutton Court in Somerset. But he took far greater pride in the position of power and influence that he and his brother, John, had reached in India through their own abilities, or in his standing in the scientific community, than he did in either his own or his wife's genteel heritage. He was both an illustration of and a strong believer in the Victorian professional ideal. The rise of the professions and of a 'professional ideal', which saw training and expertise accorded high status, substantial remuneration, and a central place in all aspects of political, social, and personal life has come to be seen as an important development in modern British society. Richard Strachey was closely involved in it in a number of different ways. As a scientist and a positivist, he shared with John Stuart Mill the belief that it was scientific knowledge that should be the new basis of authority in all aspects of personal, social and political life. He was a professional soldier and engineer with an absolute belief in the importance of merit in determining standing and responsibility. He had a strong sense of the importance of adequate training for all technical, military, and administrative work, and of experience and expertise. He was strongly committed to the view that the British administration of India needed to be made more professional through competitive examination and through the requirement that those in positions of responsibility had expert knowledge of India. Professional-ism was important to him even in the area where he remained essentially an amateur, in the natural sciences, and he played a significant role in the establishment and development of the scientific bodies that sought to set down the principles and ensure the standing of particular sciences. Thus while Lytton Strachey bewailed the decline the status of the family across the previous century, what concerned Richard Strachey was rather the possibility of its decline in the present through the apparent lack in his sons of the intellectual ability, administrative talent, capacity for hard work, and sense of imperial mission that had earned him his professional and social position. The older Strachey sons were well aware that India was the place in which their father had made his name and set a pattern that they were expected to follow. They were destined from childhood to follow him into Indian service. None of them, however, approached his success or felt as closely connected to India as he had done.

Lytton's nostalgia for the family's landed past might also be seen as a symptom of the development that caused his father to fear that the 'Strachey tendency' was dying out. Richard was essentially correct and one might well argue that the decline in both status and income of the Strachey family accelerated far more in the later nineteenth and twentieth centuries than it had between the eighteenth and the mid-nineteenth. Not only were the twentieth-century Stracheys unable to match the landed estate of their forebears, but none of them had the capacity to live on the scale or with the degree of comfort of their parents. In looking at the careers of Dick and Ralph Strachey, however, it sometimes seems that they suffered greatly in their professional lives through the constant comparison with their overwhelming father. Both appear in many ways as failures within the family, but this is not to say they achieved nothing. The brief entry on Dick Strachey in *Who's Who*, for example, makes it clear that his military career, while not outstanding, did not go unremarked. He retired as a colonel in 1919, was awarded a CMG the year before and had previously been awarded a medal and clasp both for his service in Burma from 1887–9 and for the Tochi Valley expedition in 1897.[2] It is the contrast with his father, Major-General Strachey KCMG that makes it look paltry. Ralph too progressed steadily through the East India Railway, and rose in time to become chief engineer in 1913. This was no mean feat in a highly competitive field. However, this crowning achievement of his career, reached after nearly twenty-five years, and just before he retired, paled into insignificance when compared with the way his father used engineering as the stepping stone to the much larger task of designing and supervising whole systems of public works.

As Richard Strachey feared, the declining earning capacity of the Strachey sons reflected their approach to work and careers as much as it did their abilities. Neither Dick nor Ralph had the ability to aim at anything like Richard's exalted heights, but Oliver, who was considerably more able than his older brothers, possibly did. Although he had not done well in India, Oliver found his *metier* during the First World War when he was recruited into military intelligence. His code-breaking capacities proved to be quite outstanding, but although he remained in intelligence for almost thirty years, he refused ever to accept promotion that would have entailed administrative tasks and senior responsibilities. James too, although passionately interested in Freud's ideas, always kept himself at arm's length from the centres of power within the organized profession of psychoanalysis—and never permitted his professional practice to interfere with his musical and other interests. It is clear that the three younger sons, Oliver, Lytton, and James, who broke decisively with their parental model of careers and professions, all achieved great success in their own fields. But only Lytton managed also to gain financial independence. The publication of *Eminent Victorians* in 1918 assured him the income he needed to maintain the way of life that he and Carrington had just devised. By that time Lytton was 38. Prior to that, he had been heavily dependent on a family allowance. Oliver, by contrast, was dependent all their married life on Ray's income to secure his domestic comfort, while James's capacity to pursue his interest in translating Freud depended first on the allowance that Alix received from her mother and then on the comfortable income he received when he inherited Lytton's copyrights in 1931.

While the Strachey sons rejected both the professional ideals and the emphasis on financial independence of their father, several of the Strachey daughters endorsed it with great enthusiasm. As we will see, in the inter-war years, Pippa and Ray spent years campaigning for the opening of more professions to women and for equal pay with men in those that already admitted them. Prior to that, however, all the Strachey daughters except Elinor had worked, three of them beginning to try to support themselves almost from the minute they finished school or university. In formal professional or career terms, it was Pernel who was the most successful of all the younger Stracheys and she too who had the highest earning power, apart from Lytton after the publication of *Eminent Victorians*. Pippa too had a distinguished career and was an important feminist organizer from 1907 until she finally retired in 1959. It is not quite clear, however, whether this work was ever paid—and the lack of information about her salary makes it appear that much of her work was done on a voluntary basis. Both Pernel and Pippa fit into the model of the single career woman. However, marriage did not preclude the need for work amongst the Strachey women. Dorothy Bussy worked and contributed substantially to her family income throughout her married life, as did Ray and Alix, the two youngest Strachey daughters-in-law.

❧ I ❧

Richard Strachey was an exemplary Victorian, not only in the seriousness with which he approached questions pertaining to his career and his income, but also in relation to his sense of his family responsibilities. He was financially independent from an early age, and apparently took it for granted that he would, in due course, support a wife and family. It seems not unlikely that his relatively late age at marriage was connected to his own endorsement of the Victorian dictum that a man should not marry until he was able, not only to maintain a wife, but to do so in the level of comfort to which she had been accustomed in her own home.[3] Once married, the size of his income was always a matter of real importance to Richard Strachey, particularly as the number of his children increased and he was required to provide them all not only with food and shelter, but also with an expensive education and with the travel and social opportunities that befitted a distinguished upper middle class family. He needed also to invest to ensure an adequate income for his wife and children after his death.

Richard Strachey worked extremely hard, but he did not devote all of his time to his formal career. In the best Victorian tradition, both he and Jane Strachey regarded it as necessary to involve themselves in public life and public affairs. Richard's area of interest was science and he devoted a great deal of time to the Royal Society and to a number of its subsidiary bodies. His scientific involvement had begun quite early in his life. His catalogue of Himalayan plants and his study of the glaciers of Kumaon on led to his election to the Royal Society in 1854. From that point on, he devoted a substantial amount of his time on a voluntary basis to the Royal Society whenever he was in England Indeed, after he finally settled back home in the early 1870s, his time was almost equally divided between that institution and the India Office. He served as member of the Council of the Royal Society for nearly ten years and, although never its president, was vice-president on four separate occasions. He was made a member of the committee appointed by the Royal Society to manage Kew Observatory and remained on it for twenty years. He was also involved in setting up the Meteorological Council, becoming its chairman in 1883, a position he retained until 1905. He was also closely involved in the Royal Geographical Society, of which he was president in 1887–9 and served in addition on the Committee of Solar Physics and the Council of the Royal Geological Society. Strachey was held in very high esteem within the scientific world, as is made evident in the award to him of the Siemens medal and by his election to learned societies in many other countries.[4]

Strachey's high scientific standing was made evident when he was chosen as one of the three representatives of the Royal Society to the 1884 International Congress at Washington that decided to accept Greenwich as the prime meridian. His role at this congress was a very significant one. He was elected a secretary and asked to record votes, but more importantly, it was he who formulated most strongly the case for Greenwich, and who overcame the French opposition to the choice of a place in Britain. Indeed, the final resolution accepted by the congress repeated both his words and his arguments.[5] Although showing here an unexpected talent for diplomacy, he had not quite lost the capacity to offend opponents that was so often evident in India. Thus in his term as president of the Royal Geographical Society, he ostensibly took up the feminist arguments of his wife and daughters and attempted to have women made eligible for membership—a move which not only failed, but resulted in considerable bitterness and acrimony within the society. The records of this episode are not clear as to whether it was the issue itself that aroused bitterness, but there is certainly a suggestion in some of the comments that it was Strachey's handling of the matter that was at fault.[6]

Strachey was strongly committed to the professionalization of science. He numbered amongst his close friends the first group of men to designate themselves as 'scientists', as a means of distinguishing themselves from the natural philosophers of old.[7] These men, especially Hooker, Huxley, and Tyndall, all played a significant role in the setting up of the major nineteenth-century scientific institutions including the Museum of Natural Sciences at South Kensington, the Royal School of Mines, the Herbarium at Kew gardens, and Imperial College. Strachey furthered this goal himself in his work for the Royal Society, and especially in his contribution to the establishment of the specialist societies that sought to demarcate their area of knowledge as the basis of new specialist professions. There is an irony in the way that he, as one of the last Victorian polymaths, sought to end the amateur approach to science that was the basis of his own scientific reputation. Even in an age when scientific specialities were just beginning to develop, Strachey's range of interests, including as it did geology, botany, mathematics, astronomy, meteorology, and geography, was regarded as exceptional.[8] His approach to science: his constant, even obsessive note-taking, his fascination with measurements, his love of collecting specimens and of sketching what he saw, resembled that of the amateur natural philosophers of the eighteenth century in many ways. He was, moreover, able to make important contributions to so many fields precisely because they were too new to have been established formally as disciplines with clear requirements for training, or an extensive body of accepted knowledge. He acquainted himself with the basic principles of botany and geology just months before he made his journey to survey and collect botanical samples in the Himalayas in 1846. In a similar way, he delivered geography lectures at Cambridge, and became concerned about Indian meteorology, without any formal training in those fields.[9]

✋ II ✋

Just as Richard Strachey grew up assuming that he would make his career in India, so too did his oldest sons. It was clear from the start, however, that none of the Strachey sons would reach the heights of their father. Failure had dogged their steps even before they left England or began to prepare for imperial lives and they continued in India. Dick's letters from India tell a story of ongoing difficulties, with limited promotional opportunities, advancement sought but not granted, apparent openings which did not materialize, and expectation denied. Rules seemed to keep changing in ways that disadvantaged him. Thus, for example, in 1884, Dick sought admission as probationer to the Staff Corps—only to discover that he was no longer eligible as a new order had just come out saying that in future no one could become a probationer with more than four years service. He would have just five years service when he wished to be admitted.[10] A few years later, in 1887, he was promised a job in the intelligence branch. However, shortly after he received the initial offer, another letter came apologizing for the mistake, but indicating that in fact there was no vacancy for a paid attaché. Instead, he was offered a job as an unpaid attaché for six months.[11] Dick undoubtedly suffered from the rigidity of structure and the limited opportunities available to junior officers in the Indian army. Salaries were low, promotion was difficult and often involved training of a kind that took people away from the troops they would command and the kind of work they would be required to do.[12] He began his military life in India on an income of 200 Rs (or £20) a month, barely enough, he explained to his father, to cover his mess bills.[13] Richard Strachey supplemented this by £240 per annum until 1899 when at the age of 39, Dick was promoted to major and began to earn 1,000 Rs (or approximately £100 per month).[14]

Dick was singularly unable to utilize or take advantage of his family connections. There were times when letters from his father resulted immediately in his being offered a new post—but somehow, after a few months, the offered position seemed to disappear. Despite their own misgivings about Dick, Richard and Jane Strachey concurred with his sense of being ill-used by the army. Reading his letters, however, one is hard pressed to see his lack of success as entirely unwarranted. While filled with complaints about the shabby treatment he received, they suggest a lack of any capacity to think strategically or critically, or indeed to voice independent views at all. Moreover, he had a pronounced dislike of any form of office or administrative work and hence was never sure he wanted to be involved in intelligence or staff training.

His letters home make it very clear that Dick's life in India was almost entirely bounded by the activities and the outlook of the Indian Army. One of his nephews later suggested that Dick's love of and interest in classical literature made him unsuited to military life.[15] His own letters suggest rather that, while he tried to maintain some connection with the familial reading habits, he did so with difficulty and that he greatly enjoyed the world of leopard hunting, pig sticking, and amateur theatricals that dominated his various military stations. His colonel wanted to keep him at the regiment's headquarters in Thansi, he wrote to his father a few months after he had arrived in India, 'probably because I am band president and he doesn't want another one'.[16] Meanwhile army life was filled with excitement. 'Colonel Dremsky's Raja has won the Ganges Cup which is a pigsticking race', he reported in another letter, 'beating all the sporting talent of India—I think everyone is pleased as he is a very nice young chap.'[17]

Dick's military role included a range of different tasks: he participated in surveys of the local area, worked sometimes in stores, and seems to have occasionally done some intelligence work. There is no question, however, that he was happiest planning or engaging in combat, particularly against the bands of thieves known as 'dacoits' in the north of India. 'They have telegraphed from Mandalay', Dick wrote to his mother, 'asking if we have one or 2 young officers who have some knowledge of native troops and can be sent in command of a party of 100 Ghookas [sic].'

I was offered this and accepted with pleasure . . . we start tomorrow. It is rather funny sending officers from a British Regt to command native troops, but I suppose they are very short of officers. I was not at all sorry to be given this job as it will probably be a sort of separate command and the Ghookas are splendid little chaps & are much more likely to see sport in these jungles than our men who, with the best intentions, are apt to be a little slow in getting through a green bamboo bush.[18]

The letter points not only to his racial views, but to an almost infantile approach to battle. Unfortunately for him, the dacoits seemed to disappear and, as there was no promise of advancement, Dick went home for a holiday. He handed his bearer over to his brother Ralph who was about to arrive in India. The bearer, Dick explained to his mother, is 'an excellent man, very honest and moderate. Besides, as his knowledge of English is limited his master has to exercise his Hindustani daily.'[19]

Just as Dick's career offers a strong contrast to that of his father, so too did his income and scale of life. Much of his life seemed to involve some kind of financial struggle. There was a sufficient salary to enable Dick and Grace to live very comfortably in India and sometimes to enter into the elite life of the Raj, as they did for a while in Simla. Dick's salary went down rather than up in subsequent years, however. He was put on half-pay when his regiment was disbanded in 1907, leaving him insufficient even to pay for his passage home. He tried hard to augment his small military pay when he returned home, finding work first in the War Office and then in the Department of Military Pensions. The work was never particularly lucrative unfortunately, and as had happened in India, he constantly found himself being passed over for promotion by younger men. 'I have now been told officially that as I reach the age limit of my rank on 19th of this month', he wrote to his mother in May 1915.

I shall be placed on retired pay when someone else can be found to replace me but am to 'carry on' until my successor arrives . . . I have nothing really to complain of about being retired, as I am not to be promoted, as I quite realize that it is necessary to make way for a younger man. Of course I am a bit disappointed that they wouldn't or couldn't give me advancement that would have kept me on, & I think I have been treated rather scurvily in not having had my past work recognised in any way officially, but I don't want to figure as a man with a grievance, & if I *am* to go then the sooner the better, as I may have a chance of getting something else to do now, which I should probably not get if I waited till after the war.[20]

Dick moved on to work with Lord Derby, first on the voluntary recruitment scheme Derby favoured, and then helping plan the conscription that was introduced in 1916. As we will see, this work put him even more at odds with his younger brothers. From his own point of view, however, what mattered more was the lack of public reward. Dick was working very hard, Grace wrote to Jane Strachey early in 1916, but was enjoying it. Nonetheless Grace, and one assumes Dick too,

was very disappointed at not seeing Dick's name in the New Year Honours—very nearly every other man at the War Department has either had promotion or an order. Dick has fallen between all the stools by having had 7 heads over him since war began—each one goes as soon as he has gained enough knowledge of the work to see how much valuable work Dick does, and once he has left the War Department his recommendation is useless, so I don't see how Dick is ever to get on unless Lord Derby stays long enough to be useful. There is so much luck in these things.[21]

Dick moved from the War Department to Pensions, but decided to retire in 1919 when he was in his late 50s. 'I have resigned from Ministry of Pensions as from the end of this year', he wrote to his mother.

I have been getting £315 a year for slaving from 10 to 7 every day with 18 days leave in a twelve month. Now under the new Royal Covenant my army pension is to be raised by £300 so we can just manage to get along on the new pension alone and came to the conclusion we should be justified in giving up uncongenial industry and trying to get some pleasure out of life before we lose the desire for it.[22]

Dick had earlier estimated his military pension at £500 per annum, so the additional amount made it up to £800, an adequate, but not a lavish middle-class income.[23] Their income was never sufficient to enable Dick and Grace to live in the same style as either of their families, nor were they able to enter into—or even contemplate—the casual and bohemian life of their younger siblings. In 1917, Dick wrote to Pippa that they had been 'to a dinner party last night at Sir John Marshall's—the first in I don't know how many years. So I put on my costume fresh from the tailors, and Grace hoisted out her ancient finery and diamonds and cut a dash!'[24] For reasons that were never explained, Dick was omitted from his mother's will and thus received no augmentation to his income after her death in 1928.[25]

Ralph Strachey also had initial difficulties in getting to India. His scholarly results were not the problem. On the contrary, as he was gifted in mathematics and science, they were a constant source of pleasure to his parents. He failed to gain admission to the army, however, because of his poor eyesight and weak spine. He trained at Cooper's Hill, an engineering college set up to provide expertise for India, and went out not as a soldier, but rather as an engineer on the East Indian Railway. Although always financially comfortable and gaining promotions with ease, Ralph was never happy in India. This was not because he had any objections to the life of the Raj. On the contrary, unlike his father, he thoroughly enjoyed being in Calcutta or Allahabad. 'There seem to be some nice people about', he wrote to Pippa when he first reached Allahabad in 1890, and 'I have called on 27 people out of about 80 and as they are fearfully particular about calling, it will probably be some time till I am fairly launched.' Once launched, he thoroughly enjoyed 'the gaieties' including dances, drawing rooms, horse races, and so on.[26]

Ralph's problem was that, as an engineer often charged with designing and overseeing the construction of new railway lines and bridges, he spent much of his time in isolated spots, far from any large urban centre, where the only other inhabitants were Indians whom he regarded as completely alien. In 1893, he was sent to Barakan. The following year, he spent many months in Chirulia and went from there to the Shahabad region of Bengal and then Gya. Churulia, he wrote to Pippa, was

the vilest hole yet seen on this unpleasing planet. It is the disgustingest dreariest desert in the solar system . . . The bungalow is planted on a desolate and arid rocky place; the chosen home of the centipede, the scorpion and the caterwampus, seven hundred miles from the nearest human, who is a coal heaver of the deepest dye.[27]

He spent most of 1898 and some of 1899 working on the Dehri Bridge in the Shahabad District of Bengal. When it was nearly finished, he wrote to Pippa that he was 'heartily sick of living in the wilderness and am beginning to feel appallingly like Eckhart In *Borkman*—I want to live my life mother and see bright happy faces round me—which things are not to be found here'.[28] In March 1899, he was sent to Gya which was 'full of black ladies and gentlemen . . . in fact rather a hole'[29] and later that year he went reluctantly to Lillooah. There at least he was part of a railway colony and was given a comfortable and spacious house.

When Ralph escaped to any of the large cities, he seems thoroughly to have enjoyed the mindless and frivolous social activities indulged in by other young English men—and which drove his father to distraction. In Cawnpore in 1896, he explained to Pippa, his day began 'at 6 or earlier so I can finish outdoor work in the morning. Then breakfast at 12, then 40 winks till 5 or so', when he would 'dress in English clothes and go to the club to play whist till 8, then home to dinner and whisky and soda.'[30] The days were varied slightly when he was in Calcutta: after morning work, he and his friends would 'drive round in the tum-tum. The great thing is to drive up and down the red road, trotting one way and walking the other. Everybody in Calcutta acts in this idiotic manner and it makes a most amusing entertainment.'[31]

By contrast with Dick, Ralph Strachey seems to have managed very well financially, although there are few precise figures available. He began to earn what he regarded as 'a vast salary' when he became associate engineer on the EIR in the mid-1890s, and it obviously went up as he was promoted through the ranks until he finally became chief engineer in 1913.[32] His income enabled him to maintain a home for his wife in England, to send his sons to public schools, and even in 1920 to invest £1,000 in an ill-fated plan of Ray Strachey's to set up a firm of women builders. Both his personal circumstances and his personality ensured that Ralph lived always in a very modest way, however, often in lodgings, and without the kind of home in which social activities could take place. At the same time, he seems to have had no interests outside his family and his work and to have litle interest in pursuing a social life.

The real change in the family's approach to India as providing the framework for their son's careers was made evident in the case of Oliver, the third Strachey son. Oliver was a clever and imaginative child, with a talent for musical composition and crosswords. Although it is not clear why this was the case, there seems to have been no thought of his going to India as a soldier. Hence, as we have seen, he was sent instead to Balliol to prepare for the Indian Civil Service entrance exam. He gave this up and ultimately went to India with no qualifications only because he had no alternative. There was thus nothing remotely connected with personal duty, family heritage, or imperial glory in Oliver's approach to India. He went because it was the only place in which his father had the capacity to organize him a job. His work consisted of sorting out railway schedules and costings. It required him, as he explained to Lytton, 'to study a work called the East India Railway Goods tariff. This consists of a volume 3 miles thick on tissue paper, showing the rates for every conceivable—and inconceivable—commodity from every station in India to every other.'[33] It also involved much travel as he had to acquire knowledge particularly about the transporting and the rates applied to coal. When he had mastered the rates, he became personal assistant to the general traffic manager with responsibility to supervise all work regarding rates and tariffs. In October 1899, he wrote to his mother from Assansole in the north of India that he spent his days

knocking about pilot and trolleys, interviewing colliery managers etc., I generally get up at 4.30 and go to bed at 9. I sleep on a stretcher on the platform of whatever station I am on. Curiously I like it—its a better kind of life than vile Calcutta ... Assansole is my headquarters, but I'm only there from Saturday evening until Sunday evening and roam about all week. My face is black with sun and coal, and I feel as fit as anything.[34]

Unlike Ralph, Oliver did not like Calcutta. His dislike arose in part from a combination of his own snobbery and his sense of the social snobbery of the Raj, on the one hand, and from the lack of interest in music and culture more generally which he found there. 'I feel no desire to prance about in Society', he wrote to his mother shortly after he arrived. 'I'm sorry to say it rather vexes, what I've seen of it. It appears to me to contain too many housemaids in duchesses feathers. Its a very odd system to my mind, all this kowtowing to nobodies—I daresay I shall get used to it. If only they had some idea of civilisation it would be better.'[35] He found the philistinism of the British in India hard to tolerate. 'The great pain of this place', he wrote to his sister Pernel, 'is that nobody in India has ever read a book or looked at a picture, or heard a piece of music, or ever thought, or ever spoken to anyone who has ever thought about anything but horses. The only exception to this that I have met is Ralph whom it is a pleasure to meet!'[36] His own fastidious literary and musical tastes were constantly offended by meeting people who loved Marie Corelli (whom Jane Strachey once described as 'a literary scullery maid') and found it tiring to listen to Beethoven. 'I try to make whisky and bridge into substitutes for friends and life', Oliver wrote to Lytton, 'but really they are not successful—though of course when one's drunk it's all right.'[37]

While Oliver disliked being in India, Ralph often felt that he fitted in and was much more comfortable there than Ralph was himself. Oliver's easy charm and musical talents made him a popular figure in many different situations. In 1903, Ralph paid a visit to Oliver and Ruby and reported to Pippa that Oliver was very cheerful and important, as he had been left in charge of the whole district around Assansole for three months. 'He has made great friends with the people in the cantonments and is considered the wit of the age. Every remark he makes is greeted by all the captains and majors with yells of joy and no party is complete without him.' He had been adopted by the local regiment which had 'the best string band in the world and Oliver has taken charge of it, orders all their music, and is writing a song to be sung at some function with full orchestral accompaniment'.[38]

Oliver managed one or two promotions, but his Indian salary, like that of his brother Dick, was inadequate for him to live on and it too was supplemented by an allowance from his father. His wife Ruby later insisted, moreover, that his excessive drinking and constant absence from work made his position precarious, even in a railway of which his father was the

1. The Stracheys and friends in Simla, c.1860s. Jane Strachey is seated on the left and Richard on the right

2 (*a*). John and Richard Strachey

(*b*). Sir Richard Strachey in full dress uniform, *c*.1870s

(*c*). Portrait of Sir Richard Strachey by Simon Bussy, *c*.1900

3 (*a*). Jane Strachey, *c.* 1860

(*b*). Portrait of Jane Strachey by
Dora Carrington, 1920

4 (*a*). Four generations of women: Jane Strachey with her mother, daughter, and grand-daughter, *c*.1880s. Left to right: Lady Henrietta Grant, Betty Rendel, Jane Strachey, Elinor Rendel

(*b*). Richard Strachey and his daughters, *c*.1890s. Left to right: Elinor, Marjorie, Pernel, Dorothy, Pippa

5. The Strachey family, c.1890s. Left to right standing: Dick, Lytton, Dorothy, Jim Rendel, Pippa. Left to right seated: Ralph, Pernel, Richard, Jane, James, Elinor Rendel, Oliver. In front: Marjorie

6 The Strachey children, c.1890s. Left to right: Marjorie, Dorothy, Lytton, Pernel, Oliver, Dick, Ralph, Pippa, Elinor, James

7 (a). Dick Strachey

(b). Ralph Strachey

(c). Margaret Strachey with her sons, Dick and John, 1908

(d). Ralph Strachey with the same sons, Dick and John, c.1911

8 (*a*). Dorothy, Simon, and
Jamie Bussy, *c*.1912

(*b*). Dorothy Bussy, *c*.1930

(*c*). Simon Bussy, *c*.1930.

9 (*a*). Pippa Strachey in the Women's Land Army outfit she
loved to wear in the country, *c*.1918

(*b*). Pippa Strachey in more formal attire

10 (*a*). Pernel Strachey

   (*b*). Pernel and Pippa Strachey,
      c.1930s

11 (*a*). Ray Strachey (nee Costelloe), 1911

(*b*). Oliver Strachey, 1911

(*c*). Ray Strachey, self-portrait

(*d*). Oliver Strachey, playing solitaire *c*.1914

12 (*a*). Lytton Strachey as a child

(*b*). James Strachey as a child

(*c*). James and Lytton Strachey, *c*.1905

13 (*a*). Marjorie Strachey *c*.1900

(*b*). Marjorie and Lytton Strachey playing chess, 1920s

14. Ray Strachey's sketches
   (*a*). Lytton Strachey

(*b*). Alix Strachey

15 (*a*). Alix Strachey, *c*.1960s

(*b*). James Strachey, *c*.1960s

16 (*a*). Lytton and Pernel Strachey

(*b*). Jane Strachey with her granddaughter, Barbara

chairman. Oliver left India when his marriage came to an end in 1909, with nothing definite to go to—but a determination not to return. Luck was on Oliver's side, however, and both financial security and a career came to him unbidden after he returned home and lasted throughout his life. From the family's point of view, Oliver's financial future was secured from the moment he married Ray Costelloe. Ray did attempt to augment the income that she already received from the family trust and from the allowances paid to her by the Berensons by establishing Oliver as a writer. As the niece of the writer, Logan Pearsall Smith, and the step-daughter of Bernard Berenson, and already a published author herself, Ray saw writing as a natural avenue for an able young man. Becoming self-supporting was something else, however, and Ray's scheme for Oliver required financial support from her stepfather. She insisted that his Indian experience suited him well to become an expert in Indian history. The Berensons, however, sensibly took 'Indian history . . . to mean a grand name for idleness on Oliver's part', and refused to support him in it.[39] Ray did manage to get Oliver to do some historical research while they were in India in 1912. Working together, they produced a slim volume on *Keigwin's Rebellion*, a small-scale revolt against the British that occurred in India in the mid-eighteenth century. The Strachey connections even enabled them to bring it out under the prestigious imprint of the Clarendon Press in the Oxford Historical and Literary Studies series.[40] Oliver's interest in historical research soon flagged, however, and for some time he seemed quite unable to work at all. Ray's letters to her mother suggest that Oliver required a month's rest every time he even contemplated taking a job!

Things changed during the First World War and Oliver fell into a new career with the same lack of effort that had been required by his second marriage. He shared the patriotic fervour of the older members of his family and had begun doing unpaid work in the Staff Office with his older brother, Dick, as soon as the war began. Within a few weeks, however, Ray wrote to Jane Strachey in a state of some excitement, to say that Oliver had been offered a proper job at the War Office. While he was working with Dick,

a rumour reached him via Dominic Spring-Rice that the War Office was looking for someone with an ingenious head for puzzles and acrostics to decipher codes & piece together scraps of wireless messages picked up from the enemy. Dominic said he had suggested Oliver. Oliver inquired about it, and was taken by Dick to see General Anderson who took him at once.[41]

Oliver regarded this work as great fun and seemed to need far fewer rest breaks than had been the case previously. His new life was interesting, exciting, and even dangerous. He was sent out to Egypt in 1916 and on his return, the ship he was travelling on was torpedoed. He lost all his possessions, but was unharmed and soon rescued by another ship. His ability was widely acknowledged. Dick, who must have felt a little envy at the success of his younger brother, wrote to Pippa of a conversation he had had with one of Oliver's bosses in the War Office. Oliver was seen as 'invaluable to them in his particular sphere . . . his analytical mind and clear intelligence were exactly what was wanted for his job.' The War Office regarded themselves as 'very lucky to have got him'.[42] While Dick struggled in vain to be noticed and bitterly resented the fact that he was not granted any title, Oliver's was awarded an OBE in the New Year's Honours list of 1917.[43]

Although it was not clear at the time that this would be the case, Oliver's career in intelligence lasted nearly forty years. At first he doubted that his job would even last the duration of the war and both he and Ray were convinced that it would come to an end as soon as the war was over. The value of code-breaking to intelligence and military operations during the First World War, however, led to a decision by the British Cabinet to establish a permanent code-breaking agency. Veterans of both naval intelligence (from the Navy's 'Room 40') and of the War Office's MIB (where Oliver had been) were brought together after the war in the somewhat oddly named General Code and Cipher School. Initially under the First Lord of the Admiralty, the school was transferred to the Foreign Office in 1922. Oliver Strachey and Dillwyn Knox were regarded as the two most able men there, and each headed a team which was identified by their initials: ISOS, the acronym for Intelligence Services Oliver Strachey, and ISDK for Intelligence Services Dillwyn Knox.[44] Although there are no records available concerning his activities in intelligence, published memoirs and recent studies of British code-breakers suggest that Oliver turned out not only to be an extremely good code-breaker, but also to have considerable abilities in the recruitment and training of new staff.[45]

Oliver Strachey was one of the very few to work in intelligence and cryptography in both the First and Second World Wars. When Bletchley Park was set up as the main decoding centre in 1938, he was moved there and seems to have continued working even after his formal retirement date of 11 November 1939. Although never taking part in work on the Enigma machines, Oliver's language skills continued to be necessary because, even when the German codes were broken numerically, language experts were needed to work out the actual content of messages. One of the young men recruited to Bletchley later recalled being 'assigned to assist one of elder statesmen, Oliver Strachey' in the autumn of 1940. He was then working on German Abwehr translations. 'This involved writing out messages in columns of overlapping consecutive segments of text in a pattern resembling the gable end of a house . . . and juggling with them until fragments of words began to appear in each line: this was in fact a far more difficult operation than anagramming the police double-transposition depths.' Strachey's team was credited with breaking the code that enabled MI5 to keep track of the messages of double agents and to spot German spies arriving in Britain.[46] Oliver Strachey's name continued to be an integral part of the work at Bletchley Park because all the decoded Abwehr messages continued to be classified under the general heading ISOS. Oliver himself continued to be involved either at Bletchley or with Allied military intelligence until 1943 when he suffered a heart attack and finally retired.

Oliver had found a niche which he thoroughly enjoyed and at which he was exceptionally able, but his was never really a lucrative job. His starting salary was £400 a year, an amount that continued throughout the war.[47] In the inter-war period, the location and status of the General Code and Cipher School was a matter of contention—and so too was the question of how its salaries should be graded and matched with those in the civil service. As a result, salaries remained relatively low—and were the source of constant complaint. Oliver's salary went up after the war. By 1924, Ray Strachey informed her mother, he earned £650 per annum after tax.[48] He could have earned more if he had chosen to: his daughter, Barbara Strachey, maintains that he was offered promotion several times after the war, but refused as this would have involved giving up the cryptography, which he loved, in favour of administration, which he loathed.[49] Thus in 1939, he was still was one of the three chief assistants in the general Code and Cipher School.

Fortunately for Oliver, neither he nor his family were tied to what he earned: the £650 that he earned in the early 1920s, as Ray explained to her mother, was about one-quarter of what their family spent. She supplied the remaining three-quarters, some of it from the interest she received on her Marconi and other shares, some from the family trust—and the rest paid to her as an allowance by Berenson and by her mother.[50] The £2,200 that Ray regarded as the minimum for normal life meant that she and Oliver had and spent far more than most of the other young Stracheys. Ray, as her daughter Barbara, her mother, and her aunt Alys Pearsall Russell all noted, was both extravagant and irresponsible when it came to money.[51] She took no interest in clothes, but her passion for motor cars, opera, holidays, her garden—and for engaging in wildly impractical schemes which others were expected to fund—all required constant financial support. There was a constant flow of cheques from Mary Berenson, with money being sent every time a child had a birthday or needed a holiday or a new coat, or indeed when Ray decided to stand for Parliament.[52] Berenson paid Ray an annual allowance, but he too was appealed to for extra money, not only to support Oliver as a writer, but again in 1921 when Ray decided to set up a company of women builders. He refused, and a few months later Ray wrote to say how sensible of him it had been, and how much more difficult it was to set up a business than she had realized.[53] Berenson and Ray were fine—but Ralph Strachey, whom Ray had persuaded to invest £1,000 in this scheme, lost all of his money.[54]

All of this came to an end in 1931. The Depression and Berenson's difficulties with some of the regular clients for whom he had bought paintings meant that he was no longer able to pay Ray her allowance.[55] Mary continued to provide some money, but she too had less at her disposal. Fortunately for herself and her children, Ray Strachey was an immensely competent woman and she immediately set about earning the money that she needed. As a first step, she went back to working for Nancy Astor. She had been Astor's unpaid parliamentary adviser in the early 1920s, but now became her full-time paid parliamentary secretary, on a salary of £500. She continued to do this until 1935, when she became the paid organizer of the Women's Employment Federation. Ray supplemented her income through her books and through a series of radio programmes for the BBC.[56]

III

While the older Strachey sons struggled to find or to make their way in careers, a couple of the single daughters found them with ease and took to them with great enthusiasm. Pernel was the first, following her success at Cambridge with academic positions that eventually took her to the position of principal at Newnham. Although older than Pernel, Pippa followed after her in developing a desire for a career and in working out what she wanted to do. It is interesting to see here too, that while the Strachey name and the example of Richard Strachey weighed heavily on his older sons, but brought them little help, both the family name and connections played an important part in assisting the Strachey daughters. This is made most evident in regard to Pippa, for whom Richard's imperial reputation and the family's Indian connections provided the springboard into an independent and successful life. She was one of many British women for whom imperial travel and experience was both exhilarating and empowering.[57] Nothing could have been more different from the Indian experiences of the Strachey sons than that of Pippa. She was determined to make the most of her time there and mobilized every family resource in order to do so. India thus provided her not only with a range of new experiences, but with a sense of power that enabled her to change her life quite dramatically.

The different approaches to India between Pippa and her brothers were evident from the moment that she arrived there in 1900. Her brothers had settled as quietly as they could into their new surroundings, but Pippa had no inclination to do so. As the daughter of the chairman of the East India Railway, she believed strongly that she and the uncle who was accompanying her were entitled to special treatment. When her brothers would not help, she appealed to her father. 'Dearest Papa,' she wrote shortly after her arrival. 'This is the cry of the outraged Chairman's daughter. No carriage—no pass for Uncle Trevor. Ralph says it is quite out of the question his mentioning such things to Douglas & that unless you write to ask them to be polite to me they will continue to ignore me.'[58] Pippa was far too impatient to wait for letters and had already 'despatched a telegram to Douglas demanding the carriage and the pass'.[59]

Pippa's impertinence worked and two months later she wrote with great delight to tell her parents that her demands had been met.

I am sure you will all be pleased to hear that I'm at last firmly established in my rightful position upon the East Indian Rly. That's to say in complete control. I won't say that the cause has been won without a struggle but all that is now entirely an affair of the past & I can contentedly retire into the background and smile with conscious power. What Mr Douglas thinks in his heart of my proceedings I should be sorry to say but whether (as some suppose) his acts are prompted by sarcasm or whether he is simply amused & wants to see what pitch I shall go to the result is highly satisfactory & not only is the railway placed at my disposal but his private goods as well so that at the end of my time in Calcutta I had a luxurious brougham at my orders. I left Howrah on Tuesday evening in a most exquisite brand new compartment replete with every luxury & was seen off by a bevy of bowing dignitaries ranging from Agent to Station Master. As for the arrangements for my journey to Rawal Pindi they are of the most elaborate & magnificent description including special unhitching etc., on a foreign line.[60]

Pippa was given Carriage no 859, the one used by the senior executive of the EIR. She thought it delightful. It was 'elegant white with shining brass trimmings and *Reserved* painted in large letters where 1st class normally is', and contained a small verandah, a vast saloon freshly painted in white and pale green furnished with two large couches, a massive dining room table, and a soft downy leather armchair, which still left 'room to dance a figure eight'. There was also a bedroom and a bathroom with a 'real enamel bath with a lid'. Once on the train, she was treated like an important official: railway employees bowed as she went past—and, if the train to which her carriage was attached arrived at any station at an uncivil hour, her carriage was placed in a siding so that her sleep was not disturbed![61]

Pippa traversed much of North India in her carriage, even going into Malakand which was regarded as unsafe for women. She was not prepared to confine herself to areas where there were rail tracks, however, and purchased a rickshaw to go further afield. This of course entailed the employment of rickshaw men or *jamponees*. As an employer of male Indian labour, she not only increased her own sense of power, but also rendered herself masculine. She lost no time in feminizing and infantilizing 'her men'. 'I must tell you about my *Magnificent* jamponnees', she wrote to her mother.

I have five (most people have 4 and some degraded beings 3) delightful retainers exquisitely dressed in beautiful new blue serge suits & putties, brown leather belts, white puggarees with scarlet pointed tops & scarlet and gold bands across. I'm sure I have no right to this grandeur of scarlet and gold but I wouldn't give it up for anything, & sat gloating over the whole spectacle the whole afternoon. As for the men I am already devoted to them & have turned them into ladies maids. Isn't it a good idea? I was going quite mad with anguish this afternoon because the Barnes' vile servants wouldn't bring me any bath water but my cries of distress reached the ears of my faithful followers who at once leaped to their feet & hurried to the rescue bringing cans.[62]

Unlike her brothers, Pippa had both her parent's sense of social standing and entitlement, and much of her mother's charm and social skill. Thus she made sure it was her cousin Arthur Strachey, the chief judge of Bombay, and his wife Nellie, rather than her brothers, who organized her entry into Raj society. The Arthur Stracheys ensured that she met everyone who counted in Bombay and enjoyed all that city had to offer. While Pippa was in Bombay, Queen Victoria died—and both she and Nellie had to ensure that they had appropriate mourning dress to undertake all the social activities that made up their daily life. There was some compensation, however, in terms of how the Indians responded: 'The queen's death is the most dismal thing that could have happened. The natives are much impressed and Arthur is much pleased with their behaviour. With one accord every single shop in the native town was shut up & in the evening all lights were extinguished & the streets perfectly deserted and empty.'[63]

That Pippa was made of stronger stuff than her brothers was already clear and it became even more so when she was forced to manage a family tragedy. While she was staying with Arthur and Nellie Strachey in Simla in 1901, Arthur contracted enteric fever and died quite suddenly. Nellie was prostrate and it fell to Pippa to manage all the details of the funeral and then to deal with Arthur's estate. The funeral was particularly complicated because Arthur had stated in his will that he wished to follow Hindu custom and be cremated. His wife insisted that his wishes be carried out, but it was Pippa not Nellie who had to make arrangements in the face of the fierce opposition to this request that came from the rest of the British community of Simla. Lord Curzon, the viceroy, agreed that Arthur's wishes be followed—and he was the only member of the British community to accompany Pippa and the coffin to the chapel where it spent the night before the cremation. Pippa insisted that Arthur Strachey's Indian bearer, Tulsi, also be admitted to the chapel—and it was he who had to organize the cremation. Tulsi later accompanied Pippa to Allahabad to clear out Arthur's home and pack up all his and Nellie's effects.

In dealing with this crisis, Pippa had been heavily dependent on Arthur Strachey's Indian servants. Tulsi had not only organized the cremation, but had been her mainstay in packing up the household, dealing with bills, and paying off all the other servants. Pippa was well aware of all that he did, and became very fond of him. But her discussions of him, as of other Indian servants, never fully acknowledge his abilities or recognize him as an adult. Indian servants in her letters are constantly referred to as children, and as totally malleable beings. She became very friendly with Azerat Ram, the leader of her team of jamponees, and spent much time chatting to him. But nothing could dispel her sense of the unreliability of orientals—and she refused to believe his statement that he was a high-caste Brahman, although this turned out to be the case. Occasionally she was forced to recognize that her assumptions about the ignorance and docility of her servants were erroneous, but in her mind, they remained less than fully human. 'Just now I find my retinue of servants a great drain on the resources,' she wrote to her parents in July 1901,

the wretched creatures are always having to be provided with something or other. They have all had to be given blankets for the wet weather but I must admit I don't grudge them their blankets much—a very different matter to my frenzy when I found they had all worn enormous holes in their 'pantlums' as they call them! My jamponees really are rather dears—they run like mad by the hour together without minding in the least & they combine an exaggerated sense of humour with an appearance of portentous solemnity which is rather pleasing. The other day I remarked in a peevish voice . . . a propos of some curious performance by one of them 'What is that child doing now?' whereupon to my intense horror he went off into a complicated convulsion of some sort & concealing his face in his hands fled like the wind to some retreat from which stifled gasps and groans of laughter were heard to proceed. This curious episode led me to conclude that the creature understood English which was rather a shock to the feelings.[64]

Pippa's Indian experiences opened up a new world of authority and independence. By having to negotiate the structures of the Raj, on the one hand, and infantilizing and feminizing her Indian male servants, on the other, she seemed to have found a way of assuming certain masculine prerogatives without ever having to challenge the social and familial structures in which she lived. Her life in India unquestionably made her see herself as independent and as needing a sphere of action beyond that of home.

Lacking formal qualifications, and with the assistance of her mother, she gathered a series of testimonials from relatives and family friends. Jane Strachey was particularly important here, drafting the testimonials that the distinguished Strachey relatives signed. It was she who suggested to Pippa's uncle, Sir John Strachey CGSI, the terms he should use to indicate his belief that her activities in India demonstrated that she could take on any kind of work. 'Although my niece, Miss Philippa Strachey, has not been employed in any professional work', wrote Sir John on Jane's instructions, 'I have had personal experience which enables me to speak with confidence of her remarkable business capacity.'

At the death of my son in India, Sir Arthur Strachey, late Chief Justice of the north western provinces, she was the only member of my family on the spot, and she undertook, in circumstances of very unusual difficulty, the duty of winding up his affairs. The manner in which she dealt with the business which thus devolved upon her was so thoroughly satisfactory and complete that I feel I can recommend her with the utmost confidence for a post in which intelligence, judgement, method and tact are necessary.[65]

It was not only the support of her uncle that helped Pippa, but also the immediate friends and contacts of her mother. Emily Davies recruited Pippa to work for the London Society for Women's Suffrage in 1907.[66] There were a number of paid suffrage organizers at the time. For the most part, however, these positions seem to have been offered to the working-class women who could not have continued their involvement without being paid, rather than to the middle-and upper middle-class women on whose unpaid labour the movement had always depended.[67] The lack of any record of a salary amongst Pippa's papers supports the idea that she worked without any form of payment. The idea that Pippa worked in a voluntary capacity is further re-enforced by a letter Nancy Astor wrote Pippa in 1953, announcing to her that she was going to make out a seven-year covenant for the sum of £100 'for you to spend on yourself... You can't know what a joy this is for me', Lady Astor continued, 'to give you this—you who have done so much for me and for others.'[68] As we have seen, moreover, Pippa lived at home and continued both to look after her parents and to manage her mother's finances. She was a woman of very modest demands, unlike her sister-in-law, Ray. She lived extremely frugally at home, didn't drive or want a car, spent little on clothes and tended often to holiday with family or friends. Hence her family allowance was perfectly adequate, as was her inheritance after Jane Strachey died.

It is interesting to note the contrast between Pippa and her mother, as volunteer workers. While Jane Strachey was always the *grande dame* of any feminist organization she was connected with, Pippa took the role of 'organizing secretary'. This reflected her dislike of the limelight in which her mother shone with such ease, but it also pointed to a different attitude to work. Jane Strachey mostly thrived on meetings and public occasions. Sometimes she did correspondence for her various organizations at home, but equally often directed unpaid secretaries to do it for her. Her involvement was very much a part-time thing, fitted into the spaces in her busy family and social life. By contrast, Pippa saw herself as a full-time worker and attended her office almost every day. Both she and Ray Strachey behaved like paid employees, seeing themselves as responsible for every aspect of the work they undertook. Pippa's contribution was acknowledged in the award to her of an OBE. Ironically, while neither Pippa nor Ray (at least in the 1920s) were themselves professionals, the feminist cause with which they were most concerned was precisely that of opening professions to other women.

If Pippa Strachey continued the endeavours of nineteenth-century feminists, including her mother, Pernel was one of their beneficiaries, establishing a successful career in those very educational institutions for which nineteenth-century feminists fought so hard. Pernel stands out amongst the younger Stracheys for the focus and dedication with which she pursued her career. She was the only one of the younger Stracheys who seemed to have a clear idea of what she wanted to do, and of the best way to do it. While her siblings—and at least one of the university-educated women who married into the family—all drifted aimlessly after they left university, Pernel embarked immediately on postgraduate study in France. This led in 1900 to a position as lecturer in French at Royal Holloway College, and then in 1905 took her back to Newnham. She was appointed first as a lecturer and then in 1917 as the director of studies in modern languages. Finally in 1923 she became principal of Newnham College.

Pernel's working life was a source of some comment amongst her Bloomsbury friends, none of whom were quite certain of the merits of an academic career—and all of whom saw it as inferior to the life of a creative writer or artist. After Pernel had visited her in 1918, Virginia Woolf commented on what a pleasure her company always was. It was possible, she felt, that Pernel had a certain 'faintness, remoteness, & donnishness', but 'she is too sensible, humorous & indolent to have taken the shape of a professor, or indeed to believe heartily in Newnham or education, or anything but books & ideas & poetry & so on. A more unambitious person does not live; but she has not the dullness & flatness which generally exists in these self-effacing, unselfish old maids.'[69] Woolf's contempt for academic work is evident in her summation of Pernel and her insistence that, although Pernel read widely and had an intense curiosity about many things, her knowledge was slightly limited. Unlike a creative writer, she knew everything from books and 'lacked the power and perhaps ambition to handle the things in themselves'.

While Pernel read widely, she published very little. Indeed, her only publication was one edited poem. Nor did she work continuously on her lectures. The notes for them now held in the Women's Library certainly give evidence of careful thought and preparation. Once prepared, however, they seem to have lasted throughout her career.[70] Some of her friends, most notably Jane Ellen Harrison, were distinguished scholars, but she seems not to have desired this reputation for herself. At the same time, she was widely recognized as a gifted debater and public speaker, and as one who brought to this task wit, elegance, and considerable intellectual skill. On one occasion, she was apparently asked in her capacity as college president to participate in a solemn debate on the relative merits of eastern and western civilization, and agreed to do so. The night before the debate occurred, however, someone removed the original topic from the board and replaced it with a very different one, namely, 'That the red Queen is a higher type of womanhood than the White Queen'. Pernel appeared completely unfazed and, drawing on her extensive literary knowledge, 'delighted her audience by comparing the Red Queen to the ideal of womanhood expressed in some of Wordsworth's noblest lines'.[71]

Her successful career depended very much on her capacity to fit into college life and to be liked and admired by her colleagues. This is made abundantly clear through the process by which she became principal of Newnham. The minutes of the governing body of Newnham report that, in January 1923, Athena Clough announced her resignation as principal. After some discussion, it was agreed that the vacancy should be advertised and that both the names of those who applied and those suggested by members of the board would be considered at the next meeting. Pernel Strachey was herself a member of the Newnham Governing Board and sat through a couple of meetings during which a series of names were brought forth, discussed, and discarded. At one meeting, that of 15 March, Pernel was not present. Presumably she had been asked not to attend. At this meeting, the final two applicants were rejected and, without any prelude, Pernel Strachey was nominated. There was no discussion, and certainly no suggestion that she be asked formally to apply or to attend an interview. On the contrary, immediately after she was nominated, she was declared to have been unanimously elected by the twenty-four members of the board who were present.[72] There was much elation amongst members of the college at the idea that it would remain in the hands of one who had been so long connected to it and who would be sure to maintain its values and traditions.[73]

Pernel Strachey did not become principal of Newnham until the 1920s, but there is something in the report of college meetings that is very reminiscent of the battles fought by Emily Davies and Anne Clough when women's colleges first opened at Cambridge in the 1860s and 1870s. As principal she was involved in constant and often difficult negotiation between a staff with very decided and conservative ideas on how young women should behave and a student body expecting a wide range of freedoms, some of which were truly shocking to much of the college staff. From the reports of the meetings, Pernel emerges as a woman of good sense who understood the wishes of the students, but who respected her older women colleagues and dealt with their concerns with immense patience. Occasionally one feels that her conversations with her colleagues repeated similar ones and revealed ideas and attitudes that existed in her own home—and that she treated her older colleagues with something of the immense patience that all the Strachey children showed Jane Strachey in her declining years.

There were several related issues that brought to the fore the difference in expectation of college life between young women students and their older women teachers. Sometimes the question centred on technological change. Thus student use of radios was a subject of extensive debate. Many students wanted to listen to a 'wireless' in their college rooms, as they would have done at home. The dons, none of whom had this opportunity in their own youth, felt that radios in student rooms would be noisy and disruptive. Political developments in Europe in the 1930s assisted the student cause, as even the most conservative don was forced to acknowledge that serious young women might wish to keep abreast of the threatening developments in Germany. In 1938, after several years of debate, it was finally agreed that, for an experimental period, students could use their wireless 'for serious purposes', in hours not designated specifically as silent ones—and providing that no one else was disturbed.[74] Women students did not only want to listen to the serious news, however. They also demanded the right to entertain young men and to have evening parties in their rooms. Here too, Pernel's good sense prevailed: small parties were allowed, provided that there were no more than eight in the college on any one evening, and that no student attended more than two per week, and that no more than two young men could be present at any party.[75] College records suggest that Pernel worked patiently to gain agreement on both of these issues. There was one issue, however, on which even she found it hard to be accommodating. This involved the question whether students who married should be allowed to complete their university course. Some members of the governing board felt they should not, arguing that once a woman married, the college was unable to guarantee that she would have adequate time or facilities to study—and moreover that married female students should expect to fulfil the normal duties of a wife, and to give domestic responsibilities precedence over their own work. This is the only time that the college minutes suggest a sharp speech from Pernel, and one can almost see her hackles rise as she insisted that she had always 'taken it for granted that a student who married should finish her course'. And doubtless to her relief, the motion 'that it should be the policy of the College to discourage undergraduate students from continuing their work for the tripos after marriage' was convincingly lost.[76]

In addition to helping to modernize some of the Newnham regulations, Pernel also worked extremely hard to expand the college building and improve its facilities. She devoted years of her life to organizing the building appeal, fighting a committee that wanted only to allow for the smallest possible changes, as she insisted on a substantial and well-designed new wings with sitting rooms and dormitories. She battled also for the installation of a new hot water system, central heating, and eventually in the 1930s even electric light. The building fund required her to take a higher public profile than she liked, meeting the Queen and many visiting dignitaries whose aid she had enlisted. Like others in the family, she was assisted by Maynard Keynes. He was then a fellow at King's and persuaded the provost to offer a very generous donation to the Newnham building fund.[77]

For all this, Pernel did not enjoy administrative work. The other Stracheys all pitied her for having to devote so much time to such a tedious activity. Newnham students were well aware of her lack of interest in many day-to-day matters—including the quality of college food. Virginia Woolf provided a memorable description of Newnham food in *A Room of One's Own*, with its description of her Newnham dinner of dried-out meat, potatoes, and sprouts, and stewed prunes and custard followed by cheese and biscuits, all washed down with water, contrasted to the glorious lunch of partridges and iced desert, accompanied by excellent wine, that she had been given at King's College earlier in the day. Woolf's description of Newnham food has long been the subject of debate, with some old Newnham students arguing that she was late for dinner on the night she described—and hence caused the food to be more tasteless and dried out than usual.[78] But no one questions the idea that Newnham food was endured rather than enjoyed.

It is hard to assess precisely how successful Pernel was as principal of Newnham. Comments from Newnham students vary, with some recalling her humour, common sense, and lightness of touch—while others noted rather her distance and inability to engage with students or to put them at their ease. She never pretended to enjoy student activities. One old pupil remembered years later,

going to Miss Strachey to ask permission to produce a play in College. Miss Strachey acquiesced, but said in tones of anguish (she knew she would have to be present), 'keep it short: oh *do* keep it short'. Miss Strachey sometimes forsook her exquisite remoteness to condescend to very minute personal counsels. I remember a composition of hers pinned up on the notice-board in Clough, which described in exact detail how to get out of one's bath in such a way as to leave a minimum amount of water on the floor.[79]

III

While Pernel was the most successful of the Strachey daughters, she was not the first who had sought paid work. Dorothy began doing so almost as soon as she left Allenswood—and indeed was offered her first position there. In the first instance, the offer of work seems to have come as something of a surprise. 'Miss Souvestre has offered me a salaried post as teacher of literature at Allenswood. What do you think of it?' Dorothy wrote to her mother in 1888, 'I shall have to go twice a week probably. But as the railway is to be opened in the autumn it shouldn't be such a business. The sum has not been mentioned.'[80] The amount was never made clear in family letters, but the position was clearly acceptable as Dorothy took it on and continued to teach literature at Allenswood almost until she married.

Working at Allenswood did not divert all Dorothy's attention from the family. Unlike Pernel's later position at Royal Holloway, it was only a part-time job which allowed Dorothy time to oversee all domestic affairs and contribute to the care and the education of her younger siblings. She also found time to coach Pernel in Latin and Greek for her Cambridge entrance examination in the late 1890s. Nor was the Allenswood job a sufficient paid occupation for Dorothy, and after a few years, she extended her teaching by setting up private classes at home. Dorothy has started classes for 'some girls who have come out and need to improve their general knowledge', wrote Pippa to Pernel in 1895.[81] Dorothy offered these girls French language and English literature, as well as some general studies.

Dorothy's marriage and her move to France of course put an end to all of this, but not to her need to earn. Marie Souvestre tried to assist by finding her translating work to do and Dorothy also earned money in other ways. There are no extant records of the Bussy finances. But Dorothy's letters home suggest that they just managed, with the occasional sale of one of Simon's paintings supplemented by paying guests, the lessons she gave to the children of French neighbours and of English friends, and her own translations. The Bussys were always described as poor, but theirs was a relative poverty that has to be seen in terms of Dorothy's own expectations. Thus the Bussys were never without servants, for example. Indeed, although she grew up in a small French village, Janie, their only child, always had an English nurse. Moreover, living as they did amidst a community of other artists, and in a home with a vegetable garden that provided much of their food, the Bussys managed their life with a fair degree of comfort.

The other sister for whom life was a constant financial struggle was Marjorie. Her professional life, like her personal life, never quite came together. Just as Dick Strachey suffered by constant comparison with his father, so Marjorie suffered in comparison with her older sisters. Whatever they did together, she was outshone by them. This was evident early in her school and university days, in relation to Pernel, and in her adult ones in relation to Pippa. Like so many of the younger Stracheys, Marjorie left university with no idea what she wanted to do. The fact that both her mother and Pippa were then working in the suffrage campaign made it natural that she would be drawn into it too and she spent a couple of years organizing suffrage caravans. The work never appealed to her and, as we will see, unlike Pippa, she never seemed to establish a place or identity of her own within it. Marjorie was not particularly enthusiastic about women's suffrage and within a couple of years had begun to explore the possibilities of training as a teacher. She seems to have taught small classes in private schools for a couple of years before deciding that what she really wanted to do was to study music and movement at the Dalcroze-Schule in Dresden. Jane Strachey provided money for her fees, and while there Marjorie also seems to have given some private lessons. Marjorie began her work at the Dalcroze-Schule in August 1913. She lodged at a hostel, ate meals at a cheap cafe, and spent the days working at gymnastics, rhythmic gymnastics, improvisation, and solfege. The work was arduous and exhausting, she complained to her mother, especially for one accustomed to sedentary life; although the mixture of people was fascinating. 'The companions of my labour seem even more extraordinary than they were in summer,' she wrote in her second term there. 'They include an English girl of 16 without a word of German or a note of music and a Japanese philosopher. In the house next to me are a French countess and her daughter. I don't like them but they may improve.'[82] The school seemed to her rather badly organized and she had to battle to gain promotion at the end of her first year. This was to little avail as the war began shortly after and she had to leave Germany and go home.

Once back home, Marjorie again gave private lessons to the children of an acquaintance, and then decided to undertake training as a primary school teacher. 'There is a great demand for better educated women in the work', she explained to her mother,

and I believe there is scope for new and intelligent ideas. I don't think it would be hard to get a Headmistress-ship so one could live on salary. I would have to train for a year at a college. One, at Darlington, has for its head a sister of Lytton's friend Hawtrey and I have talked to her about it. Training would cost only £12.10 pa, including tuition, board and lodging as the Board of Education makes a grant to the College for each student they train.[83]

She went to Darlington later that year, working as a teacher of young children at the same time as she received her training. She obtained a position as a trainee teacher in a local school the following year. She wrote cheerful letters to her mother about her classes, but indicated to Lytton that the students with whom she lived were all 'imbecile' and that her practical teaching was dreadful. 'I spent an appalling fortnight with class of nearly 50 boys and girls trying to teach them half the subjects of the curriculum', she wrote. 'It was incredible and shattering to the nerves—harder than anything I have done.' She was pleased after that to have a 'pleasant class of 20 girls'.[84] Her life was also socially isolated, she noted and 'I have not spoken to a man for 3 months'.

Marjorie continued seeking work as a teacher, but in September 1917 announced that she was now going to change her plans. 'Mr Boyde, the Secretary of the Education Committee, has been urging me to come into the office for good—and I have decided that I will. It means giving up teaching which is a pity, but I believe it is a better opening and has more to offer.'[85] Jane Strachey was unimpressed with this idea, indicating to

Marjorie that she had shown little interest in or aptitude for routine work or administration.[86] She did undertake the office work, but it did not lead to permanent employment and Marjorie was looking for a school job the following year.

Marjorie's infrequent correspondence with her family makes it hard to trace every step of her working life, but it is clear that the hoped-for post of principal did not eventuate. For the rest of her life, she seems to have alternated short-term teaching contracts in public and private schools with periods of time working as a resident governess for particular families, or organizing small classes of her own. Even when she had a full-time position, as a woman teacher, her salary was lower than that of her siblings. She never earned more than £250 per annum, the sum she had in 1920 as an employee in the Education Department. Teaching salaries were generally low, often around £100 or £150 per annum—and she earned even less than this when working privately. Her income was sometimes supplemented by the family, often by Lytton who offered her money on a fairly regular basis. Marjorie occasionally stayed at the Strachey flat in Gordon Square, but more often lived alone until the Second World War. Her domestic circumstances were humbler than any of her siblings—and she seems to have been the only one who did her own domestic work and did not always employ a servant.

Marjorie's difficult and marginal life as a teacher contrasts strongly with that of Pernel. This was clearly so in the view of Jane Strachey, whose letters suggest a sense that Marjorie herself was the problem: that her constant changing of her mind about what she wanted to do meant that she never settled down to anything. Clearly there is some truth in this, but it does not tell the whole story. Sometimes the fates seemed to conspire against Marjorie too, bringing to an end activities or forms of training or employment that she was herself very much engrossed in. Thus, for example, her training at the Dalcroze-Schule in Dresden was terminated abruptly by the outbreak of war.[87] In a similar way, some of the private schools where she was employed closed suddenly, bringing to an end what had appeared to be permanent work. Quentin Bell, who had lessons from Marjorie, regarded her as a brilliant teacher.[88] It is clear too that her teaching career was made more difficult still because of her poor eyesight—and that she was not good at dealing with school authorities. As a result, Marjorie lived a rather hand-to-mouth existence, moving from one place to another, never establishing either a career or a comfortable home.

❧ IV ❧

Despite her deep affection for her two youngest sons, and her sense of their exceptional and unusual abilities, Jane Strachey wanted both of them to follow the family tradition by gaining employment in the ICS. Both Lytton and James rejected this idea. Not only did they dislike the idea of working in India, but they feared the restrictions and demands that might be imposed by any career. Writing essays and reviews for the 'higher' or serious journals and weeklies had provided career opportunities for large numbers of intelligent university graduates throughout the nineteenth century, and both thought about this, but without enthusiasm. The starting up of new magazines or reviews to reflect new ideas and critical approaches continued well into the twentieth century, and many of the friends of Lytton Strachey were engaged in such endeavours and sought his input and support. The family had its own literary organ too, *The Spectator*, which was owned and edited by a nephew of Richard's, St Loe Strachey.

The question of what he should do, or rather of how best to enable him to finance the life of reading, writing, and sociability that he wanted to pursue, was a constant source of concern to Lytton Strachey. A Cambridge fellowship would have been the ideal solution. But when this did not materialize, journalism seemed the only answer. Lytton had contributed a number of articles to both *The Spectator* and to the *Independent Review* in his last two years at Cambridge.[89] Holroyd estimates that for the next two years he wrote an article every six weeks for *The Spectator*, earning 3 guineas a time. This kind of activity did not appeal to him particularly. 'I spend my days trying to be a journalist', he wrote to a friend in 1905 'but I seem to lack the conviction and energy which I feel are necessary. Other things are more interesting than reviews, but daily bread must be earned somehow.'[90] Lytton was an excellent and punctual reviewer, managing so successfully to contain his own rather more radical and subversive views within the solid conservative framework required by *The Spectator* that he was offered not only the position of a regular reviewer (which he accepted in 1907) but also that of editor, which he declined. Journalism of this kind, he felt, did not pay sufficiently nor would it leave him to time to follow his own desires and to write what he wanted.[91] In 1912, he published his first volume of essays, *Landmarks in French Literature*, which was well-received and was an epoch-making event for him. After this, as Holroyd shows, he determined to cease either hankering after Cambridge, or devoting his time to journalistic writing, and began to plan the historical and biographical works which he really wanted to write. He ceased writing for *The Spectator* in 1914 and, although he wrote occasional critical essays after that, he devoted his working time to his own research and writing.

The question of earning an income and of being able to live an independent life continued to be a matter of concern for Lytton. The small amounts he earned through his writing were supplemented by a small family allowance. However taking the family money became harder when the Stracheys were facing the straitened circumstances that followed Richard's retirement from the East India Railway in 1907—just about the time that Lytton refused the editorship of *The Spectator* and indicated his desire to reduce the number of articles and reviews he was writing. He often felt that he should give up the £50 allowance he received each year, but, as he explained to Leonard Woolf, he felt equally that it was his duty to write plays in the hope that he would one day have enough money to live on.[92] This struggle came to an end with the publication of *Eminent Victorians* in May 1918.

Lytton Strachey's literary earnings were substantial throughout the 1920s. Holroyd estimates that *Eminent Victorians* sold approximately 35,000 hardback copies in Britain during his lifetime and 55,000 in the US.[93] The publication of *Queen Victoria* brought still more financial rewards. Maynard Keynes, whom Lytton like the other Stracheys, consulted on all financial matters, sold the US rights of *Queen Victoria* for $10,000.[94] In the last decade of his life, Lytton was very comfortable financially and subsidized other members of the family too. Both Dorothy and Marjorie benefited from his largesse. His success subsequently provided James with financial security as he inherited all Lytton's copyrights in 1932.

James Strachey took at least as long to decide what he was going to do as did Lytton. Jane Strachey had taken active steps to establish a career for her younger son, but to no avail. When James left university his mother persuaded St Loe Strachey, who was both James's cousin and his godfather, to find him work on *The Spectator*. St Loe, who was extremely fond of Jane, agreed to do so and created a position for James as his own personal secretary. The work was not taxing. 'What you would have to do', St Loe explained to James, 'would be to come down here [to the Spectator office] every Tuesday, Wednesday, Thursday and Friday mornings to see what was wanted. It would be very seldom that you would have to be at the office in the afternoon.'[95] James received £50 for the first six months apprenticeship, but after that he was paid £400 per annum, enough, he commented to Lytton, to enable him to lunch at Simpson's every day and to go to all the ballet and opera he desired, provided that he remained living at home. St Loe's letters to James suggest that he saw him as talented and was keen to offer all the support he could. For James, however, even regular lunches at the Savoy did not make working at *The Spectator* tolerable. He hated 'bolstering up the ruling class', he complained to Lytton.[96] St Loe's homophobia, his social and political conservatism, and his tendency to rewrite articles which did not appeal to him were all hard for James to endure, and he was constantly advised by Lytton to resign. James became deeply depressed in 1913, and took several months leave. His position at *The Spectator* became increasingly difficult once the First World War began. James was a conscientious objector and his stance was absolutely antithetical to that of St Loe. James struggled on, but finally resigned in 1916.

During the First World War, James was involved in voluntary relief work amongst refugees, apparently with some success. Shortly after, he turned his attention to psychoanalysis, the field to which he devoted the rest of his life. James had been introduced to the ideas of Freud at Cambridge through F. W. Myers and the Society for Psychical Research.[97] Alix too came to psychoanalysis through Myers, as she had planned to study psychology with him when she finished her degree in modern languages.[98] Myers had discussed some of Freud's ideas at meetings of the Society for Psychical Research, arranged for Freud to be made an honorary member of the society and published one of his papers in 1912. By 1915, Alix and James were both reading and discussing one of the earliest English translations of Freud, Brill's *Interpretation of Dreams*.[99] It is not quite clear exactly how and when they decided to take this interest further, but they agreed to include a visit to Vienna to see Freud in the course of a European trip in 1920.[100] Although James later insisted that it was Freud who had first suggested that he and Alix translate some of his writings into English, his correspondence with Ernest Jones indicates that he had already begun translating Freud before going to Vienna. The Stracheys arrived with the first translation of *Group Psychology* almost complete.[101] Jones, who was the leading British psychoanalyst and maintained close contact with Freud, wrote a letter of introduction for the Stracheys in which, moreover, he made clear to Freud that James was interested in psychoanalysis as a profession and wanted to translate Freud's work. As a result, Freud accepted James for considerably less than he would have required from an ordinary patient because 'the case of a man who wants to be a pupil and become an analyst' was above financial considerations.[102]

James and Alix spent eighteen months in Vienna and left early in 1922 with letters from Freud indicating that they were now fully qualified as analysts. Their training, however, had been extraordinarily limited. James's training analysis with Freud lasted for just over a year before being terminated abruptly when Alix suffered a severe lung ailment that made them leave Vienna for a warmer climate in 1921. Alix had not planned to go into analysis when they arrived in Vienna, and began only when she had a recurrence of her earlier symptoms of anxiety and palpitations. As James explained to Lytton, after Alix 're-developed her palpitation attacks at a performance of Gotterdammerung, and subsequently couldn't face theatres and concerts without awful qualms', he poured the story out to Freud, who agreed to see her, but did not have sufficient time available to undertake a proper analysis and planned to refer her to someone else. 'After a certain number of hours', however, James explained to Lytton,

he became fascinated, partly by her case, & partly by the effect of the actions and re-actions caused by taking both of us at once. (He had in fact begun by thinking it almost a technical impossibility) unluckily he then became full up, so had to drop her for a time; but he appears most unwilling to hand her over, and expects to be able to take her on again shortly.[103]

Freud was clearly very taken with James and Alix, whom he regarded as 'exceptionally nice and cultured people though somewhat queer' and directed Jones, who was often critical of them, to treat them with sensitivity and respect.[104] At Freud's insistence, and despite his own desire that all analysts should be medically trained, Jones organized the Stracheys' admission to the British Psychoanalytic Society.

For the rest of their lives, James and Alix combined translation with practice as psychoanalysts. James was the more prominent of the two, both as a translator and an analyst. He took an active role in the British Psychoanalytical Association as a member of the training committee, a contributor to a number of congresses and symposia, and for some years editor of the *International Journal of Psychoanalysis*. He always held himself somewhat aloof from the psychoanalytic community, however, disliking strongly the political battles in which psychoanalysis seemed always to be engulfed. From the start, he was interested primarily in translating Freud's work and he was Freud's favourite English translator. On several occasions, Freud insisted on giving James work to do, despite the opposition voiced by Ernest Jones, who felt that James was extremely slow and disinclined to work hard. 'Your 2 wishes, that Strachey should do the translation himself and that it be done quickly, have a certain incompatibility', he wrote to Freud in 1927.

His intolerance of work, about which you doubtless know more than I do, has not been improved by his having 8 patients a day. Recently he ungraciously objected to being put on the James Glover memorial Sub-Committee, because it would involve giving up part of an evening every two or three months and it is hardly possible to get out of him a book review or other contribution.[105]

As this letter suggests, however, James soon had a quite substantial practice. His most celebrated patient was Donald Winnicott, whom he saw inconclusively for many years. James's treatment of Winnicott has been the subject of some discussion. Winnicott's biographer questions both the ethics of James's behaviour (in discussing Winnicott's analysis with Alix) and James's capacity to understand or treat Winnicott's sexual and personal problems.[106] Winnicott himself eventually terminated this analysis, although he remained on very affectionate terms with both James and Alix.

James's dislike of psychoanalytic politics was made more evident in his response to the 'controversial discussions' between the followers of Anna Freud and those of Melanie Klein that tore the British psychoanalytic community apart in the late 1930s and 1940s. While others saw these debates as fundamental to the meaning and future of psychoanalysis, James saw them as involving questions of dogma that had no place in the scientific discipline of psychoanalysis.[107] At the same time, as the major English translator of Freud, James became one of the central figures in British psychoanalysis, establishing and in some ways creating the language of psychoanalysis and the ways in which it was read and understood in the English-speaking world. Despite, or perhaps because of, his aloofness from the daily life and the intense political struggles of the British psychoanalytic community, James always had a special place within it.

James's Bloomsbury associations played a role here, but they were augmented by his vast knowledge of and passionate interest in music, literature, and ballet, his sense of humour, and his absolute intellectual honesty. He was seen as one who brought his broad cultural knowledge to psychoanalysis and who gave it a distinctive cast through doing so. His dry humour and his refusal to take the movement as seriously as it sometimes took itself was evident also in the very charming and ironic piece he wrote on being made an honorary life member of the British Psychoanalytic Society at the celebration of its fiftieth anniversary in 1963. He managed in it to deal in a very humorous fashion with the complete domination of British psychoanalysis in its first few decades by Ernest Jones, to appreciate the new procedures and protocols for training—while recognizing that, had they existed at the start, neither he nor several others would ever have become analysts—and to ask whether, despite the need for method and system, it was 'worth while to leave a loophole for an occasional maverick'.[108] James's speech was much praised by those attending the dinner.[109] Martin James, a practising analyst regarded it as the high point of the night—and saw it as illustrative of James's broader role within the profession. 'Quite apart from saving the anniversary dinner at the Savoy by your whiff of British Grape shot I feel sure you have exerted the same influence for years at the society and deserve its midget honours for that too.' It was the lightness of touch evident in James's speech that he especially admired—something singularly lacking in their European colleagues. He hoped that James 'would come and show us how to do it again'.[110] A similar view of James was expressed by Donald Winnicott. In the obituary he wrote for James, he commented on James's detachment and intellectual honesty, on the importance of his cultural inheritance, and the richness that it gave his life, and on his charm. James, he insisted, 'will always be my favourite example of a psychoanalyst'.[111]

Alix Strachey shared James's interest in psychoanalysis, but played a rather smaller role both in the profession and in the Freud translation. She was very active in psychoanalytic circles in Berlin in the mid-1920s, when she was there without James, undergoing analysis with Karl Abraham.[112] However, she seemed unable or unwilling to establish a central place for herself within psychoanalytic circles when she returned to London after Abraham's death in 1925. She rarely attended psychoanalytic meetings or congresses and certainly did not ever hold any kind of office in the British Association of Psychoanalysis. Moreover, although the Strachey house was set up with consulting rooms, she seems only to have had one or two patients.[113] Alix continued to work alongside James in translating Freud, although here too she took a subordinate role, working on the glossary of psychoanalytic terms that James and Ernest Jones devised and taking on the specific tasks that James wanted her do. She did also do some major translations of her own, working first on Melanie Klein's *Psychoanalysis of Children* and then on the papers of Karl Abraham. As we will see, after the Second World War, Alix also attempted to apply psychoanalytic concepts to questions about peace and international relations, although her success in this endeavour too was limited.[114] For many of those around, Alix, while charming and extremely intelligent, always had about her the air of a perpetual student, with a passion for reading and for argument, but a low tolerance of boredom and routine, and no inclination to engage in regular work. She saw herself as far more of an emancipated woman than were her Strachey sisters-in-law, but in this respect at least, she fell back easily into the leisured life of a middle-class Victorian and Edwardian woman rather than accepting the need for financial or professional independence.

10

Gender Transformations and the Question of Sexuality

Just as the Stracheys serve to illustrate broader trends in relation to education, marriage, and single life in the late nineteenth and early twentieth centuries, so too one can see a reflection of these trends in their understanding of gender and their approaches to sexuality. Several of the Stracheys participated in the late nineteenth-century discussions about sexuality, arguing strongly for the need to understand it in new ways and to accept new codes of sexual behaviour. Indeed, the whole family serves to illustrate in an extremely concentrated form the changes in sexual behaviour and outlook that were the source of such anxiety in Britain. As a happy, monogamous, and extremely fertile couple, well able to support their many children, Jane and Richard Strachey epitomize the mid-Victorian sexual ideal. By contrast, their children illustrate almost all the developments that caused such anxiety later in the century. As we have seen, relatively few of them followed their parents' marital example, and even fewer produced children. This family that had been so very prominent and well-known in the nineteenth century had almost died out completely by the mid-twentieth. At the same time, several of the younger Stracheys completely rejected or overturned the sexual and moral world of their parents. They engaged openly in sexual infidelity and experimentation and were deeply interested in questions about sexual identity and behaviour, rarely mentioned by their parents. This was the case not only with Lytton and James, whose preoccupation with homosexuality is well known. Oliver Strachey, by contrast with his brothers, saw heterosexual

263

desire, expression, and fulfilment as deeply problematic, as did his sister, Dorothy. At the same time, the fact that the Strachey family in its Victorian form existed at least until the death of Jane in 1928 involved the younger members of the family in a constant need for secrecy and subterfuge.

The interest in sexual questions and the changing approaches of Lytton and James across the turn of the nineteenth and twentieth centuries illustrates in microcosm a number of the new approaches to sexuality that were so significant in the wider social world. Lytton Strachey and his friends were by no means unique in their interest in questions of how best to understand sexual desire and behaviour, or their assumption that homosexuality was not only acceptable but superior to heterosexuality. On the contrary, they were but one amongst a number of groups of lawyers, doctors, philosophers, writers, and artists preoccupied with questions about sexuality in the final decades of the nineteenth century.[1] The general question of how best to classify sexual behaviour or to regulate and police it was subject to constant debate at this time. The traditional role of religion and of morality in determining appropriate and acceptable sexual behaviour that was widely accepted in the early and mid-nineteenth centuries was being challenged by those who argued that sexual matters involved medical rather than moral questions and needed to be investigated and understood in scientific or medical terms. Medical control of sexual behaviour was challenged in turn by legislators who, in 1885, for the first time in Britain, outlawed sexual relations between adult men. This new legislation replaced earlier laws that had not focused only on same-sex relationships, but rather proscribed 'unnatural' sexual acts like buggery, by whoever they were committed.[2] Hence it too reflected a new understanding of sexuality and sexual identity and a new sense of its importance.

Feminism too played a significant role in much of the nineteeth-century debate about sexuality and marriage. From the late eighteenth century onwards, feminist demands for legal and political rights and economic independence had aroused hostility and anxiety about the future of family life and of motherhood. While many Victorian feminists had done their best to counteract such concerns and to stress the feminist commitment to womanly duty, the 'new woman' evident both in literature and sometimes in society in the 1890s depicted both marriage and family life as institutions that preyed on and often destroyed women. Some even suggested that women should not only be able to live independently of marriage, but even that, like men, they should be able to engage in sexual activity outside marriage.[3] The 'new woman' of the later nineteenth century was accompanied by several different forms of 'new man'. On the one hand, imperial expansion in the later nineteenth century brought with it a new ideal of masculinity, embodied by the imperial rulers and adventurers who eschewed marriage and family life in favour of exploration and adventure, military activity, and the subduing of foreign lands and peoples.[4] On the other hand, modern urban life in metropolitan centres seemed to bring with it a variety of apparently effeminate men whose lives centred on the illicit and decadent pleasures to be found in major cities.[5]

Sexual freedom was of great importance to Lytton Strachey and to James and Alix, all of whom believed that their understandings of sexuality and of sexual behaviour were part of a new movement that was bringing new sexual freedoms after a period of intense sexual silence and repression. The whole question of nineteenth-century sexuality has been the subject of extensive study and exploration recently by historians and cultural theorists, some of whom have questioned the insistence by Freud, Ellis, and even Edwardian Bloomsbury, that they were the harbingers of a new sexual freedom after decades of Victorian repression. There was unquestionably greater tolerance of certain forms of sexual behaviour, but this was accompanied by new forms of sexual classification and regulation. In the course of this recent historical discussion, moreover, the interpretation of Victorian sexuality so widely accepted in the late nineteenth and early twentieth centuries has also been questioned as historians and cultural theorists have insisted on the need to recognize the complexity of Victorian approaches not only to sexuality, but also to questions of gender. The discrepancies evident between the formal codes and moralistic discourse so characteristic of the Victorians, on the one hand, and the extensive evidence of widespread illicit and perverse sexual activity, on the other, has long been a source of fascination. While some writers have sought to expose the sexual hypocrisy evident throughout nineteenth-century society, others have attempted rather to explore the reasons why sexual propriety and constraint seemed so inordinately important in an age of rapid industrialization with a growing market economy.

In the past three or four decades, there have been a range of rather different approaches to the question of Victorian sexuality. In the 1970s, Michel Foucault questioned the very idea that the Victorians used silence as a way to repress sexual activity, pointing to the vast range of discussions and discourses about sexual desires and behaviour that filled Victorian medical, educational, and even general periodical literature.[6] More recently, increasing attention has been paid to this general discussion of sexuality and to the ways in which it brought to the fore contemporary anxieties about declining rates of marriage and childbirth, the increasing numbers of single women and men, and the relationship between sexual behaviour, gender identity, and mental health.[7] The centrality of questions of gender has also been stressed. Indeed, it seems scarcely surprising that questions about gender identity and sexual desire should become matters of serious social and political concern at a time when an apparent disinclination to marry and a falling birthrate seemed to threaten Britain's imperial status and economic power. In the final decades of the century, sexual scandals and an increasingly radical critique of heterosexual relations brought a new prominence to homosexuality and seemed to suggest that the very institution of marriage was under threat.

One can see very clearly amongst the Stracheys some of the changes in masculinity that have come to be identified by historians across the nineteenth and early twentieth centuries. There are obviously significant shifts in the forms of masculinity evident in a family that prided itself on its military tradition and imperial distinction in the mid-nineteenth century, while producing in Lytton Strachey one of the most self-conscious dandies and homosexuals of his day some decades later. The pattern of masculinity across these two generations of Stracheys is, however, far more complex than one that simply involves the rejection by the two younger sons of the masculine codes and traditions of their family. For Richard Strachey too deviated from some Victorian and imperial masculine norms, in terms of his stature, his frequent ill health, and sometimes also his nerves. Moreover, one could argue that none of his sons accepted or replicated his version of masculinity in either their public or private lives. None of them saw themselves as a paterfamilias or shared Richard's understanding of the role and duties of husband and father. Thus James and Lytton, although very different from their older brothers, were following rather than inventing a familial trend in their rejection of Victorian masculinity.

A similar point can be made about the Strachey women, none of whom really accepted or endorsed prevailing norms of femininity. Jane Strachey was a happy and devoted wife and mother, but never a typical one. She was not in any obvious way masculine, but certainly eschewed most feminine interests and activities. A tall and rather clumsy woman, she adored reading and discussing public affairs and took no more interest in dress or in her appearance than she did in housekeeping or nursing her young. Several of her daughters were considerably more skilled in domestic management than she, and kept her out of kitchens and bedrooms whenever they could. Nonetheless only Elinor lived within the conventional constraints of a married woman. All the others rejected the marital ideals and pattern of feminine life accepted by their parents and society, either seeking careers or a range of unconventional relationships. All of them engaged in complicated negotiations with prevailing norms of femininity while seeking to lead independent lives.

Nowhere was this sense of the importance of sexuality more evident than in the new sciences, psychoanalysis and sexology, that came into being at this time and took sexuality as their central object of investigation. For both sexologists and psychoanalysts, sexuality was the central core of individual life and identity. 'Few people ever fully appreciate the powerful influence that sexuality exercises over feeling, thought and conduct', wrote the Austrian pioneer of sexology, Richard von Krafft-Ebing, in the preface to his encyclopedic study of perversion, *Psychopathia Sexualis*. Like other proponents of the new 'science of sexuality' that came into existence in the 1870s and 1880s, Krafft-Ebing insisted that the importance of sex in every aspect of life could only be properly understood when it was recognized as a distinct domain of scientific inquiry.[8] It was to this domain that James and Alix Strachey committed themselves, through their study and translation of Freud. In the process, they came to endorse an entirely new understanding of what sexuality meant.

I

The changing pattern of masculinity in the nineteenth century has recently been the subject of extensive discussion and debate. Many historians of gender have suggested that there was a shift away from the 'domestic masculinity', evident amongst those middle-class men who focused their attention on work, family life, and society within Britain in the first half of the nineteenth century, towards an 'imperial masculinity' that emerged in the later decades of the century, as imperial expansion and military engagements brought an apparent rejection of family life in favour of male camaraderie and sexual adventure.[9] This chronological pattern has been disputed by others who seek to elucidate quite different patterns of masculinity amongst professional men or in particular sections of the middle class. Nor is it particularly helpful in thinking about those like Richard Strachey whose involvement in imperial administration began early in the nineteenth century—and was always integrally connected to family traditions and family life. Richard Strachey's India was closely bound up with his family relations, first through his father and brothers and then through the extended familial networks created by his own and his siblings' marriage. Although he was distinguished as a soldier, Richard Strachey loathed military life and gained no pleasure from its masculine codes or rituals. Like most upper middle-class professional men, he participated in a number of all male groups, belonging to several scientific and other learned societies, and dining frequently with male friends at the Athenaeum or the Oriental club. But he rarely did this in India. Moreover, the centre of his world was always his family and it is a moot point as to whether it was his brother John or his wife Jane who shared most closely his ideas, thoughts, and concerns. This is not to suggest that imperialism was unimportant either to Richard Strachey's sense of his own masculinity, or to the ways he was seen by others. On the contrary, it was central to it. But its role was extremely complex—and his imperial calling was not something that provided an alternative to, or an escape from, his family.

Strachey was very much a self-conscious maker of empire, and shared many of the qualities that Mrinalinhi Sinha has seen as so important to the 'manly Englishman' of the mid and later nineteenth century. In Sinha's view, the ideal of English manliness was based on moral and intellectual qualities quite as much as on physical ones, and involved self-discipline and restraint rather than the physical strength so prized in a later age.[10] This ideal was constantly contrasted with the lack of intellectual strength and moral restraint evident amongst Indian men. Richard Strachey certainly saw himself as an educated, rational, self-disciplined man with a strong sense of duty, a capacity for hard work, and a preparedness to bear discomfort and emotional isolation if his work demanded it. Both he and his brother John constantly contrasted the decent and straightforward English manliness they shared with their colleagues and admired, with the self-indulgence, sensuality, and weakness of the Bengalis, whom they despised. Not all Indians were Bengalis, of course, and the Strachey brothers often contrasted the strong and fearless Sikhs and Pathans whom they respected for their military prowess with the weak and 'effeminate babus'.[11] Military prowess was not enough, however, and they insisted that Sikhs and Pathans lacked the intellectual and administrative capacities necessary to exercise political authority.[12] Hence it was only the 'manly Englishman' who combined all the qualities necessary for both conquest and rule.

While his intellectual capacities and self-discipline served well, in Richard Strachey's mind, to differentiate him from the Indians whom he helped to rule, they could not disguise the fact that, like many British women, his health was not sufficiently robust to manage the fierce Indian heat. He suffered bouts of severe fever in the summers and, like the women of the Raj, was sometimes sent to the hills to recover. Of course, he did not behave like a Raj wife once he was there: on the contrary, it was when recovering from fever in the Himalayas that he began working on botany and geology. As his obituary in *The Times* commented, he was one of the men whose ill health made an important contribution to the work he did in India.[13] His health was always an issue that crossed gender boundaries, however. His anxiety about it, as we have seen, was recognized both within his family and in the army as having something almost hysterical about it— and it required constant management by his family.

Imperial life may have enhanced Richard Strachey's sense of masculinity in certain respects, but it diminished his capacity to carry out properly all his masculine duties. It interfered constantly with the role he played in parenting his sons, for example, and reduced his ability to establish and transmit what he saw as a desirable form of masculinity for the next generation. This transmission of masculine values, that John Tosh has seen as a major concern to many Victorian fathers, was impossible for imperial administrators.[14] Strachey's many years in India kept him away from his older sons and meant that he was so old when the younger ones were born that they thought of him as a benign and aged grandfather rather than a father. His parental anxieties are evident both in many of his letters to his sons and in his discussions with Jane about them. Letters, however, allowed for little beyond exhortation and their very formality showed his incapacity ever to reach into the lives of his sons or to enter their world and their interests. Some of these letters serve also to make clear his recognition of the extent to which he and many of his scientific friends contravened accepted masculine norms. Norma Clarke has pointed to the difficulties that those men engaged in literary pursuits in the nineteenth century had in establishing their masculinity. Thomas Carlyle in particular struggled to fit the literary, and often fragile, 'man of letters' into his rugged masculine ideal.[15] Science, unlike literature, demanded masculine reason rather than feminine sensibility, so that Richard Strachey did not have quite the same difficulty as Carlyle. Nonetheless he was aware that he needed to make a special case when demanding that his sons admire the scientists of whom he thought so very highly. 'Your Mama tells me that you are going to hear Mr Tyndall's lectures', he wrote to his oldest son, Dick, in 1868.

You must try to remember what he says, & to understand it all, & some day perhaps you may be a very wise man like him. It is much better to be wise than strong and indeed the wisest men are often a little weak. An elephant is much stronger than fifty men, but a wise little boy will make him do whatever he wants.

He could not let the opportunity pass to relate this discussion to Dick himself, so he stressed that 'the only way to become wise is to be industrious and to attend to your lessons. Boys who are idle never become wise, and neither I nor your Mama would be happy of we thought you would be a dunce.'[16]

Richard Strachey may not have met all the masculine norms of mid-Victorian society. Nonetheless, he was not only successful in his career, but managed also to father a large family over whom he ruled as a benign patriarch. None of his older sons followed him in this regard. Fatherhood eluded Dick and neither Ralph nor Oliver exhibited any capacity for the government of their families. This was not because the Strachey sons embraced the values of the imperial adventurer and hunter who looms so large in the recent literature on late nineteenth-century imperialism. There is perhaps a hint of this new form of military and imperial masculinity in Dick Strachey's enjoyment of military life, especially his enthusiasm for hunting dacoits and pig-sticking. Certainly, Dick seemed to enjoy the daily routine and male camaraderie of military life far more than his father had done. But Dick showed no wish to continue this kind of life and sought to exchange it for marriage and a home as soon as he could and his inability to marry until the mid-1890s was a source of acute distress.

Dick Strachey clearly had far greater problems than his father had done in complying with the most important standards or expectations of the masculinity of his own class and time. His difficulties in gaining promotion meant that he was quite unable to meet that most basic masculine requirement, financial independence, and depended on financial help from his father until he was 40. Even after that, he lived a far humbler life than that of either his parents or the parents of his wife. Dick's inability to keep his wife in the standard of comfort that she had had in her father's home was compounded by his inability to have children. There is no discussion in the Strachey correspondence of the cause of Dick and Grace's childlessness. Its consequence nonetheless was to deprive Dick of the authority of fatherhood or of the position of head of his own family. It is notable that, after the death of Richard Strachey in 1908, despite some correspondence with Dick as to where his mother and sisters should live, there was no suggestion that he might assume the position of head of the Strachey family.

Ralph, the next Strachey son, was even further removed than Dick from the normal masculine expectations and standards of late nineteenth-century imperial life. The spinal weakness and poor eyesight that precluded him from entering the army made this clear. His life as a railway engineer in itself was often a solitary one and excluded him not only from imperial adventure, but even from normal social life. Even in Calcutta, although he enjoyed a game of whist at 'the club', this was often followed by a solitary dinner at home and an early bedtime. Nor did India spell personal or sexual freedom to him. Like Dick, he saw it as a form of exile both from Britain and from a beloved family at home. 'I enjoyed being at home so much, it was hateful having to come back,' he wrote to his mother after a trip home in his seventh year of Indian service. 'I have got such a nice family I am sure it was worse for me than for most people.'[17]

Like Dick, Ralph married in his early 30s, although it seems to have been shyness and an incapacity to relate to women outside the family, rather than financial difficulties, that delayed his marriage. Marriage did not, however, bring him either comfort or independence from his earlier family and home. Ralph did manage to father three children. As one of them recalls, however, he was never able to assert any form of paternal authority. His mildness and dislike of conflict meant that he always gave way before his rather more quarrelsome wife. Moreover, at the first sign of her emotional instability, he turned back to his sister, Pippa, for help. It was Pippa and their sister-in-law, Ray, rather than Ralph, who managed his wife, his children, and his finances. After his death, Ray Strachey described Ralph as 'Christ-like', but in ways which emphasize his lack of direction, decisiveness, or strength.[18]

While Dick and Ralph Strachey clearly struggled in their attempts to meet the masculine norms and expectations of late nineteenth-century Britain, Oliver Strachey rejected many of them out of hand. Oliver made clear at an early age his lack of interest in pursuing any kind of profession or career. He took what came his way in terms of work, but never felt called upon to exert himself to get on or to seek any form of financial independence. He married early and at a time when he had no capacity to support his wife or child. His lack of financial independence was a source of concern to his family, but Oliver clearly felt no responsibility in this regard. He and Ruby got by as best they could, assisted by regular cheques from Richard Strachey. To the great relief of his mother and sisters, Oliver's second marriage to Ray Costelloe provided him with a regular source of income. Ray assumed the management of all financial and family matters. Even when she and Oliver were no longer living together, Ray oversaw his financial and domestic arrangements. Indeed, her sense of Oliver's incompetence was such that, shortly before her death, she wrote to their son Christopher explaining all of Oliver's financial affairs—and indicating even where Oliver's cheque book was.[19] Nor had fatherhood any meaning to Oliver. He brutally exerted what he saw as his paternal right to Julia, his first daughter, when he removed her from her mother after they divorced. But he took little interest in Julia after that, leaving it up to his sisters and to Ray's relatives to provide her with a home and care.[20] Although affectionate to them, he had little to do with the upbringing or education of the two children of his second marriage. They regarded him as a charming companion, but it never occurred to them to seek his aid or support.[21]

❧ II ❧

The Strachey women came no closer to meeting the accepted gender ideals of their time than did their menfolk. Although a devoted wife and mother, Jane Strachey had always been unconventional in her behaviour and in her approach to marriage and motherhood. Nonetheless, she had managed very well to combine marriage and motherhood with her interest in public affairs and her active engagement in feminism. In the next generation, it was only Elinor who followed this course. The other Strachey daughters engaged to a greater or lesser extent in a revolt against many of the conventions of Victorian and Edwardian femininity. The term 'revolt' is a strong one, but it is hard not to see something of it in the refusal of either Dorothy or Pippa to take any notice of the attentions of the many eligible young men who sought to marry them, in Pernel's determined move away from home and her choice of a career and a life spent amongst women friends and colleagues, or in Marjorie's unseemly party behaviour and passion for telling obscene nursery rhymes. It was evident also in the two youngest Strachey daughters-in-law: in Alix Strachey's cultivation of masculine dress and her refusal to be involved in home-making or domestic management, and in Ray Strachey's determination to organize the life she chose centred on a London-based career, on the one hand, and a rural retreat in the mud house she built herself, on the other.

In the most obvious way, the Strachey women signalled their rejection of prevailing norms of femininity in their carelessness about dress and appearance. Here too, Jane Strachey led the way. To the great consternation of her own mother and sister, Jane Strachey had never paid much attention to her own appearance. She prided herself on her capacity to devise ingenious outfits for balls at little expense and took no notice at all of fashion. She was, however, prepared to let her sister dress her or oversee her wardrobe when the occasion absolutely demanded it. Her daughters were subject to no such restraint. Pippa often prided herself on her 'unkempt appearance' while Marjorie took positive pleasure in shocking people with what she wore.[22] The lack of concern for appearance amongst the younger Strachey women was a subject of comment amongst their friends. 'How curiously untidy all Strachey women become at the least provocation', Virginia Woolf noted after a visit from Pippa. 'Without a certain degree of good looks it isn't worth being vain—that's their reasoning, I always suppose.'[23] Even here, though, there were differences amongst the Strachey women. Marjorie relished being outrageous—and enjoyed shocking her family in the process. 'Marjorie is expected here tomorrow', Jane wrote to James in 1913. 'I suppose she will prance down the high street in black satin tights & bare feet, to 4 different and simultaneous tunes. What will your aunt Lell say!'[24] Pippa, by contrast, accepted the need for some moderation in dress. Although she took no interest in clothes, she did not reject feminine dress and demeanour completely. She loved wearing the uniform of the Women's Land Army during the First World War, but indulged this passion only in the country. When in town, she wore the skirts and coats that seemed more appropriate feminine garb, *albeit* in an extremely dishevelled way.

The youngest Strachey sisters-in-law, Ray and Alix joined enthusiastically in this rejection of feminine dress. In Ray's case, this issue was a rather more fraught and important than it was for the other Stracheys. Her mother and stepfather, Mary and Bernard Berenson, lived in the midst of elegant and wealthy expatriate circles in Florence and regarded fashion and elegant living as matters of the utmost importance. Ray happily accepted their generous allowance, but rejected utterly their values or approach to life— and did her best to show this through her dress, on the one hand, and her enthusiasm for sport and for politics, on the other. In her student days at Newnham, Ray had been happy with the tailored skirts with shirts and ties that were adopted by many women students. From quite early on in her married life, however, and particularly after her second pregnancy when she gained a great deal of weight, she refused to take any notice of her appearance at all. She made a point of wearing whatever was comfortable— taking so little notice of her clothes that she sometimes discovered she had put on dresses inside out or back to front!

Alix Strachey differed from both Ray and her other sisters-in-law in the marked interest she took in clothes. She rejected anything that could be deemed 'feminine', refusing ever to don a dress, but opting instead for stylish trousers. Alix often noted her liking for 'turd coloured' trousers, shirts, and jackets. But the comments in themselves make clear the importance of her own sense of style—and the many photographs of her in these outfits demonstrate that she was keen on good quality and cut and wore her clothes extremely well. On occasion, she also donned a black leather jacket and cap—garments which looked wonderful when she posed on a motor bike. These clothes suited her well and Virginia Woolf, who certainly included Ray in her critical comments on the badly dressed Strachey women, never included Alix in this general condemnation. Laura Doan has recently explored the fashion for masculine clothing in the 1920s, arguing that it was a style and not a sexual statement, and cautioning against reading too much into the sexuality involved in women's wearing of masculine clothes.[25] In Alix Strachey's case, however, it is interesting to note that, while her enjoyment of masculine clothing did not signify an absolute rejection of heterosexuality, her wearing of it was accompanied by a determined pursuit of lesbian relationships. Her clothes were one of the many things that Alix discussed with her husband, James. Her appearance, however, unquestionably contributed to the sense shared by family and friends that Alix was the masculine one in her partnership with James.

Their rejection of feminine clothing was a signal of other and more significant desires to reject feminine norms amongst the Strachey women. All of them were constantly involved in negotiating their desire for independence and a new kind of life with their sense of the importance of certain familial duties. These negotiations were stressful and all of them developed strategies of their own for dealing with them. Pippa is perhaps the most interesting here. As we have seen, Pippa Strachey's trip to India in 1900 required her to assume the role of family head when her cousin, Arthur Strachey, died. She clearly relished the authority that that she now wielded, but seems to have felt some anxiety about asserting it within the family. She seems to have taken care to refrain from any suggestion that she was now in full command, engaging rather in a kind of subterfuge in which she exercised power without seeming to do so. Pippa sent daily letters home from India, explaining what was happening and seeking advice from her parents as to what to do next. But of course the letters took weeks to be answered and she had always acted decisively before there was any response. Moreover in some instances, such as insisting on carrying out her cousin's wish to be cremated, although this was seen as a heathen Indian rather than a British practice, one has a sense that Pippa may well have acted in ways that her family would not have condoned.

Although she never sought analysis and manifested few signs of emotional or psychic disturbance, Pippa's conduct sometimes does show qualities that Joan Riviere later incorporated in her discussion of 'femininity as masquerade'. Like the women Riviere describes, Pippa constantly sought approval and support from her parents and later her siblings after she had taken assertive and decisive actions—as if to reassure herself and them of her own femininity.[26] When she returned home after her trip to India, Pippa resumed her role of family housekeeper, looking after her ageing and infirm father and then doing the same for her mother. But she was far from being a Victorian single daughter or drudge. On the contrary, Pippa effectively became the family head, deciding where she and her parents would live and managing the family finances. She was constantly called on to resolve family problems and difficulties, especially when anything needed to be made known to her mother, or when anyone sought financial support. As her older brothers realized, it was she and not they on whom their mother depended and they too turned to her for help, support, and advice, as their younger siblings did. She managed not only her mother's money, but also the terms of her will—thus determining how the family money was distributed. This exercise of power was always accompanied by the asking of advice, although in effect she was simply seeking confirmation of decisions she had already taken. This is not to suggest in any way that she was hypocritical. Just as Pippa eschewed the limelight in her feminist work, so too she was clearly uncomfortable appearing in any way as the family head. She exercised power in an indirect way, but she was no less powerful for that. Pippa Strachey was patient and sometimes long-suffering, but as she made clear in regard to Ralph's wife, she enjoyed her exercise of authority. She was able also, we have seen in her relationship with Lytton, to extract a high price for hurt suffered at the hands of members of the family who demanded perhaps more than she could give—or who slighted her.

While Pippa worked out a new kind of role within the very bosom of the family, Pernel seemed determined to work out her life far away from it. Pernel seems never to have been involved in any form of domestic management or support—and she never sought to undertake it. In her early years, it was her education that took her away from the family, and when it was finished, Pernel took up easily and quickly the role of an independent professional woman, too busy to offer family support during term time—and entitled to use her vacation time precisely as she chose. Occasionally Pernel was prevailed upon to take her younger siblings with her, as she did Lytton when she and Jane Ellen Harrison travelled to Sweden in 1912. But it was others who fitted into her plans, rather than she who accommodated them.

Pippa and Pernel Strachey worked out new ways to organize their lives, but without coming into significant conflict with either family or friends. By contrast, Marjorie Strachey frequently transgressed the boundaries of feminine propriety in ways that were both public and shocking. In part this was a result of the fact that, while the two older Strachey sisters sought personal independence, neither of them sought in any way to challenge prevailing sexual norms. Marjorie Strachey belonged to a younger generation for whom an active sexual life was deemed considerably more important. Unlike Pernel, moreover, she apparently had wanted to marry and have a family. Her tragedy, as she portrayed it to friends like Virginia Woolf was that she never succeeded in finding a possible partner and her only sexual relationship ended in a very distressing way. Yet, despite her apparent desire to marry Josiah Wedgwood, Marjorie never showed either any interest in or any capacity for domestic or family life. Unlike her older sisters, she rarely participated in housekeeping for her parents and siblings, and there was a general sense that starvation would ensue if she ever had. As a lowly paid teacher, Marjorie lived in a very simple way. Her confrontations with femininity and propriety occurred primarily in the form of the entertainments that she offered. Marjorie was renowned throughout

Bloomsbury and beyond for her party performances. These consisted of dances—in which she sometimes wore tights, but also performed nude—and recited nursery rhymes in ways that made them both menacing and obscene. Quentin Bell, who firmly believed that all Marjorie's difficulties arose from her lack of physical charm, argued that she showed great courage in exploiting her very ugliness to hold and enrapture an audience.

That she could sing, dance and recite proves her courage, but there was something almost inconceivably brave about her resolve to make herself look really atrocious. I once saw her rehearse a performance clad in black tights into which she had forced a bright scarlet cushion suggestive of some indecent deformity. Thus clad she danced across the floor and sang nursery rhymes, or what had been nursery rhymes, until Marjorie converted them by her manner and innuendos, into something unspeakably sinister and macabre. When, in the middle of this outrageous performance, a corner of the scarlet cushion began to slip down between her silk-stockinged legs the effect was overwhelming.[27]

This particular performance apparently took place before an audience of 'cultivated ladies from Hampstead and Kensington' who had expected something very different when they came to be entertained by Miss Strachey—and left the room horrified. Marjorie's dances and nursery rhymes were greatly enjoyed at Bloomsbury parties, however, and were sought after as far as Cambridge, although Pernel sometimes refused to permit her to perform there!

While engaging in performances that depended on sexual innuendo and double entendres, Marjorie Strachey did not share Bloomsbury's openness about sexual matters. She was certainly more inclined to discuss sex than her older sisters: in her early adult years, she shocked both James and Lytton by announcing that she had 'almost decided to copulate with some woman or other'. James, who found any reference to women's sexuality at this point disgusting, complained to Lytton about the way that 'women always make things so indecent'.[28] But there is no evidence that Marjorie actually carried out this plan. She maintained a rigidly conventional approach to sexual misdemeanours which was equally appalling to Lytton and James. Oliver's divorce was a source of horror to her—and she embarrassed her brothers intensely by her refusal to talk to, or even to acknowledge, known adulterers like H. G. Wells, even when they attended the same dinner parties.[29] She seemed to ricochet backwards and forwards between Victorian assumptions and those of the Bloomsbury world without ever working out any form of accommodation between them.

❧ III ❧

While questions of gender preoccupied the Strachey women, few of them actively interrogated questions of sexuality or transgressed sexual norms. The reverse is true of their brother Oliver Strachey, for whom questions of gender were apparently unproblematic, but who was both fascinated and troubled about sex. Sex was clearly not something Oliver could discuss with his sisters, Pernel or Pippa, nor does he seem to have discussed it with Ralph. It comes to the fore primarily in his correspondence with Lytton. The relationship between Oliver and Lytton Strachey was a markedly asymmetrical one. In the late 1890s and the early 1900s, Oliver seems to have admired Lytton and to have sought some connection with his intellectual and literary world and with the sexual freedoms that that world offered. Lytton had no such interest in Oliver. Like James, he regarded him as boring and old-fashioned, and as lacking the intellectual capacity and distinction evident amongst his friends. From the start of his Cambridge years, moreover, Lytton had found many others with whom to discuss his own sexual preoccupations. He felt little interest in Oliver's heterosexual concerns—and Oliver in turn showed little sympathy for Lytton's anxieties about his own homosexuality. Nonetheless, and despite his complaints about Lytton's lack of response, Oliver wrote to Lytton for several years while he was India and his letters offer a rare insight into heterosexual male desire in the early twentieth century—and into the difficulties of finding ways to articulate it.[30]

While Oliver Strachey was clearly promiscuous, engaging in many different sexual relationships both simultaneously and serially, his letters to Lytton suggest that it was emotional rather than sexual intimacy that he sought. 'Have you ever thought of fornication for fornication's sake?', he asked him in 1906.

I expect really it's the right thing; but I'm afraid I'm not up to it. With me it's always the relation that is exciting—the being on fornicating terms with someone is so tremendous, & the wonderful gradual exchange of mentality . . . what I mean is that its neither the copulation nor the desire to copulate that is the great thing for me, but the being on copulating terms and the arrival at that point.[31]

It was 'not that I don't like copulation', he added, 'but I believe I like the relation more . . . Don't you find new friends more exciting than old? Mama had a good phrase for that: she said that with new friends you have your

278

capital to draw on, but with old friends only your interest.'[32] Doubtless Jane Strachey would have been horrified to see her comment on friendship applied to sexual relationships!

Unfortunately Oliver did not retain Lytton's replies to his letters. One has a sense that Lytton rejected his approach to copulation, preferring the spiritual and emotional intimacy so important to his ideal of the 'higher sodomy'. Oliver in turn rejected the view that what mattered most was the spiritual intercourse of souls. 'Bodily love,' he argued, 'is not an expression of soul's love, but just bodily love.' He preferred to recognize the importance and benefits of lust. Both love and lust, he argued 'seem to me to be a desire for contact, & the thing is that lust gets it, whereas love only glimmers towards it . . . If the real *I* could touch the real *you* of course it would be infinitely finer than copulation . . . but meanwhile there is much to be said in favour of a successful bookmaker as against the incomplete artist.' He felt, moreover, that it was necessary to recognize 'the extraordinary intenseness of purely sensual feelings as compared with mental', and hence to acknowledge the intensity of sexual passion.

This correspondence came to an end in 1908. Oliver returned to England after his divorce from Ruby and certainly never wrote to Lytton in the course of his second marriage. There are a few other sources of information about him, however, that are interesting. He was clearly much more at ease both with his sexuality and indeed with his body than was Lytton. He allowed Duncan Grant and Vanessa Bell to photograph him naked—something his younger brothers would never have done.[33] Moreover, Oliver was also very open with his sexual knowledge. In 1911, he supplied James Strachey with detailed information on different forms of contraception, which James in turn sent on to Rupert Brooke, with a series of drawings to ensure that Brooke could purchase what he needed at a chemist. Oliver's information included descriptions of French letters, pessaries, and syringes intended to be used with spermicides containing quinine. Oliver's continued ambivalence about actual intercourse was evident in the advice he gave to James. 'My dear boy', James quoted him as saying, 'I recommend you to content yourself, if you're dealing with a girl with "playing about" with her—you can get plenty of pleasure that way. But if you *must* block someone, my final advice to you is—let it be a married woman.'[34]

Unfortunately for feminist biographers, there are few reflections from Oliver on his sexual life after he married Ray, nor did she ever comment on his sexual history and attitudes, or on their sexual life. There was one final comment from Oliver on sexual matters that is a rather curious one. It is a letter to Havelock Ellis written in 1921. Oliver was reading one of Ellis's works, he explained, and felt the need to tell him how important his work had been in his life. He regarded Ellis as a 'dear friend', he wrote, and indeed felt he had been one for a very long time. Far from revealing anything about Oliver himself, however, the letter is rather a bluff and chatty one—similar, as Oliver himself noted, to many that Ellis probably received. But one feels Oliver here reverting to Strachey sociability and good manners, rather than taking the opportunity to write of anything that really was important to him. 'I like you my dear sir—Immensely,' he wrote, 'I like your intelligence, your feeling, your sympathy, your unaffected humanity, your reality—why I even like your opinions on Schubert and Beethoven, and what could be rarer than that?' Oliver's history was 'not among your dossiers', he concluded, but if he had written Oliver's history, Ellis would have found his own name playing a prominent part.[35]

IV

Lytton Strachey may not have shown any interest in writing to his older brother about his sexuality, but it was certainly something he discussed in immense detail both with his younger brother, James, and with many of his friends. His own sense of gender identity and his sexual life and writings have in turn been the subject of much recent scrutiny, although there is still considerable debate about how to interpret Lytton Strachey's approach to sexuality—and particularly his sense of his own sexual modernity. While his father and older brothers may have had some difficulties in living up to the dominant masculine norms of their society, Lytton Strachey rejected them entirely. He chose an altogether different model in Oscar Wilde. It was from Wilde, many recent commentators argue, that Lytton 'learned the style and performance of gender ambiguity', and he emphasized his frailty and effeminacy in ways that made him the antithesis of virile Victorian masculinity.[36] Lytton greatly enjoyed several of Wilde's plays, sometimes offering 'queer' readings of them to his cousin, Duncan Grant. In the privacy of his rooms at Cambridge, he affected the clothes and posture of a Wildean dandy, donning pale yellow gloves, or silk pyjamas, while he entertained friends to decadent evenings. His Cambridge performances,

Michael Holroyd argues, consciously brought Wilde to mind as Strachey too sought to use elegance and wit to challenge conventional morals.[37] In his performances and his letters, Lytton serves well to illustrate what many historians of sexuality have seen as one of the most significant developments of the late nineteenth century: the emergence of homosexuality as a particular sexual identity and of homosexual subcultures that emphasized the importance of homosexuality in every aspect of artistic, social, and personal life.[38] At the same time, of course, Lytton was appalled by Wilde's fate, which kept ever before him the knowledge that his own sexual desires were deemed criminal.

While Strachey's desire to question accepted gender boundaries and to proclaim himself a homosexual are not open to question, this is not the case when it comes to his approach to sexual behaviour, which has been seen in very different ways by recent historians. For Linda Dowling, Lytton Strachey marks a clean break with an older Victorian tradition, prevalent particularly at the universities, in which intense romantic intellectual and spiritual friendships between men were seen as the highest form of relationship—and as something that connected the nineteenth century with classical Greece. These relationships, Dowling argues, were rarely consummated. Indeed, both at Oxford and Cambridge intense male friendships flourished, but sexual activity between men was usually regarded as morbid or diseased.[39] The very fact that there was no physical consummation was seen as showing the superiority of these intellectual and spiritual bonds to any form of relationship with women. Many of the men who had been involved in university brotherhoods married, but marriage was seen as involving a 'lower self', while the 'higher self' continued to engage in the supreme pleasure of celibate male friendships.

When Lytton Strachey first went to Cambridge in the 1890s, the whole question of how to view and interpret male friendships was undergoing change. The mid-nineteenth-century ideal of chaste but loving same-sex relationships was no longer possible. By the 1880s and 1890s, Hellenic ideals that earlier generations had seen as spiritual were understood to have involved explicitly sexual feelings and relationships between men. At the same time, sexology had brought with it a new awareness and a new language of 'sexual inversion' and deviance. Lytton Strachey has long been credited with bringing a new openness to the discussions of sexuality, particularly homosexuality, both in Cambridge then in Bloomsbury. He insisted on the importance of homosexual desire at meetings of the

Apostles, and sought to remove the cloak of brotherly love from earlier male friendships by pointing to what he saw as the obvious homosexuality of many members of the society. Strachey's frankness was evident also in his correspondence, especially with Maynard Keynes and with his brother James. Their letters talk not only of love and longing, but also of homosexual marriage and divorce and, more confrontingly, of buggery and rape.

The openness of this discussion has led many to assume that Strachey was the leading figure in a sexually free community, in which the open practice of homosexuality was not only allowed but encouraged. And yet, for Lytton Strachey himself, as several recent writers have argued, sex was something to be talked about rather than performed. While scorning the evasions of some of the earlier Apostles, Julie Taddeo has argued, Strachey and his friends were themselves very much immersed in the ideal of the 'higher sodomy', and sought even in their 'new style of love' to ensure that restraint was always exercised over 'the impetuosity of . . . desires.'[40] Like earlier generations of Apostles, they drew on Plato and classical Greece in an endeavour to exalt themselves and their friendships. Their verbal violence was thus accompanied by considerable physical timidity. Thus the 'rape' referred to in the Keynes/Strachey letters usually meant a kiss, while buggering someone meant kissing them in a bedroom. Even Strachey's pornographic poems were concerned to laud the 'holy and essential' over the 'body's flesh'. Taddeo points to the severe constraints that both Lytton Strachey and Maynard Keynes imposed on the beautiful young men with whom they fell in love. Preoccupied as they were with their own physical inadequacies, both Strachey and Keynes often resisted physical involvement, insisting that their younger partners accept and live up to their own high and spiritual Grecian ideals. Men, like Duncan Grant, who felt no guilt about sex and thoroughly enjoyed their own physical being, were extremely hard for them to deal with.

This emphasis on restraint and on a particular set of 'high' ideals was evident also in James Strachey. Lytton Strachey and Keynes sometimes expressed shock at the overt forms of sexual display evident amongst James and his younger friends, but James's letters to Rupert Brooke suggest that for him too, unrequited desire, on the one hand, and gossip and intrigue, on the other, were the main ingredients in sexual life. James pursued Brooke, but it was his love he wanted. 'Really, you know,' he wrote to Brooke on one occasion, 'its only in the most *special* circumstances that copulation's tolerable'.[41] Both Strachey and Brooke followed with interest

a discussion amongst some of the other Apostles as to whether relationships between men should ever be consummated. For James, as for Lytton,
it was the freedom to discuss sexual feeling and desire that mattered—
rather than any actual form of sexual expression.

Lytton Strachey's interest in and preparedness to talk openly about
sexuality was as important in the world of Bloomsbury as it had been at
Cambridge. It was he whom Virginia Woolf regarded as the person who
broke down the final conversational taboo amongst the inner core of
Bloomsbury when, shortly after the marriage of Vanessa Bell and Clive
Bell, he asked Vanessa if a stain on her dress was semen. In a moment,
Woolf insisted, 'all barriers of reticence and reserve' were broken.

A flood of the sacred fluid seemed to overwhelm us. Sex permeated our conversation. The word bugger was never far from our lips. We discussed copulation
with the same excitement and openness that we had discussed the nature of
good... All this had the result that the old sentimental views of marriage in
which we were brought up were revolutionised... Perhaps the fidelity of our
parents was not the only or inevitably the highest form of married life... So, there
was now nothing that one could not say, nothing that one could not do at 46
Gordon Square. It was, I think a great advance in Civilization. It may be true that
the loves of buggers are not... of enthralling interest or paramount importance.
But the fact that they can be mentioned openly leads to the fact that no one minds
if they are practised privately.[42]

As Woolf makes clear, this free discussion of sexuality, and the recognition
of homosexual desires, was seen by Lytton and his Bloomsbury friends as a
key part of their own modernity. Amongst some in Bloomsbury, of course,
it was also accompanied by considerable sexual experimentation and
freedom, both in heterosexual and in homosexual terms. This approach
to sexuality served to differentiate the modern young inhabitants of
Bloomsbury from their elders and from the rest of society, few of whom
were prepared openly to acknowledge their own or other people's sexuality. The open discussion of sex also allowed the kind of intimacy amongst
friends that was so central to Bloomsbury. Vanessa and Clive Bell entertained their friends while they were in bed, breaking down instantly the
barriers between drawing room and bedroom that were so important in
Victorian homes, and by implication inviting friends to share their intimate
life.[43]

While Lytton Strachey could discuss sexual questions openly with
James and with his other friends, his domestic life remained subject to

the constraints of any Victorian home. The death of Leslie Stephen freed Vanessa Bell and Virginia Woolf to live where and how they pleased. However, both Sir Richard and Lady Strachey were still alive when Lytton and James were at Cambridge and indeed for many years after. Hence Lytton's homosexuality and indeed his entire private life required a certain amount of care and negotiation within the family. Several of his siblings seem to have been very much aware of his inclinations and of his life. James and Oliver both were, as indeed were Dorothy and Marjorie. Lytton's letters to Dorothy, especially those from just after the First World War, describe in detail his life, his parties with young men, and his emotional states and relationships quite clearly.[44] Ray Strachey too was in the know. Her own friendships with Keynes and Virginia Woolf would have made it hard for this not to be the case. Mary Berenson was a little shocked when she visited Ray in London in 1910, and Ray after taking her to several Bloomsbury gatherings explained that the men 'were all sods'.[45]

The two people from whom Lytton's life had to be kept hidden were Jane Strachey and Pippa.[46] It was Pippa who seems to have posed the greatest difficulty for Lytton. She was the sister to whom he was closest and on whom he depended most. She was also the one who most resembled their mother in her sexual attitudes and reticence. Hence his homosexuality was never openly broached with her. One has a sense that Pippa had taken on some aspects of the persona of the 'new woman' of the 1890s, but was not prepared to move any further than that. She was prepared to discuss prostitution and to encompass a range of heterosexual possibilities, but she seems not to have been ready to engage with homosexual ones. This is nicely illustrated in a report Lytton sent James concerning a conversation he had had with Pippa just after she returned from a visit to Bertie and Alys Russell's. Maynard Keynes had been a fellow guest. Pippa, Lytton reported,

thought that nowadays women were so sensible that there was nothing in the conversation of young men which they couldn't hear with equanimity. It would be impossible for people in the [suffrage] Society to feel any strain when they were talking to people at Newnham, whatever the subject. 'For instance no one, I'm sure, would ever be shocked by Keynes.' Colossal! What a vision she must have of the world. It's really too terrific.[47]

Pippa, who saw Keynes on his best behaviour, had of course no idea of the correspondence he constantly exchanged with Lytton and James in which buggery, sodomy, and rape were constant themes.

Pippa's own views are hard to ascertain. On the one hand, it seems possible that the deep hurt she felt she had suffered at Lytton's hands had something to do with discovering his sexuality. But there is no direct evidence to support this view. On the other hand, one does have a sense that, while Pippa maintained a Victorian reticence about sex, she did not necessarily share the sexual attitudes of her mother. Unlike Jane Strachey, for example, she had no difficulty in accepting Lytton's domestic arrangements with Carrington. On the contrary, as we have seen, she was a frequent and very welcome visitor to their home and much beloved by Carrington. Lytton's own behaviour in regard to Pippa too is rather curious. He was never frank with her—but he seems to have gone out of his way to be 'discovered'. James worked hard to protect his sisters from any unsought sexual knowledge, but not Lytton. He frequently wrote and received sexually explicit letters in the Strachey home without remembering to seal the envelope. In response to his frequent expressions of anxiety lest his letters be read, Keynes insisted that their provocative letters were deliberately written with a view to their possible discovery.[48] In an even more direct way, Carrington commented on the 'Freudian' aspect of Lytton wanting her to hide an indecent drawing by Augustus John when Pippa came to visit, while 'forgetting even the name of the book he put it into'.[49]

There was never any open acknowledgment from Pippa during his lifetime. However it does seem likely that she was well aware of her brother's life. Just as Jane Strachey, despite her own reticence, acted decisively and sensibly to defuse family hysteria when Duncan Grant was found by an aunt and uncle to have nude pictures in his luggage, so too Pippa seems to have lived comfortably in a world dominated by sexual discussion, homosexuality, and extra-marital relations, without ever expressing disapproval or indeed feeling the need to take up any position at all. Frances Partridge confirms this view in a rather wonderful anecdote concerning Pippa in her final years. When the sexual life of Bloomsbury was first clearly exposed in Holroyd's *Lytton Strachey* in 1968, Pippa was still alive. Oliver's daughter, Julia Strachey, went to visit Pippa in her nursing home and pointed out that Lytton had slept with Duncan Grant while the family was still living at Lancaster Gate. Julia, who had hoped to shock Pippa, was rather taken aback when Pippa replied 'Well, you know he was very beautiful!' Frances herself was rather appalled that Julia had 'forced Pippa to admit that she had known about Lytton's tendencies, that she remembered an Eton boy going to his bedroom, and that she was shocked by it', but Julia showed no remorse 'for badgering this poor old lady on the brink of the tomb, and forcing her to face what James tried his best to shield her from'.[50]

V

By the 1920s, James and Alix Strachey were beginning to develop an approach to questions about sexuality quite unlike that of anyone else in the Strachey family. It derived from their translation and study of the writings of Freud. In James's view, Freud's *Three Essays on Sexuality* stand alongside his *Interpretation of Dreams* 'as his most momentous and original contribution to human knowledge'.[51] When he translated this essay, James provided an editorial note explaining both his sense of what was most important in Freud's discussion of sexuality and a brief history of the development of Freud's ideas about it. In the 1890s, he explained, Freud's recognition of the importance of sexual factors in anxiety neuroses, neurasthenia, and then of psychoneuroses led him to a more extensive investigation of sexuality. Work done in the course of his early partnership with Fleiss made Freud aware of the importance of bisexuality in infants and of erotogenic zones that are liable to stimulation in infancy, but later suppressed. This question of erotogenic zones and infantile pleasures also led to a recognition of the development of perversions, on the one hand, and of the 'repressive forces' of disgust, shame, and morality, on the other. In what has come to be a widely accepted account of the development of Freud's ideas, James insisted that, while all the elements of the theory of infantile sexuality existed by the mid-1890s, they still required the keystone that was provided when Freud abandoned his seduction theory and accepted that sexual impulses operated autonomously in young children without any need for adult stimulation or interference. Freud was led to this in part by his own self-analysis which revealed to him the Oedipus complex, the means by which infantile sexual desires can be contained and resolved within the familial setting.[52]

In the course of the 1920s, as Alix and James Strachey worked on translating the writings of both Freud and Melanie Klein, they struggled to comprehend some of their ideas, especially those dealing with the unconscious sexual desires of children. This was not because they had any disinclination to accept the connection between sexuality and the unconscious or the existence of infantile sexuality, but rather because they had difficulty in understanding precisely how the Oedipal situation worked. When exactly was it, they pondered, that a little boy became sufficiently aware of female anatomy to be able to desire, or to imagine, even unconsciously, any form of genital contact with his mother?[53] Their correspondence illustrates well the novelty of a psychoanalytic approach to sexuality in the 1920s, and how difficult it was to understand, even for those who helped develop the language in which this approach became known in the Anglophone world.

Although James and Alix shared some of their new insights into sexuality with Lytton, their growing interest in the unconscious and its importance in every aspect of life often made them impatient with him, as with their other friends. After lunching with Lytton at the Oriental Club in 1925, James wrote to Alix about how difficult it was either to gossip about the private lives of friends or even to discuss general questions about religion or asceticism. 'I find I have to suppress almost everything that it occurs to me to say. Why can't these asses read the Professor's works?'[54] This comment contrasts sharply with the earlier ease James had felt in discussing sexual questions with his older brother. During their Cambridge days in the 1890s and the early twentieth century and later in Edwardian Bloomsbury, James and Lytton had written about sex constantly, seeking not only to articulate their own wishes and desires, but also to transgress and undermine the Victorian sexual norms that dominated their familial and social lives. The naming and bringing into open discussion of much that had continued to be hidden or frowned upon by respectable society was for them an important act of resistance and subversion. However, the language in which they discussed sexual desire and behaviour was one that would have been easily understood by their contemporaries. Their constant reference in talk and in correspondence to buggers and sodomites, to homosexual marriage, to rape and other forms of sexual intercourse, would have shocked and offended their parents and families, but in part this was precisely because the language they used was so familiar. Lytton Strachey and his friends sought both new approaches to sexual morality and new forms of sexual identity. The importance of the unconscious in sexual desire, however, and the place of sexuality in other aspects of emotional life was almost as foreign to them as it was to their parents. Theirs was essentially a pleasure in dirty talk of a particular kind and the constant exaggerations, whereby a kiss became 'rape', simply provided added frisson.

James and Alix had to come to terms with Freud's views, because their work as his translators required a very sophisticated understanding of his ideas. In the course of these translations, they played a significant part in devising what became the English psychoanalytic terminology. Their correspondence provides a wonderful insight into the difficulties they faced in translating Freud at a time when even most basic terms such as 'sex' and 'sexual' required definition. This is well illustrated in a letter James wrote to Alix, discussing a disagreement between himself and the leading English analyst, Ernest Jones. Jones, who was often critical of the Stracheys, checked all their early translations of Freud. James and Alix in turn were often scathing about Jones's ideas, and critical of his approach to translation and his capacity as a proof reader. On this particular occasion, they had disagreed about the meaning and use of the term 'sexual'. In a passage that James translated as 'the ego has no sexual currents', Jones had crossed out the term 'sexual' and written in the margin, '*Sex* ... (my distinction between sex & sexual comes in well here). Adj. Sex=section=division between 2 sexes. Sexual=pertaining to sexuality in general.' Jones, James explained to Alix, 'uses the *noun* "sex" to mean the quality of being either m(ale). or f(emale)., and the noun "sexuality" to mean everything connected with the Libido. And the *adjective* "sexual" corresponds to the *noun* "sexuality", and the adjective "sex" to the *noun* "sex".' Using an illustration taken from Lytton Strachey's *Queen Victoria*, James went on further to explain Jones's use of the terminology.

Thus he would say:
(1) The Prince Consort's sex is male.
(2) He was not interested in questions of sexuality.
(3) His sex characteristics were strongly developed.
(4) His sexual desire was repressed.[55]

James regarded this account as 'intelligible, if frothing'. But he continued to feel that, in the passage in question, his use of the word 'sexual' was correct.

The German 'Sexualstrebengen' is the same word Freud's used several times before ... I think if you read the whole passage through, it's fairly clear that he must mean the ego has no sexual currents *uberhaupt* and not that the ego is not specifically masculine or feminine (which is what Jones must be suggesting). But I admit the whole passage is involved ... and I stand to be corrected.[56]

Ultimately James's rendition of the passage was the one that was published. What is important here is not the resolution of the translation of a particular word, but rather the sense that this correspondence offers of how very novel and complex this language about sexuality that has since come to be taken for granted, was in the 1920s.

This interest in infantile sexuality and the new language of sexuality that accompanied it went along with a quite new way of seeing and understanding the behaviour of those around them. This was particularly noticeable in relation to their family. Thus, for example, playful behaviour in younger relatives was seen in more explicitly erotic terms. In 1925, James described to Alix an evening he had spent at his mother's, in the company of Ray Strachey and her adolescent daughter. Barbara Strachey was

practically grown up . . . most attractive I thought—and frantically coming on. I suppose she's just still absolutely in the latency period. Her one idea to 'rag' (physically) all the time: filch things out of uncle James's pockets—or to filch his specs and false beard. At the end there was a most affecting scene of theatrical embrace. Ray seemed to me decidedly uneasy and stiff about it.[57]

As we have seen, the first of Freud's works that the Stracheys began to translate was not any of the writings specifically on sexuality, but rather his 'Group Psychology and the Analysis of the Ego'. This work, too, is very interesting in terms of its discussion of the relationship between individual sexual development and identity and the behaviour of crowds. In it, Freud outlined briefly his understanding of libido in a way that both stressed the sexual basis of all forms of love and connected political and social behaviour with unconscious erotic feelings in ways that the Stracheys probably found extremely revealing and significant, especially after they had just lived through the First World War. This work served also to show the importance of the unconscious and of sexuality in every realm of life, something which both Alix and James strongly believed. It remained a very important work for them, providing the framework for Alix's one significant monograph, *The Unconscious Motives of War*, that was published in 1957.[58]

In taking up the question of crowd psychology, Freud was addressing an issue of considerable interest and concern amongst late nineteenth-century psychologists and sociologists who sought to analyse the new forms of political behaviour that seemed to be emerging with mass society. His own work was strongly influenced by the French sociologist Gustave le Bon, who argued that individuals ceased to act consciously or on the basis of their own will in crowds, acting rather unconsciously, on suggestions almost as if they were hypnotized. Freud regarded le Bon's analysis of the group mind and of the importance of the unconscious in it as brilliant, but felt that his approach failed to analyse the connection between the leader and the crowd.

To explain the feelings of the crowd for their leader, Freud first felt it necessary to explain his understanding of libido and of the complexities of sexual development and sexual object choice. Some of these ideas had already been enunciated in his 'Essays on Sexuality', but they appeared in 'Group Psychology' in a summary and rather more definite form. His definition of libido emphasized the sexual element in all forms of love. We call by the name libido, he explained,

the energy . . . of those instincts which have to do with all that may be comprised under the word 'love'. The nucleus of what we mean by love naturally consists (and this is what is commonly called love in what the poets sing of) in sexual love with sexual union as its aim. But we do not separate from this—what in any case has a share in the name 'love'—on the one hand, self-love, and on the other, love for parents and children, friendship and love for humanity in general, and also devotion to concrete objects and abstract ideas. Our justification lies in the fact that psychoanalytic research has taught us that all these tendencies are an expression of the same instinctual impulses; in relations between the sexes these impulses force their way towards sexual union, but in other circumstances they are diverted from this aim or are prevented from reaching it, although always preserving enough of their original nature to keep their identity recognisable.[59]

In the process of explaining how groups came to be formed, he insisted also on the importance of understanding a range of different forms of sexual identity and of emotional development, and particularly the genesis of homosexuality. The issue that was most significant for him centred on identification, and on the different forms it could take. Identification with a parent, he insisted, was the original form of emotional tie. Normally, the child after some struggle replaced the parent with another sexual object. This did not always happen, however, and excessive identification with a parent could quite often be seen as providing the genesis of male homosexuality.

A young man has been unusually long and intensely fixated upon his mother in the sense of the Oedipus complex. But at last, after the end of puberty, the time comes for exchanging his mother for some other sexual object. Things take a sudden turn: the young man does not abandon his mother, but identifies himself with her; he transforms himself into her, and now looks about for objects which can replace his ego for him, and on which he can bestow such love and care as he has experienced from his mother ... A striking thing about this identification is its ample scale; it remoulds the ego in one of its important features—in its sexual character—upon the model that of what has hitherto been the object. In this process the object itself is renounced.[60]

The final point for Freud centred on the ways in which groups involved the sublimation of the sexual drive of their members, as each one came to internalize their desire for the leader and to turn the leader into their own ego ideal. The formation of a group thus rested on his ideas about sexual identity, erotic displacement, and about the ways in which sexual feelings could be sublimated and removed from any direct sexual object and channelled towards a beloved leader. In the case of some individuals, he argued, one could see complex and regressive forms of identification in which there was no direct desire for a particular sexual object, but rather an internalization of the qualities of the desired person and a sense of identification with others who shared that same ideal. The sublimation of sexual feelings that was required for the formation of a group, dedicated to its leader and with each member identifying with each other because of this shared ideal, left no place for other forms of sexual life. The army and the church provided Freud's two main examples, and he insisted that neither allowed any place for women or for what Freud referred to as 'the aims of the genital organisation of the libido'.[61]

The question of homosexuality, and the sublimation of homosexual desires, features largely in Freud's analysis of group psychology. The account he offers there, and the assumption that homosexuality is connected to irrational group behaviour, does raise some of the questions that have been widely debated recently concerning Freud's evaluation of different forms of sexuality. His significance in establishing as separate categories 'homosexuality' and 'heterosexuality' has been widely recognized, but many questions have been raised about the extent to which he contributed to a homophobic discourse through his emphasis on heterosexuality as 'normal', not just in a statistical sense, but also as something equated with psychic maturity, in contrast with homosexuality which often seems to appear as abnormal and immature. The idea that psychoanalysis could 'cure' homosexuality was certainly around in some advanced circles in Britain in the early 1920s—and underlay some of Lytton Strachey's early hostility to Freud. 'Psycho-analysis is a ludicrous fraud,' he wrote to Carrington in 1920 not only Ottoline has been cured at Freiburg. The Sackville-West youth was there to be cured of homosexuality. After 4 months & an expenditure of £200, he found he could just bear the thought of going to bed with a woman. No more. Several other wretched undergraduates have been through the same 'treatment'. They walk about haggard on the lawn, wondering whether they could bear the thought of a woman's private parts, and gazing at their little lovers, who run round and round.[62]

Neither James nor Alix Strachey seem to have read psychoanalysis in this way, however, and Lytton too became rather more sympathetic after they took it up. It is hard not to see their attraction to it as being connected in some way to their awareness of their own complex sexual and emotional lives. Both were very much aware of the extent to which they transgressed accepted gender boundaries, with the tall, strong, trouser-clad Alix always markedly in contrast to the slight, silent, and apparently frail James. Alix took no interest in feminine pursuits and exuded a form of masculine power. The tom-boyishness and passion for cricket evident in her adolescence transformed itself in her early adult years into a need to be the one who pursued her male lover and rejected the advances anyone made to her. James in turn was an often silent and inert man. His passive suffering under the weight of his infatuation with Rupert Brooke had been a great source of anxiety to Lytton. Even when James's sexual orientation had shifted from homosexual to heterosexual, and his attention shifted from Rupert Brooke to Noel Olivier, he continued to play a passive and even masochistic role. In their initial coming together, Alix had played the active and aggressive role with James. These transgressions of gender and sexual norms had been accompanied by periods of acute emotional and nervous distress for both Alix and James during and after their student days. James's unhappiness and passivity at Cambridge was a source of constant comment from Lytton and Duncan Grant. He was aware of it too and, in 1913, felt too debilitated by depression to carry out his duties at *The Spectator*. Alix too had suffered from nervous complaints. She had some kind of breakdown while at Newnham in 1912 and 1913. Although regarded as a cardiac weakness at the time, it seems in retrospective to have been a nervous condition that left her thin, weak, and apparently anorexic.[63]

Whatever its impact on others, psychoanalysis did nothing to reduce the sexual tolerance or the interest in different forms of sexual behaviour that James and Alix had exhibited in their Bloomsbury days. On the contrary, although James seemed to have established a heterosexual identity for himself, he retained a strong sense of commitment to homosexual free-dom—joining Alix in regular donations to the movement for homosexual law reform.[64] Alix, on the other hand, began to engage in lesbian relation-ships in the same decade as she took up psychoanalysis. She spent much time in the 1920s questioning whether she should or would have a lesbian relationship. She was distressed by the obsessive attention of her old university friend, Josephine Dellisch, and did attempt to persuade her to undergo analysis as a way to deal with it. But she bewailed her own inability to fall in love with a woman quite often throughout the 1920s, rather than seeing it as 'normal'. While in Berlin in 1925, for example, she wrote to James about an episode at one of the many balls she attended where 'I was led round by a Saph. [sic] of an ultra masculine character, tho' feminine appearance. She went so far as to seize my hands & kiss them & invite me to her studio to tea. Shall I go? I appear to be as repressed as ever in that direction'.[65] As we have seen, in 1929 Alix does seem finally to have embarked on a lesbian relationship with a woman called Nancy M that satisfied her curiosity without disrupting her marriage.

11

A Feminist Family

Feminist activity and commitment was an important thing within the Strachey family, spanning almost a century and including both generations. Jane Strachey first took an interest in the movement for women's suffrage in 1867 and the family's involvement continued until Pippa Strachey resigned as 'organizing secretary' of several feminist groups in 1951. It was the question of women's suffrage that was of greatest interest and importance, dominating Strachey family life and conversation in the decade or so before the First World War, where it jostled with imperial and artistic concerns. 'I feel very homesick for you all just now,' Dorothy Bussy wrote to the family from her home in France early in 1914, 'and wish I was at Belsize Park Garden—in the delightful atmosphere of Suffrage and Russian ballet.'[1]

The close connection between feminist and imperialist concerns that has been explored recently by Antoinette Burton and several others was very evident amongst the Stracheys, although the particular form it took in this family was unusual.[2] Unlike many of their contemporaries, the Strachey women showed no interest in the sufferings of their 'little Indian sisters'. India and their own imperial experience offered them rather an insight into major political developments and a sense of their own power. Thus it was the pleasure she took in commanding her Indian servants and organizing the family affairs in India that led Pippa Strachey to discover the administrative abilities that led her to become a suffrage organizer. At the same time, for her, as for her mother and her sister-in-law Ray, commitment to the continuation of the British Empire, and the belief in the superiority of Britain and British institutions to all others gave feminism additional weight: Britain, in their view, had the responsibility to set the

294

pattern and standard for all other women in the empire. Indian expertise also gave them a special place in the suffrage movement. At a time when opposition to women's suffrage became highly organized and included amongst its leaders several ex-viceroys, all of whom argued that enfranchising women would lead to the destruction of the British Empire, women with direct imperial experience that enabled them to counter these views were extremely valuable to the suffrage movement.

Although several of the Stracheys made important contributions to the women's movement, none were charismatic leaders like Josephine Butler, Emmeline Pankhurst, or even their friend Millicent Fawcett, whose names have become synonymous with particular feminist campaigns. Ray Strachey's history of the women's movement, *The Cause*, continues after many decades to make her a familiar figure to feminist historians. As a feminist activist, however, she like Jane and Pippa Strachey belonged in the second rank of the movement, amongst those women whose organizing capacity and constant effort, while rarely being publicly noticed or acknowledged, enabled the women's movement to survive. The lives of these feminists are just beginning to be explored. It is their stories, as Sandra Holton has argued, that enable us to understand the texture of feminist activities, the nature of feminist lives, and the ways in which feminist beliefs and activities fitted into family lives and social networks.[3]

In their approach to feminist causes, one can see the playing out of familiar traits amongst the Strachey daughters. Here, as elsewhere, Elinor followed her mother both in the kinds of activities that she undertook and in the way her feminism fitted into her marriage and family life. Dorothy took little part in any organized feminist campaign, but expressed herself much more passionately about the importance to her of feminism and insisted that it was integral to her sense of her own identity. Pippa, whose immense organizing and interpersonal skills led to a full-time career in the suffrage campaign and later in the movement to extend women's employment, took little interest in any kind of feminist theory. Pernel's feminist activity was mainly undertaken away from the family at Cambridge, where she was actively involved in the campaigns to have women admitted to Cambridge degrees, while Marjorie participated in the suffrage campaign in the years when she had nothing else to do, but never quite established a position for herself within it.

The growing importance of the suffrage movement within the Strachey family in the early twentieth century illustrated the broader British pattern.

There was little suffrage discussion amongst the Stracheys in the 1890s and the early years of the twentieth century, when the suffrage movement was very much in the doldrums. After a half-century of drawing-room meetings and occasional public lectures, and despite the existence of many local suffrage societies recently joined together in a National Union of Women's Suffrage Societies, little seemed to have been achieved. Some women had become prominent in national and imperial politics: in the battles over Irish Home Rule and in the controversy over the concentration camps set up by the British in 1899, during the Anglo-Boer War.[4] But there was little public suffrage activity until the advent of the militant campaign in 1905. All the other suffrage societies were revitalized by the spate of publicity generated by the first militant demonstration organized by the Women's Social and Political Union: the interruption of a Liberal Party campaign meeting by Christabel Pankhurst and Annie Kenney—and their subsequent arrest and trial. This led to a number of similar activities by the WSPU and to the organization of public meetings by other suffrage groups. The Strachey family was interested in all of these developments, but they first entered the suffrage movement *en masse* in 1907 when Pippa was called upon to help organize the first major demonstration of the NUWSS. It is interesting to note here that the younger Strachey women all called themselves 'suffragettes'. Later historians, while recognizing that there was a considerable overlap between moderate and militant suffrage supporters, have still tended to stress the demarcation evident in nomenclature between the militant *suffragettes* who followed the Pankhursts, and the moderate *suffragists* of the NUWSS. But despite their lack of sympathy with the militants, and their absolute adherence to the moderates, Dorothy and Pippa both used the term 'suffragette' to describe the very moderate Stracheys and indeed anyone engaged in a suffrage campaign. 'We were all with you in spirit at the Suffragette dinner party last night', she wrote to her mother in 1910—at a time when relations between the moderate and the militant suffrage supporters were at a very low ebb—and no one contradicted her.[5]

The Stracheys also offer an insight into the changing place of feminism within the broader pattern of British cultural life. In the nineteenth century, feminist demands fitted as easily into the framework of advanced liberals or radical political ideas as they did into the general framework of progressive causes and beliefs, or indeed into new literary and artistic ideals. Jane Strachey's feminism was thus buttressed by her reading of Mill and George Eliot, or in the later nineteenth century of Ibsen. In the early twentieth century, however, this harmony was disrupted. The new interest in sexuality, particularly homosexuality, evident within Bloomsbury and the growing criticism that emerged during the First World War of the whole framework of political and social institutions led to a questioning of the desirability of political involvement and an emphasis on the importance of individual life, small communities, and personal rebellion. The feminist commitment to gaining entry for women into existing political institutions often seemed outmoded and old-fashioned to those engaged in the pursuit of literary and artistic modernism, or of a 'modern' social and sexual life. The clash is illustrated by the complex and sometimes uncomfortable relationship that Pippa and Ray Strachey had with Lytton Strachey and his Bloomsbury friends. Although they enjoyed quite close friendships with Virginia Woolf, Maynard Keynes, and Roger Fry, both Pippa and Ray rejected or ignored the new ideas and codes of personal and sexual behaviour that were so important in Bloomsbury generally and were brought into the family by Lytton and James. By the end of the First World War, the devotion of Pippa and Ray to public service, patriotic causes, and family duty made them seem to Virginia Woolf like members of another generation who had nothing in common with her or her world.[6] In a similar way, the younger women in the family, like Alix Strachey, who embraced sexual experimentation, psychoanalysis, and new patterns of domestic life, regarded organized feminism as boring and irrelevant. At the same time, of course, the awkward place of the Strachey women within the world of Bloomsbury serves to underline the ambivalence about women's autonomy that ran right through the ideas and beliefs of these pioneers of British modernity.

I

Jane Strachey, the first feminist in the family, fitted easily into the common pattern amongst the nineteenth-century British upper-middle-class women who devoted themselves to the cause of women's emancipation.[7] She became interested in the suffrage question early in her married life, apparently when she came to see the ways in which familial and social expectations thwarted the capacity of individual women to follow their own talents and inclinations. In common with many Victorian feminists, she saw herself as a happily married and comfortably situated woman with an obligation to support and assist her less fortunate sisters. But this was combined with a sense of grievance, even distress, about the inadequacy of her own education. Like many other mid-nineteenth-century feminists, she took a great interest in contemporary politics generally, and insisted on the close connection between the demand for women's rights, the American abolitionist campaigns, and the demands of Italian nationalists. All of these ideas are neatly encapsulated in a letter she wrote to her husband after meeting a young woman in difficult personal circumstances in the late 1860s.

It is heart-breaking to think of the sufferings in intellect and affection which hundreds of women endure from their socially-enslaved position; one so exceptionally placed as I am (I—who have been thinking my walls were narrow, & knocking my head against them!) is startled when brought into actual contact with this position, the paramount duty of such a one is to use every advantage she has got, & devote her energies in the cause of their freedom—it is everyone's duty to strike for it as their slavery is a gigantic obstacle to the progress of humanity, but what the freedom of Italy is to an Italian, such ought to be the cause of women to a woman.[8]

The very terms of this comment point to the importance for Jane Strachey of the ideas of John Stuart Mill. She later explained to Lytton that Mill was 'the guiding star of my youth, giving one a coherent scheme of thought and an intellectual basis for conduct, when all one had been brought up to believe lay shattered, & with it an enthusiasm & emotions which vitalised it all'.[9] He was the author she turned to in the years immediately after her marriage in an effort to make up for the inadequacies of her own schooling and to learn what she felt she needed to know if she was properly to undertake her role both of mother and of wife. When Richard Strachey returned to India in the mid-1860s, she worked her way methodically through Mill's *Political Economy*, as well as his works on *Liberty*, *Utilitarianism*, and *Representative Government*.[10] She became something of a proselytizer, giving lectures on Mill's ideas to her friends, and insisting that her sister, Elinor Colevile, also study him. The Strachey daughters were initiated into the ideas of Mill and their mother's feminism at an early age. Elinor 'had decided views on women's rights' by the age of 7, doubtless because she was already becoming familiar with Mill.[11] 'Almost the first serious book my mother read aloud to me', Dorothy Bussy later recalled, was Mill's *On Liberty*. 'I was about 15 and I suppose it coloured me for life.'[12]

298

Mill was central also to her first active engagement in the women's movement. She signed the petition supporting women's suffrage which he presented to Parliament in 1867—and was amused in later years by the fact that she could sign the petition while Millicent Garrett Fawcett, her close friend and later leader of the suffrage movement, who was only 18 at the time, could not. She avidly read his speech in support of women's suffrage in 1867, and made sure that Richard did so too.[13] There is an irony in the way Jane Strachey's commitment to the cause of women's emancipation was connected to her intense adulation of this great man. One has a sense that she felt he had become in her adult life what her father had been in her youth—and she herself drew this connection by hanging Mill's portrait next to that of her father in her drawing room in 1869.[14]

Although she took some part in feminist activities in the 1860s, subscribing to Newnham College as well as supporting the suffrage, Jane Strachey's involvement in feminism at that time was minimal. She commented herself that there was little point in taking up the question while she was spending so much time in India, and as we have seen, she took no interest in the situation of women there. But of course she was also engaged in almost continuous child bearing throughout the 1860s, 1870s, and even 1880s. It was not until after the birth of her last child in 1887 that Jane Strachey began seriously to devote her time to the women's movement. She was by then a well-established figure in London society, with extensive familial and social connections. In 1897, moreover, Richard Strachey became a GCSI. Jane Strachey had not welcomed the title, but as Lady Strachey she was much in demand on feminist committees. The fact that she had left the Liberal Party and become a Conservative after Gladstone declared his support for Irish Home Rule in the mid-1880s made her particularly attractive to a movement that insisted that it was above party loyalties, but often found it hard to find women outside the Liberal Party for its various boards and committees. The Women's Local Government Society, established in 1888, was one such body that had had great difficulty in finding women not associated with the Liberal Party and, as Patricia Hollis has argued, 'head hunted' Lady Strachey as its president in 1903.[15] She was delighted and devoted a great deal of time to developing its policy, chairing meetings, and giving speeches both at small local meetings and at large public ones.

As her fellow Tory, Emily Davies, had done in her educational campaigns, Jane Strachey attempted to maximize support for women in local government by insisting that this particular campaign was not necessarily connected to the wider demand for women's suffrage. In 1902, for example, she wrote firmly to the Hampstead Branch of the Women's Local Government Association to disabuse them of the idea that the Women's Local Government Society only supported candidates who were in favour of women's suffrage. On the contrary, from the viewpoint of the central committee, Lady Strachey insisted, 'the only matter to take into consideration is whether the candidate is qualified to perform the duties she undertakes ... to reject a well-qualified candidate on grounds which are altogether outside our sphere of action would be neither just nor politic'. In this case she felt it imperative to avoid 'the withdrawal from the Society of many valued members whose views are in favour of women in Local Government, but opposed to giving them the Parliamentary franchise'.[16]

Jane Strachey's period of greatest involvement with the women's movement coincided with the renewal of energy in the suffrage campaign that accompanied the emergence of the Women's Social and Political Union in 1903. She joined the London Society for Women's Suffrage and through that became active in the National Union of Women's Suffrage Societies. Here too, her title and her social prominence were important. There was never any suggestion that she would do routine work: her role was rather to provide a public face and she often stood beside Millicent Garrett Fawcett, the president of the NUWSS, on stage or at the head of processions. Her picture featured frequently on the front page of the *Common Cause*, the NUWSS weekly paper. Her papers in the Women's Library suggest that she was in constant demand all round the country as a lecturer both on women's participation in local government and on women's suffrage. She sometimes felt ambivalent about making public speeches and chairing large meetings, although, as she confided to Lytton in 1902, 'I had long wanted to know whether my voice could fill St James Hall, & it can. I could give a fine reading in it.'[17]

In the years between 1900 and 1914, she was occupied writing letters, making appearances at meetings, participating in deputations to the prime minister. Although her disagreement with the policies of the militants was well-known, even they sought her support: on one occasion, she was invited to attend a militant deputation to the prime minister, Asquith, and on another, she was asked by the Women's Freedom League to endorse their campaign to have women boycott the census of 1911. Needless to say, she declined.[18] At the same time, she refused publicly to condemn the militants. Like Millicent Fawcett, she recognized the great boost in interest and enthusiasm for the suffrage movement generated by the suffragettes. Even when the militants began their campaign of breaking the windows of West End shops, Lady Strachey refused to participate in the condemnation of them and the expressions of support for shopkeepers amongst other Conservative and Unionist women.[19]

In all her feminist activity, one can see the importance of her adherence to the Conservative Party. She was absolutely committed to the ideal of slow political change. Her goal was not universal suffrage, but rather the admission to the franchise of women with property and education. She was opposed to adult suffrage when it surfaced as a demand in the early twentieth century, not, as was the case with some younger suffragists, for fear that it might lead to universal manhood suffrage and thus maintain the exclusion of women, but rather because it threatened to enfranchise too many people. 'Every extension of the franchise hitherto has been gradual and partial', she wrote in response to a letter seeking her opinion on this matter, 'and to bring in at one stroke so large a body of inexperienced voters would probably be damaging both to the country and to women themselves.'[20] What was needed was the enfranchisement of a small number of propertied women. But her conservatism did not mean that she was happy with the Conservative Party. On the contrary, like many of her contemporaries, Jane Strachey found herself becoming increasingly angry about the behaviour of her own political party. By 1910 she decided that that the refusal of the Conservative Party to endorse women's suffrage made her 'consider it worse than futile to support with our time, our energy, our money those who while accepting these to the full, deny us direct political power on the plea that women are incapable of forming a reasonable judgement on political matters, & that their interference in them would be injurious to the State'.[21] Following the line that had been taken by the National Union of Women's Suffrage Societies Electoral Fighting Fund, she planned henceforth 'to give all the support I can to candidates of either party who are in favour of it [admission of women to citizenship]'.

In a similar way, although a devout supporter of empire, she would have nothing to do with those imperial organizations that omitted women. The secretary of the Church Lads Brigade received a sharp response to a request for a donation in 1914. 'After the refusal to admit girls to participate in the Empire Day Celebrations in Hyde Park,' she wrote,

I am surprised at any appeal being made to women by your society for funds in connection with a movement for the better training of citizens for the British Empire. It has been quite clearly stated that women are considered to stand outside it; and if none but men have a place in representing the Empire, none but men should be expected to keep up the cost.[22]

Jane Strachey's involvement in the women's movement was not confined to the question of suffrage or of women's involvement in local government. Perhaps the organization which bore her most distinctive stamp was the Lyceum Club, of which she was a founder member in 1904 and which she served for many years as president. Intended as a club that would encourage debate and discussion on many different issues and serve as a meeting place between its members and men and women prominent in the world of politics, literature, and science, the Lyceum Club was intended to enhance both feminist activities and the social and cultural world of women. On its tenth-anniversary celebration, Jane Strachey spoke in glowing terms of her pride in the club, and especially of the way in which it combined cultural and political discussion and gave women the opportunity to participate in the public world. 'Here in our magnificent installation we find rest and ease and comfort . . . here women representing every civilised and social interest, and of every nationality, meet in a freedom of intercourse hitherto unattainable; here we receive Ministers of State, Ambassadors, leading men of science and art and literature as our guests.'[23]

While welcoming the discussion of new ideas at the Lyceum, Lady Strachey was adamant about the need to maintain the strictest of moral values. She insisted, for example, on the exclusion of divorced women from the club. Her own inclinations were all towards tolerance, she wrote in response to an appeal to reconsider this decision in regard to one particular woman who had ended a terrible marriage,

But I cannot overlook the fact that the Committee are the trustees of the Club, and that an overwhelming public opinion is against being forced into association with ladies whose experience has been so unfortunate. General rules are apt to come hard on particular cases; but if the Committee were to relax such a rule as this in one instance it would mean nothing less than having to become a court for the re-trial of every lady who thought she could plead extenuating circumstances.[24]

Her involvement in the women's movement ensured that Jane Strachey enjoyed a vigorous old age. She was at her most active, in the suffrage movement, in local government, and in the Lyceum Club when she was in her 70s and continued this well into her 80s. The deterioration in her eyesight that occurred in the course of the First World War, however, made her reduce her activities and she resigned first from the Lyceum Club and then—after several attempts—from the Women's Local Government Society in 1920.[25]

❧ II ❧

Although all the Strachey women kept up with and took an interest in the suffrage campaign and in a range of other feminist issues, they did not all devote much time and effort to them. Feminism seems to have mattered very little to the two older sisters, Elinor and Dorothy. Elinor Rendel seems only to have been initiated into suffrage activity through the suffrage marches and demonstrations of 1907-8, when she was already 47. As the mother of five children, she, like her own mother, may have felt it necessary to wait until her child-bearing years and major family responsibilities were over before entering into feminist campaigns. Prior to this, she had certainly demonstrated her convictions about the importance of women's education by sending her two daughters to the Kensington Girls School, and then to Newnham College. But she was never an ardent suffragist, and seems not to have engaged in any suffrage activities that were not family events. In so far as she was interested in feminist campaigns, she followed her mother again in taking a special interest in encouraging women's participation in local government. 'I am rather busy just now over the borough council elections which take place on Nov 1st', she wrote to her mother in 1919. 'There are at least 15 women candidates standing—possibly there may be more eventually—10 Conservatives and 5 Labour Party.'[26]

Dorothy Bussy, while keeping a close eye on the activities of her mother and sisters, took even less part in feminist campaigns. She wrote regretfully about missing out on suffrage marches in England, but never thought of participating in the women's movement in France. She once found herself staying in a holiday home with the 'chief mainstays of women's suffrage in France'.[27] But this did not lead to any activity in the women's movement in her adopted country. Nonetheless, Dorothy always called herself a feminist and saw her commitment to women's rights as integral to her life. One can see its importance in her assumption that she would participate in earning an income and that her marriage was a working partnership. It was the subject of extensive argument and discussion later, in her correspondence with André Gide and with his friend, the editor of the *Nouvelle Revue Française*, Roger Martin du Gard. Like Pernel, Dorothy protested vehemently against what would later come to be called sexism and often felt that she was subjected to hostility by Gide and his friends because of it. She often commented on the hostile and neurotic approach to women amongst Gide's friends. This was so of Roger Martin du Gard, for example, whose 'worst and most neurotic complexes are mixed up with the subject of women'.[28] She liked the work of Jules Romain, but was 'terribly shocked by his attitude to women'. He was an intelligent man with an encyclopedic knowledge, but he treated women in a way which put them 'outside the pale of humanity'—and showed a shocking blindness to the modern world.[29]

It was ironic that Dorothy insisted on her feminism and spelt out her ideas about the need for women's independence and freedom in the very relationship in which she was most abject. Thus her strongest feminist claims appear alongside her frequent declarations of love for Gide, pleas for his attention, and statements making it clear that without Gide, her life had little meaning. One could argue that Dorothy's very insistence on her entitlement to express her feelings and her demand that they be acknowledged and accepted by Gide has in it a feminist component. Like some of the women writers of the late eighteenth and early nineteenth centuries, she was asserting the right of women to love as they chose, rather than to accept the convention that women should be chosen and should respond to the feelings of others.[30] She was emphatically the subject of her own desire and rather than suffering in silence, she made her desire a dominating feature both of her own world and of Gide's.

While Dorothy's analysis of sexism has a very modern ring to it, some of her ideas about English women and the benefits they derived from being enfranchised, hark strongly back to nineteenth-century feminism in their emphasis on responsibility, duty, and virtue. In England in 1946, after an absence of several years necessitated by the Second World War, she told Gide that her deepest impression was

the magnificent development which the improvement in their position has brought to English women . . . Responsibility has been given them and a very near approach to equality. My admiration for the way in which they have borne the frightful test of the last terrible years is unbounded and the virtues they have displayed are those which men used to claim as exclusively their own . . . You who believe in progress should open your eyes and see what changes may be worked in the constitution of a slave population by opportunity and education.[31]

Dorothy's sense of the importance and the impact of women's rights in England was doubtless enhanced by her closeness to her younger sister Pippa and their sister-in-law Ray, and her knowledge of the importance of their contribution to the cause. Both Pippa and Ray Strachey were heavily involved in the suffrage movement before the war, played an important part in organizing women's work during it, and campaigned afterwards to extend women's employment and to gain equal pay, particularly in the civil service and the professions.

As the older of the two, Pippa became a significant figure in suffrage organization before Ray. Her mother's involvement made the women's movement an obvious place for her to begin working after she returned from India in 1902. Although it was her Indian experiences that led her into feminist activism, Pippa Strachey took no more interest in Indian women at the turn of the century than her mother had done earlier. She met and became friendly with several women while she was in India, but all of them were British. As a single woman, she had not even the limited contacts with female servants that her mother had had in the process of running a home. As with Jane Strachey, Pippa's lack of interest in the situation of Indian women is not entirely easy to explain. In the decade before she went to India, British feminists had become involved in two major campaigns centring on Indian women: one directed against the regulation of prostitution through the Cantonment Acts, and the other seeking to end the practice of child marriage.[32] Both were explicitly concerned with sexual questions and Pippa Strachey, like her mother, preferred not to discuss such distasteful matters. In regard to the question of prostitution in India, moreover, one can see that, as an essentially dutiful daughter and one who shared the family outlook on imperial and social questions, she would not care to take up a campaign that involved criticism of British administration—and about which her father had already expressed his strong opposition. Nonetheless, there were other questions also being addressed in India, concerning women's education and their need for access to women doctors, which she also ignored.

One has a sense that questions about the fate of Indian women were seen by both Jane and Pippa Strachey as marginal and as being of less importance than were those dealing with suffrage for white women in Britain. There was nothing philanthropic about the Stracheys and they never

305

expressed any kind of concern about the suffering of those located outside their own privileged world. As we have seen, Richard Strachey expressed nothing but scorn and contempt for the philanthropists who sought to ameliorate the conditions of Indian famine victims—and Jane never demurred from this view. John Stuart Mill too disliked philanthropy, arguing that philanthropic women were particularly damaging in their lack of understanding of the importance of independence for the poor. Thus it is not surprising that for both Jane Strachey and her favoured daughter, feminist activity centred on the needs of privileged women and on activities that kept them within mainstream politics.

Only one member of the Strachey family was ever in close contact with Indian women. This was Ralph's wife, Margaret. Margaret Strachey was a woman with little education and few interests, to whom Jane Strachey had once suggested that there would be lots to do with zenanas.[33] When Margaret was in India with Ralph in 1908, she began to meet some Indian women. 'Until lately, I have *never* come in contact with native life at all,' she wrote to Jane Strachey.

However one of my greatest friends here, the wife of one of the high Court judges, is very interested in what is called the 'National Association' of the East and West. I have been to gatherings at her house, where even Purdah ladies have come, & where in consequence no men, not even the husbands and brothers were allowed. I liked many that I met and found it quite easy to converse on any subject with them. I was astounded several times at their knowledge. I am not clever myself, but I can easily recognise it in others. One gets the idea that these ladies having been shut up all their lives lacked educational advantages but when one talks to them, one realises that either they have learnt in a few years, what it has taken a generation to learn, or else a very high standard of education has been carried on behind the purdah. Of course some are very parrot-like repeating little sentences off by heart, on any subject you introduce, in a monotonous voice until they reach the full-stop.[34]

Several of the Bengali women that she met invited her to their homes, and invited her to join their society. Although interesting, these meetings and the possibilities they raised filled her with alarm. One should not, she felt, enter into Indian society lightly.

I am not sure yet of the Government's views on the subject, and I feel one's individual ideas might do much more harm than good. All the English women ought to uphold all the same views in accordance with Government views I think, & ought not to join unless they could do so with judgement should any vital discussion arise. Personally when I first went I meant to talk only on ordinary topics, such as the weather, one's children's upbringing, gardening & music and such harmless subjects, *but they* invariably introduce the one subject of the government, sailing as near the wind as possible, so far I have let it pass pretending not to see the swadasheeness of their remarks. But I shall have to be prepared sooner or later. India is intensely interesting to me . . . [35]

A month later, when she was already on her way home to England, Margaret commented on the seething unrest evident in India—and made one of the most critical comments about India ever to be seen in Strachey correspondence. 'I fear there are many years of great trouble before poor India & there are so many side issues & the great question, it makes it all seem hopeless just now', she wrote. 'But the *hatred* of the native all over India for the white races is very strong and most marked, & our government & its mistakes is encouraging this feeling all it can!'[36]

Margaret Strachey's marginal status within the Strachey family serves only to underline how little importance the others attached to the question of Indian women. Thus, although Pippa always regarded her trip to India as the great point of change in her life, she did not associate this in any way with developing any kind of feminist concern there. It was rather the case that she began looking for an activity on her return—and, as she later recalled, was discovered by 'Miss Emily Davies, in her bonnet and shawl, who with unerring instinct discovered my existence and caught me in her net and changed a butterfly into a caterpillar.'[37] Davies had been the founder of Girton College in the 1860s and the mainstay of the nineteenth-century campaign to improve secondary education and extend tertiary education to women.[38] By the early twentieth century, she had retired from Girton and was devoting her formidable energy to the suffrage cause. At Davies's suggestion, Pippa joined the committee of the London Society for Women's Suffrage in 1906 and became its secretary the following year. Despite her own high regard for Pippa, Jane Strachey took it for granted that Pippa's election was the result of her 'respectable name', rather than for any qualities of her own.[39]

Shortly after assuming the role of secretary, Pippa was called upon to organize the first major public demonstration that the National Union of Women's Suffrage Societies had ever held. The demonstration came about, she later recalled, because

[t]he two Secretaries Miss Palliser and Miss Sterling were seized with the idea of arranging a procession in imitation of the Trade Unions. It was considered a wild

idea, as ladies parading in the Streets had never yet been seen but no one wanted to damp their ardour & the plan was approved and dates and some preliminaries fixed when both the originators were taken ill & vanished completely from the scene leaving myself and another junior Committee member to deal with the situation as best we could.[40]

Pippa and her colleague had to make all the arrangements including organizing bands and marshals and providing the carriages needed to transport many elderly women, liaising with the police, coordinating all the participating societies, and publicizing the event. So little serious thought had been given to the event, Pippa recalled that the date had been set for February. As might have been expected, 'it poured with rain in the morning of the day but mercifully cleared up at lunch time & what came afterwards to be known as the Mud March went off successfully'.[41] The march was in many ways a family affair: Lady Strachey walked at the head of the procession, followed by Elinor, Pernel, Marjorie, Elinor's two daughters, and Ray. Two of the Rendel sons, Dick and Andrew, however, disapproved, walking alongside their mother and sisters, protesting all the while that that they didn't believe in women's suffrage.[42]

Pippa even demanded help from her brothers and their friends. 'Won't you and Norton put on angelic pinions & fly to the assistance of a suffering suffragette?', she wrote to James.

The grand demo takes place next Saturday & I am Commander in Chief for Hyde Park . . . My hair is turning grey with the thought of the scene. My days are divided between Cannon Row Police Station & the telephone mount. Bands, brakes, & badges are provided. Trained gymnasts with trumpet voices are engaged. Police in their thousands will attend us. Meetings are organised in Exeter Hall & Trafalgar Square. But further assistants are much wanted & if you two would come it would be glorious and would amuse you very much.[43]

James was reluctant, but Maynard Keynes came to the rescue. Not only did he act as a steward helping to maintain order, but over the next few years, he provided Pippa with cash when she needed it, and helped her out of many tight spots—including arranging for the instant delivery of the 520 lanterns that she needed for the great suffrage pageant in 1909.[44]

In the course of the first demonstration in 1907, Pippa showed her great administrative talents. She was not only very efficient, combining imagination and vision with an eye for detail, but she also had wit, immense tact, and great interpersonal skills. 'The grand procession on Saturday is the universal topic of conversation', Lytton wrote to Duncan Grant a day or two before it occurred:

Pippa will of course be the central figure, on a white charger. She controls all, and interviews police and Scotland Yard daily. The other day Superintendent Wells said, 'Well, Madam, is there anything else we can do for you?' She replied—'Only one thing. If you could give orders that the Metropolitan Police Band could walk at the head of the procession.' The Superintendent gasped, and then realised it was a joke. He nearly died of laughter and has been her bond slave ever since.[45]

The day after the demonstration, Lytton reported again. 'The Suffrage Procession went off without a hitch—I believe entirely owing to Pippa's astounding management. The Police were dazzled and Chief Inspector Wells said in his final speech—"Dear madam if you are ever in difficulty or danger, you have only to apply to us!" '[46] Thus, while the militants were frequently engaged in battle with the police, Pippa regarded them—and was treated by them—as a trusted friend. She went on to organize the giant suffrage pageant and several other major demonstrations before the war put an end to such displays. Through all of this, Pippa played a part in the feminist transformation of political campaigning that Lisa Tickner shows was a significant contribution to British political life.[47] Although many others commented on the sharpness of Pippa's mind and her letters make quite clear her wonderful turn of phrase and literary skills, she did her best to eschew publicity and to keep out of the public gaze, preferring the role of organizing secretary.

The ease with which Pippa managed the suffrage movement depended not only on her efficiency and administrative skills, but also on the ability she shared with Pernel to maintain an easy relationship with the older women who continued to dominate the suffrage movement and whose insistence on maintaining the forms and the decorum that had been appropriate in their youth sometimes caused tension with younger women. Davies had been renowned as a stickler for propriety even in the 1860s, doing her best to rid societies with which she was involved of anyone with a taint of radicalism. Now she was concerned to ensure that the suffrage campaign was carried out with due moderation, and that her suffrage society had nothing to do with the militant suffragettes. Jane Strachey and Millicent Fawcett insisted also on the maintenance of established moral and behavioural codes and on dignity and decorum. There was tension between these older women and younger ones who felt more enthusiasm for the militants or who sought a closer connection with the Labour Party.[48] But such tensions did not occur with Pippa. The ease with which she related to these older women and handled their demands says much both about her tact and about the nature of her own feminism, which always had an air of the nineteenth century about it. She shared the belief held so strongly by Jane Strachey and Millicent Fawcett that women could only progress through slow and considered actions and needed always to show their good sense, responsibility, and fitness and capacity for citizenship. Thus while she called herself a suffragette, Pippa seems never to have had even the slightest interest in the militants. Their technique of interrupting the meetings of government ministers and thereby courting arrest and imprisonment, their flair and energy, and their genius for gaining public attention entranced some other moderates, at least for a time, but never her.

Pippa's desire to eschew the limelight was evident even when it came to writing. In the midst of her suffrage organizing, she wrote a short play entitled 'The Fair Arabian: An Old Story'. This was a slight orientalist comedy about a beautiful young woman, Zuleika, who is caught between— and outsmarts—both her jealous husband, 'Abdulla The Lion of the Desert', and a rather unpleasant visitor to the desert called Leo, 'a philosopher'.[49] The play is a short one act, amusingly written and light of touch. It was presented as a suffrage money-raiser along with a private reception at the Royal Court Theatre on Friday 9 July and Monday 12 July 1909. On the programme, however, the author's name is given as Sydonie Colton.[50]

While Pippa was busily engaged in suffrage activities in London, Ray Costelloe (as she then was) was taking up the cause at Newnham. She too came from a family of devoted feminists. Both her grandmother, Hannah Whitall Smith, and her aunt, Alys Pearsall Russell, had long been dedicated to women's rights.[51] Ray's mother, Mary Berenson, had strong feminist inclinations in her youth, and lectured on the 'woman question' in London. Mary Berenson's feminism, however, had about it something of the romantic revolt that characterized Mary Wollstonecraft. As a young woman, Mary Berenson had fought strongly against the constraints she faced. In opposition to her own parent's wishes she had cut short her university education in order to marry. Soon, however, she found the demands of motherhood and the constant need to assist and support the political ambitions of her lawyer husband, Frank Costelloe, impossible. Rejecting the normal path of wifely and maternal duty, she left her husband and young children to go off to Italy, seeking intellectual, emotional, and sexual fulfilment with her lover, Bernard Berenson. She kept in close contact with her daughters, and sought to make Ray share her beliefs in the importance of passion, and that the highest form of life was one dedicated to the pursuit of culture and civilized society.[52]

Ray never commented on the pain of her mother's departure when she was a child of 4. However, she rejected her mother's ideas and values entirely, refusing to take any interest in fashion, high culture, or elegant society, and devoting herself even in adolescence to politics and to sport.[53] Against her mother's wishes, she rejected any suggestion that she study languages or history and enrolled in mathematics at Newnham. Once there, she became caught up in women's suffrage. Ray had become close friends with Ellie Rendel, the oldest daughter of Elinor Strachey when they were both pupils at the Kensington Girls' School, and their friendship deepened when they were at Newnham. It was Ellie who took Ray to her first suffrage meetings and demonstrations. For a short time, Ray was smitten by the militant approach. 'You may be thankful I'm not of age', she wrote to her mother in 1907, 'or I should be marching off to prison. As it is I can only get excited and talk grand—and perhaps interrupt a Liberal meeting if I get a chance.'[54] But this enthusiasm was short-lived. Soon she and Ellie were attending meetings of the moderate National Union of Women's Suffrage Societies, and working under its auspices to organize their own meetings and debates in Cambridge. They invited speakers, including Ray's aunt, Alys Russell and the North of England suffrage organizer and campaigner, Sarah Reddisch, and for a time established their own group, the Younger Suffragists, for women under the age of 30.[55] Ellie was the more prominent activist at this time, and was often invited to speak at suffrage meetings both in England and at an International Suffrage Alliance meeting in Amsterdam in 1908 to which Ray accompanied her. Their suffrage activity came to a halt in 1908, when both of them went to the United States to spend a year at Bryn Mawr. But it resumed as soon as they returned and in 1909 Ray was very involved in the International Suffrage Congress being held in London. She was even, to her great disgust, called on to organize a suffrage dance!

It was through Ellie that Ray became friendly with the Stracheys. From the start, she was entranced by their intelligence, their casualness, their sense of humour—and their lack of interest in fashion or in the kind of conversation that Mary Berenson valued so highly. By 1910, Ray was a regular visitor to the Strachey home at Belsize Park Gardens, often sleeping there when there were suffrage activities in London. As Ray's daughter Barbara and others have commented, it was as if Ray had fallen in love with a family—and was simply waiting for an opportunity to join it when she met and married Oliver. However, while she liked all of the family, it was clearly Pippa, described often in Ray's diary as 'a delightful person' who was the centre of her interest.[56] Working with Pippa clearly gave Ray's suffrage work an added zest. Work was so important to Ray that she refused to interrupt it either for her engagement or even her marriage. 'I am so busy with suffrage work', she wrote to her mother shortly after her wedding, that 'I hardly have time for Oliver'.[57] The visit that Ray and Oliver made to Italy and then India after their wedding brought a short interruption. But on their return to England shortly before the outbreak of war in 1914, even though Ray was pregnant, she threw herself immediately back into the fray. The birth of her first child and then another pregnancy and miscarriage took her away from suffrage work briefly, although Oliver attended meetings in her stead and brought back all the gossip![58] Early in 1915, however, Ray was back at work with an official position as parliamentary secretary of the National Union of Women's Suffrage Societies.[59]

During the First World War, the partnership between Ray and Pippa became closer than ever. They worked together organizing the relief efforts undertaken by the National Union of Women's Suffrage Societies and in the area of women's employment. By this time, Ray had become the more prominent of the two. It was she who always took the position of president or chairman of the organizations they ran, and who delivered the public lectures and speeches. Ray adored lobbying and the busyness that her work as parliamentary secretary of the NUWSS involved. She raced around London in her motor car, going from one meeting to another, filled with a sense of importance and excitement. Pippa continued to prefer the role of secretary, keeping out of the limelight and undertaking all the day-to-day administrative tasks. Ray was as different in personality and approach to Pippa as she was in her preferred mode of operation. Where Pippa got on with everyone, Ray regarded those with whom she disagreed as enemies and treated them always with hostility. She adored intrigue and often seems to have fomented it. She always saw herself as cold and unsociable, keeping her warmth and concern only for those few people whom she truly liked. Nonetheless her efficiency and her enthusiasm were often remarkable and effective. Despite her much greater public role and prominence, Ray herself regarded Pippa as the leader.

The extent to which both Pippa and Ray sympathized with the views of the nineteenth-century suffrage pioneers was emphasized during the First World War. Within the women's movement, as in the Strachey family, the war brought to the fore conflicting views and values over questions about patriotism and the importance of supporting the British war effort. Millicent Garrett Fawcett, like Jane Strachey, was passionately patriotic and totally committed to the British war effort.[60] So were Pippa and Ray. There were many suffragists, however, with pacifist sympathies. Some wanted to express their opposition by participation in an international feminist peace conference to be held at the Hague in 1915. Fawcett was totally opposed to their doing so. Not only was it unquestionably women's duty to support the war effort, and to refuse to meet members of enemy states, but she also saw it as strategically necessary for women to demonstrate their understanding of the obligations of citizenship by participating as extensively as possible in relief work. Pippa and Ray were trusted Fawcett allies. Ray, who dearly loved a good fight, relished the battle against the 'poisonous pacifists' and was exultant when those with pacifist sympathies resigned from the executive of the NUWSS—even though they made up a significant majority of the NUWSS office-bearers. She wrote to her mother in high excitement in April 1915 of 'the great cataclysm' in the suffrage world.

We have succeeded in throwing all the pacifists out. They wanted us to send a delegate to the Women's Peace Conference at the Hague, & we refused. Then they resigned in a body—and they included the majority of our officers and committees! It is a marvellous triumph that it was they who had to go out and not us—and shows that there is some advantage in internal democracy, for we only did it by having the bulk of the stodgy members behind us.[61]

Ray was particularly pleased to be able to rid the suffrage movement of those feminists who had sympathized with the labour movement, including the editor of *The Common Cause*, Helena Swanwick, Catherine Marshall and Kathleen Courtney. Pippa was slightly less exultant—but her distaste for pacifists is equally clear in the violence of her language. A few months after this great cataclysm, she made a trip to Birmingham during which she had tried to negotiate between other pacifist sympathizers, and to bring them behind the NUWSS war effort. 'I have spent 3 days in Birmingham sweeping away pacifists', she wrote to Roger Fry,

or as my mamma orders me to say—pacifist propagandists. They were like straws in a whirlwind which was satisfactory but boring. I found myself forced to my annoyance to figure several times as a sort of Christian knight in armour to defend them at the expense of my cherished schemes & I had the revolting experience of seeing my life long foe licking my boots with a face black with various emotions.[62]

Once they had dealt with the pacifists, Ray and Pippa turned their attention to the question of women's employment. Together they ran an organization called Women's Service, dedicated to finding employment and voluntary work for women who wanted it, and to finding and training the women needed to fill the new positions being set up by both government and industry. In the course of their work, they were often critical of government, employers, and unions who left women out of account in planning, paid them inadequately, and gave no thought to their immediate needs or their future careers.[63] But they also castigated women themselves, who showed a disinclination to undertake training that would qualify them for new positions. 'We have any amount of openings for training in work that will have an after-the-war value', wrote Ray in 1916, 'but an insufficient number of applications in dental mechanics, dispensing, massage, welding, and engineering . . . We can't get women for the many posts we have vacant on the land.' To her great regret, there continued to be surplus women in welfare, but very few woman willing to engage in other industries.[64]

Running Women's Service was arduous and demanding. Early in 1917, for example, Pippa and Ray were asked to assist the War Office in finding hundreds of women to be involved in military support positions—'a sort of "Kitcheners' army" of women', Ray wrote to her mother—and they had also to work out all the questions concerning what the women would need in terms of training, discipline, and pay. To Ray's great indignation, the women once selected were placed under the command of a colonel, which seemed completely inappropriate as the women had no previous military training or experience. Ray and Pippa, with their old friend Thena Clough, 'have been going about like the three black ladies in the *Magic Flute*', Ray wrote to her mother, trying to make the War Office see sense, and provide a more suitable supervisor.[65]

The question of women's suffrage also began to demand more time and attention after the Speaker's Conference of 1916. The government plan to pass a new representation of the people bill in 1917, made necessary to ensure that soldiers serving away from their homes were to able to vote, brought the question of votes for women back on to the agenda. The suffrage organizations had suspended agitation during the war, but made it clear that campaigning would resume unless the government agreed to include women in the new bill. Ray took a major part both in lobbying Members of Parliament and in bringing together many different suffrage societies to ensure that they made a concerted effort to gain the vote. 'It's no joke', she wrote to her mother, 'to combine 24 suffrage and 10 other big women's societies into one basket together, and to make them all know what line is to be taken and to agree to it. It's like trying to harness a pack of wild elephants—and wild elephants with years of private conflict behind them.'[66] In the midst of all of this, Ray had to have a bladder operation, but it slowed her up only briefly. As the months went on, she lobbied and organized her own supporters and attended debates until finally in February 1918, she sat first in the visitors gallery in the House of Commons, then raced to the House of Lords, to watch the final speeches and the vote that brought the first measure of women's suffrage in Britain. As she wrote to her mother, 'the final ceremonies' with 'Black Rod and the Ushers and the clerks, with the wigs and the bowing and the walking backwards and the French words and the rolling periods: it seemed really quite impressive, perhaps because the occasion was really a great one in its way, and we were all moved by it'.[67]

Late in the evening, Ray 'skooted off in the car to tell Mrs Fawcett, who hadn't stayed so long', and they sat together in front of the fire, neither of them being able to believe it was true. Pippa, whose health was always fragile, was recuperating at *La Souco* at the time. The restrictions on women's suffrage, as the vote was only granted to propertied women over 30, meant that, while her mother was enfranchised, she was not. 'Dearest Pippa I can't bear the idea of your not having a vote,' her mother wrote, 'after all you have done for the cause, it is simply ridiculous.'[68]

Once the first measure of women's suffrage was gained, the whole women's movement had to face the question of how to reformulate their goals. Through the 1920s, there were debates about what feminism meant, and how feminist aims could best be pursued. In 1919, the National Union of Women's Suffrage Societies changed its name to National Union of Societies for Equal Citizenship, discussed the question of what 'equal citizenship meant', and tried to articulate a 'new' feminism. There has been much debate about the nature of feminism in the 1920s. Some historians have argued that, in the inter-war period, feminism lost its radical capacity to criticize prevailing institutions and ideas through their demand for sexual equality. Others have argued rather that it was in the 1920s that important questions concerning sexuality and birth control came to the fore, and when feminism took up the issues that have been of concern ever since.[69]

Neither Ray nor Pippa Strachey were interested in theoretical debates or in the attempt to formulate a broad new feminist programme. They both believed that, once the vote was won, the important question for women centred on economic independence. In their view, other issues, such as birth control or family endowments, had nothing to do with feminism at all. Thus they gradually withdrew from NUSEC, focusing their energies on their old society, the London Society for Women's Suffrage, which was now renamed the London Society for Women's Service (later to become the National Society for Women's Service when it ceased to be affiliated with NUSEC). There they continued the work they had been doing during the war, battling to extend women's access to new professions, setting up training schemes, and campaigning for equal pay. They were concerned almost entirely with professional and skilled women, campaigning for the entry of women to the legal profession, and to all grades of the civil service, on the one hand, and to the engineering trades on the other. Ray chaired the NSWS and its various committees, while Pippa was always their secretary. Ray also chaired the Women's Service Bureau which campaigned for equal pay for professional women.

Although employment was their major concern, neither Pippa nor Ray devoted their time to it exclusively. Ray was very involved in the League of Nations' Union in the early 1920s, sharing the view of many of her contemporaries that questions such as married women's citizenship needed to be dealt with on an international as well as a national basis.[70] She also maintained a close interest in politics. Although she often said she found parliamentary politics boring, Ray stood unsuccessfully as an Independent candidate for Bromford and Bow in 1918, 1920, and 1922. She also acted as an unpaid parliamentary adviser to Nancy Astor, the first woman elected to Parliament—and one whose ignorance of parliamentary procedure filled all the veteran feminists with horror.

Throughout the 1920s, both Ray and Pippa were immensely busy, juggling family responsibilities with their feminist work. Ray added another activity: writing. 'Messrs Bell and Co wrote yesterday,' she told her mother, in February 1924, 'asking me to undertake for them a History of the Women's Movement. 100,000 words. I am to go and talk over terms. If they'll give me £150 I'll do it, boring though it will be.' Ray's habitual negative response hid her real enthusiasm—and ten days later she reported that the terms were favourable and that she had now begun to be interested in the project and to find it both easy and entertaining for 'no arguments or disquisitions are needed, just the journey of a people battling against ridiculous taboos'.[71]

While it remains a wonderful, energetic, and heroic account of the nineteenth- and early twentieth-century British women's movement, *The Cause* too illustrates the way that Ray Strachey's approach to feminism mirrored that of an older generation of women. Millicent Garrett Fawcett is the central figure here. Ray was devoted to Fawcett and had long wanted to write her biography. Indeed, one of the reasons she agreed to write *The Cause*, as she explained to her mother, was that while writing it, 'I could write Mrs Fawcett's life *pari passu* so to speak'.[72] Fawcett read *The Cause* in manuscript and her influence can be seen throughout. As a result, it is in some ways anachronistic. One has no sense in reading it that is a product of the late 1920s, a period when the meaning, the programme, and the concerns of feminism were the subject of intense debate between 'old' and 'new' feminists; between those concerned with sexual purity and those insisting on sexual freedom; between those who felt that citizenship erased much of the earlier feminist programme and those who believed it impera-tive to establish what women's citizenship was. Rather the book, as Rosalind Delmar suggests, is very much 'the product of the mainstream feminism of the turn of the century', offering a story of steady gain in terms of legislative change and access for women to social, political, and educa-tional institutions.[73] Echoing the feelings of Fawcett and Jane Strachey, Ray gave pride of place to John Stuart Mill as the intellectual giant of modern feminism, providing a brief summary of his education, his early life, and his relationship with Harriet Taylor before going on to look briefly at *On Liberty*, *Representative Government*, and *The Subjection of Women*.[74] Although this was a standard nineteenth-century view, by the 1920s, Mary Wollstonecraft had begun to assume a more important place in the history of feminism. As Mary Stocks argued in *The Woman's Leader*, Wollstonecraft's *Vindication of the Rights of Woman* was still 'alive and irritating', while Mill's seemed to address 'a chapter of grievances that . . . may now be said to be closed for the English-speaking world'. Ray Strachey in her discussion could not quite avoid this 1920s viewpoint. Mill, she says,

took the ground that Mary Wollstonecraft had taken before him, and that every defender of the cause has taken since. *The Subjection of Women*, indeed is more coloured with logic and less with passion than the *Vindication*, more clearly

317

arranged, more philosophical—and less eloquent. It bears, however, the stamp of full conviction, and of deep and serious thought. Mill had pondered, as no man had pondered before, over the implications and the results of the subjection of a whole sex . . . It was the removal of the age-long subjection and submission of women from which he hoped so much.[75]

Ray and Pippa Strachey continued to work closely together throughout the 1930s. As we have seen, the Berenson financial difficulties meant that Ray lost much of her allowance in 1930 and had to seek paid work. She returned to Nancy Astor as a paid parliamentary secretary for a few years, making this a part-time position in 1934 in order to become the head of the newly established Women's Employment Federation.[76] Pippa was the honorary secretary of the executive committee—and so the two were again involved in daily contact. Ray's work required her to explore and promote careers and professions for women, establishing databases and registers of all women workers and attempting to set standards for pay and conditions. Pippa and Ray campaigned constantly throughout the decade for equal pay. They concentrated on the civil service, believing that, once the principle was established here, it would then extend to teaching and to other public services.[77] The efficiency and negotiating skills of both women were evident, not only in their dealings with treasury and in their responses to the Royal Commission on the Civil Service, but also in their bringing together of a broad coalition of women's groups all supporting this measure of equality.[78]

At the start of the Second World War, Pippa and Ray were again closely involved in organizing women's labour and their support for the war effort. Ray was hard pressed, as funding for the WEF was reduced, while demands for its services were constantly increasing. Although their work was connected, they were responsible for different organizations. Ray ran the WEF from Bedford College, while Pippa took over the primary responsibility for Women's Service which had its headquarters in Victoria. 'Closely as we work,' Ray explained to her mother, 'hers is a different organisation. But it is a loss to me, her being in a different place.'[79] This important feminist partnership which had kept so many employment campaigns active between 1919 and 1940 came to an end suddenly in July 1940, with Ray's death after an operation for ovarian cancer.

Pippa Strachey never commented on the impact of Ray's death on her life and continued her work as a feminist organizer. To the great concern of her family, she remained in London during the Blitz, keeping everyone else apprised of the damage done—and working hard to deal with the impact of the bombing both on Bedford College and on the headquarters of the LSWS in Victoria.[80] She was particularly concerned to protect its library. Pippa had played a major role in establishing the Fawcett Library in the late 1920s, persuading Virginia Woolf to donate copies of her own works to it and also to write to other women authors asking them to follow suit. With the bombing of London, she sought to protect the library from the ravages of war by arranging for the books to be given safe haven in Lady Margaret Hall. 'The L. M. H. Librarian', she wrote to Pernel, '(who turns out to be a member of the Society) has displayed some good will in offering not only space for packing cases but a present of six of these precious jewels.'[81] Pippa carried some of the books that did not fit in these cases in her own luggage on the train.

Her major work continued to involve organizing women's war service and the campaign for equal pay. She was a significant figure in the establishment of the Equal Pay Campaign Committee which was set up with some hundred affiliated women's organizations in 1943. Her commitment to equal pay was recognized by others—and indeed by Pippa herself—in her agreeing to deliver a speech at the Milestone dinner held to celebrate the acceptance of equal pay in the civil service in 1955. Her speech on this occasion was a characteristic one, harkening back to the nineteenth-century women's movement and to the women like Barbara Bodichon, Emily Davies, Harriet Martineau, and Millicent Fawcett, who 'started forth on the road that has taken us to the Milestone we are celebrating tonight'.[82]

It was not only Pippa's own sense of connection with an earlier generation of feminists that increased as she aged, but others too who saw her as a representative of the great Victorian feminist pioneers. In 1944, Pippa described to Pernel a hilarious few days she had spent with an air force group in Windermere where an earnest squadron commander was attempting to provide some education in the history of feminism for young women.

At times I feel as though I were taking part in a musical comedy, though the other characters would die of the shock if they could possibly imagine there was such a thought in my head. My own role in the affair is unhinging to begin with: I am regarded as a sort of museum piece carefully assisted up and down stairs & provided with large arm chairs etc & have to play the part to the best of my ability & attempt to figure as Mary Kingsley, Emily Davies and Mrs Fawcett rolled into one in their declining years. In addition I have to deliver unprepared lectures at all hours to earnest air women of diverse ages interspersed with occasional school masters disguised as flight commanders.

'The fact of everyone else being dressed up helps,' she added, and so does 'the supply of cocktails which I snatch up whenever offered though I doubt whether this is entirely in keeping with the part'.[83]

Pippa's activities in her final years in the women's movement are hard to establish clearly. The death of Ray and then the fact that she was now living with her sister Pernel mean that there are no letters describing her activity. She formally retired as organizing secretary of the LSWS in June 1951. But she did not retire from all activity. On the contrary, she is credited with suggesting the name 'Fawcett Society' which was adopted by the LSWS to reflect its shift in direction away from employment and back towards legislative reform. This was of course a final act of commemoration on her part, and she proceeded to act as secretary of that organization at least until 1956.[84] By this time her eyesight was failing, and she had become so slow in her movements and her work as to make her departure necessary for all.

V

While Ray and Pippa were completely absorbed in the women's movement, it proved less attractive to younger members of the Strachey family. Pernel identified with it, to some extent, but took little active part in feminist campaigns. Like Dorothy, she became 'enraged', to use a favourite Strachey term, when confronted by overt sexism and misogyny. 'I cannot restrain frenzied screams of passion,' she wrote to Lytton in 1900, after reading 'the most impudent article in the Spectator called "Women and Culture" '.

It beats everything for pompous folly and crass ignorance. Women are meant by nature to be wives and mothers, you will be glad to hear: and in so far as higher education will enable them to manage their households between and with more intelligence, we have no objection to it. We should, however, be sorry to see any increase in Bohemian ladies with latch keys; beware also of becoming cynical, hard-hearted: Senior wranglers we can do without but not the love of a mother.[85]

The reference to 'Senior wranglers' of course points to her interest in universities. And it was there, and in relation to women's education, that she concentrated both her professional and her feminist energies. It was she, after all, who issued the invitation that led Virginia Woolf to write *A Room of One's Own*, still regarded by many as the most significant feminist text of the first half of the nineteenth century. Pernel campaigned several times for the admission of women to Cambridge degrees, both as an undergraduate and in her capacity as tutor and then principal at Newnham. But her dedication to this cause was not matched by interest in the suffrage. She took her place in the large demonstrations that Pippa organized, but never seems to have attended a suffrage meeting of her own accord.

Marjorie Strachey, by contrast, worked full-time in the suffrage campaign for some years. One cannot help feeling, however, that she did this only because, when she left Somerville in 1906, she could think of nothing else to do. It was the ever resourceful Jane Strachey who seized on Marjorie as another worker for the cause. Marjorie was compliant, but the moment she began to think about teaching as a possible career she gave up suffrage work entirely—and thereafter took absolutely no further interest in it.

It is indicative of the vitality of the suffrage movement in these years that it proved a possible avenue of employment for Marjorie. No one ever suggested that she might like the routine of office work that suited Pippa so well. Marjorie's own vitality and enjoyment of public display suggested that she might be better suited to the newer and more adventurous task of travelling around England with a suffrage caravan, holding meetings, distributing pamphlets, and making speeches. This idea of providing education and propaganda throughout the country in a novel and eye-catching way was one the suffrage movement had borrowed from the late nineteenth-century socialists. It suited Marjorie well, combining as it did a rather bohemian lifestyle and a great deal of public performance. In February 1908, she wrote from Worcester to report on progress to her mother.

We have 2 meetings everyday in the Committee Rooms at 3 and 8 and as many as we can manage—one or two—in the dinner hour outside the factories. I have just made my first speech to the girls of a ready-made clothes factory. Our meetings in halls begin tomorrow and go on till polling day. Mrs Bertie Russell is coming tomorrow and Mrs Rackham the day after.[86]

The feminist world also offered Marjorie the opportunity to explore her interest in writing. From the mid-nineteenth century, British feminists had produced a range of different kinds of magazines and newspapers which included original fiction and poetry, literary reviews, historical pieces on women artists or political figures in the past, as well as articles on the current status of women and the progress of the women's movement. In 1909, the London Society for Women's Suffrage began a new one, *The English-woman*, which sought 'to reach the cultured public and bring before it in a convincing and moderate form, the case for the enfranchisement of women'. Dedicated to no party, but only to women's enfranchisement. *The Englishwoman* sought to further its aim 'by securing the sympathy and holding the attention of that public which is interested in letters, art, and culture generally—by a wise, fair and decorous marshalling of fact'.[87] Its editorial committee included the veteran moderate suffragists Lady Stra-chey and Frances Balfour as well as the writers, Cicely Hamilton and Mary Lowndes. It ran for several years and shortly after it began Marjorie had a regular theatre column in it. She wrote reviews and a number of general articles on acting as a profession and on the state of the theatre.

For all of this, it is hard not to feel that Marjorie's feminist activity was a way for her to fill in time—in a manner that won family approval—rather than something to which she was seriously committed. She gave speeches as required, but was reluctant to take on any more onerous role. She refused to organize the caravan tours, for example. She wrote for *The Englishwoman*, but would not participate in editing it. Unlike Pippa, although she was active in the women's movement for several years, she never established her own position within it. In her own eyes and in those of others, she was always the daughter of Lady Strachey. Given the difficulties she had always experienced with her mother, it is not surprising that she found it much harder than Pippa did to manage the complications that came from Jane Strachey's prominence in the movement. In August, Emily Gardner, who was organizing the caravan journey around the north of England, asked if she could 'skilfully & tactfully convey to Lady Strachey that the N. U. Will be making a very serious mistake if they insist on sending it (the caravan) to residential and Mining places in August rather than to holiday resorts'. Everyone who can goes away in August, she argued—and hence the numbers in residential areas were reduced—while the NU was paying the holiday rate to hire caravans.[88] There was nothing 'skilful or tactful' about Marjorie, who simply forwarded the letter to her mother without comment.[89]

As soon as the opportunity offered, Marjorie moved on to do other things. In 1913, Ray noted that Marjorie wanted to go to the Gordon Craig acting school and later that year, Marjorie left England to attend the

Dalcroze Schule in Dresden.[90] As we have seen, her course of study there was interrupted by the war and when she returned to England she moved, with some difficulty, into teaching. What is significant here is Marjorie's complete lack of interest in the suffrage movement—or indeed in any aspect of women's rights—in subsequent years. She never addressed any questions about women in the histories and novels that she wrote in later years, nor did she take any interest in the final stages of the suffrage campaign. 'I expect you are walking with your head higher than usual!', she wrote when the first measure of women's suffrage was introduced in 1918. Then she added a request that shows just how far from the suffrage campaign she was. 'I have been asked to join the Women's Suffrage Committee here, & they all want to do something to celebrate the passing of the Bill, but don't know what. Can you make any suggestion?'[91]

Just as Marjorie was effectively conscripted into the suffrage cause, so too at various times were Oliver, Lytton, and James. In Oliver's case this was a rather late development that followed his marriage to Ray in 1911 and didn't involve much except attending occasional meetings on her behalf. By this time both Lytton and James had been involved for some time. Their letters are filled with information and discussion about precisely what was happening in the suffrage campaign and about their own activities. They also suggest a degree of scepticism, amusement, and apprehension about what the feminist cause entailed. Disparagement and even contempt for women's intellectual capacity was certainly an issue here for Lytton Strachey, and he and Leonard Woolf pondered the question of what the woman's vote might mean—or be worth.[92] Lytton was also concerned about the high moral tone of the suffrage movement, and about the desire of some feminists to impose their own moral standards on society at large. 'I've joined the men's league for the promotion of female suffrage,' Lytton wrote to James in 1904, 'And now I really doubt whether the whole thing isn't . . . very alarming. I believe the ladies will try to forbid prostitution & will they stop there?'[93] Lytton let his sisters put on a production of his play 'A Son of Heaven' as a suffrage benefit, but ironically, as Julie Taddeo has argued, the play was a deeply misogynist one![94] The irony that is always evident in Lytton's discussions of suffrage, on the one hand, and his constant expectations that his sisters and women friends would pander always to his needs, while he offered little support in return, make it hard to see him as a serious supporter of the cause. Nonetheless, he made all the public protestations and shows of support that were required.

James seemed to take the suffrage cause rather more seriously than Lytton—and indeed was generally more sympathetic to the whole question of women's desire for independent professions and for personal autonomy. He held dances to raise funds for the suffrage cause, and sometimes went to Pippa's aid when she was organizing marches and demonstrations. But he too was amused by the intensity of feeling shown by his mother and sisters, as a letter he wrote to Lytton in the midst of the battle over the Conciliation Bill demonstrates. This bill was seen by the moderate suffragists as their last hope of gaining the suffrage. The militants had agreed to stop their agitation if the government agreed to allow the issue to be debated. If they did not do so, wrote James,

The outburst will be awful. We shall be *en pleine* revolution. At a meeting at the Exhibition today, Mrs Fawcett said that if facilities were refused, 'some of us will feel that the time has come for rougher methods.' The whole audience rose and cheered. At the end, Pippa went up & said 'When will you give the word Mrs Fawcett? I'm only waiting for it before I draw my sword.' Madame replied: 'We shall all of us have to draw our swords very soon.' She then announced in confidence that facilities have been refused... Mama has declared that if Mrs Fawcett orders it she will go to any lengths... I'm really most deeply alarmed.[95]

James also managed to devise forms of support that met other of his interests. Thus, for example, around 1910, he and Marjorie together organized a dance to raise funds for the cause. It was a fancy dress occasion and all those invited were required to be dressed as *Negres Enflammes*. David Garnett, who attended, described it as an entertaining affair. All the guests wore fancy dress, but none—except James and Marjorie—in accordance with the proposed theme. James, however, had managed neatly to combine his enthusiasm for Diaghilev and the Ballets Russes with his suffrage duties. His dress

was based on Bakst's design for the negro slave danced by Nijinsky in *Scheherezade*. That is to say, he was chiefly grease-paint from the hips upwards, but wore full Turkish trousers of blue gauze or butter-muslin, cut low enough at the waist to reveal his navel. On his head was a black astrakhan wig, and around his neck a big gold or silver-gilt necklace in the form of a cobra with jewelled eyes.[96]

Despite their splendid garb and the jollity of the evening, both James and Marjorie seemed to Garnett to be 'inspired by a mysterious sense of duty', which was evident in the intensity with which they danced.[97]

The ambivalence of Lytton and James towards organized feminism was shared by the young women to whom they became close when they left the family home, particularly James's wife, Alix Sargant-Florence, and her close friend and Lytton's companion, Dora Carrington. Like Ray and Pippa, Alix was potentially a second-generation feminist. The daughter of an ardent feminist, the painter Mary Sargant, she had attended the progressive private school Bedales before reading modern languages at Newnham in 1911. Alix reacted with hostility to anyone who questioned women's intellectual capacity or entitlement to autonomy and to work out a career. But she had no interest in campaigning to extend women's freedom. In her university days, she seemed singularly unaware of the suffrage meetings in Cambridge that had been matters of such moment to Ray. She travelled in Europe after leaving university in 1914, and was in Russia when war broke out. Her mother suggested that she devote her time to studying the Russian women's suffrage movement. But to Alix, who was learning the Russian language and dancing, this idea did not even bear contemplation. Her desire for emancipation was expressed by undertaking 'a chauffer's training course here in Petrograd; with the idea, on our return of hiring or buying a motor vehicle suitable for carting about wounded people, and presenting ourselves at the Red Cross Society for any kind of use they can make of us'.[98]

When she returned to England, Alix rejoined her young women friends, including Dora Carrington, the group Virginia Woolf described as the Bloomsbury 'cropheads'. All of these women saw themselves as emancipated. Their understanding of this concept, however, had only a limited connection with feminism and women's rights: Alix, like Pernel Strachey was angered by men who regarded women as stupid and as destined primarily for domesticity. Sexual freedom and the ability to live as they chose, however, were far more important than the vote. Alix took a vague interest in the Fabian Society, attended the meetings of the 1917 club, carried on affairs with David Garnett and Harry Norton and thought about what she would do next. But engaging in the suffrage movement did not occur to her. She thought its ideas, behaviour, and attempts at gaining attention with eye-catching colours and styles ludicrous. For both her and Dora Carrington, suffragette colours, especially as worn by waitresses in suffragette tea rooms, were the epitome of bad taste. But in general, Alix's lack of interest in the women's movement is notable. Her letters to her mother deal with her loathing of conventional ideas about marriage and sexual relationships, but she made no comment on the gaining of the first measure of suffrage for women in 1918.

Alix occasionally discussed feminism after the war when she was becoming more and more involved in psychoanalysis. She was often intrigued by the contradictory and complex ways in which feminism was played out amongst women. She wrote to James, for example, about how odd she found it that many domineering and passionate women who opposed women's rights hated men unconsciously. She pictured herself as the opposite of this: liking men, but supporting women's emancipation.[99] Nonetheless, she took little part in the arguments about femininity which were so prominent in psychoanalysis in the 1920s, and had no sympathy at all for Helene Deutsch who sought to include the social position of women in her analysis of femininity. On the contrary, in her own later work, Alix seemed rather to feel that what psychoanalysis served best to demonstrate was the many difficulties women faced—and the almost impossible task involved in the idea of women's emancipation.[100]

12

Continuity and Change

One of the most interesting questions when looking at the Strachey family over two generations centres on the extent to which it is possible to identify in detail the shared familial characteristics and attitudes that David Garnett referred to as the distinctive Strachey 'atmosphere'.[1] There is a question also about the impact of the strong sense of family tradition and of a shared outlook amongst the Stracheys on the desires of some members of the family to espouse new ideas, beliefs, and ways of life. These questions arise most particularly in relation to Lytton, James, and Dorothy, the three members of the family whose intellectual interests, activities, and personal lives diverged most noticeably from the family's Victorian heritage. New pathways were followed by others as well, of course. Pernel had a very new kind of career for a woman, while Pippa forged a distinctively modern life as a full-time feminist organizer. Their feminist beliefs and goals, however, diverged very little from those of their mother and of her previous generation. By contrast, Dorothy, Lytton, and James all became involved in new developments in art and literature, in political and intellectual debates, and in approaches to sexuality and personal life, which were in direct conflict with family tradition, and thus were distressing and incomprehensible to the older members of their family.

Despite their engagement in new ideas and new life patterns, none of the Stracheys ever sought to repudiate their family heritage. On the contrary, even while engaged in his most outspoken critique of Victorian ideas about duty, morality, religion, and empire, Lytton Strachey continued to take pride in his family and its name. Indeed, in 1918, Virginia Woolf commented somewhat acidly that Lytton Strachey's family pride had 'reached almost a religious pitch, a bad sign'. She found his attempt to argue that his younger brother, James, the mildest and most indecisive of men, had an iron will and was a great administrator laughable.[2] Moreover, while Lytton Strachey attacked Victorian values fiercely in *Eminent Victorians*, his subsequent work on Queen Victoria and Queen Elizabeth, as both Leon Edel and Michael Holroyd argue, point to his affection for and his continued immersion in the world of his mother.[3] One can see something similar in James's approach to psychoanalysis. It brought him an entirely new way of thinking about individual actions, identities, and subjectivity, introducing the whole question of the unconscious and the need to understand sexuality in a way that was completely foreign to his Victorian world. And yet James's unease about the debates and battles within the psychoanalytic community, and his insistence on the need to see psycho-analysis purely as a science point to a continuation of some of the attitudes and approaches of his father.[4] Dorothy, too, although she married a man completely outside the world of her parents, and devised a life with him quite unlike that she had known before, retained an intense sense of family tradition and worked hard to maintain her close family bonds.

Both the importance of continuity across the two generations and the extent of change are illustrated well by the relationship of the Stracheys to both the term and the general idea of modernity. James and Lytton referred often to the term 'modern' as one that served to differentiate themselves and their Bloomsbury world from their Victorian family and from those older friends whose political ideas, sexual practices, values, and general ap-proach to life they regarded as outmoded. And there is no question that the term did serve to suggest a new demand for intimacy that encompassed an unprecedented openness about sexuality, especially homosexuality, on the one hand, and a whole set of ideas about art and aesthetics, on the other. Yet even here, one can see more continuity within the Strachey family than Lytton or James quite recognized or acknowledged. For the concept of modernity had been a very important one within their family to the previous generation. Although he did not use the term in the way his sons did, half a century earlier, Richard Strachey had regarded himself and been seen by others as a distinctively 'modern' figure. He was a leading representative of the new breed of modernizing imperial administrators, seeking to break with tradition in their approach to administration and more particularly in their application of science and technology to the rule of India. In a similar way, Jane Strachey was very conscious of herself as a progressive modern woman, with her passionate interest in politics and public affairs, her feminist commitment, and her determination to be a new kind of wife and mother—quite unlike the one she had known in her own familial home.

Moreover, while for Lytton and James it was their modernity that served to differentiate themselves from other members of the family, one could argue that some of the very concepts that constituted their understanding of modernity were shared by their parents. Richard Strachey's belief in science as the only way to combat religion and obscurantism, for example, and the adulation of scientists that was so evident both in him and in Jane were to a marked extent accepted and continued by all their children—and most emphatically by Lytton and James. In a similar way, all the Stracheys accepted some part of the family's imperial tradition and values. Lytton and James might have questioned the desirability of imperial careers and seen imperial involvement as immersing people in a world completely out of touch with their own. Nonetheless, like their parents, they called upon an imperial framework and saw the lack of civilization in much of the empire in ways that helped to define the modernity of their own metropolitan world. This is not to suggest that they did not have very different ideas from their parents and older siblings about sexual behaviour and personal life, or indeed about politics and art. But it is to argue that even these new ideas were often contained within a traditional and familial framework.

I

Although Richard Strachey did not use the term 'modern' in as explicit a way as his youngest sons, the term serves in many ways to encapsulate his approach to his profession and his life—and it is in some ways easier to articulate the meaning of modernity for him and to show how it influenced his intellectual outlook and approach than is the case with either Lytton or James. For Richard Strachey, as indeed for many contemporary historians, modernity was clearly and unambiguously associated with the Enlightenment and articulated directly in the terms of mid-Victorian rationalism, positivism, and science.[5] He believed absolutely that scientific principles had to be applied not only to the management of the natural world, but also to government and administration. Thus he strongly supported the application of utilitarian principles to institutions and administration, seeing in Bentham's 'rational calculus' not an impossible desire to quantify human happiness or misery, but rather the only possible means to govern rationally or to overcome pointless traditions.[6]

Strachey's education had occurred in the 1830s, the decade in which John Stuart Mill in his essay on 'The Spirit of the Age' had asserted the importance of science as the appropriate basis of certainty in a new age in which traditional beliefs and traditional authority had disintegrated. Science for Mill was replacing religious and customary authority, both through its capacity to provide new information and because all the truths it discovered could be demonstrated to and understood by anyone (with an adequate education).[7] Hence it was the appropriate basis of knowledge and belief in a democratic age. Strachey was an avid reader of Mill and also, as we have seen, in the 1860s and 1870s, of Auguste Comte, the French positivist by whom Mill had himself been so strongly influenced. He shared the impatience and even hostility to religious thought and belief evident in Mill and amongst other contemporary advocates of science, especially T. H. Huxley and John Tyndall. In their view, science could take over from religion not only in the area of knowledge, but of morality, as scientific endeavours required and developed important moral and social qualities including care, patience, honesty, generosity—and humility.[8] There was no reason to fear overthrowing superstitious beliefs and restraints, Richard Strachey argued.

Human society is in truth constituted as it now is in consequence of *real* causes not of imaginary ones. If as a fact there is no such being as a personal deity then the elimination of the *idea* of such a power cannot affect human affairs, unless the idea of such a being has in effect equal power with such a being if he had exis-ted . . . The real spring to our existing social and moral system is a very high standard of human morality . . . The true '*grand etre*' who rules us is without question this great force of the combined instincts, appetites, capacities & so forth of the human being . . . So far as I can see the real power will come out with greatly increased majesty & authority when the shreds of rags and tissue with which it has been encased by the superstition of our ancestors shall be firmly torn down.[9]

Richard Strachey's belief in the importance of science and in its power to end superstition and transform the world had a counterpart in the 1860s and 1870s in the political radicalism of his wife. While he attempted to imbue Jane with his scientific ideals, she tried to sweep him up in her republican enthusiasm and desire for political reform. In the months leading up to the 1867 Reform Act in particular, Jane Strachey's letters to her husband are filled with discussion of the politics of reform—and the games that her young children devised in which they campaigned for reform—and with her general sense of the connection between her hostility to religion, her belief in positivism, and her desire for reform of the suffrage that would enfranchise women and working men.[10] For some time, Jane was also a convinced republican, regarding the monarchy as unnecessary and even dangerous.[11] Her radicalism was enhanced by her enthusiasm for Italian freedom. Like many feminists and upper middle-class English men and women, she was intensely sympathetic to Mazzini.[12] In 1870, Jane went to live in Italy for a few months with her mother and children. She had lessons to brush up her language skills 'with an Italian master who gave me my first lesson yesterday, & is to come three times a week. He is an oldish creature, & fancy my joy when I discovered that he is a genuine Republican, a friend of Mazzini! & a quondam conspirator!'[13]

Richard Strachey, while inherently more cautious than Jane, often attempted to echo her tone and views—and while he was in India, made a point of reporting conversations in which he had taken a line that she would have approved. In 1868, for example, he wrote to her from India about a discussion he had had with one of his visitors about land and land holding, in which there had been agreement that the continental approach to subdividing land was preferable to the British system of primogeniture. 'I of course went on the democratic side,' Richard assured Jane, 'asserting that a landlord was of no use excepting to himself, and as you were not there to go beyond me, I rather adopted your tone.'[14] A decade later, when he was again in India without Jane, he told her that he 'had a great burst of eloquence a few evenings ago at dinner . . . in favour of women's rights and generally I behave well in such respects, and support my character of red republican philosopher'.[15]

The political world of the senior Stracheys changed in the 1880s. While opposing the Tories and supporting Gladstone on many specific measures, as devotees of the British Empire, Jane and Richard Strachey could not accept Gladstone's proposal for Irish Home Rule in 1885—and they left the Liberal Party in disgust. They regarded Gladstone himself as absolutely wicked, and were delighted whenever they thought he was looking old or frail.[16] Their path after that seems to have followed a familiar one through the ranks of the Liberal Unionists in the 1890s and then finally to the Tories. This was never a comfortable home for Jane who, like her friend Millicent Garrett Fawcett, always resented the Conservative position on women's suffrage. Her republicanism certainly came to an end, however, and she seems to have come increasingly to feel the importance not only of Queen Victoria, but also of many of the other royal houses of Europe. Thus, as Lytton noted in his memoir 'Lancaster Gate', her sense of what was 'right and proper' included the idea that it was essential for her daughters to wear mourning for the German emperor.[17]

Both Jane Strachey's radicalism and Richard Strachey's belief in science were closely integrated into their imperial outlook. In Richard's case, one can see well how they came together, not only in his work in India, but also in the important role he played at the Prime Meridian Conference held in Washington in 1884. The aim of the conference, as far as the British and American delegates were concerned, was to propose to the governments represented 'the adoption as a standard meridian that of Greenwich passing through the centre of the transit instrument at the observatory at Greenwich'.[18] That this was a political as well as a scientific issue was made very clear by the French delegation which refused to accept that Britain should be the country through which the prime meridian passed. They questioned even whether or not it was desirable to fix upon a common longitude for all nations. When they were defeated on that point, they sought to establish the principles upon which such a common longitude should be based—arguing that it might be best to have different measures of longitude, or to distinguish between 'meridians of a geographical or hydrographical nature and meridians of observatories'.[19] Nations required accurate meridians acquired through observatories as the basis for geodetic and topographical operations, but these matters were of importance only to the country in which they belonged. Meridians for geographical purposes did not require quite such a degree of accuracy—and therefore did not need to privilege a particular observatory. The French delegation was quite prepared to accept that many navies utilized English charts and recognized the importance of Greenwich. However, once this accepted superiority of the British was 'transformed into an official and compulsory supremacy', they feared it would 'suffer the vicissitudes of all human power and . . . become the object of burning competition and jealousy among nations'.

Strachey was a vocal delegate at the conference where he was also elected as one of the secretaries, required to keep a tally of votes. He was unusually tactful, moreover, doing his best to assuage French anxieties and to show concern for French sensibilities—while pushing hard for a single meridian to be based at Greenwich. 'Longitude was longitude', he argued in response to the French idea of different longitudinal measure. 'It would never do if for geographical purposes we are to have second or third class longitude and for astronomical purposes a first-class longitude.' It was absurd to argue that a ship needed less accuracy than did astronomy—if its captain wanted it to arrive at a precise port! It seemed to him essential to fix an initial meridian through an astronomical observatory which could be connected with other places through other observatories and telegraphy wires.[20] For all the scientific arguments he could mount, Strachey's insistence on the need for the prime meridian to be based at Greenwich was deeply imbued with his imperialism and his sense that longitude and universal time needed to be devised in the way best suited to the convenience of 'the civilised world'. It was impossible to vote on a meridian without setting up a universal day, he insisted, and no matter how the longitude was calculated, there would be discontinuity at some point on the globe. It would be sensible if a system of counting was introduced that counted longitude in both directions from Greenwich and produced discontinuity in both longitude and time at the same place—at the meridian 180 degrees from Greenwich. 'It would be very inconvenient if the resolution . . . adopted . . . caused discontinuity both in longitude and local time in Europe.' It would be far better to have the international and universal day settled as the 'Greenwich civil day', and to have the discontinuity over New Zealand and Fiji—in part of the 'uninhabited world'.[21]

The belief that Richard Strachey shared with many of his contemporaries that their scientific approach would ensure that their knowledge was accurate and their approach to all matters free of bias has been extensively criticized recently in terms of the racism and the sexism that were both incorporated in and supported by their understanding of science. For Strachey and his colleagues, Darwin's theory of evolution could be applied not only to the natural, but also to the social world. Societies moved from one stage to another and could be classified according to their level of complexity, and races could be similarly analysed and classified.[22] It was to Darwin, Strachey argued in his lectures on geography, that science was indebted for its understanding of the differences amongst the races of men in terms of the regions they inhabited and their descent and current development.[23] Evolutionary theory, as expounded by other followers of Darwin including T. H. Huxley, produced the hierarchy of races that Strachey described in the long essay on 'Asia' that he contributed to the *Encyclopaedia Britannica* in 1880. The original peoples of Asia came from four different racial groups: Mongolian (the largest in number), Caucasian (whom, following Huxley, he divided into Melanochroic and Xanathocroic), Australoid and Negroid. The Aryans of India, those speaking languages derived from or akin to the ancient form of Sanskrit are 'the most settled and civilised of all Asiatic races'.[24]

Strachey's scientific views and approaches may be subject to criticism today, but they were strongly endorsed by his family. The continuing importance of science within the Strachey family is demonstrated most clearly in the ideas of Lytton and of James. Although the older Strachey sons, particularly Ralph and Oliver, shared Richard's interest in mathematics and some of his skill in physics and engineering, neither ever wrote anything general about science, nor were they preoccupied with it as in any way an intellectual problem. Nor was it a matter of great concern to the Strachey daughters, for whom languages and literature were of more consuming intellectual interest. Both Lytton and James, however, were interested in science, albeit in rather different ways. In Lytton's case, one can see it in the accolade he offered G. E. Moore after his first reading of *Principia Ethica*. Moore's book, he wrote, had shattered all earlier writers on ethics and laid the true foundation. What was most important about Moore's work was 'the establishment of that Method which shines like a sword between the lines. It is the scientific method deliberately applied for the first time to reasoning.' In a line strongly echoing late eighteenth- and nineteenth-century ideas about the capacity of science to root out error, and even with a possibly unintended echo of his parents' interest in Comte who had also defined an age of reason, Lytton insisted that, with Moore's book, 'the truth, there can be no doubt, is really now upon the march. I date from Oct. 1903 the beginning of the Age of Reason.'[25]

While his response to Moore celebrated the rise of a new science, Lytton Strachey always retained a fascination with some Victorian scientists as well. It was they who enabled him to express his sense of nostalgia for what had been lost between the Victorian period and his own. In 1906 he began reading Darwin, working his way through the *Origin of Species*, *The Descent of Man*, and finally, the *Autobiography*. He was instantly smitten both with Darwin's style and with his character. Indeed, Michael Holroyd regards his discovery of Darwin as 'the single bright spot' in a year in which there was much confusion and anguish about both Lytton's personal life and his professional prospects.[26] 'Did you realize that he was one of our greatest stylists?', he asked his sister Dorothy

Bussy.[27] He waxed more lyrical in letters to Duncan Grant to whom he praised the many good stories about parrots, butterflies, peacocks and Barbary apes in *The Descent of Man*. 'But the chief charm', he added, 'is Darwin's character which runs through everything he wrote in a wonderful way . . . He was absolutely good—that is to say, he was without a drop of evil; though his simplicity makes him curiously different from any of us. And, I suppose, prevents him from reaching the greatest heights of all.'[28]

Even more than Lytton, James Strachey shared the approaches and values evident in his father's understanding of science and applied them in his own intellectual world. James's sense of the importance of science is most evident in his approach to Freud and in the framework he established for the translation of Freud's work. The summary of Freud's life and thought that is included in each volume of the collected works of Freud makes this clear, with its heavy emphasis on Freud's medical training and scientific method. Freud's discoveries, James explained, using a terminology that his father would have approved entirely, 'may be grouped under three headings—an instrument of research, the findings produced by the instrument, and the theoretical hypotheses inferred from the findings'. He was, first and foremost, 'the discoverer of the first instrument for the scientific examination of the human mind. Creative writers of genius had had fragmentary insight into mental processes, but no systematic method of investigation existed before Freud'.[29] Through self-analysis, Freud discovered

the nature of the unconscious processes at work in the mind and . . . why there is such a strong resistance to their becoming conscious; it enabled him to devise techniques for overcoming or evading the resistance in his patients; and, most important of all, it enabled him to realize the very great differences between the mode of functioning of these unconscious processes and our familiar conscious ones.[30]

James's desire to emphasize the scientific aspect of Freud's thought led him to seek a new scientific language, devoid of other associations, for his English translation. As we will see, in recent years, this has made his translation of Freud extremely controversial as many of those who are interested primarily in the ways in which Freud's thought can be applied to culture, or who want to stress the breadth and expansiveness of his approach, argue that Strachey produced a particularly narrow version of Freud's thought.[31]

❧ II ❧

While Richard and Jane Strachey did not use the language of modernity to define themselves, their two youngest sons, Lytton and James, most emphatically did. The term 'modern' appears frequently in their correspondence with each other, especially around 1909–10, and it was used not so much to point to particular ideas or beliefs or values as to designate a whole new approach to life. This approach was one that Lytton and James shared with their Bloomsbury friends, but emphatically not with their family. The intellectual approach, the insistence on clarity, honesty, precision, and the freedom to discuss anything that Lytton and his friends had learnt from G. E. Moore and the Apostles at Cambridge was important here, but it served primarily as a background. What mattered was the application of this honesty and openness of discussion to sexual questions and to intimate feelings, in ways that had been unthinkable in Cambridge. It was this freedom of discussion that seemed to break every Victorian taboo that defined the understanding of modernity shared by Lytton and James Strachey in the years leading up to the First World War. The use of the term 'modern' in their correspondence refers both to the open acceptance and discussion of homosexuality, and to the broader sense that close personal relationships required intimacy in terms of the sharing of emotions, experiences, and domestic life in ways quite unknown to the world of the Victorian upper middle class. The appearance of the term coincided with the new kind of social life that became available to Lytton and James and their friends with the marriage of Vanessa Stephen and Clive Bell in 1907. Bloomsbury gatherings had occurred before this, and both Lytton and James had regularly attended Virginia and Adrian Stephen's regular Thursday night 'at homes' at which close friends consumed whisky and buns and discussed every topic they cared for. But, as we have seen, the marriage of the Bells brought something different. In Frances Spalding's view, as a married woman, Vanessa Bell was consciously 'making social history' through her bawdy talk and insistence on her right to discuss anything and everything with male friends. The marriage of the Bells also brought a new sense of informality, marked most clearly by the use of first names. When 'Mr Strachey' became 'Lytton' in the Bell household, it was a sign that many formal social barriers were to be removed. Lytton was admitted to the Bell home whenever he chose to call—and entertained while the married couple lay in bed.[32]

The importance of new approaches to intimacy and sexuality is under-scored by the way in which both Lytton and James Strachey used the term 'modern' primarily to apply to relationships. In 1909, for example, when Bloomsbury talk about sex was at its height, Lytton used the term 'mod-ernity' to indicate his growing sense of distance from his old friend Dickinson, with whom it was not possible to discuss homosexuality.

Speaking of modernity, I had tea with Dickinson today and suffered acutely. I found it impossible to be at my ease. We of course discussed America; But I couldn't ask the one question I wanted to—whether there were many sods at Harvard—because I felt it would be out of key. Why should it be? Dear dear, leagues apart we were, and yet—ave maria! we date back from the poor fellows, but its no good.[33]

Amongst the rest of the Strachey family, discussion of sexual questions was completely taboo—and intense emotion was avoided whenever possible. This was the case even with Marjorie, although she was younger than Lytton. In James's view, Marjorie had her first encounter with modernity at the hands of Virginia Woolf. 'There seem have been some doings between Marjorie and Virginia,' he wrote to Lytton in 1909.

Marjorie stayed the night with Virginia and told Duncan she could never go there again. It seems that while they were talking, M told V that she was too literary and never had any real feelings. V broke out into paranoid tirade 'No feelings? Its you that have no feelings—you don't know what feelings are. How dare you come here and despise me? I despise you, if you only knew the unfathomable horrors in which I pass my life.'[34]

Marjorie was really alarmed and told Duncan that she would write and say 'that I can never go there again unless she guarantees that such a scene shall not be repeated'. This, James thought, was Marjorie's 'first introduc-tion . . . to *la vie moderne*,' and he wondered whether she would 'break under it'.[35] Sexuality and intimacy were not the only thing that defined Lytton Strachey's sense of the modern. Like Baudelaire and Benjamin, he felt very strongly that there was something fragile and evanescent about modern life that contrasted strongly with the permanence and stability of the Victor-ians. Interesting people, he told James, were bound 'in time to collapse or simply vanish—which seem the inevitable alternatives of modern life'.[36]

This sense of fragility and emotional vulnerability was closely con-nected, in Lytton's view to a new sense of the importance of art, aesthetics, and domestic design.[37] Our fathers, he thought, would have laughed at the idea that a house has an influence on its occupants, for to our fathers the visible conformations of things were unimportant; they were more interested in the mental and moral implications of their surroundings than in the actual nature of them; and their spirits, so noble and oblivious, escaped the direct pressure of the material universe . . . Our view is different. We find satisfaction in curves and colours, and windows fascinate us, wc are agitated by staircases, inspired by doors, disgusted by cornices, depressed by chairs, made wanton by ceilings, entranced by passages, and exacerbated by a rug.[38]

It is interesting to note, however, that while he enjoyed being surrounded by modern things, Lytton Strachey took relatively less interest in modern art than did many of his Bloomsbury friends. He was relatively unmoved by the epoch-making exhibition 'Manet and Post-Impressionism' that was organized by Roger Fry at the Grafton Gallery in November 1910 and was so significant an event to many of his friends.[39] This exhibition was central to the understanding of modernity and to a new sense of freedom to experiment with artistic forms for Virginia Woolf, as for Vanessa Bell and Duncan Grant. It attracted extensive and hostile publicity. The paintings of Manet, Gauguin, Cezanne, Matisse, and others, with their lack of interest in any form of realistic representation, their dramatic approach to colour, and their apparent casualness of execution caused outrage amongst English art critics and journalists—many of whom felt that this revolutionary new art contained the same seeds of revolt and subversion as were evident in the trade union battles and strikes that were currently occurring and with the militant campaigns of the suffragettes.[40] While the rest of Bloomsbury felt that life was being transformed by this exhibition, it seems to have had little impact on the Stracheys. It does not rate even a mention in Holroyd's biography of Lytton Strachey and, although he visited it and commented on some of the paintings in his letters to Dorothy Bussy, he was far from overwhelmed. He attended the second of Fry's Post-Impressionist exhibitions in 1912 but, as Holroyd comments, 'seemed more interested in the effect produced by Post-Impressionism than in the pictures themselves'.[41]

The year 1910 was significant for Lytton Strachey too, but for reasons that had nothing to do with the post-impressionists. It was the year that he received his first major literary commission for *Landmarks in French Literature*, which in turn saw him give up his research on Warren Hastings. It was also the year in which he became friendly with Ottoline Morrell, thus gaining access to Garsington as a regular rural retreat. He was able to spend more and more time away from his family and home and became known to a much wider world. But the changes for him in that year were of a very different kind from the 'liberation and encouragement to feel for oneself' that Vanessa Bell described as the major impact of the post-impressionist exhibition.[42]

While Lytton and James Strachey had no doubts about their own modernity, others have not been quite so sure. Amongst contemporary scholars, this is a matter of some debate. Michael Holroyd certainly supports Lytton's claims, arguing that he introduced a 'modern' approach to sexuality and to personal life, both in Cambridge and later in Blooms-bury.[43] Peter Stansky agrees, seeing the approach both to the Victorians and to biography that Lytton took in *Eminent Victorians* as a major step in the development and the documenting of modernism in Britain.[44] Others disagree. Writing in the 1930s André Maurois questioned whether one might not rather think of Lytton Strachey himself as the last eminent Victorian in his outlook and his mode of life.[45] More recently this point has been elaborated at length by Julie Anne Taddeo who argues that even in his sexual ideas and beliefs, Strachey had considerably more in common with his Victorian forebears than with any notion of the modern. His advocacy of the 'higher sodomy' on the one hand, and his oriental erotic fantasies, on the other, were all derived from and closely connected to the Victorian imperial world of his youth. His way of life replicated many aspects of Victorian patriarchy, dependent as it was on constant female service and self-sacrifice which Lytton, in light of his own patriarchal assumptions and sense of female inferiority, took as his due.[46]

The ambiguity of Lytton Strachey's approach to modernity, and the extent to which he continued to maintain the attitudes of his family, can be seen particularly in his attitude to imperialism. For both Leonard and Virginia Woolf, criticism of and indeed outright rejection of European imperial aspirations were integral to a sense of the new political, social, and aesthetic possibilities that constituted modernity.[47] But this was not the case for Lytton Strachey. On the contrary, he incorporated both a residue of his family's imperial values and a new form of oriental erotic imagining quite easily into his own 'modern' outlook. The start of what Virginia Woolf later called 'Old Bloomsbury', with its sexual openness and its G. E. Moore-inspired talk about the beautiful and the true, did not in any way undermine Lytton Strachey's interest in the life of Warren Hastings.[48] He had first attempted to vindicate Hastings in an essay-writing competition in 1901. But he also chose him for the theses he submitted for the Trinity College fellowship in 1904 and again in 1905. Even when he failed to gain the fellowship, he continued to work on Hastings until 1910, incorporating as he did so many of the Victorian imperial values of the Strachey family.[49]

Lytton Strachey's acceptance of the India of his parents and of their imperial values and beliefs was made even more evident in 1907 when he reviewed *The Letters of Lord Lytton* for the *Independent*.[50] He could not accept his mother's views concerning the merits of Lytton's poetry, but he greatly admired his role in India. 'His Lordship thought he was a poet manqué—nothing more mistaken. He was simply a great statesman.'[51] Strachey's review was sufficiently laudatory to please even the Lytton family. 'Was that wonderful review of the book in the *Independent* by one of your sons?' Edith Lytton wrote to ask Jane Strachey? 'I can't tell you how perfect I think it and it is so well written and so understanding of my dear husband.'[52] Lytton in turn was pleased by her response. 'Lady Lytton's letter was touching,' he wrote to Dorothy, 'and I think she really did like it which is something.'[53] In subsequent reviews in the *Spectator*, he extended his defence of empire, endorsing the view that English discipline converted Indians from savage barbarism to noble virtue.[54] These essays, as S. P. Rosenbaum comments, suggest Kipling's India rather than even hinting at the critical view of the Raj offered by E. M. Forster.[55]

This continued fascination with India and with the empire more broadly throughout these years is in many ways surprising. In late 1904, Lytton's close friend, Leonard Woolf, went to Ceylon. Woolf himself later accepted that he went out to Ceylon with an unquestioning acceptance of the merits of British imperial power, but was aware that a new and more critical approach to the empire had begun to emerge in 1905.[56] The regular letters that he sent Strachey from Ceylon do not contain the clear and focused criticism of imperialism that Woolf published in the early 1920s.[57] Rather they suggest his sense that imperial rule was hopeless and chaotic, with vast authority given to people ill-equipped to exercise it and waste, muddle, and brutality evident everywhere. Strachey did not really pick up on this critique. Indeed, one of the noticeable features of the Woolf/Strachey correspondence of these years is the insight it offers into how these two young men, who had been so close at Cambridge, became more and distant. Woolf, who was often unhappy in Ceylon, disliking much of what he had to do and feeling completely cut off from his own world, wrote at length of his surroundings, his administrative and judicial tasks, and his frequent distaste for all the people he had to deal with, British and Sinhalese alike. Strachey, who was engrossed in his own sexual life, took little note of Woolf's imperial problems. When he commented on Woolf's specific stories, it was often through a very explicit eroticizing of imperial life. Thus Woolf's painful letters explaining his horror at having to condemn men to death or to witness executions were incorporated into Strachey's sexual fantasies. 'I long to pay you a visit,' he wrote, 'I could be so lazy while you were condemning blacks to death, dreaming every kind of wonder and writing poetry in the intervals.'[58] Far from making Strachey recognize the bleak side of imperialism, Woolf's letters reinforced his sense of an erotic imperial world offering a limitless supply of nubile black male bodies.

This creation of an erotic orientalist fantasy world was a central part of Lytton Strachey's own sense of modernity. It certainly transgressed all the boundaries evident in the Indian stories that he heard at home and it involved a dramatic shift away from any Victorian notion of duty and into a world of limitless indulgence and pleasure. His imaginary empire centred rather more on North Africa and Arabia than on India, informed perhaps by the visit Lytton had made to Egypt in his early adolescence. In the tales that he produced for friends, the published stories such as 'An Arabian Night', and the letters to Woolf and other friends, Strachey elaborated his sense of the erotic possibilities of a world beyond 'civilization', where the prejudices of his own society could be ignored or suspended and new sexual possibilities explored.[59] Although intrigued by the idea of a sexual empire, and willing often to articulate his fantasies about nubile black bodies, Lytton Strachey did not ever enter into a relationship with or indicate that he felt any desire for someone from another race.[60] Unlike E. M. Forster, for example, he had no close Indian or African friends, nor did he engage in sexual adventures while travelling. His frequent illnesses and his shyness both militated against sexual conquest when he was away from home, and despite his letters to Leonard Woolf, he seems to have lacked the desire evident in so many British and French writers who travelled to 'the east' in search of sexual adventure. 'My tastes are not at all in the direction of blacks,' he explained to Leonard Woolf, after a trip to Algiers in 1913, 'The more black they are, the more I dislike them'.[61] Julie Taddeo has critically analysed Lytton Strachey's orientalist fantasies. She argues that they are grounded in his childhood reading and understanding of India, and that they undermine any claim that can be made about his modern identity. Rather, she argues, they involve a firm endorsement of his family's imperial values. While seen by himself and others as 'liberating', and as part of his own 'modern' outlook, Lytton's imperial vision offered only limited scope for himself while constantly re-enforcing his sense of white superiority and dominance.[62]

While Lytton Strachey continued to share something of his family's imperial outlook, he differed strongly from his parents and older siblings when it came to other political questions. Although evident before, this became inescapable in the course of the First World War during which Lytton and James Strachey took up a position completely antithetical to that of the rest of the Stracheys. In the course of the war itself, as in the years leading up to it, it was James who took the lead in formulating a new political opinion. He had attended Fabian Society summer schools in 1910 and for a few subsequent years with Rupert Brooke and a group of other friends.[63] Their political commitment did not meet the exacting standards of Beatrice Webb, who regarded James and his friends as self-indulgent dilettantes, treating the summer schools as a vacation rather than engaging in serious political study.[64] Nonetheless, he did take a serious interest in political and social questions. Lytton, who had few political interests at the time, endorsed some of James's Fabian sympathies, which put them both at odds with the rest of the family. Lytton's support for Beatrice Webb's minority report on the Poor Law Commission put him on opposite sides of the political fence from his sister, Pippa. Like James, he felt that the Poor Law and the workhouse system should be replaced by a completely new approach to welfare payments. Pippa did not agree, believing that the old Poor Law should be retained, but modified. Lytton was horrified by Pippa's response.[65]

Of course Lytton himself was selective in the reforms he advocated. Thus while he welcomed a new approach to the Poor Law, he was much less certain when it came to the question of divorce. Some of the recommendations of the 1912 Royal Commission on Divorce seemed to him completely incomprehensible. He was understandably horrified at the idea that 'unnatural vice' be accepted as a cause for divorce. But he was extremely puzzled about 'the unanimity over what they call "the equality of the sexes." '

If a woman commits adultery its surely far more serious from the point of view of marriage, the home, etc., than if a man does. So far as I can see, the only reason why divorce was ever recognised as the proper thing for adultery at all was because the family system would be wrecked if promiscuous fucking on the part of wives was allowed. One can understand a man objecting to bringing up other peoples children.[66]

These differences of political outlook became more and more pronounced with the outbreak of war in 1914. Here, too, James led the way. Having just come back from an extended European trip that had taken him to Berlin, Vienna, Moscow, and St Petersburg, he was appalled by the prospect of war. 'It seems to me that every possible effort ought to be made to prevent Grey from letting us in,' he wrote to Lytton in July 1914. 'There must surely be a chance of voting him down in the House of Commons.'[67] While working at the *Spectator*, James was made aware of what he saw as a number of quite ridiculous ideas that made British involvement in the war appear essential. One such scenario involved the possibility that, if Britain were not involved, Russia and France might combine to crush Germany—and then all three might patch up their quarrels and attack Britain in concert. James thought this view nonsensical, but was convinced that it was what his cousin St Loe believed. When the war began, James became increasingly despondent as British jingoism became more and more vehement. 'Did you see that German composers were to be left out of the Promenade concerts?', he wrote to Lytton in August 1914, 'I've written a frantic letter to the manager and thought of another to the press. Are our doctors to give up using salvarsan?'[68]

Lytton, while listening closely to James, was not immune to war fever. While agreeing that the situation and the state of the country were awful, he did admit to an occasional 'desire to go out there and fight myself'. He could understand people being overcome by enthusiasm for war and 'at any rate one would not have to think any more'.[69] His opposition centred largely on his sense of the need to protect intellectuals like themselves. He was unable to 'see the sense of intellectual persons' engaging in combat, 'so long as there are enough other men and the country is not in danger'. In the first couple of years of the war, then, as James became a more and more committed pacifist, Lytton prevaricated over how to respond. James was always aware that Lytton's hostility to the war and his pacifism lacked the intensity of his own—and he felt himself to be far more at one with other convinced Tolstoyans and pacifists like Harry Norton and Bertrand Russell.[70] He met Russell at a friend's house in September 1914 'and we fell into one another's arms as co-workers in a great cause'.[71]

Lytton's opposition to the war, like that of his Bloomsbury friends, grew stronger as he watched the pointless slaughter. Quentin Bell later recalled that there had been some optimism amongst his parents and their friends during the first decade of the twentieth century, and a belief that 'the forces of unreason' might be vanquished, and that Britain might ameliorate the conditions of its imperial dominions, concede some of the demands of the labour movement—and move away from the nineteenth-century adulation of Empire, Nation, Home, and Moral Cleanliness.[72] The war made clear that this was not the case. For Clive and Vanessa Bell and their friends, the war was considered to be a period of 'National Insanity' and they did their best especially after 1916 to make clear their opposition to it.

James and Lytton had said little to their mother about their sexual preferences or about the other aspects of their lives of which she disapproved. On the question of the war, however, some of their differences had to be confronted. Jane Strachey's passionate patriotism and imperial fervour made it unthinkable that she should be anything but an ardent supporter of the war, and she was supported in her stance by Pippa, Ray, and all her other children. Oliver and Dick, although too old to fight, were both actively engaged in the war effort. Indeed, Dick was directly involved in the plan which brought the different positions within the Strachey family to a head. Dick worked in the War Office for several years and in October 1915, became involved in the administration of the new Derby Scheme. This scheme was an attempt to increase the number of men available for war in a voluntary way, by persuading all those of serviceable age to 'attest' to their willingness to join up whenever they were called to do so. James refused to 'attest' and as a result was forced to resign from the *Spectator*. He was compelled to inform his mother of these developments. 'I am sorry to send disturbing news', he wrote to her in December of 1915:

St Loe has come to the conclusion that it would be wrong of him to keep on in his employment any one of military age; and he consequently felt obliged to ask me either to join the army under Lord Derby's scheme or to leave the *Spectator*. I imagine I should in any case have been rejected on physical grounds (my eyes alone would probably be enough); but I felt it would hardly be decent to get out of it in that way, as I have such very strong objections to having anything to do with the business at all.[73]

Jane Strachey, who was then staying with Dorothy in France, was greatly distressed by this event. She was concerned about James's loss of secure employment (especially as her own investments had suffered heavily during the war and there was now less for the family to live on). But this was of less significance than their differences in outlook. However, she was not prepared to allow political differences to destroy her relationship with her beloved youngest son—and she held to the hope that he might change his mind. 'What I really regret more than anything is that our views in this tremendous crisis should be in disagreement', she wrote,

but even here my dear, we hold one opinion in common, & that the most important of all—viz to stick by whatever we do think right. And here I should just like to add a remark as the fruit of my experience; keep an open mind; don't let anything you have sincerely held at one time keep you chained if you *should* see a different vista opening out as you walk uphill.[74]

Of course James did no such thing. On the contrary, both he and Lytton became more and more opposed to the war and to the ways it was being run. The introduction of conscription in January 1916 was the final straw. It was this that made Lytton become publicly active, as both he and James joined the No Conscription Fellowship, helping to disseminate its message in a variety of ways, extending from the drafting of pamphlets to the licking of stamps. In one of his pamphlets, Lytton argued that conscription was wrong in itself and was being introduced as a way of crushing both Labour and any other form of opposition in Britain. What was the point of going to war with Germany, he wondered, if the British government was itself introducing so many policies that had typified the German authoritarianism that was ostensibly being fought against?[75]

While none of the other members of the family supported the position taken by Lytton and James, all of them agreed with Jane Strachey that what mattered was that everyone followed their own conscience. Not only did they not see this disagreement as a reason for any kind of breach, but most of them attended when Lytton and James had to face conscription tribunals in 1916. Even St Loe, strongly as he disapproved of James's stance, appeared as a character witness on his behalf. James refused to undertake any form of civilian service, insisting before the tribunal that he held it wrong 'to take any part in the war; and my objection applies not only to combatant service but to any action which is likely to assist in its prosecution'.[76] Once the tribunal was over, James began to work with the Quaker organized Emergency Committee for the Assistance of Germans, Austrians, and Hungarians in distress. James's sense of opposition to established British society continued—and made him the one member of the family to welcome the Russian Revolution in 1917.[77] His mother appears to have taken some comfort from the fact that his work for the Emergency Committee was excellent. In 1918, she wrote with great pride to her sister, Elinor, of a comment about James made by someone on her daughter,

Elinor Rendel's relief committee. 'She said that she had never known anyone to equal him for tact, kindness, capacity and organising power, and that he had saved a hundred women and children from starvation.'[78]

After appearing before the tribunal in January 1916, Lytton Strachey was required to present himself for a medical examination in June where he was finally declared unfit for military service. Thus there was no further question of his being called up. He continued his own battle against the war through support for the No Conscription Fellowship and through his own writings. He produced columns in the *New Statesman* in which he criticized and condemned the barbaric situation and demanded a return to civilized standards of behaviour. More importantly, he devoted himself to writing *Eminent Victorians*, a work planned before the war, but altered during it so that, as Michael Holroyd argues, 'its theme became an ironic sifting of those Victorian pretensions that seemed to have led civilization into a holocaust of unparalleled magnitude'.[79]

While *Eminent Victorians* retains a very significant place in the history of biography, its intellectual standing as a critique of Victorian values, and its connection with modernism are rather more open to question. The book itself, as Michael Holroyd suggests, occupies a somewhat anomalous place in modern literature. Its ease and polish prevented it from indicating adequately the struggle involved in throwing off the weight of Victorian tradition, while at the same time ensuring that it did not suggest ways of seeing the world anew. Gerald Brennan wrote to Lytton, suggesting that it provided a border between the old world and the new, rather than taking its readers on to new horizons.[80] It went as far as Lytton Strachey was prepared to go. His subsequent works offered far less either in the way of critiquing earlier generations or in terms of offering new intellectual approaches or new world views. *Queen Victoria* was far gentler in its approach both to the monarch and her reign than *Eminent Victorians* had been, suggesting that the intensity of Lytton's hostility to the Victorians was already spent. Nor did Strachey engage passionately in either the politics or the literary developments of the 1920s. Robert Skidelsky is surely right in insisting that Lytton Strachey caught a temporary mood with *Eminent Victorians*, but that his voice was not one that was heard in any significant way throughout the 1920s. For him, as for his Bloomsbury friends, it was the Edwardian period that was the high point of existence—and the First World War brought to an end the world in which they felt most at home.[81]

❦ III ❦

Lytton's capacity to retain old values and assumptions while engaging in a world of modern art, society, and politics can be seen also in regard to the Bussys in France. As we have seen, Lytton Strachey regarded Dorothy's marriage to Simon Bussy in 1903 as an event that shook the Strachey edifice to its foundations, bringing as it did an unprecedented connection with a family of French artisans of very limited means. The life the Bussys organized in France was also in many ways quite unlike that of any other members of the Strachey family. *La Souco*, their idyllic house on the French Riviera, became a holiday retreat for the others, but for Dorothy and Simon it was the centre of a new life dedicated to art, work, and to a quite new community. Like many middle-class women in the nineteenth century, but unlike anyone known to the Stracheys, Dorothy also turned her home into a workplace, taking in paying guests who enabled her and Simon to eke out a modest subsistence.

The tenor of life at *La Souco* owed much to Simon Bussy. He was a quiet and unassuming man, considerably less imposing than his father-in-law or indeed than some of the Strachey sons. He was nonetheless determined to maintain his own culture and values and to dedicate his life absolutely to his art.[82] Indeed, Bussy's passion for painting and his approach to it dominated every facet of his and of Dorothy's life. Bussy had trained originally in the studio of Gustave Moreau and his early work shows clearly the influence both of Moreau's symbolism and of his very dark palette. Although devoted to his teacher, Bussy had decided in the 1890s that he needed to leave both Moreau's studio and Paris and to find a new source of inspiration in the natural world. He left on a walking tour with a large backpack and covered a considerable distance, walking across the Jura, through Switzerland, and finally into Germany. His most successful exhibition ever, that of 1897, was a result of this journey and included many landscapes of the areas he had seen. On his return to Paris in 1898, Bussy shifted gear once again. He began painting at the Academy Carmen, recently founded by Whistler. Bussy admired Whistler and was intrigued by his work. As Philip Loisel argues, one can see something of Whistler's influence in Bussy's subsequent work, in his use of a palette with far more grey and lilac, in his approach to the human figure, and in the increasingly abstract approach to landscape evident in the paintings that he did between 1899 and about 1910.[83]

Simon Bussy had a complex relationship with contemporary developments in French art. He was regarded as a very promising young painter in the 1890s. Indeed, Matisse, who was a close friend, saw him as a leader and frequently sought his advice. But Bussy felt himself less and less in tune with French impressionism or with any of the major forms of post impressionism that replaced it. He did not hold Cezanne in high regard, nor was he interested in Braque or Picasso or in the paintings of Matisse. This was made very clear when he made the final shift in 1912 that determined his subsequent work as a painter. In that year, while visiting the London zoo, Bussy suddenly came to see, he wrote later, a way of synthesizing his earlier landscape studies and those he wished now to do by focusing on the animals and birds at the zoo. He began working on detailed animal studies, which he saw almost as portraits of animals, to which he devoted the rest of his life.[84] He simplified his palette, choosing often to undertake studies that were almost monochrome, in the belief that emotion could best be expressed in this simplified approach to colour. He ceased trying to paint directly from nature, feeling rather that he needed to compose his work in a studio from the many detailed studies that he undertook.[85] He was aware that this approach and his determination to follow a path so different from that of his contemporaries involved resolutely turning his back on success. But he felt unable to proceed in any other way.[86]

Roquebrunne, where Simon and Dorothy settled, proved ideal for this approach. Over the years, a community of artists settled there, with Jean Vander Eeckoudt as the central figure, all of whom shared with Bussy a desire to emphasize precision, on the one hand, and the need to simplify and limit their use of colour, on the other.[87] The Bussys thus lived in the midst of a very engaged artists' colony in Roquebrunne that was passionately interested in all facets of art—and determinedly experimental despite in its opposition to the directions that were fashionable in Paris or indeed London. Their life was very sociable and their home always full of people. Simon also became quite involved in local government.

In the period after the war, the Bussys were introduced to a new range of artistic, political, and personal issues largely through their close friendship with André Gide. They had met Gide in England in 1918, and continued to see and to correspond regularly with him after that. As we have seen, Dorothy's passionate involvement with Gide made the relationship always somewhat awkward and intense. Nonetheless, her work as his translator led into a range of other kinds of contacts with his friends and with his political and intellectual world. It was she rather than Simon who became involved with Gide's world, although for Gide himself one of the great charms of the Bussys was Simon, of whom he became immensely fond.

There were many different ways in which Gide drew the Bussys into modern approaches to literature, culture, and politics. One of the most important was their inclusion in the annual retreats at Pontigny at which a range of philosophical issues were discussed.[88] Gide also opened a new range of political ideas to the Bussys. Unlike James, they showed no particular enthusiasm for the 1917 Russian Revolution. Gide's interest and involvement in the Soviet Union in the 1920s and 1930s, however, brought it more closely into their frame of reference. Janie Bussy had strong sympathies with communism and Dorothy became increasingly interested and supportive too.

Gide's writing was also important to Dorothy, especially those works that dwelt in detail on sexual questions and on his own homosexuality. While Dorothy, and presumably Simon too, were well aware of Lytton Strachey's sexuality and knew about several of his relationships, Lytton had written only occasionally about sex in any explicit way, and about homosexuality only obliquely and in works for his friends. The openness of Gide's account of his own sexual development, and his detailed exposition of his ideas about the sexual attractions of older men for younger men and boys, was unprecedented. Dorothy Bussy was thrown into a state of some anguish when Gide preferred her not to be the translator of his most explicitly sexual works, finding it hard to acknowledge his sense that this work needed a male translator. 'How can you', she wrote, 'who pride yourself particularly on imitating a woman's, a young girl's voice, think that the opposite impersonation—especially in a translation is impossible?'[89] But these writings were clearly familiar to her. Gide's openness and his approach to sexuality in literature were also important for her, not least in providing a kind of model and a silent encouragement for her to explore the sexual feelings of an adolescent girl at school in *Olivia*.

Dorothy Bussy's involvement in the intellectual and political debates of the inter-war years did little to shake her strong sense of connection to her Strachey family roots or heritage. Back in England, after the horrors of the Second World War, she came increasingly to feel a sense of pride in her roots. 'I am very little Scottish', she wrote to Gide,

Just a touch of the Highlands—nothing at all of the Lowlands. I am really good English stock—My forbears Somersetshire Squires since the 16th century, one of my ancestors an intimate friend of Locke's (no fanatics we). And during this last stay in England, I have come to admire or rather respect the English more than I did when it was the fashion to look down on one's countrymen.

She was very impressed by the new Labour government. Its members were ignorant of parliamentary etiquette, but would doubtless soon learn all they needed to know about government. When confronted by the demise of the British Empire, however, her response was couched completely in terms of her family tradition. Indian independence in 1947 and the demand by Egypt for its independence in 1950 were to her rather shocking. 'It now remains to be seen', she wrote to André Gide,

whether our 'slave dominions', Egypt and India, have learnt enough from us of the art of government to manage for themselves without too great a fiasco. Anyway I think the decline and fall of the English Empire is honourable on the whole. But as you imagine, there is a good deal in the present goings on of Congress and the Muslim League which is pretty irritating to a member of a great Anglo-Indian family of civil servants.[90]

IV

Like Dorothy, James and Alix Strachey became involved in new ideas and a whole new intellectual world after the First World War. As we have seen, they had both expressed an interest in abnormal psychology and had begun to read Freud in the years leading up to the war. But it was in 1920 that they began to translate Freud and to think about undergoing analysis and becoming analysts themselves.[91] Both James and Alix suffered from what are now thought of as a range of emotional and nervous disorders and clearly their attraction to psychoanalysis related in some way to their own desires for a cure. James had suffered from severe depression both as a student and when he was working for the *Spectator* in 1913. Alix too suffered some kind of collapse while at Cambridge, which is now seen very much as a nervous one, and she suffered intermittently from depression and from a range of phobias, experiencing severe palpitations in theatres or crowded places or in trains throughout her life. She appears also to have been anorexic. Thus while they had already begun to do some work on the translation of Freud when they went to Vienna in 1920, the question of being analysed was also an important one.

James's admiration for Freud grew immensely when his analysis began. Freud, he explained to Lytton, was a dazzling artistic performer who made every hour 'into an organic aesthetic whole'.

Sometimes the dramatic effect is absolutely shattering. During the early part of the hour all is vague—a dark hint here, a mystery there—then it gradually seems to get thicker; you feel dreadful things going on inside you, and can't make out what they can possible be; then he begins to give you a slight lead; you suddenly get a clear glimpse of one thing; then you see another; at last a whole sense of light breaks in on you; he asks you one more question; you give a last reply—and as the whole truth dawns upon you the Professor rises, crosses the room to the electric bell, and shows you out at the door.

That's on favourable occasions. But there are others when you lie for the whole hour with a ton weight on your stomach simply unable to get out a single word. I think that makes one more inclined to believe it all than anything. When you positively feel the 'resistance' as something physical sitting on you, it fairly shakes you all the rest of the day.[92]

Alix, however, did not share this view. She disliked Freud as an analyst, which is hardly surprising in view of the shabby treatment she received from him. But her lung ailment in 1921 also brought James's analysis to an end. He was very distressed at the abrupt termination of his analysis, but could do nothing about it. This experience of the sudden loss of an analyst was to be repeated for both of them. On Freud's advice, Alix resumed analysis with Karl Abraham, whom she greatly liked and admired, in Berlin a few years later. Abraham, however, died suddenly, before her analysis was complete. Shortly after this James went into analysis with James Glover, but Glover too died suddenly in 1926. While James seems not to have attempted analysis again after this, Alix did, becoming a patient of Edward Glover when she returned to London. It is not clear how long this analysis lasted, but it did not help with her phobias. She managed them, she later explained to Donald Winnicott, with the help of occasional drugs—and the support of friends.[93]

It is ironic, in view of this experience, that James constantly insisted that it was as a therapeutic agency that psychoanalysis was most significant. His sense of what had happened in his sessions with Freud seem to have stayed with him, and to make him believe that it was transference and a 'mutative interpretation' that allowed a patient to become aware of and redirect some of their unconscious infantile aggression that were the core of psychoanalysis.[94]

While James always regarded Freud as one of the greatest thinkers ever, he was not entirely uncritical. Friends, like Frances Partridge, insisted that Freud (like Lytton Strachey) was one of James's household gods about whom he could bear no criticism.[95] However, James's correspondence with both Ernest Jones and Alix Strachey suggest that this is not the case. He admired Freud greatly, but he was often unsettled by the interpersonal relations and the politics evident both within Freud's own circle and in the British psychoanalytic community—and pondered from time to time whether Freud himself was responsible for the breaks with disciples and the general tension that surrounded him. Like Ernest Jones, he was puzzled at Freud's lack of knowledge of Darwin, and by the Lamarckianism of his approach. He was also concerned at some of the post-war developments in Freud's thought. The turn to metapsychology bothered him and 'the death instinct business . . . always seemed to me a lamentable muddle'.[96]

While devoting themselves to the works of Freud, both James and Alix tended to keep the psychoanalytic world at a remove. Alix became completely absorbed in it for a short time while she was in Berlin, being analysed by Abraham in 1925-6. During this time, she combined her regular analytic sessions with attending the 'sitzungs' or lectures and seminars that were held on six nights of the week at the Berlin Polyclinic. This left one night each week during which she and many of her colleagues attended balls or dances where they often remained until 6 a.m.[97] Alix Strachey's enjoyment of popular music and dancing was frowned upon by Virginia Woolf and others, who saw it as a common and unintellectual activity. Alix missed the kinds of conversation that characterized Bloomsbury parties while she was in Berlin, but adored everything about the dances, including the dressing up, the dancing itself, the different people that one met and could analyse in a dance hall. Although James was interested in what Alix did, he did not really share her love of African art any more than her pleasure in parties, dancing, and popular music. On the contrary, for him, even Lytton's parties were a trial. 'I suppose if one isn't a bugger & doesn't dance all parties are *dull*', he wrote rather disconsolately after one.[98] He loved music, but his tastes were classical. Mozart ranked as his favourite composer—indeed, as one of his household gods.[99] James regularly attended classical concerts and operas, and sometimes writing programme notes for Glyndebourne. Alix too liked classical music, but for her it fitted easily alongside her taste for lighter and more modern fare.

While undergoing analysis, Alix also developed a passion for African art. James had to send her volumes on the history and art of Benin from the London Library and Alix bought as many books on African art as she could. She also had a pronounced preference for those European painters who were influenced by African art, especially Picasso, over others like Cezanne who were more favoured by Bloomsbury.[100] The connection between psychoanalysis and these other interests was always made clear in Alix's letters. 'Has it ever struck you', she asked James,

what the 2 main differences between African and Australian civilization are? (1) The Africans are horribly bloodthirsty & sacrifice thousands of human beings in a religious way, whereas the Australians never do, & their avenging expeditions & wars are extremely dim. 2) The Africans are the best artists there have ever been & everything they produce is simply an amazing work of genius (in sculpture & ornament etc., I mean), whereas the Australians are negligible in that line. The connection may be this:
cruelty   Art (modelling one's turds)
          anal-erotism
          (sadism)
But then where do the Mexicans & Peruvians come in? Perhaps as mediumly cruel and mediocre artists.[101]

While James was very conscious of the new insights offered by psycho-analysis, and often felt that it drew him away from family and old friends, he continued to share many family interests and past-times. His love of music was certainly shared by the family, and so too was his passion for cross-words and other puzzles. In the midst of a series of discussions about the glossary that he was preparing to accompany the translations of Freud in 1925, he explained to Alix that

all my real energies just now go to a ghastly X-word competition. It's an elimin-ation competition. Viz they go on setting more and more difficult puzzles until someone wins the £2500 prize. We've just got the third, & it's the first really hard one there's ever been. Eg 'Reverse a word which might indicate the trend of the affections of a great king during the years 1509, 1540 and 1543.' Answer 'SYT-TIK'—because Henry VIII was in love with three people called Katharine in those years. And so on.[102]

The following day, he intended to send her various things associated with the glossary, but explained that 'none of this can be done today. I'm in a nightmare over the £5000 Cross Word Comp. But by God I've done the Third round puzzle (I shudder to think what the next one'll be like.)

But I must go to the BM now for a final check of my results.'[103] In their psychoanalytic mode, James and Alix were both prone to commenting on the unconscious cause of the behaviour of those around—but it never occurred to James to analyse the obsessiveness with which he undertook these puzzles. They had been part of his life as a Strachey child and they remained so until the end of his days.

A Literary Family

Literature was important to the Stracheys in many different ways. Every member of the family read voraciously, and several of them had marked literary talent. This is evident obviously in their published works, but also in the absolutely wonderful letters that some of them wrote. Pippa's letters from India, for example, were rightly cherished by the family, and read aloud in a similar way to Lytton's diary of his trip to Egypt and South Africa. Throughout the nineteenth and the early twentieth century, their love of reading, their shared sense of literary history, and their communal literary activities, including the acting of plays by favourite authors, helped bind the Stracheys closely together. In later years, however, and especially after the First World War, literature also served to divide them, or at least to mark divisions that were becoming increasingly prominent. This was obviously true of those essays and erotic writings of Lytton that were kept away from the family and read only to close friends. But even his major work, *Eminent Victorians*, like James's translations of Freud, were unpalatable or incomprehensible to their older siblings. This was true also of some of Dorothy Strachey's translations of the writings of André Gide.

The family's literary interests were a Grant rather than a Strachey inheritance. They derived very much from Jane Strachey who, as Virginia Woolf commented, was 'an omnivorous reader', with an extensive literary knowledge. 'She had her hands upon the whole body of English literature, from Shakespeare to Tennyson,' Woolf noted, 'with the large loose grasp that was so characteristic of the cultivated Victorian. She had a special love for the Elizabethan drama, and for English poetry'.[1] Her love of reading aloud was augmented by her capacity to quote by heart much of the work of her favourites, and Woolf recalled that 'when she was past eighty, she stopped one summer evening under a tree in a London square and recited the whole of "Lycidas" without a fault'.[2]

The younger Stracheys may not have had at their disposal quite as rich a repository as Virginia Woolf found in Leslie Stephen's library, but they certainly grew up surrounded by all the standard English authors and with a strong sense that the collected volumes of Scott and Swift and Milton were a necessary part of any home. These books were regarded almost as treasured family friends. In 1919, when she was packing up the house at Belsize Park Gardens to move to the final family home in Gordon Square, Pippa decided that it was essential that some of the family books be replaced. 'Dearest Mama', she wrote to Jane.

Lytton & I have taken a terrific liberty in regard to your Scotts. We went into the question of mending their bindings and found it would cost 7/- a volume—or 16 guineas at the lowest. We inquired from Edwards about a new set—and finally found one of the same edition, 1829 in quite nice binding for 5 guineas from which something will be deducted for the old set. What do you think about the Swift? It is another case like the Scott, & one of the volumes is missing. Shall we again try & get another set of the same edition to replace it? It seems bad not to have a Swift in the house but the poor creature is in a deplorable state.[3]

The absence of books and of any knowledge or interest in the literature that they deemed significant was one of the things that the Strachey sons found hardest to cope with while they were in India. Both Jane and Pippa seemed always to be dealing with requests to send out works like Daudet's *Sapho* (in French) to distant sons and brothers.[4] And Oliver needed to say nothing more to indicate his disgust for those he met in India than that they enjoyed reading Marie Corelli, an author whom Jane Strachey always described as 'a literary scullery maid'.[5]

While many of the Stracheys published books, not all were celebrated writers. On the contrary, Lytton was really the only one to make a significant mark on British literary history. But others were notable in their own particular fields. Richard Strachey wrote not only scientific reports, but also lectures on geography and general articles on Asia in the *Encyclopaedia Britannica*.[6] Jane Strachey's love of poetry resulted in a volume of her own *Nursery Lyrics*.[7] In addition, she edited a couple of works, a collection of poetry and prose for young readers, and the work for which she was best known, her edition of the *Memoirs of a Highland Lady*, the autobiographical writings of her aunt, Elizabeth Grant, published in the

1890s.[8] In the next generation, Lytton began to make his name seriously as an essayist with his *Landmarks of French Literature* in 1913, and of course became a celebrated author with the publication of *Eminent Victorians* in 1918.[9] His work was followed shortly after by the translations of Freud done by James and Alix,[10] and by Dorothy's first translations of Gide.[11] Dorothy's novella, *Olivia*, did not appear until 1949, but it was widely acclaimed than and has been almost continuously in print since.[12] Marjorie wrote too in many different forms, but her numerous novels, biographies, and essays never succeeded in gaining any form of critical acclaim.

I

Although the Strachey's literary interests are always associated with their mother, Richard Strachey deserves some mention here too. This is not because of his own literary talent. On the contrary, we have already seen the extreme formality of his letters, and when it came to his lectures and other writings, even his scientific colleagues regarded his style as excessively dry. One has always a sense that words were to him an inferior method of communication to either numbers or sketches. His diaries and notebooks, for example, are filled with figures and notations. Where others might have described people they had met or significant conversations or events in their daily life, he noted temperature, barometric pressure and altitude, the gradient of a slope he climbed, or the rainfall of a region that he visited, as the things that were significant and memorable. He was also quite talented artistically. His notebooks also contain many sketches and his watercolours were greatly appreciated as gifts by members of the family. But it was this very passion for science that was significant, as it enabled him to introduce his family into the world of scientists and of scientific writing which, as we have seen, was so important to both Lytton and James.

Jane Strachey's knowledge and her love of literature were widely known and much admired. Her readings were sought after, not only by her children and their friends, but by Mlle Souvestre for her school, and by groups of young women willing to pay her to take classes in which she read and discussed literature. Her literary interests and her choice of material to read aloud encompassed not only poetry, drama, fiction, and essays, but also the philosophical and political and historical works of Hume and

Adam Smith and John Stuart Mill. Despite the breadth of her literary range, there was always something strongly didactic in Jane Strachey's approach. This was evident even in the title of her first published work, *Lay Texts for the Young in English and French*, intended as an inspiration and guide for young people.[13] It was equally evident in the collection of her own verse published as *Nursery Lyrics* first in 1893, and then in a revised edition in 1922.[14] The lyrics are readable and sometimes engaging, but they did not, as both she and her family knew, warrant serious attention as poetry. It is particularly interesting here to see the calls to duty and the imperial echoes that are evident in the language that she used even for poems with no ostensibly imperial theme. One entitled 'Forestalled' begins as follows:

> Up the pallid arch of heaven sprang the golden horses beating
> With their crystal hoofs a pathway for the day,
> All the air broke into colour, dewy-cool, and gay with greeting
> From the myriad forces waking into play;[15]

It was not for her own writing that Jane Strachey became known in literary circles, but rather for her work in arranging the publication of *The Memoirs of a Highland Lady* in 1897. These were the memoirs of her great aunt, Elizabeth Grant. Jane had read them in the early 1890s while holidaying at Rothiermurchus and decided to edit them for publication. To her delight John Murray agreed to publish them.[16] The book instantly became popular. 'There is a regular boom of the Highland Lady', she wrote to Pernel, a year after it had first appeared. 'Everyone is talking about it and it can't be got at libraries. I believe Murray is bringing out a second edition. *The Spectator*, *Academy*, *Blackwoods* and *Literary Times* have all had excellent articles.'[17] Murray published several more editions and the work has remained in print ever since.[18]

Jane Strachey may not have written *Memoirs of a Highland Lady*, but it certainly bears her mark. She edited the text extremely carefully to ensure that her aunt presented both herself and the Grant family in the best possible light. A new edition of these *Memoirs* has been published recently which shows clearly the very extensive cuts that she made to the original manuscript.[19] Elizabeth Grant's frank and informal memoirs were written initially, apparently, not for publication, but rather to entertain her family. They were filled with gossip and with amusing and sometimes malicious comments on the dress and behaviour of the people that she met or observed. Jane Strachey carefully removed anything that even suggested questionable morals or conduct by members of the Grant family. Thus, for example, while Elizabeth herself described at length a journey to Holland in which her father ran up substantial debts—and after which he smuggled out some china. Jane Strachey's version makes no reference to either event. In a similar way, she removed all reference to the family's financial difficulties or to the amorous dalliances of Elizabeth Grant's brother William, both of which were discussed at some length in the original. Nor would she permit any mention of the sexual misdemeanours of acquaintances that so amused her great aunt. Elizabeth Grant, for example, described in some detail a European trip during which the queen of Sweden and the Duc de Richelieu 'crossed our path in almost every direction', apparently, or so she thought, because the duc had tired of his affair with the queen and was constantly moving to escape her attentions, while she pursued him relentlessly. But none of this could be allowed. Finally, in an effort to represent her great aunt as a courteous woman with good manners and delicate feelings, Jane Strachey removed many passages in which Elizabeth's acerbic wit and sharp tongue seemed too evident. Thus, for example, Elizabeth described an evening when neighbours had been invited to dinner who turned out to be impossible. The wife was incredibly dull and boring, and the husband 'a great big and ungainly man with head and face and teeth of the "Wolf of Badencih" ', but all these comments were removed by Jane Strachey whose edition simply indicates that the hospitable Grants entertained their neighbours at dinner.

Jane Strachey's deep sense of commitment to family, nation, and empire was evident in every aspect of her life—and in some of the suggestions for reading and for writing that she made to her children. In 1896, for example, while trying to devise an almanac, she read a history of the British Navy, and wrote at once to tell Lytton that it was, 'the most fascinating subject it is possible to imagine. I strongly advise you to study it when you get the chance.'[20] A few years later, when Lytton was beginning to establish his own literary credentials, she appealed to him to refute an argument recently put forward by Edmund Gosse in which he argued that the English were an unpoetic unimaginative nation. Jane Strachey was deeply offended and wanted Lytton to point out the 'dominating power of imagination in the English character, even in our non-literary achievements. Nelson & Clive & Pitt, & all the leaders and trainers of alien races are as much evidence that we are an imaginative race as are Shakespeare & Keats & Jeremy Taylor'.[21]

❦ II ❦

The literary interests and activities that Jane Strachey shared with her children established particular bonds between some of them. Lytton, whom she regarded as the cleverest and most talented of her offspring, was the one drawn most closely to his mother in this regard. From his earliest years, they engaged in literary games. Their letters to each other always began with the quoting of consecutive lines of Ben Johnson's poem, *Buzz quoth the blue-fly* serving both as a private talisman and a way to indicate a sequence.[22] Jane Strachey enjoyed and encouraged Lytton's early experiments: his attempt to render 'Little red Riding Hood a la Gibbon', for example, despite the fact that 'the wolf of style has almost devoured the little lamb of a story!'[23] Their literary contact remained close and very important for several decades. Not only did she introduce Lytton to English and French literature as a child, but she continued to share his interests into his adulthood. Few of Lytton's close Cambridge friends read as widely as he, and it is notable that the person with whom he discussed his early literary essays in most detail was his mother. From about 1904 until 1916, their regular letters were filled with detailed discussion of all the works he was reading and writing about. They wrote to each other at length about Shakespeare, Milton, Fletcher, Dryden, and Beddoes and of course about many French writers. Lytton recognized his debt to his mother and acknowledged it in a number of different ways, most notably the dedication of his first major work, *Landmarks in French Literature* to 'J.M.S.'

Lytton's writing was not only of interest to his mother, but became very much a family affair. His sisters were closely involved as Pippa got him books from the library and typed his manuscripts, while Dorothy offered critical appreciation. Dorothy's knowledge of French literature was at least as extensive as Lytton's, and her understanding of the French language considerably greater. She shared his passion, not only for the Elizabethans, but also for the eighteenth century. She was one of his most appreciative readers and amongst the family probably the one whose views he took most seriously. He was very pleased to receive her letter praising his first book, *Landmarks in French Literature* in 1912. 'It seems to me quite phenomenally good', she wrote. 'The striking thing about it is the ensemble. It sweeps on with such a rush and is informed with such a spirit of unity— something like the Progress of Poesy.' It was exactly what such a book ought to be. Dorothy thought the 'Age of Louis XIV' inspired and was especially pleased with his essays on Corneille, Voltaire, and Saint-Simon, although she thought he was 'rather stiff to poor old Montaigne'.[24] 'I'm glad you pass the book', Lytton replied. 'I feel that I can rely on your judgement.'[25]

Family influence was evident also in Lytton Strachey's decision to write a series of essays on the Victorians. He was strongly imbued with the idea of himself as a 'modern', and was beginning to develop a critical approach to the imperial world of his parents when he began to plan his *Victorian Silhouettes* (the first title suggested for the work). But his adherence to family values is nonetheless clear. At the start, he envisaged about a dozen essays, including not only Nightingale, Manning, Gordon, and Thomas Arnold, but also the philosopher and educator, Henry Sidgwick, the painter George Watts, and Darwin, Mill, Carlyle, and Benjamin Jowett. Strachey was already beginning to feel some horror and disgust at the Victorians. After reading the letters of the novelist, George Meredith, he wrote to Virginia Woolf that the Victorians seemed to him 'a set of mouthing bungling hypocrites'. Nonetheless, while some of the sketches were intended as critical ones, Lytton's adulation both of his father and of Victorian science was very much evident. Thus Darwin was to be a central figure in the book.

It was the First World War that changed both the title and the content of these essays. Lytton Strachey's growing sense of revulsion at the carnage and the chaos of the war, and his outrage at government attacks on workers and on those who opposed the war profoundly changed his attitude to the nineteenth century. In its final form, his *Eminent Victorians*, as Michael Holroyd comments was 'an ironic meditation on those nineteenth-century values that led civilization into such slaughter'.[26]

The family response to *Eminent Victorians* is hard to ascertain. Lytton gave copies of it to several of his sisters, all of whom were delighted— although only Dorothy wrote to say how very much she had enjoyed reading it. It was probably Dick, to whom Jane Strachey sent a copy of the book, who found it hardest to take. 'Thanks for sending Lytton's book', he wrote after reading it. 'I enjoyed it immensely and am glad it is such a success, though I'm afraid it won't please everyone!'[27] It certainly seems not to have pleased Dick's wife, Grace. Jane Strachey's feelings are harder to gauge. Lytton did not pick on any of her favourite Victorians in this first book, but his general approach clearly made her uneasy. This was made very clear in her response to his plan to tackle Queen Victoria as his next subject. Lytton seems to have been aware of this, and found it hard to discuss it with her. He had been working on his biography of Queen Victoria for several months before he finally told his mother about it. She was not pleased. 'My dearest Lytton', she wrote in response to his letter,

I don't quite fancy your taking up Queen Victoria to deal with. She no doubt lays herself open to drastic treatment, which is one reason I think it better left alone. She could not help being stupid; but she tried hard to do her duty; & considering the period she began in, her up-bringing, hereditary associations, and her position, this was a difficult matter & highly to her credit. She has won a place in public affection & a reputation in our history, which it would be highly unpopular & I think not quite fair to bring down.[28]

In the place of Queen Victoria she offered another sacrificial lamb. 'What about Disraeli? He is near enough our own time to be topical & too near to have been thoroughly dealt with yet?'[29]

Lytton Strachey did not accede to his mother's request in any obvious way. He continued to work on this biography, commenting to several of his siblings about the stupidity evinced in the queen's journals. Jane Strachey was probably increasingly apprehensive as anticipation about the book's publication mounted. 'We're looking forward with the greatest excitement to the arrival of Queen Victoria', Lytton's brother James had written from Vienna in March 1921. 'I wonder whether Lytton's read it to you yet, and whether its very shocking. Will the whole family be involved in disgrace.'[30] But when *Queen Victoria* was finally published later in 1921, it was clear that Strachey had not done what his mother most feared. Instead of being caustic, he was genial and even affectionate. His book, wrote Ivor Brown in his introduction to the Collins Classic Edition, 'surprised by its warmth of tone . . . Following the queen herself down the decades, he found himself at last engaged in a sentimental journey.'[31]

Strachey's sentimentality and the appearance of something even approaching fondness for Queen Victoria has been a source of constant comment since the publication of this book. Michael Holroyd, who seems to have been slightly discomfited by Strachey's refusal to pillory Queen Victoria, finds it only possible to explain the 'tenderness' evident in the book, by arguing that 'can partly be attributed to Strachey having associated the Queen with his mother'.[32]

This leap from Queen Victoria to Lady Strachey is an easy one to make. Jane Strachey was 80 when Lytton was working on this book. Like the queen, she had been a deeply loving wife, and a devoted if somewhat erratic mother. In her widowhood, too, Jane Strachey seemed to resemble Queen Victoria. Like the queen, she withdrew from her former life and seemed to be completely out of touch with her time. She knew little of the lives of her children, hated and feared the new world of popular activities—day trippers were to her an abomination—and held with passion to her earlier imperial ideals and her memory of the exciting and exotic years she and her husband had spent in India. She had also recently lost the sight of one eye and was threatened by loss of the other as well.

Lytton Strachey's writings in the course of the 1920s also drew on the ideas and the experience of James and Alix Strachey. James was in Vienna undergoing analysis with Freud when Lytton first began working on Queen Victoria, and James's accounts of his analysis certainly seems to have reduced Lytton's earlier hostility to Freud. 'Does he ever make jokes?', Lytton asked, 'Or only German ones? And in what language does it all go on? I wish to God he could have analysed Queen Victoria. Its quite clear, of course, that she was a martyr to anal eroticism: but what else? what else?'[33] Lytton Strachey's knowledge of psychoanalysis seems to have expanded when James and Alix returned to England in 1921. He did not read much of Freud, but Alix in particular explained to him some of the fundamentals of psychoanalysis.[34] His interest and his growing acceptance that the unconscious was an important factor in writing lives was evident in *Elizabeth and Essex* which he dedicated to James and Alix. This long awaited book received a rather mixed reception. Although some members of the family regarded it as his greatest work, friends were disappointed. Virginia Woolf, while recognizing that her own jealousy of Lytton's fame might have given her a subtle pleasure in his failure, was depressed by it. It reduced her respect for him or her concern about his opinions. It was a 'lively, superficial meretricious book', she thought, feeble and shallow. But if Lytton could 'palm it off on us after years of effort . . . I feel no bite in his disapproval.'[35] Later critics, while not as damning as Woolf, have agreed that this was certainly greatly inferior to his two major biographical works. His inability to encompass or depict the world of Elizabethan England was a particular problem, and offered a sharp contrast to his incisive sense of and his extraordinary capacity to depict the world of the Victorians. One of the other difficulties with this work centres on its attempt to combine fiction and history in a rather more obvious way than his early works—but, as Woolf recognized, far less successfully than she did in *Orlando*.

363

⚜ III ⚜

While Lytton's work was widely read and much praised within the family, James did not seek any such recognition for his. 'I hope, by the way, that our literary efforts in this field won't be too closely followed by an admiring family', he wrote to Lytton in 1921, when the family was in the midst of its excitement about *Queen Victoria*.

The first article must almost be published by now and is devoted entirely to the question of forthing—and the next one is all about torturing small boys. All of these however are anonymous; but our magnum opus, which we've not yet begun, and which is to be a book of the Prof's own clinical papers, will have our names largely printed all over it. I'm afraid Grace will be even more pained by it than by Queen Victoria.[36]

The response of the rest of the family to Alix and James's translations of Freud seem not to have been recorded. Marjorie seems to have been the only one who read their work—and while often asking them to send her books, she never said anything about them.

Their translations of Freud, however, ensured that, next to Lytton, James was the best known of all the younger Stracheys. This was the case particularly after the appearance of the *Standard Edition of Freud*. Indeed, in recent years, James Strachey has become considerably more controversial than Lytton, as the question of how Freud's work should be translated has become the subject of heated debate, not only amongst psychoanalysts but also amongst many literary critics, historians, and scholars engaged in cultural studies. It was largely James who determined the English form of Freud's key psychoanalytic concepts, choosing terms quite unlike their German original. Where Freud wrote *Ich*, *Es* and *Uberich*, which translate literally as 'me', 'it', and 'above-me', James Strachey chose rather to use 'ego', 'id', and 'super-ego'. Sometimes, if an important term had no direct English equivalent, James and Alix Strachey followed the well-established practice in the natural sciences of developing an entirely new Latin-based term. Thus, for example, the Stracheys devised the term 'cathexis' to render in English the German word *besetzen*, although literally this would be translated as 'engagement', or 'investment'. Freud's term *anlehnung*, literally meaning 'leaning on' or 'attachment', was translated by James as 'anaclisis'.

James saw this deliberate attempt to develop a new, specialized, and technical language for psychoanalysis as a way to make people decide for themselves exactly what these terms meant. His correspondence with Ernest Jones make it very clear that he had no wish to close discussion about the meanings of important concepts by establishing new terms. On the contrary, he saw his approach as one that would keep debate and discussion about the meaning of terms open. In regard to 'cathexis', he explained to Jones, that not only was there no English equivalent of *besetzen*, but the concept itself was a very complex one. Moreover, Freud used the term both as a process and as an end-state. Rather than attempting to find a variety of English terms for each of Freud's different usages, Strachey suggested that the English translation provide a new and completely artificial term. In his view, this very artificiality would leave the meaning of the term open as people would have to work hard trying to discover what its meaning really was.[37]

Whatever differences of opinion there are about the merit of James's translation of Freud, no one doubts its importance. Indeed, some would even suggest that James Strachey is almost as important as Freud in the Anglophone world because it is through his interpretation and his words that psychoanalysis has come to be known. Many recent critics argue that his approach involved excessively and even falsely 'scientizing' Freud's work. James does have defenders, however, who point out that the translation was overseen by a committee that included both Ernest Jones and Anna Freud, and that they like James were committed to building on Freud's own attempts to establish psychoanalysis as a science. Some even argue that the work, while not perfect, serves to underline the problems that are integral to the very task of translating psychoanalysis— which itself is constantly involved in translating feelings and fragments that are not immediately accessible into an intelligible language that is useable by practitioners.[38]

However critical recent writers have been of James's translation, it was thought of very highly by contemporaries, especially in the 1940s and 1950s, when the *Standard Edition* was appearing. In these years, James often felt besieged by requests for translations that he was unable to do. He was awarded the prestigious Schlegel-Tieck prize for translation, an indication that his work was recognized outside the confines of the psychoanalytic profession. James Strachey's work on Freud involved considerably more than translation. He provided an introduction to each volume and sometimes to each essay, along with scholarly notes that traced the history and development of ideas and concepts though Freud's work. Ernest

Jones, the leader of the British psychoanalytic community at the time regarded James's introductions as being major contributions to the field. When he received volume II of the *Standard Edition*, he wrote to congratulate James. 'Now I understand why it took so long. Apart from its quite staggering thoroughness I think that your sections (2) and (3) of the Introduction are the most valuable and original contribution you have ever written. They are really of fundamental historical and scientific importance.'[39]

It is interesting here also to note James's decision to devote himself primarily to the tasks of translation and editing, rather than to undertaking his own analysis or writing. James was not an inexperienced writer. He had written quite a lot of music criticism in his time at the *Spectator*, and later contributed programme notes for the operas at Glyndebourne.[40] But he wrote very little of his own within the field of psychoanalysis. He contributed an occasional conference paper, often on rather technical questions about the meaning of transference or on particular issues in Freud's thought.[41] The one time he stepped outside this framework was in an unusual and quite amusing piece called 'Some Unconscious Factors in Reading'.[42] The essay began with him insisting that there were unconscious factors that explained the differences in reading capacities, reading techniques, and in the kind or extent of pleasure that different people took in reading. In order to explore this idea further, he looked at 'the oral influences to be found in a large number of metaphors applied to reading' and at the ways in which the eating especially of sweets, or the drinking of whisky, was often an accompaniment to the pleasures involved in 'devouring' literature. Through this discussion, James sought to establish a connection between reading and the oral stage of infant development. At the same time, he argued, one gained different insights if one turned 'from the unconscious *aim* of reading . . . and consider the *object* concerned'. James took up both Freud's statement that books and paper are female symbols, and Ernest Jones's suggestion that books and other printed matter 'are a curious symbol of faeces'. This in turn led to a discussion of 'the remarkable and widespread habit of reading while defecating'. James illustrated this point with a discussion of one of his patients, who spent considerable time reading in toilets, deriving much of his knowledge from the small squares of newspaper placed in some toilets instead of toilet paper. This patient also enjoyed eating while defecating—and James argued that those who read while defecating 'are performing the same coprophagic act in a still more disguised fashion'. Indeed, James insisted, a 'coprophagic tendency lies at the root of all reading. The author excretes his thoughts and embodies them in a printed book: the reader takes them, and after chewing them over, incorporates them into himself.'[43] James insisted that his approach to reading fitted in also with some of the theories of infancy held by Melanie Klein. The oral sadistic phase which he saw as the basis in reading was consonant with her insistence that there was a connection between the destructive impulses and the beginning of intellectual development. Finally, James argued that his pathway through this subject allowed one to put together the apparently incompatible statements of Freud concerning how books could be interpreted as faeces.

For if the book symbolises the mother, its author must be the father; and the printed words, the author's thoughts, fertilising and precious, yet defiling the virgin page, must be the father's penis or faeces within the mother. And now comes the reader, the son, hungry, voracious, destructive and defiling in his turn, eager to force his way into his mother, to find out what is inside her, to tear his father's traces out of her, to devour them, to make them his own, and to be fertilised by them himself.[44]

While this essay clearly addresses points in psychoanalytic theory which James strongly believed, it is hard not to see something slightly tongue in cheek in this analysis of reading. James was at one and the same time seeking to turn a psychoanalytic gaze on questions about reading and culture which were of such importance within his own family and in Bloomsbury, and managing in the process to stress the connection between enjoyment of high culture and very fundamental bodily processes. He managed also to encompass the ideas not only of Freud, but also of Karl Abraham, Ernest Jones, and Melanie Klein—the analysts who were probably most important to him and to Alix. The tone of the piece does seem to show both James's profound seriousness about psychoanalysis and his continual slight sense of scepticism about it.

While James Strachey always retained his sense of humour around psychoanalysis, Alix seemed less able to do so. Although she and James were equally committed to psychoanalysis, from the start he had taken the lead while she had adopted a subsidiary role. James made this clear in his first letter to Jones in 1920 in which he broached the possibility of doing some Freud translation. He would, he assured Jones, have 'the help of a German collaborator'.[45] Alix's role was that of assistant and collaborator in all the joint Strachey translations. She worked without James on translating some of the essays of Karl Abraham, who had been her own analyst in Berlin, and on translating some of Melanie Klein. But she never established herself as an independent translator and her major role was that of James's assistant.

While assisting and taking second place to James, Alix Strachey certainly aimed to be an independent writer. She spent many years working on a book that finally appeared as *The Unconscious Motives of War* in 1957.[46] Although scarcely known now, it did receive some attention when it was first published. Not all of it was favourable: Frances Partridge quoted one review that began 'this is a very bad book'—and was relieved that Alix was able to laugh at it.[47] But it was taken up by the United Nations Association and the Institute of Public Affairs which sought further articles from Alix on the psychological barriers to disarmament and on questions about psychology and nationhood,[48] and a second edition was published in 1960.[49] As this suggests, this book is not the hidden masterpiece that Alix's friends hoped for, although it is an extraordinarily interesting work— and one which might well bear the title already given to Alix and James's letters: *Bloomsbury/Freud*. The central purpose of the book is to introduce the main ideas in Freudian psychoanalysis to a lay audience in order to demonstrate the important insights which psychoanalysis can offer in dealing with questions of war and national aggression.[50] The summary nature of the account of psychoanalysis, presented as a science completely developed by Freud, makes the book appear rather dogmatic. But there are small sections where Alix's own political and social radicalism—and her sense of humour—appear briefly, most often in her application of psycho-analytic ideas to particular social groups. Alix placed great emphasis on the importance of childhood development, stressing the fact that the kind of adult anyone became was determined by the ways in which a child dealt with the Oedipal phase and with their own bisexuality. She took a certain pleasure in stressing the extent to which children and adults had to deal with homosexual impulses and in pointing to the homosexual desires which underlay many types seen as particularly masculine. The 'clubbable' man is thus shown as one who was not particularly masculine, but whose friendliness to his own sex resulted from the sublimation of his homosexual impulses,[51] while the 'Nazi type in the making' is the boy who develops an excessive masculinity as a way of rejecting his own female desires and feelings.[52] She tended to describe women in terms of literary or biblical characters. Thus she wrote about the Delilah type, who never surmounted her phallic phase, remaining envious of men and unconsciously seeking to deprive them of their penis; or the Dora-type in *David Copperfield*, the epitome of helpless femininity, who, as a result of her original sadism and envy of the penis, adopted an ultra-passive position in childhood, renouncing all activity.[53]

While everyone assumed that *The Unconscious Motives of War* was the work to which Alix had devoted all her time, her papers at the Institute of Psycho-Analysis contain many handwritten and typed draft chapters which were not included in this book and suggest that she was planning another one as well. The two projects were similar: both involved providing an outline of the main concepts of psychoanalysis. But the chapters that were not published also include ones on the history of psychoanalysis and some rather amusing chapters on the ways in which literary figures illustrate psychoanalytic concepts and on the insights that psychoanalysis offers into everyday life.[54]

IV

Dorothy Bussy was the third person amongst the younger Stracheys to make an impact on the literary world. She only became known as a translator in the 1920s and as an author after the Second World War, although she had been engaged in literary activity for a long time before that. Dorothy had turned to translation as a way of earning money shortly after she and Simon moved to France in 1903. Her translations of Auguste Breal's *Velasquez*[55] and of Camille Mauclair's *Antoine Watteau 1864–1721*[56] were published in England in 1904 and 1906, as part of series of popular works on French artists. She also produced a small work on *Eugene Delacroix*,[57] and attempted unsuccessfully to publish critical essays on French literature. The birth of her daughter, Janie, in 1907 seems to have put an end to this kind of work, and to have encouraged her to fall back rather on taking in paying guests at La Souco, and offering classes in French to the children of family and close friends.

It was Dorothy's meeting with André Gide in 1918 that brought her a new career in translating. Almost from the moment that Dorothy began to give Gide lessons in English conversation, she started to translate his work, beginning with *La Porte Etroite* before she had a contract—and indeed before she had even discussed doing these translations with Gide. She told him about it only when it was already finished, and when the question of publication arose. Although the translation was done in 1919, it did not find a publisher until 1924. Initially, Dorothy's work met some hostility from Gide's American publisher, but she was soon accepted as his major English translator and, indeed, her versions of some of Gide's best-known works remain the standard English ones. The *Immoralist* has been translated again, but the Bussy translations of *Strait is the Gate, The Counterfeiters, and The School for Wives*, remain in print.[58]

Dorothy Strachey had very strict views about translation. She had a vast knowledge of both English and French literature, a frequent subject in her correspondence with Gide. But like Pernel, she felt an awe for creative writers and always referred to herself as the 'careful craftsman' labouring on and attempting to render as accurately as possible Gide's words. She felt there was a great distance between herself as a translator and Gide as an artist. To the criticism that her translation of *La Porte Etroite* was too literal, she responded that she could not and would not do anything other than attempt to render Gide's French as closely as possible into English. 'Of course I am not so stupid as not to know that fidelity to the letter may betray the spirit', she wrote to him.

But I know too that the spirit is very often inherent in the letter. I tried to be faithful to both. I tried to give the book's intensity, its acuity, its aridity and I knew these things depended also on the severity, the nudity, the purity of the langua-ge . . . It is odd in French. Why shouldn't it be odd in English?[59]

Her approach to translation, she insisted, was necessarily different from that of Gide.

When *you* translate Conrad or Shakespeare, or Fitzgerald's Omar Khayam, you may allow yourself liberties—that is another affair . . . But when M. Cornaz [the French translator of *Eminent Victorians*] & I set out to translate Lytton & you, our chief merits must be first *comprehension*—and then *respect, fidelity* & *abnegation* (It really sounds like advice to the newly married instead of to translators.)[60]

It was this literalness that brought hostile criticism in the United States. But when Gide sought the opinion of Arnold Bennett on the quality of her work, Bennett insisted that, although not perfect, she was likely to be the best translator he would find. There were occasional errors and inelegant phrases in her work, but on the whole he ranked her next to Scott Moncrieff, the translator of Proust.[61]

Dorothy did not confine her attention to translation, however. In a postscript to a letter to Gide in 1933, some ten years after she had enumerated the rules she followed as a translator, she confided, 'A *deadly* secret. I have written a book.'[62] No one else had been told—and she asked him never to refer to it. Apprehensive and lacking in self-confidence as she was, Dorothy sent Gide a copy of her manuscript seeking his comments. It dealt with a passionate schoolgirl infatuation for her headmistress, and with the destructive force which the lesbian entanglements amongst the teachers in a girls school unleashed on the whole school. In view of the very open discussion of homosexuality and indeed of pederasty in Gide's work, Dorothy had hoped for a sympathetic response. But this was not forthcoming. To be fair to Gide, Dorothy sent her novel to him at a time when he was preoccupied with political developments in Germany. The Nazis had recently come to power, and an augury of what was to come was already evident in the Reichstag fire and the imprisonment of the Bulgarian Dmitrov. Gide had been involved in the campaign for the liberation of Dmitrov, and just before receiving Dorothy's manuscript had travelled with André Malraux to Berlin to try to persuade Goebbels to release him. Nonetheless, his response was less than encouraging. He read the work with keen emotion, he told Dorothy, spending three evenings delving into those 'pathetic reminiscences' and hearing her voice clearly in them.[63]

Later, when the book was about to be published, she reproached both herself and him. She had been stupid, she wrote, to send her work to a male writer who would have no sympathy with women's creative aspirations. Fifteen years after she had shown the manuscript to Gide, she reread it, thought it quite good, and took it to London where she showed it to three women, all of whom liked it a great deal. Rosamund Lehmann, one of the women who read it, passed it on to her publisher brother, John. But Dorothy, who dedicated the book 'to the beloved memory of V. W.', sent her manuscript to Leonard Woolf. To her surprise, for she now felt that her work would be of no interest to men, 'he was more enthusiastic than anybody else'. Hogarth Press had recently merged with Chatto & Windus, and the partners immediately offered her a contract.[64] When *Olivia* was finally published, Dorothy sent it again to Gide. He too was greatly taken with it—and embarrassed by his earlier response. He had read it immediately, he wrote, 'hungrily, delightedly, with anguish, intoxication . . . Freud alone could say what scales covered my eyes the first time I read it.'[65] He proceeded to praise it very highly indeed.

Your Olivia seems to me an extraordinary tale, as accomplished and perfect as possible in its feeling, its decorum and tact, its secret lyricism, its *restraint* in indiscretion, its wisdom acquitted through reflection, in the moderation of its ardour (without the ardour being in any way diminished) in its eloquent reserve, in its quality at the same time of modesty and candour.[66]

Olivia was published anonymously and was an immediate success. Within two years of its publication, there was an American edition as well as translations into French, German, Norwegian, Finnish, and Japanese. In 1951, it was made into a film in France by Jacqueline Audry.[67] It remains in print, in constant demand in courses on gay studies. The fact that it was published anonymously meant that Dorothy's life was affected little by its success. She enjoyed the reviews—and was rather delighted that the Catholic Church thought the book of sufficient significance to ban it.

One of the questions about this book that has been asked ever since centres on the extent to which it was autobiographical. As we have seen, it evokes the atmosphere of Mlle Souvestre's schools extremely well, but it does not actually tell Dorothy's own school story. Nonetheless, many people refused to accept this.[68] Dorothy herself argued the case in greatest detail with the Roger Martin du Gard, whom she had come to know well through André Gide, and who translated the book into French. Martin du Gard admired *Olivia* greatly, but took it as absolutely autobiographical. Indeed, from the moment he read it, he began to address his letters to 'chère Olivia' rather than to Dorothy. He insisted that it was autobiography and that she should claim and acknowledge it as such. Dorothy resisted, insisting that she had sought to do something more than write the memoirs of one individual. She explained to him that there were a number of little books of a special genre that she had always greatly admired. These were: *The Princess of Cleves*, Benjamin Constant's *Adolphe*, Goethe's *Sorrows of Young Werther*, and Gide's *Straight is the Gate*. All of these books had dealt in intimate detail with a youthful and painful past, but managed to become very popular. Dorothy had wanted *Olivia* to be the fifth in this company. There were no such books in English—and she sought to write the first. She wished people to understand that the author of the book was not (if she ever had been) the simple, passionate, and ignorant young girl that she had drawn in Olivia. She had used her memory, but like all artists had carefully searched, filtered, transfigured, condensed, and composed it.[69] Martin du Gard accepted some of this, but argued that there was no need to insist on its fictional status—and made the rather odd suggestion that readers be allowed to decide for themselves.[70] The sticking point for him was ultimately the similarity between Olivia's early descriptions of herself—and his knowledge of her passionate love of Gide. The apparent confession from Olivia that love had always been the chief concern of her life, and that this school episode was followed by others, seemed to him extraordinarily frank and indiscreet, but also somehow to make the picture of Olivia into one of Dorothy. He and Dorothy never saw eye to eye on this matter, but it fortunately had no bearing in his translation of her work.

Although *Olivia* has continued to be a widely read book, in part because it continues to be issued as *Olivia by Olivia*, it has never made Dorothy Bussy into a prominent author. Indeed, when Penguin decided to include it in their modern classics series in 1966, they seem to have known neither the correct title of the book, nor how to spell the name of its author. Leonard Woolf, to whom they wrote seeking assistance, pointed out rather tartly that 'the book's title is Olivia, not Olivier, and her name is Bussy, not Bussey'.[71]

IV

Several of the other Stracheys also wrote, although none of them achieved the degree of recognition accorded to Dorothy, James, or Lytton. Some of this writing no longer seems to exist. Elinor, for example, apparently wrote poetry, which she regarded as having insufficient merit to warrant publication.[72] In some cases, writing was done as an adjunct to other activities, rather than as something valued in itself. However, even here there was a Strachey twist. Thus, as we have seen, Pippa in her capacity as a feminist activist wrote not only reports on women's employment, but also a short play that was produced as a suffrage benefit. This play, called *The Fair Arabian: An Old Story,* was one dealing with a beautiful young woman caught between, but able also to outsmart, her jealous husband, Abdulla, the Lion of the Desert, and a very patronizing and rather stupid European philosopher, named Leo. One day when Abdullah is away, Leo who is travelling in the area arrives and attempts to seduce her. Abdullah returns while Leo is still there—and Zuleika has to get him away before her very jealous husband sees him. She does so by playing on Abdullah's jealousy, and thereby making him forget an important ritual that he and she always observed, the omission of which gave the other a winning point. Abdullah storms out of the tent, furious both that she has incited his jealousy and won a point in their other game—and while he is gone, Zuleika sends Leo away. The play was obviously written for a feminist audience, and it does contain some amusing comments linking orientalist assumptions with sexist ones. Thus Leo, on first meeting Zuleika, offers some observations both on Arab women and more generally on the intellectual differences between men and women. 'My studies have taught me', he explains to her, that though women

lack profundity & the power of grasping abstractions, still you cannot with justice be termed fools. Your wit, though superficial, is keen and brilliant & it is probable that your intelligence differs no more from the highest type of masculine intellect than the intelligence of a native M.A. of Calcutta from a native M.A. of Heidelberg[73]

Leo is ultimately absolutely shocked by Zuleika's wit and cunning—and her capacity, as she says, to get the better of both him and her husband. *The Fair Arabian* was never published, but it was performed in 1911 at the Court Theatre—and Jane Strachey was delighted by the enthusiasm for it shown by both George Bernard Shaw and Thomas Hardy.[74]

While Pippa's minor literary work achieved considerable acclaim, Marjorie tried unsuccessfully for much of her life to establish herself as a writer. Her literary aspirations were always something of a joke to Lytton and James. When he was ill in 1910, James told Lytton that Marjorie had visited his sick room saying, ' "at Last I've written a *really* great poem. Shall I read it to you?" How could I say it seemed to be merely by Lord Henry Somerset? But I did murmur the useful foreign vocable "imitatif" And she's not been here since.'[75] In that same year, Jane Strachey offered a slightly more constructive approach, getting Marjorie to write the theatre columns and dramatic criticism for *The Englishwoman*, a short-lived periodical established by the London Society for Women's Suffrage. Marjorie's articles make very clear the extent to which she was writing under the supervision, if not the thumb, of her mother and older sisters. Thus her longest essay was an obligatory feminist piece, criticizing the theatre as a very conservative institution, reflecting in regard to women a life that is 'fading from our immediate consciousness' and that reflects the world of our mother and grandmothers rather than our own. There are almost no accurate depictions of modern women, she insisted, 'and hundreds of the professions occupied by women are still awaiting their dramatist. So far, indeed, educated women have hardly been touched. There is the singularly disagreeable figure of Vivie in *Mrs Warren's Profes-*

sion . . . but no one of any experience would accept Vivie as a representative Newnham student.'[76] Indeed, one of the things most needed, she insisted, was a good play about a women's college. Anticipating Virginia Woolf's comments in *A Room of One's Own*, she commented also on the absence of women's friendship on the stage—and the ways in which this lack re-enforced a sense of the inferiority of women.

The dismissive attitude of James and Lytton to Marjorie's efforts unques-tionably contain something of their general contempt for all their sisters at this stage in their lives. At the same time, Marjorie's actual writings, and her constant entreaties to Lytton to help her to become a member of the Society of Authors, to find her a publisher—or let her use his name to find one herself, make one more than a little sympathetic to their viewpoint. Moreover, although Marjorie wanted to be a writer, she never decided what exactly she wanted to write. In this, as in every other aspect of her life, Marjorie found it hard to decide on any particular path. She adapted folk tales, and wrote one novel, a couple of biographies, and a study of *Saints and Sinners of the Fourth Century*. Her long biography of Chopin, and the shorter biograph-ical studies published as *Mazzini, Garibaldi and Cavour*, seem to have been written as introductions for students interested in these men, rather than as serious works offering new research or anything new in approach. In a similar way, her novel, *The Counterfeits*, published in 1927, is very deriva-tive both in its style and in its humour.[77] The novel is very conventional and, despite its rather heavy attempt at risqué humour, its style bears witness more to Marjorie's passion for Charlotte Yonge than to her reading of Freud or Virginia Woolf. Intended as a spoof on Bloomsbury, it lacks either the irony or the humour that such a piece would need and ends up being both lame and pedestrian. The first scene occurs in a house in Fitzroy Square and the characters have names that seem intended both to suggest and to send up the Bloomsbury group, such as Volumnia Fox, and Clyte-mnestra and Agamenon Arnold Brown! It tells the story of a woman who goes out to Bessarabia as a VAD during war and once there, falls in love with a Russian—who is himself in love with his sister-in-law and manages to kill both his brother and himself. Both amongst the London group and their Russian counterparts, there is a constant succession of mixed and changing partnerships as husbands and wives go off with other partners and everyone is both hysterical and theatrical. The book received few reviews and was rarely commented upon at all either by the family or their friends.

Marjorie's inability to establish herself as a writer contrasts most conspicuously with the ease of Ray Strachey, who was remarkably successful, despite the fact that her writing came second to her feminist activism. Ray had begun writing while very young, publishing her first novel—one based very closely on an episode in her life—at the age of 20.[78] She wrote a couple of other novels after this, which resemble Marjorie's in the obvious influence of Charlotte Yonge, a favourite author of them both, and in their resolute refusal to engage with any aspects of modernism in style, language, or plot. James found Ray's novels quite as hard to deal with as Marjorie's writings—and dreaded having either of them ask him about them.

In Ray's case, however, it was not the novels that were significant, but rather her biographical and historical works. Unlike Marjorie, Ray chose to write about women she knew well and understood. Her portraits of Frances Willard, and of her grandmother, Hannah Whitall Smith, are enlivened by her deep knowledge of and affection for these women. Her interpretation of Willard, she made clear, was greatly indebted to Hannah Whitall Smith, 'whose stories of Miss Willard and faith in her, have enabled me to read her life rightly'.[79] This book was followed by her study of Hannah Whitall Smith herself, which stressed the generosity and warmth of her grandmother and the affection and support she offered her grand-daughters.[80]

While Marjorie had to look for publishers, Ray Strachey's best known work, *The Cause*, was one that she undertook entirely because a publisher requested it. Messrs Bell and Co. wrote yesterday, she told her mother, in February 1924, 'asking me to undertake for them a History of the Women's movement. 100,000 words. I am to go and talk over terms. If they'll give me £150 I'll do it, boring though it will be. But I could write Mrs Fawcett's life *pari passu* so to speak, though it would be tedious job I could very easily do it, having all the facilities at hand'.[81]

Some ten days later, Ray wrote to her mother to say that the terms were favourable and that she had now begun to be interested in the project. Indeed, she became more and more engrossed in it, finding it both easy and entertaining, for 'no arguments or disquisitions are needed, just the journey of a people battling against ridiculous taboos'.[82] This very readable book remains the most energetic and heroic account of the successes and triumphs of the nineteenth-century women's movement, and essential reading for any historian of feminism. It is a testimony to Ray's energy and efficiency, and her capacity to throw herself fully into any project at hand.

14

Old Age and Death

Although the history of old age is attracting an increasing amount of scholarly attention, the question of how precisely to define this stage of life remains a difficult one.[1] This is particularly so for a family like the Stracheys. Unlike other life stages, old age lacks clear or unequivocal markers. In some periods and for some groups, it is seen as commencing at a formal age of retirement or when one becomes entitled to a pension or specific welfare benefit—around 60 or 65 today. This is of little help in regard to a family to whom state provision was of little significance, and whose members often remained active long beyond the normal age of retirement. Richard Strachey after all, was 71 when he became chairman of the East India Railway and he did not retire until he was almost 90. Things changed for the next generation, but not in a uniform manner. Thus while Oliver was formally required to resign from his intelligence work at Bletchley Park at the age of 65 in 1939, in fact he continued to work there until he had a heart attack in 1943.[2] By contrast, Pernel departed from Newnham College in 1941, when she was 65. For those working informally, like Marjorie, however, there was no retirement age and she continued to take on individual pupils until she was well into her 70s. Pippa, too, who was essentially engaged in voluntary work, only relinquished her role as organizing secretary of the London Society for Women's Service in 1951—at the age of 80.

For the most part, the Stracheys were remarkable both for their longevity and for the duration of their active lives. Many did not see or think of themselves as 'old' at ages which others would have regarded as requiring that designation. Each individual had in some measure to decide when they were old enough either to limit their work and other commitments or to require some form of additional support and assistance. The rest of the family also had to make decisions about this in order to establish what form of additional support might be necessary. In some cases, old age seemed to come suddenly. Thus Richard Strachey apparently began to seem old and in need of special care and attention towards the end of the 1890s. James Strachey later insisted that it was the severe attack of dysentery he experienced in 1897 which marked the decline for him from an active and relatively youthful life to an aged and semi-invalid one.[3] In a similar way, Jane Strachey's loss of one eye in 1915 precipitated her withdrawal from feminist and other activities and the start of old age.[4]

Both Jane and Richard Strachey remained at home until they died, lovingly cared for in their final years by Pippa with some support from their other children. Few of the younger Stracheys experienced that level of domestic care and attention. It was obviously impossible for the childless ones and Elinor, the only one who had a large family, lost both her daughters while she was still alive. Although she had two remaining sons, no one suggested that they should care for her and she was seen by the others as being very much alone towards the end. The other siblings depended on a spouse or on each other. Pippa and Marjorie, the last to die, clung together, with some support from rather impatient nieces, until they went into nursing homes. In their later years in the 1950s and 1960s, James, the youngest of them all, attempted to keep an eye on his older sisters.

As one might expect, there was a close parallel between the general pattern of life of the younger Stracheys and their experiences of old age. Thus Dick Strachey seems to have had a singularly miserable time, while Pippa after the final break up of Gordon Square and her own move to a nursing home seems to have retained her grace and high spirits to the end.

❦ I ❦

Of all the Stracheys, and despite his long history of ill health, Richard was the most remarkable in terms of the level of activity and vigour that he maintained until he was almost 90. He fathered his last child at the age of 71, at which point he also took up a major new professional position. Throughout his 70s and 80s, he continued to be active in the scientific world through

378

his extensive involvement in the Royal Society and especially its meteorological office, and to be closely involved with Indian administration, first
through his place on the India Council and then through his chairmanship
of the East India Railway. Although he remained active, it is clear that he was
increasingly coming to be seen as old and as needing care by his family for
some time prior to his final retirement. Despite James's insistence that it was
only in 1897 that he became an old man, family letters suggest that throughout this decade there was a general sense of his becoming frail and in need of
additional care. His health was a matter of increasing concern. To the long-
standing problem of constipation were added periodic attacks of gout and a
variety of other gastric problems.[5]

The family's sense of Richard Strachey's physical frailty and vulnerability was exacerbated by his inability to cope with London traffic. He was, as
Michael Holroyd says, a 'dangerous pedestrian' and seems to have collided
with or been run over by cabs and carriages on several occasions.[6] He was
never seriously harmed. However, these accidents caused great anxiety to
his family—and increased the sense his younger children had of his
belonging entirely to an earlier time and place.

While he remained in control of his business affairs during the 1890s,
Richard Strachey handed more and more authority over domestic and
familial affairs to others. It was in this period that Jane Strachey's literary
and musical interests came to dominate family life and her friends to fill the
house, while Pippa and Dorothy took over the responsibility for sorting out
major domestic problems. It was they, for example, who dealt with the
great drain crisis in 1896, when it was discovered that the drains in the
house were in an appalling state and needed to be replaced.

Although no one ever actually said anything about this, one does have a
sense that Richard became increasingly irascible in this decade, and prone
also to making sudden decisions that caused Jane and the family some
difficulties. Jane Strachey never dreamt of criticizing her husband, but
occasionally in her letters to the children, one has some sense of mild
exasperation. In 1893, for example, she wrote to Lytton of the change in
family plans for the summer.

It was first of all settled that we should not go into the country this year but take
little excursions in small parties; but a few days ago your papa suddenly announced that he could not bear it and that we must find a house instantly! Whereat
a great bustling and hustling. We have now heard of a most magnificent place in
the Mendip Hills that sounds too good to be true.[7]

proceedings in silent anxiety, never wanting to order her husband about in any semi-public forum.[12]

Richard Strachey died at home on 12 February 1908. Jane was very distressed that she had hardly seen him at the end: she had herself been ill when he suffered his final illness, and by the time that she was better, and everyone realized that he was nearing the end, he was barely conscious.[13] Thus after almost half a century of a very happy marriage, she was not properly able to say goodbye. She took some consolation, however, in the widespread recognition of his death. A memorial service held for him at Christ Church, Lancaster Gate, was extremely well attended and there were at least two dozen obituaries in daily papers and in the specialized journals of the many scientific bodies with which he had been involved. All were carefully recorded in a notebook. As she had done after the death of her father, Jane also took some solace from being involved in writing some of the tributes to him.

While Richard Strachey was declining gently in these final years, Jane Strachey who was still in her 50s was extremely active and energetic. She had only begun to emerge as a public figure in the late 1880s and the 1890s and continued to relish this new life until the war. Jane's love of social life was very evident in the 1890s, and despite Richard's frailty her letters record a ceaseless round of dinners, garden parties, and 'at homes'. She was engaged in many different activities, increasing her range as her children became more and more independent. Her major literary activities were undertaken in the course of the 1890s and in that decade she also began to learn Spanish, to take a course in book-binding, and to devise an almanac. She continued to be a celebrated reader, extending the reading aloud that had been so important to her family into the public world. She read both English and French drama, not only at her daughter's schools, but also to groups of women who formed classes to hear her, and to have her assist them in their reading. She also became a public speaker on both feminist and literary subjects. 'I read my lecture on Sydney and the Elizabethans at Toynbee Hall', she wrote to Lytton in 1908, and it was 'much applauded. It was an audience of artisans, but they were very well up on Elizabethan literature.'[14] In these years she emerged also as a leading figure in the women's movement, becoming president of the Women's Local Government Society, engaging actively in the suffrage movement, and taking a leading role in the Lyceum Club. She greatly enjoyed this expanding public role, which continued until the First World War.

For all her engagement in contemporary life, there was a distinct change in Jane Strachey's relationship with the rest of her family in 1897 when she became 'Lady Strachey'. This was associated with age, although not directly caused by it. Richard Strachey's relationship with the family seems not to have changed when he was awarded CGSI and became 'Sir Richard', perhaps because there was already some formality and some distance in his relationship with his children. When it came to Jane, however, the change is very noticeable. Although she complained about becoming 'just another Lady Strachey', she took to the title with ease and played the role of *grande dame* with great gusto.[15] This is very evident in all of her feminist activity. She immediately assumed a position of authority while never dreaming that she would be expected to do any routine work. The change was reflected also in the family by the use of her title, rather than 'mama', to refer to her. The title came at a time when there was a marked and growing conservatism in Jane Strachey's social attitudes and beliefs, and the constant reference to her in family letters as 'Her ladyship' or 'Lady S' serves to underline this development. It was Oliver, Lytton, and James who used the title most often, and it illustrated not only their growing sense of distance from her, but a sense also of the need to negotiate her particular crotchets. From the late 1890s, she appeared to some of the family to be more and more out of touch with their world. This view of her was constantly re-enforced by her hostility to new social customs and anxieties, thus for example she warned Ray not to let Julia, Oliver's daughter, play barefoot in the park, for fear of the debris left around by day trippers.[16] Her passion for jokes and for repeating stories about Indian life became increasingly irritating, especially to Lytton and James, to whom her inability to understand anything about their personal or sexual lives— or to countenance anything unconventional—was very distressing.

The death of Richard Strachey was a profound loss to Jane, but it was in some measure assuaged by her relationships with her two favourite siblings, Trevor Grant and Elinor Colevile, who were also widowed by this time. Jane went, accompanied by Trevor, to Mentone to be with her sister, Elinor, a month after Richard's death and she subsequently spent a considerable amount of time either there or in Ledbury at Elinor's country home. Although she was still very active, her health, which had been fairly robust for much of her life, became more problematic. After Richard's death, Jane seems to have been subject to increasingly severe colds and attacks of lumbago, and to feel the need for rest, for country air, and for

more limited movement. Both her sight and her hearing began to deteriorate, and she had considerable trouble with her teeth as well. There was
little that could be done to help. 'I began my deaf cure yesterday,' she wrote
to James in 1909, '& it made me so ill that if there are the same results today
I shall have to drop it.'[17] Her deafness did not prevent her from singing,
however, and she wrote songs for and organized a choir. 'We had a choir
rehearsal on Friday', she told James, 'and my songs went very well and
caused great amusement. I have now got nearly 60 singers together! I *shall*
be thankful on Pippa's account when it is over.'[18]

It was the First World War that really signalled the start of Jane
Strachey's old age. She was in her early 70s at this point, and her health
seems to have deteriorated quite rapidly, exacerbated one would assume by
the anxieties and problems of the war. At its start, Marjorie was in Germany
and there was much concern about her and how to ensure that she had the
money that she needed and indeed could be brought home.[19] The Bussys
also had a difficult time at the start of the war, as Simon was required to
spend time in a military camp, even though he was recognized as unfit for
military service.[20] Money was a major problem. After the drastic reduction
in family income that accompanied Richard's retirement in 1907, there was
the additional question of how badly Jane's investments would be affected
by the war. She was extremely anxious both about herself and about
her many still dependent adult children—which included James as well
after 1915—all of whom seemed to be 'screaming for money'.[21] She went to
the investment registry to make inquiries in October of 1914. 'Their
opinion was better than Expected', she wrote to Lytton.

They consider the Capital I have invested in Hungarian & Mexican bonds to be
quite safe certain to be repaid in any eventuality—Of course no dividend will be
paid except in the case of one of the Mexicans, which are paid through America,
Altogether I calculate that my income will be reduced by about £200 pa; but as
long as the capital is secure, that is a small matter.[22]

Pippa suggested that they economise by reducing the number of servants
they employed—especially as one left early in the war and hence the
reduction could be made by not replacing her, rather than sending anyone
away—and this in due course was done.[23]

The great change really came in 1915 when Jane lost one eye. Jane was
staying with Dorothy when it happened and remained there for some time.
In her period of recuperation, she was allowed to read for ten minutes a

time for up to an hour a day—very little for as passionate and inveterate a reader as she had been.[24] Jane began to withdraw from her public role at this time. She did not cease to be interested in public affairs, but everything she did now required care. On Armistice Day 1918, for example, accompanied by her maid Ellen, she went on a bus to share the festivities at Piccadilly. 'I durst not go in the very crowded streets', she told her sister, 'but I was able to see much that was thrilling.'[25]

In the final years of her life, Jane Strachey was surrounded by the Bloomsbury world of her younger children. In 1920, she moved with Pippa to 51 Gordon Square and thus became part of the Bloomsbury enclave. Other members of the Strachey family were very near, with Alix and James Strachey at no. 41, and Oliver and his daughter Julia at no. 42. Vanessa Bell, Duncan Grant, Maynard Keynes, and several of Lytton's other friends lived close by.[26] This move entailed a further reduction in the Strachey's scale of life. Much of the family furniture was disposed of and even the library was reduced in size.

In Lytton's view, Gordon Square was 'a good deal more comfortable & convenient than Belsize'.[27] The move to Bloomsbury allowed Jane Strachey to participate in some of the social activities of her children and she attended a number of Bloomsbury gatherings. 'She forges about a room like a clumsy three decker, benignant, and yet easily morose', wrote Virginia Woolf after a party in 1920 during which she had sat in a corner with Jane Strachey talking of their Anglo-Indian relatives and the Indian Mutiny. Woolf felt that she hoarded 'some grievance against her family, like most old people, for not reading aloud to her', but was still very easy with strangers.[28]

In her final years, between 1920 and her death in 1928, Jane Strachey's life was increasingly miserable. Her remaining eye began to deteriorate, making her dependent on others not only for her basic care, but also to read to her and to help with her beloved crossword puzzles. She attempted to learn Braille, but never became proficient in it. Her health became more and more frail. In 1921, Virginia Woolf noted in her dairy that Lytton was being called on to stay with his mother more often, as she was having fainting fits. She was often hard to deal with because of her incessant need to be entertained. The whole family was somewhat gloomy in these years, reflecting the growing social tensions and economic concerns of the 1920s and the many losses they experienced amongst their friends during and after the war. This is not to say there were no light moments: at the small family gathering held to celebrate her 85th birthday, Jane managed to sing one of her favourite songs, ' "My mother bids me bind my hair" to great applause'.[29] But this was a high point. The year of Jane Strachey's death, 1928, was also the one in which Pernel's old friend, Jane Harrison, died, which was a blow to all. Dorothy Bussy, who continued to visit every summer, found London hard to manage in that year. 'As usual when I am staying in London I feel as if I were living in a charnel house surrounded by aging friends, illness, madness, operations and death', she wrote to André Gide. 'And this year I see very little youth to counterbalance the impressions'.[30] She felt more than a little guilty as she was about to return to *La Souco* in September. 'I leave my mother in good health and spirits—considering', she wrote to Gide. 'Pippa is not very well, but there is nothing serious the matter. But I always have a violent feeling of remorse when I leave them all at the beginning of winter to wrestle with cold, anxiety, poor health and general gloom—while I go off to sunshine and happiness.'[31]

After Jane Strachey's death, Ray Strachey reflected on her final years. She had been a remarkable person, she thought, although miserable since she went blind.

It was strange how very little interest she took in her children. I don't think this was the result of age at all, though I daresay that increased it. What she enjoyed was using her brains—& then last year and more, when she couldn't do much else, she spent all the time she could doing crossword puzzle games. It was wearing and rather difficult for those who had to do them, partly because she was so deaf, & partly because she was so unexpected—and after about half an hour of it one got very tired.[32]

The younger Stracheys were nonetheless profoundly affected by their mother's death. 'It is impossible to escape the grief, though one has discounted it so long', Lytton wrote to Topsy Lucas.[33] Dorothy Bussy was as ever the most articulate about the continuing sense of loss. She was saddened also by the impossibility of discussing it with the others. 'I miss Mamma out of the house, out of my life dreadfully', she wrote to Gide during the course of her first summer in London after Jane Strachey's death.

It seems impossible to speak about it to anybody. Just with Pippa for a second. Pippa feels it more. She has not the consolations I have and the distractions. It is true she has her work in which she is interested and which is more 'serious' than anything I do. She has had to take a long rest from it, but I think her health is better and hope she will go back to it before the autumn.[34]

Jane Strachey's death brought another epoch of the Strachey family to an end, but Pippa who had been so pivotal in the family in earlier years, insisted on retaining the family home in Gordon Square and holding it together. Dorothy never failed to feel the maternal presence when she was there.

❦ II ❦

Not all the younger Stracheys enjoyed the family tradition of longevity. Ralph and Lytton both died in their 50s, the former in June 1923, a few years before Jane Strachey's death and the latter three years after. Nothing illustrates more clearly the different place of these two brothers within the family than the impact of their death. Ralph's death was a source of considerable distress to Pippa, and was certainly a loss to Oliver and Ray, but it seems to have had almost no impact on anyone else. Ralph, although nice, was 'extraordinarily unlike a Strachey in most ways', Duncan Grant had noted on one of Ralph's visits home—and in part as a consequence his connections with the others were quite distant.[35] He had been closely involved with Ray in the years prior to his death, having invested £1,000 in her building company, and applying his engineering skills to the design of the mud brick houses that she wished to make.[36] He lost all his money when the project was given up, but it is at least possible that it was worth it in some ways, as it gave him an occupation after he returned to England and an office in which to spend his days. Margaret Strachey's inability to keep house seems to have meant that both she and Ralph lived in boarding houses during those years and hence his domestic comfort was limited. The cancer from which Ralph died was hard to diagnose. 'Ray says, and I agree with her, that it has been going on for years and that in reality he is dying of Margaret', Marjorie Strachey wrote to Lytton, 'The whole thing is a nightmare.'[37]

Dorothy Strachey echoed this view. The summer of 1923, she told Gide, was one of miserable darkness. 'On just one single day the sun has shone— and that was the day of my brother's funeral—so even that was wasted—as far as I was concerned. Not that the funeral affected me much. I think they are indecent and disgusting affairs. But I have been affected—for it has been a pathetic—a tragic business.' This was because Ralph's life was sad and not, she hastened to assure Gide, because 'it is a loss I feel in my own life. It is not that.'[38] Marjorie too attended the funeral, suggesting to Lytton that he invite Pippa to Tidmarsh after it to recover.[39] Ralph's death led to a very considerable and prolonged battle with his widow, Margaret, concerning his estate, and especially the provision for his children and the mementoes he had left for Oliver and Pippa, which Margaret refused to give them.[40] After his death, however, he faded out of the family picture very quickly indeed.

By contrast, Lytton's death, also from cancer in 1931, was a catastrophic and traumatic event for his family as well as for his Bloomsbury friends. Lytton's literary status and the family's pride in his achievements were important here. But he had also maintained closer contact with many of his siblings, including not only James and Pippa, but also Dorothy, Oliver, Pernel, and Marjorie, than had Ralph. Michael Holroyd has written in some detail of the last weeks of Lytton Strachey's life, with the alternating period of hope and despair as his health waxed and waned.[41] The difficulties of gaining a medical diagnosis of his condition added to everyone's uncertainty. Lytton's death was a terrible thing for his domestic companions, Carrington and Ralph Partridge, but also for his siblings. Most of the younger Stracheys spent time with him or at least were close by in his final weeks. Pippa and James stayed in his house, Ham Spray, sharing the nursing and care with Carrington and Ralph Partridge. Oliver, Pernel, and Marjorie stayed at the local hotel. Ray Strachey too became deeply involved 'in the awful waiting down at Hamspray with all those miserable unhappy friends of his'. As ever, she had gone there to keep an eye on Pippa and to provide her with whatever support she could. But Ray's immense competence meant that Carrington immediately handed over all domestic responsibility, while after Lytton's death, James got her to arrange the funeral.[42] Dorothy's letter to Gide describing the impact of Lytton's death contrasts markedly with her letter about Ralph.

It is dreadful and such an unexpected gap in our lives. He was the centre and pivot of so much in our private family life as well as in his larger circle. He was our most beloved brother long before he was a famous man. And all the salt and zest of life seemed to come from him. I can't take a step in my mind (not to speak of my affections) without meeting his figure . . . I shall never be able to read Shakespeare again or Racine without a pang . . . He was the first child I ever loved. Affectionate, witty, happy responsive creature. He never changed.

Poor Pippa. To have struggled so hard and to have failed at last. Everybody else will recover, but she won't. I hope she will come and rest with us here, but I don't think she will.[43]

In the event, the Bussys helped several of the Stracheys to recover. Pippa went to stay for some time and was followed by Marjorie and then by James and Alix. Pippa was a physical wreck, Dorothy told Gide, 'but outwardly composed'. She was quite different from Marjorie who, Dorothy noted, 'as usual can't open her mouth without making us all laugh—something of a clown. Stimulating, however, though sometimes to the point of exhausting her public.'[44] By contrast, Dorothy regarded James as 'rather a tragic character—left more lonely than ever by Lytton's death'.[45]

While Ralph and Lytton both died much too young, their oldest brother, Dick Strachey seems to have hung on to his life for much longer than he wanted. The lack of close contact between Dick and his siblings makes it hard to ascertain the details of his final years. He resigned from the Ministry of Pensions in 1919 at the age of 59, in a somewhat disconsolate state because he felt that he was yet again being required to work excessively hard for little reward or recognition.

The following year, Dick and Grace travelled to Europe, and enjoyed their time in France and Spain immensely.[46] After that, there is an almost total silence about them in the family correspondence. This does not necessarily mean that there was no contact. It is more than likely that Dick remained in touch with Elinor, the sister to whom he was closest and possibly also with Ralph. However, after 1920. there are few letters from him amongst Pippa Strachey's papers. Shortly before Jane Strachey's death, Pippa and Lytton had agreed to change her will so that Dick, who had been omitted from her latest will, should receive the same amount as the other sons.[47] There is no indication, however, of whether or not Dick saw his mother before her death, of his response to that death, or of any role he might have taken in her funeral.[48] He had not cut all ties with the family. Thus James wrote to him in 1932, after the death of Lytton. But the letter is extremely brief, intended simply to inform him that Pippa had gone off to Roquebrunne to stay with the Bussys and 'seemed fairly all right', and that James and Alix too were managing, after a week at Bournemouth.[49] When Dick died in 1935, it was Pippa who notified the others. The only response to this amongst the family's papers is a letter from Dorothy confirming one's sense that Dick's final years were not happy ones. 'Dearest Pippa,' she wrote, 'Your telegram about Dick has just come. Poor dear Dick. But his last few years must have been miserable. I feel a horrid kind of remorse about him. He was hardly treated by fate ... One was dreadfully sorry for him.'[50]

❧ III ❧

The remaining Stracheys stayed in close contact with each other during their final years, and for much of the time their life continued to revolve around the family home in Gordon Square. Pernel moved in with Pippa when she retired from Newnham in 1941 and remained there until her death ten years later. Oliver too made a home in Gordon Square in 1944, and the Bussys spent as much time there as they could. Marjorie lived quite close by in her own small apartment in Taviton Street. She visited Gordon Square regularly and moved in with Pippa some time after Pernel's death. For several years, James and Alix lived just a few doors away and saw the others frequently.

Elinor Rendel, who from the time of her marriage had a series of grand homes of her own, was never part of the Bloomsbury world of the Stracheys. But she was in constant contact with Dorothy, Pippa, and even more with Marjorie. Elinor had mothered Marjorie when she was young and, especially after the death of Elinor's husband, James Rendel in 1937, Marjorie took her place beside Elinor's daughter Ellie, helping to look after her oldest sister until Elinor died in 1944.

This closeness amongst the Stracheys was particularly evident during the Second World War, a time of considerable difficulty and stress for all of them. There was no thought of anyone being engaged in active service, of course. Even James, the youngest, was 50 when the war began. Oliver, however continued to be actively engaged in code-breaking and was stationed at Bletchley Park until 1943 when he had a heart attack and finally had to retire.[51] All the Stracheys worried about where and how to live, especially during the Blitz when their London homes became dangerous and evacuation seemed necessary. The Bussys had the added difficulty of the German occupation of France.

While the war years were difficult for them, several of the Stracheys remained extremely active. Dorothy Bussy had commented to Gide in 1937 that Pippa and Pernel were 'beginning to look a little battered by the waves of life', but Pippa continued to engage in a ceaseless round of activity.[52] She was very active in several feminist campaigns, especially those directed to equal pay. She also emptied the offices of the London Society for Women's Service in order to save money, helped move the Women's Employment Federation into Bedford College, and moved the books from the Fawcett

Finding the right summer house, one that was both sufficiently capacious and accessible, was a major trial for the rest of Richard's life. 'The terrible question of the summerhouse looms,'[8] Jane wrote to Lytton in 1903—and it was a significant item in much of her correspondence around these years.

Richard Strachey's irascibility was also evident when he travelled to Europe. Pippa accompanied him to France in 1898, and although her report home is characteristically light and humorous, one senses that it was not entirely an easy trip. 'Papa had a quarrel on the Channel boat with an old lady on the verge of apoplexy', she wrote to her mother,

she accused him of taking away her air to which he replied 'nonsense' & refused to move. It was most brutal. His next piece of wickedness was at one of the railway stations in France when a very grand general with his staff of officers was seen on the platform, & it was with the greatest difficulty that I prevented the villain from putting his head out the window and shouting 'viva Zola!'[9]

Towards the end of the 1890s, Richard's decline into semi-invalidism became more pronounced. He continued to be employed, but often delegated the day-to-day work to others. This was so both at the East India Railway and in the Meteorological Office of the Royal Society. 'I am still a semi-invalid', he wrote to Pippa in 1901,

and Betty Hill is still in attendance. I am able to get to Nichols Lane (where the EIR Office was located) on Board Days & also to the Meteoric Office once a fortnight. Still, however, I get Mr Colvin to the greater part of the routine work of the EIR and the benevolent Mr Shaw saves me all trouble at the 'Weather bureau'. I have been turned out of my room by Pernel's essays—but this seems a reasonable excuse for not doing EIR work.

Richard felt that Pippa, who was then in India, would be able to judge 'how far this system of governing the EIR is practically successful'.[10]

Richard Strachey's deafness made him increasingly withdrawn within the family circle at this time, and he took little part in domestic or family affairs. He was remembered by friends of the younger Stracheys as 'a silent man, who listened with interest and amusement to the verbal hurricane around him', and much of his domestic pleasure seemed to centre on the novels that were presented to him each evening on a silver tray.[11] He needed to be helped into bed—and was taken up at about 10 each evening by Ellen, the family maid, although even this could become something of a trial: if he were enjoying his book, he would ignore Ellen entirely, until one of his daughters insisted that it was bedtime. Jane Strachey watched the

Library to Oxford.[53] Pippa spent some of her time with Pernel in Cambridge and some in London, writing wonderful letters about the many adventures she had each day. Oliver had suggested in 1939 that Pippa should have a dug-out built in her home. She had resisted this idea, however, preferring to make her home in the bomb shelter already in Gordon Square.[54] 'I feel very much reassured about my two shelters into which I betake myself at the sound of the Siren as they call it,' she wrote to Pernel from Gordon Square in August 1940.

I have sampled Gordon Square by night and morning and it is quite a pleasant resort with rather a high class clientele supplemented by a few taxi drivers & other passers by—it has never been anything but sparsely inhabited and if you select your seat plenty of light for reading. The library for the blind where I go from the office is supposed to be one of the strongest places to be found as it was originally planned for a garage designed to bear the weight of countless motor cars with steel girders . . . Just outside is the soldiers post manned by imposing grenadier guards who take the greatest interest in the proceedings and guide the wanderers to the door in the most charming manner & I think there is a great advantage in public shelters from the certainty of their being looked after if anything does go wrong.[55]

'With a cushion & rug', she told James, 'it's not impossible to get some sleep. But a whole night in bed has now become a luxury.'[56] She saw a great deal of the damage done in London as she travelled on her daily round, sometimes commenting that she was the only spectator and that others already took the devastation for granted. The Strachey houses sustained some damage, but never became uninhabitable.

Pernel remained at Cambridge until 1941 and then moved to Gordon Square with Pippa. There is a singular absence of letters about how she occupied herself or what she did during the remaining period of the war. Pippa's wartime letters are concentrated in the period 1939–41 and there is no information as to how exactly these sisters lived through the final years of the war.

In Marjorie's case, there is a little more information. She was in her late 50s when the war broke out and clearly felt no reason to alter her pattern of life. Marjorie did not have a formal full-time position at that point, but devoted herself rather to teaching small groups of children, sometimes in private homes. During the Blitz, there had been some plan for her to go to the United States with a small family whose parents wanted them evacuated from England. But that scheme came to nothing. She continued to teach the children of friends and acquaintances, however. 'She has a class of very small children to teach at Hindhead,' Pippa told James in 1941, 'which sounds most exhausting and altogether trying.'[57] In the years after that, Marjorie devoted herself to the care of her oldest sister, but seems to have continued teaching at the same time.

While Pippa determined not to leave London, during the Blitz, Alix and James chose to go. Early in 1940, they decided to make their home with Alix's mother at Lord's Wood in Marlow. Although they were safe there, they had little domestic comfort or ease. The relationship between Alix and her mother had always been a difficult one and deteriorated during the war. Pippa who visited them there early in 1941 wrote to Pernel that Alix had been 'so affectionate and charming that I can't get over it. Unluckily the same can hardly be said of the relationship between her and her ma but Mrs S. F. is always very friendly to me and didn't seem to object to my appearance.'[58] The few letters that Alix wrote in these years suggest that her mother was suffering from dementia. She was terrified of her servants, insisted on locking herself in her room at night, and precipitated terrible scenes in the daytime. The domestic drama, though exhausting, did not interfere with Alix or James's work, however, and they went on determinedly translating and editing the *Standard Edition* of Freud's work. James was also editor of the *International Journal of Psycho-Analysis*, a position he maintained throughout the war. Alix was his most prolific reviewer, contributing several reviews of new works on psychoanalysis to every issue.

While those Stracheys who were in England kept in close touch with each other, it was not possible to maintain the same level of contact with the Bussys during the war. Visits were impossible and mail services irregular. For some months in 1939-40, and then again later, there were long periods in which no letters moved between Britain and France. In October 1944, Dorothy Bussy wrote to tell Gide that she had received her first letter from England in more than a year—and this meant that she had not heard of the death of her oldest sister, Elinor, until three months after it occurred.[59] The lack of contact also meant that Dorothy's allowance could not be sent and the Bussys were often in very difficult financial situation.

Overall, the war years were ones of very severe difficulty for the Bussys. Some years prior to the war, they had decided that they should leave *La Souco*. Despite its charm, its isolation made it increasingly difficult for them and it was also very expensive for them to live there. As early as 1931, Dorothy Bussy had explained to Gide that their financial prospects made it imperative for them to think of selling *La Souco*. They seemed to have almost no other prospect of earning an income. 'A considerable source of our income was English boarders and pupils', Dorothy wrote, 'but there is no chance of that now.' They had sent away one maid, but intended to keep the other.[60] Their move did not eventuate until 1936 when Dorothy wrote to tell Pippa that they had bought a small flat in Nice. The flat was smaller than the house, but in a new block with central heating. 'The point is of course we shall be able to live in Nice much more cheaply than in *La Souco*. We will have a charwoman for four hours per day instead of 2 expensive servants eating us out of house and home; will spend half as much on heating and food as we do now.' The purchase was made possible because Dorothy had a small amount of English capital and the devaluation of the franc enabled her to use it to get the flat and to move.[61]

Moving from their home of many years was hard, although it did bring them into closer contact with old friends including Roger Martin du Gard and Henri Matisse. At the start of the war, it even facilitated their close contact with André Gide who stayed with them for seven months from October 1939 until May 1940. The war years, however, were extremely difficult. The Bussys were not certain that Nice was safe, and spent some months each year in Vence and Cabris. They endured several years of marked financial hardship, isolation, and intense fear. The German occupation added not only anxiety and constant danger, but also a sense of hostility and alienation as everyone was suspicious of everyone else. When she went to London in 1945, Dorothy commented on the friendliness and the new spirit of camaraderie that seemed to have emerged in Britain, which was in marked contrast to the lack of common purpose or endeavour or of community life in France.[62] The German occupation and the Vichy government made these things impossible. The Bussys moreover had a far deeper sense of the horrors of Nazism than did their England relatives. They had a number of Jewish friends who were sent to concentration camps. Some survived, but their fate was a constant source of anxiety. Food shortages in France were also very severe—and Dorothy hated seeing her daughter 'starved, overworked and growing old'.[63] When Dorothy and Janie managed to get to England in July 1945, Dorothy commented on the fact that, while the English complained of food rations, they had no understanding of what food shortages were—and their problem really was an inability to cook.[64] It was on her return to Nice after that trip to London that Dorothy articulated most clearly what the war had been like. It was horrible being in Nice, she told Gide.

The atmosphere was overpowering. 'I am back again in those frightful war years; every step, every glance, every object reminds me of that hideous time—solitude, fear, horror . . . then came the nightmare of the occupation, growing fear, growing starvation, growing despair.'[65]

In addition to its other hardships, The war brought several devastating and unexpected deaths. Ray Strachey's was the first. She died suddenly in July 1940 after an operation for what was thought to be a fibroid. There had been a some anxiety before the operation, and questions raised about whether it was malignant, but this had been allayed by the doctors involved. 'The past week was filled with alarm about Ray', Pippa wrote to Pernel on 7 July. However,

the uncertainty was to exist for such a short time that I didn't write & now she has had an operation that showed the necessity of removing the organ but gave no suspicion whatever of anything malignant in her condition. Ellie and the surgeon agree—but this will be verified later after examination. But even if they were found to be mistaken it wouldn't be important because there is 100% safety if this portion of the anatomy is removed in the early stages of cancer.[66]

Ellie Rendel, who remained the family's medical adviser, came to report that the operation was successful and that everything was going as well as possible. Ray, however, died nine days later. She clearly had some sense that this might happen, as she had sent her son Christopher a detailed letter before she went into hospital explaining her and Oliver's financial affairs. In characteristic unsentimental style, Ray insisted that she neither expected nor intended to die—and that deathbed sentiments were quite uncalled for. But it is hard not to see some premonition in this letter.[67] There is no other comment amongst Pippa's papers concerning Ray's illness or death. But after all the years of Ray's devotion and with their shared feminist interests and occupations, it must have been a terrible blow.

This was followed by the death of Virginia Woolf in April 1941, which came as another terrible and unexpected loss. Both Leonard and Virginia Woolf had been friends of the Stracheys for almost half a century, and even if rarely seen were an intimate part of their world. The Woolfs had visited Pernel in Cambridge only a couple of weeks before Virginia's death, and Pippa had debated whether or not to go there as well to see them. Pippa felt completely shattered by this death, she told James, and Dorothy and Pernel clearly felt the same.[68]

Not very long after this, Elinor's daughter, Ellie Rendel was found to be suffering from inoperable cancer and died in September 1942. She had always been an integral part of the Strachey family. 'She was greatly beloved by us all', Dorothy Bussy explained to André Gide, 'and more than beloved—for her profession had made her the intimate friend, counsellor, support of us all, always understanding, devoted, helpful and regardless of self.'[69] Dorothy was particularly concerned about how Elinor would fare after the loss of her daughter. She still had two married sons, but it was the single daughter, Ellie, who had been her companion and carer. Marjorie stepped into the breach. When Elinor's London home had been bombed in 1941, and she and Ellie had moved to Ray Strachey's home, the mud house at Fernhurst. Marjorie had gone too. Feeling greatly concerned about the demands on Ellie, she had, as Pippa explained to James, nobly given up her own home to go with them.[70] When Ellie died, Marjorie took over the care of her oldest sister. Elinor, who was then 82, was becoming increasingly frail. Like the other Stracheys, she had problems with her eyes. She suffered from cataracts and feared losing her sight. Elinor had always shared much of her mother's mid-Victorian approach to life—and this caused considerable difficulties now. It was particularly hard to find servants who treated Elinor with the kind of deference she expected. After a long search, Marjorie told Pippa that they had at last found 'what seems very hopeful in Florence. She is over 60, accustomed to old ladies and says ma'am instead of Mrs Rendel. So she is coming on June 1st.'[71] Elinor was not able to enjoy Florence for long, however as she died in July of that year.

❦ III ❦

At the end of the Second World War, there were still six Stracheys left, but their declining years were dominated by illness and death.

Pernel was the first to die after the war, apparently in Gordon Square. There are no extant letters that describe her final years. Her obituary in the Newnham College Roll suggests that her health was poor. She had planned to extend her study of French literature, but 'war-time distractions and impaired health did not permit of prolonged study'. The college that had been her home and the centre of her life for decades continued to be important and she visited it frequently, sometimes staying for several weeks over the long vacation. Pernel remained at home until the end, dying there on 19 December 1951.[72] Her loss was a great sorrow to Pippa, who carefully stored all the letters of condolence that she received. It made her also reach out a little to earlier friends, particularly to Duncan Grant and Vanessa Bell with whom the Stracheys still sometimes shared a house. 'One clings to the treasures one has left', Pippa wrote to Duncan in response to his letter of condolence, 'and you are one of those few most precious treasures of my heart.'[73]

Oliver was the next of the Stracheys to die, and although one cannot follow his final years in detail, the comments of his daughter, Julia, and her friend, Frances Partridge, provide some vivid sketches of them. Oliver had suffered a very severe heart attack in 1943 and continued to be ill and in hospital intermittently until his death. The selfishness and need for constant amusement that had always characterized him continued, and this meant that he was often bored and could be very trying for others. Julia Strachey who stayed with him for a couple of weeks after his heart attack made it clear that she found him impossible. 'You must know that one of the things I suffered greatly with in my childhood', she wrote to her future husband, Lawrence Gowing,

was Oliver's forcibly feeding me with uplift and culture. Now of course his passion for 'educating' people against their wills is given full reign. Yesterday afternoon he rang his bell , and when I appeared before him looked at me with demonic triumph in his face. At last he said: 'NOW! Shall we try and give you a little education in decent music?'. He then played Delius' Appalachia saying 'You certainly won't like it' with roars of happy laughter.[74]

Oliver remained in hospital until May 1944. There was a flurry of correspondence amongst his siblings about him and many expressions of concern that he was in such a bad way. Boredom, Marjorie felt, was his major problem—but there was little that could be done about it. 'It is, however, as you say a comfort that he is being well looked after', she wrote to Pippa. 'In these days it is almost a miracle'.[75]

When he came out of hospital, Oliver made his home in Gordon Square. Julia Strachey noted that he had 'complete and majestic comfort there', in two large rooms. With his cheerful red face and white hair, he looked 'like a twinkling Anglo-Indian God of some sort'.

He is utterly cheerful and well, and really does seem to have bobbed up on to the top of the wave again: it is such a mercy. His talk is all about wanting to write a work on 'aesthetics' if you please! He who hasn't looked at anything but detective stories or 'memoirs from the highlands' for twenty years now! He is as naive as a Robin redbreast.[76]

While Oliver might have been in majestic comfort, he was often very depressed. His daughter Barbara maintains that he attempted suicide twice—only to be nursed back to life by Pippa.[77] He drank heavily and although he seems sometimes to have visited the Oriental Club, he was increasingly incapacitated. His sisters, moreover, had no idea how to look after him. Julia Strachey's descriptions of Oliver during the 1950s point also to the increasing chaos of Gordon Square and the growing inability of the remaining Stracheys to manage their lives. In 1958, she described to Frances Partridge the nightmare that she had encountered at Gordon Square, after receiving a *'coupe de telephone* telling me that Oliver was dangerously ill with pernicious anaemia, and that the whole Strachey tribe had gone down like ninepins with flu'.

I hadn't the face, or heart really, to allow that to go on, so I . . . went down . . . for a fortnight. Oliver is considered to have 'turned the corner', and the Stracheys are beginning to stumble to their feet again. It reminds me of a French poem Aunt Dorothy used to make me recite as a child, in the manner of the Comedie Francaise:
   'Hajlmar se souleve entre les morts sanglants . . . '
And now about Oliver, I dread going into all the pathos and horror, but will just say that I was reminded of Rake's Progress. Those four bottles of neat whisky a week, which he has accustomed himself to consuming, had resulted in his system being unable to manufacture Vitamin B 12—in other words developing pernicious anaemia. This has been cured by injections. But Marjorie and Pippa, when they hear the word 'Vitamin' think it refers to some modern quack religion like Mrs Besant or nudism, so they wouldn't believe me when I told them what the disease really was. I do think I have got a most *inhuman* family![78]

Oliver survived this crisis, but died in a nursing home two years later in 1960. That year saw also the end of the entire Bussy family after a very trying few years. The Bussys remained based in Nice for a few years after the war, making frequent visits to London in the summer. Both Dorothy and Janie loathed Nice and wanted to go back to *La Souco*. Their tenant, however, refused to leave and they were only able to go back to their home when they finally managed to get a legal settlement that forced him out in 1951. But their years of being able to enjoy their old home were limited. The Bussys had worked throughout the war and continued to do so afterwards. Simon and Janie painted and planned exhibitions, while Dorothy although in her 80s, continued both to do some translation and to work on her own books. It was in the years immediately after the war that she published her novel, *Olivia*, to great and unexpected acclaim. After a considerable struggle, she also published her *Fifty Nursery Rhymes—with a Commentary on English Usage for French Students*.[79] Their period of active life was limited, however. In 1953, Simon Bussy suffered what appeared to be a stroke. It left him physically able to move, but completely senile. The attack occurred at *La Souco*, but Janie and Dorothy immediately took him to England where he went into a nursing home and remained there until his death in 1954. Janie had a nightmare trip escorting her father across the channel as he had no idea what he was doing and attempted to open the aeroplane door. She feared that if his true state were known, he would not be allowed to fly—and so had to find ways of controlling him without alerting the flight crew.[80]

Dorothy, too, was becoming senile at this time. Frances Partridge noted that when Dorothy and Janie had visited them in May 1953, Dorothy was 'as fragile looking as something made of matchsticks, and as alarming to be with as a young baby. One moment she is completely on the spot, sharp as needles. The next she says "Indian" when she means "Chinese" or begins telling us who Beckford was.'[81] The life of Janie Bussy, as all her friends were only too aware, was a very hard one. Like her father, she was a painter, but her artistic work often had to take second place to caring for her elderly parents. 'I must say I often think females are down trodden even now', Vanessa Bell wrote, after seeing Janie one day in London. 'If Janie were a son no one would ever have expected her to do anything but paint—and the poor creature hasn't children to make any of it worthwhile. She can only have real freedom after all her relations have died, it seems.'[82] This sense of Janie as been enslaved to all her elderly Strachey relations was expressed by others as well. In March 1960, Julia Strachey wrote to Frances Partridge about the declining state of the Stracheys. 'Oliver is in frightful trouble, oh dear, oh dear—behaved abominably, then broke his poor old leg, and has spent the last two weeks screaming at the top of his lungs like a—well, I'll make no comparisons. Pippa now blind, Marjorie's legs gone. Dorothy alone rides over Janie triumphant. What a world.'[83]

Janie's irritation with her mother and her frustration were palpable, and often commented on by her friends, but there was nothing she could do. Unfortunately she never lived to enjoy the freedom that might have been hers once her relatives were dead, for Janie herself died in April 1960, from a gas leak in the bathroom at 51 Gordon Square.

Janie's death was a horrifying tragedy to both her family and her friends. Frances Partridge reported that Marjorie Strachey seemed almost to hold herself responsible. Marjorie's comments suggest that Dorothy was in a dangerous state of senile dementia at this stage. 'Dorothy had been getting weaker and also madder,' Frances Partridge reported, 'and Marjorie and Pippa decided they must never leave Janie in the house alone with her mother.'[84] They did so, however, for a few days when they arranged to go and stay with Alix and James at Marlow. There was a clear implication in Marjorie's account either that Dorothy harmed Janie—or that Janie might have committed suicide. Frances Partridge did not accept this, recalling that she and her husband had smelt gas in the Strachey home some years earlier, in 1953, and that it was this faulty geyser that had killed Janie. After Janie's death, Dorothy was placed in a nursing home where she died a few months later with no knowledge of what had happened.

The Strachey house in Gordon Square was clearly becoming more and more chaotic. The ageing Stracheys were constantly anxious that London University would evict them and take back the house. This did not happen, although some of their younger relatives sometimes wished it would, for the house and its state were a source of great concern. The faulty geyser that killed Janie Bussy—and that Frances Partridge had smelt seven years earlier—was a case in point, for nothing in the house was attended to or repaired. Pippa, who maintained charge, had never been particularly concerned about her physical comfort or her surroundings and she became less and less so as she aged. Her nieces, including Janie Bussy and Oliver's two daughters, Julia and Barbara Strachey, all became more and more irritated at Pippa's refusal either to let them look after the house or to do so herself. Broken furniture was not mended, newspapers piled up in every conceivable place, and the house became more and more shabby. Nor was Pippa concerned about food. She was always very thin and seemed to regard eating as a chore. Barbara Strachey recalled that Pippa would cut even a pea into four pieces and take some time to swallow them.[85]

While careless of her physical surroundings, Pippa had by no means lost her zest for life. She retired in 1951, the year that Pernel died, and it is impossible to tell how she occupied her days after that. She seems, however, to have remained healthy and active for some time. In 1960, accompanied by James and Duncan Grant, she made a last trip to Aviemore in Scotland with a view to seeing the Grant family estate of Rothiemurchus where they had all had such happy childhood holidays. Even on the train, Pippa managed very well. They discovered that the dining car was nine carriages away from their seats, James told Alix. Pippa, however 'negotiated the fearful cross overs between coaches quite successfully'.[86] In reply to this latter, Alix commented on what a good thing it was that Marjorie, who had become quite stout, had not come on this trip. For 'she never could have got back from her meal'.[87]

Once they arrived at Aviemore, James was in a state of constant anxiety about Pippa, who 'rushes about by herself in the most alarming manner—climbing stiles and plunging into ravines. My worst phantasy is that she'll break a leg & have to be kept in an Inverness hospital for 6 weeks.'[88] No such thing happened as Pippa was well able to look after herself—although sometimes in unexpected ways. They had a bit of excitement on one particular day, James wrote to Alix.

Pippa went out by herself in her usual way. She constantly wanders out on walks in various directions. But when at 8 o'clock she hadn't returned, we became more and more uneasy and sent people out to look. Finally at 9.15 she turned up quite calmly having walked at least 5 miles over mountain paths, lost her way, knocked up a native (whose grandfather she had of course known intimately) been led by him on the right path and carried bodily over a burn ('the bridge is away' is what he said). It was all in broad daylight and she may not have realised how late it was. It has left her completely unscathed.[89]

Pippa also insisted on making contact with the current laird at Rothie-murchus, John Peter Grant VI, whom none of the Stracheys actually knew. The Stracheys seem not to have had anything to do with the Grants after Janie's death while Duncan had become *persona non grata* amongst his Grant relations when he declared that he was a conscientious objector during the First World War. Thus both he and James were extremely anxious when Pippa insisted on phoning the laird at Rothiemurchus. The old animosities, although still part of family lore, had ceased to be import-ant, however. 'The Laird and Mrs came yesterday evening,' James reported to Alix, 'full of tumultuous affection—embraces and strawberries and invitations and offers to drive us round. Duncan was included in general jubilations and is now convinced that he was paranoiac about his relations. We are all invited to tea on Monday.' When they went to tea, the Grants and their circle had many stories about India, all of which were familiar to Pippa and 'floods of anecdotes' were exchanged between her and the laird.[90]

Marjorie had not come on this trip, but one has a sense that her slightly marginal status within the family changed a little in these years and that she settled into a companionable relationships with Pippa and also with Alix and James. Her feelings seem to have become a matter of more importance. Thus, for example, James wrote anxiously to Alix when he and Pippa were in Scotland to tell her that they had 'made the most frightful discovery. *Neither* of us remembered Marjorie's birthday on the 20th—and according to you she'll be cut to the heart. What can be done?'[91] There is no record of how the crisis was resolved.

Pippa's health did begin to deteriorate seriously after this trip. A couple of years later, Julia Strachey phoned Frances Partridge and told her that Pippa, who was by then almost 90 was crippled by arthritis and unable either to fend for herself or to be cared for at home. Julia arranged for her to go to a nursing home, but was angry that Pippa was resentful when she did so.[92] Pippa's eyesight had been failing too, but she managed to teach herself Braille before becoming completely blind. Although not looking forward to going into a nursing home, her characteristic humour asserted itself when she did, and old friends commented on the fact that they would feel very cheerful after visiting her, and indeed that these visits were a delight.[93]

Marjorie Strachey went into the same nursing home as Pippa in 1963. Julia Strachey who visited her there noted that she had not lost her sense of humour. Her letter describing a visit there to her friend Frances Partridge is headed 'a lighter note'. 'When I last visited Aunt Marjorie in her nursing home', she wrote,

she said to me, 'Sometimes at nights I feel quite mad. But they don't manage these things well here. The other night I was so confused I thought I was Nelson at the Battle of Trafalgar—in fact dying. So I rang the bell and the Nurse came and told me always to ring the bell if I felt worried. But if one's Nelson—and dying—how *can* one ring an electric bell?'[94]

Julia asked how the nurse was supposed to know that Marjorie was Nelson. Marjorie replied 'she might at least have *asked*'. Marjorie died in the nursing home the following year.

James, as the youngest member of the family, took a considerable measure of responsibility for his older sisters, visiting them regularly in their nursing homes and looking after their affairs. In a rather touching way, he continued to the very end to try to ensure that members of the family were protected from knowing anything about each other that would cause them distress. He did his best to ensure that sexual information, including anything about Lytton's homosexuality, was kept securely hidden away from any of his older sisters. Sometimes this desire to prevent distress involved going to quite extraordinary lengths. Thus, for example, in 1963,

Frances Partridge recorded a conversation she had had with James about the correspondence between Dorothy Bussy and André Gide, which was to be sold by Sothebys—and was expected to fetch a vast amount of money.

The complication is that Pippa long ago told Marjorie to burn it, as it too plainly revealed Dorothy's being in love with Gide. Marjorie pretended she had done so, but gave it to a friend to hide. Now Pippa is blind she will not see if the sale is reported in the papers, but James, with characteristic Strachey *folie de grandeur* thinks it may be on the wireless, and plans to disconnect Pippa's transistor at the time![95]

Pippa remained in the nursing home for a number of years, finally dying there in 1968.

❧ IV ☙

The final years of James and Alix Strachey are much better documented than those of their siblings, partly because they continued to correspond with other members of the psychoanalytic community, and also because Frances Partridge continued to visit them regularly and to record these visits in her diaries.

James and Alix both continued to work on their Freud translations until their respective deaths. In James's case, this was severely interrupted from time to time by eye trouble. He had to cut short a visit to South Africa in 1949 when the vision in one of his eyes suddenly deteriorated. A near catastrophe occurred a few years later when the other too was damaged. 'Poor James', wrote Frances Partridge. 'A fearful disaster has befallen him. After months of planning for their winter in Ceylon they set sail, but he suffered a slipped retina in his good eye on the voyage and after seeing specialist in Colombo they took the next boat home—a dismal journey, ending in a desperate attempt to save his sight by operation.'[96] When Frances Partridge visited him at Middlesex Hospital she found him lying 'flat on his back . . . like a wonderfully distinguished marble effigy, waving one long beautiful hand'. There was no knowing whether the operation would be successful, or whether he would suffer partial or even total blindness. 'Yet so wonderfully calm, serene, even gay did James manage to be . . . that I began to see how courage can turn horrible events into inspiring ones'. James did recover, although the process was slow. He did not write anything for more than a year after the operation—and even then his large and untidy letters bore witness to his poor sight. It did improve, however, and the following year he was back at work.

The question of where to live was a major preoccupation of James and Alix in the 1950s. When their lease at 41 Gordon Square came to an end in 1956, and London University, the owner of the building, raised their rent from £250 to £900 per annum, James and Alix decided to move to the country. They looked around the New Forest, but decided that 'house hunting was so unproductive' that they would move permanently to Lord's Wood. Alix's mother had died by then and her house had been left jointly to Alix and her brother, Phillip Sargant-Florence. He had no wish to live there and was happy for Alix and James to do so. They had the house altered so that it made two separate apartments and moved there early in 1957. Frances Partridge regarded this house as their womb. She visited shortly after they moved in and described the decidedly eccentric life they lived there.

A huge central-heating plant has been installed in the cellar, large enough to heat a battleship or blow up the house, and it makes the rooms far too hot, as even Alix allows . . . In this large house with a sitting-room for each (Alix's containing a frigidaire in case she should fancy a cool drink) as well as several communal ones, they lead a fairly ramshackle life, and feed off tinned soups and carrots. Alix does all the housework such as it is so the beds are never made, and she looked at the floor and said thoughtfully: 'I've not swept it for a month and I'm wondering when I shall have to.'[97]

Although Alix initially maintained that the windows at Marlow did not open because they had been badly painted, when on a subsequent visit Frances managed to open her own window slightly, it caused great distress. What, she wondered, could the meaning of fresh air be in analytic terms. Michael Holroyd, who spent nearly five years working on the papers of Lytton Strachey that were at Lord's Wood, also commented both on the heat of their dwelling, kept at 80 degrees Fahrenheit, and on the elaborate measures they took to keep fresh air out. 'No windows were open', he noted, 'and, to prevent the suspicion of a draught, cellophane curtains were drawn against them . . . I felt I had entered a specially treated capsule where some rare variety of *homo sapiens* was being exquisitely preserved'.[98] Frances Partridge found 'the highly irrational life led by these two highly intellectual and rational people' a source of constant amusement and pleasure. She continued to visit them regularly, always noting their eccentricities and sometimes also their lack of ordinary human feeling. Thus, for example, when she went there after the sudden, unexpected, and to her devastating death of her only child, they talked continuously, but, she noted, never mentioned this death that obsessed her—'not even as ordinary non-analytical people do with accurate instinctiveness have they opened the subject'.[99]

James and Alix remained at Marlow for the rest of their lives. James suffered a heart attack and died suddenly in 1967. Alix was devastated. Shortly after James's death, she wrote a sad letter to Frances Partridge. 'I cannot disguise the fact that I am quite sick with misery—with the dreadfulness of James being dead and that I shall never see, or hear, or touch him again.'[100] She continued to work on the Freud translation, however, trying to bring James's great project to an end until her death in 1972.

Afterword

The death of Pippa Strachey in 1968 brought to a close the group of Stracheys with whom I have been concerned. It is fitting that she was last of the family to die, because Pippa serves almost better than anyone else to exemplify the very idea of the Strachey family in both its Victorian and its later forms. She illustrates well both the character of the Stracheys, and the dominant themes of this book in her sense of family and empire, her intelligence, her feminism—and her complex relation to the modern world. For if any one theme has dominated this work, it is that of the relationship between the Stracheys and modernity. The relationship of the Victorian world of their parents to their own modern one was a question of immense importance to both Lytton Strachey and Virginia Woolf. Their ideas on this question, and more particularly their interest in exploring its importance and its working out in particular lives has been very important in this work. Both Strachey and Woolf were adamant abou the superiority of the 'modern' world to its 'Victorian' antecedent aesthetically, morally, and socially—although both were deeply imbued with Victorian literature and history, and bound closely to that Victorian world through both intellectual and familial ties.

As the final chapters of this work make particularly clear, while drawing much from the works of Lytton Strachey and Virginia Woolf, I want to question their reading both of the 'Victorian' and of the 'modern' world. For the Victorian world of Richard and Jane Strachey, as their letters and other writing makes clear, was also a self-consciously 'modern' one, although its understanding of modernity was very different from that of the next generation. Richard Strachey and his brother John were in the forefront of the modern approaches to the government of India introduced in the mid-nineteenth century. They were imbued with utilitarian ideas and a sense of the need to transform Indian physical and material life as well as to develop new institutions and modernize British administration. When they married in 1859, Richard and Jane Strachey made a self-consciously modern and progressive couple, eschewing superstition and religion, and following the ideas of J. S. Mill and Auguste Comte and the teachings of science. Their companionate marriage, based on mutual respect as well as love, on shared views and values, and on constant discussion of public as well as private matters, made them very different from their own parents and relatives. Inevitably, Jane and Richard Strachey became more conservative as they aged. Nonetheless, the differences between the approach to life of Richard and Jane Strachey and those of some of their children points to the multiplicities of ways of life and outlook which fit under the general heading of 'modernity' rather than allowing one simply to see the older Stracheys as upholders of Victorianism or tradition.

Just as I have sought to emphasize the modernity of the older Stracheys, so too the close focus on family life and relationships that has been offered here leads one to question that of some of the younger ones. Lytton and James Strachey might well have been able to insist on the modernity of their approach to questions of art, sexuality, and ethics, in comparison with that of their parents and older siblings. But Lytton's 'modernity', while evident in his aesthetic tastes, his approach to sexuality and in some aspects of his private life, was not always evident in his own literary work—and was certainly not evident in his expectations and demands of, or in his dependence on, his sisters. On the contrary, one can see clearly how he assumed his entitlement to devotion, self-sacrifice, and care from his women folk with all the ease of a Victorian patriarch.

Moreover, although he bewailed the conservative and even reactionary beliefs and values of his older sisters, some of them too were very much engaged in modern life. Pernel and Pippa Strachey may not have experienced the complex sexual lives or emotional entanglements which dominated their brothers' lives or constituted *la vie moderne* in the eyes of Bloomsbury. Nonetheless, both of them were modern career women, following their professional and political interests and leading autonomous and busy lives. In a similar way, their sister-in-law, Ray Strachey, at whom Lytton and James always looked askance, pioneered another modern way of life, which involved the combination of marriage and motherhood with a career and a very independent and unconventional social and domestic life. Ray Strachey found little enjoyment in Bloomsbury parties or smart dinners, but she found immense enjoyment in building herself a mud brick house with a swimming pool in which she could swim naked and where she could relax in a completely uninhibited (and utterly un-Victorian) way.

The relationship of imperialism to modernity is important here too, for while Lytton, like Virginia Woolf, sometimes seemed to feel that imperial lives were completely antithetical to modernity, this did not mean that modernity necessarily entailed a critique or a rejection of imperialism. On the contrary, while the Strachey family makes clear the way in which the life pattern of the Victorian Raj came to an end in the later nineteenth century, it also serves to show the continuation of imperial beliefs and values and the ways in which they could be bent to new and different ends. For Lytton Strachey, the empire became a source of sexual fantasy in which complex patterns of domination and desire could be worked out imaginatively—if not in terms of actual experience or relationships. Turning the family pattern on its head, Pippa Strachey's life illustrates the ways in which imperial connections and experience could empower women and give them the self-confidence to seek new and independent public lives. Moving one stage further on, and while maintaining many of the racial and hierarchical values connected to imperialism, Alix Strachey drew on psychoanalysis to explain why imperialism would inevitably bring resistance and resentment—and probably come to an end.

Questions about modernity and its importance are evident in other ways as well. This study has shown very clearly the very short time that it took for this branch of Stracheys to cease being a large, affluent, and powerful Victorian family—and effectively to disappear. As Leonard Woolf commented in his autobiography, the Stracheys were not only a most remarkable family, but also 'an extinct phenomenon which has passed away and will never be known again'. There were few Stracheys left when Woolf was writing his own autobiography and almost none when he died. The Stracheys were by no means the only large Victorian family to die out within two generations, but their size and prominence in the nineteenth century makes this disappearance particularly striking. That one is chronicling their demise adds a slightly dirge-like quality to the final stages of this study—and makes it hard always to resist the language of decline. Just as the life of Mary Wollstonecraft at the end of the eighteenth century served for many conservatives as an illustration of the appalling consequences of a belief in the rights of women including suicide attempts, illegitimate children, and an irregular family life, so the Stracheys could serve as an illustration of the demographic catastrophe that would result from espousing careers for women, and new forms of sexual and intimate domestic life. At the same time, of course, there is no question that the pattern of life seen as so satisfying by Richard and Jane Strachey depended not only on assumptions, codes, and values that their children rejected, but also on very different feelings and desires. Even had it been possible to achieve, the life that so suited them would have been stifling and destructive for many of their children.

What becomes very clear through the combination of biography and history in this study is the marked changes between the older and the younger Stracheys, not just in intellectual outlook, but also in emotional make-up. While the family name and traditions remained important to them all, many of the younger Stracheys would have found it intolerable to attempt to lead lives similar to those of their parents. For some it was their sexuality, for others their desire either for more intimate relations with friends and companions or for greater autonomy and independence, that made a new way of life imperative. In a sense, then, one of the major things this study serves to illustrate is the connection between changes in individual feeling and desire, on the one hand, and broader historical patterns, on the other. One can see this at least as much in the shifts evident in sibling relationships across the generations as one can in terms of concepts of gender, or approaches to sexuality, or marital patterns. It is as evident in Dorothy's marriage and articulation of her feelings about Gide or in the ways in which Pippa dealt with her feelings about Lytton as it is in the emotional life of Lytton himself. Not all of these things would have been included by Lytton Strachey in his concept of 'modernity', but, taken together, they point to the extent and the magnitude of the internal shifts that accompanied the move of the Strachey family from Bombay to Bloomsbury.

Notes

INTRODUCTION

1. Virginia Woolf, *The Diary of Virginia Woolf*, ed. Anne Olivier Bell, iv (Harmondsworth: Penguin Books, 1983), 140.

2. I will throughout this book use the term 'Anglo-Indian' in its 19th-century sense of British families who lived and served in India, rather than in its current sense as applying to those born in India of mixed British and Indian parents. The Stracheys themselves frequently used the term about themselves and it is important in establishing their sense of identity.

3. Oliver Strachey to Richard Strachey, just dated 'Tuesday 1 1889', IO, Eur F 127/133. 'Uncle John' was Richard Strachey's brother, Sir John Strachey, GCSI, CIE. (1823–1907)

4. Lytton Strachey to Bernard Swithinbank, 21 Sept. 1908, cited in Julie Anne Taddeo, *Lytton Strachey and the Search for Modern Sexual Identity: The Last Eminent Victorian* (Binghamton, NY: Haworth Press, 2002), 57.

5. Ibid.

6. 'Lancaster Gate' in Lytton Strachey, *Lytton Strachey by Himself: A Self-Portrait*, ed. Michael Holroyd (London: Heinemann, 1971).

7. It was difficult, Oliver explained, 'as you're not an Anglo-Indian'. Oliver Strachey to Lytton Strachey, 22 July 1922, BL, Add Mss 60723.

8. Leonore Davidoff, Megan Doolittle, Janet Fink, and Katherine Holden, *The Family Story: Blood, Contract and Intimacy, 1830–1960* (London: Longman, 1999), 92.

9. 'Lancaster Gate', 21.

10. Virginia Woolf, 'Lady Strachey', *The Nation and Athenaeum* (22 Dec. 1928), 441–2.

11. Eric Stokes, *The English Utilitarians and India* (Oxford: Oxford University Press, 1959).

12. Michael Holroyd, *Lytton Strachey* (London: Vintage, 1995), 56–71.

13. Ray Strachey, *The Cause: A Short History of the Women's Movement in Great Britain* (London: Virago, 1978; first published 1928).

14. Leonard Woolf, *Sowing: An Autobiography of the Years 1880–1904* (London: Hogarth Press, 1970), 190.

15. Woolf, *Diary*, i. 236.

16. Quoted in Keith Hale (ed.), *Friends and Apostles: The Correspondence of Rupert Brooke and James Strachey 1905–1914* (New Haven: Yale University Press, 1998), 3–4.

17. David Garnett, *The Golden Echo* (London: Chatto & Windus, 1954), 257–8.

18. Woolf, *Sowing*, 187.

19. See e.g. Amabel William-Ellis, *All Stracheys are Cousins: Memoirs* (London: Weidenfeld & Nicolson, 1983), pp. ix–xii.

20. Woolf, *Diary*, i. 132.

21. Dorothy Bussy, *Olivia* (London: Virago, 1987; first published 1949), 13.

22. *Virginia Woolf and Lytton Strachey: Letters*, ed. Leonard Woolf and James Strachey (London: Hogarth Press, 1956); Hale, *Friends and Apostles*; Richard Tedeschi (ed.), *Selected Letters of André Gide and Dorothy Bussy* (New York: Oxford University Press, 1983).

1. AN ANGLO-INDIAN FAMILY

1. Jane Strachey, handwritten notes for speech on a debate 'That India should not be allowed self-government' at the Lyceum Club, 15 Mar. 1910. Papers of Jane Maria Strachey, WL.

2. Henry Strachey (1732–74). See Barbara Strachey, *The Strachey Line: An English Family in America, in India and at Home, 1570 to 1902* (London: Victor Gollancz, 1985).

3. John Strachey, *India: Its Administration and Progress* (London: Macmillan & Co., 1911), pp. x–xi.

4. 'Death of General Sir Richard Strachey', *The Times* (13 Feb. 1908), 12.

5. R. Dione and R. Macleod, 'Science and Policy in British India, 1858–1917: Perspectives on a Persisting Belief', in *Asie de Sud: Traditions et changements* (Paris: Éditions du Centre National de la Recherche Scientifique, 1979), 55–68.

6. Ian Stone, *Canal Irrigation in British India: Perspectives on Technological Change in a Peasant Economy* (Cambridge: Cambridge University Press, 1984), 4–15.

7. Lord Cross to Richard Strachey, 1 June 1881, IO, Eur F 127/178.

8. Mike Davis, *Late Victorian Holocausts: El Niño Famines and the Making of the Third World* (London: Verso, 2001), 12.

9. Ibid.

10. Jean Dreze, *Famine Prevention in India* (New York: World Institute for Development Economic Research of the United Nations, 1988).

11. Thomas Holditch, 'Richard Strachey—Obituary', *Geographical Journal* (Mar. 1908), 343.

12. G. H. D., *Lieutenant-General Sir Richard Strachey, G.C.S.I., 1817–1908* (London: privately published, Harrison and Son Printers, 1908).

13. Bernard S. Cohn, *Colonialism and its Forms of Knowledge: The British in India* (Princeton: Princeton University Press, 1986).

14. See e.g. Betty Askwith, *Two Victorian Families* (London: Chatto & Windus, 1971), 36–7; Elizabeth French Boyd, *Bloomsbury Heritage: Their Mothers and their Aunts* (London: Hamish Hamilton, 1976), 48–60.

15. See Jane Strachey, letter to *The Times* (11 Jan. 1911). She frequently made speeches on this theme as well. See Papers of Lady Strachey, WL.

16. Antoinette Burton, *Burdens of History: British Feminists, Indian Women, and Imperial Culture, 1865–1915* (Chapel Hill, NC: University of North Carolina Press, 1994); Nupur Chaudhuri and Margaret Strobel (eds.), *Western Women and Imperialism* (Bloomington: Indiana University Press, 1992); Clare Midgley (ed.), *Gender and Imperialism* (Manchester and New York: Manchester University Press and St Martin's Press, 1995).

17. See correspondence between Richard Strachey and Chief Engineer, IO, Eur F 127/164.

18. Richard Strachey to Jane Strachey, 15 May 1862, IO, Eur F 127/315.

19. D. A. Washbrook, 'India, 1818–1860: The Two Faces of Colonialism', in Andrew Porter (ed.), *The Oxford History of the British Empire*, iii (Oxford: Oxford University Press, 1999), 395.

20. See Javed Majeed, *Ungoverned Imaginings: James Mill's* History of British India *and Orientalism* (Oxford: Clarendon Press, 1992).

21. For discussion of his reforms see Eric Stokes, *The English Utilitarians and India* (Oxford: Oxford University Press, 1959); Burton Stein, *A History of India* (Oxford: Blackwell, 1998), 221–7; Washbrook, 'India, 1818–1860'.

22. Zaheer Baber, *The Science of Empire: Scientific Knowledge, Civilisation and Colonial Rule in India* (Delhi: Oxford University Press, 1998), 207.

23. Benita Parry, *Delusions and Discoveries: Studies on India in the British Imagination 1880–1930* (Bristol: Penguin, 1972).

24. The India Council acted as an advisory and review body to the Secretary of State for India, often exercising considerable authority over Indian policy.

25. Letter from the Directors of the Agra and Masterman Bank Ltd to Investors, 6 June 1866, IO, Eur F 127/116.

26. Edward Strachey to Richard Strachey, 25 May 1866, IO, Eur F 127/114.

27. John Strachey to Richard Strachey, 16 June 1866, IO, Eur F 127/116.

28. Jane Strachey to Sir John Peter Grant, 1 Nov. 1866, IO, Eur F127/7.

29. Richard Strachey to Lord Cranbourne, 2 Feb. 1867, IO, IOR Neg 11672.

30. 'Functions of the Inspector general of Public Works', dated Simla 2 July 1867, copy in IO, Eur F 127/167.

31. Richard Strachey to Lord Cranbourne, 3 Sept. 1867, IO, IOR Neg 11672.

32. Richard Strachey to Jane Strachey, 15 Feb. 1868, IO, Eur F 127/319.

33. Richard Strachey to Lord Lytton, 19 Aug. 1878, IO, Eur E 128/34.

34. Bartle Frere to Sir Charles Trevelyan, quoted in John Martineau (ed.), *The Life and Correspondence of Sir Bartle Frere, BART., G.C.B., F.R.S.*, i (London: John Murray, 1895), 421.

35. Ibid. 423. Bartle Frere to Richard Strachey, 12 Oct. 1863.

36. Jane Strachey to Richard Strachey, 21 Aug. 1874, IO, Eur F 127/127.

37. Lord Salisbury to Richard Strachey, 23 Dec. 1874, IO, Eur F 127/178.

38. Anil Seal, *The Emergence of Indian Nationalism* (Cambridge: Cambridge University Press, 1970), 3.

39. Lord Salisbury to Richard Strachey, 23 Dec. 1874, IO, Eur F 127/178.

40. Richard Strachey to Lord Salisbury, 26 Dec. 1874, IO, Eur F 127/178.

41. Lord Lytton to Lord Cranbrook, 2 June 1878, IO, Eur 218/518.

42. My discussion of this episode is based largely on L. Brennan, 'The Development of the Indian Famine Codes: Personalities, Politics, and Policies', in Bruce Currey and Graeme Hugo (eds.), *Famine as a Geographical Phenomenon* (Dordrecht: D. Reidel, 1984), 91–113.

43. Richard Strachey to Jane Strachey, 4 Jan. 1878, IO, Eur F 127/322.

44. John Strachey, *The Indian Famine of 1877, Being a Statement of the Measures Proposed by the Government of India for the Prevention and Relief of Famine* (London: Kegan Paul & Co, 1878).

45. Ibid. 17.

46. Richard Strachey to Jane Strachey, 15 Feb. 1878, IO, Eur F 127/322.

47. George Huddleston, *History of the East Indian Railway* (Calcutta: Thacker Spink & Co., 1906), 268–72.

48. Ibid. 270.

49. Board of Directors of the EIR to Sir Richard Strachey, 1 Jan. 1907, IO, Eur F 127/78.

50. Huddleston, *East Indian Railway*, 273.

51. Richard to Jane Strachey, 15 July 1862, IO, Eur F 127/315. On one current estimate, this income would have the purchasing power of £280,000 today.

52. Richard to Jane Strachey, 18 May 1860, IO Eur F 127/315.

53. Secretary to the Government of India to Richard Strachey, 18 July 1866, IO, Eur F 127/180.

54. 'Appointment of an Inspector General of Irrigation Works', 22 Jan. 1867, IO Eur F 127/178.

55. Richard Strachey to Sir John Peter Grant, 16 Jan. 1871, IO, Eur F 127/9.

56. His total salary and allowances, including both the £1,200 he received as a member of Council and the £556.6 he received as retirement pay and 'good service pension' from the army, gave him a total income of £1756.5. Paper presented to Parliament, 'Payment of Members of Council', IO, Eur F 127/178.

57. Ibid.

58. Richard Strachey to Pippa Strachey, 6 Nov. 1893, BL, Add Mss 60729.

59. C. Hobhouse to Secretary of EIR, 21 June 1907, IO, Eur F 127/178.

60. Jane Strachey, 'Some Recollections of a Long Life', *Nation and Athenaeum* (5 Jan. 1924), 514.

61. Jane Strachey to Richard Strachey, 26 May 1862, IO, Eur F 127/125.

62. Jane Strachey to Elinor Colevile, 29 June 1863, IO, Eur F 127/82.

63. Jane Strachey to Elinor Colevile, 29 July 1863, IO, Eur F 127/82.

64. Jane Strachey to Elinor Colevile, 2 Nov. 1863, IO, Eur F 127/82.

65. Jane Strachey to Dick Strachey, 26 Jan. 1869, IO, Eur F 127/439.

66. Jane Strachey to Dick Strachey, 13 Dec. 1869, IO, Eur F 127/439.

67. See the series of letters from Jane Strachey to Elinor Colevile, May–Nov. 1863, IO, Eur F 127/82.

68. Lord Lytton to Jane Strachey, 13 Mar. 1881, IO, Eur F 127/361.

69. Dorothy Bussy to André Gide, 20 Sept. 1942, Lettres de Dorothy Bussy à Andre Gide, Bibliothèque Nationale, NAF 15631

70. Virginia Woolf, 'Lady Strachey', in Mary Lyon (ed.), *Books and Portraits* (London: Hogarth Press: 1977), 208. Originally published in *The Nation and Athenaeum* (22 Dec. 1928), 358.

71. Virginia Woolf, *The Diary of Virginia Woolf*, ed. Anne Olivier Bell, i (Harmondsworth: Penguin Books, 1979), 107.

72. Thomas Metcalfe, *Ideologies of the Raj*, The New Cambridge History of India, 3 (Cambridge: Cambridge University Press, 1994), 28–57.

73. Mrinalinha Sinha, *Colonial Masculinity: The 'Manly Englishman' and the 'Effeminate Bengali' in the Late Nineteenth Century* (Manchester: Manchester University Press, 1995), 102.

74. John Strachey, *India* (London: Macmillan, 1888), 360.

75. John Strachey, *The Finances and Public Works of India from 1869 to 1881* (London: Kegan Paul Tench, 1882), p. viii.

76. Richard Strachey to Jane Strachey, 18 Jan. 1867, IO, Eur F 127/114.

77. Richard Strachey, *The Physical Causes of Indian Famine* (London: Royal Institution of Great Britain, 1877), 20.

78. For a discussion of British civil servants who did attempt to question these values and to make close friendships amongst Indians, see Clive Dewey, *Anglo-Indian Attitudes: The Mind of the Indian Civil Service* (London: Hambledon Press, 1993).

79. Jane Strachey to Dick Strachey, 2 Sept. 1868, IO, Eur F 127/439.

80. Jane Strachey to Dick Strachey, 18 Nov. 1868, IO, Eur F 127/439.

81. William Dalrymple, *White Mughals: Love and Betrayal in Eighteenth-Century India* (London: Harper Collins, 2002).

82. See Pat Barr, *The Memsahibs: The Women of Victorian India* (London: Secker & Warburg, 1976) and Margaret Macmillan, *Women of the Raj* (London: Thames & Hudson, 1988).

83. Quoted in Michael Mason, *The Making of Victorian Sexual Attitudes* (Oxford and New York: Oxford University Press, 1994), 1.

84. Jane Strachey to Richard Strachey, 25 May 1867, IO, Eur F 127/126.

85. Jane Strachey to Sir Peter Grant, 23 Sept. 1860, IO, Eur F127/7.

86. Thomas Carlyle, *Reminiscences* (London: Macmillan, 1887), 243.

87. Dalrymple, *White Mughals*.

88. Ibid. 336–40.

89. Ibid. 489–95.

90. The Strachey Papers in the India Office Library contain a large collection of the documents she collected concerning not only Stracheys and Grants, but also the Plowden, Frere, and Kirkpatrick families into which various Stracheys or Grants married. See IO, Eur F127/478a.

91. Jane Strachey to Edward Strachey, 3 April 1886, IO, Eur F 228/96.

92. Edward Strachey, 'The Romantic Marriage of James Achilles Kirkpatrick, Sometime British Resident at the Court of Hyderabad', *Blackwood's Magazine* (July 1893).

93. John Strachey, *The End of Empire* (London: Victor Gollancz, 1961), 55.

94. Trevor Grant to Jane Strachey, 2 Dec. 1859, IO, Eur F127/302.

95. Trevor Grant to Jane Strachey, 28 Dec. 1859, IO, Eur F127/302. Unfortunately Jane's original letter no longer exists.

96. Elinor Colevile to Jane Strachey, 9 Feb. 1860, IO, Eur F127/306.

97. Elinor Colevile to Jane Strachey, 6 Oct. 1867, IO, Eur F 127/306.

98. Jane Strachey to Richard Strachey, 6 Jan. 1870, IO, Eur F 127/127

99. Richard Strachey to Jane Strachey, 8 Mar. 1867, IO, Eur F127/319.

100. John Strachey, 'Note on the Question of the Appointment of Indians to the Covenanted Civil Service', n. d., IO, Eur E2/8/117a.

101. Ibid.

102. For a detailed analysis of this issue, see Edwin Hirschmann, *White Mutiny: The Ilbert Bill Crisis in India and the Genesis of Indian National Congress* (Delhi: Heritage Publishers, 1990) See also Mrinalini Sinha, 'Reconfiguring Hierarchies: The Ilbert Controversy, 1883–4', in her *Colonial Masculinity*.

103. Strachey, *India*, 364–6; for a discussion of this view, see Stokes, *English Utilitarians and India*, 282–6.

104. See the *Chairman's Address to the Proprietors of the East India Railway*, no. 45, 4 Jan. 1893. IO, Eur F 127/218.

105. For the debate over the Contagious Diseases Acts in India, see Philippa Levine, *Prostitution, Race and Politics* (London: Routledge, 2003).

106. Arnold P. Kaminsky, 'Military Legislation and British Troops in Late Nineteenth Century India', *Military Affairs*, 43/2 (1979), 79.

107. *Woman Suffrage and India*, pamphlet no. 26 of the Anti-Suffrage League, copy in the Papers of Jane Maria Strachey, WL.

108. Lady Strachey, draft letter to *The Times* (30 Dec. 1908), copy in Papers of Lady Jane Strachey, WL.

109. Jane Strachey to Richard Strachey, 2 May 1867, IO, Eur F 127/318.

110. Lady Strachey, handwritten notes for her 'Speech on the Debate "That India should be Allowed Self-Government" ' at the Lyceum Club, 15 Mar. 1910, Papers of Jane Maria Strachey, WL.

2. AN IMPERIAL MARRIAGE

1. See e.g. Patrica Branca, *The Silent Sisterhood: Middle-Class Women in the Victorian Home* (London: Croome Helm, 1975) and Martha Vicinus (ed.) *A Widening Sphere: Changing Roles of Victorian Women* (London: University of Chicago Press, 1977), but see also Jim Hammerton, *Cruelty and*

Companionship: Conflict in Nineteenth-Century Married Life (London: Rou-tledge, 1995).

2. John Tosh, *A Man's Place: Masculinity and the Middle-Class Home in Victor-ian England* (New Haven: Yale University Press, 1999); see also the discus-sions of marriage in Alice Jenkins (ed.), *Rethinking Victorian Culture* (London: Palgrave Macmillan, 2000).

3. Jane's cousin, Kate Batten, had married Richard Strachey's younger brother, John, three years earlier.

4. Jane Strachey to Richard Strachey, 2 Aug. 1867, IO, Eur F 127/126.

5. Jane Strachey to Richard Strachey, 4 Jan. 1869, IO, Eur F 127/126.

6. Richard Strachey to Jane Strachey, 4 Jan. 1878, IO, Eur F 127/320.

7. Jane Strachey to Pernel Strachey, 24 Oct. 1897, BL Add Mss 60717.

8. Richard Strachey to Jane Strachey, 20 Apr. 1859, IO, Eur F 127/315.

9. Richard Strachey to Sir John Peter Grant, 4 May 1859, IO, Eur F 127/9.

10. Sir James Colvile to Richard Strachey, 5 July 1859, IO, Eur F 127/310.

11. See the folder of letters to Richard Strachey from his sister, Jane Hare, IO, Eur F 127/113.

12. Sir John Grant to Jane Strachey, 19 May 1859, IO, Eur F 127/299.

13. Dorothy Bussy, *Olivia*, 14. There is some dispute about extent to which this novel was autobiographical—but this picture of Olivia's mother resembles descriptions of her own mother that Dorothy sent to André Gide, especially those describing her love affair with her cousin, Sydney Forster. See Richard Tedeschi (ed.), *Selected Letters of André Gide and Dorothy Bussy* (New York: Oxford University Press, 1983), 71-4.

14. Jane Strachey to Richard Strachey, 26 June 1859, IO, Eur F 127/126.

15. Jane Strachey to Richard Strachey, 28 Jan. 1862, IO Eur F 127/126.

16. Jane Strachey to Richard Strachey, 17 Jan. 1867, IO, Eur F 127/126.

17. Richard Strachey to Jane Strachey, 13 Feb. 1867, IO, Eur F 127/316.

18. Lytton Strachey to James Strachey, 9 Apr. 1909, BL, Add Mss 60707.

19. Bussy, *Olivia*, 13; 'Lancaster Gate', in Lytton Strachey, *Lytton Strachey by Himself: A Self-Portrait*, ed. Michael Holroyd (London: Heinemann, 1971), 18.

20. Richard Strachey to Jane Strachey, 24 Feb. 1862, IO, Eur F 127/315.

21. Jane Strachey to Richard Strachey, 28 Jan. 1862, IO, Eur F 127/125.

22. Richard Strachey to Jane Strachey, 23 Mar. 1862, IO, Eur F 127/315.

23. Richard Strachey to Jane Strachey, 28 Feb. 1867, IO, Eur F 127/318.

24. Nupur Chaudhuri, 'Bloomsbury Ancestry: Jane Maria Strachey, Feminism and Younger Strachey Women', in Wayne K. Chapman and Janet M. Manson (eds.), *Women in the Milieu of Leonard and Virginia Woolf* (New York: Pace University Press, 1998), 59–75.

25. Jane Strachey to Richard Strachey, 18 Sept. 1867, IO, Eur F 127/126.

26. Richard Strachey to Jane Strachey, 26 Nov. 1866, IO, Eur F 127/318.

27. Richard Strachey to Jane Strachey, 23 Mar. 1862, IO, Eur F 127/315.

28. Quoted in Betty Askwith, *Two Victorian Families* (London: Chatto & Windus, 1971).

29. Richard Strachey to Jane Strachey, 15 Oct. 1880, IO, Eur F 127/323.

30. Jane Strachey too had a very strong sense of her own social skills. See her letters to Richard Strachey written from Italy between November and December 1870, 10 EUR F 127/127.

31. At the time, Galton, a prominent theorist of eugenics, was attempting to use a statistical method to work out the pattern of inheritance, particularly of intellectual qualities, amongst 'able families', or ones who had made a mark in politics, business, science, and literature. For a discussion of his approach to eugenics, see Daniel Kevles, *In the Name of Eugenics* (Cambridge, Mass.: Harvard University Press, 1985). Richard Strachey's comment was in a handwritten list attached to a letter from Richard Strachey to Francis Galton, 29 Sept. 1900, Galton Papers, UCL.

32. See e.g. John Strachey to Richard Strachey, 7 May 1855, IO, Eur F 127/115.

33. Richard Strachey to Jane Strachey, 3 June 1862, IO, Eur F 127/315.

34. Jane Strachey to Richard Strachey, 25 May 1867, IO, Eur F 127/126.

35. For a discussion of the nature of Victorian feminism, see Philippa Levine, *Victorian Feminism, 1850–1900,* (London: Routledge, 1987) and Barbara Caine, *Victorian Feminists* (Oxford: Oxford University Press, 1992).

36. Jane Strachey to Henrietta Grant, 9 June 1869, IO, Eur F 127/67. The baby referred to was Roger, who lived only a few hours. Jane's count includes the two babies who had died.

37. Kate Strachey to Jane Strachey, 22 April (no year—but presumably 1876, the year of Pernel's birth), IO, Eur F 127/348. The child's full name was Joan Pernel Strachey, but she was never referred to by her first name.

38. Henrietta Grant to Jane Strachey, 21 Oct. 1887, IO, Eur F 127/300.

39. Jane Strachey to Richard Strachey, 28 Jan. 1862, IO, Eur F 127/125.

40. Jane Strachey to Elinor Colevile, 22 Nov. 1862, IO, Eur F 127/82.

41. Richard Strachey to Jane Strachey, 27 Nov. 1862, IO, Eur F 127/315.

42. Jane Strachey to Richard Strachey, 17 Jan. 1867, IO, Eur F 127/126.

43. Lytton's poem is quoted in Michael Holroyd, *Lytton Strachey* (Harmondsworth: Penguin, 1979), 18. Dorothy Strachey's *Olivia by Olivia* was first published in 1949.

44. Jane Strachey to Sir John Grant, Nov. 1869, IO, Eur F 127/7.

45. Jane Strachey to Richard Strachey, 2 July 1867, IO, Eur F 127/125.

46. Jane Strachey to Sir John Grant, Nov. 1869, IO, Eur F 127/7.

47. Richard Strachey to Jane Strachey, 3 Dec. 1869, IO, Eur F 127/319.

48. Richard Strachey to Jane Strachey, 1 Mar. 1878, IO, Eur F 127.

49. Edith Lytton, wife of the viceroy, Lord Robert Lytton (after whom the baby was named), to Jane Strachey, 16 Apr. 1880, IO, Eur F 127/366.

50. Jane Strachey to Sir John Peter Grant, 1 Nov. 1866, IO, Eur F 127/7.

51. Richard Strachey to Jane Strachey, 21 Dec. 1870, IO, Eur F 127/319.

52. See Askwith, *Two Victorian Families*.

53. Jane Strachey to Sir John Grant, 15 Aug. 1866, IO, Eur F 127/7.

54. Jane Strachey to Sir John Grant, 8 Dec. 1860, IO, Eur F 127/7.

55. Jane Strachey's 'Memoirs', quoted in Elizabeth French Boyd, *Bloomsbury Heritage: Their Mothers and their Aunts* (London: Hamish Hamilton, 1976), 64.

56. Ibid.

57. Strachey, 'Lancaster Gate', 20–1.

58. Jane Strachey to Lytton Strachey, 19 Oct. 1894, RC.

59. Strachey, 'Lancaster Gate', 17–18.

60. Douglas Blair Turnbaugh, *Duncan Grant and the Bloomsbury Group* (Secaucus, NJ: Lyle Stuart Inc., 1987), 18–19.

61. Sir James Colevile to Richard Strachey, June 1862, IO, Eur F 127/310.

62. Jane Strachey to Richard Strachey, 4 Aug. 1862, IO, Eur F 127/125.

63. Jane Strachey to Richard Strachey, 9 Apr. 1862, IO, Eur F 127/125.

64. Sir James Coleville to Richard Strachey, 16 June 1862, IO, Eur F 127/310.

65. Jane Strachey to Richard Strachey, 6 Sept. 1862, IO, Eur F 127/125.

66. John Grant to Richard Strachey, 2 Mar. 1891, IO, Eur F 127/68.

67. Agnes Grant to Mr Grant, 21 June 1892, Grant Papers, Rothiermurchus, bundle 214; see also the series of letters from Elinor Colevile to Jane Strachey in the 1880s dealing with the ongoing tension between the Grants. IO, Eur F 127/308.

68. John Grant to Richard Strachey, 3 Mar. 1873, IO, Eur F 127/68.

69. John Grant to Richard Strachey, 24 Mar. 1873, IO, Eur F 127/68.

70. Sir James William Colevile (1810–1880) was appointed chief justice of the supreme court of Bengal. He retired to England in 1859 and became a member

of the Privy Council. He married Elinor Grant in 1857. 'Sir James William Colevile', *Dictionary of National Biography*, xi (London: Smith Elder & Co., 1887).

71. Sir James Coleville to John Peter Grant, 25 Jan. 1862, IO, Eur F 127/27.

72. Jane Strachey to Pippa Strachey, 10 Feb. 1898, BL, Add Mss 60717.

73. Jane Strachey to Elinor Colevile, 19 Feb. 1908, IO, Eur F 127/83.

74. G. H. Lewes to Jane Strachey (envelope dated 26 Nov. 1872), BL, Add Mss 54338.

75. Jane Strachey, 'Recollections', *Atheneaum*, 3 (12 July 1924), 474.

76. J. W. Cross to Jane Strachey, 26 Dec. 1880, BL, Add Mss 54338.

77. Jane Strachey to Lytton Strachey, 3 July 1889, RC, Box 5.

78. Jane Strachey to James Strachey, 19 Mar. 1898, BL, Add Mss 60717.

79. Jane Strachey to Richard Strachey, 25 Nov. 1870, IO, Eur F 127/127. See also Anon., *Some Memories of Marie Souvestre* (privately printed at Oxford University Press by John Johns, n.d.), copy in British Library.

80. This correspondence can be seen in the Papers of Jane Maria Strachey, WL.

81. Jane Strachey to Lytton Strachey, 15 June 1892, RC.

82. Jane Strachey to James Strachey, 16 Mar. 1898, BL, Add Mss 60717.

83. Mrs Richard Strachey, *Lay Texts for the Young in English and French* (London: Cassell & Co., 1886), xii.

84. Jane Strachey to Lytton Strachey, 5 Oct. 1890, RC.

85. Jane Strachey to Lytton Strachey, 6 July 1890, RC.

86. Jane Strachey to Lytton Strachey, 15 Oct. 1896, RC.

3. STRACHEY CHILDHOODS

1. See the letters from Jane Strachey to Richard Strachey describing the children in 1862, IO, Eur F 127/125.

2. 'Lancaster Gate', in Lytton Strachey, *Lytton Strachey by Himself: A Self-Portrait*, ed. Michael Holroyd (London: Heinemann, 1971).

3. Jane Strachey to Richard Strachey, 27 Apr. 1862, IO, Eur F 127/125.

4. See BL, Add Mss 60640–8.

5. Leonard Woolf, *Sowing: An Autobiography of the Years 1880–1904* (London: Hogarth Press, 1970), 192.

6. Jane Strachey to Lytton Strachey, 13 July 1896, RC.

7. Virginia Woolf, 'Lady Strachey', *The Nation and Athenaeum* (22 Dec. 1928), repr. in Mary Lyon (ed.), *Books and Portraits* (London: Hogarth Press: 1977), 210.

8. Strachey, 'Lancaster Gate', 13.

9. See Michael Mason, *The Making of Victorian Sexual Attitudes* (Oxford and New York: Oxford University Press, 1994).

10. For an excellent discussion of these changing views, see George K. Behlmer, *Friends of the Family: The English Home and its Guardians, 1850–1940* (Stanford, Calf.: Stanford University Press, 1998), 121–45.

11. See e.g. Alfred Adler, *Understanding Human Nature* (Oxford: One World, 1992; 1st published 1927); and more recently Juliet Mitchell, *Mad Men and Medusas: Reclaiming Hysteria and the Effects of Sibling Relations on the Human Condition* (London: Allen Lane, 2000).

12. Anne McClintock, *Imperial Leather: Race, Gender, and Sexuality in the Colonial Contest* (New York: Routledge, 1995).

13. Jane Strachey to Richard Strachey, 18 Apr. 1862, IO, Eur F 127/125.

14. Jane to Elinor Colevile, 29 June 1863, IO, Eur F 127/82.

15. Jane Strachey to Richard Strachey, 28 Jan. 1862, IO, Eur F 127/125.

16. Jane Strachey to Richard Strachey, 18 Apr. 1862, IO, Eur F 127/125.

17. See series of letters from Jane Strachey to Richard Strachey written in 1862, IO, Eur F 127/125.

18. Richard Strachey to Jane Strachey, 13 Feb. 1867, IO, Eur F 127 /318.

19. Richard Strachey to Dick Strachey, 9 Mar. 1867, IO, Eur F 127/438.

20. Jane Strachey to Richard Strachey, 2 July 1867, IO, Eur F 127/318.

21. Elinor Colevile to Jane Strachey, 24 Dec. 1867, IO, Eur F 127/306.

22. Elinor Colevile to Jane Strachey, 20 Mar. 1868, IO, Eur F 127/307.

23. Jane Strachey to Dick Strachey, n.d. but presumably early 1868, IO, Eur F 127/439.

24. Jane Strachey to Dick Strachey, 3 Oct. 1868, IO, Eur F 127/439. 2 sept 68

25. Jane Strachey to Richard Strachey, 4 Dec. 1870, IO, Eur F 127/127.

26. Lytton Strachey, *Queen Victoria* (New York: Harcourt, Brace & Jovanovich, 1921), 8–21.

27. Jane Strachey to Richard Strachey, 2 July 1867, IO, Eur F 127/126.

28. Jane Strachey to John Peter Grant, Nov. 1869, IO, Eur F F 127/7.

29. Jane Strachey to John Peter Grant, 1 Nov. 1866, IO, Eur F 127/7.

30. Jane Strachey to Richard Strachey, 17 Jan. 1867, IO, Eur F 127/126.

31. Jane Strachey to John Peter Grant, Simla, Nov. 1869, IO, Eur F 127/7.

32. Henrietta Grant to Jane Strachey, 28 Apr. 1871, IO, Eur F 127/300.

33. Jane Strachey to Ralph Strachey, n.d., IO, Eur F 127/443.

34. 'Knoll' was the family nickname for Oliver Strachey.

35. 'Our Pippa' by Norile and Lodley (Elinor and Dolly) 'Our paper', no. X, n.d., BL, Add Mss 60645.

36. Letters from Elinor Colevile to Jane Strachey from May to July 1878, IO, Eur F 127/307.

37. Elinor Colevile to Jane Strachey, 27 June 1878, IO, Eur F 127/307.

38. Elinor Colevile to Jane Strachey, 5 Sept. 1878, IO, Eur F 127/307.

39. Elinor Colevile to Jane Strachey, 10 Jan. 1879, IO, Eur F 127/307.

40. See Jane Strachey to Lytton Strachey, 3 Nov. 1890, 19 Oct. 1891, 9 Feb. 1893, RC.

41. Jane Strachey to Lytton Strachey, 3 Nov. 1890, 19 Oct. 1891, 9 Feb. 1893 RC.

42. Jane Strachey to Lytton Strachey, 5 June 1890, RC.

43. The letters from Oliver to Pernel are in BL, Add Mss 60723.

44. Lytton Strachey to Jane Strachey, 3 Nov. 1896, RC.

45. Michael Holroyd, *Lytton Strachey* (London: Vintage, 1995), 19-25.

46. Dorothy Strachey to Jane Strachey, 25 Feb. 1884, IO, Eur F 127/331.

47. Elinor Rendel to Jane Strachey, 31 Mar. 1891, IO, Eur F 127/307.

48. Jane Strachey to Lytton Strachey, 24 Feb. 1895, RC.

49. Marjorie Strachey to Jane Strachey, 2 June 1895, IO, Eur F 127/342.

50. Marjorie Strachey to Jane Strachey, 30 Mar. 1898, IO, Eur F 127/342.

51. Jane Strachey to Lytton Strachey, 19 Oct. 1891, RC.

52. Jane Strachey to Lytton Strachey, dated Mar. 1893, RC.

53. Jane Strachey to Lytton Strachey, 24 Feb. 1895, RC.

54. James Strachey to Jane Strachey, 22 May 1898, IO, Eur F 127/344.

55. Dorothy Strachey to Pippa Strachey, 3 Mar. 1903, WL, ALC 27E.

4. SCHOOL DAYS

1. Michael Holroyd, *Lytton Strachey* (London: Vintage, 1995), 23-41.

2. For the debates about education and the movement for the reform of girls' education in Britain, see J. S. Pederson, *The Reform of Girls' Secondary and Higher Education in Victorian England: A Study of Elites and Institutional Change* (New York: Garland, 1987); F. Hunt (ed.) *Lessons for Life: The Schooling of Girls and Women 1850-1950* (Oxford: Basil Blackwell, 1987) and June Purvis, *A History of Women's Education in England* (Milton Keynes: Open University Press, 1991).

3. See Sheila Fletcher, *Feminists and Bureaucrats: A Study in the Development of Girls' Education in the Nineteenth Century* (Cambridge: Cambridge University Press, 1980).

4. Blanche Wiessen Cooke, *Eleanor Roosevelt*, i (New York: Penguin Books, 1992), 109–25.

5. There are no clear records about the start or end dates of the school life of the Strachey daughters and I have worked out their school years from their letters home.

6. Edith Lytton to Jane Strachey, n.d., IO, Eur F 127/366. Constance Lytton, who later became a militant suffragette, suffered under and struggled against this domestic atmosphere. See Patricia Miles and Jill Williams, *An Uncommon Criminal: The Life of Constance Lytton, Militant Suffragette 1869–1923* (Knebworth: Knebworth House Education and Preservation Trust, 1999).

7. See e.g. the letters sent by Rosalind Potter (later Dobbs) to her sister Beatrice Webb. Barbara Caine, *Destined to be Wives: The sisters of Beatrice Webb* (Oxford and New York: Clarendon Press, 1986).

8. Dorothy Bussy, *Olivia by Olivia* (Harmondsworth: Penguin Books, 1949), 30.

9. Jane Strachey to Richard Strachey, 22 July 1868, IO, Eur F 127/126.

10. John G. Gresson to Jane Strachey, 6 May 1873, IO, EUR F 127/308.

11. Ibid.

12. L. Davenport to Jane Strachey, 4 Nov. 1873, IO, Eur F 127/308.

13. Jane Strachey to Richard Strachey, 4 Jan. 1878, IO, Eur F 127/126.

14. Richard Strachey to Jane Strachey, 1 Feb. 1878, IO, Eur F 127/321.

15. V. S. Davenport to Jane Strachey, 4 Oct. N.Y., IO, Eur F 127/308.

16. Jane Strachey to Strachey, 24 Feb. 1895, HRC.

17. Dick Strachey to Richard Strachey, 6 Feb. 1879, IO, Eur F 127/131.

18. Dick Strachey to Jane Strachey, 21 Aug. 1879, IO, Eur F 127/326.

19. Dick Strachey to Jane Strachey, 14 June 1878, IO Eur F 127/326.

20. Jane Strachey to Richard Strachey, n.d., IO, Eur F 127/128.

21. Elinor Rendel to Ralph Strachey, n.d., IO, Eur F 127/444.

22. Jane Strachey to Ralph Strachey, 4 Feb. 1884, IO, Eur F 127/444.

23. Jane Strachey to Ralph Strachey, 19 Oct. 1885, IO, Eur F 127/443.

24. Mr Bartholomew to Jane Strachey, Clifton College, Bristol, 8 Feb. 1885, IO Eur F 127/145

25. Ralph Strachey to Jane Strachey, Oct. 1886, IO, Eur F 127/333.

26. Only part of this letter remains—and the teacher is not named. The letter is dated 10 Nov., and is addressed 'Dear Sir'. IO, Eur F 127/145.

27. Virginia Woolf, *Roger Fry: A Biography* (London: Hogarth Press, 1940).

28. Oliver Strachey to his mother, n.d., IO, Eur F 127/337.

29. Jane Strachey to Richard Strachey, 27 Nov. 1892, IO, Eur F 127/126.

30. Bussy, *Olivia*, 15.

31. See the letters from Marie Souvestre and from Caroline Dussant to Jane Strachey, WL, ALC, 27 G.

32. See the letters from Elinor Strachey to Jane Strachey written in 1874–5, IO, Eur F 127/323.

33. Elinor Strachey to Jane Strachey, n.d., IO, Eur F 127/323.

34. Elinor Strachey to Jane Strachey, 19 Mar. 1884, IO, Eur F 127/323.

35. Caroline Dussant to Jane Strachey, 13 Jan. 1883, WL, ALC 27 G.

36. Marie Souvestre to Jane Strachey, 10 Nov. 1882, WL, ALC 27 G.

37. Marie Souvestre to Jane Strachey, 17 Aug. 1883, WL, ALC 27 G. By this time, Marie Souvestre was settled in London.

38. Jane Strachey to Caroline Dussant, 27 Apr. 1884, WL, ALC 27 G3. It is interesting to note that Jane Strachey felt it important to keep a copy of this letter.

39. Jane Strachey to Caroline Dussant, 27 Apr. 1884, WL, ALC 27 G3.

40. Marie Souvestre to Jane Strachey, 9 May 1883, WL, ALC 27 G3.

41. 'Tiendra de moi quelque chose qui ajoutera pour elle un prix de la vie'. Marie Souvestre to Jane Strachey, 10 Nov. 1882, WL, ALC 27 G3.

42. Ibid.

43. One of the other pupils at Les Ruches in 1883 was Beatrice Webb's youngest sister, Rosalind Potter. She wrote home at least three times a week throughout the year and never once mentioned any quarrels, or distress or uncertainty. See Caine, *Destined to be Wives*.

44. Dorothy Strachey to Roger Martin du Gard, 26 July 1948, Lettres du Roger Martin du Gard à la Famille Bussy, BN, NAF 15758.

45. Dorothy Bussy to Pippa Strachey, 24 Jan. 1905, WL, ALC 27 E.

46. Dorothy Bussy to Pippa Strachey, 14 Jan. 1905, WL, ALC 27 E.

47. Dorothy Bussy to Pippa Strachey, 25 Mar. 1905, WL, ALC 27 E.

48. Marjorie Strachey to Pippa Strachey, 14 May 1944, BL, Add Mss 60722.

49. Handwritten paper entitled 'My Life' in the Papers of Philippa Strachey, WL.

50. Betty Askwith, *Two Victorian Families*, 71.

51. Pippa Strachey to Jane Strachey, 26 Jan. 1888, IO, Eur F 127/335.

52. Pernel Strachey to Jane Strachey, 5 Feb. 1891, IO, Eur F 127/339.

53. Pernel Strachey to Jane Strachey, series of letters from 1892, IO, Eur F 127/339.

54. Pernel Strachey to Jane Strachey, 6 Mar. 1893, IO, Eur F 127/339.

55. Marjorie Strachey to Jane Strachey, 20 June 1895, IO, Eur F 127/342.

56. Marjorie Strachey to Jane Strachey, letter dated Allenswood 1898, IO, Eur F 127/342.

57. Marjorie Strachey to Jane Strachey, May 1898, IO, Eur F 127/342.

58. Marjorie Strachey to Jane Strachey, 22 Nov. 1896, IO, Eur F 127/342.

59. Marjorie Strachey to Jane Strachey, Allenswood, May 1896, IO, Eur F 127/342.

60. Natania Rosenfeld, *Outsiders Together: Virginia and Leonard Woolf* (Princeton: Princeton University Press, 2000), 15–18, 47–8. See also Frederick Spotts (ed.), *The Letters of Leonard Woolf* (London: Weideneld & Nicolson, 1989), 570–1.

61. Marjorie Strachey to Jane Strachey, 6 July 1898, IO, Eur F 127/342.

62. Head, Hyde Park Kindergarten, to Jane Strachey, Xmas 1887, IO, Eur F 127.

63. Quoted in Holroyd, *Lytton Strachey*, 23.

64. This account is drawn from Holroyd, *Lytton Strachey*, 28–35.

65. Ibid. 45–40.

66. Lytton Strachey to Jane Strachey, 15 Feb. 1897, HRC.

67. Holroyd, *Lytton Strachey*, 42–8.

68. James Strachey to Jane Strachey, 20 Oct. 1897, IO, Eur F 127/344.

69. James Strachey to Jane Strachey, 5 Feb. 1899, WL, ALC 27 D.

70. H. J. Edin to Jane Strachey, 8 Aug. 1899, WL, ALC 27 D.

71. Mr Colmely to Jane Strachey, 25 Sept. 1899, WL, ALC 27 D.

72. I am very grateful to the archivist of St Paul's School for finding and sending me copies of James's school reports.

5. UNIVERSITY LIFE

1. Barbara Strachey, *The Strachey Line: An English Family in America, in India and at Home, 1570 to 1902* (London: Victor Gollancz, 1985).

2. See C. N. Brooke, *A History of the University of Cambridge* (Cambridge: Cambridge University Press, 1993), 82–91.

3. Ibid. 151–73.

4. Harold Perkin, *The Rise of Professional Society: England since 1880* (London: Routledge, 1989), 369.

5. Brooke, *History of Cambridge*, 151–75.

6. J. M. Compton, 'Open Competition and the Indian Civil Service', *English Historical Review*, 83 (1968), 265–84.

7. Richard Strachey to Jane Strachey, Sept. 1881, IO, Eur F 127/323.

8. Jane Strachey to Lytton Strachey, 15 June 1892, HRC.

9. For some, e.g. Tennyson, it was rather a nightmare! See John Kilham, *Tennyson and* The Princess: *Reflections of an Age* (London: Athlone, 1958).

10. See Barbara Stephen, *Emily Davies and Girton College* (London: Constable & Co, 1927); Rita McWilliams-Tulberg, *Women at Cambridge: A Men's University—Though of Mixed Type* (London: Gollancz, 1975); Barbara Caine, *Victorian Feminists* (New York: Oxford University Press, 1992).

11. Lytton Strachey to James Strachey, 17 Sept. 1910, BL, Add Mss 60708.

12. C. J. Dewey, 'The Education of a Ruling Caste: The Indian Civil Service in the Era of Competitive Examinations', *English Historical Review*, 88 (1973), 262–85.

13. Martha Vicinus, *Independent Women: Work and Community for Single Women, 1850–1920* (Chicago: University of Chicago Press, 1985), 130–5; Caine, *Victorian Feminists*, 98–9.

14. See letters from Oliver Strachey to Jane Strachey, Oct. 1892–Mar. 1893, IO, Eur F 127/133.

15. Jane Strachey to Lytton Strachey, 9 Feb. 1893, HRC.

16. Conversation with Barbara Strachey, 24 Oct. 1997.

17. I am grateful to John Jones, the archivist at Balliol College, for sending me information about the entry on Oliver on the Balliol Register.

18. Arthur Hobhouse was sent on a similar trip some years later when his mother discovered something about his homosexual liaisons at Cambridge—with Lytton and James Strachey, amongst others. See Barbara Caine, *Destined to be Wives: The Sisters of Beatrice Webb* (Oxford and New York: Clarendon Press, 1986).

19. G. Bushnell to Richard Strachey, 18 Aug. 1893, IO, Eur F 127/152.

20. Oliver Strachey to Jane Strachey, 26 May 1896, IO, Eur F 127/337.

21. Jane Strachey to Lytton Strachey, 13 July 1896, HRC.

22. Oliver Strachey to Jane Strachey, 9 Oct. 1896, IO, Eur F 127/337.

23. Jane Strachey to Pippa Strachey, 10 Feb. 1898 , BL, Add Mss 60717.

24. Jane Strachey to Richard Strachey, 16 Oct. 1895, IO, Eur F 127/126.

25. Richard Strachey to Pernel Strachey, 28 Oct. 1895, BL, Add Mss 60729.

26. Oliver Strachey to Pernel Strachey, n.d., BL, Add Mss 60723.

27. For the development of Newnham and for wider discussion of the lives of women at British universities, see McWilliams-Tulberg, *Women at Cambridge*; Carol Dyhouse, *No Distinction of Sex? Women in British Universities, 1870–1939* (London: UCL Press, 1995), and Vicinus, *Independent Women*.

28. See Brooke, *History of Cambridge*, 311–18.

29. Pernel Strachey to Pippa Strachey, 2 Oct. 1895, BL, Add Mss 60724.

30. This was Thena Clough, the niece of the founding principal, Anne Jemima Clough.

31. Pernel Strachey to Pippa Strachey, 2 Oct. 1895, BL, Add Mss 60724.

32. Pernel Strachey to Pippa Strachey, 3 Oct. 1895, BL, Add Mss 60724.

33. Pernel Strachey to Pippa Strachey, 24 Oct. 1895, BL, Add Mss 60724.

34. Pernel Strachey to Dorothy Strachey, 26 Oct. 1897, BL, Add Mss 60724.

35. Pernel Strachey to Pippa Strachey, 2 Nov. 1898, BL, Add Mss 60724.

36. Ralph Strachey to Pippa Strachey, 13 Sept. 1898, ALC, WL.

37. Pernel Strachey to Lytton Strachey, 14 Oct. 1897, BL, Add Mss 60724.

38. Pernel Strachey to Lady Jane Strachey, 3 May 1897, IO, Eur F 127/339.

39. McWilliams-Tulberg, *Women at Cambridge*.

40. Pernel Strachey to Lytton Strachey, 23 Jan. 1898, BL, Add Mss 60724.

41. Jane Strachey to Pernel Strachey, 17 Feb. 1897, BL, Add Mss 60717.

42. Pernel Strachey to Pippa Strachey, 24 Oct. 1895, BL Add Mss 60724.

43. Pernel Strachey to Lady Jane Strachey, 8 Aug. 1897, IO Eur F 127/339.

44. Pernel Strachey to Lytton Strachey, 14 Oct. 1897, BL, Add Mss 60724.

45. Pernel Strachey to Lytton Strachey, 20 Jan. 1898, BL, Add Mss 60724.

46. Pernel Strachey to Pippa Strachey, 20 May 1898, BL, Add Mss 60724.

47. Ibid.

48. Miss J. M. Tuke to Jane Strachey, Newnham, 21 June 1898, IO, Eur F 127/165.

49. Pernel Strachey to Pippa Strachey, 26 Feb. 1899, BL, Add Mss 60725.

50. Pernel Strachey to Lytton Strachey, 4 Nov. 1899, BL, Add Mss 60725.

51. Pernel Strachey to Pippa Strachey, 19 Jan. 1900, BL, Add Mss 60725.

52. Lytton Strachey to Jane Strachey, 3 Oct. 1899, HRC.

53. Cited in Michael Holroyd, *Lytton Strachey* (London: Vintage, 1995), 73.

54. Holroyd, *Lytton Strachey*, 56–74; Robert Skidelsky, *John Maynard Keynes*, i. *Hopes Betrayed, 1883–1920* (Harmondsworth: Penguin Books, 1994), 106–32;

Leonard Woolf, *Sowing: An Autobiography of the Years 1880–1904* (London: Hogarth Press, 1970), 160–95; S. P. Rosenbaum, *Victorian Bloomsbury: The Early Literary History of the Bloomsbury Group* (New York: St Martin's Press, 1987).

55. See Woolf, *Sowing*, 197–9; Phyllis Rose, *Woman of Letters: A Life of Virginia Woolf* (London: Routledge & Kegan Paul, 1978), 21.

56. See Paul Levy, *G. E. Moore and the Cambridge Apostles* (London: Macmillan, 1989); and W. C. Lubenow, *The Cambridge Apostles, 1820–1914: Liberalism, Imagination and Friendship in British Intellectual and Professional Life* (Cambridge: Cambridge University Press, 1998).

57. Holroyd, *Lytton Strachey*, 82.

58. Jane Strachey to Lytton Strachey, 3 Feb. 1902, HRC.

59. Holroyd, *Lytton Strachey*, 81.

60. Warren Hastings was the first governor-general of India, from 1773 to 1784. He exerted British power by removing all powers from the Nawab of Bengal, ended the tribute that the East India Company had been paying to the Mughals, and engaged in a number of wars to extend the sway of the company. In order to fight these wars, he extracted considerable amounts of money from a number of Indian rulers. Hastings's conduct of Indian affairs led to his impeachment in Parliament after he had returned to England in 1784. The prosecution lasted ten years. Hastings was eventually found innocent—but was financially ruined and thus divested of his Indian fortune in the process.

61. Woolf, *Sowing*, 131.

62. Holroyd, *Lytton Strachey*, 91.

63. Woolf, *Sowing*; Jane Strachey to Lytton Strachey, 18 June and 16 July, 1898, HRC.

64. Julie Anne Taddeo, *Lytton Strachey and the Search for Modern Sexual Identity: The Last Eminent Victorian* (Binghamton, NY: Haworth Press, 2002), 15–50.

65. James Strachey to Jane Strachey, 9 Mar. 1906, IO, Eur F 127/345. Lytton was presumably referring to the memoir of the philosopher and Apostle, Henry Sidgwick, written by his brother, Arthur, and his wife Eleanor: *Henry Sidgwick: A Memoir* (London: Macmillan, 1906).

66. See letters from James Strachey to Jane Strachey, IO Eur F 127/345.

67. Lytton Strachey to Leonard Woolf, 25 Oct. 1905, HRC.

68. Lytton Strachey to J. M. K., 21 Nov. 1905, KC.

69. Lytton Strachey to J. M. K., 21 Nov. 1905, KC.

70. For the relationship between Rupert Brooke and James Strachey, see Keith Hale (ed.), *Friends and Apostles: The Correspondence of Rupert Brooke and James Strachey 1905–1914* (New Haven and London: Yale University Press, 1998).

71. Lytton Strachey to Duncan Grant, 6 Mar. 1907, BL, Add Mss 57932.

72. Lytton Strachey to Duncan Grant, 6 Mar. 1907, BL, Add Mss 57932.

73. James Strachey to Lytton Strachey, 9 Aug. 1907, BL, Add Mss 60708.

74. James Strachey to Lytton Strachey, 3 June 1907, BL, Add Mss 60708.

75. Skidelsky, *Keynes*, i. 235.

76. Ibid.

77. Hale, *Friends and Apostles*, 34–5.

78. Ibid.

79. For the history of Royal Holloway, see Caroline Bingham, *The History of Royal Holloway College, 1886–1986* (London: Constable, 1987).

80. Marjorie Strachey to Jane Strachey, 10 Oct. 1902, BL, Add Mss 60722l.

81. Marjorie Strachey to Jane Strachey, 19 Oct. 1902, BL, Add Mss 60722l.

82. Marjorie Strachey to Jane Strachey, 20 Oct. 1904, BL, Add Mss 60722l.

83. Marjorie Strachey to Jane Strachey, 30 Oct. 1904, BL, Add Mss 60722l.

84. Ibid.

85. Marjorie Strachey to Jane Strachey, 6 Nov. 1904, BL, Add Mss 60722l.

86. Marjorie Strachey to Jane Strachey, 9 June 1906, IO, Eur F 127.

6. MODERN MARRIAGES

1. 'Lancaster Gate', in Lytton Strachey, *Lytton Strachey by Himself: A Self-Portrait*, ed. Michael Holroyd (London: Heinemann, 1971).

2. Jane Strachey to Lytton Strachey, 8 Feb. 1903, HRC.

3. Strachey, 'Lancaster Gate', 26–7.

4. Mary Lyndon Shanley, *Feminism, Marriage and the Law in Victorian England, 1850–1895* (Princeton: Princeton University Press, 1989).

5. B. H. Lee, *Divorce Law Reform in England* (London: Owen, 1974); Lawrence Stone, *Road to Divorce: England 1530–1987* (Oxford and New York: Oxford University Press, 1990). Although it was not until 1923 that the Child Custody Act recognized mothers as custodians, divorce cases prior to this even amongst Anglo-Indians show a preparedness amongst judges to allow women access. See e.g. IO, Eur E 333/17.

6. Richard Strachey, *A Strachey Child* (Oxford: privately published, 1979), 7–13.

7. John Tosh, *A Man's Place: Masculinity and the Middle-Class Home in Victorian England* (New Haven: Yale University Press, 1999).

8. Jane Strachey to Ralph Strachey, 3 Feb. 1882, IO, Eur F 127/443.

9. He was also active in British local government, as a member of the Metropolitan Asylums Board and for many years chair of the Kensington Board.

10. Conversation with Frances Partridge, 27 Oct. 1997.

11. Elinor Rendel to Jane Strachey, 12 Mar. 1912, IO, Eur F 127/324.

12. James Rendel to Jane Strachey, 20 Mar. 1908, IO Eur F 127/324.

13. Jane and Richard Strachey Wills, IO, Eur F 127/288.

14. Dorothy Bussy to André Gide, 5 Aug. 1931, Correspondence of Dorothy Bussy and André Gide, BN, NAF 15631.

15. Jane Strachey to Pippa Strachey, 18 Nov. 1883, BL, Add Mss 60717.

16. Ray Costelloe described a suffrage meeting at 'sister Rendel's' in a letter to her family on 26 Oct. 1912, LL.

17. Elinor Rendel to Jane Strachey, 16 Nov. 1919, IO, Eur F 127/324.

18. Dick Strachey to Jane Strachey, 16 Sept. 1892, IO, Eur F 127/327.

19. Dick Strachey to Jane Strachey, 10 Feb. 1895, IO, Eur F 127/328.

20. Dick Strachey to Richard Strachey, 24 May 1897, IO, Eur F 127/131.

21. Grace Norman to Jane Strachey, 14 Feb. 1867, IO, Eur F 127/328.

22. Grace Strachey to Jane Strachey, Abbingdon (n.d.), IO, Eur F 127/328.

23. Grace Strachey to Jane Strachey, 2 Jan. 1916, IO, Eur F 127/328.

24. Oliver Strachey to Richard Strachey, 22 Aug. 1900, IO, Eur F 127/133.

25. Ralph Strachey to Pippa Strachey, 23 Aug. 1900, WL, ALC 27 B 2.

26. Strachey, *Strachey Childhood*, 10–12.

27. Ibid. 16.

28. Pippa Strachey to Jane Strachey, 31 Oct. 1901, BL, Add Mss 60727.

29. Pippa Strachey to Jane Strachey, 7 Nov. 1901, BL Add Mss 60727.

30. Ralph Strachey to Pippa Strachey, 24 Nov. 1905, WL, ALC 27 B 2.

31. Diary of Ray Strachey, 25 June 1924, LL.

32. Dorothy Bussy to André Gide, 5 July 1921, in Richard Tedeschi (ed.), *Selected Letters of André Gide and Dorothy Bussy* (New York: Oxford University Press, 1983), 71.

33. Pernel Strachey to Pippa Strachey, 6 Jan. 1892, WL, ALC 27 D.

34. Dorothy Bussy to André Gide, July 1921, in Tedeschi, *Letters*, 71–4.

35. Pernel Strachey to Lytton Strachey, 4 Nov. 1899, BL, Add Mss 60725.

36. Dorothy Strachey to Pippa Strachey, 21 Nov. 1901, BL, Add Mss 19909.

37. Pernel Strachey to Pippa Strachey, 8 July 1902, BL Add Mss 60725.

38. See Phillipe Loisel, *Simon Bussy (1870–1954) L'Esprit du trait: du zoo à la gentry* (Paris: Somogy d'éditions d'Art, 1996).

39. Dorothy Bussy to Richard Strachey, 15 May 1903, BL, Add Mss 60661.

40. Dorothy Bussy to Jane Strachey, 6 June 1903, BL, Add Mss 60661.

41. Ibid.

42. Lytton Strachey to Leonard Woolf, Wed. 25th (1902), HRC.

43. Lytton Strachey to Leonard Woolf, 18 Apr. 1904, HRC.

44. Dorothy Bussy to André Gide, 5 July 1921, in Tedeschi, *Letters*, 74.

45. Zoum Walter, *Pour Sylvie* (Paris: Jaques Antoine, 1975), 65.

46. Ibid. 166.

47. See e.g. Alan, Sheridan, *André Gide: A Life in the Present* (London: Hamish Hamilton, 1998).

48. Jean Lambert, 'Introduction', in Tedeschi, *Letters*, p. xix.

49. Eric Marty, 'Gide at Dorothy Bussy', in Patrick Pollard (ed.), *André Gide et l'Angleterre* (Birkbeck: Le Colloque Gide, 1986), 87–94.

50. Oliver Strachey to Pernel Strachey, 8 Mar. 1900, BL, Add Mss 60723.

51. Ibid.

52. Oliver Strachey to Pernel Strachey, 10 Apr. 1900, BL, Add Mss 60723.

53. Ralph Strachey to Pippa Strachey, 22 Oct. 1908, WL, ALC 27 C.

54. James Strachey to Lytton Strachey, 9 Nov. 1908, BL, Add Mss 60707.

55. Oliver Strachey to Pippa Strachey, 20 Jan. 1909, WL, ALC 27 C.

56. Ruby Strachey to Pippa Strachey, 7 Jan. 1909, WL, ALC 276.

57. See Jane Strachey to Jack Strachey, 23 Oct. 1909, IO, Eur F 127/483. This whole file deals with Oliver's divorce and the family's concerns about its consequences.

58. See Frances Partridge and Julia Strachey, *Julia* (London: Gollancz, 1983); and Barbara Strachey, *Remarkable Relations: The Story of the Pearsall Smith Women* (New York: Universe Books, 1982). For a discussion of Ray as a mother in regard to her own two children, Barbara and Christopher, see Johanna Alberti, *Beyond Suffrage: Feminists in War and Peace, 1914–28* (Basingstoke: Macmillan, 1989).

59. Ruby Hunter to Julia Strachey, 25 Mar. 1932, UCL.

60. Ruby Hunter to Julia Strachey, 21 Nov. 1934, UCL.

61. See e.g. Ray Costelloe to her family, 9 Dec. 1906, LL.

62. Ray Costelloe to Oliver Strachey, 5 May 1911, LL.

63. Oliver Strachey to Karen Costelloe, 18 May 1911, LL.

64. Ray Strachey to Karen Costelloe, 18 May 1911, LL.

65. Jane Strachey to Elinor Colevile, 19 May 1911, IO, Eur F 127/83.

66. Mary Berenson to Alys Russell and Logan Pearsall Smith, 17 Oct. 1911, in Barbara Strachey and Jayne Samuels (eds.), *Mary Berenson: A Self-Portrait from her Letters and Diaries* (London: Hamish Hamilton, 1983), 173–4.

67. Mary Berenson to Bernard Berenson, 2 July 1913, in Strachey and Samuels, *Mary Berenson*, 190–1.

68. Mary Berenson to Alys Russell, 22 May 1914, in Strachey and Samuels, *Mary Berenson*, 196.

69. Ray Strachey to Oliver Strachey, 25 May 1911, LL.

70. Alys Russell to Mary Berenson, 26 Feb. (no year given, however it was shortly after the birth of Barbara Strachey, so presumably 1912), UCL.

71. See e.g. Ray Strachey to Mary Berenson, 9 July 1911, LL.

72. Oliver Strachey to Jane Strachey, 12 May 1912, IO, Eur F 127/338.

73. Oliver Strachey and Ray Strachey, *Keigwin's Rebellion (1863–4)* (Oxford: Clarendon Press, 1916). The book was vol. 6 in a series of Oxford Historical and Literary Studies issued under the direction of C. H. Firth and Walter Raleigh (who was a relative of the Stracheys).

74. Ray Strachey to Mary Berenson, 7 Jan. 1917, LL.

75. Ray Strachey to Pippa Strachey, 7 July 1921, BL, Add Mss 60729.

76. Conversation with Barbara Strachey, 24 Oct. 1997.

77. Diary of Ray Strachey, 24 March 1924, LL.

78. Diary of Ray Strachey, 22 July 1929, LL.

79. Ray Strachey to Mary Berenson, 8 Apr. 1928, LL.

80. Ray wrote to her mother every two or three days and described her daily life in considerable detail. See the letters from Ray Strachey to Mary Berenson throughout the 1920s and 1930s, LL.

81. Strachey and Samuels, *Mary Berenson*, 256–87. Ray described the Berenson difficulties in some detail in her letters to Pippa. See BL, Add Mss 60729.

82. Diary of Ray Strachey, 2 June 1929, LL.

83. See Pippa Harris (ed.), *Songs of Love: The Letters of Rupert Brooke and Noel Olivier* (London: Crown, 1991), 101–46.

84. Their relationship is clearly documented in her letters to James which he assiduously kept. See BL, Add Mss 60684–9.

85. For Alix Strachey see Barbara Caine, 'The Stracheys and Psychoanalysis', *History Workshop Journal*, 45 (1998), 145–69; Perry Meisel and Walter Kendrick (eds.), *Bloomsbury/Freud: The Letters of James and Alix Strachey 1924–1925* (London: Chatto & Windus, 1986), 8–11; and Lisa Appignanesi and John Forrester, *Freud's Women* (London: Virago, 1993), 352–71.

86. Meisel and Kendrick, *Bloomsbury/Freud*, 25.

87. See BL, Add Mss 65158.

88. Dora Carrington to Lytton Strachey, 29 Mar. (1918), BL, Add Mss 65158.

89. Dora Carrington to Alix Strachey, 9 Oct. 1920, BL, Add Mss 65158.

90. Virginia Woolf's Diary, 18 May 1920, in Anne Olivier Bell (ed.), *A Moment's Liberty: The Shorter Diary of Virginia Woolf* (London: Hogarth Press, 1990).

91. Alix to James Strachey, Lord's Wood, Marlow, 24 Sept. (no year but presumably 1922, as James was travelling in Germany with Lytton), BL, Add Mss 60701, 224.

92. Many of these letters have been published in Meisel and Kendrick, *Bloomsbury/Freud*.

93. Alix Strachey to James Strachey, 11 Sept. 1925, BL, Add Mss 60703.

94. Alix Strachey to James Strachey, 25 Nov. 1924, BL, Add Mss 60702.

95. Frances Partridge suggests that 'Nancy M' was Nancy Morris, the sister of Sir Cedric Morris. Letter from Frances Partridge to the author, 9 Mar. 1997.

96. Carrington's Diary, entries for 12 and 20 Jan. 1928, BL, Add Mss 65159.

97. Frances Partridge, *Memories* (London: Phoenix, 1988), 223.

98. James Strachey to Noel Olivier, 3 Aug. 1938, BL, Add Mss 60716.

99. Noel Olivier to James Strachey, 18 June 1935, BL, Add Mss 60686.

100. Few of James's letters survive, but one can chart the relationship through Noel's letters to him. BL, Add Mss 60686–8.

101. There was some tension involved in finalizing the Freud translations after James's death. This is detailed in a number of letters to and from Alix in the Correspondence Files at the British Institute of Psychoanalysis, see CSC/F18/01–19 and CSF/F04/05–35. Alix also seems to have taken on James's concern about Angela Richards. She left her £2,000 as well as her radiogram, records, and tapes. See Papers of Alix Strachey, BIP, Box 4 'Wills and Codicils'.

7. SINGLE LIFE

1. Martha Vicinus, *Independent Women: Work and Community for Single Women, 1850–1920* (Chicago: University of Chicago Press, 1985); Barbara Caine, *Victorian Feminists* (New York: Oxford University Press, 1992), 20–42.

2. 'The Spinster by One', *The Freewoman* (23 Nov. 1911), cited in Leonore Davidoff, Megan Doolittle, Janet Fink, and Katherine Holden, *The Family Story: Blood, Contract and Intimacy, 1830–1960* (London and New York: Longman, 1999), 221; see also Lucy Bland, *Banishing the Beast, English Feminism and Sexual Morality* (Harmondsworth: Penguin, 1995).

3. Jane Strachey to James Strachey, 13 Feb. 1914, BL, Add Mss 60719.

4. Pamela Diamand (née Fry); Hugh Lee and Michael Holroyd, *A Cezanne in the Hedge and Other Memories of Charleston and Bloomsbury* (Chicago: University of Chicago Press, 1992), 58.

5. Jane Strachey to Lytton Strachey, 22 July 1899, HRC.

6. Dorothy Bussy to Pippa Strachey, 2 June 1903, WL, ALC

7. Dorothy Bussy to Pippa Strachey, 20 Oct. 1892, WL, ALC.

8. Dorothy Bussy to Pippa Strachey, 19 Oct. 1892, WL, ALC.

9. Pippa Strachey to Jane Strachey, 14 May 1896, IO, Eur F 127/335.

10. Jane Strachey to Pippa Strachey, l7 May 1896, BL, Add Mss 60717.

11. Pippa Strachey to Roger Fry, 20 Oct. 1918, WL, ALC.

12. Pippa Strachey to Jane Strachey (dated just 'Easter Monday', but written in the holiday Pippa had at La Souco from Apr. to May 1928), IO, Eur F 127/336.

13. Janie Bussy to Pippa Strachey (the letter is undated, but it is possible that it was written in 1932, shortly after Lytton Strachey's death), BL, Add Mss 60661.

14. Pippa Strachey to Jane Strachey, 1 Apr. 1913, IO, Eur F 127/336. Pippa does not name the man.

15. Mary Stocks, *My Commonplace Book* (London: Peter Davies, 1970), 13.

16. Lytton Strachey to Leonard Woolf, 15 Feb. 1904, HRC.

17. Roger Fry to Pippa Strachey, 16 June 1915, WL.

18. Frances Spalding, *Roger Fry: Art and Life* (London and New York: Elek, 1980).

19. Pippa Strachey to Roger Fry, 25 Aug. 1916, WL, ALC.

20. Diaries of Ray Strachey, Mar. 1924, LL

21. Pippa Strachey to Roger Fry, 21 Nov. 1915, WL.

22. Pippa Strachey to Jane Strachey, 26 June 1928, IO, Eur F 127/336.

23. Diaries of Ray Strachey, 31 May 1929, LL.

24. Vicinus, *Independent Women*, 38–40.

25. See Michael Holroyd, *Lytton Strachey* (London: Vintage, 1995), 214–15.

26. See Pernel Strachey to Lytton Strachey, 9 Nov. 1901 and 6 Aug. 1915, and Pernel Strachey to Jane Strachey, 19 Aug., no year, BL, Add Mss 60726.

27. E. E. Duncan-Jones, '1929', in Anne Phillips (ed.), *A Newnham Anthology* (Cambridge: Cambridge University Press, 1979), 173.

28. Entry for 3 Sept. 1918, Virginia Woolf, *The Diary of Virginia Woolf*, ed. Anne Olivier Bell, i (Harmondsworth: Penguin Books, 1979), 189.

29. See Mary Beard, *The Invention of Jane Harrison* (Cambridge, Mass.: Harvard University Press, 2000); Annabel Robinson, *The Life and Work of Jane Harrison* (New York: Oxford University Press, 2002).

30. Quentin Bell, *Elders and Betters* (London: John Murray, 1995), 153–4.

31. Jane Strachey to Pippa Strachey, 18 Apr. 1908, BL, Add Mss 60717.

32. Jane Strachey to James Strachey, 4 Sept. 1913, BL, Add Mss 60717.

33. Dorothy Bussy to Jane Strachey, 30 Oct. 1905, IO, Eur F 127/331.

34. Entry for 12 Mar. 1919, Virginia Woolf, *Diary*, ed. Anne Olivier Bell, i (Harmondsworth: Penguin Books, 1977), 252.

35. Pernel Strachey to Lytton Strachey, 6 Aug. 1915, BL, Add Mss 60726.

36. James Strachey to Alix Strachey, n.d. (Dec. 1924), BL, Add Mss 60714.

37. Ibid.

38. Entry for 13 Dec. 1924, Virginia Woolf, *Diary*, ed. Anne Olivier Bell, ii (Harmondsworth: Penguin Books, 1978), 323.

39. Ray Strachey to Mary Berenson, 11 Mar. 1929, LL.

40. See particularly Julie Anne Taddeo, *Lytton Strachey and the Search for Modern Sexual Identity: The Last Eminent Victorian* (Binghamton, NY: Haworth Press, 2002); and Holroyd, *Lytton Strachey*.

41. Lytton Strachey to James Strachey, 19 May 1904, BL, Add Mss 60706.

42. Lytton Strachey to James Strachey, 3 Oct. 1912, and 30 Oct. 1905, BL, Add Mss 60708.

43. Lytton Strachey to James Strachey, 9 Apr. 1909, BL, Add Mss 60707.

44. Lytton Strachey to Leonard Woolf, 22 May 1906, BC.

45. Lytton Strachey to Leonard Woolf, 16 Jan. 1907, BC.

46. Holroyd, *Lytton Strachey*, 408.

47. Ibid. 401.

48. Woolf, *Diary*, i. 236.

49. Holroyd, *Lytton Strachey*, part 4.

50. L. Woolf, *Diary*, ed. Anne Olivier Bell, iii (Harmondsworth: Penguin Books, 1980), 108, 130.

8. SIBLING TIES

1. The person who used this language most extensively was Pernel. See her letters in BL, Add Mss 60724.

2. Frances Spalding, *Duncan Grant: A Biography* (London: Pimlico, 1998), 20.

3. Dorothy Strachey to André Gide, 8 Sept. 1946, BN, NAF 15631.

4. Frank Sulloway, *Born to Rebel: Birth Order, Family Dynamics, and Creative Lives* (New York: Pantheon Books, 1996).

5. Alfred Adler, *Understanding Human Nature* (Oxford: One World, 1992; 1927).

6. Sulloway, *Born to Rebel*, 95–9.

7. Juliet Mitchell, *Mad Men and Medusas: Reclaiming Hysteria and the Effect of Sibling Relations on the Human Condition* (London: Penguin, 2000).

8. For more discussion of this issue, see George Behlmer, *Child Abuse and Moral Reform in England, 1870–1908* (Stanford, Calif.: Stanford University Press, 1982)

9. See Spalding, *Duncan Grant*, 11–14.

10. Richard Strachey to Jane Strachey, 15 Mar. 1878, IO, Eur F 127/321.

11. Richard Strachey's letters to the press and to prominent individuals are all in the Strachey Papers. IO EUR F 127/149

12. Richard Strachey to Jane Strachey, 1 Mar. (1877/8?), IO, Eur F 127/321.

13. For a description of the Strachey drawing room at Lancaster Gate as a 'family room' designed to contain the extended family that gathered there every Sunday afternoon, see 'Lancaster Gate' in Lytton Strachey, *Lytton Strachey by Himself: A Self-Portrait*, ed. Michael Holroyd (London: Heinemann, 1971), 22. On the importance of extended family to the older Stracheys, see Barbara Strachey, *The Strachey Line*, 120–70.

14. James Strachey to Lytton Strachey, 20 Mar. 1911, BL, Add Mss 60708.

15. James Strachey to Lytton Strachey, 22 Mar. 1911, BL, Add Mss 60708.

16. James Strachey to Lytton Strachey, 14 May 1912, BL, Add Mss 60709.

17. The nature of Dorothy's close relationship with Elinor is set out most clearly in her letters to André Gide. BN, NAF 15630–1.

18. James Strachey to Lytton Strachey, 4 Jan. 1915, BL, Add Mss 60708.

19. See e.g. Lytton Strachey to Dorothy Bussy, 25 Feb. 1909 and 12 Nov. 1930, PUL.

20. James Strachey to Lytton Strachey, 13 June 1911, BL, Add Mss 60709.

21. James Strachey to Lytton Strachey, 2 Dec. 1913, BL, Add Mss 60709.

22. Dora Carrington to Lytton Strachey, 26 Oct. 1920, BL, Add Mss 62891. Inez Ferguson was Oliver's current mistress.

23. Dora Carrington to Lytton Strachey, 1 Nov. 1920, BL, Add Mss 62891.

24. Julie Anne Taddeo, *Lytton Strachey and the Search for Modern Sexual Identity: The Last Eminent Victorian* (Binghamton, NY: Haworth Press, 2002).

25. Lytton Strachey to Dorothy Bussy, 22 Oct. 1931, and Dorothy Bussy to Lytton Strachey, 30 Oct. 1931, PUL.

26. Dorothy Bussy to André Gide, 18 Sept. 1919, in Richard Tedeschi (ed.), *Selected Letters of André Gide and Dorothy Bussy* (New York: Oxford University Press, 1983), 31.

27. See Lytton Strachey to Dorothy Bussy, 22 Nov. 1921, PUL.

28. Margaret Strachey to James Strachey, n.d., BL, Add Mss 60722.

29. Pippa Strachey to Roger Fry, Aug. 1917, WL, ALC.

30. Lytton Strachey to James Strachey, 17 Sept. 1910, BL, Add Mss 60708.

31. The importance of Pippa in Lytton's life is made particularly clear in his letters to James Strachey from about 1905–13. See BL Add Mss 60706 and 60707.

32. Pippa Strachey to Roger Fry, n.d. (early 1918), WL, ALC.

33. Pippa Strachey to Lytton Strachey, 25 Feb. 1919, BL, Add Mss 60728.

34. Lytton Strachey to Pippa Strachey, 27 Feb. 1919, BL, Add Mss 60721.

35. Pippa Strachey to Lytton Strachey, 3 Mar. 1919, BL, Add Mss 60728.

36. Leonore Davidoff and Catherine Hall, *Family Fortunes: Men and Women of the English Middle Class 1780–1850* (London: Routledge, 1992).

37. Lytton Strachey to Dorothy Bussy, 5 Feb. 1929, PUL.

38. Duncan Grant to Lytton Strachey, 9 Feb. 1906, BL, Add Mss 57933.

39. Jane Dunn, *Virginia Woolf and Vanessa Bell: A Very Close Conspiracy* (London: Cape, 1990).

40. Frances Partridge, *Everything to Lose: Diaries 1945–1960* (London: Gollancz, 1985), 306.

41. J. D. Schvaneveldt and M. Ihinger, 'Sibling Relationships in the Family', in W. R. Burr, R. Hill, F. I. Nye, and I. L. Reiss (eds.), *Contemporary Theories about the Family*, i (New York: Free Press, 1970), 367–453.

42. Thomas H. Powell and Peggy Ahrenhold Gallagher, *Brothers and Sisters: A Special Part of Exceptional Families* (London: Paule Brookes Publishing Co., 1993), 16–19.

9. WORK, INCOME, AND CHANGING CAREER PATTERNS

1. 'Lancaster Gate', in Lytton Strachey, *Lytton Strachey by Himself: A Self-Portrait*, ed. Michael Holroyd (London: Heinemann, 1971).

2. 'Colonel Richard Strachey', *Who was Who*, iii (London: Adam and Charles Black, 1967).

3. J. A. Banks, *Prosperity and Parenthood: A Study of Family Planning among the Victorian Middle Classes* (London: Routledge & K. Paul, 1969).

4. See W. N. Shaw, 'Sir Richard Strachey, G.C.S.I., F.R.S.', *Nature* (27 Feb. 1908), 373–95; and the collection of documents entitled 'Correspondence and Papers on Honours', IO, Eur F 127/180.

5. See the copy of the Report by the Committee on the International Congress at Washington, 1884, IO, Eur F 127/188.

6. See folder, 'Royal Geographical Society', IO, Eur F 127/190.

7. James E. McClellan and Harold Dorn, *Science and Technology in World History: An Introduction* (Baltimore: Johns Hopkins University Press, 1988).

8. See e.g. Shaw, 'Sir Richard Strachey'.

9. See 'Sir Richard Strachey', *Dictionary of National Biography* (Supplement, Jan. 1901–Dec. 1911), 439–42.

10. Dick Strachey to Richard Strachey, 17 Nov. 1884, IO, Eur F 127/131.

11. Dick Strachey to Richard Strachey, 9 May 1887, IO, Eur F 127/131.

12. See T. A. Heathcote, *Indian Army: The Garrison of British Imperial India, 1822–1922* (Newton Abbot: David & Charles, 1974).

13. Dick Strachey to Richard Strachey, 3 June 1881, IO, Eur F 127/131.

14. Dick Strachey to Richard Strachey, 26 Feb. 1899, IO, Eur F 127/131.

15. Richard Strachey, *A Strachey Child* (London: Owen, 1979), 22.

16. Dick Strachey to Richard Strachey, 2 June 1887, IO, Eur F 127/131.

17. Ibid.

18. Dick Strachey to Jane Strachey, 3 Mar. 1889, Eur F 127/326.

19. Dick Strachey to Jane Strachey, 10 Apr. 1889, IO, Eur F 127/326.

20. Dick Strachey to Jane Strachey, 15 May 1915, IO, Eur F 127/329.

21. Grace Strachey to Jane Strachey, 2 Jan. 1916, IO, Eur F 127/329.

22. Dick Strachey to Jane Strachey, 12 Nov. 1919, IO Eur F 127/329.

23. See Dick Strachey to Jane Strachey, 15 May 1915, IO, Eur F 127/329.

24. Dick Strachey to Pippa Strachey, 24 Oct. 1917, WL, ALC 27 C.

25. Pippa Strachey to Lytton Strachey, 19 Feb. 1927, BL, Add Mss 60728.

26. Ralph Strachey to Pippa Strachey, 23 Aug. 1900, WL, ALC 27 B 2.

27. Ralph Strachey to Pippa Strachey, 23 July 1894, WL, ALC 27 B 2.

28. Ralph Strachey to Pippa Strachey, n.d., letter number 35, WL, ALC 27 B 2.

29. Ralph Strachey to Pippa Strachey, 24 Mar. 1900, WL, ALC 27 B 2.

30. Ralph Strachey to Pippa Strachey, 12 Mar. 1896, WL, ALC 27 B 2.

31. Ralph Strachey to Pippa Strachey, Sept. 1894, WL, ALC 27 B 2.

32. Ralph Strachey to Jane Strachey, 29 May 1913, IO, Eur F 127/333.

33. Oliver Strachey to Lytton Strachey, 2 Feb. 1899, BL Add MSS 60723.

34. Oliver Strachey to Jane Strachey, 5 Oct. 1899, BC Add MSS 60723.

35. Oliver Strachey to Jane Strachey, 16 Mar. 1895, BL, Add Mss 60723.

36. Oliver Strachey to Pernel Strachey, Allahabad, Nov. 1899, BL, Add Mss 60723.

37. Oliver Strachey to Lytton Strachey, 11 July 1907, BL, Add Mss 60723.

38. Ralph Strachey to Pippa Strachey, 1 Jan. 1903, BL Add Mss 60723.

39. Ray Strachey to Mary Berenson, 20 May 1912, LL.

40. It is hard not to believe that the Strachey family connection with Professor Walter Raleigh, one of the directors of the series, had something to do with this.

41. Ray Strachey to Lady Strachey, 27 Sept. 1914, IO, Eur F 127/338.

42. Dick Strachey to Pippa Strachey, 18 Sept. 1916, BL, Add Mss 60729.

43. Jane Strachey to Elinor Colevile, 12 Dec. 1916 and 27 Dec. 1917, IO, Eur F 127/83.

44. Peter Twinn, 'The Abwehr Enigma', in F. H. Hinsley and Alan Stripp (eds.), *The Inside Story of Bletchley Park* (Oxford: Oxford University Press, 1994), 123–5.

45. See A. G. Denniston, 'The Government Code and Cypher School between the Wars', *Intelligence and National Security*, 1/1 (1986), 48–70; David Kahn, *Seizing the Enigma: The Race to Break the German U-Boat Codes, 1939–1943* (Chatham: Souvenir Press, 1991), 82–8.

46. Henry Dryden, 'Recollections of Bletchley Park', in Hinsley and Stripp, *Bletchley Park*, and Enigma transcripts in the Public Record office suggest that language-based decoding at Bletchley Park continued to appear under the title of ISOS even after Oliver left in 1943.

47. Ray Strachey to Jane Strachey, 27 Sept. 1914, IO, Eur F 127/338.

48. Ray Strachey to Mary Berenson, 8 Apr. 1924, LL.

49. Barbara Strachey, *Remarkable Relations: The Story of the Pearsall Smith Women* (New York: Universe Books, 1982).

50. Ray Strachey to Mary Berenson, 8 Apr. 1924, LL.

51. Strachey, *Remarkable Relations*, 299.

52. Ray wrote to her mother two or three times per week, and there are very few letters which do not deal either with cheques received, money needed, or purchases made.

53. See Ray Strachey to Bernard Berenson, 18 Dec. 1920; Ray Strachey to Mary Berenson, 25 Jan. 1921; and Ray Strachey to Bernard Berenson, 10 Jan. 1922, LL.

54. Ibid.

55. Strachey, *Remarkable Relations*, 297–9.

56. Ibid. 299–300; and letters from Ray Strachey to Mary Berenson throughout 1932: see in particular, 26 May 1932, LL. Ray frequently mentioned her radio broadcasts in the early 1930s. See Ray Strachey to Christopher Strachey, 25 Feb. 1932, in which she talks of having to sit up all night to write a programme for which she was paid £8.8.0. The BBC archives have no record of these broadcasts so it is not possible to establish precisely how many there were.

57. Other instances of the ways in which imperialism empowered British women are discussed in Nupur Chaudhuri and Margaret Stroble (eds.), *Western Women and Imperialism; Complicity and Resistance* (Bloomington: Indiana University Press, 1992); Antoinette Burton, *Burdens of History: British Feminists, Indian Women, and Imperial Culture, 1865–1915* (Chapel Hill, NC: University of North Carolina Press, 1994) and Julia Bush, *Edwardian Ladies and Imperial Power* (London: Leicester University Press, 2000).

58. Trevor Grant was her mother's brother and her travelling companion for part of this trip.

59. Pippa Strachey to Richard Strachey, 2 Nov. 1900, BL, Add Mss 60653.

60. Pippa Strachey to Richard and Jane Strachey, 14 Mar. 1901, BL, Add Mss 60653.

61. Pippa Strachey to Jane Strachey, 27 Mar. 1901, BL, Add Mss 60727.

62. Pippa Strachey to Jane Strachey, 8 May 1901, BL, Add Mss 60727.

63. Pippa Strachey to Jane Strachey, 25 Jan. 1901, BL, Add Mss 60727.

64. Pippa Strachey to Jane Strachey, 18 July 1901, BL, Add Mss 60727.

65. Testimonial dated 15 Dec. 1904, BL, Add Mss 60717. There is a letter in the Strachey Papers in which Sir John makes clear its origin. 'Here is the testimonial—except that I have added a few adjectives. It is the same as your draft no 1. It is, I suppose, wise to speak only of business capacity for if I were to say that Pippa is an angel of goodness it might make my testimonial

suspected of partiality.' Sir John Strachey to Jane Strachey, 15 Dec. 1904, IO, Eur F 127/349.

66. Speech at a dinner in honour of Pippa held in June 1951; Papers of Pippa Strachey, WL.

67. Jill Liddington and Jill Norris, *One Hand Tied Behind: The Rise of the Women's Suffrage Movement* (London: Virago, 1978).

68. Nancy Astor to Philippa Strachey, 29 Aug. 1953, Papers of Philippa Strachey, WL.

69. Entry for 3 Sept. 1918, Virginia Woolf, *The Diary of Virginia Woolf*, ed. Anne Olivier Bell, i (Harmondsworth: Penguin Books, 1979), 188.

70. See St Elizabeth, Abbess of Schonau, *Poem on the Assumption*, ed. J. P. Strachey (Cambridge: Cambridge Anglo-Norman Texts, 1924). Some of her lecture notes are included in the papers of Pernel Strachey at the Women's Library.

71. Clara D. Rackham, 'Joan Pernel Strachey, 1875–1951', *Newnham College Roll* (Jan. 1951), 32.

72. The election process is described in some detail in the Minutes of the Governing Body of Newnham College for 26 Jan., 27 Feb., 15 Mar. 1923, Newnham College Archives.

73. Several members of the college wrote to Jane Strachey to express their delight. See in particular Katherine Stephen to Jane Strachey, 16 Mar. 1923, and Fanny Stanley to Jane Strachey, 18 Mar. 1923, IO, Eur F 127/372.

74. See Minutes of Meetings of the Governing Board of Newnham College, 29 May 1936; 28 Jan. 1938; 1 Dec. 1939, NC.

75. This matter was the subject of a special meeting of the governing board. See Report of the Special Meeting of the Governing Board of Newnham College, 7 Mar. 1941, NC.

76. See Report of the Special Meeting of the Governing Board of Newnham College, 24 Nov. 1922, NC.

77. Pernel Strachey to J. M. Keynes, 9 May 1937, KC, PP/45/318/2.

78. E. E. Duncan-Jones, '1929', in Anne Phillips (ed.), *A Newnham Anthology* (Cambridge: Cambridge University Press for Newnham College, 1979), 174.

79. Ibid. 173.

80. Dorothy Strachey to Jane Strachey, 11 July 1888, IO, Eur F 127/331.

81. Pippa Strachey to Pernel Strachey, 6 Nov. 1895, BL, Add Mss 60653.

82. Marjorie Strachey to Jane Strachey, 1 Oct. 1913, IO, Eur F 127/343.

83. Marjorie Strachey to Jane Strachey, 19 Apr. 1916, IO, Eur F 127/343.

84. Marjorie Strachey to Jane Strachey, 12 Dec. 1916, IO, Eur F 127/343.

85. Marjorie Strachey to Jane Strachey, 9 Sept. 1917, IO, Eur F 127/343.

86. Marjorie Strachey to Jane Strachey, 16 Sept. 1917, IO, Eur F 127/343.

87. See letters from Marjorie Strachey to Jane Strachey throughout 1913 and 1914, IO, Eur F 127/343.

88. Quentin Bell, *Elders and Betters* (London: John Murray, 1995), 153.

89. Michael Holroyd, *Lytton Strachey* (London: Vintage, 1995), 122.

90. Quoted Ibid.

91. Ibid. 168.

92. Lytton Strachey to Leonard Woolf, 16 Jan. 1907, BC.

93. Holroyd, *Lytton Strachey*, 427.

94. See correspondence between Lytton Strachey and Maynard Keynes, Jan. 1920 to Jan. 1922, KC, JMK/pp/45/316-5.

95. St Loe Strachey to James Strachey, 30 Sept. 1909, BL, Add Mss 60738.

96. James Strachey to Lytton Strachey, 14 Apr. 1910, BL Add Mss 60707.

97. In 1912, the Society for Psychical Research elected Freud as an honorary member and included in its proceedings for that year a paper he wrote in English, 'A Note on the Unconscious in Psychoanalysis'. See Ricardo Steiner, 'To Explain our Point of View to English Readers', *International Review of Psychoanalysis*, 18 (1991), 352–3.

98. Alix Sargent-Florence to Mary Sargent-Florence 7 June 1914, BL, Add Mss 60701, 72.

99. A. A. Brill, *The Interpretation of Dreams* (New York: Macmillan, 1913).

100. Perry Meisel and Walter Kendrick (eds.), *Bloomsbury/Freud: The Letters of James and Alix Strachey 1924–1925* (London: Chatto & Windus, 1986), 29–30.

101. James Strachey to Ernest Jones, 18 Apr. 1920, BIP, CSD/F03/01.

102. Freud to James Strachey, 7 June 1920, Meisel and Kendrick, *Bloomsbury/Freud*, 28–9.

103. James Strachey to Lytton Strachey, 6 Nov. 1920, BL, Add Mss 60712.

104. Sigmund Freud to Ernest Jones, 14 July 1921, in R. A. Paskauskas (ed.), *The Complete Correspondence of Sigmund Freud and Ernest Jones 1908–1939* (Cambridge, Mass.: Harvard University Press, 1993), 431. 'Queer' in this context means strange.

105. Ernest Jones to Sigmund Freud, 5 Dec. 1927, in Paskauskas, *Complete Correspondence*, 638.

106. Brett Kahr, *D. W. Winnicott: A Biographical Portrait* (London: Karnac, 1996).

107. See D. W. Winnicott, 'James Strachey, 1887–1967', *International Journal of Psycho-Analysis*, 50/129 (1969), 131; Pearl King and Ricardo Steiner (eds.), *The Freud–Klein Controversies 1941–45* (London: Tavistock/Routledge, 1993).

108. James Strachey, untitled, in *The British Psycho-Analytical Society Fiftieth Anniversary* (London: privately printed, Mansfield House, 1963), 22–4.

109. See letters from Bion and others in James Strachey's papers, BIP, CSF/F09/28.

110. Martin James to James Strachey, 11 Dec. 1963, BIP, CSF/F09/28.

111. Winnicott, 'James Strachey', 130–1.

112. This is shown clearly in Kendrick and Meisel, *Bloomsbury/Freud*. But see also Peter Gay, *Freud: A Life for our Time* (London: J. M. Dent & Sons, 1995), 461–8; and Lisa Appignanesi and John Forrester, *Freud's Women* (London: Virago, 1993), 352–71.

113. There is no documentation concerning Alix's patients. Frances Partridge, who shared the Stracheys' house for many years, however, recalls that Alix had two patients. Letter to the author from Frances Partridge, 4 Mar. 1997.

114. Alix Strachey, *The Unconscious Motives of War* (London: George Allen & Unwin, 1957).

10. GENDER TRANSFORMATIONS AND THE QUESTION OF SEXUALITY

1. See e.g. Elaine Showalter, *Sexual Anarchy: Gender and Culture at the Fin de Siècle* (London: Virago, 1992); Lesley A. Hall, *Sex, Gender and Social Change in Britain since 1880* (New York: St Martin's Press, 2000); Lucy Bland and Laura Doan (eds.), *Sexology in Culture* (Oxford: Polity Press, 1998).

2. Jeffrey Weeks, *Sex, Politics and Society: The Regulation of Sexual Crime since 1800* (London: Longman, 1989); Frank Mort, *Dangerous Sexualities: Medico-Moral Politics in England since 1830* (London: Routledge, 1987).

3. There is an extensive literature on the 'new woman'. See e.g. Sally Ledger, *The New Woman: Fiction and Feminism at the Fin de Siècle* (Manchester: Manchester University Press, 1997); Lucy Bland, *Banishing the Beast: English Feminism and Sexual Morality, 1885–1914* (Harmondsworth: Penguin, 1985); Ruth Brandon, *The New Woman and the Old Man: Love, Sex and the Woman Question* (London: Secker & Warburg, 1990); Angelique Richardson, *Love and Eugenics in the Late Nineteenth Century: Rational Reproduction and the New Woman* (Oxford: Oxford University Press, 2003).

4. See e.g. Jonathan Rutherford, *Forever England: Reflections on Maculinity and Empire* (London: Lawrence & Wishart, 1997); J. A. Mangan and James Walvin, *Manliness and Morality: Middle-Class Masculinity in Britain and America 1800–1940* (Manchester: Manchester University Press, 1987) and George Mosse, *The Image of Man* (Oxford: Oxford University Press, 1998).

5. See e.g. Alan Sinfield, *The Wilde Century: Effeminacy, Oscar Wilde and the Queer Moment* (London: Cassell, 1994).

6. Michel Foucault, *The History of Sexuality, i.: An Introduction*, tr. Robert Hurley (London: Penquir, 1979).

7. See e.g. Bland and Doan (eds.), *Sexology in Culture*.

8. Richard von Krafft-Ebing, *Psychopathia Sexualis*, tr. F. J. Rebman, ed. Brian King (Burbank: Bloat 1999), pp. ix–x.

9. See Catherine Hall, *White, Male and Middle-Class: Explorations in Feminism and* History (Cambridge: Polity, 1992) and John Tosh, *A Man's Place: Masculinity and the Middle-Class Home in Victorian England* (New Haven: Yale University Press, 1999).

10. Mrinalinha Sinha, *Colonial Masculinity: The 'Manly Englishman' and the 'Effeminate Bengali' in the Late Nineteenth Century* (Manchester: Manchester University Press, 1995).

11. John Strachey, *India* (London: Macmillan, 1888), 364–6.

12. Ibid. 380.

13. 'Death of General Sir Richard Strachey', *The Times* (13 Feb. 1908), 12.

14. Tosh, *A Man's Place*, 84.

15. Norma Clarke, 'Strenuous Idleness: Thomas Carlyle and the Man of Letters as Hero', in Michael Roper and John Tosh (eds.), *Manful Assertions: Masculinities in Britain since 1800* (London and New York: Routledge, 1991), 24–43.

16. Richard Strachey to Dick Strachey, 22 Jan. 1868, IO, Eur F 127/439.

17. Ralph Strachey to Pippa Strachey, 30 Oct. 1895, WL, ALC.

18. Ray Strachey's Diaries, vol. i, 25 June 1924. Ray Strachey Papers, LL.

19. Ray Strachey to Christopher Strachey, 3 July 1940, LL.

20. See Julia Strachey, *Julia: A Portrait by Herself and Frances Partridge* (London: Victor Gollancz, 1983), 45–8.

21. Interview with Barbara Strachey, 24 Oct. 1997.

22. Pippa Strachey to Pernel Strachey, 21 Nov. 1940, BL, Add Mss 60728.

23. Virginia Woolf, *The Diary of Virginia Woolf,* ed. Anne Olivier Bell, i (Harmondsworth: Penguin Books, 1979), 117.

24. Jane Strachey to James Strachey, 4 Sept. 1913, BL, Add Mss 60719.

25. Laura Doan, 'Passing Masculinities: Reading Feminine Masculinities in the 1920s', *Feminist Studies*, 24 (1999), 663–700.

26. Joan Riviere, 'Womanliness as Masquerade', in Russell Grigg, Dominique Hecq, and Craig Smit (eds.), *Female Sexuality* (London: Rebus Press, 1999), 172–82.

27. Quentin Bell, *Elders and Betters* (London: John Murray, 1995), 154–5.

28. James Strachey to Lytton Strachey, 4 May 1910, BL, Add Mss 60706.

29. James Strachey to Lytton Strachey, 17 Mar. 1910, BL, Add Mss 60708.

30. See letters from Oliver Strachey to Lytton Strachey, BL, Add Mss 60723.

31. Oliver Strachey to Lytton Strachey, 18 Jan. 1906, BL, Add Mss 60723.

32. Ibid.

33. See Richard Shone, 'Bloomsbury Nude: Some Hitherto Unpublished Photographs', *The Charleston Magazine*, 16 (1997), 30–2.

34. James Strachey to Rupert Brooke, 10 Apr. 1911, in Keith Hale (ed.), *Friends and Apostles: The Correspondence of Rupert Brooke and James Strachey 1905–1914* (New Haven and London: Yale University Press, 1998), 170–2.

35. Oliver Strachey to Havelock Ellis, 2 July 1921, BL, Add Mss 70555.

36. Julie Anne Taddeo, *Lytton Strachey and the Search for Modern Sexual Identity: The Last Eminent Victorian* (Binghamton, NY: Haworth Press, 2002), 125.

37. Michael Holroyd, *Lytton Strachey* (London: Vintage, 1995), 102.

38. See Jeffrey Weeks, *Coming out: Homosexual Politics in Britain from the Nineteenth Century to the Present* (London: Quartet Books, 1977).

39. Linda Dowling, *Hellenism and Homosexuality in Victorian Oxford* (Ithaca, NY: Cornell University Press, 1994).

40. Taddeo, *Lytton Strachey*, 15–40.

41. James Strachey to Rupert Brooke, 13 Sept. 1909, in Hale, *Friends and Apostles*, 78.

42. 'Old Bloomsbury', in Virginia Woolf, *Moments of Being*, ed. Jeanne Schulkind (St Albans: Triad/Panther Books, 1978), 200.

43. Frances Spalding, *Vanessa Bell* (London: Weidenfeld & Nicolson, 1983), 62–84.

44. See the letters from Lytton Strachey to Dorothy Bussy, Strachey Papers, PUL.

45. Mary Berenson to her family, 10 June 1910, LL.

46. The extent of Pernel's knowledge of Lytton's life is impossible to discern—although one would assume that her life in Cambridge would have made her fairly well aware of it.

47. Lytton Strachey to James Strachey, 27 Oct. 1909, BL, Add Mss 60706.

48. J. M. Keynes to Lytton Strachey, 10 Jan. 1906, KC.

49. Dora Carrington to Julia Strachey, n.d., UCL, Box 7/A.

50. Frances Partridge, *Good Company: Diaries January 1967–70* (London: Orion, 2001), 67.

51. See James Strachey, 'Editor's Introduction' to 'Three Essays on Sexuality', in Sigmund Freud, *On Sexuality*, ed. James Strachey, The Pelican Freud Library, 7 (Harmondsworth,: Penguin, 1977), 34.

52. Ibid. 35–7.

53. James Strachey to Alix Strachey, 16 Dec. 1924, in Perry Meisel and Walter Kendrick (eds.), *Bloomsbury/Freud: The Letters of James and Alix Strachey 1924–1925* (London: Chatto & Windus, 1986), 147.

54. James Strachey to Alix Strachey, 9 Dec. 1924, BL, Add Mss 60714.

55. James Strachey to Alix Strachey, 16 Feb. 1925, in Meisel and Kendrick, *Bloomsbury/Freud*, 201–2.

56. Ibid.

57. James Strachey to Alix Strachey, 4 Jan. 1925, BL, Add Mss 60714.

58. Alix Strachey, *The Unconscious Motives of War* (London: George Allen & Unwin, 1957).

59. Sigmund Freud, 'Group Psychology', in *The Penguin Freud library*, ed. Albert Dickson, xii (London: Penguin, 1985), 119.

60. Ibid. 138.

61. Ibid. 145.

62. Lytton Strachey to Dora Carrington, dated 'Sunday 7.15' but sent from Garsington Manor, BL, Add Mss 60721.

63. See Meisel and Kendrick, *Bloomsbury /Freud*, 6–7.

64. Alix Strachey's will, dated 22 Oct. 1965 left £1,000 each to Homosexual Law Reform Society; Family Planning Association; Abortion Law Reform Association. The Papers of Alix Strachey, BIP, Box 4.

65. Alix Strachey to James Strachey, 25 Feb. 1925, in Meisel and Kendrick, *Bloomsbury/Freud*, 218.

11. A FEMINIST FAMILY

1. Dorothy Bussy to Jane Strachey, 1 July 1914, IO, Eur F 127/332.

2. See Antoinette Burton, *Burdens of History: British Feminists, Indian Women, and Imperial Culture, 1865–1915* (Chapel Hill, NC: University of North

Carolina Press, 1994); Vron Ware, *Beyond the Pale: White Women, Racism and History* (London: Verso, 1992); Kumari Jayawardena, *The White Woman's Other Burden: Western Women and South Asia during British Rule* (London: Routledge, 1995).

3. The most extensive work on this has been done by Sandra Stanley Holton, *Feminism and Democracy: Women's Suffrage and Reform Politics in Britain, 1900–1918* (Cambridge: Cambridge University Press, 1986); but see also June Hanham, *Isabella Ford* (Oxford: Blackwell, 1989).

4. See Julia Bush, *Edwardian Ladies and Imperial Power* (London and New York: Leicester University Press, 2000); and Paula M. Krebs, *Gender, Race and the Writing of Empire: Public Discourse and the Boer War* (Cambridge: Cambridge University Press, 1999), 32–54.

5. Dorothy Bussy to Jane Strachey, 12 Dec. 1906, IO, Eur F 127/332.

6. Virginia Woolf, *The Diary of Virginia Woolf*, ed. Anne Olivier Bell, i (Harmondsworth: Penguin Books, 1979), 117–18.

7. Philippa Levine, *Feminist Lives in Victorian England: Private Roles and Public Commitment* (Oxford: Blackwell, 1990); Barbara Caine, *Victorian Feminists* (New York: Oxford University Press, 1992).

8. Jane Strachey to Richard Strachey, 2 May 1867, IO Eur F 127/126. On the general question of the relationship between feminism and abolitionism, on the one hand, and Italian nationalism on the other, see Claire Midgley, *Women against Slavery: The British Campaigns* (London: Routledge, 1992) and Barbara Caine (ed.), *Women and the Flight to Italy*, special issue of *Women's Writing*, 10/2 (2003).

9. Jane Strachey to Lytton Strachey, 23 May 1910, HRC.

10. See her letters to Richard Strachey throughout 1867, IO, Eur F 127/126.

11. Jane Strachey to Richard Strachey, 1 Oct. 1867, IO, Eur F 127/126.

12. Dorothy Bussy to André Gide, 22 Nov. 1944, BN, NAF 15631.

13. Jane Strachey to Richard Strachey, 25 May 1867, IO, Eur F 127/126.

14. Jane Strachey to Richard Strachey, 13 Nov. 1869, IO, Eur F 127/126.

15. Patricia Hollis, *Ladies Elect: Women in English Local Government, 1865–1914* (New York: Oxford University Press, 1987), 323; see also the letter Jane Strachey received on her resignation, Marian Berry to Lady Strachey, 24 Mar. 1920, Papers of Jane Maria Strachey, WL.

16. Jane Strachey to Mrs Cowles, 13 Dec. 1902, Papers of Jane Maria Strachey, WL.

17. Jane Strachey to Lytton Strachey, 19 Oct. (envelope 1902), HRC.

18. This correspondence is in the Papers of Jane Maria Strachey, WL.

19. See her correspondence with Louise Samuel, Mar. 1912, Papers of Jane Maria Strachey, WL.

20. See Jane Strachey to Lady Selbourne, 23 Jan. 1912, Papers of Jane Maria Strachey, WL.

21. Lady Strachey to Miss Hope, July 1910, Papers of Jane Maria Strachey, WL.

22. Jane Strachey to the Sec Church Lads Brigade, 11 July 1914, Papers of Jane Maria Strachey, WL.

23. Jane Strachey, presidential address, *The Lyceum* (Monthly Journal of the Lyceum Club), 118 (1908), 5.

24. Lady Strachey to Miss Smedley, 25 May 1907, Papers of Jane Maria Strachey, WL.

25. Annie Leigh Browne to Lady Strachey, 20 Jan. 1915, Papers of Jane Maria Strachey, WL.

26. Elinor Strachey to Jane Strachey, 20 Oct. 1919, IO, Eur F 127/323.

27. Dorothy Bussy to Jane Strachey, Montana 1910, IO, Eur F 127/332.

28. Dorothy Bussy to André Gide, 13 Mar. 1931, BN, NAF 15631.

29. Dorothy Bussy to André Gide, 7 Mar. 1936, BN, NAF 15631.

30. On this question see Barbara Caine, *English Feminism, 1780–1980* (Oxford: Oxford University Press, 1997), 43–50.

31. Dorothy Bussy to André Gide, n.d. (seems to be 1946), BN, NAF 15631.

32. See Burton, *Burdens of History*, 127–70.

33. Margaret Strachey to Jane Strachey, 11 Apr. 1908, IO, Eur F 127/326.

34. Ibid.

35. Ibid.

36. Margaret Strachey to Jane Strachey, 12 May 1908, IO, Eur F 127/326.

37. Pippa Strachey, handwritten speech at a dinner in her honour held in June 1951, Papers of Pippa Strachey, WL.

38. Barbara Stephen, *Emily Davies and Girton College* (Westport, Conn.: Hyperion Press, 1976); Daphne Bennett, *Emily Davies and the Liberation of Women: 1830–1921* (London: André Deutsch, 1990); Caine, *Victorian Feminists*, 54–102.

39. Jane Strachey to James Strachey, 5 Nov. 1906, BL, Add Mss 60717.

40. Pippa Strachey, handwritten speech for a dinner in her honour held in June 1951; Papers of Pippa Strachey, WL.

41. Pippa Strachey, handwritten speech for a dinner in her honour held in June 1951; Papers of Pippa Strachey, WL.

42. Ray Costelloe to Mary Berenson, 10 Feb. 1907, LL.

43. Pippa Strachey to James Strachey, 4 Feb. 1907, BL, Add Mss 60728.

44. Pippa Strachey to Maynard Keynes, 11 Feb. 1907, 2 Dec. 1907, and 13 Apr. 1909, KC, JMK/PP/45/317.

45. Lytton Strachey to Duncan Grant, 5 Feb. 1907, BL, Add Mss 57932.

46. Lytton Strachey to Duncan Grant, 11 Feb. 1907, BL, Add Mss 57932.

47. Lisa Tickner, *Spectacle of Women: The Imagery of the Suffrage Campaign, 1907–1917* (London: Chatto & Windus, 1987).

48. See Holton, *Feminism and Democracy*.

49. The text is discussed in Ch. 13

50. The typescript for the play, 'The Fair Arabian' is in the Women's Library in London. It is given three pseudonyms: Marie Caine on the front, Paul Strachey on the back, and Sydonie Colton in the advertising flier.

51. See Barbara Strachey, *Remarkable Relations: The Story of the Pearsall Smith Women* (New York: Universe Books, 1982).

52. Barbara Strachey and Jayne Samuels (eds.), *Mary Berenson: A Self-Portrait from her Letters and Diaries* (London: Hamish Hamilton, 1983).

53. Barbara Caine, 'Mothering Feminism, Mothering Feminists: Ray Strachey and *The Cause*', *Women's History Review*, 9 (1999).

54. Ray Costello to Mary Berenson 17 Dec. 1907, LL, 18.

55. There is a cutting from the *Daily News* (12 Nov. 1909) describing the new group in the Hannah Whitall Smith Papers, Box 18, fo. 3.

56. Diary of Ray Strachey, 20 Aug. 1910, LL.

57. Ray Strachey to Mary Berenson, 30 May 1911, LL.

58. Ray Strachey to Mary Berenson, 19 Feb. 1915, LL.

59. Ray Strachey to Mary Berenson, 22 May 1915, LL.

60. See David Rubinstein, *A Different World for Women: The Life of Millicent Garrett Fawcett* (New York: Harvester Wheatsheaf, 1991); Jill Liddington, *The Long Road to Greenham: Feminism and Anti-Militarism in Britain since 1820* (London: Virago, 1989).

61. Ray Strachey to Mary Berenson, Aug. 1914, LL.

62. Pippa Strachey to Roger Fry, 22 June 1915, WL. Unfortunately, Pippa does not identify who the person was.

63. For an extensive and critical analysis of government policies and of the hardships women workers faced in the course of the First World War, see Gail Braybon, *Women Workers in the First World War* (London: Croom Helm, 1981). For a more general discussion of women's involvement in the war, and of the impact of war on women's lives, see Susan R. Grayzel, *Women*

and the First World War (Harlow: Longman, 2002); Angela K. Smith, *The Second Battlefield: Women, Modernism and the First World War* (Manchester: Manchester University Press, 2000).

64. Report in *The Times* (13 June 1916), 8.

65. Ray Strachey to Mary Berenson, 26 Jan. 1917, LL.

66. Ray Strachey to Mary Berenson, 1 Apr. 1917, LL.

67. Ray Strachey to Dear Family, 11 Feb. 1918, LL.

68. Jane Strachey to Pippa Strachey, 14 Feb. 1918, BL, Add Mss 60719, 1908–19.

69. See Johanna Alberti, *Beyond Suffrage: Feminists in War and Peace, 1914–28* (Basingstoke: Macmillan, 1989); Susan Kingsley Kent, *Making Peace: The Reconstruction of Gender in Inter-War Britain* (Princeton: Princeton University Press, 1993); Harold L. Smith (ed.), *British Feminism in the Twentieth Century* (Aldershot: Elgar, 1990).

70. See Janet M. Manson Clemson, 'Practical Idealists: The League of Nations and the 1923 American Tour of Robert Cecil and Ray Strachey', *Passport: Newsletter of the Society for Historians of American Foreign Policy* (June 2001).

71. Ray Strachey to Mary Berenson, 26 Feb. 1924, LL.

72. Ray Strachey to Mary Berenson, 20 Mar. 1924, LL.

73. Rosalind Delmar, 'What is Feminism?', in Juliet Mitchell and Ann Oakley (eds.), *What is Feminism?* (New York: Pantheon Books, 1986).

74. Ray Strachey, *The Cause: A Short History of the Women's Movement in Great Britain* (London: G. Bell & Sons, Ltd., 1928), 64–70.

75. See Barbara Caine, 'Victorian Feminism and the Ghost of Mary Wollstonecraft', *Women's Writing*, 4/3 (1997), 261–75.

76. See Brian Harrison, *Prudent Revolutionaries* (Oxford: Clarendon Press. 1987), 174–80.

77. Harold L. Smith, 'British Feminism and the Equal Pay Issue in the 1930s', *Women's History Review*, 5 (1996), 97–110.

78. Smith, 'British Feminism', 98.

79. Ray Strachey to Mary Berenson, 15 Jan. 1940, LL.

80. See her letters to James and Pernel Strachey for 1941–4 in BL, Add Mss 60653.

81. Pippa Strachey to Pernel Strachey, 16 Jan. 1941, BL, Add Mss 60728. There is no information about this apart from Pippa's letters. However I am grateful to Julie Courtney, the archivist at Lady Margaret Hall, for establishing that Library Committee Meeting of 4 February 1940 notes that 'Storage room for packing cases was being offered to the Library of the National Society for Women's Service'.

82. Pippa's handwritten speech (without either a heading or a date) is in the Papers of Philippa Strachey, WL.

83. Pippa Strachey to Pernel Strachey, 13 July 1944, BL, Add Mss 60728.

84. Mary Stott, *Before I Go: Reflection on my Life and Times* (London: Virago, 1985), 28–9.

85. Pernel Strachey to Lytton Strachey, 9 Sept. 1900, BL, Add Mss 60725.

86. Marjorie Strachey to Jane Strachey (on NUWSS letterhead), 3 Feb. 1908, IO, Eur F 127/343.

87. 'Manifesto', *The Englishwoman*, 1/1 (1909), 1.

88. Marjorie Strachey to Jane Strachey, 26 July 1908, IO, Eur F 127/342.

89. Marjorie Strachey to Jane Strachey, 28 July 1908, IO, Eur F 127/342.

90. Ray Strachey to Mary Berenson, Feb. 1913, LL.

91. Marjorie Strachey to Jane Strachey, 11 Feb. 1918, IO, Eur F 127/343.

92. See letter of Leonard Woolf to Lytton Strachey, 3 Mar. 1907, in Frederick Spotts (ed.), *The Letters of Leonard Woolf* (London: Weideneld & Nicolson, 1989), 124.

93. Lytton Strachey to James Strachey, 19 May 1904, Lancaster Gate, BL, Add Mss 60706.

94. Julie Taddeo, 'A Modernist Romance? Lytton Strachey and the Women of Bloomsbury', in Elizabeth Harrison and Shirley Peterson (eds.), *Unmanning Modernism: Gendered Re-Readings* (Knoxville, Tenn. University of Tennessee Press, 1997), 134.

95. James Strachey to Lytton Strachey, 9 June 1910, BL, Add Mss 60708.

96. David Garnett, *The Golden Echo* (London: Chatto & Windus, 1954), 208.

97. Ibid. 209.

98. Alix Sargant-Florence to Mary Sargent, 24 Dec. 1914, BL, Add Mss 60701.

99. Perry Meisel and Walter Kendrick (eds.), *Bloomsbury/Freud: The Letters of James and Alix Strachey 1924–1925* (London: Chatto & Windus, 1986), 78.

100. For an extended discussion of Alix Strachey, see Barbara Caine, 'The Stracheys and Psychoanalysis', *History Workshop Journal*, 45 (1998), 158–64.

12. CONTINUITY AND CHANGE

1. David Garnett, *The Golden Echo* (London: Chatto & Windus, 1954), 257.

2. Virginia Woolf, *The Diary of Virginia Woolf*, ed. Anne Olivier Bell, i (Harmondsworth: Penguin Books, 1979), 132.

3. Leon Edel, *Bloomsbury: A House of Lions* (Harmondsworth: Penguin, 1979), 229–30; Michael Holroyd, *Lytton Strachey* (London: Vintage, 1995), 489–96. Unless otherwise indicated, this is the edition of Holroyd I have used.

4. See Barbara Caine, 'The Stracheys and Psychoanalysis', *History Workshop Journal*, 45 (1998), 145–69.

5. For a discussion of these issues, see Mark S. Micale and Robert L. Dietle (eds.), *Enlightenment, Passion, Modernity: Historical Essays in European Thought and Culture* (Cambridge: Cambridge University Press, 2000) and Charles Taylor, *Philosophy and the Human Sciences* (New York: Cambridge University Press, 1985).

6. See Eric Stokes, *The English Utilitarians and India* (Oxford: Oxford University Press, 1959), 282–6.

7. John Stuart Mill, '*The Spirit of the Age*', in *Essays on Politics and Culture*, ed. Gertrude Himmelfarb (Garden City, NY: Doubleday, 1963).

8. T. H. Huxley, 'Scientific Education: Notes of an After Dinner Speech' (1869), in his *Collected Essays* (London: Macmillan, 1894), 111–34.

9. Richard Strachey to Jane Strachey, 16 June 1867, IO, Eur F 127/318.

10. See in particular Jane's letters during 1866–7, around the Second Reform Act. IO, Eur F 127/126.

11. Jane Strachey to Richard Strachey, 25 Jan. 1878, IO, Eur F 127/129.

12. Jane Strachey to Richard Strachey, 8 June 1867, IO, Eur F 127/126.

13. Jane Strachey to Richard Strachey, 4 Dec. 1870, IO, Eur F 127/127.

14. Richard Strachey to Jane Strachey, 11 Feb. 1868, IO, Eur F 127/321.

15. Richard Strachey to Jane Strachey, 17 Dec. 1878, IO, Eur F 127/321.

16. Jane Strachey to Richard Strachey, 30 Jan. 1890, IO, Eur F 127/129.

17. 'Lancaster Gate', in Lytton Strachey, *Lytton Strachey by Himself: A Self-Portrait*, ed. Michael Holroyd (London: Heinemann, 1971).

18. *Protocols of Proceedings of the International Conference in Washington for the Purpose of Fixing a Prime meridian and a Universal Day* (Washington, DC, 1884) in IO, Eur F 127/188, p. 23.

19. Ibid. 45.

20. Ibid. 49.

21. Ibid. 108.

22. For a discussion of 19th century attempts to classify races and to establish a pattern of social evolution, see Stephen Jay Gould, *The Mismeasure of Man* (New York: Berg, 1983) and E. Nathaniel Gates, *Racial Classification in History* (New York: Garland, 1977).

23. See report on Strachey's lectures entitled 'Scientific Geography', *The Times* (13 Feb. 1877), 8.

24. Richard Strachey, 'Asia', in *Encyclopaedia Britannica*, 9th edn., ii (Edinburgh: Adam and Charles Black, 1880), 697.

25. Lytton Strachey to G. E. Moore, 11 Oct. 1903, quoted in Holroyd, *Lytton Strachey*, 89–90.

26. Holroyd, *Lytton Strachey*, 150.

27. Lytton Strachey to Dorothy Bussy, 10 May 1907, PUL.

28. Lytton Strachey to Duncan Grant, 30 Dec. 1906, BL, Add Mss 57932.

29. James Strachey, 'Sigmund Freud: Sketch of his Life and Ideas', in Sigmund Freud, *Two Short Accounts of Psychoanalysis* (Harmondsworth: Pelican Books, 1962). This sketch was included in every volume of the Penguin Freud Library.

30. Ibid.

31. For an excellent summary of the issues—and a strong defence of the Stracheys—see Mark Solms, 'Controveries in Freud Translation', *Psychoanalysis and History*, 1/1 (1998), 28–43.

32. Frances Spalding, *Vanessa Bell* (London: Weidenfeld & Nicolson, 1983), 63–7.

33. Lytton Strachey to James Strachey, 16 Nov. 1909, BL, Add Mss 60707.

34. James Strachey to Lytton Strachey, 6 Dec. 1909, BL, Add Mss 60707.

35. Ibid.

36. Lytton Strachey to James Strachey, 16 Nov. 1909, BL, Add Mss 60707.

37. Regina Gagnier, 'Modernity and Progress in Economics and Aesthetics', in Juliet John and Alice Jenkins (eds.), *Rethinking Victorian Culture* (London: Macmillan, 2000), 224.

38. Strachey, 'Lancaster Gate', 16.

39. See Peter Stansky, *On or about December 1910* (Cambridge, Mass.: Harvard University Press, 1996), 174–237.

40. For a detailed discussion of responses to the exhibition, see ibid. 204–14.

41. Holroyd, *Lytton Strachey*, 271.

42. Spalding, *Vanessa Bell*, 92.

43. Holroyd, *Lytton Strachey*, 101–10, 171–3.

44. Stansky, *On or about December*, 186.

45. André Maurois, 'Lytton Strachey', in *Points of View from Kipling to Graham Greene* (London: Muller, 1969), 241.

46. Julie Anne Taddeo, *Lytton Strachey and the Search for Modern Sexual Identity: The Last Eminent Victorian* (New York: Harrington Park Press, 2002).

47. See Kathy J. Phillips, *Virginia Woolf against Empire* (Knoxville, Tenn.: University of Tennessee Press, 1994); and Natania Rosenfeld, *Outsiders Together: Virginia and Leonard Woolf* (Princeton: Princeton University Press, 2000), 19, 33–5.

48. 'Old Bloomsbury', in Virginia Woolf, *Moments of Being*, ed. Jeanne Schulkind (St Albans: Triad/Panther Books, 1978), 200.

49. See S. P. Rosenbaum, *Edwardian Bloomsbury: The Early Literary History of the Bloomsbury Group* (New York: St Martin's Press, 1994), 129.

50. Lytton Strachey, 'Lord Lytton', in Michael Holroyd and Paul Levy (eds.), *The Shorter Strachey* (Oxford: Oxford University Press, 1980).

51. Lytton Strachey to Leonard Woolf, 16 Jan. 1907, BC.

52. Lady Edith Lytton to Jane Strachey, 21 Apr., no year, IO, Eur F 127/366.

53. Lytton Strachey to Dorothy Bussy, 10 May 1907, PUL.

54. Lytton Strachey, *Spectatorial Essays*, ed. James Strachey (London: Chatto & Windus, 1964).

55. Rosenbaum, *Edwardian Bloomsbury*, 129.

56. See Frederick Spotts (ed.), *The Letters of Leonard Woolf* (London: Weidenfeld and Nicolson, 1989), 'Introduction'; Leonard Woolf, *Growing: An Autobiography of the Years 1904–1911* (London: Hogarth, 1961), 3–17.

57. See Leonard Woolf, *Economic Imperialism* (New York: Howard Fertig, 1970; 1st publ. 1920).

58. Lytton Strachey to Leonard Woolf, 11 Dec. 1905, BC.

59. See e.g. 'The Curious Manuscript' and 'An Arabian Night,' in Lytton Strachey, *The Really Interesting Question and Other Papers*, ed. Paul Levy (London: Weidenfeld & Nicolson, 1972).

60. My account is heavily indebted to Julie Taddeo's chapter, 'Ploughboys, Postboys and the Arabian Nights: Lytton Strachey Explores the Sexual Empire', in her *Lytton Strachey*, 51–76.

61. Lytton Strachey to Leonard Woolf, 23 Apr. 1913, quoted in Taddeo, *Lytton Strachey*, 60.

62. Taddeo, *Lytton Strachey*, 56–61.

63. James Strachey to Lytton Strachey, 12 Sept. 1910, BL, Add Mss 60708.

64. Keith Hale (ed.), *Friends and Apostles: The Correspondence of Rupert Brooke and James Strachey 1905–1914* (New Haven and London: Yale University Press, 1998), 34.

65. Lytton Strachey to James Strachey, 17 Sept. 1910, BL, Add Mss 60708.

66. Lytton Strachey to James Strachey, 12 Nov. 1912, BL, Add Mss 60709.

67. James Strachey to Lytton Strachey, 31 July 1914, BL, Add Mss 60710.

68. James Strachey to Lytton Strachey, 18 Aug. 1914, BL, Add Mss 60710.

69. Lytton Strachey to James Strachey, 18 Aug. 1914, BL, Add Mss 60710.

70. James Strachey to Lytton Strachey, 2 Sept. 1914, BL, Add Mss 60710.

71. James Strachey to Lytton Strachey, 15 Sept. 1914, BL, Add Mss 60710.

72. Quentin Bell, *Bloomsbury* (London: Weidenfeld & Nicolson, 1968), 135.

73. James Strachey to Jane Strachey, 1 Dec. 1915, IO, Eur F 127/345.

74. Jane Strachey to James Strachey, BL, Add Mss 60717.

75. See the selection of Lytton Strachey's letters and wartime diaries in Strachey, *Lytton Strachey by Himself.*

76. James Strachey to Lytton Strachey, 29 Feb. 1916, BL, Add Mss 60710.

77. James Strachey to Lytton Strachey, 1 Mar. 1918, BL, Add Mss 60710.

78. Jane Strachey to Elinor Colevile, 12 Nov. 1918, IO, Eur F 127/83.

79. Holroyd, *Lytton Strachey*, 136.

80. Quoted in Michael Holroyd, *Lytton Strachey: A Critical Biography*, ii (London: Heinemann, 1968), 325.

81. Robert Skidelsky, *John Maynard Keynes, ii. The Economist as Saviour* (Harmondsworth, Penguin Books, 1992), 13–18.

82. Bussy's life is outlined in Francois Fosca, *Simon Bussy*, Pentres Nouveau, 43 (Paris: Gallimard, 1930); and Phillipe Loisel, *Simon Bussy (1870–1954) L'Esprit du trait: du zoo à la gentry* (Paris: Somogy d'éditions d'Art, 1996), 22–38.

83. Loisel, *Simon Bussy*, 28–9.

84. Lawrence Gowing later claimed that each animal study was really a self-portrait of Bussy in animal form. See Frances Partridge and Julia Strachey, *Julia* (London: Gollancz, 1983), 269.

85. Fosca, *Simon Bussy*, 8–9.

86. Ibid.

87. See André Gide et al., *Jean Vander Eeckhoudt* (Brussels: Éditions de la Connaissance, 1948), 6–7.

88. See François Chaubec, *Paul Desjardins et les decades de Pontigny* (Paris: Presses Universitaries du Septentrion, 2000); Alan Sheridan, *André Gide: A Life in the Present* (London: Hamish Hamilton, 1998).

89. Dorothy Bussy to André Gide, n.d., BN, NAF 15631, fo. 278.

90. Dorothy Bussey to André Gide, 28 June 1951, BN, NAF 13651.

91. James raised the possibility of doing translations of Freud for the first time in a letter to Ernest Jones, 28 Apr. 1920, BIP, CSD/F03/01.

92. James to Lytton Strachey, 6 Nov. 1920, BL, Add Mss 60711.

93. Draft letter from Alix Strachey to Donald Winnicott, 5 Dec. 1969, BIP, Papers of Alix Strachey, Box 2.

94. James Strachey, 'The Nature of the Therapeutic Action of Psycho-analysis', *International Journal of Psychoanalysis*, 15 (1934), 127–59.

95. Frances Partridge, *Everything to Lose: Diaries 1945–1960* (London: Gollancz, 1985), 32.

96. James Strachey to Ernest Jones, 11 Sept. 1925, BIP, CSD/F02/17.

97. Alix's letters to James contain a mixture of English and German as well as a number of their own private terms. She always referred to 'sitzungs' rather than using the correct German plural 'sitzunger'.

98. James Strachey to Alix Strachey, 22 Dec. 1924, BL, Add Mss 60714.

99. Partridge *Everything to Lose*, 306.

100. Alix Strachey to James Strachey, 30 Mar. 1925, Perry Meisel and Walter Kendrick (eds.), *Bloomsbury/Freud: The Letters of James and Alix Strachey 1924–1925* (London: Chatto & Windus, 1986), 245.

101. Alix Strachey to James Strachey, 16 Nov. 1924, Meisel and Kendrick *Bloomsbury/Freud*, 118.

102. James Strachey to Alix Strachey, 25 Feb. 1925, Meisel and Kendrick *Bloomsbury/Freud*, 220.

103. James Strachey to Alix Strachey, 26 Feb. 1925, BL, Add Mss 60714.

13. A LITERARY FAMILY

1. Virginia Woolf, 'Lady Strachey', *The Nation and Athenaeum* (22 Dec. 1928); repr. in Virginia Woolf, *Books and Portraits*, ed. Mark Lyon (London: Hogarth Press, 1977), 209.

2. Ibid. 210.

3. Pippa Strachey to Jane Strachey, 15 Oct. 1919, IO, Eur F 127/336.

4. Dick Strachey to Jane Strachey, 24 Apr. 1889, IO, Eur F 127/326.

5. Jane Strachey to Lytton Strachey, 5 Oct. 1890, HRC.

6. Richard Strachey, 'Asia', in *Encyclopaedia Britannica*, 9th edn. (Edinburgh: Adam and Charles Black, 1880), 697.

7. Jane Strachey, *Nursery Lyrics* (London: Bliss & Co, 1893).

8. Jane Strachey (ed.), *The Memoirs of a Highland Lady: The Autobiography of Elizabeth Grant of Rothiermurchus, Afterwards Mrs Smith of Baltiboy, 1797–1830* (London: John Murray, 1899).

9. Lytton Strachey, *Eminent Victorians* (London: Chatto & Windus, 1918).

10. James's first published work was the translation of Freud's *Group Psychology and the Analysis of the Ego* (London and Vienna: International Psycho-Analytical Library, 1922), no. 6.

11. Dorothy's first translation of Gide was *Strait is the Gate* (London: Jarrolds, 1924).

12. Dorothy Bussy, *Olivia by Olivia* (London: Hogarth Press, 1949).

13. Jane Maria Strachey, *Lay Texts for the Young, In English and French* (London: Cassell & Co., 1887).

14. Jane Strachey, *Nursery Lyrics* (London: Bliss & Co., 1893; 2nd edn., London: Chatto & Windus, 1922).

15. Strachey, *Nursery Lyrics* (1922), 34.

16. Its full title was as noted in n. 8.

17. Jane Strachey to Pernel Strachey, 1 Apr. 1898, BL Add Mss 60717.

18. The Murray 2nd edn. was issued as *Memoirs of a Highland Lady: The autobiography of Elizabeth Grant of Rothiemurchus, afterwards Mrs Smith of Baltiboys, 1997–1830*, ed. Lady Strachey (London: John Murray, 1911).

19. *Memoirs of a Highland Lady: Elizabeth Grant of Rothiemurchus*, ed. with an introd. by Andrew Tod (Edinburgh: Canongate, 1988).

20. Jane Strachey to Lytton Strachey, 15 Oct. 1896, HRC.

21. Jane Strachey to Lytton Strachey, 11 Feb. 1904, HRC.

22. '*Buzz quoth the blue-fly,* | Hum quoth the bee, | Buzz and hum they cry, | And so do we: | In his ear, in his nose | Thus do we see | He ate the dormouse, | Else it was thee'.

23. Lytton Strachey to Jane Strachey, 15 Feb. 1897, HRC.

24. Dorothy Bussy to Lytton Strachey, 31 Jan. 1912, PUL.

25. Lytton Strachey to Dorothy Bussy, 6 Feb. 1912, PUL.

26. Holroyd, *Lytton Strachey*, 269.

27. Dick Strachey to Jane Strachey, 29 June 1918, IO, Eur F 127/327.

28. Jane Strachey to Lytton Strachey, 10 Jan. 1919, HRC.

29. Ibid.

30. Michael Holroyd, *Lytton Strachey: A Critical Biography*, ii (London: Heinemann, 1968), 433.

31. Cited ibid. 432.

32. Holroyd, *Lytton Strachey*, 495.

33. Lytton Strachey to James Strachey, 24 Nov. 1920, BL Add Mss 60712.

34. Holroyd, *Lytton Strachey*, 610.

35. Entry for 28 Nov. 1928, Virginia Woolf, *The Diary of Virginia Woolf*, ed. Anne Olivier Bell, iii (Harmondsworth: Penguin Books, 1980), 208–9.

36. James Strachey to Lytton Strachey, 16 Feb. 1921, BL Add Mss 60712.

37. James Strachey to Ernest Jones, 27 Nov. 1921, BIP, CSD/F03/03A. See also Darius Gray Orniston, 'The Invention of "Cathexis" and Strachey's Strategy', *International Review of Psycho-Analysis*, 12 (1985), 391–9.

38. This debate is not only about James or the Strachey translation, but also about what psychoanalysis is and means, and about whether it is best seen as a framework that provides the basis for professional training and practice, or more broadly as an approach to culture, subjectivity, and meaning. The two approaches are in many ways incompatible, and each refers to a different Freud. This incompatibility is currently made absolutely clear by the fact that there are two new editions of Freud currently being published. The Institute of Psycho-Analysis in London with the Hogarth Press are bringing out a revised edition of the *Standard Edition of the Complete Psychological Works of Freud*, using the Strachey translation and language, which will also be used for a new edition of *The Complete Neuroscientific Works of Sigmund Freud* to be published by the Institute of Psycho-Analysis in conjunction with Karnac Books. See Mark Solms, 'Controveries in Freud Translation', *Psychoanalysis and History*, 1/1 (1998), 28–43. At the same time, Penguin is bringing out a quite new edition of the Penguin Freud Library, under the general editorship of Adam Phillips, which involves new translations of all the works. In this case, there are a number of different translators, each of whom is free to translate in accordance with their own understanding of the text. The essays have been recombined, moreover, to fit a new set of thematic volumes—one of the first of which is significantly titled 'Wild Analysis'.

39. Ernest Jones to James Strachey, 11 Nov. 1956, BIP, CSD/FO2/24.

40. James's correspondence suggests that he wrote programme notes earlier, however the Glyndebourne archives only contain two articles that he wrote in the 1950s, one to commemorate the conductor, Fritz Busch, for the Glyndebourne Festival Programme in 1952, and another on 'Mozart and Glyndebourne' for the Festival Programme in 1956.

41. James Strachey, 'The Function of the Precipitating Factor in the Aetiology of the Neuroses: An Historical Note', *International Journal of Psycho-Analysis*, 12 (1931), 326–30.

42. James Strachey, 'Some Unconscious Factors in Reading', *International Journal of Psycho-Analysis*, 11 (1930), 322–31.

43. Ibid. 330.

44. Ibid. 331.

45. James Strachey to Ernest Jones, 28 Apr. 1920, BIP, CSD/FO3/01.

46. Alix Strachey, *The Unconscious Motives of War* (London: George Allen & Unwin, 1957).

47. Partridge, *Everything to Lose*, 278.

48. Letter from Hugh Thomas to Alix Strachey, 6 Sept. 1960, BIP, Papers of Alix Strachey, Box 4. Alix published an article on 'Psychological Problems of Nationhood', *The Year Book of World Affairs* (London, 1960), 261–85.

49. Strachey, *Unconscious Motives*.

50. Ibid. 3–7.

51. Ibid. 126.

52. Ibid. 127.

53. Ibid. 127–8.

54. See e.g. *Times Literary Supplement* (26 July 1957); *Sociological Review*, 5 (1957), 301–2; *Political Science Quarterly*, 2 (1958), 314–5.

55. Auguste Breal, *Velasquez*, tr. Mme Simon Bussy, The Popular Library of Art (London: Duckworth & Co., 1904).

56. Camille Mauclair, *Antoine Watteau 1864–1721*, tr. Mme Simon Bussy, The Popular Library of Art (London: Duckworth & Co., 1906).

57. Dorothy Bussy, *Eugene Delacroix* (London: Duckworth & Co., 1907).

58. See André Gide, *The Immoralist*, tr. David Watson (New York, Penguin, 2001), but see also André Gide, *Strait is the Gate*, tr. Dorothy Bussy (Cambridge, Mass.: R. Bentley, 1980), *The School for Wives,* tr. Dorothy Bussy (Cambridge, Mass.: R. Bentley, 1980), *The Counterfeiters,* tr. Dorothy Bussy (New York: Vintage Books, 1973).

59. Dorothy Bussy to André Gide, 22 Nov. 1922, in Richard Tedeschi (ed.), *Selected Letters of André Gide and Dorothy Bussy* (New York: Oxford University Press, 1983), 94.

60. Ibid.

61. See *Correspondence André Gide–Arnold Bennett: Vingt ans d'amitié littéraire (1911–1931)*, introduction by Linette F. Brugmans (Geneva: Textes Litteraires Français, Librarie Droz, 1964), 157–64.

62. Dorothy Bussy to André Gide, 5 Dec. 1933, in Tedeschi, *Selected Letters*, 153.

63. André Gide to Dorothy Bussy, 15 Jan. 1934, ibid. 155–6.

64. Dorothy Bussy to André Gide, 23 Feb. 1948, ibid. 277–8.

65. André Gide to Dorothy Bussy, 5 June 1948, ibid., 284.

NOTES

66. Ibid.

67. See Erica Foulkes, 'Esquisse bibliographique de l'œuvre de Dorothy Bussy', *Bulletin des Amis d'André Gide*, 17 (1989), 481-6.

68. See e.g. the 'Afterword' by Susannah Clapp to Dorothy Bussy, *Olivia by Olivia* (London: Virago, 1987; 1st publ. 1949), 111-14.

69. Dorothy Bussy to Roger Martin du Gard, 26 July 1948, Lettres de Roger Martin du Gard à la famille Bussy, BN, NAF 15758.

70. Roger Martin du Gard to Dorothy Bussy, 8 Aug. 1948, Lettres de Roger Martin du Gard à la famille Bussy, BN, NAF 15758.

71. Leonard Woolf to Anthony Godwin, 12 Jan. 1966, SUL, I Q 3c 9.

72. Frances Partridge (ed.), *Julia* (London: Gollancz, 1983), 35.

73. See Philippa Strachey, 'The Fair Arabian: An Old Story in 1 Act' by Marie Caine, n.d., WL. The play only exists in a typescript. It has the name 'Marie Caine' on the front—and 'Philippa Strachey' on the back.

74. Jane Strachey to Elinor Colevile, 14 July 1909, IO, Eur F 127/83.

75. James Strachey to Lytton Strachey, 29 Jan. 1910, BL, Add Mss 60708.

76. Marjorie Strachey, 'Women in the Modern Drama', *The Englishwoman*, 29 (May 1911), 186-9.

77. Marjorie Strachey, *The Counterfeits* (London: Longmans Green & Co, 1927).

78. Ray Strachey, *The World at Eighteen* (London: T. Fisher Unwin, 1907).

79. Ray Strachey, *Frances Willard: Her Life and Work* (London: Fleming H. Revell Company, 1913), i.

80. Ray Strachey, *A Quaker Grandmother: Hannah Whitall Smith* (New York: Fleming H. Revell Co., 1914).

81. Ray Strachey to Mary Berenson, 26 Feb. 1924, LL.

82. Ray Strachey to Mary Berenson, 20 Mar. 1924, LL.

14. OLD AGE AND DEATH

1. Pat Thane, *Old Age in English History: Past Experiences, Present Issues* (Oxford: Oxford University Press, 2000), 5-12.

2. There are no official records dealing with this. However, Frances Partridge notes that he was still working in the War Office Cipher Department until his heart attack on 9 Feb. 1943. Frances Partridge and Julia Strachey, *Julia* (London: Gollancz, 1983), 183.

3. Michael Holroyd, *Lytton Strachey*, 707.

4. Dorothy Bussy to Lytton Strachey, 5 Feb. 1916, BL Add Mss 1990.

5. His health problems were discussed in detail by Elinor Rendel when she stayed with him at Lancaster Gate while her mother went away in 1892. See the letters from Elinor Rendel to Jane Strachey, Jan. to Mar. 1892, IO, Eur F 127/323.

6. Holroyd, *Lytton Strachey*, 5–6. See also Jane Strachey to Lytton Strachey, 19 Oct. 1894, HRC.

7. Jane Strachey to Lytton Strachey, 21 July 1893, HRC.

8. Jane Strachey to Lytton Strachey, 3 June 1903, HRC.

9. The Stracheys were vehement Dreyfusards and extremely critical of the French army's treatment of Dreyfus. Zola's 'J'accuse', which served to mobilize support for Dreyfus, was highly regarded by them. Pippa Strachey to Jane Strachey, 1 June 1898, IO, Eur F 127/335.

10. Richard Strachey to Pippa Strachey, 12 Apr. 1901, BL, Add Mss 60729.

11. Leonard Woolf, *Sowing: An Autobiography of the Years 1880–1904* (London: Hogarth Press, 1970), 188.

12. Holroyd, *Lytton Strachey*, 5.

13. Jane Strachey to Elinor Colevile, 19 Feb. 1908, IO, Eur F 127/83.

14. Jane Strachey to Lytton Strachey, 8 Nov., no year, HRC.

15. Betty Askwith, *Two Victorian Families* (London: Chatto & Windus, 1971), 39.

16. Jane Strachey to Pippa Strachey, 1 Sept. 1912, BL, Add Mss 60719.

17. Jane Strachey to James Strachey, 2 Feb. 1909, BL, Add Mss 60719.

18. Jane Strachey to James Strachey, 24 Apr. 1909, BL, Add Mss 60719. There is no other information about this choir, but Pippa's involvement makes it likely that it was a suffrage choir.

19. Pernel Strachey to Jane Strachey, 17 and 19 Aug. 1914, BL, Add Mss 60726.

20. Dorothy Bussy to Jane Strachey, 5 May 1915, BL, Add Mss 19909.

21. Pernel Strachey to Jane Strachey, n. d., BL, Add Mss 60726.

22. Jane Strachey to Lytton Strachey, 22 Oct. 1914, HRC.

23. Pippa Strachey to Jane Strachey, 28 Sept. 1914, IO, Eur F 127/336.

24. Jane Strachey to Lytton Strachey, 24 Feb. 1916, HRC.

25. Jane Strachey to Elinor Colevile, 12 Nov. 1918, IO, Eur F 127/83.

26. Holroyd, *Lytton Strachey* (1995), 462–3.

27. Lytton Strachey to James Strachey, 27 Jan. 1921, BL, Add Mss 60712.

28. Virginia Woolf, *The Diary of Virginia Woolf*, ed. Anne Olivier Bell, ii (Harmondsworth: Penguin Books, 1981), 54.

29. James Strachey to Alix Strachey, 14 Mar. 1925, in Perry Meisel and Walter Kendrick (eds.), *Bloomsbury/Freud: The Letters of James and Alix Strachey 1924–1925* (London: Chatto & Windus, 1986), 233.

30. Dorothy Bussy to André Gide, 19 Apr. 1928, BN, NAF 15631.

31. Dorothy Bussy to André Gide, 18 Sept. 1928, BN, NAF 15631.

32. Diary of Ray Strachey, 31 May 1929, LL.

33. Cited in Holroyd, *Lytton Strachey*, 604.

34. Dorothy Bussy to André Gide, 15 June 1929, BN, NAF 15631.

35. Duncan Grant to Maynard Keynes, 10 June 1910, BL, Add Mss 58210

36. Ray Strachey to Mary Berenson, 12 Dec. 1920, LL.

37. Marjorie Strachey to Lytton Strachey, 25 May 1923, BL, Add Mss 60722.

38. Dorothy Bussy to André Gide, 30 June 1923, BN, NAF 15631.

39. Marjorie Strachey to Lytton Strachey, 20 June 1923, BL, Add Mss 60722.

40. See the series of letters from Margaret Strachey to Pippa Strachey, IO, Eur F 127/450.

41. Holroyd, *Lytton Strachey*, 669–81.

42. Ray Strachey Diary, 2 May 1932, LL.

43. Dorothy Bussy to André Gide, 23 Jan. 1932, in Richard Tedeschi (ed.), *Selected Letters of André Gide and Dorothy Bussy* (New York: Oxford University Press, 1983), 44.

44. Dorothy Bussy to André Gide, 5 Apr. 1932, in Tedeschi, *Selected Letters*, 149.

45. Ibid.

46. Dick Strachey to Pippa Strachey, 16 May 1920, WL.

47. Lyton Strachey to Pippa Strachey, 22 Feb. 1927, BL, Add Mss 60721.

48. There is no discussion of Jane Strachey's funeral in the Strachey Papers.

49. James Strachey to Dick Strachey, 10 Feb. 1932, BL, Add Mss 60716.

50. Dorothy Bussy to Pippa Strachey, 23 Oct. 1935, BL, Add Mss 60661.

51. Barbara Strachey, *Remarkable Relations: The Story of the Pearsall Smith Women* (New York: Universe Books, 1982), 303.

52. Dorothy Bussy to André Gide, 3 Jan. 1937, in Tedeschi, *Selected Letters*, 171.

53. Pippa Strachey to Pernel Strachey, 4 Oct. 1939, BL, Add Mss 60727.

54. Pippa Strachey to Pernel Strachey, 14 May 1939, BL, Add Mss 60727.

55. Pippa Strachey to Pernel Strachey, 25 Aug. 1939, BL, Add Mss 60727.

56. Pippa Strachey to Pernel Strachey, 1 Sept. 1940, BL, Add Mss 60727.

57. Pippa Strachey to Pernel Strachey, 21 Nov. 1940, BL, Add Mss 60727.

58. Pippa Strachey to Pernel Strachey, 26 Feb. 1941, BL, Add Mss 60727.

59. Dorothy Bussy to André Gide, 30 Oct. 1944, BN, NAF 15631.

60. Dorothy Bussy to André Gide, 29 Sept. 1931, BN, NAF 15631.

61. Dorothy Bussy to André Gide, 18 Nov. 1936, BN, NAF 15631.

62. Dorothy Bussy to André Gide, 16 July 1945, in Tedeschi, *Selected Letters*, 242–3.

63. Dorothy Bussy to André Gide, 19 Nov. 1944, BN, NAF 15631.

64. Ibid.

65. Dorothy Bussy to André Gide, 29 Oct. 1946, in Tedeschi, *Selected Letters*, 257.

66. Pippa Strachey to Pernel Strachey, 7 July 1940, BL, Add Mss 60727.

67. Ray Strachey to Christopher Strachey, 3 July 1920, LL.

68. Pippa Strachey to James Strachey, 3 Apr. 1941, BL, Add Mss 60727.

69. Dorothy Bussy to André Gide, 20 Sept. 1942, in Tedeschi, *Selected Letters*, 221.

70. Pippa Strachey to James Strachey, 21 Nov. 1940, BL, Add Mss 60728.

71. Marjorie Strachey to Pippa Strachey, n d, BL, Add Mss 60722.

72. Clara D. Rackham, 'Joan Pernel Strachey, 1875–1951', *Newnham College Roll* (Jan. 1951), 29–31.

73. Quoted Frances Spalding, *Duncan Grant A Biography* (London: Pimlico, 1998), 411.

74. Julia Strachey to Lawrence Gowing, 26 Feb. 1943, in Partridge, *Julia*, 185–6.

75. Marjorie Strachey to Pippa Strachey, 14 May 1944, BL, Add Mss 60729.

76. Julia Strachey to Frances Partridge, 30 Oct. 1944, in Partridge, *Julia Strachey*, 194.

77. Conversation with Barbara Strachey, 24 Oct. 1997.

78. Partridge and Strachey, *Julia*, 253.

79. Dorothy Bussy, *Fifty Nursery Rhymes—with a Commentary on English Usage for French Students* (Paris: Gallimard, 1956).

80. The best account of this is provided by Frances Partridge, *Everything to Lose: Diaries 1945–1960* (London: Gollancz, 1985), 172–3.

81. Ibid. 79.

82. Vanessa Bell to Angelica Garnett, 6 Sept. 1954, cited in Frances Spalding, *Vanessa Bell* (London: Weidenfeld & Nicolson, 1983), 359.

83. Julia Strachey to Frances Partridge, 1 Mar. 1960, in Partridge, *Julia Strachey*, 266.

84. Partridge, *Everything to lose*, 357–8.

85. Conversations with Barbara Strachey, 24 Oct. 1997, and with Frances Partridge, 23 Oct. 1997.

86. James Strachey to Alix Strachey, 7 July 1960, BL, Add Mss 60716.

87. Alix Strachey to James Strachey, 8 July 1960, BL, Add Mss 60704.

88. James Strachey to Alix Strachey, 11 July 1960, BL, Add Mss 60716.

89. Ibid.

90. Ibid.

91. James Strachey to Alix Strachey, 25 July 1960, BL, Add Mss 60716.

92. Frances Partridge, *Hanging On: Diaries December 1960-December 1963* (London: Collins, 1990), 14 Mar. 1963, 103.

93. Mary Stocks, *My Commonplace Book* (London: Peter Davies, 1970), 14.

94. Julia Strachey to Frances Partridge, 23 Aug. 1963, in Partridge, *Julia*, 281.

95. Frances Partridge, *Other People: Diaries September 1963-December 1966* (London: Harper Collins, 1992), 18 Nov. 1963, 25–6.

96. 12 Jan. 1953, in Partridge, *Everything to Lose*, 172.

97. 20 Apr. 1957, in Partridge, *Everything to Lose*, 277–8.

98. Holroyd, *Lytton Strachey* (1995), p. xiii.

99. 18 Nov. 1963, Partridge, *Other People*, 25.

100. Partridge, *Good Company*, 69.

Bibliography

COLLECTIONS

Bibliothèque Nationale (BN)

Gide Papers
Papers of Dorothy Bussy
Correspondence of Roger Martin du Gard

British Institute of Psychoanalysis (BIP)

Papers of Alix and James Strachey
Correspondence Files

British Library Manuscript Collections (BL)

Strachey Papers
Dora Carrington Correspondence
Keynes Papers
Havelock Ellis Papers

British Library Oriental and India Office Collections (IO)

Lytton Papers
Salisbury Papers
Strachey Papers

Women's Library (WL)

Papers of Pippa, Pernel, and Jane Maria Strachey
ALC (Autograph Letter Collections)

Harry Ransom Center (HRC)

Strachey Papers

King's College (KC)

Keynes Papers

Lilley Library, University of Indiana (LL)
Hannah Whitall Smith Papers: Letters of Ray Strachey

New York Public Library, Berg Collection (BC)
Strachey Papers

Newnham College Archives (NC)

Princeton University Library (PUL)
Strachey Papers

Sussex University Library (SUL)
Woolf Papers

University College Library (UCL)
Galton Papers
Papers of Julia Strachey

PUBLISHED WORKS

Adler, Alfred, *Understanding Human Nature* (Oxford: One World, 1992; 1st published 1927).

Alberti, Johanna, *Beyond Suffrage: Feminists in War and Peace, 1914–28* (Basingstoke: Macmillan, 1989).

Anon., *Some Memories of Marie Souvestre* (privately printed at Oxford University Press by John Johns, n.d.).

Appignanesi, Lisa, and Forrester, John, *Freud's Women* (London: Virago, 1993).

Askwith, Betty, *Two Victorian Families* (London: Chatto & Windus, 1971).

Baber, Zaheer, *The Science of Empire: Scientific Knowledge, Civilisation and Colonial Rule in India* (Delhi: Oxford University Press, 1998).

Banks, J. A., *Prosperity and Parenthood: A Study of Family Planning among the Victorian Middle Classes* (London: Routledge & Kegan Paul, 1969).

Beard, Mary, *The Invention of Jane Harrison* (Cambridge, Mass.: Harvard University Press, 2000).

Behlmer, George K., *Friends of the Family: The English Home and its Guardians, 1850–1940* (Stanford, Calif.: Stanford University Press, 1998).

Bell, Anne Olivier (ed.), *A Moment's Liberty: The Shorter Diary of Virginia Woolf* (London: Hogarth Press, 1990).

Bell, Quentin, *Bloomsbury* (London: Weidenfeld & Nicolson, 1968).

—— *Elders and Betters* (London: John Murray, 1995).

Bennett, Daphne, *Emily Davies and the Liberation of Women: 1830-1921* (London: Andre Deutsch, 1990).

Bland, Lucy, *Banishing the Beast: English Feminism and Sexual Morality* (Harmondsworth: Penguin, 1995).

Boyd, Elizabeth French, *Bloomsbury Heritage: Their Mothers and their Aunts* (London: Hamish Hamilton, 1976).

Brandon, Ruth, *The New Woman and the Old Man: Love, Sex and the Woman Question* (London: Secker & Warburg, 1990);

Breal, Auguste, *Velasquez*, tr. Mme Simon Bussy, The Popular Library of Art (London: Duckworth & Co., 1904).

Brennan, L., 'The Development of the Indian Famine Codes: Personalities, Politics, and Policies', in Bruce Currey and Graeme Hugo (eds.), *Famine as a Geographical Phenomenon* (Dordrecht: D. Reidel Publishing Co., 1984).

Brooke, C. N., *A History of the University of Cambridge* (Cambridge: Cambridge University Press, 1993).

Burton, Antoinette, *Burdens of History: British Feminists, Indian Women, and Imperial Culture, 1865-1915* (Chapel Hill, NC: University of North Carolina Press, 1994).

Bush, Julia, *Edwardian Ladies and Imperial Power* (London and New York: Leicester University Press, 2000).

Bussy, Dorothy, *Eugene Delacroix* (London: Duckworth & Co., 1907).

—— *Olivia by Olivia* (London: Hogarth Press, 1949; repr. London: Virago, 1987).

Caine, Barbara, *Destined to be Wives: The Sisters of Beatrice Webb* (Oxford and New York: Clarendon Press, 1986).

—— *English Feminism, 1780-1980* (Oxford: Oxford University Press, 1997).

—— 'Mothering Feminism, Mothering Feminists: Ray Strachey and *The Cause*', *Women's History Review*, 8 (1999), 295-310.

—— 'The Stracheys and Psychoanalysis', *History Workshop Journal*, 45 (1998), 145-69.

—— 'Victorian Feminism and the Ghost of Mary Wollstonecraft', *Women's Writing*, 4/3 (1997), 261-75.

—— *Victorian Feminists* (New York: Oxford University Press, 1992).

Chaubec, François, *Paul Desjardins et les decades de Pontigny* (Paris: Presses Universitaires du Septentrion, 2000).

Chaudhuri, Nupur, 'Bloomsbury Ancestry: Jane Maria Strachey, Feminism and Younger Strachey Women', in Wayne K. Chapman and Janet M. Manson (eds.), *Women in the Milieu of Leonard and Virginia Woolf* (New York: Pace University Press, 1998).

—— and Strobel, Margaret (eds.), *Western Women and Imperialism* (Bloomington: Indiana University Press, 1992).

Clarke, Norma, 'Strenuous Idleness: Thomas Carlyle and the Man of Letters as Hero', in Michael Roper and John Tosh (eds.) *Manful Assertions: Masculinities in Britain since 1800* (London and New York: Routledge, 1991).

Cohn, Bernard S., *Colonialism and its Forms of Knowledge: The British in India* (Princeton: Princeton University Press, 1986).

Compton, J. M., 'Open Competition and the Indian Civil Service', *English Historical Review*, 83 (1968), 265–84.

Cooke, Blanche Wiessen, *Eleanor Roosevelt*, (New York: Penguin Books, 1992).

Correspondence André Gide–Arnold Bennett: Vingt ans d'amitié littéraire (1911–1931), introduction by Linette F. Brugmans (Geneva: Textes Littéraires Français, Librairie Droz, 1964).

Dalrymple, William, *White Mughals: Love and Betrayal in Eighteenth-Century India* (London: Harper Collins, 2002).

Davidoff, Leonore, and Hall, Catherine, *Family Fortunes: Men and Women of the English Middle Class 1780–1850*, (London: Routledge, 1992).

—— Doolittle Megan, Fink Janet, and Holden Katherine, *The Family Story: Blood, Contract and Intimacy, 1830–1960* (London and New York: Longman, 1999).

Davis, Mike, *Late Victorian Holocausts: El Niño Famines and the Making of the Third World* (London: Verso, 2001).

Delmar, Rosalind, 'What is Feminism?', in Juliet Mitchell and Ann Oakley (eds.), *What is Feminism?* (New York: Pantheon Books, 1986).

Denniston, A. G., 'The Government Code and Cypher School between the Wars', *Intelligence and National Security*, 1/1 (1986), 48–70.

Dewey, C. J., 'The Education of a Ruling Caste: The Indian Civil Service in the Era of Competitive Examinations', *English Historical Review*, 88 (1973), 262–85.

Dione, R., and Macleod, R., 'Science and Policy in British India, 1858–1917: Perspectives on a Persisting Belief', in *Asie de Sud: Traditions et changements* (Paris: editions du Centre National de la Recherche Scientifique, 1979).

Doan, Laura, 'Passing Masculinities: Reading Feminine Masculinities in the 1920s', *Feminist Studies*, 24 (1999), 663–700.

Dowling, Linda, *Hellenism and Homosexuality in Victorian Oxford* (Ithaca, NY: Cornell University Press, 1994).

Dreze, Jean, *Famine Prevention in India* (New York: World Institute for Development Economic Research of the United Nations, 1988).

Dunn, Jane, *Virginia Woolf and Vanessa Bell: A Very Close Conspiracy* (London: Cape, 1990).

Edel, Leon, *Bloomsbury: A House of Lions* (Harmondsworth: Penguin, 1979).

Fosca, François, *Simon Bussy*, Pentres Nouveau, 43 (Paris: Gallimard, 1930).

Foucault, Michel, *The History of Sexuality, An Introduction*, tr. Robert Hurley (London: Penguin, 1979).

Foulkes, Erica, 'Esquisse bibliographique de l'œuvre de Dorothy Bussy', *Bulletin des Amis D'André Gide*, 17 (1989), 481–6.

Freud, Sigmund, 'Group Psychology', in *The Penguin Freud Library*, ed. Albert Dichson xii (London: Penguin, 1985).

G. H. D., *Lieutenant-General Sir Richard Strachey, G. C. S. I., 1817–1908* (London: privately published, Harrison and Son Printers, 1908).

Gagnier, Regina, 'Modernity and Progress in Economics and Aesthetics', in Juliet John and Alice Jenkins (eds.), *Rethinking Victorian Culture* (London: Macmillan: 2000).

Garnett, David, *The Golden Echo* (London: Chatto & Windus, 1954).

Gay, Peter, *Freud, a Life for our Time* (London: J. M. Dent & Sons, 1995).

Gide, Andre, et al, *Jean Vander Eeckhoudt* (Brussels: Éditions de la Connaissance, 1948).

Hale, Keith (ed.), *Friends and Apostles: The Correspondence of Rupert Brooke and James Strachey 1905–1914* (New Haven and London: Yale University Press, 1998).

Hall, Lesley A., *Sex, Gender and Social Change in Britain since 1880* (New York: St Martin's Press, 2000).

Hammerton, Jim, *Cruelty and Companionship: Conflict in Nineteenth-Century Married Life* (London: Routledge, 1995).

Hanham, June, *Isabella Ford* (Oxford: Blackwell, 1989).

Harris, Pippa (ed.), *Songs of Love: The Letters of Rupert Brooke and Noel Olivier* (London: Bloomsburg, 1991).

Harrison, Brian, *Prudent Revolutionaries* (Oxford: Clarendon Press, 1987).

Henry Dryden, 'Recollections of Bletchley Park', in F. H. Hinsley and Alan Stripp (eds.), *The Inside Story of Bletchley Park* (Oxford: Oxford University Press, 1994).

Holditch, Thomas, 'Richard Strachey—Obituary', *The Geographical Journal* (March 1908), 343.

Hollis, Patricia, *Ladies Elect: Women in English Local Government, 1865–1914* (New York: Oxford University Press, 1987)

Holroyd, Michael, *Lytton Strachey* (London: Vintage, 1995).

—— *Lytton Strachey: A Critical Biography* (London: Heinemann, 1968).

Holton, Sandra Stanley, *Feminism and Democracy: Women's Suffrage and Reform Politics in Britain, 1900–1918* (Cambridge: Cambridge University Press, 1986).

—— *Suffrage Days: Stories from the Women's Suffrage Movement* (London: Routledge, 1996).

Huddleston, George, *History of the East Indian Railway* (Calcutta: Thacker, Spink & Co., 1906).

Jayawardena, Kumari, *The White Woman's Other Burden: Western Women and South Asia during British Rule* (London: Routledge, 1995).

Kahn, David, *Seizing the Enigma: The Race to Break the German U-Boat Codes, 1939–1943* (Chatham: Souvenir Press, 1991).

King, Pearl and Steiner, Ricardo (eds.), *The Freud–Klein Controversies 1941–45* (London: Tavistock/Routledge, 1993).

Krafft-Ebing, Richard von, *Psychopathia Sexualis*, tr. F. J. Rebman, ed. Brian King (Burbank: Bloat, 1999).

Krebs, Paula M., *Gender, Race and the Writing of Empire: Public Discourse and the Boer War* (Cambridge: Cambridge University Press, 1999).

Ledger, Sally, *The New Woman: Fiction and Feminism at the Fin de Siècle* (Manchester: Manchester Univesrity Press, 1997).

—— 'The New Woman and the Crisis of Victorianism', in Sally Ledger and Scott McCracken (eds.), *Cultural Politics at the Fin de Siècle* (Cambridge: Cambridge University Press, 1995).

Lee, B. H., *Divorce Law Reform in England* (London: Owen, 1974).

Lee, Hugh, and Holroyd, Michael, *A Cezanne in the Hedge and Other Memories of Charleston and Bloomsbury* (Chicago: University of Chicago Press, 1992).

Levine, Philippa, *Feminist Lives in Victorian England: Private Roles and Public Commitment* (Oxford: Blackwell, 1990).

Levy, Paul, *G. E. Moore and the Cambridge Apostles* (London: Macmillan, 1989).

Liddington, Jill, *The Long Road to Greenham: Feminism and Anti-Militarism in Britain since 1820* (London: Virago, 1989).

—— and Norris, Jill, *One Hand Tied Behind* (London: Virago, 1978).

Loisel, Phillipe, *Simon Bussy (1870–1954) L'Esprit du trait: du zoo à la Gentry* (Paris: Somogy d'éditions d'Art, 1996).

Lubenow, W. C., 'Authority, Honour and the Strachey Family, 1817–1974', *Historical Research*, 76: 194 (Nov. 2003), 512–34.

—— *The Cambridge Apostles, 1820–1914: Liberalism, Imagination and Friendship in British Intellectual and Professional Life* (Cambridge: Cambridge University Press, 1998).

McClintock, Anne, *Imperial Leather: Race, Gender, and Sexuality in the Colonial Contest* (New York: Routledge, 1995).

McWilliams-Tulberg, Rita, *Women at Cambridge: A Men's University–Though of Mixed Type* (London: Gollancz, 1975).

Majeed, Javed, *Ungoverned Imaginings: James Mill's History of British India and Orientalism* (Oxford: Clarendon Press, 1992).

Mangan, J. A., and Walvin James, *Manliness and Morality: Middle-Class Masculinity in Britain and America 1800–1940*, (Manchester: Manchester University Press, 1987).

Martineau, John (ed.), *The Life and Correspondence of Sir Bartle Frere, BART., G.C.B., F.R.S.* (London: John Murray, 1895).

Marty, Eric, 'Gide and Dorothy Bussy', in Patrick Pollard (ed.), *Andre Gide et l'Angleterre* (Birkbeck: Le Colloque Gide, 1986).

Mason, Michael, *The Making of Victorian Sexual Attitudes* (Oxford and New York: Oxford University Press, 1994).

Mauclair, Camille, *Antoine Watteau 1864–1721*, tr. Mme Simon Bussy, The Popular Library of Art (London: Duckworth & Co., 1906).

Maurois, André, *Points of View from Kipling to Graham Greene* (London: Muller, 1969).

Meisel, Perry, and Kendrick, Walter (eds.), *Bloomsbury/Freud: The Letters of James and Alix Strachey 1924–1925* (London: Chatto & Windus, 1986).

Metcalfe, Thomas, *Ideologies of the Raj*, The New Cambridge History of India (Cambridge: Cambridge University Press, 1994).

Midgley, Clare (ed.), *Gender and Imperialism* (Manchester and New York: Manchester University Press and St Martin's Press, 1995).

Mitchell, Juliet, *Mad Men and Medusas: Reclaiming Hysteria and the Effects of Sibling Relations on the Human Condition* (London: Allen Lane, 2000).

Mort, Frank, *Dangerous Sexualities: Medico-Moral Politics in England since 1830* (London: Routledge, 1987).

Mosse, George, *The Image of Man* (Oxford: Oxford University Press, 1998).

Orniston, Darius Gray, 'The Invention of "Cathexis" and Strachey's Strategy', *International Review of Psycho-Analysis*, 12 (1985), 391–9.

Parry, Benita, *Delusions and Discoveries: Studies on India in the British Imagination 1880–1930* (Bristol: Penguin, 1972).

Partridge, Frances, *Everything to Lose: Diaries 1945–1960* (London: Gollancz, 1985).

—— *Good Company: Diaries January 1967–70* (London: Orion, 2001).

—— *Hanging On: Diaries December 1960-December 1963* (London: Collins, 1990).

—— *Memories* (London: Phoenix, 1988).

—— *Other People: Diaries September 1963-December 1966* (London: Harper Collins, 1992).

—— and Julia Strachey, *Julia* (London: Gollancz, 1983).

Paskauskas, R. A. (ed.), *The Complete Correspondence of Sigmund Freud and Ernest Jones 1908–1939* (Cambridge, Mass.: Harvard University Press, 1993).

Perkin, Harold, *The Rise of Professional Society: England since 1880* (London: Routledge, 1989).

Phillips, Anne (ed.), *A Newnham Anthology* (Cambridge: Cambridge University Press, 1979).

Phillips, Kathy J., *Virginia Woolf against Empire* (Knoxville, Tenn.: University of Tennessee Press, 1994).

Powell, Thomas H., and Gallagher, Peggy Ahrenhold, *Brothers and Sisters: A Special Part of Exceptional Families* (London: Paule Brookes Publishing Co., 1993).

Richardson, Angelique, *Love and Eugenics in the Late Nineteenth Century: Rational Reproduction and the New Woman* (Oxford: Oxford University Press, 2003).

Riviere, Joan, 'Womanliness as Masquerade', in Russell Grigg, Dominique Hecq and Craig Smit (eds.), *Female Sexuality* (London: Rebus Press, 1999).

Robinson, Annabel, *The Life and Work of Jane Harrison* (New York: Oxford University Press, 2002).

Rosenbaum, S. P., *Victorian Bloomsbury: The Early Literary History of the Bloomsbury Group* (New York: St Martin's Press, 1987).

Rosenfeld, Natania, *Outsiders Together: Virginia and Leonard Woolf* (Princeton: Princeton University Press, 2000).

Rubinstein, David, *A Different World for Women: The Life of Millicent Garrett Fawcett* (New York: Harvester Wheatsheaf, 1991).

Rutherford, Jonathan, *Forever England: Reflections on Masculinity and Empire* (London: Lawrence & Wishart, 1997).

Schvaneveldt, J. D., and Ihinger, M., 'Sibling Relationships in the Family', in W. R. Burr, R. Hill, F. I. Nye, and I. L. Reiss (eds.), *Contemporary Theories about the Family* (New York: Free Press, 1970).

Seal, Anil, *The Emergence of Indian Nationalism* (Cambridge: Cambridge University Press, 1970).

Shanley, Mary Lyndon, *Feminism, Marriage and the Law in Victorian England, 1850–1895* (London: Taurus, 1989).

Shaw, W. N., 'Sir Richard Strachey, G.C.S.I., F.R.S.', *Nature* (27 Feb. 1908), 373–95.

Sheridan, Alan, *André Gide: A Life in the Present* (London: Hamish Hamilton, 1998).

Shone, Richard, 'Bloomsbury Nude: Some Hitherto Unpublished Photographs', *The Charleston Magazine*, 16 (1997), 30–2.

Showalter, Elaine, *Sexual Anarchy: Gender and Culture at the Fin de Siècle* (London: Virago, 1992).

Sinfield, Alan, *The Wilde Century: Effeminacy, Oscar Wilde and the Queer Moment* (London: Cassell, 1994).

Sinha, Mrinalinha, *Colonial Masculinity: The 'Manly Englishman' and the 'Effeminate Bengali' in the Late Nineteenth Century* (Manchester: Manchester University Press, 1995).

Skidelsky, Robert, *John Maynard Keynes, Hopes Betrayed, 1883–1920* (Harmondsworth: Penguin Books, 1994).

—— *John Maynard Keynes, The Economist as Saviour* (Harmondsworth, Penguin Books, 1995).

Smith, Harold L., 'British Feminism and the Equal Pay Issue in the 1930s', *Women's History Review*, 5 (1996), 97–110.

Solms, Mark, 'Controveries in Freud Translation', *Psychoanalysis and History*, 1/1 (1998), 28–43.

Spalding, Frances, *Duncan Grant. A Biography* (London: Pimlico, 1998).

—— *Roger Fry: Art and Life* (London and New York: Elek, 1980).

—— *Vanessa Bell* (London: Weidenfeld & Nicolson, 1983).

Spotts, Frederick (ed.), *The Letters of Leonard Woolf* (London: Weideneld & Nicolson, 1990).

Stansky, Peter, *On or about December 1910* (Cambridge, Mass.: Harvard University Press, 1996).

Stein, Burton, *A History of India* (Oxford: Blackwell, 1998).

Steiner, R., 'To Explain our Point of View to English Readers', *International Review of Psychoanalysis*, 18 (1991), 351–92.

Stephen, Barbara, *Emily Davies and Girton College* (London: Constable & Co., 1927; repr. Westport, Conn. 1976).

Stocks, Mary, *My Commonplace Book* (London: Peter Davies, 1970).

Stokes, Eric, *The English Utilitarians and India* (Oxford: Oxford University Press, 1959).

Stone, Ian, *Canal Irrigation in British India: Perspectives on Technological Change in a Peasant Economy* (Cambridge: Cambridge University Press, 1984).

Stone, Lawrence, *Road to Divorce: England 1530–1987* (Oxford and New York: Oxford University Press, 1990).

Stott, Mary, *Before I Go: Reflection on my Life and Times* (London: Virago, 1985).

Strachey, Alix, 'Psychological Problems of Nationhood', *The Year Book of World Affairs* (London 1960).

—— *The Unconscious Motives of War* (London: George Allen & Unwin, 1957).

Strachey, Barbara, *Remarkable Relations: The Story of the Pearsall Smith Women* (New York: Universe Books, 1982).

—— *The Strachey Line: An English Family in America, in India and at Home, 1570 to 1902* (London: Victor Gollancz, 1985).

—— and Samuels, Jayne (eds.), *Mary Berenson: A Self-Portrait from her Letters and Diaries* (London: Hamish Hamilton, 1983).

Strachey, Edward, 'The Romantic Marriage of James Achilles Kirkpatrick, Sometime British Resident at the court of Hyderabad', *Blackwood's Magazine* (July 1893), 356–64.

Strachey, James, 'Editor's Introduction' to 'Three Essays on Sexuality', in Sigmund Freud, *On Sexuality*, ed. James Strachey, The Pelican Freud Library, 7 (London & Penguin, 1977).

—— 'Sigmund Freud. Sketch of his Life and Ideas', in Sigmund Freud, *Two Short Accounts of Psychoanalysis* (Harmondsworth: Pelican Books, 1962).

—— 'Some Unconscious Factors in Reading', *International Journal of Psycho-Analysis*, 11 (1930), 322–31.

—— 'The Function of the Precipitating Factor in the Aetiology of the Neuroses: An Historical Note', *International Journal of Psycho-Analysis*, 12/1 (1931), 326–30.

—— 'The Nature of the Therapeutic Action of Psycho-Analysis', *International Journal of Psychoanalysis*, 15 (1934), 127–59.

Strachey, Jane, *Nursery Lyrics* (London: Bliss & Co., 1893).

—— 'Recollections', *Atheneaum*, 3 (12 July 1924), 474.

—— 'Some Recollections of a Long Life', *Nation and Athenaeum* (5 Jan. 1924), 514.

—— (ed.), *The Memoirs of a Highland lady: The Autobiography of Elizabeth Grant of Rothiermurchus, Afterwards Mrs Smith of Baltiboy, 1797–1830* (London: John Murray, 1899).

Strachey, John, *India* (London: Kegan Paul & Co., 1888).

—— *India: Its Administration and Progress* (London: Macmillan & Co., 1911).

—— *The End of Empire* (London: Victor Gollancz, 1961).

—— *The Finances and Public Works of India from 1869 to 1881* (London: Kegan Paul Tench, 1882).

—— *The Indian Famine of 1877, Being a Statement of the Measures Proposed by the Government of India for the Prevention and Relief of Famine* (London: Kegan Paul & Co, 1878).

Strachey, Julia, *Julia: A Portrait by Herself and Frances Partridge* (London: Victor Gollancz, 1983).

Strachey, Lytton, *The Shorter Strachey* (eds.) Michael Holroyd and Paul Levy (Oxford: Oxford University Press, 1980).

—— *Lytton Strachey by Himself: A Self-Portrait*, ed. Michael Holroyd (London: Heinemann, 1971).

—— *Queen Victoria* (New York: Harcourt, Brace & Jovanovich, 1921).

—— *Spectatorial Essays*, ed. James Strachey (London: Chatto & Windus, 1964).

—— *The Really Interesting Question and Other Papers*, ed. Paul Levy (London: Weidenfeld & Nicolson, 1972).

Strachey, Marjorie, *The Counterfeits* (London: Longmans Green & Co, 1927).

—— 'Women in the Modern Drama', *The Englishwoman*, 29 (May 1911), 186–9.

Strachey, Mrs Richard, *Lay Texts for the Young in English and French* (London: Cassell & Co., 1886).

Strachey, Oliver, and Strachey, Ray, *Keigwin's Rebellion (1863–4)* (Oxford: Clarendon Press, 1916).

Strachey, Ray, *A Quaker Grandmother: Hannah Whitall Smith* (New York: Fleming H. Revell Co., 1914).

—— *Frances Willard: Her Life and Work* (New York: Fleming H. Revell Co., 1913).

—— *The Cause: A Short History of the Women's Movement in Great Britain* (London: G. Bell & Sons, 1928; London: Virago, 1978).

—— *The World at Eighteen* (London: T. Fisher Unwin, 1907).

Strachey, Richard, *A Strachey Child* (Oxford: Privately published, 1979).

Strachey, Richard, 'Asia', in *Encyclopaedia Britannica*, 9th edn., ii (Edinburgh: Adam and Charles Black, 1880).

Strachey, Richard, *The Physical Causes of Indian famine* (London: Royal Institution of Great Britain, 1877).

Sulloway, Frank, *Born to Rebel: Birth Order, Family Dynamics, and Creative Lives* (New York: Pantheon Books, 1996).

Taddeo, Julie, 'A Modernist Romance? Lytton Strachey and the Women of Bloomsbury', in Elizabeth Harrison and Shirley Peterson (eds.), *Unmanning Modernism: Gendered Re-Readings* (Knoxville, Tenn.: 1997).

—— *Lytton Strachey and the Search for Modern Sexual Identity: The Last Eminent Victorian* (New York, NY: Harrington Park Press, 2002).

Tedeschi, Richard (ed.), *Selected Letters of Andre Gide and Dorothy Bussy* (New York: Oxford University Press, 1983).

Thane, Pat, *Old Age in English History: Past Experiences, Present Issues* (Oxford: Oxford University Press, 2000).

Tickner, Lisa, *Spectacle of Women: The Imagery of the Suffrage Campaign, 1907–1917* (London: Chatto & Windus, 1987).

Tosh, John, *A Man's Place: Masculinity and the Middle-Class Home in Victorian England* (New Haven: Yale University Press, 1999).

Turnbaugh, Douglas Blair, *Duncan Grant and the Bloomsbury Group* (Secaucus, NJ: Lyle Stuart Inc., 1987).

Twinn, Peter, 'The Abwehr Enigma', in F. H. Hinsley and Alan Stripp (eds.), *The Inside Story of Bletchley Park* (Oxford: Oxford University Press, 1994).

Vicinus, Martha, *Independent Women: Work and Community for Single Women, 1850–1920* (Chicago: University of Chicago Press, 1985).

Walter, Zoum, *Pour Sylvie* (Paris: Jacques Antoine, 1975).

Ware, Vron, *Beyond the Pale: White Women, Racism and History* (London: Verso, 1992).

Washbrook, D. A., 'India, 1818–1860: The Two Faces of Colonialism', in Andrew Porter (ed.) *The Oxford History of the British Empire*, iii (Oxford: Oxford University Press, 1999).

Weeks, Jeffrey, *Sex, Politics and Society: The Regulation of Sexual Crime since 1800* (London: Longman, 1989).

Weeks, Julie, *Coming out: Homosexual Politics in Britain from the Nineteenth Century to the Present* (London: Quartet Books, 1977).

William-Ellis, Amabel, *All Stracheys are Cousins: Memoirs* (London: Weidenfeld & Nicolson, 1983).

Winnicott, D. W., 'James Strachey, 1887–1967', *International Journal of Psycho-Analysis*, 50/129 (1969), 130–1.

Woolf, Leonard, *Economic Imperialism* (New York: Howard Fertig, 1970; first published 1920).

—— *Growing: An Autobiography of the Years 1904–1911* (London: Hogarth, 1961).

—— *Sowing: An Autobiography of the Years 1880–1904* (London: Hogarth Press, 1970).

—— and Strachey James, (eds.), *Virginia Woolf and Lytton Strachey: Letters* (London: Hogarth Press, 1956).

Woolf, Virginia, *Books and Portraits*, ed. Mary Lyon (London: Hogarth Press, 1977).

—— *Moments of Being*, ed. Jeanne Schulkind (St Albans: Triad/Panther Books, 1978).

—— *Roger Fry: A Biography* (London: Hogarth Press, 1940).

—— *The Diary of Virginia Woolf,* ed. Anne Olivier Bell, 5 vols. (Harmondsworth: Penguin Books, 1979–85).

Index